A dictionary of modern painting

A DICTIONARY

of

MODERN PAINTING

General Editors

CARLTON LAKE
and
ROBERT MAILLARD

METHUEN AND CO. LTD
36 ESSEX STREET · STRAND · LONDON WC2

Translated from the French
Dictionnaire de la Peinture Moderne
(Fernand Hazan Éditeur, Paris)
by LAWRENCE SAMUELSON, KATIE KAPLAN,
MARY HART, BARBARA MARCHUTZ
and BETTINA WADIA.

3. 1.

CATALOGUE N° 2/5822/28

First published in 1956
Second edition 1958
Third edition 1964

LIST OF CONTRIBUTORS

John Ashbery	J. A.	Frank Mc Ewen	F. MC E.
Alan Bird	A. B.	Franz Meyer	F. M.
Françoise Choay	F. C.	Michael Middleton	M. M.
Raymond Cogniat	R. C.	Raoul-Jean Moulin	R.-J. M.
Pierre Courthion	P. C.	Joseph-Emile Muller	J.-E. M.
Bernard Dorival	B. D.	Mathilde Pomès	M. P.
Frank Elgar	F. E.	Eva Rapsilber	E. R.
Florent Fels	F. F.	Maurice Raynal	M. R.
Dino Formaggio	D. F.	John Rewald	J. R.
Maurice Gieure	M. GI.	Henri-Pierre Roché	H.-P. R.
Marina Grey	M. GR.	Claude Roger-Marx	CL. R.-M.
Jacques Lassaigne	J. LA.	Denis Rouart	D. R.
André Lejard	A. L.	G. di San Lazzaro	S. L.
Jean Leymarie	J. LE.	Michel Seuphor	M. S.
Bo Lindwall	B. L.	Philippe Soupault	PH. S.
Edwin Livengood	E. L.	Claude Spaak	C. S.
Jerome Mellquist	J. M.	Bettina Wadia	B. W.

PREFACE

The aim of this book is to give a simple and reliable account of modern painting from the Impressionists up to our own time. It is the joint work of a number of art critics, mostly French; but though it comes from Paris, the vital centre of most modern movements in art, the editors have been at pains to maintain a broad outlook and describe painting activities outside France.

This is a dictionary in the sense that two hundred and fifty entries follow one another in alphabetical order; but they are not simply dry recitals of dates and facts. Each entry is a considered essay on its subject, a critical and sympathetic appraisal of the artist or movement in question. In this sense we believe the book to be unique, and we hope it will prove an illuminating guide to all interested in modern painting.

The editors were faced with the problem of where to start and where to end. The Impressionists were chosen as a convenient starting-point, but what was to be the closing date? It was finally decided that the only living painters to be included should be those who had made their mark before the outbreak of the Second World War.

In addition to the names of painters and art movements, the reader will find accounts of men of letters such as Apollinaire and André Breton who influenced the development of painting in their time. There are also descriptions of places such as the Slade School and the Bateau-Lavoir, where painters assembled and worked.

In this English version, which has been done by five translators in Paris working closely with the original publisher, a number of additional entries have been inserted in their appropriate places, and the number of illustrations has been increased.

For this third edition the book has been completely revised and enlarged. It now affords a detailed panorama of world painting from 1850 to 1950. There are 100 new articles and 110 new illustrations.

A

ABSTRACT ART Discussion of abstract, non-representational art has generally led to controversy rather than to any real clarification of the subject. Fanatical opponents and supporters reach a deadlock, because it is as useless to deny the legitimacy of abstract art as to try and impose its principles as absolute dogma. No artistic formula can be justified or condemned in itself; it must be judged by reference to the quality of the works that exemplify it. After half a century of vicissitudes, and despite its present widespread acceptance, abstract art still presents difficulties of an historical and aesthetic nature which no article on the subject, no matter how brief and objective, can ignore. Architecture and music are naturally admitted to be abstract arts, not required to 'represent' something, and subject to their own laws, whereas poetry, painting and sculpture are considered arts of representation. Ought this traditional distinction to be maintained or, aesthetics being universal, can all arts claim the same inherent autonomy as music and architecture ? It does seem that abstract art was born from the very desire to emulate music and architecture, with a freedom and discipline of its own. Kandinsky, with his suggestions of music, and Mondrian, with his ideal of architecture, demonstrate the limitations and, at the same time, the achievement of abstract art. In the general process of abstraction that characterizes modern art, is there a line of demarcation between the domains of representational and non-representational art ? And if so, where should it be drawn ? Can one speak of relative and absolute abstraction, and where does absolute abstraction begin ? Finally, is abstract art in its various manifestations a truly original creation of the twentieth century, the outcome of historical conditions, or is it a cyclic phase whose equivalent is to be found in the arts of the past ?

The term 'abstract' itself is equivocal and invites discussion. For one could easily claim that all art is abstract, just as one might follow Picasso in declaring that there is no abstract art. Attempts to substitute other terms for it have failed. One interpreter of the movement, Michel Seuphor, had said: 'I call abstract art all art that does not recall or evoke reality, regardless of whether that reality be the point from which the artist started, or not'. Abstract art falls into two historically defined periods: an initial period (1910-1916) when abstraction was the result of an anti-naturalist process, and a second period that began in 1917 with the *De Stijl (*)* movement and is still going on, in which abstraction for abstraction's sake is the absolute principle from which the artist starts. It might perhaps be clearer, as is becoming the accepted practice to do, to call the first 'abstract art' and the second 'non-representational art'.

Fauvism *(*)* and Cubism *(*)* certainly favoured the autonomous development of forms and colours, and every kind of artistic experiment was tried during the extraordinary outburst of activity that preceded the 1914-1918 war. The first deliberately abstract water-colour by Kandinsky (spots of colour in dynamic juxtaposition without any representational purpose) dates from 1910, the same year that he wrote his fundamental work *Concerning the Spiritual in Art*, one of the basic books on abstract art. What shocked him into this new technique was a brilliantly coloured dress and the sight of one of his pictures standing on its side. But it was in referring to music that he discovered his aesthetic principle. Significantly, he called his sketches 'Improvisations' and his finished works 'Compositions'. The value of his abstract imagination rests on his genius as a colourist and the quality of his lyricism (*vide* Kandinsky). In 1912 the Czech Kupka also exhibited some abstract canvases directly inspired by music: *Fugue in Two Colours*, *Warm Chromatic*, etc (*vide* Kupka). He was the forerunner of the Musicalists, who, about 1920, formed a group with Blanc-Gatti and Valensi. Picabia,

KANDINSKY. FIRST ABSTRACT WORK. WATER-COLOUR. 1910.

subject (a tree, or the façade of a cathedral), purging it bit by bit of all natural appearance until it became no more than a diagram. This experiment, conducted systematically with that austere and methodical application so characteristic of puritan Holland, reached the same impasse as did Malevitch's, although Mondrian's approach was from the opposite direction. With Neo-Plasticism *(*)*, Mondrian started from abstraction, from absolute plastic relationships, in order to attain the purity and universality of mathematics. He has had an influence on modern contemporary architecture and, through the Bauhaus *(*)*, has left his mark on the development of Kandinsky (*vide* Mondrian, Van Doesburg).

About the same time that Mondrian laid the foundations of the new art, a few artists at Zürich, Jean Arp and Sophie Taeuber among them, quite unaware of this sudden departure, launched into their experiments with free, irrational forms, which were to be the essential contribution of Dadaism *(*)* to abstraction. From Magnelli at Florence, about 1915 came a series of strictly abstract paintings in flat areas of strong colours.

A glance at the situation of painting as a whole at the end of the First World War suggests that Abstract Art was on the point of spreading everywhere. In fact, it is interesting to notice that painters as different as Matisse, Léger and Villon felt its attraction. Anyway, a pause was soon apparent and, after some of the great Cubists had given up abstraction, it was clear that its general acceptance had not yet come. More significant than this was the rise of Surrealism *(*)* in 1924, which made the existence of Abstract Art even more uncertain and the period between the wars was one of alternating eclipse and resurgence. While Picabia and Delaunay, for instance, returned to figurative painting, new abstract artists appeared after 1920

whose *Rubber* (1909) was non-representational, joined the movement while Delaunay, the founder of Orphism *(*)*, exalted to abstraction the lyricism of pure colour, which, he said, was both 'form and subject' (*vide* Picabia, Delaunay). But it was in Russia that experimentation in abstract art was carried to its extreme limits, beginning in 1913: the Rayonism *(*)* of Larionov and Nathalie Gontcharova, the Constructivism of Tatlin (revived in 1920 by the Pevsner brothers and Gabo), the Nonobjectivism of Rodchenko, and the Suprematism *(*)* of Malevitch, which gave us the celebrated black square on a white ground. Most of the pioneers of abstract art are of Russian origin and the real precursor of it was the Lithuanian Tchurlianis, in 1906-1907. The Slav sensibility is haunted by the fascination of non-existence, the anguished flight from reality (*vide* Larionov, Gontcharova, Malevitch).

Another country in which abstract art has thrived is Holland. There Mondrian and the *De Stijl* movement (Van Doesburg, Van der Leck), in opposition to the lyrical tendencies which Kandinsky inherited from Fauvism and Expressionism, crystallized the intellectual and geometrical tendencies derived from Cubism and transformed abstraction into non-representation. Before *De Stijl* Mondrian's method was to make successive abstractions of a given

among whom were the Germans, Freundlich and Vordemberge-Gildewart, the Hungarian, Moholy-Nagy who taught at the Bauhaus, the Dutchman, Domela, who rejoined the *De Stijl* group, the Belgians, Servranckx and Peeters; after 1923, Schwitters and Baumeister; in 1926, the painter-typographer, Werkman; in 1933, former Cubists, such as Charchoune, Reth, Herbin and after 1933, Magnelli in geometric and Hartung in a lyrical style. The first international exhibition of Abstract Art was organised in April 1930 at Paris by Michel Seuphor and Torrès Garcia and sponsored by the review, *Cercle et Carré (*)*, founded the same year. The Abstraction-Création *(*)* group, which continued the work of Cercle et Carré, was founded in 1932 and, like its predecessor, published an annual volume until 1936, while it too organised regular exhibitions. This group consisted of about four hundred members. Nevertheless, Abstract Art then seemed to suffer a set-back. With the outbreak of the Spanish Civil War, then the beginning of the Second World War, Expressionism regained its vitality and became predominant.

Obviously, the war marked a break even in the world of the arts, and when it ended, a completely new scene is revealed to an attentive observer. Klee died in 1940, Delaunay in 1941, Freundlich in 1943, Kandinsky and Mondrian both in 1944. Names, unknown till then, made their appearance and, after 1945, helped to spread Abstract Art in each country. This explains the importance of the Salon des Réalités Nouvelles, which, when it was inaugurated at Paris in 1946, assembled more than a thousand contributions and became the first official Salon of non-figurative art. Then the publication of Michel Seuphor's book, *Abstract Art: its Origins and First Masters*, in April 1949, was a sort of recognition of the historical importance of the movement and its creators.

An exhaustive account of recent developments in abstract painting is beyond the scope of the present article. Although too many works are only intellectual exercises or purely decorative, academic vulgarisations of abstraction, some, on the other hand, are the response to a profound desire to escape from a worn out reality and master a 'new reality', a realm of pure painting that expresses the continuum of the inner life or patterns itself on the structure and rhythm of the universe. It is only possible to mention the outstanding personalities and movements of an eventful and still too familiar present. In France it must suffice to record names as different and contradictory as Hartung and Bissière, Fautrier and Bazaine, Manessier and Lanskoy, De Staël and Vieira da Silva, Estève and Wols, Poliakoff and Soulages, Atlan and Bram van Velde. In 1955, the term 'Tachisme' was coined to describe the work of painters such as Mathieu and Riopelle. In Belgium the leading artists are Van Lint, Anne Bonnet, Gaston Bertrand and Delahaut. Alechinsky settled in Paris after joining in the Cobra movement with the Dane, Jorn, and the Dutchman, Appel. Although the Nazis had condemn-

MONDRIAN. COMPOSITION. 1913.   *Kröller-Müller Museum, Otterlo.*

ed all avant-garde art, a school of abstract painting has grown up today in Germany with artists such as E. W. Nay, Theodore Werner, Fritz Winter, Julius Bissier and Sonderborg.

In Italy, after the experiments of Balla and Magnelli about 1915, which seem so far away, non-figurative art did not reappear until the work of Soldati first, then Prampolini and Reggiani about 1931-1934. It was only at the end of the Second World War that Italy returned to the main stream of European art that a coherent movement can be traced with the work of Afro, Vedova, Corpora, Capogrossi, Burri and Santomaso. Abstraction then spread over Spain, Scandinavia, Yugoslavia, Poland and even reached Brazil and Japan.

The first American practitioners of abstract art were Stanton MacDonald-Wright and Morgan Russell. Calling themselves 'synchromists', they made a stir in Paris and Munich in 1913. That same year they were represented in New York's Armory Show *(*)*. Both, however, returned to a naturalistic style, MacDonald-Wright about 1919, Russell in the early 'thirties. Russell died in 1953. Wright has just recently

gone back to abstraction with a brilliantly lyrical style (*vide* MacDonald-Wright and Russell).

Miss Katherine Dreier was the first to introduce to America the work of the leading European abstract artists, in an exhibition held at the Brooklyn Museum in 1926. A little later A. E. Gallatin followed her lead, in setting up his Gallery of Living Art (now at the Philadelphia Museum), and Baroness Hilla Rebay founded in 1937 the Museum of Nonobjective Painting (now the Solomon R. Guggenheim Museum). But these steps in themselves did not bring about a full-fledged abstract art movement in America. Such painters as Max Weber, Marin, Feininger, Stuart Davis and Marsden Hartley flirted with abstraction but never gave themselves over to it wholly. During that post-World War I period only Covert (*Brass Band*) and Miss Dreier herself (*Abstract Portrait of Marcel Duchamp*) produced works which are completely abstract. It was not until 1935 that American artists threw themselves wholeheartedly into abstraction. The pioneers were Harry Holtzman and Burgoyne Diller, who widened the scope of Mondrian's influence. They were followed by Fritz Glarner, Charmion von Wiegand, and others.

With the Association of American Abstract Artists, founded in 1936, abstract art entrenched itself in New York. Among the participants in the group's first annual exhibitions were: George L. K. Morris, Holtzman, Holty, Ferren, Albers, Cavallon, Gallatin, McNeil, Reinhardt, and Charles Shaw. After the Second World War many others joined the group, among them von Wicht, Bolotovsky, Sennhauser, Alcopley, Wolff, Xceron, Frelinghuysen, Slobodkina, Perle Fine; more recently still, Beate Hulbeck and Ado Fleischmann. But since 1950 the ranks of American abstract artists have swelled far beyond this group to cover the entire country. Pure abstraction, particularly in the manifestation termed Abstract Expressionism, which Jackson Pollock spearheaded, has its devotees in every state in the Union.

PICABIA. UDNIE OR THE DANCE. 1913.
Musée d' Art Moderne, Paris.

4

KUPKA. PHILOSOPHICAL ARCHITECTURE. 1913.
Galerie Louis Carré, Paris.

In the 'official' exhibitions put on by the Metropolitan Museum, abstract works are as numerous as representational ones. One notes frequently an emphasis on calligraphy, in the Oriental sense of the word. This art of the sign goes from an extreme of finesse in the work of Mark Tobey to an extreme of power in that of Franz Kline, passing, meanwhile, through the tortured meanderings of Pollock. Another form of abstraction, built aroun the 'spot', and hence closer to Impressionism, is encountered in the work of such painters as Clifford Still and Mark Rothko. Arshile Gorky, who died in 1948, worked a very individual abstract vein stemming from Surrealism. Other abstract expressionists include Tworkow, Stamos, Donati, Hans Richter, Motherwell, Gottlieb, Congdon, Baziotes and Willem de Kooning. De Kooning, however, has veered away from abstraction in the past few years and gone over to a more pronounced expressionism. One of the stronger influences on the work of many of these painters has been Hans Hoffmann, whose school has helped to develop a number of remarkable artists (*vide*

Gorky, Hoffmann, Kline, Pollock and Tobey).

In Great Britain pure abstraction, in the sense that Mondrian or Kandinsky, for example, gave it, has never had much of a vogue. Even Ben Nicholson, who, over the past twenty years, has been the standard-bearer of English abstract art, returns frequently to a figurative style of painting, and is even so unorthodox as occasionally to group within the bounds of one canvas a purely abstract motif and a recognizable landscape—and successfully (*vide* Nicholson).

The magazine *Axis*, founded by Myfanwy Evans in 1935, was the first British review to speak out on behalf of abstract art. It carried articles by Sir Herbert Read, Geoffrey Grigson, James Johnson Sweeney, George L. K. Morris, and Roland Penrose, and reproduced works by the leading Continental artists and, along with them, those of English abstractionists Ben Nicholson, Winifred Dacre, Ivon Hitchens, Arthur Jackson, Henry Moore, Edward Wadsworth and John Piper. Piper was at that period the great hope of the new English abstract art, but he later abandoned abstraction completely and returned to his personal landscape style.

About this time Paule Vezelay (***), an independent English artist, began painting abstract canvases. She has a very individual style, with crisply distinguished forms, sometimes close to Arp's, and a subtle palette. Toward the end of the 'twenties Miss Marlow Moss, working in Paris, was a fervent disciple of Mondrian.

In 1937 Ben Nicholson, Naum Gabo, and the architect J. L. Martin, brought out an important book, *Circle, An International Survey of Constructivist Art*, but it was not until 1951 that there was a real spurt of activity in the abstract domain. In that year a new convert, Victor Pasmore, had his first exhibition of purely abstract work. Other young abstract painters followed his example and their activity was summarized in a book by Lawrence Alloway, *Nine Abstract Artists, their Work and Theory* (1954). These nine include, along with Pasmore, Robert Adams, Terry Frost, Adrian Heath, Anthony Hill, Roger Hilton, Kenneth Martin, Mary Martin, and William Scott. In addition to these artists there are Stephen Gilbert, Vera Spencer, and William Gear, each of them pursuing a different path toward abstraction. The latter three are shown more frequently on the Continent than in England. But over all his countrymen the figure of Ben Nicholson looms, internationally, as by far the most important among British abstract painters.

There is no longer any need to prove the vitality of abstract art. Perhaps there is all the more reason to fear an academic proliferation. In fact, Abstract Art is always in danger from dry formality, facility or mere decorativeness. Kandinsky already gave a warning about this when he said, 'The most important thing about form is to know whether it is the result of an inner necessity or not'.　　　　J. LE.

ANDRÉ. THE SQUARE AT DEAUVILLE. *Private Collection, Paris.*

ABSTRACTION-CRÉATION

At the beginning of 1931, the Belgian painter and sculptor, Georges Vantongerloo, decided to found a new group that would revive and carry on the aims of Cercle et Carré *(*)*, which no longer existed. The original members were Herbin, Béothy, Valmier, Kupka, Gleizes and nearly all those who had belonged to Cercle et Carré, as Vantongerloo had the records of the group in his possession. But over the next five or six years, Abstraction-Création expanded and developed considerably. From 1932, an illustrated volume was published annually with the title, *Abstraction-Création art non-figurative* and from 1933 onwards, exhibitions of members' work were held in a small gallery in the avenue de Wagram. None of them, however, attained the importance of the Cercle et Carré shows. In its heyday, Abstraction-Création had some four hundred members of whom about half lived in France. The last annual appeared in 1936, but ten years later, it found a natural continuation in the yearly volumes published by the Salon des Réalités Nouvelles in exactly the same style. The series of fifteen volumes are a mine of information on international abstract art from 1932 to 1956.

ACADÉMIE JULIAN

Founded in Paris in 1860 by Rudolph Julian, this was the first Academy to be formed in the shadow of the École Nationale des Beaux-Arts. It was never a rival institution but served from the beginning as a kind of preparatory studio for those waiting to enter the École Nationale. After some initial difficulties, involving several moves, from the Faubourg Montmartre to Montparnasse before eventually setting itself up in the Rue du Dragon, it finally became very successful when, about 1888, Bonnard, Vuillard, Denis, Ibels, Ranson, Roussel and Vallotton–later to become the Nabis *(*)*–began to meet there. Some years later, in 1892, Matisse came also, to work mainly under the guidance of Bouguereau, an honest painter though devoid of originality, who once said to him: 'You rub out your charcoal with your finger, which shows that you are a slipshod person . . . You will never know how to draw.' La Fresnaye and Segonzac came to work at the Academy in 1903, Derain and Léger in 1904. Marcel Duchamp also found his way there and stayed just long enough to contract that profound aversion for the semi-official conception of art represented by Bouguereau that prompted him to start his pre-Dada revolt.

ACADÉMIE RANSON In order to provide a centre of activity for the Nabi movement, founded under Gauguin's influence, Paul Ranson and his wife France, founded an Academy in Paris in 1908. They had been acquainted for some time with Gauguin's ideas through Sérusier, who had met Gauguin in Brittany in 1888 and been immediately carried away with enthusiasm for his art and perhaps even more for his theories. These Sérusier transmitted to Ranson as well as to his other friends at the Académie Julian *(*)*: Pierre Bonnard, Maurice Denis, X.-K. Roussel, Édouard Vuillard. These young artists, who called themselves the Nabis, propounded a new type of painting characterized by the simplification of line and colour with a view to achieving the decorative effect which was their main preoccupation. But they needed a headquarters where they could teach the results of their research. This they found at the Académie Ranson. Maurice Denis and Sérusier (who had La Fresnaye and Goerg among his pupils) taught there in 1908, as did Vuillard and Roussel. Later, such different artists as Vallotton and La Patellière, Kisling and Maillol, Christian Bérard and Gromaire, Le Moal and Manessier, frequented the school. Closed during the Second World War, the Academy reopened in 1951, and is now continuing its work, still faithful to the principles of independence and liberty.

ACADÉMIE SUISSE In wretched premises on the Quai des Orfèvres, some time between 1825 and 1830, a former model by the name of Suisse (whom they used to call *le Père Suisse*) opened a free academy, provided with models if not with instructors. There one could meet, in 1842, Bonington, Delacroix and Courbet. The Académie Suisse was at its zenith in about 1860, when the future Impressionists frequented it. It was there that Pissarro made the acquaintance of Monet and Guillaumin in 1859, and in April 1861 met Cézanne, who had just arrived from Aix-en-Provence. Cézanne was then twenty-two years old, Pissarro thirty-one. The friendship that immediately sprung up between the two artists was a particularly fertile one, for it was to his contact with Pissarro that Cézanne owed his initiation into the Impressionist technique during his stay at Auvers-sur-Oise in 1872-1874. Among the regular models of the Academy was a Negro by the name of Scipion, who figures in Cézanne's famous canvas now in the São Paulo Museum *(see* illustration, page 59). For a long time the Académie Suisse constituted the antechamber of the very official École Nationale des Beaux-Arts to which, as is well known, admission was not easily gained by avant-garde painters.

ANDRÉ Albert (1869-1954). French painter; born in Lyons, died at Laudun. When he was twenty, he went to Paris on the advice of his brother to do commercial designing, but he soon left this work to join the Académie Julian, where he met Valtat, Ranson, Henry Bataille. When he exhibited for the first time in 1894 at the Salon des Indépendants, Renoir discovered him and introduced him to Durand-Ruel, who remained his dealer until he died. Durand-Ruel introduced him to a new public by selling the greater part of his work to the most important American collections and the Museums of

ANGRAND. THE VALLEY. 1907.

New York, Washington, Chicago, Philadelphia, which is the reason he is still less known in France than other painters of the same standing.

André was not Renoir's pupil, but an intimate friend and the only one in whom he would confide completely. From 1894 until his death in 1919, André took the intensest interest in his life, noted down his remarks and described his way of living and painting in a book (1918), which was a revelation of Renoir's familiar world. The portraits he did of Renoir during the same period, at work or surrounded by his friends, appeal to us through their sincerity and simplicity; they are not paintings of a historical moment, but records of human life. He never had any intention of distorting what he could see and, except for his Bathers—peasant women whose size had nothing symbolical about it—his art is unassuming, confidential and rooted in the details of life. 'He can only paint what he sees,' George Besson, said of him. Like many painters of his generation who followed the Impressionists, Albert André was not influenced by a technique, but learned from his experience in the open air, how to establish a close bond with nature, seize and communicate the sensuousness of light on a naked body. The visits he made on his travels to the museums of Germany, England, Italy and Spain were made into opportunities for working. He painted the lively port at Marseilles, the place Pigalle, which he could see in winter from his studio in the rue Duperré and sometimes he framed the hurried movement of the passers-by on a closer plane. He painted sensitive landscapes of Bagnols-sur-Cèze and the surroundings of Laudun, where he stayed from spring to autumn. Nothing could be calmer or more orderly than the southern sky-line and its warm, harmonious light or the gatherings of friends, who are never posed in a formal group, but whose attitudes seem so familiar to the viewer that he almost feels one of them. 'Albert André's work,' Marius Mermillon wrote, 'was a faithful and trusting dialogue with people and things to whom he was always the truest friend'. He was made curator of the museum at Bagnols-sur-Cèze in 1918 and enriched it with gifts from his numerous friends (Renoir, Monet, Signac, Bonnard, Marquet, Matisse).   R.-J. M.

ANGRAND Charles (1854-1926). French painter; born at Criquet-sur-Ouville, died at Rouen. He was a clever pupil at school and worked as an assistant master at Rouen, then at Paris. He had a wide circle of friends who included Cross, Luce, Pissarro, Van Gogh, Verhaeren and, through his friendship with Seurat and Signac, was represented at the first Salon des Indépendants in 1884, and took an active part in the exhibitions of the Neo-Impressionist group. His friend, Félix Fenéon, wrote of his work from 1881 to 1885: 'the skill of his brush works and breaks down the thick, malleable pigment, in rich, skilful colouring, and fashions it into impasto relief.' After 1886, Angrand, like Seurat and Signac, adopted the technique of division of tones and simultaneous contrasts. He painted orchards, harvesting and other scenes from country life and attracted attention by his very personal interpretation of Divisionist theories. Large pastels, of the same period, showed the strength of his draughtsmanship. Towards the end of the century, he gave up his stippling technique and allowed the intensity of pure tones to vibrate in large rectangular brush-strokes. In his graphic work,

MODIGLIANI. PORTRAIT OF APOLLINAIRE.

Angrand refined his draughtsmanship and used it as a means to technical experiment. Charcoal, particularly, enabled him to deepen his space and produce extremely fine contrasts. 'His subject —the crystallisation of appearances—emerges from a halo of light, shaping and disintegrating through its waves into rich shadows.' (Georges Besson). He fled from the artistic life of Paris in 1913 to work alone in the path he had traced for himself, with a quiet determination that had made him a subtle draughtsman and a rich colourist. He exhibited pastels at the Société des Artistes Rouennais. A year after his death, in 1927, a retrospective exhibition of his work was shown at the Salon des Indépendants, which illustrated the qualities of the man as much as the artist.   R.-J. M.

ROBERT DELAUNAY. WINDOWS. 1912.
Jean Cassou Collection, Paris.

APOLLINAIRE Guillaume de Kostro-witsky (born in Rome 1880, died in Paris 1918). Born of a Polish mother and a Swiss-Italian father, Apollinaire used to like to pass himself off as the son of an Italian prelate. An extraordinary character and an inordinate hoaxer, but at the same time a poet of captivating charm and sincerity, Apollinaire played a most important role in the history of modern art. One of his claims to distinction–and by no means the least–stems from his having perpetuated the tradition started by the nineteenth-century French poets headed by Baudelaire of devoting some of their finest work to the exaltation of the plastic arts, particularly the new painting of their time. Apollinaire's poetic temperament, his constant preoccupation with creativity, his enlightened faithfulness to the art of the past, destined him for the role that he was to play as the standard-bearer of Cubism. This taste for the plastic arts, far from being gradually acquired, as it was with many poets and writers, was marked in Apollinaire from an early age, the product of a mind 'ardent in its search for beauty'. Apollinaire was passionately drawn to any work of art that tended to give Nature the aspect of something outside the bounds of reality. He was inordinately sensitive to all subjects or objects that in any way transfigured our all too humdrum lives. Hence that love that he manifested for odd curios, for the arts of primitive peoples, of Negroes, for children's drawings;

that enthusiasm for the unexpected, the esoteric and the rare.

When, in 1904, he first came in contact with Derain, Vlaminck and Matisse, he was completely staggered by the apparently anarchical riot of colour in the work of the future Fauvists and by their ambition to conjure up a reality more authentic than mere appearances. That was something that matched his penchant for the unknown and the bizarre. It did not take him long to discover that these painters' ideas also had something stirring and true in them. Soon, through his writing, he was giving his new friends every support in their efforts.

At this point Apollinaire met Picasso, whose blue period opened up new and somewhat conflicting vistas before him. Apollinaire emerged considerably shaken by the totally contradictory things he had seen. Confronted with Picasso's work, he could not have reacted otherwise. He never gave lightly his support to any of the evolutions of the art of his day. Only after careful analysis – *méditations esthétiques*, to quote from the title of one of his books – did he permit himself to be drawn into the art movements of which he was a witness. He never, for example, concealed the fact that *Les Demoiselles d'Avignon* (*see* plate, page 77) had disconcerted him at first. He was always honest in his criticism, both of himself and of those he championed.

It was not until 1913 that he came out with a passionate defence of Cubism in his book on the Cubist painters, *Les Peintres Cubistes*. From then on he did not hesitate to recognize in the new aesthetic movement a revolution 'renewing the plastic arts' and once more respecting discipline and craftsmanship. Rereading this book, which is full of prophetic insight, makes one appreciate the intelligence and sensitiveness of the way Apollinaire could define and single out the characteristic feature of a painter's style, as when he wrote of Picasso: 'He is a newborn child: he imposes order on the universe for his own ends and as an easier means of communication with his fellows.' But besides the different studies of individual painters, he was particularly concerned with the conflict in painting between the processes of the mind and the senses. But what he extolled in Cubism was the idea of creation, which formed its core. Cubism is 'not an imitative art but a conceptual art that aspires to creation', he wrote. The same year, 1913, his instinct and his enthusiasm led Apollinaire to take over a review, *Les Soirées de Paris (*)*, which became the paragon of avant-garde reviews under his editorship, where poets and painters appeared side by side. He further strengthened the new links he had made between painting and poetry, when he coined the term, Orphism *(*)*, to describe the art of Robert Delaunay. The glittering enchantment of this artist's *Windows*, opening out on to a world of pure colour, actually had a far greater effect on Apollinaire's sensibility than the austere dialectics of the Cubist compositions ever had, although Apollinaire took over some daring examples of Cubist syntax which, transposed into the sphere of poetry, inspired him to a totally new way of writing (as evidenced in his ellipses, his omission of punctuation and his *calligrammes*). One of his finest poems, *Windows*, was written under the inspiration of Delaunay's picture.

Because of his insatiable curiosity, Apollinaire allowed himself to be charmed by the Futurist adventure, from 1912 on. The surmise is, however, that he was attracted more by its scintillating dynamism that tended to convert painting

CHIRICO. PROPHETIC PORTRAIT OF APOLLINAIRE
1914. WOOD ENGRAVING BY P. ROY.

into a kind of cinematography than by its negation of all tradition and the advice given by the Futurists to set fire to all museums. Apollinaire soon gave up his collaboration with the Futurists. But it was with profound conviction that he upheld the metaphysical conceptions of Chirico, in his opinion 'the most astonishing painter of his time'. The search for unsuspected relationships between objects, propounded by Chirico, led Apollinaire to stress the importance of dreams and to throw light on certain elements of the subconscious which were to be the basis of Surrealism (a name which he invented in 1917). We have been left an extremely disturbing testimony of the friendship between the two men at that time: the portrait of Apollinaire, dated 1914, in which Chirico gives a silhouette of the poet as a human target with a bullet-hole in his head. The portrait was indeed prophetic. Apollinaire died in 1918, an easy prey to the flu epidemic, after being wounded in the forehead by a German bullet in the war.

Apollinaire applied his initiative to the most decisive and daring art movements of his time. The close union between poets and painters which he promoted created a kind of poetic effervescence around the plastic arts which has gone far towards placing their creations on a radically new plane. It is to Apollinaire's courage, his convictions and, above all, to the confidence which his culture and genius inspired, that painting of the first half of this century owes the audacity and the daring of its concepts, if not the actual creation of its general aesthetic doctrine. Apollinaire's work has, in addition, the merit of having enabled artists to overcome, with surprising rapidity, the inevitable opposition and fatal incomprehension that this most sensational revolution in art history was bound to stir up.   M. R.

ARMORY SHOW An international exhibition of modern art held in February 1913 in New York. Coming after the first exhibitions of Matisse (1908) and Picasso (1911), both arranged there by Alfred Stieglitz (*vide* this name) in his Gallery 291, it has remained famous in the annals of artistic life in the United States. On the initiative of an artistic avant-garde which had already got itself talked about, a number of artists such as Matisse, Picasso, Braque, Léger, Derain, Vlaminck, as well as Kandinsky, Brancusi and Marcel Duchamp, were invited to exhibit their works, under prudent cover of some paintings by Courbet, Ingres, Delacroix and several of the leading Impressionists. The works of a number of young American painters were also on exhibit, chaperoned, so to speak, by a few artists of long standing such as Whistler, Ryder and Twachtman. Thus, every trend was represented: Classicism, Romanticism, Realism, Impressionism, Fauvism, Cubism, Expressionism and Abstract Art. The exhibition showed a perfect unity, the canvases having been selected with care. There seemed to be every reason to hope that it would be a success. Eleven hundred works were assembled in the armory of the 69th Cavalry Regiment, hence the name 'Armory Show'. The experiment was received with scandalous demonstrations unprecedented in the United States. Amid howls of derision and laughter, the Cubist room and, in

particular, Marcel Duchamp's *Nude Descending a Staircase*, were attacked by a frenzied mob that threatened to destroy the canvases it considered offensive to good taste. The Press, as was to be expected, endorsed the public's hostile attitude. Nevertheless, the exhibition was a great success, stirring up curiosity if nothing else. It moved to the Chicago Art Institute, where it was received with similar scenes. Boston showed the same disapproval, but with more restraint. Every-

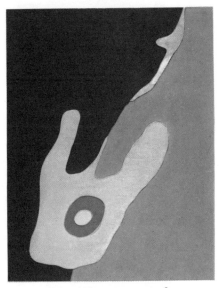

ARP. CONFIGURATION. 1928.
Kuntsmuseum, Basel.

where the exhibition provoked the same reaction. The Armory Show did, nevertheless, manage to find a few supporters and became the subject of somewhat penitent comment from its critics after it closed. But from then on modern art found a large audience in the United States.

ARP Jean (or Hans). French painter, sculptor, poet, born in Strasbourg in 1887. The part that Arp has played, and continues to play, in the sphere of the arts is considerable. Like his antithesis Mondrian, he has not set up a school but has followers of varying degree of skill. But

ARP. ARRANGEMENT ACCORDING TO THE
LAWS OF CHANCE. CUT OUT PAPER.

Apollinaire and Delaunay. When war broke out, he returned to Switzerland, and in December 1915 he exhibited his first abstract works at the Tanner Gallery, Zürich, paintings in generally rectilinear forms. But he gave up ordered movement almost immediately, in order to give preference to objects 'arranged according to the law of chance, rudimentary, irrational, mutilated, broken', already heralding Dadaism *(*)*, which he founded at the beginning of 1916, together with Tzara, Janco, Ball and Hülsenbeck. The movement held its noisy sessions at the Cabaret Voltaire *(*)* in Zürich, and Arp remained one of its central figures, contributing to all its publications. In 1916 he illustrated Hülsenbeck's *Phantastische Gebete (Fantastic Prayers)* with a series of abstract woodcuts which he called studies in symmetry. In 1917 he brought out his first polychromatic reliefs and, the following year, his first woodcuts in the form of spots to illustrate Tzara's *Cinéma Calendrier du Cœur Abstrait*. Meanwhile he had made the acquaintance of Sophie Taeuber, who later became his wife, and he was for a while influenced by her more severe art. Together they created large collages of geometrical, rectilinear cutouts (1918).

In Cologne, in 1920, he collaborated with Baargeld and Max Ernst in new Dadaist enterprises. He met Schwitters in Hanover in 1923, and contributed to the *Merz (*)* review, which published, among other things, a series of his lithographs entitled *7 Arpaden*. In 1925 he published, together with El Lissitzky, *The Isms of Art*, a survey of all the movements then in existence. The following year he went to live at Meudon, near Paris, with his wife, Sophie Taeuber, and became a member of the Surrealist group (1926-1930). At the same time, in collaboration with Sophie Taeuber and Theo van Doesburg, he undertook the decoration of the *café dansant* 'L'Aubette', in Strasbourg, an important piece of work which has since been destroyed. Arp was a member of the *Cercle et Carré (*)* group, and took part in its international exhibition in April 1930. The following year he became a member of the *Abstraction-Création (*)* group. This was the period of pictures made out of bits of twine and torn paper, and of the first sculptures in full relief, in which Arp accentuated more and more that supple and clear-cut style which has earned him universal renown. All this time he continued

the catalytic action of these two pioneers is such that they find themselves, often unwittingly, in the midst of every controversy and every advance in art today.

Very much attracted to painting, and considerably shaken by his first contacts with modern art in Paris in 1904, Arp managed to prevail on his parents to send him to Weimar to study at the Academy (1905-1907), and then to Paris, where he attended the Académie Julian in 1908. But this official instruction failed to appeal to him, and he retired to meditative isolation in Weggis, Switzerland. There he met Klee in 1909. In 1912 he paid a visit to Kandinsky in Munich, and took part in the famous *Blaue Reiter (*)* exhibition. The following year he went to Berlin where, together with the leading Expressionists, he took part in the *Erste Herbstsalon* (First Autumn Salon) organized by Walden, who, in his magazine *Der Sturm*, had already published some curious drawings by Arp, human figures sketched in undulating lines. In 1914 he was back in Paris, where he met Max Jacob, Modigliani,

to write poetry, sometimes in German, sometimes in French. He is equally well versed in both cultures. In 1940, fleeing before the invading Germans, Arp and Sophie Taeuber took refuge in Grasse, without interrupting their poetic or plastic work. In the course of a clandestine journey to Switzerland his wife was killed in an accident in January 1943. After the Liberation several important exhibitions of his work were held in New York, where his monograph *On My Way* appeared in 1948. In 1949 and 1950 Arp himself went to the United States, where he enjoys a considerable reputation. A collection of his poems in French, *Le Siège de l'air*, was published in Paris in 1946. In 1952 Curt Valentin published his *Dreams and Projects* in New York. In 1953 two collections appeared in Germany: *Word Dreams and Black Stars* in Wiesbaden and *Hairy Hearts* in Frankfurt. In the same year Arp executed a large bronze for the university city of Caracas, which he entitled *Cloud Shepherd*. Retrospective exhibitions of his work followed in several cities until the most comprehensive took place in the Musée d'Art Moderne, at Paris in 1962. Arp is a sensitive artist, but one who seeks clarity of line and original purity of form. He likes to compare art to a fruit that has to be born of man, in the same way that other fruits

grow on trees. In fact, much of his work reflects the suppleness of the plant world without, however, any attempt at imitation or description. Arp's constant concern is to create as easily as he walks, to model as freely as he breathes. His ideal is natural simplicity linked with perfection of organic form. This very Greek love of perfection combined with lack of artifice explains the admirable unity of his work, which cannot be compared with any other of this century. In between the various currents of Dadaism, Surrealism and Abstract Art, Arp has created a kind of cross-roads that is his exclusively, and can be defined only by using his name. Whether it be poetry, collage, relief, sculpture, or torn bits of paper, Arp brings into modern life an element of simplicity and calm, always tinged with humour. His work is a kind of new Arcadia, a soothing haven in the midst of a frenzied, machine-age world.   M. S.

ART NOUVEAU *See Jugendstil.*

ATELIER GLEYRE If the name of Gleyre, a painter of Swiss origin (1808-1874), is remembered at all, it is because he opened a studio to which Monet, Bazille, Sisley and Renoir used to come in 1862. According to Renoir, who considered him an admirable person, Gleyre used to give his pupils a certain freedom. All the same, he one day asked Renoir, 'Do you paint to amuse yourself?' To which Renoir replied, 'Of course, and if it didn't amuse me, believe me, I shouldn't do it.' The teaching of the Atelier Gleyre was complementary to that of the École des Beaux Arts, which was not as important as it was soon to become. Monet has described what happened in the live model class. Each Monday, Gleyre used to correct the week's work and the very first week, Monet was the object of the following remark, which is a perfect summary of the principles of the official teaching: 'Remember, young man, when you paint a figure, you should always think of antiquity. Nature is all very well as an element in your study, but it is not interesting in itself. There's nothing like style, you know!' It is easy to imagine the effect the Swiss teacher had on the Impressionists, who did not submit to it for long – in all, about one year, just long enough to save his name from oblivion.

ARP. PAINTING ON CRUMPLED PAPER. 1942.

B

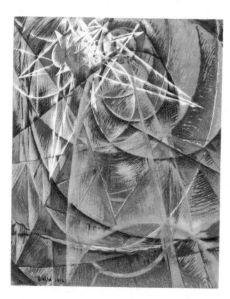

BALLA. MERCURY PASSING BEFORE THE SUN. 1914.
Private Collection, Milan.

BACON Francis (born Dublin in 1909).
English painter. His parents were
English and he is a descendant of the Elizabethan
philosopher and essayist, Francis Bacon. His
father retired from the army to train horses on a
farm near Dublin. Bacon received no formal
education, except for about a year at Dean Close
School, Cheltenham, after his parents' return to
England. He left home when he was sixteen and
went to London, where he had a variety of odd
jobs, including work in a Lyons restaurant and
as a. valet. He travelled across France and
Germany and lived for a time in Berlin, before
settling in London in the late 'twenties, where
he earned his living as a interior decorator.

Bacon is entirely self-taught. He began painting in the late 'twenties, helped in some of the

elementary technical problems by his friend,
Roy de Maistre, the Australian painter. Bacon
has always destroyed a great deal of his work
and nothing appears to survive of his early paintings. It seems from the reports of those who
knew him at the time that he experimented with
a number of styles and at one point was influenced by Souverbie and Lurçat. He eventually evolved an abstraction, similar to the
rugs he designed, but by 1932, the date of Roy
de Maistre's painting, *Francis Bacon's Studio*, he
had moved away from this and the works, stack-
ed against the studio wall, contain a disturbing
dream-like imagery. It developed into the contorted half-human, half-animal creatures of
Three Studies for Figures at the Base of a Crucifixion
(1944, Tate Gallery, London) and the incongruous imagery of *Painting 1946* (Museum of
Modern Art, New York) where a cleric under an
umbrella stands in front of a couple of butcher's
carcasses. Towards the end of the 'forties, the
violent juxtaposition of images disappeared, but
the incongruity remained to give a nightmare
irreality to ordinary subjects. He has rarely
painted directly from nature. The starting points
of his works are press photographs, often re-
cording violent events or public figures, snapped
in dramatic postures, reproductions of paintings, stills from films (the close-up of the
screaming nurse, in the Odessa steps sequence
from Eisenstein's *Battleship Potemkin* is one of his
his favourites) and Eadweard Muybridge's books
of artists' photographs. The single human
being, isolated with his pain and fear, is the
almost invariable subject of paintings, except
for a few studies of animals which express the
same emotions. The three recurrent themes of
his work are studies for the Crucifixion (all
single figures, except one), Popes (many based
on Velasquez's portrait of Pope Innocent X,
which he has only seen in reproductions) and
portraits of executives or politicians. His figures
are frequently enclosed by the lines of a cube,

which are intended according to Bacon merely as a device to focus the figure, but which create depth and suggest the vacuity beyond. Isolated in space or placed in empty rooms, their mouths opened on a soundless scream, vaporising heads and imprecise features, fluid lines of bodies that never seem supported by the floor or furniture beneath them, they are creatures of a macabre fantasy. Yet, like the press photographs and films that inspired so many of them, they are projections of an infernal darkness that is also a part of life.   B. W.

BALLA Giacomo (1871-1958). Born in Turin; died in Rome. Italian painter. Balla is Futurism's (*) most astonishing manifestation. He made himself known through academic paintings, which were thought highly of by the critics of the time. During a brief stay in Paris, he discovered Impressionism and Divisionism and developed a passion for problems of light and colour. On his return to Rome he made the acquaintance of Severini and Boccioni, and imparted the new creed to them. In 1901 he was converted to Futurism by Marinetti. Three years later his picture *Dog on a Leash*, now in the Museum of Modern Art, New York, was received with derision by a public still hostile to avant-garde tendencies. In this rather childish analysis of movement he reproduced the mechanics of walking by depicting on the canvas the successive positions taken up by a woman's legs and a little dog's paws, in the manner of a film in slow motion.

Of the five signers of the Futurist manifesto, he was the only one who did not take part in the Paris exhibition. He never really understood the meaning of Futurism until he saw Severini's *Spherical Expansion in Space*. From 1913 to 1916 he painted a whole series of pictures, among them *Mercury Passing Before the Sun*, which are reckoned among the most abstract works that Futurism has given us, although they are inspired by Nature. Balla succeeded in giving an original and finished plastic form to the sensations, the movement, and the 'states of the soul' which Futurism, at first analytical, afterwards sought to synthesize in a single and unique expression, taking its example from Cubism. If we consider not the intention but the results, it must be recognized that Balla, unwittingly perhaps, went beyond the limits of Futurism to take his place alongside the leading masters of abstract art. Unfortunately, this period of authentic invention, which found no response in a world entirely preoccupied with war at the time, was of brief duration. His pioneering work remained almost unknown for a long time, and has only recently been brought to light, thanks to a number of exhibitions and some very just writing on the subject.   S. L.

BALLETS RUSSES Serge de Diaghilev (1872-1929), that 'impresario of contemporary art in all its forms and expressions', applied his genius not only to the dance but also to music and painting. He converted the ballet, hitherto nothing more than a danced interlude confined within narrow, fixed rules, into a spectacle in which everything was united to delight the eyes, ears and mind. Under his influence ballet became a synthesis of the arts of the theatre, in which music and painting were no longer embellishments but essential elements integrated into the performance and an indispen-

PICASSO. DIAGHILEV AND SALISBURG. 1917.

BAKST. DECOR FOR 'SHEHERAZADE' . 1910.   *Musée des Arts Décoratifs, Paris.*

sable part of it. With Diaghilev the word 'décor' lost its traditional meaning. It no longer signified that artificial setting, as false as a photographer's back-cloth, the aim of which was simply to limit the spectator's range of vision. Henceforth, form and colour were made to harmonize with the movement of the dancer, and become an integral part of it. The first artistic events arranged in Paris by Diaghilev were not ballet performances but an exhibition of Russian art at the Salon d'Automne in 1906, and a performance of *Boris Godounov*, with Chaliapin in the leading part. In his youth Diaghilev was at first inclined towards music and painting. While studying Law at the University of St Petersburg he attached himself to a group of painters and became friendly with Benois. Under the editorship of Diaghilev and Benois the group started a publication called *The World of Art*, whose aim was to reform painting. The main plank in its platform was individualism, and through it Diaghilev attacked what he called sterile academicism, and made a plea for the recognition of individuality, defining art as a 'free and disinterested act taking place in the soul of the artist', its only function being pleasure, and its

only instrument beauty. Ballet struck him as an ideal medium for such reform, and one in which the quickest results could be obtained. One of the reasons for the founding of his ballet troupe was to give the new painting a platform. Thus it was Diaghilev's passion for music and painting that led him to ballet. In 1898 he had organized an exhibition of international art, where some important works by the French Impressionists were presented, and caused a considerable stir in Russia.

Having staged a dance performance in St-Petersburg in 1907, with Fokine, Nijinsky and Pavlova, which encountered considerable opposition, Diaghilev decided to take his troupe to Paris. They gave their first performance at the Théâtre du Châtelet on the 19th of May, 1909, with a programme consisting of *Le Pavillon d'Armide*, *Polovtsian Dances* from *Prince Igor*, and *Le Festin*, with décors by Alexandre Benois, Roerich and Korovine. This performance was one of the most extraordinary events of the early years of the twentieth century. The novelty of the spectacle, the lavishness and magnificence of the costumes and décors, and the quality of the dancers, aroused a feeling of utter bewilderment which soon changed to delirious enthusiasm. Nijinsky astounded the spectators with his prodigious leaps. The following year Diaghilev presented *Schéhérazade*, a fantasy of movement, colour and light. The richness of Bakst's décor, the like of which had not been seen before, filled, the audience with wonder and amazement. It seemed as though all the barbarism of the Orient was tempestuously sweeping away a theatrical tradition which was to be, from then on, nothing but a futile survival. *Schéhérazade* was followed by the *Fire Bird* (décor by Golovine, costumes by Golovine and Bakst).

Until 1914 the Ballets Russes had a Paris season every year. Among the most celebrated works presented during that period were *Le Spectre de la Rose* (1911, décor and costumes by Bakst); *Petrouchka* (1911, décor and costumes by Benois); *L'Après-midi d'un Faune* (1912, décor and costumes by Bakst), one of the most outstanding ballets of the first period, which provoked a scandal, Nijinsky's performance having stressed the erotic aspect; *The Rite of Spring* (1913, décor and costumes by Roerich). *Le Coq d'Or* (1914, décor and costumes by Gontcharova) marks the end of this period. The novelty of these productions can be gauged if we bear in mind the fact that at that time an exaggerated, almost religious, feeling for *trompe-l'œil* was current in the theatre. In real life, as on the stage, half-tones and pale colours were the mode. Dim light, a mysterious melancholy, even dust, had become in some way indispensable to any theatrical production. The works produced for the Ballets Russes by the painters with whom Diaghilev surrounded himself played a decisive role. Although they used only a few colours, these were generally extremely vivid: orange, black, pink, blue, white, emerald or Veronese green. The painter had full say in all matters affecting not only the décors but also the costumes and other accessories. For *Jeux* (music by Debussy, 1913) Léon Bakst used only three colours: against a décor of blue and green, flashes of white provided by the dancers themselves, dressed as tennis-players. In *Petrouchka* Alexander Benois depicted white-shuttered windows in a blue wall, with painted flags and banners waving in the sky; in the background a merry-go-round with wooden horses in a blaze of colour, not far from a big, yellow wall with the outline of a

staircase sketched on it. When the fantastic motley crowd invaded the stage the frame was there, ready to hold it and transform it into an ordered and harmonious whole.

The second period of the Ballets Russes began in 1917. It was marked by the creation of some forty ballets of extraordinary diversity. Until then Diaghilev had drawn primarily on Russian artists: musicians like Stravinsky and painters like Benois, Bakst, Larionov and Gontcharova. Now he began to turn to French and other foreign artists for their collaboration. Among the musicians that he enlisted, apart from his compatriots Stravinsky and Prokofiev, were Satie, Auric, Milhaud, Poulenc, Manuel de Falla and Rieti; among the painters were Picasso, Derain, Matisse, Braque, Marie Laurencin, Gris, Utrillo, Max Ernst, and Miró. The new trends in French painting were well suited to his purpose of

BENOIS. COSTUME FOR THE MOOR IN 'PETROUCHKA'. 1911.

providing something surprising, and he sensed so exactly the value of the enrichment that the painters brought to the theatre, that he made a point of reproducing their décors without any modification of his own, respecting even the tiniest details of the artist's model. He wanted from these non-specialists a new outlook that could not come from professional theatre designers, who were too tied to rules that had by then become habit.

The first ballets that marked the resumption of Diaghilev's activities in 1917 were *Contes Russes* (décor and costumes by Larionov), *Les Femmes de Bonne Humeur* (décor and costumes by Bakst), and Cocteau and Satie's *Parade* (décor and costumes by Picasso), which created another scandal. Satie's music was accompanied by the noise of sirens and typewriters. The audience was so incensed that it hissed not only at the music but also at the splendid costumes designed by Picasso. In 1919 came the *Boutique Fantasque* (décor and costumes by Derain) and the *Three-Cornered Hat* (décor and costumes by Picasso), followed in 1920 by *Pulcinella*, also designed by Picasso, and *Le Chant du Rossignol* (décor and costumes by Matisse). The year 1924 saw the creation of

Les Fâcheux by Georges Auric, with décor and costumes by Braque, who also did those of *Zéphyr et Flore* in 1926, *Les Biches* (décors and costumes by Marie Laurencin), and *La Tentation de la Bergère* (décor and costumes by Juan Gris).

Later, Diaghilev presented *Le Train Bleu*, an 'opérette dansée' by Jean Cocteau and Darius Milhaud (décor by Laurens, costumes by Chanel), *Les Matelots* by Georges Auric (décor and costumes by Pedro Pruna), *Barabau* (décor and costumes by Utrillo), *Apollon Musagète* (décor by André Bauchant, costumes by Chanel) and *Le Fils Prodigue* (décor and costumes by Rouault). Two ballets testify to Diaghilev's constant search for novelty: *Roméo et Juliette* (1926), with décor and costumes by Max Ernst and Miró, and *Le Bal* (1929), with décor and costumes by Chirico. Both of them, the latter in particular, caused minor scandals. This list would be incomplete without mention of the constructivist ballets: *La Chatte* (costumes and constructions by Pevsner and Gabo), presented in 1927, *Pas d'Acier* (costumes and constructions by Jacoulov) and *Le Renard*, previously performed in 1922 with décor and costumes by Larionov, but this time (1929) with constructivist décors by the

PICASSO. DECOR FOR 'PULCINELLA'. 1920.

same artist. From this rich and impressive list one can see to what an extent the indefatigable impresario of the Ballets Russes, by giving painters a platform worthy of their talent, helped them to overcome the indifference, sarcasm and opprobrium that still threatened their art.

The death of Diaghilev, which resulted in the dispersal of the Ballets Russes company, marked the end of an exceptionally happy and fertile period in the history of the arts. But the fact remains that the brief sojourn of this impresario of genius in the world of the theatre turned upside down and inside out all the ideas then existing about production and the use of the stage. From then on the names of such painters as Matisse, Derain, Chagall, Bérard, Miró and Dufy began to figure on the posters of ballet companies, to look no farther than that. Then, too, Diaghilev started the tradition that painters be asked to supply not only a model of the décor and the costumes for any particular ballet, but also production ideas. The painter's role was now considered a key one. Throughout the life of the Diaghilev ballet the décor maintained an exceptionally high standard. Ballet after Diaghilev has had little to show in the way of discovery, and there has been a tendency to neglect décor (and music) and develop choreography. This is particularly true of England, where the choreographer is the leader of the creative team (and sometimes the whole of it) instead of being but one of the four partners that went to make a Diaghilev ballet. The result is that England's record in scenic design is not very impressive, whereas her record in choreography and dancing is outstanding. Ballet in England, as in France, derives directly from Diaghilev, whose company included a number of English dancers. His company died with him, but through the dispersed members his inspiration was carried to all the leading countries of the world, where it dominates ballet to this day.

Ballet in the United States is also descended from the Ballets Russes, although Diaghilev was almost unknown there. A number of Russian dancers settled there as teachers, but were for a long time quite unable to implant the idea that ballet was an art form and not merely a technique. This changed only with the visits of Colonel de Basil and his troupe in 1933-1934. The seeds of a sound tradition that is today growing and developing were planted by Balanchine, who founded the American School of Ballet in 1934, and whose work is often featured by the New York City Ballet. A. L.

BALLETS SUÉDOIS The Swedish Ballet first appeared in 1920. It was founded by a wealthy patron named Rolf de Maré and Jean Borlin, dancer and choreographer. It roused fierce controversy, sometimes even caused a scandal. Each new creation was a thoroughly Parisian event and the young troupe found an invaluable friend in Jacques Hébertot, who gave them a home in the Théâtre des Champs-Élysées. The programme of their first performance, 25th October, 1920, consisted of three very different ballets: Debussy's *Jeux* (décor by Bonnard), Albeniz's *Iberia* (décor by Steinlen), and *La Nuit de la Saint-Jean*, drawn from Swedish folklore. Although somewhat disconcerted by this new ballet form, which was primarily a mimed transcription of a pictorial motif, the public gave the troupe a warm reception. The dancers were, on the whole, rather mediocre, and Jean Borlin's choreography was unimaginative. He had the good fortune, however, to find some first-rate collaborators among whom the most distinguished were, besides the members of the *Groupe des Six*, Jean Cocteau, Blaise Cendrars, Jean Hugo, Chirico and above all Fernand Léger. During the four years of their existence, the Ballets Suédois created about twenty ballets of which the most distinguished were *L'Homme et son Désir* (1921) by Claudel; *Les Mariés de la Tour Eiffel* (1921) by Cocteau, with décors by Irène Lagut, costumes and masks by Jean Hugo; *La Jarre* (1924) by Pirandello, with décors and costumes by Chirico; *Relâche* (1924) by Picabia and Erik Satie and *La Création du Monde* (1923) by Cendrars and Milhaud, with a magnificent curtain and brilliant costumes by Léger. A. L.

BATEAU-LAVOIR In the early years of the century the poet Max Jacob gave this name to a strange conglomeration of artists' studios in Montmartre, at the top of the steps leading to No. 13 Rue Ravignan. They were situated in a modestly shaded square which later took the name of the singer Émile

LAURENCIN. THE GUESTS (PICASSO, FERNANDE OLIVIER, APOLLI-
NAIRE, THE ARTIST). 1908. *Museum of Modern Art, Baltimore.*

Goudeau. It was a gloomy heap of dark and dirty premises made of beams and planks that had all the appearance of scrap. On stormy days they swayed and creaked so dangerously on their uncertain foundations that they reminded one of the washing-boats on the Seine–hence the name. There are all sorts of conjectures as to the origins of the Bateau-Lavoir. It has even been suggested that it was once a factory. In any case, the painter Maufra appears to have been its first artistic tenant, about 1890. When Van Dongen, and later Picasso, came to live there, that is to say between 1900 and 1904, the tenants included a costermonger, a washerwoman, and a restorer of old pictures, a solemn gentleman with a white beard who was introduced to the Douanier Rousseau as the Minister of Fine Arts, on the occasion of the famous banquet given for him by Picasso in 1908 in his studio. The Douanier presided over the banquet, while poems and speeches extolled him in uproarious though kindly vein. The Douanier sang some compositions of his own, and played the violin. That was the occasion when, a little intoxicated by so much unaccustomed attention, he confided to Picasso: 'Actually, you and I are the two greatest painters: I in the modern *genre*, you in the Egyptian'. The function ended with everyone

drunk, but it was certainly the most wonderful day in the life of the pathetic Douanier.

Beginning in 1904, there was a change in the social status of the tenants of the place. Little by little, writers and artists began to take it over. Among those who came to live there, at one time or another, were Pierre Mac-Orlan, Juan Gris, André Salmon, Gargallo, Max Jacob and Pierre Reverdy. It became a kind of club that had its *habitués*–artists like Matisse, Braque, Derain, Dufy, Marie Laurencin, Modigliani, Laurens, Utrillo, Lipchitz, Maria Blanchard, Metzinger, Marcoussis; poets and writers like Apollinaire, Jarry, Cocteau, Coquiot, Cremnitz, Paul Fort, Warnod, Radiguet, Gertrude Stein; actors like Dullin, Harry Baur, Gaston Modot; and dealers like Vollard, Sagot, Kahnweiler and Berthe Weill; not to mention inquisitive strangers. It was with this outstanding group that Picasso first discussed Cubism (*). Few places have been so full of historical associations as this Bateau-Lavoir and it was in the midst of this artistic and intellectual effervescence that Picasso laid the foundation of Cubism, when he finished the *Demoiselles d'Avignon* in the spring of 1907. From 1908 on, daily discussions took place, either in the studios of Picasso or Juan Gris or in the neighbouring cafés, with a passion that never abated. The new aesthetic doctrine slowly took shape around Picasso in the course of discussions that went on night and day between Braque, Derain, Gris, Marcoussis and Metzinger, joined later by Guillaume Apollinaire, Maurice Raynal and the mathematician Princet. It goes without saying that the relations between so many different kinds of temperament were not always idyllic, but the history of art certainly knew, then, some of its greatest moments. When war broke out in 1914 painters left the Bateau-Lavoir and Montmartre for more comfortable lodgings. M. R.

BAUCHANT André (1873-1958). Born at Châteaurenault, Indre-et-Loire; died at Montoire. This inspired market-gardener was like a figure out of Genesis, a veritable patriarch. He started to paint at the age of forty-six. Immediately he proved himself a prodigious portrayer of Biblical, mythological and even historical scenes. He had a certain Franciscan grace about him, and it was as a lover of flowers that he composed his hymn to Nature. His father was a gardener, and as soon as the boy was old enough to do so he helped his father with his work. He married in 1900, and visited the Exposition Universelle in Paris on his honeymoon. After the First World War he left his flower-beds and devoted himself to art. In 1921 he exhibited nine paintings at the Salon d'Automne. He attracted the notice of Le Corbusier, Ozenfant, Lipchitz and Diaghilev, for whom he painted the décor for *Apollon Musagète*. His career as a painter had begun. After trying a number of salons, Bauchant confined himself to the Salon d'Automne and that of the Surindépendants from 1929 on. In the winter of 1949 he had a big retrospective exhibition at the Galerie Charpentier, with 215 of his pictures on view.

With Bauchant our eyes seem to be present at the creation of the world. Everything vibrates in his painting: everything has the glittering purity of the first days of the world. It is wonderful to see how the painter arranges his colours on the canvas: dahlias, magnolias, narcissus spring up, the sea teems with fish, and all the birds of the air are in flight. There is abundance everywhere. Apples, pears and grapes fill the dishes, crowned by flowers. In his best work the paint is applied smooth and shining and not too thick, covering the white of the canvas without any preparation. His colours are sharp, and at the same time delicately shaded. Bauchant is more than an illustrator. He is an illuminator of life and vision who paints as a warbler sings in the hawthorn. It is good, it is tonic for us, in the midst of disputes about the spirit of form and the psychology of colours, to pause before this elderly child of grace. Here is a world glorified by a brush that revels in profusion. The sky is full of birds, the sea full of fish, and the slopes thick with trees and houses. Everything is fertile in these compositions that burst with harmonious and exciting discoveries. Here is all the joy of Nature, disturbed only by the flames and battles of history and legend. P. C.

BAUHAUS In 1919 Walter Gropius, one of the leading contemporary German architects, founded in Weimar the *Staatliches Bauhaus* (State Building House), a grouping together of the schools of fine arts and crafts. The inaugural manifesto concluded with these words: 'We seek to form a new body of craftsmen who will no longer know that pride of class that erects a high wall between artisans and artists. We must desire, devise and work together to prepare the new edifice of the future, which will harmoniously unite architecture, sculpture and painting. This edifice will be raised by the hands of millions of workmen–a crystalline emblem of the new faith in the future.' Stemming from the historical and social conditions of defeated Germany, the Bauhaus showed a desire for positive, rational reorganization, as a reaction against expressionist individualism. Its conscious ambition was to revive the lost unity of all the arts, in relation to modern architecture on the

BAUCHANT. FATHER TRUFFAUT. 1925.
Private Collection, Paris.

one hand and the concrete needs of our industrial civilization on the other. The 'Bauhaus', according to its programme, 'wishes to re-establish the harmony between the different artistic activities, between craftsmanship and artistry, and bind them all together in a new conception of building. Our final but still distant aim is one unified work of art–the *magnum opus*–where there will no longer be any distinction between monumental and decorative art.' It was at the same time a School of Fine Arts, and a School of Arts and Crafts, with a broader and more modern spirit than the old, backward-looking institutions of the same name. It was a self-contained centre of artistic instruction and culture, with tremendous breadth of scope.

The leading teachers, together with Gropius, were artists of the first rank: Lionel Feininger (from 1919 to 1933), Paul Klee (from 1920 to 1929), Oskar Schlemmer (1921 to 1929), Wassily Kandinsky (from 1922 to 1932), and Ladislaus Moholy-Nagy (from 1923 to 1928). Klee taught theory, then painting on glass and tapestry. He summed up the basic essentials of his method in his book *Pedagogical Sketchbook*, published in 1925. Kandinsky gave lessons in general theory, but concentrated more on abstract composition and monumental painting. The influence of these two great artists was tremendous at the Bauhaus but, despite their will to discipline, there was a certain contradiction between their romantic instincts and the clearly architectural and purist tendencies which dominated the group and which suited Feininger, Schlemmer and Moholy-Nagy better. In the spirit of the Bauhaus the latter two renewed the technique of working in metal and plastic materials, the arts of the theatre and the ballet, photography, typography, publicity, and so on. But it was undoubtedly Feininger, faithful to the Bauhaus from its first day to its last, who best exemplified the constructivist aesthetic doctrine in its flexibility and its purity (*vide* Feininger, Kandinsky, Klee, Moholy-Nagy, Schlemmer).

In 1929, under reactionary pressure, the Bauhaus moved to Dessau where, a victim of National Socialism, it had to close down in 1933.

Gropius, who gave up the management of the Bauhaus in 1928, and Feininger settled in the United States in 1937, where their work and influence continue. Moholy-Nagy joined them there, and tried to revive the tradition of the group, founding a New Bauhaus in Chicago. Two complete retrospective exhibitions have been held, one in New York in 1938, the other in Munich in 1950. J. LE.

BAUMEISTER Willi (1889-1955). Born and died in Stuttgart. He is the least German and, possibly, the most European of the German painters. At a time when all modern German painters are more or less strongly attached to Expressionism, which is a specifically German movement, Expressionism is almost nonexistent in Baumeister. Instead, one can notice Neo-Plasticism, Constructivism, Negro or Aztec art, speleology, prehistory and calligraphy; that is to say, universal rather than national influences. Baumeister is eminently a painter of today, and his art shows the major themes, the fleeting loves, as well as the nostalgia and secret desires of this highly complex era. The variety of his work, the sudden changes, his heaviness and his lightness, sometimes coupled together, could easily baffle the spectator; yet the work as a whole remains one of the most curious of our time by reason of its explorations in unexpected

BAUMEISTER. GOUACHE. 1923.
Private Collection.

places, and one of the most moving by reason of its varied themes, each one revealing a new style, each one bringing something surprisingly novel into the plastic arts. The logical evolution of these themes is in itself significant. After canvases offering nothing but horizontal and vertical lines, from 1920 on he began to paint his *Mauerbilder*, mural paintings, in which curved and sloping lines are again admitted. About 1928

BAZILLE. FAMILY GATHERING. 1867. *Musée du Louvre.*

he began the series entitled *Painter with His Palette*, in which undulating lines appear together with rectilinear planes, with vivid touches of colour in the palette. At the same time he developed the sports theme (*Tennis Players, Runner*) which, towards 1933, changed to a simple ideogram (*The Jumper, Homo Footballensis*).

During the war, prohibited from teaching by the Hitler regime, Baumeister began to devote himself to scientific research on colour, and became passionately absorbed in the study of prehistoric archaeology. In secret he executed a series of paintings of weird, organic forms, usually in an earth colour on a white ground, which he called *African Histories*. They are very much like the *Perforations* and *Paintings in Relief* of the same period, all of them strongly impregnated with the prehistoric and the archaic. After the war these forms were made more ordered and civilized (1946-1947), and became a kind of script, not yet deciphered, according to the painter himself. After some new detours, Baumeister then produced an astonishing series of paintings with large black surfaces, which he called *Montaru*. This was in 1953. Then, almost at once, he began a new series, in which black gave way to white, and these he named *Monturi*. Such is the bewildering– and, to some, exasperating–course of Baumeister's work. Affinities with Léger and Miró are discernible at certain

points, but only in details. His work is never systematic, never hardened into any one method, and stays supple and inventive at every moment of its evolution.   M. S.

BAZILLE Frédéric. French painter born at Montpellier, 1841, died in action at Beaune-la-Rolande during the Franco-Prussian war, 1870. Bazille came of good Protestant, bourgeois stock. He was about the same age as Monet, Renoir and Sisley, whom he met shortly after his arrival in Paris, in 1862. He went there to study medicine and painting. He soon failed in medicine, which bored him, but applied himself with passion to his art studies. He enrolled as a pupil of the Swiss painter Gleyre (*vide* Atelier Gleyre) and met in his academy the three painters who were to become his friends. Very often they–Monet in particular–would appeal to his generosity, and as he was less impecunious than they, thanks to a modest allowance he received from home, he found it quite normal to come to their aid. With Monet and Renoir he often went to paint in the open. More than either of them Bazille liked to express himself in light colours and convey the limpidity of the atmosphere. Everyone recognized his merits. Thus Impressionism, which was to manifest itself some ten years later, was unconscoiusly being prepared.

But Bazille, who had a share in its evolution and was one of its most enthusiastic and gifted exponents, and–according to his friends–one of its most devout supporters, was destined not to be there when the group made its first public appearance in 1874. War had come. Bazille had enlisted in the army and was killed. Impressionism had lost at the very outset one of its finest artists. Later on, Bazille was forgotten. But time gives things their proper perspective, and now his qualities are being rediscovered. Bazille's work provided a link between Courbet, whose work he admired at Montpellier, and that of the Impressionists, whom he foreshadowed, and shows how the aesthetic revolutions of the nineteenth century formed a logical chain with classicism in a far more direct manner than was generally believed. If he had lived to become one of the great masters of the movement, perhaps the significance of his work would have seemed less exceptional. Dramatically limited to fewer than one hundred paintings, his work shows an astonishing mastery, and impresses one with its unity and firmness of style. His most significant canvas is *Family Reunion*, which seems like a summing-up of his work as a whole. All the seriousness and fervour of Bazille's character are expressed in it, and all his favourite themes are to be found there: flowers, placid portraits, landscapes with distant horizons, trees, and the peace and quiet of family intimacy. This unaffected art is neither banal nor indifferent. It seek to attain grandeur through tranquillity; and the immobility of his figures gives the composition an amazing density which never becomes overpowering. It is difficult to know what to prefer in this work: the brilliant colouring of the still-life in the middle of the picture or the intensity of the portraits. R. C.

BEARDSLEY Aubrey Vincent (1872-1898). English illustrator; born in Brighton, died in Mentone. Musically gifted, of personal charm and a notable conversationalist, Beardsley epitomized to a greater degree than any other English artist of his time the spirit of 'that strange and decorative disease known as l'*Art Nouveau*'. In its highly-wrought and sinuously intertwined patterning, his work may be compared with that of Klimt, Toorop

and others; its dainty ornamentation with running lines of little dots, its artificiality of proportion and of sentiment are his alone. In 1883 his family settled in London and in the following year he was presented to the public as an 'infant musical phenomenon'. Four years later he obtained a post in an architect's office and later again as a clerk in an insurance company. By the age of 18 he was already becoming known for his drawings and, in 1891, on the advice of Burne-Jones and Puvis de Chavannes, he abandoned his office job to attend the Westminster School of Art. His first important commission, a two-volume edition of the *Mort d'Arthur*, came from Dent the publishers. For this he produced more than 500 drawings. At the same time he was contributing caricatures, or 'portraits-charges', of Zola, Verdi and others to the *Pall Mall Budget*. On the foundation of *The*

BEARDSLEY. ISOLDE. GOUACHE. ABOUT 1890.

Yellow Book, that short-lived publication which so completely enshrined the spirit of the English 'fin-de-siècle', he became its art editor. Subsequently he joined Arthur Symons on *The Savoy Magazine*, to which he contributed, as well as many drawings, three poems and a prose fragment. Chief among the other works he illustrated were *Salomé*, *The Rape of the Lock* and, just before his death, *Volpone*.

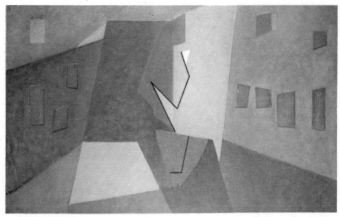

BEAUDIN. SOLITARY WINDOWS. 1950.   *Private Collection, Paris.*

He also executed posters for the Avenue Theatre and for Fisher Unwin.

Bearsley's output between 1892 and 1898 was indeed prodigious. In his feverish activity may be sensed a driving desire, conscious or unconscious, to forestall the advent of death, just as, in the capricious manner of his drawings, with their undertones of decadence and morbidity, one may sense the heated imagination of the consumptive. Three phases have been detected in his work. In the first, the influence of the Pre-Raphaelites, Burne-Jones and Puvis was pre-eminent. The second, decorative, phase in which his superb grasp of mass and scale were most clearly demonstrated, was based on Japanese influences. The third, touched by 18th century France, was more complex and suggested the beginning of what might have proved to be a new acceptance of nature.   M. M.

BEAUDIN André. French painter born at Mennecy, Seine-et-Oise, in 1895. From 1911 to 1915 Beaudin worked at the École des Arts Décoratifs. In 1921 he paid a visit to Italy. The most important factor in his formation was his meeting with Juan Gris, whose teachings he admired and understood undoubtedly better than anyone else. Like him, he considers that Cubism remains an excellent method of knowing and defining form, and organizing colour. Developing this idea to its logical conclusion, Juan Gris succeeded in humanizing to the utmost an art based on a rigid preliminary order. His followers, in their turn, resolved the problem of the apparent contradiction between construction and expression. Few solutions have the balance, elegance and solidity of that brought by Beaudin. His compositions, which were at first tormented and far too crowded with meaning, gradually grew quieter and more restrained. The canvas became the meeting-ground of opposing forces which harmonized and united. Beaudin is a painter of pure light as it appears emerging from the night. His art, in its limpidity, never escapes from honest reasoning. It is full of subtle poetry. Whether he takes as his model horses fighting, or a horse race, or the varied faces of Paris, or the flight of a bird before an open window, he liberates the universal quality, and at the same time adorns this image with the most subtle nuances of the passing moment. In a few simple lines, harmonizing with cold, vivid colours, he depicts the birth of day, or its various hours. Beaudin has illustrated the books of such poet friends of his as Paul Éluard and Francis Ponge. He has also done some important sculptural work, which, with its superimposed planes, is like a concrete representation of his painting. The dignity of this painter, his reserve, his classicism, have kept him clear of fashions and infatuations. His work has, consequently, all the more unity and lasting value.   J. LA.

BECKMANN Max. German painter; born in Leipzig in 1884, died in New York in 1950. From 1906 on Beckmann was part of the artistic life of Berlin. He remained attached to German Impressionism and also, though less openly, to the symbolism of Marées. Most of his work, however, the moving portrayal of human nature, was painted after his experiences on the battlefields from 1914 to 1918. In 1933 political persecution forced him to flee from Frankfurt, where he had been living for a long time, to Berlin and then to Amsterdam in 1936. In 1947 he left for the United States, where he died some three years later. The main subject of his work was the human figure in all the glory of its vital force, and the misery of its debasement. He was trying–to quote him–to enclose man, 'monster of such terrifying, convulsive vitality', in a structure of planes and lines. His vigorously constructed compositions of 1920 thus become nightmarish visions in which women, in all the crudity of their physique, cripples squatting on their maimed stumps, and bloated characters, jostle one another in horrible carnival masquerades. During the following years, as his memories of the war grew fainter, other human realities came to the fore: landscapes and still-lifes, portraits and nudes. These landscapes and objects also have a haunting vitality. The man in the portrait–it was his own face that Beckmann kept on scrutinizing endlessly–remains brutal and enigmatic; the woman is elemental, often brazen, sometimes tender. At this time, his increasing contact with French painters helped Beckmann to acquire a new breadth and greater simplicity of expression. A more fastidious art with freer colours and deeper blacks began in 1932 and was developed during his years of exile. The principal works of this last period were seven immense triptychs, which are stamped with a complex symbolism. In the triptychs, *Departure* (1932-1935) and *The Argonauts* (1949-1950), the enigma of our existence is expressed in allegorical language which, at times, attain an intensity and a force that actually have a physical effect on the spectator. F. M.

BÉRARD Christian (1902-1949). French painter; born and died in Paris. When he left the Lycée Janson de Sailly, he joined the Académie Ranson in 1920, where he worked under Maurice Denis and Vuillard who had a decisive influence on his development. He made friends with Léonide and Eugène Berman and in 1925 he held his first exhibition at the Galerie Pierre. The following year he was represented in a group exhibition with other painters of his own generation, the Berman brothers, Pavel Tchelitchev, Léon Zack, Hosiasson. A similarity in their styles invited a common label: neo-Romanticism and neo-Humanism were coined and finally the second caught on. Supported by the critic, Waldemar George, the aim of the movement was a return to spiritual and sentimental values as a protest against the purely aesthetic experiments of Cubism. In an attempt to restore importance to subject matter, it tried to give an image of man and the universe that would have emotive associations and would be an expression of his inner life. The movement was short-lived and broke up soon after 1930. Its members developed in different directions, except Bérard who remained faithful to its inspiration. He painted indistinct seashores and hazy landscapes from which strange figures emerged, self-contained and secretive, like his most striking portraits. During the inescapable loneliness of a stay in England, he depicted an anguished, tormented London. The great variety of his work does not succeed in concealing the persistent uneasiness of an artist whose superficial admirers nevertheless considered a capricious trifler.

Friendly first with Jean Cocteau, then with Louis Jouvet, he began a brilliant career as a theatre designer in 1930. He worked for the Ballets de Monte-Carlo (*La Septième Symphonie*, 1938), the Ballets des Champs-Élysées (*Les Forains,* 1945), the Comédie-Française (*L'Illusion Comique*, 1937; *Renaud et Armide*) as well as for Jouvet's Théâtre de l'Athénée (*La Folle de Chaillot*). There the painter found he could give free play to his sense of fantasy, his taste for improvisation and his imaginative temperament. He sometimes achieved fantastic effects by the simplest means, intensely contrived and conceived, with the light touch and fine instinct of a rare colourist. There is the same enchantment in the water-colours he did for the books of his friends: Giraudoux, Cocteau, Colette, Gide, Elsa Triolet. R.-J. M.

VAN DEN BERGHE. FLOWERS OVER
THE TOWN. 1928.

BERGHE Frits van den (1883-1939). Belgian painter; born and died at Ghent. The painter who was to become one of the leaders of Belgian Expressionism, began by painting in an impressionist manner. His style changed during the 1914-1918 war, when he was in Holland with Gustave de Smet. When he returned to his own country in 1922, he worked for some months in Ostend with Permeke, before settling at Afsné, in the River Lys region. Three years later, he returned to Ghent where he lived till his death. The painting of his Expressionist period has much in common with both Smet and Permeke, but he is less primitive and sturdier than the first, more reflective and less impetuous than the second. He did not restrain the feelings that were roused by what he saw around him; he was preoccupied by it as a moralist and the conception he had formed of men and their behaviour was projected uncompromisingly onto his painting. If, for example, he wanted to express his disgust at the sight of poverty in the midst of squandered plenty, he showed a thin, pale creature, shivering in his rags, as he passed bare-foot on a cold

night the house, where a buxom woman gently suckled a pig in the enveloping warmth. His massive forms are always closely related to the geometric composition and his colour is heavy and rather austere. His light belongs more to dreams and nightmares than to the world of common day and contrasts between light and shadow are sharp.

The fantastic element increased in Van den Berghe's art about 1927, when grotesque beings began to appear in his work, with disturbing masks that grinned derisively, and where man is in the clutches of his anxiety and erotic obsessions (already in earlier paintings women often appeared as temptresses, provocative and, at the same time, unfeeling idols). At this point his style changed too: soft, elastic bodies composed of spongey matter; drawing that lost its incisiveness; colours became lighter, more unreal and finally seemed poisonous.   J.-E. M.

BERNARD Émile (1868-1941). Born in Lille, died in Paris. The role played by Bernard was an unusual one—interesting but tragic. At the age of sixteen he already showed brilliant talent. He started work at the Cormon studio in Paris but was expelled for insubordination. He had met Toulouse-Lautrec there, and after making friends with Van Gogh and Gauguin in 1886 he decided to go and work with the latter at Pont-Aven. In collaboration with his friend Anquetin, Bernard had worked out the theory of Cloisonnism, a style which featured bold flat surfaces and vigorous colours, with black or blue contours separating the forms, like partitions (*cloisons*). In Brittany he used all his persuasive powers to advocate this theory, and succeeded to some extent in influencing Gauguin. Though this influence was later to become the cause of bitter antagonism between the two artists, Bernard's name will always be linked with this curious Pont-Aven school, which played an important part in the years around 1890. Bernard's early work was tremendously forceful. Competent and original as a painter, he also made woodcuts, sculpture, furniture and tapestries. He was also a poet and writer, with an alert mind charged with religious mysticism and predisposed to philosophical digression. Keen and unselfish in character, he was the first before 1890 to proclaim admiration for Cézanne and Redon, both of whom were partly indebted to him for their rise to fame. He was on intimate terms with Van Gogh, and here again, with utter disinterestedness, did all he could to force recognition of a genius he was practically alone in recognizing. In 1894 he visited Italy, then went to Egypt, where he stayed ten years, working out on his own a new art style inspired by the Venetian masters, for whom he had an unbounded admiration.

On his return to France in 1904 he paid a visit to Cézanne, whose pleasure at the younger painter's enthusiasm did not preclude a subsequent criticism of his work: 'He completely turns his back on all his theories; his drawing is old stuff based on a vision prompted not by a feeling for Nature but by what he has seen in museums, and even more by a philosophic turn of mind acquired through too vast a knowledge of the masters he admires'. Unfortunately, this tendency was only to increase with time.

Bernard was a tremendous worker, and found time, apart from his painting, to write articles, letters, memoirs and polemical pieces, and to give lectures and even to found and edit a review–*La Rénovation Esthétique*. Among other things, he published the extremely interesting letters he had received from Van Gogh, Gauguin, Redon and Cézanne–documents which are indispensable to an understanding of modern art.

Though his early works, full of both promise and achievement, are the only ones to attract any attention today, Bernard nevertheless holds an enviable place in art history, for he was one of the rare beings to whom the great painters of his time offered their friendship. He himself felt deeply embittered at being known only as the advocate of Cézanne, Van Gogh, Gauguin and Odilon Redon while his own later work remained permanently in the shade, from where it is unlikely ever to emerge.   J. R.

BERNARD. BRIDGE AT ASNIÈRES. ABOUT 1887.   *Private Collection.*

BERNHEIM-JEUNE Galerie. The history of this important gallery began far back in the eighteenth century with the frame and colour business, founded by Joseph Bernheim. He was succeeded by his son, Alexandre Bernheim, who was friendly with most of the artists of the Franche-Comté, most important of whom was Gustave Courbet. This friendship was to prove important, in fact, on the advice of the painter, Alexandre went to Paris in 1863, where he lived at No. 8 rue Laffitte, the centre of picture dealing at the time. It was really through Josse and Gaston Bernheim-Jeune, Alexandre's sons, that about 1900 the gallery moved first to 25 boulevard de la Madeleine, then 15 rue Richepanse, where the most brilliant period of its history began. For twenty-five years, under the direction of Félix Fénéon (*), some of the great exhibitions that made contemporary art history took place there. Notable among these were the retrospective exhibitions of Cézanne's work in 1907 and 1910 (68 oil paintings and watercolours were exhibited at this) and the Van Gogh exhibition of 1901, which was a landmark in the development of Derain and Vlaminck. The Bernheim brothers admired the Divisionists and Nabis and succeeded in making contacts with some of the leading artists at the beginning of the century: Bonnard from 1904, Vuillard from 1906 and Henri Matisse, who regularly exhibited collections of his works at the gallery between 1910 and 1926. The intelligence and experience that guided an eclectic policy made the gallery one of the artistic centres of the capital. Outstanding among the principal exhibitions were those of Cross (preface to the catalogue by Maurice Denis) and Sisley's studio in 1907; Seurat and Lautrec in 1908; Maillol in 1911; Monet (the series of *Views of Venice*), the Douanier Rousseau and the first exhibition of the Italian Futurists in 1912; Renoir and the synchromist painters, Morgan Russell and Macdonald-Wright, in 1913; Odilon Redon in 1917; Dufy in 1921. In 1924, the Galerie Bernheim-Jeune moved to the corner of the Faubourg Saint-Honoré and the avenue Matignon, where it has remained since and, after the dislocation and losses under the German occupation in the last war, it resumed its activities under the direction of Jean and Henry Dauberville.

One enterprise deserves to be specially mentioned. The gallery began issuing its own biographical and critical publications on contemporary artists, as a contribution to their documentary history. Notable among these publications were *Courbet, Manet, Van Gogh, Lautrec* by Théodore Duret, the large albums on Degas and Matisse, the writings of Gaston Bernheim de Villers, a unique collection of drawings by Seurat and the inventory of Renoir's studio by Albert André, with 800 illustrations of all the paintings left by the artist. A catalogue raisonné of the complete works of Bonnard is now in preparation.

BISSIÈRE Roger. French painter born at Villeréal in the Lot-et-Garonne in 1888. He came to Paris in 1910, and lived there for a long time in complete isolation, in so far as his art was concerned. Only in 1920 did he begin to exhibit, first at the Salon d'Automne, then at the Salon des Indépendants. He was a member of the *Esprit Nouveau (*)* group and published, in the review of that name, a series of studies on modern painting and the old masters, the result of long meditations on the problems of art. At that time Bissière was one of the painters who

were trying to humanize Cubism. His severe constructions were brightened by subtle nuances of colour. He became widely known through his many exhibitions. But far from seeking to exploit his success and develop the happy and balanced vein of his art, he broke completely with anything that threatened to become a formula. He preferred to abandon his conquests and devote himself to his still inconclusive researches into accidents of form and the secret chemistry of his materials. During a long period of inner conflict, during which he produced very little that he considered worth exhibiting, Bissière accumulated technical experience and psychological discoveries. He accepted a teaching post at the Académie Ranson *(*)*, and there found himself in contact with the best of the new generation of painters. Because he put himself on the same plane of research as they, despite difference of age and experience, he soon achieved an extraordinary influence with these painters, attracting to him the most promising and widely varied talents.

However, Bissière was then an almost forgotten painter. In 1938 he decided to retire to the country, in the Lot, where he has been living since. During the war he stopped painting altogether. Serious eye trouble gave rise to fears for his sight. Nevertheless, helped by his wife, he worked at some curious mural canvases, for which he made use of whatever he had at hand – old multicoloured materials, woollens and other fabrics – to replace the colours he did not have. These he assembled and arranged into grandiose, monumental compositions on profoundly religious themes. The result is striking, and gives an impression of extraordinary freedom. These brilliant, barbaric works, exhibited in 1947 at the Galerie Drouin, with a collection of bucolic paintings in the same spirit, immediately drew attention to a painter who could suddenly bring a completely new life to his art. Since then his work has shown a remarkable development. Not only freed from all suggestion of subject and situation, but also of the particular and accidental, it radiates joyfulness. There is no barrier between the observer and this diapered painting that is like the song of a bird, a perfumed inflorescence, a breeze-blown forest. A painting becomes a medium, a living thing, a being with a life of its own, capable of communicating directly the strong, simple virtues, which inform

BLANCHARD

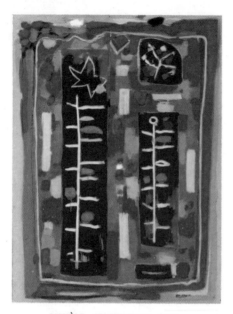

BISSIÈRE. COMPOSITION. 1952.

sense of tragedy and grandeur, a kind of coloured imagery reminiscent of popular Slav art, and finally a human presence, a restraint even in deliberate distortion, an emotional self-control which seem to come from the French side of her. To Cubism Maria Blanchard owed her method of composing a picture, of organizing the planes with a rhythm which accentuates the contour of forms. But this severity, no matter how geometrical it became, never ended in abstraction; nor did the emphasis on volume ever become mechanical: the surface is modelled with a freedom that is never brutal, the gestures of the people she depicts are full of tenderness and the impression of grandeur comes from the judicious use of plastic elements, as wells as from the sentimental expression that shines from the subject. As a painter of children she seems to have bent over their faces with a real maternal solicitude. Despite a general impression of tranquillity and contentment, very few of her canvases are free from a deep melancholy which doubtless had its origins in the sad life of the artist herself. Her palette, limited to earth colours, muted blues, olive greens, dull whites and blacks–helps to heighten this feeling. Small and hump-backed, Maria Blanchard did not sink to despair in her art, despite her physical handicap. On the contrary, her misfortune gave her a keen sense of the grandeur and tragedy of everyday life which, had it not been for her, would have been almost totally absent from the art of her time.   R. C.

it, almost without the knowledge of its creator.

The honour of the Prix National in 1952, regular exhibitions at the Galerie Jeanne Bucher, a retrospective at the Musée d'Art Moderne in Paris in 1959 and contributions to the great international exhibitions of Venice, Sao Paulo and Kassel have placed Bissière among the leading artists of the world. Unsure of himself, he is one of those men who refuse to exercise any influence or assert themselves. But his painting possesses the purity of inspiration and freshness that a work of art often only acquires after a while, when time has stripped it of its opacity and the incomprehensibility of its intentions. Behind Bissière's painting there is always a living, challenging experience.   J. LA.

BLANCHARD Maria. Born in Santander, Spain, 1881; died in Paris in 1932. Does she owe her troubled, complex art to the Spanish influence of her father and the part French, part Polish influence of her mother? These three nationalities might partly explain her painting, in which one finds the Spanish

BLAST 'Vorticism' was the only movement in Great Britain comparable in intention with Parisian Cubism (*) and Italian Futurism (*) before 1914. Wyndham Lewis (*) was the creative pivot around which Vorticism revolved, and the publication Blast, which he edited, was the group's public platform. It was a period of polemic, of artistic turmoil, of group activity and noisy manifestos. 'Putsches', Lewis has written, 'took place every month or so.' The Futurists held an uproarious exhibition at the Sackville Gallery in March 1912, and it was during this year that Lewis made his first drawings (e.g. The Centauress), which are now recognized as Vorticist. (The word was actually coined by Ezra Pound the following year.) Vorticism was abstraction, often totally non-figurative, and

30

characterized by flat, plan-like systems of arcs and angles organized radially from a particular focal point (the 'Vortex') which draws the spectator into a whirling recession. Like Cubism and Futurism, the movement was essentially anti-Impressionist; like the latter, it 'accepted the machine world . . . it sought out machine forms'. The 'political' purpose of the movement was to 'hustle the cultural Britannia' and *Blast*–or, to give it its full title, *Blast: Review of the Great English Vortex*–was to blow the cobwebs from her eyes as though with a flame-thrower. There were, in fact, only two issues, published by John Lane, The Bodley Head. The first, in a puce cover, appeared on June 20th, 1914; the second, in a white cover, the following year. The main manifesto in No. 1 was signed by R. Aldington, Arbuthnot, L. Atkinson, Gaudier-Brzeska, J. Dismorr, C. Hamilton, E. Pound, W. Roberts,

H. Sanders, E. Wadsworth, and Wyndham Lewis. Humour ('Quack ENGLISH drug for stupidity and sleepiness'), sport, and the years 1837-1900 ('curse Abysmal inexcusable middle class') were blasted; hairdressers, seafarers and ports, England were among the blessed. Reproduced were works by Gaudier-Brzeska, Epstein, Frederick, Etchells, Spencer Gore, Cuthbert Hamilton, William Roberts and Wyndham Lewis. C. R. W. Nevinson and Edward Wadsworth were among the additional names in No. 2. Between these two issues, in June 1915 at the Doré Gallery, there took place the 'First' (and last) Vorticist Exhibition. Besides the artists from the Rebel Art Centre ('the Great London Vortex') founded by Miss Lechmere and Lewis in Great Ormond Street, some half a dozen sympathisers contributed. But, as Lewis wrote nearly a quarter of a century later, 'a bigger *Blast* than mine had rather taken the wind out of my sails'. The exhibition coincided with the deaths in France of the movement's philosopher, T. E. Hulme, and its most talented sculptor, Gaudier-Brzeska. Many of its other artists subsequently employed Vorticism's precise, clearcut, sharp-edged, metallic handwriting to record aspects of the war upon which Europe was embarked, and incidentally to start the modern movement in England, but all subsequently retreated to a greater or lesser extent from Vorticism's extreme point of complete abstraction. M. M.

BLAUE REITER (Der). This name has been given to one of the most fertile artistic movements of the Germany before 1914. It was believed for a long time that the title was derived from a little picture by Kandinsky, dated 1909 and actually called 'The Blue Rider'. Now, in 1930, Kandinsky himself carefully explained in the *Kunstblatt*, how the name came to be adopted: 'Franz Marc and I chose this name as we were having coffee on the shady terrace of Sindelsdorf. Both of us liked blue, Marc for horses, I for riders. So the name came by itself.' At the beginning of the century Munich was one of the main centres of German artistic activity. When Kandinsky settled there in 1896, the Jugendstil (*) was thriving. In 1902 he opened his own school of art, and became president of the 'Phalanx' group. In 1904 all the

BLANCHARD. BOY WITH ICE CREAM.
Musée d'Art Moderne, Paris.

advanced groups of artists united, and exhibitions were arranged of works by Cézanne, Gauguin, Van Gogh and the Neo-Impressionists. In January 1909 Erbslöh, Jawlensky, Kandinsky, Kanoldt, Kubin, Gabriele Münter, Marianna von Werefkin, Schnabel and Wittenstein formed the New Artists' Federation of Munich, and held their first exhibition at the Tannhäuser Gallery from December 1909 to January 1910. Other artists joined the movement: Bechtejeff, Erma Bossi, Kogan, Sacharoff (1909), Girieud, Le Fauconnier (1910), Franz Marc, Otto Fischer (1911) and Mogilewsky (1912). In addition, Picasso, Derain, Rouault, Vlaminck, Braque and Van Dongen were invited to take part in the exhibitions.

This vast group, with no definite programme, had no aim other than to unite all the young artistic forces. To show its importance and its variety, Marc and Kandinsky took it upon themselves, in July 1911, to prepare a collective volume of aesthetic studies and numerous illustrations under the title of *Der Blaue Reiter.* But even before it appeared, in the course of the third combined exhibition (December 1911) differences of opinion arose over questions of jury, and Kandinsky, Kubin, Marc and Gabriele Münter left the Association. On the 18th of December, also at the Tannhäuser Gallery, the first exhibition of the new Blaue Reiter group was held, showing forty-three pictures by Henri Rousseau, Delaunay, Epstein, Kahler, Macke, Bloch, Schönberg, David and Wladimir Burljuk, Bloè-Nietslé, Gabriele Münter, Kandinsky, Marc and Campendonck. A second exhibition, confined to drawings and engravings (in black-and-white), 315 items altogether, took place at the Goltz Gallery three months later, in February 1912. The circle was enlarged by the inclusion of the Brücke *(*)* group of Dresden, the New Secession of Berlin, the French artists Braque, Derain, Picasso, La Fresnaye, Vlaminck, Lotiron and Véra, and the Russians Nathalie Gontcharova, Larionov and Malevitch. Paul Klee, moved by the works of Marc, Delaunay and Kan-

dinsky, joined the group and exhibited his poetic water-colours.

Tle Blaue Reiter year book gives a fairly good picture of the scope of this movement, which embraced all the arts, and its revolutionary enthusiasm. 'Traditions', said Franz Marc, 'are a fine thing, but what is really fine is to *create* a tradition, and not just live off one.' Kandinsky, prime mover and fighting theoretician, contributed an article on the problem of form, a sequel and conclusion to his basic work, *Concerning the Spiritual in Art,* which had appeared a little while before. (An English translation of this work by Michael Sadleir, under the title of *The Art of Spiritual Harmony,* was published in 1914.) Marc wrote a study of the different tendencies in modern art in Germany; David Burljuk, of tendencies in Russia. Roger Allard introduced Cubism; Erwin von Busse wrote of Delaunay. Theodor van Hartmann, Sabanjeff and Arnold Schönberg dealt with modern music. There was no formulation of any aesthetic rule, unless perhaps an aversion to academic formulas, and a faith in what Kandinsky called the 'inner necessity'. This was the simple declaration that appeared on the title-page of the inaugural catalogue: 'We do not seek to propagate any

BOCCIONI. ELASTICITY.   *Private Collection, Milan.*

32

precise or particular form: our aim is to show, through the variety of forms represented, how the inner desire of the artist expresses itself in different ways'. Expressionism (*), Cubism (*), Orphism (*) and Abstract tendencies (vide Abstract Art) were to be seen there in a generous fraternity of romantic inspiration.

The war dispersed the efforts and energy of the Blaue Reiter. Macke was killed in 1914, Franz Marc in 1916. Klee and Kandinsky went back to the Bauhaus (*) at Weimar and Dessau. A retrospective exhibition of the movement was arranged in Munich in 1949 (vide Jawlensky, Kandinsky, Klee, Macke, Marc).　　　J. LE.

BOCCIONI Umberto. Italian painter and sculptor born at Reggio in Calabria, 1882; died at Sorte, 1916. In Rome at the same time as Gino Severini, he learnt the basic rules of Divisionism (then the fashion in France) from the painter Giacomo Balla, who had just returned from Paris. He became acquainted with Marinetti at Milan in 1908 and, with Balla, Severini, Russolo and Carrà, signed the Manifesto of Futurist Painters in February 1910 and became the real theorist of the group (vide Futurism). His main preoccupation, both as painter and sculptor, was to give life to matter by translating it in terms of its movement. Above all, he struggled desperately to shake off previous influences, such as the 1900 style in particular, by which he felt poisoned. In his manifestos, and his book Futurist Sculpture and Painting (1914), he stressed the necessity of universalizing the 'impressionist moment'. 'While the Impressionists create a picture in order to render a particular moment, and subordinate the life of the picture to this moment, we synthesize all moments (time, place, form, colour-tone) and so construct a picture.' The Futurist picture was required to express, in addition, sensations and states of mind, a far cry from the objectivity of Cubism. Banishing horizontal and vertical lines, which metaphysical painting, on the contrary, glorified, Boccioni invented 'line-force'; that is, the energy with which every object reacts to light and shade, energy which creates form-force and colour-forces. His masterpiece is the canvas Elasticity, painted in 1912 after the Futurist exhibition in Paris. It is evident that if Boccioni had not seen

BOMBOIS. THE DANCER'S CURTAIN. 1926.
Private Collection, Paris.

the Cubists, he could not have painted this work, which is one of the most important of Futurist works. But *Elasticity*, the synthesis of a horse's movements in a race, nevertheless does express something more than a Cubist canvas of the same period. The same powerful lyricism is to be found in his sculptures: *Syntheses of Human Dynamism*, exhibited in 1913 with the famous *polimaterici* (sculptures composed of various elements such as iron, wood, glass, etc). Umberto Boccioni was called up when war was declared, and died in 1916, at the age of thirty-four, as the result of a fall from a horse.　　　S. L.

BOMBOIS Camille. French painter born at Venarey-les-Laumes, Côte-d'Or, in 1883. His father owned a barge, and it was on canal waters that Bombois spent his childhood. He has always retained his love for rivers and stretches of calm, moving water, and landscapes framed by the arches of a bridge. After brief

BONHOMME. SEATED NUDE. 1920.
Harry Goldschmidt Collection, Paris.

an art, an *œuvre*. Another four and a half years he spent in the trenches. Towards the end of 1922, having decided to show, at last, the results of so much labour, he put his best canvas on a chair in the street, and a few small ones on the ground around it. A passer-by, Noël Bureau, became enthusiastic and wrote the first article on him in a small review. Other buyers and admirers came forward, among them the German critic Wilhelm Uhde (*vide* this name), friend of Rousseau and Séraphine. Bombois was at last able to devote himself entirely to painting. Soon he established himself in his own house in a Paris suburb, in a studio which he filled with the landscapes of his own life. Camille Bombois's case is undoubtedly the most characteristic of the so-called naïve painters, the one that shows most clearly the path of a self-taught painter, guided from the beginning by an artistic instinct which will not be denied, which depends on no formal cultural background and is stronger than all the circumstances life puts in the way. From his youth painting has been one of the manifestation of a prodigious strength which asserts itself in

periods of schooling, the boy was sent, at the age of twelve, to Migennes, in the Yonne, as a farmhand. At sixteen he began to draw scenes from his life as a shepherd and worker in the fields. Strong and pugnacious, he loved to challenge his companions in the village square, and was soon regional champion in wrestling. He liked to pit himself against the athletes of travelling circuses. One day he left with them. The wrestlers, the female equestrians, and the country shows furnished him with new themes. Eager to see Paris, he set off on foot one day for the capital. He worked for a while as a road-mender, and then found employment as a digger in the excavations for the underground railway. Through all these vicissitudes he never stopped dreaming about painting and drawing, and, in order to be able to devote the necessary time to it, he found himself night work in a printing plant. For seven years he worked like this, snatching only a few hours' sleep, and in his free time he succeeded in elaborating a technique,

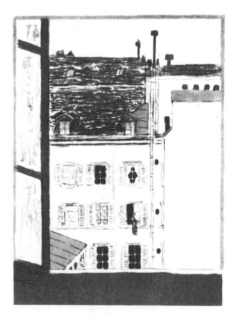

BONNARD. HOUSES ON A COURT.
LITHOGRAPH. 1895.

every sphere. When Bombois paints people he gives them extra weight and greater girth. His distortions are not dictated by plastic reasons but by his contact with the shattering realities over which he has triumphed. By his physical force Bombois has won the right to be a painter, and he has succeeded in introducing this force into his painting, using it entirely for that end. That is why, in contrast to most naïve works, his figure have weight and volume, his landscapes shape and depth. He has rediscovered the skill and distant vistas of the primitives.   J. LA.

BONHOMME Léon. French painter born in Paris in 1870, died at Saint-Denis in 1924. During the bombardment of Paris in 1870 and the Commune, Bonhomme's mother reared her infant in a cellar, while Prussian shells rained on the city. The boy who was to become the outstanding depicter of prostitute life was brought up in a working class atmosphere. He lacked Lautrec's delicacy in portraying brothel scenes, but his painting has a pathos that no other painter of the underworld has succeeded in bringing out, for he knew how to create beings addicted to debauchery, and his female animals inspire both terror and pity. His women's faces gleam like black diamonds, streaked with blood that clots in the veins. He uses remarkable blues and reds to produce these faces. He is a painter of the night and its denizens, whose sombre poetry is reminiscent of Baudelaire. Under Gustave Moreau he was a fellow-pupil of Matisse and Georges Rouault (to whom he has often been inaccurately compared). The formidable blue, black and red souvenirs that Bonhomme brings back with him from the underworld are entirely original. He died without having known the success that his work, with its exceptional violence of tone and expression, so fully deserved.   F. F.

BONNARD Pierre. French painter born at Fontenay-aux-Roses in 1867; died at Le Cannet, 1947. About 1891 Bonnard and his friends, who called themselves the Nabis (*), and whom the critics named the Symbolists or the *Revue Blanche* (*) painters, exhibited their work for the first time at the Salon des

BONNARD. BOULEVARD DES BATIGNOLLES. *Private Collection, Paris.*

Indépendants and in the small gallery of Le Barc de Boutteville. Maurice Denis was only twenty-three, Vuillard, Roussel and Bonnard were almost twenty-five, and Lautrec was three years their senior. Tall, thin, bony and withdrawn, Bonnard used to baffle people at first. He seemed to hold himself aloof from everyone and be perpetually on the defensive, even to a point of actual mistrust. Still uncertain of himself, he was first attracted by the applied arts: furniture, fans, screens, ceramics, theatre décors. In 1889 a coloured poster (*France-Champagne*) was the first to display in Paris the initials and energy of this painter, who readily accepted any kind of work that came his way. There was already a mixture of playfulness, humour and tenderness in his pictures, his first lithographs, and his sculptures. With boldness and precision, yet with the eyes of a Romantic, he explored the unknown around

BONNARD. NUDE AT THE FIREPLACE. 1917.
Musée de l'Annonciade, Saint-Tropez.

arising out of the way he deliberately forgot realities when he began to paint. But Bonnard's method of procedure was actually quite different. Suffering, like his friends Vuillard and Roussel, from the inadequacies of a technique which they were obliged to reinvent, working simultaneously on a number of different pictures, he was eternally making changes in them, sometimes for years, before he was satisfied. He would even go to retouch his canvases in the museums, much to the astonishment of the guards.

It was natural that, between the two wars, when reaction against Impressionism was so strong, Bonnard should be reproached for his lack of construction and the sketchiness of his drawing. His critics did not realize that the strength and freedom of his artistic response allowed him to carry off even the most complicated of problems. He was not a theoretician, and it was by the most contradictory–often the most paradoxical–routes that this modest explorer succeeded in fulfilling the missions he set

him, transforming everything he looked at: gardens and flower-filled rooms, the sea, the breakfast table, the boulevards, women, children, dogs. Of an extremely retiring nature, he went to live at Le Cannet, a village above Cannes, in a little villa with bare, white wooden furniture. This tiny studio, like the place he bought at Vernon in the Eure, and called 'The Trailer', testified to his profound disinterest in material comfort. He never showed his pictures in a frame to enhance their value. Water-colours, sketches, all done on any piece of paper that happened to come to hand, were carelessly tied up with string, or lay about in the dust of his studio. Humble in his methods but uncompromising in character, incapable of any concession to vanity or to money, preserving to the last his original shyness and diffidence, his ardour and his animal vitality, he always started from his own version of truth, rebelling against fashions and theories. Superficially there might be a certain similarity between some of his landscapes and still-lifes, and certain creations of the great Impressionists (particularly Claude Monet),

BONNARD. WOMAN WITH UMBRELLA
LITHOGRAPH. 1895.

himself. The constant transposition of line as well as of colour, the gift of forgetting the local tone of objects as well as the usual way of treating them, the art of considering the picture a closed universe with its own private needs–that is what is so deeply moving and charming in these miracles of invention, where fantasy becomes more true than reality. The originality and courage of this painter, who was so frail and cautious in appearance, is shown by the sense of mystery he extracts from everyday scenes. Bonnard always reminds one of a sleeper startled out of his sleep, who no longer knows either the name or the weight of things, nor even the proportions of his own room. In Bonnard, how-ever, this is never the effect of systematic or

BONNARD. BEACH AT LOW TIDE. 1932.
Musée d'Art Moderne, Paris.

deliberate confusion. Delivered from the tyrannies of perspective and lighting, Nature becomes fairylike. Where we think we should encounter a solid, there is only transparency; where we expect shade, there is only light: every assumption is foiled by a great creative vision and an intuition which reconstructs the universe. With the marvellous simplicity of a poet, he amuses himself, and wonders, and is moved by everything and nothing. Referring to one of his *Bouquets*, he confided to a critic who was interviewing him: 'The presence of the object, the motif, is disturbing to a painter. An idea being the starting-point of a picture, there is danger that he will allow himself to be influenced by the immediate, direct view of its details, if the object is there while he works. Through the sway his original idea holds over him, the painter attains the universal. If this idea fades, there remains only the motif, the object, which- overcomes the painter. From that moment he is no longer painting his own picture.' He also said: 'Defects are what gives life to a picture'.

There is no abrupt break, no inconsistency in his work, from the first small panels inspired by Paris and its suburbs–washerwomen, children, errand boys and dogs, painted on pasteboard

with a cold palette of velvety black and Watteau-like greys and whites–to the compositions of the latter part of his life: luminous bathers, fabulous animals and people, still-lifes saturated in colour, landscapes in which skies are of an opaque black, shadows of tranlucent gold, and rose-coloured meadows. Sometimes we see a glossy interior, shimmering with colour, contrasting its clarity and transparency with the resistant opaqueness of a landscape, an inert block framed by a window. There, nude bodies appear so integrated with the room that it is difficult to say whether they colour the surrounding space or take their existence from it. The pearly flesh of a thigh seems to be composed of the same substance as the furniture against which it stands out miraculously; but at the same time the back of this bathing woman, like an idol, seems part of the golden atmosphere of the room. Certain torsos, the focal point of so many reflections, seems to be marked with azure scars and pink stigmata. Some fruit baskets carry miraculous shadows. No one has ever made such a poetic fairy tale out of the most ordinary objects of our daily lives. At seventy-five, as at twenty, before woman–such a little girl in spite of the fullness of her body !–he shows the same trembling, the same love for that most mysterious of fruits, that incomprehensible and complementary being; and he feels the same sense of wonder before a dog, a child, or the sky.

Whether it be a picture, a print, a poster, an illustration, a statuette–and all these activities were complementary–Bonnard was never hampered by scene or action. He never lapsed into artificiality, sham antiquity or conventionalism if he tried to create a Greek atmosphere, and he avoided what might become outdated when he depicted the present. For he knew that the same events keep on repeating themselves under changing skies, that life will always have the same charm and the same limitations, that desire always follows the same course. No matter what he undertook, he questioned everything, re-invented the theme as well as the means of executing it, and right to the end of his life he devoted his seriousness and his experience to exploiting the most marvellous of his gifts–his youthfulness.   CL. R.-M.

BORÈS Francisco. Spanish painter born in Madrid in 1898. He began to paint at the age of seventeen in a private academy and spent long periods copying pictures in the Prado Museum. In 1922 he joined the Ultraists, a literary and artistic avant-garde group. In 1925 he exhibited for the first time: twenty canvases at the Salon of Iberian Artists. A few months later he went to Paris, where he has lived ever since. At first he was close to the young painters who made a cult of Juan Gris, and, following the latter's example, started from a plastic synthesis to find reality. But Borès by nature reacted against the rigidity of the Cubist conceptions; he refused to consider the object in itself; he feared the stagnation of forms. He broke with the geometrical spirit, and the idea of formal construction. Interested in expressing the dynamism of objects, he tried to place them in space again and evoke the surroundings that they seem to need–which led him to the practice of allusion and ellipses. Already at the time of his first exhibition at the Galerie Percier in June 1927, his work was a selection of symbols and a delicate and subtle balance of colours. From 1929 on Borès, who was interested by the Surrealist experiment, although he remained outside the movement, began to work nearer to Nature and found again a close affinity between plastic creation and the visual sensation it expressed. His scope widened. People, objects and backgrounds crowd the canvas to evoke a café terrace or a Sunday afternoon; they are sometimes treated with humour, or burlesqued, but always with the same economy of means, the same discreet detachment. They are based on reality, but they give evidence of unexpected syntheses, where imagination plays as big a role as memory. Various exhibitions in France, London and America mark this turbulent period. But very soon his work evolved

BORÈS. THE PAINTER'S TABLE. 1937.   *Private Collection, Paris.*

BOUDIN. CRI-
NOLINES ON
THE BEACH AT
TROUVILLE.
1869. *Private
Collection, Paris.*

towards a return to pure painting. More recently he has undertaken pictures which are more and more concentrated, based on the subtle play of inner relations and the skilful harmonies of minor tones. His themes are deliberately limited to simple and familiar objects, but his still-lifes, in the successive stages of their chromatic variations, are strangely alive.   J. LA.

BOUDIN Eugène. French painter born in Honfleur in 1824; died in Deauville, 1898. Two-thirds of a picture taken up with sky, the other third with the sea and a tiny fringe of sand scintillating with the fresh colours of women in crinoline–that is what the name of Boudin conjures up. But this is an unjust definition of a body of work that derives its unity from the way in which the subjects are treated, rather than from the subjects themselves. In fact, whether it be on the shores of the Channel or in Brittany or Holland, or in Brussels, Bordeaux or Venice, Boudin always looks at Nature with the tender solicitude of a lover of light. He did not paint landscapes or figures so much as the way in which they received this light, and lived on it. He did not represent volumes, but caught reflections. No more need be said to make it understood that he was one of the most obvious precursors of Impressionism (*vide* plate, page 165). Boudin, however, was not trying to do anything revolutionary when he painted those cloudy skies iridescent with an

infinite variety of greys; he exhibited very properly at the official Salon, where he won the Gold Medal in 1889, at the time of the Exposition Universelle, and the Legion of Honour in 1892. Success had come at last, to reward him for years of patient work; but, despite this official recognition that came to him so late, he thought that his young Impressionist friends (who actually owed much to him) were infinitely greater than he was. For he was as modest and quiet as his painting. However, Corot said to him 'You are the king of skies', and Courbet: 'You are a seraph; you alone know the sky'. This confirmed what Baudelaire said when he wrote that one can guess the season, the hour and the wind from Boudin's studies. This concern for exactness, which matters less to us today, was not unimportant in the eyes of artists at that time. Boudin never dreamed of denying the importance of the subject. 'Peasants', he wrote, 'hold an attraction for some painters . . . but, between ourselves, have not these bourgeois who stroll along the jetty towards the setting sun the right to be put on canvas, to be led towards the light ?' But Eugène Boudin did not deceive himself as much as might appear from that confession of faith, for he wrote elsewhere, referring to the same people: 'One feels a certain shame in painting this complete idleness. Happily, the Creator has shed a little of his splendid and warming light everywhere, and we do not reproduce the world so much as the element which envelops it.' These two quotations are contradictory, but there is one word

BOUSSINGAULT. LITHOGRAPH
FOR L.-P. FARGUE'S 'D'APRÈS PARIS'.

that figures in both: light. And that is what dominates all Boudin's work; that is how he understood the lesson of Jongkind, and proclaimed the necessity of painting in light colours and raised the curtain on Impressionism. Boudin also painted still-lifes, landscapes and even a few portraits. But he constantly came back to the seaside beneath vast expanses of sky, less to satisfy a clientèle that admired him as a 'seascape painter' than to satisfy his own longings, and doubtless because he found there what we find when we look at every one of his canvases–a sense of relaxation and peaceful expansiveness, a sweet intoxication. For in his works Nature is alive but not troubled. The vision is clear but not static, and everything is said in it without anything being affirmed brutally.   R. C.

BOUSSINGAULT Jean-Louis. French painter born in Paris in 1883; died there, 1943. He was the grandson of a famous scientist. He was a friend of Dunoyer de Segonzac, with whom he did military service in 1903, and whose studio he shared, and also of Luc-Albert Moreau at the Académie Julian. While still a young man, Boussingault, who first exhibited in 1909 at the Salon des Indépendants (*Nude Woman in a Tall Hat*), was commissioned by the couturier Paul Poiret to do a vast decoration crowded with Amazons, mannequins, swings and fabulous staircases. He was hailed as a new Constantin Guys. With a kind of suppressed humour and fundamental bluntness, this frequenter of race-courses and big bars, who had the bony features and colouring of an El Greco, took hold of the fragile present. Few pictures are as characteristic as his of the rhythms and the pleasures peculiar to the period of the Ballets Russes (*) and Poiret and the years that followed the 1914-1918 war, in which he was wounded. His faces, particularly in his lithographs and engravings, are essentially Parisian, like his landscapes (*The Champs-Élysées*), where intertwined couples and statues which seem to be made of flesh stand out clearly against the curtains of the night. Death came to the painter in the middle of his evolution. His palette, dark at first, grew richer from day to day without losing the style that characterizes all his work. The still lifes and portraits, and the decorations that he executed, particularly for the Théâtre de Chaillot in 1937, show the same sensitivity and subtlety as his drawings, his water-colours, and his illustrations for Baudelaire's *Le Spleen de Paris* and Léon-Paul Fargue's *D'Après Paris*. It is his etchings and lithographs that best demonstrate the brilliancy and sureness of his work, and make him one of the most original engravers of the twentieth century.   CL. R.-M.

BRAQUE Georges. French painter born in Argenteuil in 1882. His father was a house-painting contractor and amateur artist. Braque was eight years old when the family left the Paris region to settle in Le Havre. He became a pupil at the École des Beaux-Arts there in 1899, and also worked in his father's business. He came to Paris in 1900 and settled in Montmartre in a small, uncomfortable room, where he drew and painted with fervour. In 1902 he spent a short while in Bonnat's studio at the École

Nationale des Beaux-Arts, and then went to study at the Académie Humbert. He spent the summer of 1904 near Honfleur, returned to Paris, rented a studio–his first–and soon joined the Fauvist movement, as a result, no doubt, of his friendship with Othon Friesz, also from Havre. The two young artists travelled together to Antwerp in 1906, and to La Ciotat in 1907. He

BRAQUE. L'ESTAQUE. 1906.   *Musée d'Art Moderne, Paris.*

went three times to paint at l'Estaque near Marseilles, one of Cézanne's favourite spots. He was profoundly influenced by Cézanne in 1908. Soon moving on from Cézanne, he found himself at the head of the Cubist movement, alongside Picasso. It was in reference to Braque that Louis Vauxcelles, the art critic, made his jibe about painting in 'little cubes' in a review of the 1908 Salon d'Automne. Braque's first private exhibition took place in November of that year at Kahnweiler's, sponsored by Apollinaire. Most of the paintings were landscapes, but there was also a particularly interesting still-life; its subject, new to contemporary painting, was to be indispensable to the Cubist period, that of musical instruments. Although his stay with the Fauves was only transitory–only thirty works are known–he gave Fauvism an interesting side. Closer to Friesz, Derain and Vlaminck than to

Matisse, he disapproved, nevertheless, of their careless workmanship, their orgy of colours, and the violence of their line. With his well-balanced temperament, he did not abuse the freedom that went to the heads of most of the Fauves. Although he used the most intense colours–reds, blues, greens and orange–and placed them in little squares or sticks, like Vlaminck or Derain, he did it with more circumspection and elegance. He preferred to paint landscapes where outlines, contours and brush-strokes are used not so much to produce a brutal, decorative effect as a sense of balance and construction. He was a Fauve who thought, who worked with method, who guarded against excess; a Fauve who looked to Cézanne rather than to Van Gogh. In his Fauvism there was the impatience of the heretic. At this period he even executed several works in a single colour, which foreshadowed the monochromatic compositions of the years 1910-1911. His manner of painting soon betrayed intellectual needs foreign to his friends. At l'Estaque, in 1907, he painted landscapes strangely influenced by Cézanne, in which, along with the curves and intense colours, one can already see straight and angular lines, geometrical structures, a more subtle blending of his colours and a lighter touch. He was ushering in the Cubist movement at the time when Picasso, too, was taking a new road with his *Demoiselles d'Avignon*. Braque, however, did not disavow the conquests of Fauvism, which saved him from the austerity and dryness which Picasso has not always been able to avoid. To this influence he owes the captivating complexity and fragrant distinction of his work both then and since.

Thus we see Braque, together with Picasso, raising the insurgent flag of Cubism *(*)* in 1908, before a scandalized public–the heralds of the greatest artistic revolution since Paolo Uccello. The new aesthetic doctrine was born

BRAQUE. THE GUITARIST. 1914.
Private Collection, Paris.

work of architecture, and an object, something more real than reality itself. In this courageous enterprise Braque played a predominant role. He, more than any other Cubist–and perhaps he alone–brought to it an indomitable sense of the concrete, a keen sense of analysis, rare tonal harmonies, and a particular elegance of line–straight or curved. If Picasso showed himself particularly interested in volume, Braque knew better than anyone else how to create a plastic space and give the illusion of a new depth. On the whole, his painting of that period is distinguished by its unity, its coherence, the sobriety and, at the same time, precious beauty of its tones: blacks, greys, beiges, greens, whites, which, despite their lack of brilliance, have a mysterious vibrancy. Under these colours, ordinarily considered the most dull and lustreless, it seems as though a fire burns discreetly, slowly, without ever consuming itself. He loves precision, harmony, modulation and the subtle play of values. He detests roughness, violent contrasts, the tyranny of a method or a system, and the random outpouring of lyricism. He prefers analysis to synthesis, deduction to intuition, the decomposition of forms to their reduction or schematization. That is why Braque dominated the first phase of the movement, and it is undoubtedly to him that Cubism is indebted for its analytical character. At first he applied his research to the human figure, then to still-life. He imagined a new space; he found new forms based on a more complete, almost stereoscopic, vision of the reality around us. The combination of lines and angles, the overlapping of multiple planes, the setting out of the various parts of the object and their simultaneous projection on the surface of the picture, constitute the essential means of a method which sacrificed all previous conventions for purely plastic values. Towards 1911 Braque's art relaxed its ties with the real and became more abstract, less subject to the variable, less constructed. The subject was eliminated. It was no longer necessary to represent the object in its totality through the complex play of lines and the superimposing of planes, but to consider it as a pure sign. The works of this hermetic period suggest nothing but strictly pictorial sensations, and the picture, no longer referring to a fragment of Nature, appears as an absolute creation, a reality conceived or imagined

from the collaboration of these two opposite natures. One brought to it the intuition of the Spaniard, the concepts of the architect, the other the qualities of observation, analysis and *savoir-faire* of the French artisan.

In a manner peculiar to him in which deduction and flexible sensibility share equally, Braque has developed Cézanne's teachings with a calm coldness. He looks at Nature, dissects it and reorganizes it according to an order much less abstract than lyrical. His famous saying 'I like the rule which corrects the emotion' conveys his hostility toward excess, his innate sense of order and discipline, his taste, his prudence, his simplicity, without which Cubism might well have been a short-lived affair. Cubism made a clean sweep of all the former data of vision, and gave painting its old autonomy: a picture became a *a priori*, a reality which is sufficient in itself, and an end in itself. It was during that same year that Braque introduced, for the first time (in one of his compositions, *The Portuguese*, Kunstmuseum, Basel), an inscription in typographical letters. From then on the letters of the alphabet became a plastic element for all the Cubists. This innovation answered a need in Braque. He had already begun to feel the dangers of an art entirely cut off from the visible world, of a dialectic which might reduce painting to mere decoration. And so the letter came into his work as a reminder from the world of appearances. After the letter, the imitation wood, the imitation marble, the *trompe-l'œil* works (that Braque had seen painted as a child and had himself painted in his father's workroom) were incorporated in the picture: concrete elements opposed to the poetry of pure forms. In 1910 Braque had already painted, at the top of one of his pictures (*Violin and Jug*, Kunstmuseum, Basel) a nail which looked like a real nail and from which the picture seemed to hang. The Press openly made fun of it, but the idea was soon taken up by the other Cubists. They no longer confined themselves to imitating a nail or the grain of wood or marble; in the middle of the composition they fixed on the canvas fragments of various materials, generally paper. Thus, the technique of *papiers collés* (*) developed, initiated by Braque. The artist would fix these bits of figured or decorative paper on a sheet and

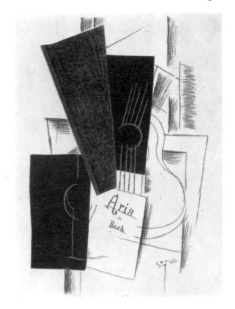

BRAQUE. ARIA DE BACH. 1914.

then trace around them, or over them, lines in pencil or ink, with touches of gouache or oil. Mixed in this way with subjectively created elements, these different substances acquired a convincing plastic and human value, entirely unexpected. Cubism now entered its synthetic period (1912-1913). The lines became less complex, the planes broadened and the small, delicate brush-strokes more flattened. The partitioning of the composition disappeared; even colour lost its austerity. Braque defined his intentions very clearly in his *papiers collés: Fruit Bowl* (1912), *Woman with Guitar* (1913), *Aria de Bach*. This form of art was carried a step farther when Braque started using, on his canvases, bits of cloth or wood, which at once lost their inert and prosaic reality, to live the same poetic life as the work of art.

BRAQUE. BOATS ON THE BEACH. 1929. *Private Collection, Paris.*

BRAQUE. STILL-LIFE. 1929.   *Private Collection.*

new space. After the more supple, more colourful, less purely intellectual *Café Bar* (1919), the *Mantelpieces* (1922-1923) and the wonderful series of *Still-lifes on a Guéridon* (1926-1930), there followed the neo-classical *Canephorae* (1923-1926), the first plaster engravings on a black background and the etchings for Hesiod's *Theogony*.

And then, towards 1930, his style changed again: line became dynamic, the arabesques more enveloping, the relief softer and (perhaps through the influence of Matisse) the palette brighter, while his drawing grew more expressive (through the influence of Picasso), notably in the *Beach* series, the *Cliffs* and the *Boats* (1928-1930) and also of the *Bathers* (1930-1931). The four or five years that followed were probably the most

Up to 1914 Braque and Picasso were inseparable. In 1911 they were seen together at Céret, in the Eastern Pyrenees, and at Sorgues, near Avignon, in 1912. When war was declared, Braque was sent to the front. He was commended for bravery. Wounded in 1915, he spent long months convalescing. When he began to paint again in 1917 he was disconcerted by the works of Picasso and his followers. From then on he was to follow the course of his own destiny. Though he still remained friendly with Picasso, he no longer worked with him. He began to turn to a relaxed and more tranquil art, closer to reality, and characterized by a less angular design and heightened colours. Though his *Guitarist* (1917) is still Cubist, his still-lifes, his landscapes and his nudes are now done in another spirit, with a freer and more supple handling. Light, so long neglected by him, claimed his attention more and more every day. His craftsmanship gained in ease and grace, though he used his talents with even stricter economy. Between 1919 and 1930 Braque seemed to be well on the way to joining the painters of the French tradition. His classicism was more evident, his audacities tempered by the well-balanced judgement which has always made us forget his virtuosity. More respectful of the subject than before, he sought to translate the freshness of his inspiration into more stable forms, set out in a

BRAQUE. IVY.

44

fertile of his career; not the most prolific, but those in which he mustered all the resources and conquests of his genius into a supremely balanced whole. Never before or since has Braque attained such harmony between inspiration and technique, intellect and sensibility, richness of expression and inner humility. He made an inventory of his acquisitions, and knew exactly where he, personally, belonged. From his Cubist past he retained principally the simultaneity of vision, the development of objects on the same plane, the inversion of space. These he used with a freedom derived from experience, giving up geometrical figures, thin colours, static constructions, and artificial disintegrations. 'I saw', he said in 1935, 'that I had taken the reflections of the world in several mirrors for the world itself.' And he applied himself to grasping the real world in all its vibrancy and fullness. He transcribed objects in cross-section and elevation; he multiplied the angles of vision; he rounded forms, displaced their axis, and modified their contours in such a way as to give the impression that they were bending. They would have tottered were it not for the mastery of the artist, who consolidated them by combining their proportions. Likewise, it was through the combination of tones that he found the most exquisite harmonies. He used the most common, the hardest and least attractive colours; yet as soon as he laid them on the canvas, white ceased to be mute, sienna was no longer dreary, black became luminous, and violet transparent. Feline elegance of line, and precision of colour; fullness, and yet lightness, of composition; knowledge that hides itself modestly behind ease of manner; an iron will that veils itself with nonchalance; boldness full of cautiousness; cold lucidity, yet so much emotion-such are the complex ingredients that consciously go into the making of a work by this man, who seems to revel in doing things the hard way.

During this period of expansion Braque produced his most concentrated and vivid still-lifes, (*Pink Cloth*, 1933; *Yellow Cloth*, 1935), his two-faced figures (*Woman with a Mandoline*, 1937, Museum of Modern Art, New York; *Duet*, 1937, Musée d'Art Moderne, Paris). He also executed limestone sculptures, fish and horses in bronze or lead, coloured reliefs in plaster . . . a happy and fertile period in which all the artist's faculties

were miraculously attuned, each contributing in equal measure to the elaboration of his work. During the war, he produced a few masterpieces, which achieved rich expression through the simplest means: *Black Fish* (1942, Musée d'Art Moderne, Paris), *Red Guéridon* (1942), *Washstand in front of the window* (1942), *Salon* (1944, Musée d'Art Moderne, Paris). Then, as his health was not good, his output lessened for some years. In 1951, he finished the *Reclining Nude*, begun in 1932, and in 1952 he completed the *Billiard Table* (Gelman collection, Mexico) which he had sketched out in 1944. Braque's style became increasingly monumental, almost as if he were afraid that refinement would turn into preciosity and a craftsman's skill into virtuosity. The group of eight *Studios* (1949-1955) was followed by the long series of *Birds* (1955-1963) where as well as a real harmony between inspiration and technique

BRAQUE. ENGRAVED PLASTER. 1948.
. *Private Collection, Paris.*

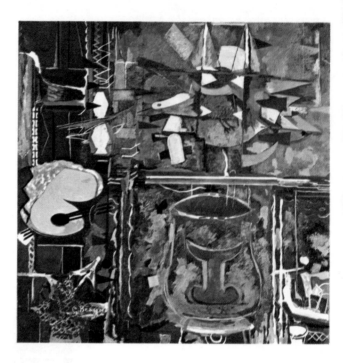

BRAQUE. STUDIO IX. 1956. *Maeght Collection, Paris.*

there is also an unexpected decorative element.

Braque, in fact, only showed a slight interest in decoration that lasted for a brief period only. In 1924, he designed the décor and costumes for Diaghilev's ballet *Les Fâcheux*. He also collaborated in two other ballets, *Salade*, which was performed in 1924 by the Soirées de Paris and the following year in *Zéphyre et Flore*, performed by the Ballets Russes. In 1948, he sculptured the tabernacle door for the church at Assy. He designed the cartoons for four tapestries on the guéridon theme. In 1952, he was commissioned to decorate the ceiling for the Henry II room at the Louvre: huge, black birds, outlined with white on a blue background on three coffered panels. The birds appear on numerous lithographs and also on two vast compositions for the Maeght foundation at Saint-Paul de Vence (1954). The same year five stained-glass windows by Braque were completed in the chapel at Varengeville, the village in Normandy where he always stays in the summer.

In all this varied work, just as in his easel painting, Braque has never for a moment betrayed the lofty consciousness that he has of his mission, expressed with such persuasive force in his *Cahiers*, written from 1917 to 1952. And in his blameless life, as well as in his exemplary work, he has never at any time lost sight of the fact that, though an artist, he is also a man.   F. E.

BRETON André. French poet born at Tinchebray, Orne, in 1896. 'To me a picture is a window that looks out on something; the question is—on what?' said Breton. Only an ardent, ascetic temperament like Breton's could organize and order a tendency capable of transcending art by denying it the power to give pleasure. Breton is primarily a poet, and once again (after Hugo, Baudelaire and Apollinaire), with Surrealism (*), the role of widening the field of knowledge has fallen to a poet. Breton began with Dada (*), that is to say, a cult of the irrational and an anarchical desire to destroy, and to undermine the conformism of logical, moral or artistic values. Out of Dada grew

Surrealism. The Surrealists' desire to reach back to the very beginning of expression and know 'what is being contrived in the depths of man's mind, unknown to him' led them, under Breton's leadership, to study dreams and to seek in the drawings of children or the art of madmen the irrefutable evidence of that primordial spontaneity which they valued above all else. But Breton did not content himself with destroying; he reconstructed. The 'Pope of Surrealism', as he has been called, required of his followers a constant fight against artistic amorality, especially against attempts that could lead them to betray, to a greater or lesser degree, the supernatural faculties he recognized in them. This uncompromising attitude could be seen when he reproached Chirico for his abdication and renunciations; when he accused Max Ernst and Miró of having collaborated with the Ballets Russes (*), or when he censured Salvador Dali for his 'deviationism' and made the famous anagram 'Avida Dollars' out of Dali's name.

The severity with which (in his writings, from *Surrealism and Painting*, 1928, to *Birth and Prospects of Surrealism*, 1941) he demanded of artists that they hew to a 'straight line' both in their work and in their way of life, shows how highly he prizes the search for an expression that will be, above all, the reflection of the most secret aspirations of the subconscious in all its primitive creative force. Unlike Dada, Breton, in his unwearying search for the supernatural, did not disdain to resort to traditional data, as when he evoked the fabulous side of certain mythologies, or the monstrous divinities of antiquity or Negro art, making use of all their spells, miracles and enchantments. Then, painters like Giovanni di Paolo, Leonardo da Vinci, Hieronymus Bosch, Blake, Goya, Fuseli and–to come closer to our own time–Redon, Chagall, Picasso and others, are considered to be, in varying degrees, precursors of Irrationalism.

In exalting the role of the subconscious, Breton proposed to the painter the discovery of an element with unsuspected resources and shock power, an element which, wherever it is given free rein, is capable of abolishing space and time. For only by starting from this abolition can one perceive, simultaneously, such contradictory notions as life and death, the past and the future, the real and the imaginary; and that, he felt, was what counted the most.   M. R.

PICASSO. PORTRAIT OF ANDRÉ BRETON.

BRIANCHON Maurice. French painter born at Fresnaye in the Sarthe in 1899. Brianchon's career has followed a straight, unswerving course without any inconsistencies: pupil at the École des Arts Décoratifs in 1915, winner of the Prix Blumenthal in 1924, teacher at the École Nationale des Beaux-Arts since 1937. There could hardly be place for daring adventures in such a life. Although he has not put forward any new theories, nor noisily associated himself with any of those elaborated in his youth, one cannot help feeling that he is complete master of himself and fully aware of what he wants to do. His work is not provocative, nor does it seek to surprise. Amidst the clamour and turbulence of the most vehement professions of faith, Brianchon plays soft music full of discreet harmonies, in which even discords lose their bite.

Sometimes he carries this discretion to extremes, with a very reduced palette: a scene in grey and green only; a landscape in grey and white, with some red and yellow to give value to the complexity of the grey or green nuances. Sometimes he does not hesitate to offer more violent contrasts: resonant reds splashed against large black surfaces. But even there he knows how to avoid extreme violence, through his refinement and astonishing sense of balance. Theatre scenes, still-lifes, portraits, compositions, form an ensemble varied in subject but with a common technique: mat painting that does not seek easy effects through the materials used or through flashy brushwork that catches the eye here and there. However, the materials and the brushwork do play an important part in Brianchon's art. No surface is completely flat or inert, no colour smooth. Everything vibrates. This art, which gives one the feeling of intimacy when a picture is hung in a room, can also adapt itself to large areas. The tapestries made from his sketches have the majesty of the great seventeenth-century wall-hangings. There, again, Brianchon is free of the fashions of our times which, in the revival of the art of tapestry, offer him a new imagery with vivid colouring, reduced to a very simple design. There is no doubt that to understand Brianchon's art well, one must bear in mind that he worked

on theatre décors in his youth. Is that where he learnt the merits of mat painting? Brianchon's art is calm, but it is also without constraint: that calm is not one of indifference; there is a human quality in even the slightest of his works.   R. C.

BRUCE Patrick Henry (1880 or 1881-1937). American painter; born in Virginia of Scottish parents. Studied with Robert Henri in New York (1902-1903), then travelled to Paris where he settled permantenly except for a few months in America just before his death in 1937. He studied with Matisse in 1908 and was associated with Delaunay's Orphist movement. Six works of this period, done apparently between 1914 and 1918, survive in the collection of the Société Anonyme *(*)* at Yale University. In them, Bruce attempts to give a feeling of structural solidity, enforced by the four sides of the canvas, to patterns of depthless planes painted brilliant, contrasting colours in a vigorous palette-knife technique. Despair at the public's estimation of them as decorated coloured surfaces caused him to cease exhibiting with the Independents. Apollinaire however seems to have caught the feeling of this work in his judgment of the 1913 Salon: 'Bruce, peintre hardi: les zones . . . (masses colorées des lumières impaires) sont presque la vivante représentation de la nature.'

Although he exhibited in the Chicago Art Institute Annual in 1905 and 1906, and in the celebrated Armory Show in New York in 1913, his work attracted little attention in America. Reviews of his first one-man show in New York in 1916 pointed out his debt to Renoir and Cézanne, saying that he 'followed his French ideal rather too closely'. Reserved and pessimistic by nature, Bruce seems to have worked in complete isolation after 1920, living with his wife and young son in the rue

BRIANCHON. THE LIBERATION. 1944.

48

de Furstenberg and supporting himself by buying antiques and re-selling them to American clients. His artistic solitude was occasionally broken by visits from his friend Henri-Pierre Roché, whose memoir of him, published in the catalogue of the Société Anonyme, contains almost all we know about his life.

Bruce's most original work dates from the decade preceding his death. Most of these canvases are abstract still-lifes of geometrical shapes derived from nature, in brilliant arbitrary colours and closely organized in a shallow, compressed space. The forms remain close to the picture-plane, but a feeling of sculptural solidity often contradicts their flatness, setting up a lively counterpoint. Their chief quality however is a feeling of almost religious austerity: the geometrical forms seem hieratic, objects of meditation. They transcend nature, and are in turn transcended by a luminous atmosphere in which formal anomalies seem on the point of dissolving into a single source of form.

In July 1933 Bruce wrote to Roché that he was moving to Versailles for his health; he had in fact been suffering for years from a grave stomach ailment. He announced that he was destroying all his paintings save 15, which he was sending to Roché: 'You are the only person in the world who likes them.' These, together with those of the Société Anonyme and some from his early Impressionist period in the collection of his widow, constitute apparently his sole surviving works.

Ignored both in his adopted country and in the land of his birth, Patrick Henry Bruce brings the lucid analytic spirit of the former to bear on the tormented metaphysics of the latter. The result is a work that is obscure, cryptic, compelling, fascinating in its very limitations, and which the public is just beginning to discover.   J. A.

BRUCE. COMPOSITION. ABOUT 1933. *Formerly in the Roché Collection, Paris.*

BRÜCKE (Die) (The Bridge). A federation of artists founded in 1905 by Fritz Bleyl and a group of pupils of the Dresden Technical School – Ernst Ludwig Kirchner, Erich Heckel and Karl Schmidt-Rottluff. One of the aims of the Brücke was to attract to itself all the revolutionary elements of the period. Thus, in 1906, Emil Nolde and the Swiss Cuno Amiet (an old friend of Gauguin at Pont-Aven), who used to exhibit at the Arnold Gallery in Dresden, were invited to join the movement. Max Pechstein and the Finn Axel Gallén joined the same year. In 1908 Van Dongen, who at the time enjoyed a prominent position in Paris, was approached, and expressed his sympathy with the cause. From 1905 on, regular exhibitions were held, and meetings took place in Kirchner's studio, a converted shop in the Berlinerstrasse, which he had adorned with frescoes, wood sculptures, and furniture made out of packing-cases, and where members worked together from the same models. The last painter to join was Otto Müller, who was admitted in 1910, a few months before the group moved to Berlin. But rifts had already begun to appear. Nolde left in 1907, Bleyl in 1909. Pechstein was expelled in 1912. The Brücke was officially dissolved in 1913 (*vide* Heckel, Müller, Kirchner, Nolde, Pechstein, Schmidt-Rottluff). This movement from which

BRUSSELMANS. THE COWS. 1929. *Private Collection, Brussels.*

that runs through all the different media: painting, sculpture and wood-engraving, posters, fabric-printing. After the transfer to Berlin of the already divided group, individual styles became more pronounced. In the nervous atmosphere of the big city, Heckel and Kirchner, the latter undoubtedly the leading figure in the Brücke, began to evolve in the direction of an expressionism intensified by sharp, broken forms and dissonant and darkened colours. On the eve of the First World War the group dispersed, each one setting out on his own artistic way.   J. LE.

one can date the beginning of modern art in Germany represented, for that country, the more or less contemporary equivalent of French Fauvism, from which it drew its main inspiration (Van Dongen was the significant link), but with an expressionist and social emphasis characteristic of the Nordic anguish. All these artists were restless creatures, over-sensitive, haunted by religious, sexual, political or moral obsessions. Dramatic landscapes and nudes, mystical and visionary compositions, scenes of the countryside, the streets, the circus, the cafés-dansants and the demi-monde were their principal themes. Their pure colours blaze in acid stridency, encompassed by rough, dry contours which show the influence of Negro art and primitive woodcuts. The first style of the Brücke group is characterized by a strong similarity of technique, made even stronger by their working together,

BRUSSELMANS Jean (1884-1953). Belgian painter; born at Brussels, died at Dilbeek. After training at the Brussels Academy, Brusselmans was attracted by Fauvism and Impressionism, before turning to that constructivist Expressionism, at the beginning of the 1920's, which was to be so characteristic of his work. Although his point of departure was always the reality around him and he never

KIRCHNER. THE PANAMA GIRLS. 1910. INDIAN INK.

ceased to refer to it, a picture was primarily for him an arrangement of forms whose regularity and severity belonged more to geometry than the world of objects. In other words, each thing—the harvester as much as the wheat sheaf, a tree in blossom, a jug or a lamp—was dominated by the overruling considerations of style and even the rays of the sun and the sea spray were surrounded by a regular outline. Obviously this severe technique did not escape the rigidity inherent in a superimposed scheme. For the same reason, it suffered from a certain dryness, all the more so that the colour, which could be as bright as a poster, added its hardness to that of the line. However, Brusselmans was not indifferent to the refinements of half-tones and could appreciate the values of brown and grey which, although they were sober, were not lacking in rarity. He did not put himself out to please: what mattered to him more than anything else was that each element of the composition should occupy its proper place in an exactly calculated work that claimed attention by its sturdiness, and consistency, its decisiveness and trenchency.   J.-E. M.

BUCHER Jeanne (1872-1946). She was an Alsatian, who had been Pitoëff's secretary in Switzerland. She went to Paris in 1920, where she opened a lending library for foreign books in the rue du Cherche-Midi, made translations and sold prints. She also got to know some artists and, on the advice of Jean Lurçat, in 1925 changed her library into a gallery for exhibiting the work of her friends. Her first show was of drawings, prints and water-colours by Gromaire, Lurçat, Pascin and Marcoussis; the second was of collages and drawings by Picasso. Later on she exhibited works by Juan Gris, Braque, Léger, Valentine Prax, Max Ernst, Klee, Kandinsky and Mondrian. Her next venture was to suggest book illustrating to some of them and the publication of their prints in book form. As a result she became the publisher of their first books by Miró, Lurçat and above all, Max Ernst (*Histoire Naturelle*, 1925; *Une Semaine de Bonté*, a collage-narrative, 1934). She gave her support to the sculptors, Lipchitz, Laurens, Arp and Pevsner. In 1927, she discovered the primitive painter, André Bauchant, and regularly exhibited his work afterwards. Finally, she contributed enthusiastically to Mme Cuttoli's work towards the revival of tapestry. In 1936, her gallery moved to 9 ter boulevard du Montparnasse where in its quiet, unassuming atmosphere, free from all prejudices, there were seen for the first time the works of Reichel, Bazaine, Vieira da Silva, Nicolas de Staël, Hajdu, Vera Pagava,

ECKMAN. PORTRAIT OF JEANNE BUCHER. 1927.

Dora Maar, Hayter and Vieillard. Until her death, Jeanne Bucher showed an unwavering courage, perception and disinterestedness.   J. LA.

C

CABARET VOLTAIRE The Dada *(*)* group, founded by the Alsatian Hans Arp, the Rumanian Tristan Tzara, and the Germans Hugo Ball and Richard Hülsenbeck, first came into the public eye when, on the 8th of February, 1916, it opened an arts club in Zurich, called the Cabaret Voltaire, with a theatre stage and an exhibition and lecture hall. On March 30th Dada inaugurated the series of entertainments that so shocked the public. In the words of the Surrealist poet Georges Hugnet: 'On the stage someone thumped keys and bottles to make music until the audience, nearly crazy, protested. Serner, instead of reciting poems, laid a bouquet at the foot of a dressmaker's dummy. A voice from beneath an énormous hat shaped like a sugar-loaf declaimed Arp's poems. Hülsenbeck bellowed his poems, while Tzara emphasized the rhythms and crescendos by banging on a bass drum.'

A slim volume entitled *Cabaret Voltaire*, to which Apollinaire, Cendrars, Marinetti, Tzara and others contributed, was published in June of that year. A performance, which degenerated into a brawl, was put on in the Kaufleute Halle in 1919, before an audience of 1,500. About that time the Dada movement developed in Berlin, Cologne, Hanover and, finally, Paris.

CAFÉ GUERBOIS Situated in Montmartre, at No. 9 Avenue de Clichy, the Café Guerbois (today the Brasserie Müller) was the meeting-place of an artistic circle which, as early as 1866 (but especially during 1868 and 1869), was frequented every Friday by Manet and the writers and art critics Zola, Duranty, Théodore Duret; the painters Bazille, Degas, Renoir, Pissarro, Monet, Sisley, Guys, Stevens; the sculptor Zacharie Astruc, the engraver Bracquemond, and the photographer Nadar. Cézanne only put in a few, brief appearances, but they drew attention to himself. At this period, Cézanne liked to behave in a rather ill-bred manner. As soon as he entered, he slipped off his jacket with a swing of his hips and hitched up his trousers, while he ostentatiously adjusted the red belt round his waist. After this, he shook hands all round, then when he reached Manet, he took of his hat and smiled, as he said in a nasal accent, 'I won't shake hands with you, Monsieur Manet, as I haven't had a wash for a week.' (John Rewald: *History of Impressionism.*)

It was at the Café Guerbois that the foundations of the Impressionist movement were laid with such enthusiasm. The discussions were mainly concerned with theoretical problems and the techniques of painting. The artists were either for or against painting in the open air. The other subject that often came up was the art of the Far East, particularly Japanese prints, which the Exposition Universelle of 1867 had given them an opportunity of studying. Inspired by the lengthy discussions that took place there, Zola enthusiastically launched his crusade for the movement, which he was soon to disavow. After the Franco-Prussian war these gatherings were resumed. Manet was always the central figure. About 1876 the group began holding its sessions at the Nouvelle Athènes *(*)*.

CAFÉ MICHELANGIOLO A Florentine café in the Via Larga that was extremely popular during the twenty years following the first Italian war of independence. From 1848/49 to 1867, it was in a way the headquarters of the most vigorous and talented among a group of painters who were searching for a new freedom of expression and manner. Until 1855, artists were to be found there like Serafino and Felice De Tivoli, Vito d'Ancona, Antonio Puccinelli and most important of all, Giovanni Fattori, the leader of the Macchiaioli group, who were to spark off the fiery discussions of the Café Michelangiolo. In fact, this became the liveliest artistic centre of the peninsula and was frequented, among others, by Vincenzo Cabianca, Odoardo Borrani, the young Diego Martelli, art-lover and enlightened critic, and finally, Signorini, the theorist of the group. The Café Michelangiolo was noted also as the meeting place for artists passing through on their way from north to south, from Milan to Naples, all involved in the most important effort to give a new life to Italian painting that the 19th century had ever known. While the group included Adriano Cecioni, Silvestro Lega and Giuseppe Abbati, other members joined it from elsewhere, Morelli and Fontanesi; some even, like Nino Costa from 1859 to 1861, or Giovanni Boldini from 1866 to 1872, came to stay in Florence. The Macchiaioli movement gained strength in the course of stormy meetings held by Morelli, Altamura and Serafino De Tivoli who brought back with them from Paris the ferment of an art of painting they had encountered at the Exposition Universelle.   D. F.

out the difficulties raised by Degas at the time of the exhibitions. When Caillebotte died, Renoir was named executor under the terms of his will. On the recommendation of the Institut de France, the Government rejected Caillebotte's donation of his collection (65 works) to the Musée du Luxembourg. As a result of protests in the Press and of the intervention of Clemenceau, the museum advisory committee finally yielded. However, they remained adamant in refusing 28 of the 65 pictures: one Manet, three Cézannes, eight Monets, two Renoirs, three Sisleys and eleven Pissarros. It is all the harder to understand this official opposition when one realizes that Caillebotte's donation included such masterpieces as *Le Moulin de la Galette* and *The Swing* by Renoir, Sisley's *Regatta Near London*, and Pissarro's *Red Roofs*. It was not until 1928 that these paintings were officially accepted by the Louvre.

CAMOIN Charles. French painter, born in Marseilles in 1879. His father, a decorator, encouraged him to paint and sent

CAILLEBOTTE Gustave (1848-1894). Born in Paris; died at Gennevilliers. He is better known as a collector than as a painter. As a former pupil of Bonnat's studio, he entered the École des Beaux-Arts in 1873. He had given up painting, when he met Monet at Argenteuil and not only became a follower of the Impressionists, but also their most important patron. Renoir painted a three-quarter length portrait of him, sitting astride a chair, in the foreground of the *Lunch of the Boating Party*. Caillebotte was represented at the second exhibition of the Impressionists in the rue Le Peletier in 1876, then at the subsequent ones in 1877, 1879, 1880 and 1882. Caillebotte's touch had a delicacy which brought him some success along with a certain amount of hostile criticism. One critic of the period accused him of having, in a picture called *Rainy weather*, depicted anything but rain; likewise, in *Pont de l'Europe*, nothing stands out but a little dog trotting along, he claimed. Through his generosity Caillebotte made many friends. He acted as buffer between the Impressionists and those around them, and he was helpful in straightening

CAMOIN. SEATED WOMAN. 1910.
Museum of Modern Art, New York.

CAMPIGLI. ON THE BALCONY. 1953.

sidered a Fauve, in so far as it became customary to include as Fauves (together with the great creators of the movement) a number of painters of the same generation who, in the early part of the century, evinced the same taste for striking colours. Their youthful enthusiasm prompted them to follow in the tracks of Matisse or Derain, but their quieter nature kept them within more restrained limits. Camoin is one of those painters for whom Fauvism was not a repudiation of Impressionism but its culmination; his sensibility places him in this tradition, rather than among the revolutionaries. Nevertheless, a certain predilection for light colours, and frequent visits to the South of France, explain his place in Fauvism (*). His nudes, interiors, and Mediterranean landscapes show that which, throughout the countless distractions of contemporary art, has managed to preserve a note of poetic freshness and a pleasing tranquillity.   R. C.

him to Paris in 1896. Camoin studied under Gustave Moreau at the École Nationale des Beaux-Arts, together with Marquet. The two of them spent a good deal of time in the Louvre, and sketched scenes from life in the streets and the music halls. From 1899 to 1902 he did military service in Arles, then Avignon, and finally Aix-en-Provence, where he visited Cézanne, with whom he kept up a correspondence from then onwards. After exhibiting at the Salon des Indépendants in 1903, he was a regular exhibitor at the Salon d'Automne until 1908. He took part in the Salon d'Automne of 1905, the year Fauvism was officially born. In 1912-1913 he went with Matisse and Marquet to Morocco. During the war, when he was serving in the camouflage section, he met Renoir, who made a deep impression on him. Renoir's influence, together with that of Bonnard, is noticeable in his post-war work. Camoin can be con-

CAMPIGLI Massimo. Italian painter, born in Florence in 1895. Campigli began to paint in Paris, working according to the plastic laws set out in Ozenfant and Jeanneret's review, L'Esprit Nouveau (*). 'In the manner of a bee,' writes Jean Paulhan, 'Campigli begins by enclosing his characters in their cells'. Certainly like a bee, also like the Cubists, although his work is more reminiscent of Etruscan and Roman painting than of Braque and Picasso. He is not insensitive, either, to metaphysical painting, and his figures have 'faces of a magical truth, as exact as anthropometric record cards, as impersonal as death masks'. His busts shaped like money-boxes, and his women shaped like amphoras, have a universal quality, as old as the earth. They are entirely different from Chirico's mannequins, whose oval skulls are full of tragic humanity, whereas Campigli's heads are empty. His women, however, have the same pleasing grace as Seurat's promenaders; their waists are extremely slender, and their arms stand out from their sides like the handles of a vase. He borrowed the anatomy of his figures from the world of childhood. At a time when the painters of his generation are constanly in search of youth, or the illusion of it, Campigli stays faithful to himself, to the poetic, painted world of his dreams.   S. L.

CARRÀ Carlo. Italian painter, born at Quargnento in 1881. Carrà was one of the signers of the Futurist Manifesto (*vide* Futurism). He borrowed from Cubism its structure and monochromes, and tried, at the same time, to insert into its austere construction the crowd movements so dear to Futurist dynamism. He introduced whole words into his compositions. (The Cubists were content with a few letters.) The words do no merely have a lyrical quality; they exercise a sort of plastic magic. When, in 1916, Carrà made the acquaintance of Giorgio de Chirico, the originator of Metaphysical Painting *(*)*, he believed he had at last found his true vocation: to rediscover the magic of painting by means of the representation of the most simple objects. He wrote: 'It is the most ordinary objects that fill the soul with grace. The artist who scorns them inevitably becomes absurd. On the artistic plane, as well as on the intellectual, his work is of no account. Ordinary things have that simplicity which is the very secret of the most sumptuous art'. When reproached for ceasing to paint that feverish life that he had exalted in his Futurist days, he replied: 'I don't see why mannequins, copper fishes, or maps, should be less worthy of study than the apples, bottles and pipes to which Cézanne owes his fame'. But for Carrà, as for Chirico, it was not just a matter of substituting dressmaker's dummies for Cézanne's apples. What they set out to find again was the magic that emanates from old paintings, and which the open-air painting of the Impressionists had dispelled. This magic was one of the effects of perspective, and the relationship between full and empty spaces in the composition of a picture. It is therefore through perspective that Chirico and Carrà wanted to renew the miracle of the Renaissance artists. Carrà's paintings of this period, less known abroad than Chirico's, are often more elaborate than those of his friend, to whom he obviously owes his first ideas. Carrà rejected everything that Chirico took from the French and the Germans. He took his inspiration from Giotto, but not without a certain heaviness; from this point of view he is much more German than Chirico. Despite his heaviness, Carrà rediscovered the beauty of paint, the density of tones, and the preciousness of colour. He, in his turn, set Chirico an example with his enchanted interiors and his enigmatic irony. A member of the Novecento *(*)* from its foundation in 1922, he was its leading figure and towered above all the other artists. Although his art lost something of its edge there still remained in his seascapes that magical feeling which, without repudiating the play of colour and light, without disregarding the problems of form and space, tries to reconcile the past and the present, the powerful art of Giotto and the living art of Cézanne. S. L.

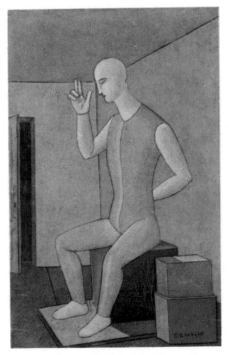

CARRÀ. HERMAPHRODITE IDOL. 1917.
Private Collection, Milan.

CARRÉ Louis (born in 1897 at Vitré, Ille-et-Vilaine). After studying law at the Faculty of Jurisprudence at Rennes University, he became an expert in antique goldsmith's work and published authoritative works on French goldsmiths' hall-marks. But he soon widened the field of his activities and in 1933 organised in Paris an exhibition of archaic sculptures from the Acropolis Museum, which was epoch-making in the simplicity and rightness of its presentation; each statue was exhibited in carefully studied lighting against light backgrounds in different colours. It was a completely fresh approach and he organised exhibitions of primitive art in the same spirit, notably the Benin bronzes, the paintings of Georges de la Tour, which were still almost unknown, and of the Le Nain brothers and Toulouse-Lautrec. In 1938, with Roland Balay, he opened a gallery, which exhibited the works of Juan Gris, Paul Klee and Le Corbusier. In spite of difficulties during the war, he gave his support to the leading French artists: Maillol, Vuillard, Matisse, Rouault, Laurens, Picasso. He made friends with a number of them, especially Bonnard, Léger, Dufy, Villon and Gromaire. He was full of enthusiasm, loved his work and had formed a high idea of it. He took a passionate interest in making the reputations of unknown artists and he organised large, meticulously prepared exhibitions for them. Among these were Kupka, Robert Delaunay and, in particular, Jacques Villon, who at last received

after the war the international reputation that was his due. At the same time, he welcomed young painters and exhibited, in his Paris gallery and the one he had opened in New York, works by De Staël, Bazaine, Estève, Lapicque, Borès, Lanskoy, Glarner, Soulages and Hartung. Notable among the sculptors were Calder, whose work he exhibited in 1946, and Gilioli.

For Louis Carré, the presentation of an exhibition is all important. He considers that the first duty towards a work of art is to enable it to be seen in the most favourable conditions possible and too much trouble can never be spent on it. His way of hanging an exhibition has a precision and perfect balance that are unequaled in bringing out the best in a painting. These exhibitions are always accompanied by publications produced, as he is always most anxious they should be, with the help of the artists themselves and the best art critics. He has been responsible for the publication of a very fine album of unpublished drawings by Dufy (1944), the first work on Jacques Villon, signed by Paul Éluard and René Jean (1948) and some interesting collections of statements by Léger and Gromaire. There is a style about all Louis Carré's activities and his way of life, even to the setting he has created for them, the harmonious modern house he had built for himself at Bazoches, near Montfort-l'Amaury, by the Finnish architect, Aalto.   J. LA.

CARRIÈRE Eugène. French painter, born at Gournay in 1849, died in Paris in 1906. Although his outspoken nature, his love of freedom and, above all, his respect for the freedom of others, made Carrière take part in the most daring enterprises and, consequently, very often associate with the most modern artists, his own art is very far from their aesthetic theories and their technical processes. His deep-rooted sense of humanity saved him from dry academism, but he was not a revolutionary by nature, nor had he any desire to shock. That is what kept him out of the various schools of painting that followed one another in quick succession at the end of the nineteenth century. One might better define him, or at least get some insight into the nature of his art, by speaking not of the painters that he knew but of the

CARRIÈRE. PORTRAIT OF VERLAINE. LITHOGRAPH.

writers who were his friends: Verlaine, Alphonse Daudet, Mallarmé, Anatole France, Edmond de Goncourt. Eugène Carrière did not believe in 'art for art's sake', he did not paint just for the pleasure of painting, but to express a sentiment, not an aesthetic sensation. Thus, what characterizes him is an intense feeling of humanity. Two themes dominates all his work, the two themes in which he could most completely show the imprint of the human soul: his pictures of motherhood and his portraits. The former show forth all the gestures of tenderness, the attitudes of hope and anxiety, the moving embraces. He did the same picture over and over again, but it was always new, because the emotion with which he contemplated his models was never exhausted. In his portraits each detail was a reflection of the artist's thought. Emerging out of the penumbra, the faces are blurred, softly receiving the light which models their features in grey monochrome. But Carrière was less interested in representing the actual features than in describing the sentiments they aroused. His drawing is as supple and sensitive as writing, and his painting has all the delicacy of a poem. He always honestly admitted that his painting had literary affinities. Perhaps that is why he had little difficulty in getting accepted, and admired. Perhaps, too, the apparent moderation of his increasingly monochromatic art served to inspire confidence. There was no reason to fear that he might spring a revolt or some other unpleasant surprise. However, on closer examination, it can be seen that Carrière had a broad manner, even very free and somewhat spirited. That was his discreet way of showing his passion. To get a real idea of its extent, one must bear in mind his last words, at the close of an exemplary life: 'Love one another with frenzy'. Carrière gave us one of today's rare examples of art put to the service of an idea, a cause. He made a point of depicting humanity in its moments of family intimacy. His dreamlike painting is, after all, the reflection of a realistic conception of life, of which his picture is always profoundly true.   R. C.

CASORATI Felice (1886-1963). Italian painter; born in Novara, died in Turin. After studying music and qualifying in law at Padua (1907), he made his first

CASORATI. STILL-LIFE.

public appearance as a painter the same year with a portrait of his sister, exhibited at the VII Venice Biennale. Versatile and highly gifted, he went his own way, working methodically at a solution of the problems of composition and colour along strictly classical lines. During the First World War, he discovered Klimt and Kandinsky whose lessons he assimilated in his own personal manner, less interested in the revolutionary element in their work than in the freedom of their rhythmic structure and harmonies. Towards the end of 1918, he settled in Turin, where he still lives and works today. There he created quite a 'school' whose severe principles exercised a profound influence on a later generation, although they rebelled against it. In his long exploration of the potentialities of painting, pursued apart from the intrigues and turmoil of theorists, Felice Casorati has acquired an unusual technical mastery and produced a skilful, soundly constructed art. His analysis of pictorial space derives from a pure Italian tradition and from a classicism that has gained new life from abstraction. It is

CASSATT. LA TOILETTE. 1891. PRINT.

concerned in turn with the refinement of form or, on a higher plane, with the metaphysical apprehension of the object.   D. F.

CASSATT Mary. Born in Pittsburg, Pennsylvania, in 1845; died in France in 1927. Predisposed in favour of French culture by her family background, Mary Cassatt spent the first few years of her childhood in Paris, then went to America. A short while before the Franco-Prussian war of 1870 she came back to Paris, no doubt in the hope of learning to paint under conditions more interesting than those then existing at the Pennsylvania Academy of the Fine Arts. Not content with studying at the Atelier Chaplin, she went to look for inspiration in the museums in Italy (where she made a study of Correggio), in Spain, and in Antwerp (where she developed an admiration for Rubens). It was in Antwerp, a few years later, that she met Degas, who suggested that she should exhibit with the Impressionists, and also gave her guidance and advice. It is wrong to conclude from this that Mary Cassatt was either a

pupil or an emulator of Degas. Although Degas, confirmed woman-hater that he was, relented a little towards her, and although she admired him greatly, and a certain kinship to Degas is discernible in the style and composition of her early work, Mary Cassatt mostly maintained a complete independence of technique and inspiration. A more obvious influence is that of the Japanese artists, particularly in her drawings and drypoints. Her precise, simplified drawing has all the skill and the impressive quality of the work of the Japanese masters. Mary Cassatt had an admirable understanding of their technique and the effects that could be obtained with it. The works she created under this influence were not pastiches but creations carefully thought out according to a definite technique. However, her art never froze into system, and she managed to escape all formulas. It is dominated far more by feeling than by technique, and the majority of her works are motherhood scenes of the most tender affection. She gave this hackneyed mother-and-child theme a new freshness by stripping it of all artifice and literature. Just as the great Impressionists show us landscapes in their everyday lighting, Mary Cassatt shows us mother and child in all their simplicity, when their gestures are not made for the purpose of being seen and reproduced. By participating in this rehabilitation of the acts of everyday life, which was a characteristic of the Impressionist movement in which she felt so much at home, Mary Cassatt made a very personal and important contributions to the body of Impressionist creation. Nearly all her energies in the last years of her life were largely absorbed in defending and making known and loved in the United States the paintings of her fellow Impressionists. She bought several paintings for herself and her family (her brother was director of the Pennsylvania railways) and persuaded her relatives to buy them too, the Stillmans, Whittemores, and particularly the Havemeyers, most of whose fine collection is now in the Metropolitan Museum of New York.   R. C.

CASSIRER (Bruno and Paul). As picture-dealers and art publishers, the Cassirer brothers played quite an important part in introducing Impressionism and neo-Impressionism in Germany. Their Berlin gallery was the first to be exclusively concerned with modern art and after 1900 they exhibited the work of several French painters. In 1903, Paul Cassirer and the art critic, Karl Scheffler, founded the review, *Kunst und Künstler* (Art and Artists) which took up the defence of the new painting. Paul was also a member of the committee of the fourth Sonderbund exhibition at Düsseldorf in 1912 and was elected president of the Berlin Secession the following year. Although their gallery also held in 1908 the first large exhibition of Matisse's works, it soon appeared rather unadventurous from the fact that it remained very largely concerned with the Impressionist masters.

CERCLE ET CARRÉ This Parisian movement originated in the meeting between the Uruguayan painter, Torrès-Garcia, and Michel Seuphor in January 1929. They thought they should try to form an international association of constructivist artists, painters, sculptors and architects, against the rising tide of Surrealism. The group had about twenty-four members whose monthly contributions soon enabled the publication of a periodical, *Cercle et Carré*, and the organisation of an international exhibition of abstract art with Constructivist tendencies. It was held in April 1930 at Galerie 23, rue La Boëtie. Mondrian, Kandinsky, Léger, Baumeister, Arp, Werkman, Sophie Taeuber, Marcelle Cahn, Schwitters, Ozenfant, Prampolini, Stazewski, Vordemberge-Gildewart, Torrès-Garcia, Gorin, Charchoune, Pevsner, Vantongerloo, Le Corbusier and many others took part. In the surroundings of the exhibition, an evening of 'verbal music' (phonetic poetry) was organised by Seuphor. The review which ran for three numbers, contained theoretical articles, notably *Realist and Superrealist Art* by Mondrian, and *In Defence of Architecture* by Seuphor, besides written statements and illustrations of their works by leading members of the group. A serious illness of Seuphor's brought the activity of the group to a sudden end. A year later, all the elements drawn together by Torrès-Garcia and Seuphor were to be found again in the Abstraction-Création *(*)* group.

CÉZANNE. THE NEGRO SCIPIO. 1866-1868. *São Paulo Museum*.

CÉZANNE Paul. French painter, born in Aix-en-Provence in 1839; died there in 1906. Cézanne came of a long line of artisans and small tradesmen of Piedmontese origin. He went to a primary school, then to a religious school, and was later sent to college by his father, who, by that time, had left his hatter's shop to become manager of a bank. Cézanne left college in 1858, with a sound education, his religious faith intact, and a close friendship with his fellow-student Émile Zola. Having done well at his studies, he entered a law school, in compliance with his father's wishes. This did not prevent him from carrying on with his drawing classes, which he had been attending since 1856. Hard-working, conscientious, but sensitive and exuberant, he was not a very gifted pupil. He was short, thick-set, very dark, with an unprepossessing face, obstinate forehead, an aquiline nose, a keen glance and quick gestures. He enjoyed swimming, hunting, and long rambles through the countryside. He was fond of music, and played the cornet in the students' orchestra, in which Zola was a flautist. In 1859 his father acquired a seventeenth-century country house,

CÉZANNE. THE HOUSE OF THE HANGED MAN. 1873. *Musée du Louvre.*

the Jas de Bouffan, on the outskirts of Aix, and spent the summers there with his wife, his son and his two daughters. There Cézanne set up his first studio. He had already made up his mind about his future: despite his father, he was going to be a painter. His father, who intended that Paul should succeed him as head of the bank, admonished him in the following words: 'Think about your future, my boy. With genius you die; it is only with money that you live'–a 'bourgeois' conception of life that irritated Paul considerably, but in which he nevertheless acquiesced. He went on painting secretly, giving his legal studies only moderate attention. Émile Zola, who had settled in Paris, urged him to come and join him there. Cézanne's father opposed the idea. But in April 1861, realizing his son's unfitness for business, and under pressure from his wife and eldest daughter, Marie, he finally gave his reluctant consent. And so Paul Cézanne went to Paris. He took lodgings in the Rue des Feuillantines, studied at the Académie Suisse (*), became friends with Pissarro and, later, Guillaumin, and resumed his former intimacy with Zola (*). He was just about able to exist on the 125 francs which his father sent him each month. The tumult of Paris was not at all to his taste,

and he was far from satisfied with the first works he produced. Eventually he was refused admission to the École Nationale des Beaux-Arts, on the ground that he had 'the temperament of a colourist' and painted 'with excess'. Discouraged, he went back to Aix, to the great delight of his father, who offered him a position in the bank. But Paul, far from sacrificing the brush to finance, went on sketching and painting with ardour. He painted four large panels, *The Four Seasons*, on the walls of the Jas de Bouffan (today in the Petit Palais Museum in Paris), parodies that he irreverently signed 'Ingres' just for the fun of it. He painted a portrait of himself and one of his father. In November 1862 he went back to Paris. He associated with the Impressionists without, however, being carried away by them. He made the acquaintance of Monet, Degas and Renoir, but the vorks he admired most were those of Delacroix and Courbet. Cézanne's own work at that period was very romantic. It pleased him no more than it did anyone else. In fact, nothing pleased him, and he was ill at ease everywhere, breaking off a budding friendship, avoiding a famous artist whose work he liked, changing his lodgings constantly, leaving Paris in disgust and going back to it out of curiosity, retiring to Aix and then leaving it soon after. When his work was rejected by the Salon in 1866, he left for Aix, disgusted. He was back in Paris in the winter of 1867-68, in new lodgings, naturally. He put in brief appearances at the Café Guerbois (*), where he met Renoir, Manet, Stevens, Zola, Cladel, Duranty. . . He never felt comfortable there. His *Grog au Vin* or *Afternoon in Naples* was rejected by the Salon in 1867. That same year he met Marie-Hortense Fiquet, a young model, whom he took with him to l'Estaque when he went there to hide in 1870, to escape the draft.

After the war, he settled in Paris. He was thirty-two years old. Until then he had indulged in a violent, sombre, and theatrical kind of painting, in which his sexual obsessions and distraught dreams figured. He painted landscapes, still-lifes and portraits–of Zola, Achille Emperaire, and Valabrègue–but also death scenes and orgies, weird, fantastic scenes with a thick impasto brutally applied, where sickly blues and livid whites slash the gloomy backgrounds. Tintoretto, Magnasco, Crespi, Goya, Daumier, all the great baroque painters, seem to preside over these lyrical effusions, these convulsed forms, these trite colours, over all the works that gave satisfaction to his turbulent nature. *The Abduction*, and *The Temptation of Saint Anthony*, *The Negro Scipio*, *The Magdalene*, or *Grief* and *The Modern Olympia* (the latter two in the Louvre)–these were the works that Manet condemned when he said to the Impressionist Guillemet: 'How can you like messy painting?'

In 1872 Hortense Fiquet bore him a son, to whom he gave his own name, Paul. He settled at Auvers-sur-Oise, where he lived for two years in the company of Pissarro and Guillaumin, who gave him advice and influenced his work. He abandoned his wild, lusty manner, his palette became lighter, his strokes gained in precision, and he employed simpler methods. *The House of the Hanged Man* (Louvre) and *Doctor Gachet's House* (Kunstmuseum, Basel) mark this renewal, brought about as much by a prolonged contact with Impressionism as by a personal need of order. Cézanne made the acquaintance of Van Gogh. Doctor Gachet (*) gave him encouragement, and some astute connoisseurs bought a few of his canvases. On his return to Paris he found the Impressionists once more, at the Nouvelle Athènes (*). He exhibited with them, although not very welcome, at the first Impressionist Salon at Nadar's in 1874, which was greeted with sarcasm and jibes. Cézanne naturally came in for his share, even more than his share. On the other hand, Count Doria bought his *House of the Hanged Man*, and a Government official, Victor Chocquet (*) became his admirer, his confidant, and, on several occasions, his model. From 1874 to 1877, in a studio that he rented at 120 Rue de Vaugirard in Paris, he enjoyed a period of tranquillity and productivity. The *Pool at the Jas de Bouffan* (1874) still belongs to his Impressionist style, but his *The Sea at l'Estaque*, painted during the summer of 1876, is constructed according to the principles of a new classicism, an evolution confirmed by the opulent still-lifes which followed, the various portraits of Madame Cézanne, and a series of *Bathers*. He gave up small brush-strokes and the division of tones, and painted in masses. He accentuated volumes, and sought unity of composition. His work gained in thought, firmness, and plastic intentity. But he was growing bitter, and found it increasingly difficult to tolerate the company of men and wordly vanities. Truly generous and kind by nature, everything–no matter how trifling–irritated him, and he suffered very much when his ingenuous pride came up against an obstacle. That is why the annual rejection of his canvases by the Salon, the raillery of the students at the École des Beaux-Arts, and the persistent incomprehension of the public, intensified his hypochondria. He sent sixteen canvases to the 1877 Impressionist exhibition. The reception was as hostile as in 1874. His father, who had never approved of his artistic career, nor of his liaison with Hortense Fiquet, reduced the already meagre allow-

CÉZANNE. SELF-PORTRAIT. 1880.
Kuntsmuseum, Bern.

ance that he made him. That made Cézanne tend to isolate himself even more, to withdraw into himself. He exasperated his mistress with his unreasonableness, his friends with his caprices. Nevertheless, many of them remained devoted, among them the painter Guillemet, who succeeded in having one of Cézanne's pictures exhibited at the Salon of 1882. From then on he lived in Provence, leaving it only for essential trips to Paris, or when he was invited to La Roche-

himself exclusively to painting. He had broken with Zola in 1886. His wife and his sister kept house for him and supervised his son's education. In 1888 he went to live in Paris for a year. He frequently met Van Gogh, Gauguin and Émile Bernard, although he did not care for them very much. He retired finally to Aix, leaving it only for brief trips to Fontainebleau, Giverny, Vichy or Paris. His irascibility increased with the first onset of diabetes. Without any

CÉZANNE. MOUNT SAINTE-VICTOIRE. 1885-1887.
Courtauld Collection, London.

Guyon by Renoir in 1885, or to Hattenville in 1886 by Victor Chocquet.

In 1883 he made the acquaintance of Monticelli. The two artists wandered through Provence on foot, haversacks on their backs, painting side by side, preferably in Gardanne, a little village in the South of France quite close to Aix-en-Provence. In 1886, in the presence of his parents, he married Hortense Fiquet, although he no longer had any feeling for her. In October of the same year his father died, at the age of almost ninety, leaving him two million francs, a considerable fortune in those days. Feeling only repugnance for human society, Cézanne devoted

serious reason, he quarrelled with several of his friends, particularly Claude Monet. He painted feverishly, but continued to have doubts about his work. Yet there never was so well-balanced and serene a period in his career as the ten years between 1885 and 1895. That was when he painted *The Chest of Drawers* (Munich), *The Blue Vase* (Louvre) and *Mardi Gras* (Moscow), the *Portrait of Gustave Geffroy*, the three versions of the *Boy in the Red Waistcoat* and the series of portraits of Madame Cézanne. He also painted five versions of the *Cardplayers*, the last of which is in the Louvre, and more than ten versions of *Bathers*, which he treated in the manner of a geometrical problem, striving to determine the laws that governed the composition of the picture. In landscapes his favourite themes at that time were the family property, Jas de Bouffan (he painted its avenue of chestnut trees several times), the village of Gardanne, the Gulf of Marseilles, as seen from l'Estaque (one version in the Louvre) and *Mount Sainte-Victoire*, notably the one with the big pine tree: in all, more than 250 canvases. His perseverance, if

independent painters and new connoisseurs voiced their appreciation. Although he was isolated within the walls of his own mistrust, and overcome with grief at the death of his mother, his lyricism increased and his art glided towards the housekeeper, Madame Brémond. In 1902 he had a studio built in the Chemin des Lauves. Age, and the suffering his illness gave rise to, made him even more suspicious and irritable. In 1905 he completed his *Grandes Baigneuses* (now in the

CÉZANNE. THE BATHERS. 1900-1905
Private Collection, Paris.

not his stubbornness, was beginning to bear fruit. This was not yet fame, but he was acquiring a reputation. One of his works was shown at the Exposition Universelle in 1889, thanks to the intervention of the faithful Chocquet. When the Théodore Duret collection was put on sale, Claude Monet bought Cézanne's *Village Street* for eight hundred francs, while the dealer Ambroise Vollard (*) exhibited 150 of his works in his gallery in the Rue Laffitte in 1895. The Press was outraged and the public incensed. The academicians turned up to voice indignant protest, but Cézanne's reputation emerged from this experience considerably enhanced. A number of

Philadelphia Museum), which he had begun seven years before. On the 15th of October, 1906, overtaken by a storm while out painting, he caught a chill and collapsed. He was brought home in a cart, and Madame Brémond hastily summoned his wife and son. They arrived too late. Cézanne died on the 22nd of October.

Despite the hostility of the public and of academic circles, Cézanne's fame had continued to grow. After Victor Chocquet's death, seven of Cézanne's canvases were sold for 17,600 francs. One of his landscapes was acquired for the Berlin Museum. He took part in the Exposition de la Libre Esthétique in Brussels in 1901, and in the

CÉZANNE. THE SEA AT L'ESTAQUE. 1883-1885.
Musée du Louvre.

Salon des Indépendants in 1899, 1901 and 1902. An entire room was reserved for him in the Salon d'Automne of 1904. He also exhibited in that Salon in 1905 and 1906. He had triumphed at last. He was accepted by the public, admired by the younger generation, and surrounded with sympathy and veneration. Painters, writers, poets came to Aix to pay homage. Nevertheless, Cézanne continued to live simply in morose and hard-working isolation, revolutionary artist and reactionary citizen; for the boldest precursor of modern art was, at the same time, the most conservative of French bourgeois. He used to go to Mass every Sunday, and scrupulously observed all the conventions of the bourgeois, conservative society to which he belonged. He had an unexpected respect for people with official standing and for State institutions. One of his lifelong desires was to be admitted to the very official Salon, already looked down upon by good painters, which kept its doors obstinately closed against him. He longed to be decorated, and the novelist Octave Mirbeau tried hard to get him the Legion of Honour, but in vain. Cézanne's reserve in matters of love was proverbial. His one sentimental venture was disappointing and abortive. In fact, women

frightened him. Timidity, clumsiness and shyness formed impassable barriers to his passionate temperament, as both his correspondence and his early works bear testimony. Violent and timid, churlish and kind-hearted, reserved and generous, passionate and level-headed, faint-hearted and proud, brimming over with affection yet distrustful of it in others, eager for honours yet indifferent to fame, small in his life yet sublime in his art, gnawed at by doubts about his work yet convinced of his superiority–such was Cézanne, the most balanced of painters and the most torn by contradictions; for, having repressed his instinct, he could feel it stirring tumultuously within him. There was a continuous struggle between the will to organize and the impulse to improvise, between the exigencies of a classical conscience and the pressure of a baroque temperament. Up to 1873 his southern impetuosity and erotic imagination, a fever of subversion and the naïveté of the self-taught, produced a pictorial licentiousness, the dangers of which Cézanne soon perceived. For a while, under the influence of the Impressionists, hoping to get rid of the waywardness of his youth, he tied himself down to a discipline, and subjected his imagination to the laws of Nature. Then began his classical period. The secret of style was no longer to be found in the delicate play of light or the banal imitation of appearances, but in the severe ordering of forms and the right distribution of colours. In his still-lifes, his portraits, his *Cardplayers*, and his views of l'Estaque or Gardanne, he resorted to an aesthetic system whose principles and appropriate means he discovered for himself; principles and means that issued from his need for perfection, his painful, groping search for an absolute. We have now to examine Cézanne's contribution to the art of painting, a contribution so rich and weighty that it has influenced the whole of modern painting, nourished all the movements that seek renewal, and inspired all the talent and genius of our century.

To understand properly the prodigious upheaval wrought by Cézanne (since, after him, a radical change occurred in the manner of seeing and in the manner of painting), he has to be seen in relation to the painting of his time. Although he is indebted to Pissarro for freeing him from the excessive romanticism of his youth, developing his gift of observation and his colour sense, nothing was more opposed to his ambition than the empiricist ideal of the Impressionists. He was a Realist as much as they were–even more so, for he wanted to go beyond the 'simple sensation' and the immediate data of the senses. 'To make of Impressionism something as solid and durable as the paintings in the museums', he once said. By sheer will-power and meditation he rediscovered the innate freshness and vigour of sensation, the fundamental sensation that he wanted to make strong and permanent. He built a world whose form, construction and colour ensure permanence and universality. Although he was an ardent admirer of Poussin, Daumier, and Courbet, he wanted none of that form drowned in chiaroscuro and modelling. On the contrary, he disengaged it, encircled it, put it in evidence and accentuated its internal structure. He gave consistency even to air, mist, vapour, to the most volatile and least palpable things in the universe. The sky and sea in his landscapes have as much breadth and solidity as the trees, rocks and houses. 'Nature must be treated through the cylinder, the sphere, the cone', he said, as the Cubists were to repeat later. But reality has three dimensions. How can it be represented on a

CÉZANNE. STILL-LIFE WITH ONIONS. 1895-1900.
Musée du Louvre.

flat surface? This is where the organizer comes in. With a firm and careful hand, he ordered and combined in the space of the picture the cubes of his houses, the architectures of his trees, the concrete blocks which are his people, the spheres that are his fruits. Verticals and horizontals intersect at right angles to give an effect of magnitude, balance and serenity. Realizing that Nature is 'more depth than surface', he suggested the third dimension by arranging planes in an unexpected manner, by displacing the visual angles, by raising the horizon line (as in *The Sea at l'Estaque* in the Louvre), without bothering about the rules of perspective as taught in the academies. But this tireless and exacting genius wanted to render Nature in its totality. How was he to express, at one and the same time, things and the air that envelops them, form and atmosphere, without resorting to the chiaroscuro of the classical painters, or the soft variegations and the shimmering glints of the Impressionists? Rejecting current conventions, Cézanne made a discovery which was to have a far-reaching effect on Western art: light and shadow no longer exist. From now on they are expressed with the aid of colours. Tone takes the place of modelling of form; the relationship of colours takes the

CÉZANNE. MAN WITH PIPE. 1890-1892.
Courtauld Collection, London.

place of chiaroscuro. He respects local tone. He substitutes pure tone, and contrasts of pure tone, for the mixture, gradations and modulations of colour. 'Model by the colours', said Antonello da Messina. This suggestion, taken up by the Venetians, has become a definite acquisition, thanks to Cézanne, who invented a pictorial light as different from natural light as a picture is from Nature itself. The difficulty lay in finding exact tones, and the exact interrelation of tones. This difficulty Cézanne triumphantly surmounted. In doing so, he arrived at a new interpretation of volume and drawing. Since form is created gradually by the brush as the artist works, it follows that drawing and painting cannot be distinct from each other. 'When colour has its richness, form has its plenitude', is his famous saying. From that time on the Impressionist division of tone began to give way to the juxtaposition of two opposite tones, the proximity of warm and cool. Each spot of paint becomes a coloured plane, a small, dense, rough-grained mass, placed there by a hand guided by reason, yet full of sensuality and flavour. Cézanne wanted to be a painter to the exclusion of everything else. Nothing counted in his eyes except painting. 'Be a painter', he wrote to Émile Bernard,

'and not a writer or a philosopher.' Disdaining literary subjects, genre scenes and allegorical compositions, he preferred to paint common objects, familiar landscapes, and portraits of humble folk. He did not create his *Bathers* to glorify the splendours of the flesh, or to follow a fashion, but in order to seek new forms and new plastic rhythms. Passionately a painter, he made the picture a concrete and complete world, a reality which is an end in itself. From this it is easy to understand the profound influence he has exercised over the generation that followed him. He brought them a method, a perfect creation, the 'picture': that is to say, an architecture of tones and forms which is not an analysis of the passing moment, does not represent an anecdote or a chance incident, but is a coherent reality, indestructible and eternal. Cézanne never wanted to betray Nature. He found in himself the heritage of the old masters, which he took and enriched with his own discoveries, and exalted to the extreme limits to which his indomitable courage and genius could bring it. 'To do Poussin over again from nature... To make of Impressionism something solid and durable like the art in the museums'–that, in short, was his credo. His work is a lesson in energy. It gives us a profound sense of comfort, religious feeling, joy mingled with sadness. For beyond this robust and balanced art his suppressed instincts rumble, and the man groans, torn between the classicism he has so patiently sought and his latent baroque tendencies. Hence the rickety tables, the crooked vases, the tottering chairs, the stiff limbs, the squint-eyed faces, the sloping postures, the forms that crumble when the vertical and horizontal break, the seeming awkwardness, the distortions that have for so long given Cézanne's hostile critics food for condemnation.

In the last ten years of his life the baroque invades his work without ever overstepping the limits laid down by a lifetime of conscientiousness and effort. He paints still-lifes swaying on slippery supports, views of Mount Sainte-Victoire shaken by internal fires, trees which seem struck by lightning, *Château Noir*'s flaming beneath stormy skies. Fauvism is already there, just as Expressionism was in the *Temptation of St Anthony* (1867), and Cubism in the *Cardplayers*. Who of the masters of modern art has not turned to him when in doubt and drawn comfort and inspiration from his example ? Matisse, Derain, Vlaminck, and many others have. 'We all start from Cézanne', Braque, Léger and Jacques Villon declared in 1953. On the other hand, the neo-classicists claim him as their model in so far as he remained faithful to the naturalist tradition. Precursor of pure painting, but also promoter of an intellectual adventure that still continues today, Cézanne is a valid source for the non-realists as well as the realists. There is not a painter today who is not indebted to him. Destiny chose this torn creature with the anguished heart and confident mind to weave the threads of a new tradition. 'I am the primitive of the way I have discovered', he wrote one day, in the full consciousness of his originality. There have undoubtedly been other innovators who have had something to give the painters of today, but they are only predecessors. He is the ancestor, the father of modern painting.   F. E.

CHAGALL Marc. Born in Vitebsk, Russia, in 1887. Marc Chagall's father, a simple, kindly soul, was employed in a herring depot. His mother, a small, lively woman, was hard put to keep her large family of eight girls and two boys, and opened a small grocery shop. In his book *My Life* Chagall writes about his home, describing the vivacity of his sisters and the eccentricity of his uncles–Neuch, who carried cattle in a jolting trap and played the violin, and Zussy, who was a hairdresser and curled his whiskers. He also tells of his grand-father's house, where animal hides hung like linen. All these were themes that inspired his first drawings and, after a number of transposi-tions, nourished his paintings. Chagall was apprenticed to a painter named Pen, an honest portraitist of the notables of the town, who showed an interest in Chagall's early works. These were on everyday, familiar subjects: water-carriers, little houses, processions over the hills. Chagall went to St Petersburg in 1907, where he went through particularly difficult times. Having failed the entrance examination to the School of Arts and Crafts, he was admit-ted to the Imperial School for the Encourage-ment of the Arts, where he even obtained a grant of ten roubles a month. But the teaching there was nonexistent, and the atmosphere

depressing and dreary. But the new school run by Bakst, the theatrical designer, had a growing reputation, increased by its contacts with France and modern art. Chagall, admitted to this studio, received a profound shock. Although the decorative research being conducted there was new to him, he found justification for his previous rebuffs and his instinctive boldness. He arbitrarily renewed his palette, discovered the expressive value of colour as such, and the distortion of line. This is to be seen in his *Red Nude*, 1908. When Chagall returned to Vitebsk, he had a style of his own, still sombre and heavy but with flashes of light. He used it in scenes that are outside and beyond direct observation, and represent the beginnings of an effort towards synthesis; these are the great themes of life: birth, marriage, death. Chagall made several versions of each, always trying to attain a more complete representation. By his side he now had an extraordinarily intuitive girl, Bella, who fired his imagination and encouraged him in his efforts. Chagall painted her in the *Portrait with Black Gloves* (1909, Kunstmuseum, Basel). When the returned to St Petersburg, with work that was quite distinct from contem-

CHAGALL. BIRTH. 1911.

porary Russian painting, he gained the patronage and friendship of a Deputy of the Douma, Vinaver, who offered him a small grant to enable him to go to Paris.

When he arrived in Paris in 1910 he took up lodgings at La Ruche, and became intimate with the poets Blaise Cendrars, Max Jacob and Apollinaire, and the painters La Fresnaye, Delaunay and Modigliani. This was a highly productive period for Chagall, during which he put all the energy that was bubbling up inside him at the service of a vision which integrated the forms of the modern world with the disciplines that stemmed from Fauvism and Cubism. It was in Paris–to use his own expression–that he washed his eyes. 'No academy could have taught me all I have found out from devouring the exhibitions, shop windows and museums of Paris.' His ideas, his instinct for geometrical composition in the construction of a picture were confirmed by the experiments he saw going on all about him. But whereas the Cubists sought to interpret objects, such as a pipe or a guitar, in their essences, Chagall applied this methodical organization to describe the elements of reality seen through his imagination or memory. Since, for him, reality always has projections into the past and the future, his work unfolds on several planes. The laws of gravity do not apply to his people and objects. Every detail keeps its full liberty and all its chances of beauty and grace. Within the solid framework created by the artist, concrete elements, becoming memories, move freely at all angles, in all dimensions. Chagall's great canvases of this period: *The Village and I* (1911), *To Donkeys and Others* (1911, Musée d'Art Moderne, Paris), *Self-Portrait with Seven Fingers* (1911, Stedelijk Museum, Amsterdam), *Drinking Soldier* (1912, Solomon Guggenheim Museum, New York), *Pregnant Woman* (1912-1913, Stedelijk Museum, Amsterdam), reveal a pure vision of an absolutely

CHAGALL. THE ANNIVERSARY. 1915.
Museum of Modern Art, New York.

unique inner world, which the artist succeeds in transmitting without spoiling or weakening, giving it an eternal existence, outside time. Almost all his canvases of this period, under (sometimes odd) names supplied by Blaise Cendrars, were selected by Apollinaire for the Chagall exhibition arranged in Berlin in 1914. This exhibition, at the Der Sturm Gallery, created a sensation and had a marked impact on the Expressionist movement after the 1914-1918 war.

Chagall had just arrived in Russia when the war broke out. Drafted into a camouflage unit, he remained in St Petersburg, and in 1915 married Bella. During this period he acquired a heightened awareness of the tragic reality of his inner world. Thus, in the *Green Rabbi* cold, strident colours and broken lines clarify his interpretation. The village, which is an extension of his own individuality, forces itself on him, no longer through the magic of memory but in naked and searing purity. It is as if the infinitely fragile and threatened world of childhood were being offered to him again. Hitherto, he had expressed its sadness, its horror and its poetry with vehemence, in intense lines and colours. Now he perceived it differently. He painted it in delicate pinks, acid greens and transparent blues.

He saved only what was essential (*The Grey House*, 1917). In this unreal atmosphere only the painter and his beloved could move, growing with their love, becoming one single, fabulous being, floating through space, above life (*Lovers over the Town*, 1917; Tretiakov Gallery, Moscow).

When the Revolution came, Chagall was appointed Commissar for the Fine Arts in the District of Vitebsk by Lunacharsky, whom he knew when the latter was in exile in Paris in 1912. The new regime encouraged the most advanced forms of modern art. Chagall founded an academy, which he opened to all art movements. He invited Lissitzky, Pougny and Malevitch to teach in it, but he had a disagreement with Malevitch, who was not so liberal, and Chagall resigned. In Moscow he joined Granowsky, director of the Yiddish Theatre, who commissioned him to paint murals for the auditorium and foyer of the theatre. When he was also asked to do the décors and costumes (notably for Sholem Aleihem's *Agents* and Gogol's *Marriage*), he helped with the production and gave the actors themselves a new dimension. He transformed them into a gallery of representative types, so complete in their portrayal of the feelings they were supposed to represent, that action became almost redundant. These décors and characters were depicted in enormous compositions on the auditorium walls, so that the audience was completely overwhelmed by a psychic world that enveloped it entirely.

In 1922 Chagall decided to return to France. It was then that Vollard (*), having noticed one of his paintings, suggested that he do some illustrating. Selecting Gogol's *Dead Souls*, he made eighty-five etchings, which were not published until 1948. In 1926 he illustrated the *Fables* of La Fontaine with one hundred etchings, published in 1952. At that time, after the severity of Cubism and the explosion of Expressionism, painting felt the need for a period of contemplation. It wanted to please, and tried numerous experiments to that end. Chagall discovered the beauty of flowers and vegetation in the South of France. He painted his first landscapes and lyrically described a new language of flowers. With unerring taste, he avoided insipidity. In 1931, invited to the opening of the Tel Aviv Museum, he went to Palestine and Syria to see the scenes of the Bible which, at Vollard's request, he later illustrated.

Beginning in 1935, profoundly affected by the atmosphere of persecution and war spreading over the world, Chagall introduced dramatic, social and religious elements into his pictures. He painted numerous Crucifixions.

In 1941 he decided to go to the United States, at the invitation of the Museum of Modern Art in New York. Tragically alert to all that was happening in Europe, Chagall found powerful and renewed inspiration in the misfortunes of his race and the threats to human liberty. In 1944 Bella Chagall died. Moving evocations of the past and the beyond began to appear in his work. He completed the great composition entitled *Around Her* (Musée d'Art Moderne, Paris), which he had begun in 1937, and which became a synthesis of all his favourite themes, grouped around the evocation of Bella. In 1945, Chagall, who had already designed the décor for the ballet, *Aleko*, under-

CHAGALL. THE GREEN EYE. 1944.

took his memorable settings of huge back-cloths, curtains and costumes for Stravinsky's ballet, the *Firebird*. Later on, he designed the décor for *Daphnis and Chloe* (1958) with music by Ravel, for the Paris Opéra. He returned finally to France in 1947 and settled in Vence in 1949. Like Renoir and Bonnard, he was captivated by the southern landscape that came alive under the vibrating light and was fascinated by the last works of Monet in which structure dissolved in colour.

His desire to possess and mould the earth that inspired him made him take up ceramics. He

CHAGALL. CLOCK WITH BLUE WING. 1949.

designed some original shapes and his experiments with glazes produced unusual colours. In 1953, he returned to some sketches he had made in America and developed them into a fantastic vision of Paris in which the monuments are personified as allegorical figures. Two visits to Greece in 1952 and 1954 at the request of the publisher, Tériade, who had commissioned him to illustrate *Daphnis and Chloe*, provided him with a new source of inspiration. Confronted with the Greek world, he felt the same shock as he had on discovering Palestine. He completed his great engraved illustrations for the *Bible*,

which he had begun for Vollard, and gave with them a remarkable vision of the ancient world. Finally, after various commissions for French churches (Assy and Metz), he designed the grand group of twelve stained-glass windows, symbolizing the twelve tribes of Israel, for the synagogue of the new Hadasseh hospital at Jerusalem, which were put in position in 1962, after being triumphantly exhibited in Paris and New York. He succeeded in giving them a remarkable richness of association, considering that his only means were the metaphorical imagery of animals, landscape and still-life.

Chagall's importance in contemporary art increases daily. In 1941 André Breton *(*)*, in search of the precursors of Surrealism *(*)*, stressed the fact that already in 1911 Chagall's work had broken down the barriers of the elements and the laws of physics. Chagall's unique and individual artistic achievement is reflected in many of the new developments of modern painting, for, with a sure instinct, he has applied himself to the problems of our times and given them an answer.   J. LA.

CHIRICO Giorgio de. Italian painter born at Volos, Greece, in 1888. His father, a Sicilian from Palermo, came to Greece as an engineer. Several years later, his family having settled in Athens, Chirico studied at a polytechnic school where both painting and engineering were taught. He devoted himself to painting and did landscapes and seascapes. In 1906 he went to Munich, attracted by the prestige of the German romantic painters (and Arnold Boecklin in particular). On completion of his studies, in 1909, he went to Italy. Turin amazed him with its rectilinear architecture, adorned with statues placed at man's height, which seemed to rise from the crowds of passers-by. In 1910 Chirico moved to Florence, where he painted his first characteristic works: *Enigma of the Oracle* and *Enigma of an Autumn Evening*, in which two people part at the foot of a white statue while, behind a wall, a sail rises on the horizon. In July 1911 he arrived in Paris with his canvases *Sabaudian Enigmas*, which he exhibited at the Salon d'Automne. At the Salon des Indépendants he also showed the first works inspired by the Gare Montparnasse in Paris. These were noticed by Picasso and Apollinaire. The latter proclaimed him the most astonishing painter of his time. Chirico made a prophetic portrait of the poet, depicting him with a bullet-hole in his skull (*see* illustration, page 10). In the works of this period Chirico strove to discover new relationships between objects, to reveal the secret connections that can exist between them. His unusual associations of images and ideas arouse in the spectator a feeling of subdued but profound anxiety. Flying lines cut the immobility of space, absent people throw shadows. Silence vibrates, waiting for the cry or whistle that will rend it. Around these cold, pure architectures the air is charged with mystery and .invention. A spatial magic is created. Chirico's objects, plaster statues or heads, vegetables or fruit, and (later)

CHIRICO. ENIGMA OF ARRIVAL. 1912.
Private Collection, Paris.

CHAGALL. THE BOY. 1952.

dressmaker's dummies, rubber gloves and dry biscuits, are all represented with absolute indifference. They are so impersonal that they lose all their natural meaning. Their grouping–which owes nothing to chance but is the result of systematic experimentation–creates limitless possibilities of elusiveness and mystery. According to his friends, Chirico had at this time prophetic and visionary powers, powers consciously created, the product of a methode which he later repudiated. Back in Italy at the outbreak of war Chirico was conscripted in 1915, at Ferrara, where he met Carlo Carrà. The architecture of this town, with its vast white, deserted perspectives, was particularly favourable to hallucination. What is termed Metaphysical Painting (*) arose from the combination of the world he had already created and this new setting. The metaphysical aspect of landscapes, objects or beings is the meaning they acquire when seen suddenly in unusual isolation or in unexpected relationships, or when seized in their nakedness, with their magical power intact. The painter made an obvious effort to define and characterize his art, and then to develop it in that metaphysical sense. That is why it soon betrayed an excess of intentions, not always clear or coherent. That probably is the origin of the crisis that destroyed the artist and his work. The composition was complicated with numerous and divergent perspectives; the dissonances between the different parts of the picture were emphasized. The picture was soon crowded with fragments of reality painted in *trompe-l'œil*.

Chirico had an enormous success at the *L'Epoca* exhibition in Rome in 1918. He was one of the leaders of the *Valori Plastici* group in 1919. While in Rome he plunged into technical researches which are, perhaps, at the root of the radical change that occurred in his work. He experimented with various old processes of painting in tempera, and, haunted by the transparent colours of the masters, tried to solve the mystery of great painting by copying Raphael, Michelangelo and Botticelli. Chirico's metaphysical universe is close to the universe of dreams, where the extraordinary precision of the details results in a new reality, secret and unpredictable. Perspective is no longer the search for the ideal line of sight, but a steep short cut leading straight into the inexplicable. The strangely grouped objects give the same bizarre sensation as the clear images of a dream. When there is a human figure, it is in the form of a clothed or plaster statue, or an articulated dressmaker's dummy. Chirico never let himself be guided by the contingencies of psychic automatism, or the dictates of his feelings: his creatures are rigorously sexless. His evolution was so rapid that when he returned to France in 1924 he was already far from the Surrealists who welcomed him as a master and made him join in their first exhibition. He executed décors for the Ballets Suédois (*) and Ballets Russes (*). He presented new themes (horses and gladiators) in a new kind of painting in which he seemed to have retained only the semblance of his former gifts. His works founder in literature and academicism, and only his novel, *Hebdomeros* (1929), reflects the grandiose visions of the Chirico of old. After 1930 he broke brutally with his past, disowned his friends and former works, and immersed himself in a feverish and frenzied exploration of empty techniques.   J. LA.

CHOCQUET Victor. This enthusiastic and keen collector ('good old Chocquet', as he was called in his time) was born in Lille about 1840. A minor Customs official, he

CHIRICO. THE GREAT METAPHYSICIAN. 1917.
Philip L. Goodwin Collection, New York.

devoted a substantial portion of his meagre income to buying Impressionist works. His first acquisitions were a small Delacroix and Manet's *Peonies*, now in the Louvre. In the little shop run by Père Tanguy (*), a dealer in art supplies and paintings, he discovered the then unknown Impressionist painters, to whom he gave at once his unqualified admiration. In 1875, at the Hôtel Drouot, the Paris auction rooms, he met Renoir at the famous sale organized there by Renoir, Monet, Sisley and Berthe Morisot. The sale was not a success, and they were not even able to pay all the expenses. In 1876 Renoir painted Chocquet's gentle, pensive face, and then made a portrait of his wife. Renoir introduced him to Cézanne, who also painted him several times: first in 1877 and again in the summer of 1889 when he was staying at Chocquet's place at Hattenville, in Normandy. It is indeed amazing that when he died the collection of this minor civil servant comprised, among others, 32 Cézannes, 11 Monets, 11 Renoirs and 5 Manets, as well as some drawings and water-colours. This collection was sold by Madame Chocquet on the 3rd and 4th of July, 1899, at a considerable profit. The famous *Mardi Gras* by Cézanne fetched 4,400 francs, a record price for the time.

CLEMENCEAU Georges (1841–1929). It was probably psychological fatalism which led Clemenceau to take up the cudgels for those who were making the Impressionist revolution. Naturally enough it was Monet, another rugged individualist, who particularly took his fancy. Years later, at the end of a turbulent political life, he could still take time to write about Monet in *The Water Lilies* (1928). He was a fervent admirer, too, of Rodin, but Rodin confided that Clemenceau made him start over again no fewer than fourteen times when he sat for his bust, apparently convinced that no material, however plastic, could adequately suggest the volcanic mobility of his feelings. There is no doubt, though, that Monet's intensity of feeling harmonized with Clemenceau's. The Tiger's enthusiasm was strong for the series of *Haystacks, Cathedrals* and *Water Lilies*–those works in which Monet pushed to its extreme consequences his single-minded passion for colour. Clemenceau took sides with most of the young talent of his day and was one of the first to demonstrate that the future is always to the avant-garde. It was by his order, as Premier, in 1907, that Manet's *Olympia*, which had been offered to the Government in 1890, following its purchase by public subscription, was finally allowed to enter the Louvre, in spite of rabid opposition from members of the Institut de France. It is thanks to Clemenceau, too, that the *Water Lilies* are now on view at the Orangerie. Monet agreed to give this famous series to the State after Clemenceau promised that it would be exhibited under the same conditions as those in which he had always seen it in the artist's studio at Giverny.

CONCRETE ART A term invented by Theo Van Doesburg in 1930 to replace the term Abstract Art. A review bearing that name, which appeared only once, was started by Van Doesburg in April 1930, lesse than a year before his death. Since then Concrete Art has been used in preference to Abstract Art in the writings of certain artists such as Arp and Max Bill. It has had a certain vogue in avant-garde circles in Switzerland and the Argentine. The term is interchangeable with Abstract Art, but it should not be forgotten that from 1910 to 1930 the masters of this art (Kandinsky, Malevitch, Mondrian and Van Doesburg himself) never used any term other than *Art Abstrait*.

CÉZANNE. LANDSCAPE. 1880-1885.   *Art Institute, Chicago.*

CONSTRUCTIVISM See Abstract Art, Suprematism, Lissitzky.

CORINTH Lovis. German painter born in Tapiau in Eastern Prussia in 1858; died in Zandvoort, Holland, in 1925. Corinth studied painting in Koenigsberg, Munich, Antwerp, and Paris. After ten years in Munich, he settled in Berlin, about 1900. From 1918 until his death he spent the summers at Urech in Bavaria, near the Walchensee, whose intense blue sings in the landscapes of his latter years. With Liebermann, Corinth belonged to what is sometimes called German Impressionism. But his heavy, sensual early work is more Naturalist than Impressionist, and the spontaneity of style to which it owes its brilliancy is inspired more by Frans Hals than by the French Impressionists. The pictures of this period were voluptuous and vivid, or else heroic allegorical scenes. This gushing creation was interrupted in 1911, when the artist had an apoplectic stroke. His painting then underwent a profound transformation: his spontaneous style lost its externally sensuous character and, instead of naïvely presenting a three-dimensional world, Corinth tried to merge the planes in a single, strong, nervous movement of colour. The vitality of his painting no longer depended on its subject: it was fully contained in the flow and intoxication of paint. Flowers and landscapes–first of the Côte d'Azur, later of the Walchensee–painted in strong, thick, luminous colours, seem born of an intimate participation in the deep and powerful song of Nature.

Before he became ill, Corinth painted some vigorous portraits, but those that came afterwards, such as that of Meier-Graefe, painted in 1914 (Musée d'Art Moderne, Paris), and the self-portraits of his latter years, have a superior emotional power. When this giant, worn down by illness and hard work, painted himself, all the strength and weakness, the reality and unreality of man, appear in this pathetic testimony. These same contrasts are to be found in his religious pictures, of which the most important is the magnificent *Ecce Homo* of 1925, now in the Basel Museum. Kirchner said of Corinth: 'In the beginning, he was only of average stature; at the end, he was truly great'. F. M.

CORRENTE This name was taken from the periodical, which was the organ of the movement, and given to one of the most interesting cultural revivals attempted in Italy before the war. Begun and continued by young artists, it left its mark, in fact, on the period from 1938 to 1940. On the 1st January, 1938, Ernesto Treccani with a group of friends founded at Milan the fortnightly, *Vita Giovanile*, which changed its title to *Corrente* in October of the same year. The new generation of critics, philosophers and artists immediately rallied to the review and its founders. Their interests were varied, but they had one common purpose: a free discussion of all cultural matters and, reacting against the long, spiritual mortification the dictatorship had imposed, on them, they felt the need to restore their link with

CORINTH. WALCHENSEE. *Dresden Museum.*

European thought. The original group consisted largely of pupils of the philosopher, Antonio Banfi (Paci, Preti, Cantoni, Formaggio, Anceschi, De Grada), who was at that time leading a vigorous campaign against Italian provincialism. Thus Corrente was a revolutionary movement with a moral rather than an aesthetic character.

Where painting was concerned it nevertheless crystallised the creative uneasiness of artists who were dissatisfied with academicism and the official art of the Novecento (*). Among these was Renato Birolli (born at Verona in 1906), whose lucid, vigorous talent could communicate the violence of feeling through the discipline of form. His writing about himself or

BIROLLI. LANDSCAPE. 1937.   *Jesi Collection, Milan.*

others, when he was endeavouring to clarify a moral or theoretical argument, revealed an exceptional polemist, sensitive to the spirit of the times and conscious of their historical significance, without losing his generous humanism. Others were Arnaldo Badodi (born at Milan in 1913; reported missing on the Russian front in 1942), whose brief life with its hallucinatory dreams—circuses, battles, dress-making workrooms—was bound up with the short blaze of Corrente: Italo Valenti (born at Milan in 1912), a magic colourist and a strange creator, during those black years, of innocent enchantment; Aligi Sassu (born at Milan in 1912), one of the most ardent and politically minded of the group and a painter of a bitter romanticism; Giuseppe Migneco (born at Messina in 1908) whose violent, disordered expressionism of those days was abandoned after the war for compositions with a quieter lyricism; Bruno Cassinari (born at Piacenza in 1912), whose highly individual manner had already, as it were by instinct, absorbed the lessons of the great European painters. To this original group, however, should be added all those who, after the first and second exhibitions of Corrente (March and

December 1939) joined the movement and, as they gradually elucidated their ideas, almost came to forming a national front of Italian painting. It will be sufficient to mention Fiorenzo Tomea, Domenico Cantatore, Gabriele Mucchi and, in the Roman group, Mario Mafai, Renato Guttuso (born at Palermo in 1912) a new and powerful artist, who produced large, boldly conceived canvases; or again, in the Venetian group, Giuseppe Santomaso and Emilio Vedova, who were both drawn along different paths towards an international abstraction. On the 10th June, 1940, the review, *Corrente,* was banned and the movement continued through the exhibitions of an art gallery and the productions of a publishing house.   D. F.

CROSS Henri-Edmond (1856–1910). Cross's real name was Delacroix. He was born at Douai, in the north of France, and he died at Saint-Clair (Var). In 1884 he was one of the founders of the *Société des Artistes Indépendants,* along with Seurat, Signac and others, and in that year he began to abandon his more or less Impressionist and rather academic style in favour of

Divisionism (*see* Neo-Impressionism). The reasons he later gave were that 'in the act of creating, will as well as instinct plays a large part; and will can only be based on exactitude. I am engrossed in this question of exactitude, seeking it in the laws of contrasting colours. Reasoning doesn't come easily to me—in fact, it is perhaps the thing I lack most; and if a painter is endowed with artistic sensibility, studying a method is not likely to hinder him in expressing what he has felt.' In fact, as he freely admitted, 'because of my temperamental make-up, my sensations are in need of grammar, rhetoric and logic'. And this was just what he found in Seurat's method disciplined by the laws of optics: simultaneous contrasts, the use of pure colours, and optical blending. However, he never became a slave to these theories, and if they enabled him to become the artist he was, they always remained a means rather than an end, and he even admitted that he would gladly abandon them if he were to find more fruitful ideas elsewhere. But the discipline of his friend's system suited his character well, helping him on what Signac called 'the road towards the logic of colour and synthesis of form'.

In Cross we find both a methodical, dispassionate thinker and a strangely troubled dreamer. His dream, quite contrary to that of Seurat, was to follow the call of his imagination more freely. He wrote to a friend: 'Can the goal of art be nothing more than to set fragments of Nature in a rectangle, with what taste the artist has at his disposal? As the starting-point, I come back to the idea of chromatic harmonies invented outside Nature, so to speak.' Of all the Neo - Impressionist group, Cross used the brightest scale of colouring, and his Pointillist technique was of almost abstract quality.

By his will to achieve a certain independence of Nature, linked with a pronounced decorative sense and a strong feeling for colour, Cross can be considered a precursor of Fauvism. In 1904 Matisse went to work with him and Signac in the South of France, fascinated by the richness of their palette, their animated way of painting, their free interpretation of what they saw. The characteristics of Fauvism–bright colouring, contrasts perhaps starting but never gaudy, synthesis of forms, a preference for flat surfaces–are all partly based on the liberties Cross took with Nature, particularly striking in his big water-colours. Less preoccupied than Signac with bringing a method to perfection, Cross made his way, in an adventurous spirit all his own, along the path opened up by Seurat; and it is just this blending of spontaneous emotional expression controlled by logic which constitutes the distinctive beauty of his work.

J. R.

CUBISM is the name given to the aesthetic and technical revolution brought about by Picasso, Braque, Juan Gris and Léger between 1907 and 1914. Matisse and Derain also contributed to the formation of this movement, which influenced the majority of the avant-garde

CROSS. THE HARBOUR AT TOULON. *Private Collection, Paris.*

artists during the years that preceded the 1914-1918 war. Like Impressionism, Cubism at first encountered nothing but general hostility, or incomprehension, and was given its name in derision. In his account of the first Braque exhibition at the Kahnweiler Gallery, the critic Louis Vauxcelles picked up one of Matisse's sallies and spoke of 'cubes' (*Gil Blas*, November 14th, 1908). The following spring, in the same paper, and again on the subject of Braque, he spoke of 'Cubist bizarreries'. The creators of Cubism accepted the term with reserve, and constantly denied they were theorists. Picasso declared: 'When we painted as we did, we had no intention of creating Cubism, but only of expressing what was inside us'. Braque said: 'For me, Cubism–or rather, *my* Cubism–is a means I created for my own use, with the aim of putting painting within range of my talents'. The vitality and fecundity of Cubism comes from the coupling of these two exceptional temperaments, who worked enthusiastically together, without surrendering their own personalities. Later, they were joined by Gris and Léger. The history of the development of Cubism falls into three phases: a Cézanne phase (1907-1909), an analytical phase (1910-1912), and a synthetic phase (1913-1914). A favourable climate for it had been prepared by the vogue of Negro sculpture and primitive art, the Seurat retrospective exhibition in the Salon des Indépendants of 1905 and, particularly, the Cézanne retrospective in the Salon d'Automne of 1907. Matisse and Derain had already disciplined Fauvism and tried to organize, methodically, the painted surface of the picture. In the spring of 1907 Picasso completed *Les Demoiselles d'Avignon*, 'hacked out with an axe', of which the right-hand section, violently simplified and constructed by drawing alone, without the use of chiaroscuro, marks the beginning of Cubism. He met Braque, whose natural evolution he speeded up. That autumn, Kahnweiler *(*)* opened, in the Rue Vignon, the gallery that was to become the home of Cubism. The famous Bateau-Lavoir *(*)* group was formed in 1908

PICASSO. LES DEMOISELLES D'AVIGNON. 1907.
Museum of Modern Art, New York.

at No. 13 Rue Ravignan, Montmartre, where Picasso, Max Jacob and Juan Gris went to live. It also included Apollinaire, Salmon, Raynal, Gertrude and Leo Stein, and others. The new aesthetic movement, intuitive with Picasso and deductive with Braque, can be clearly seen in the landscapes painted by Picasso at La Rue-des-Bois in the Oise in 1908, and at Horta de San Juan in Spain in 1909 (the latter exhibited by Vollard), as well as in the landscapes painted by Braque at l'Estaque in 1908 (exhibited at Kahnweiler's; catalogue preface by Apollinaire), and at La Roche-Guyon in 1909. Braque, fresh from Impressionism and Fauvism, controlled his colour by an austere sense of form; Picasso, the instinctive draughtsman, tried to introduce colour into his work. Each on his own was striving to find the same solutions by developing whatever quality he lacked. They made a study of the fundamental problem of painting: the representation of coloured volume on a flat surface. The history of Cubism is that of the successive solutions discovered to resolve this difficulty. The result was a new plastic language, lyrical and conceptual at the same time, which put an end to that respect for appearances which had been observed since the Renaissance. In their reaction against Impressionism and its visual spontaneity, Braque and Picasso discarded from their world all fortuitous appearances and atmospheric accidents. They tried to define the permanent properties of objects and their stability in a closed space, without perspective or light, through a geometrical crystallization inspired by Cézanne; hence the significant and very restrained choice of themes, which were limited to very simple things: trees, houses, fruit-bowls, bottles and glasses—later, small tables and musical instruments—that could

BRAQUE. HOMAGE TO J.-S. BACH. 1912.
H.-P. Roché Collection, Paris.

be reduced to geometric forms and easily identified by the spectator. They were less interested in making an inventory of the world than in creating, with a few characteristic 'signs', a language which would renew its significance. But in this initial, groping phase, in spite of their efforts, the antinomy of object and colour, local tone and volume, was overcome only by painting in monochrome, or an imitation of sculpture (*vide* Picasso, Braque).

In 1910 Braque gave up landscapes for figures and still-lifes. In his own words, he passed from visual space to tactile and manual space. Picasso left the Bateau-Lavoir for the Boulevard de Clichy, also in Montmartre, where he painted a series of heads and portraits. The second phase of Cubism, described as analytical by Juan Gris, because of the increasing breakdown of form, is characterized by the use of simultaneity. Several aspects of the same object are put together on a single canvas, rather as a child sees an object, as it exists in itself and in our minds. Thus, the object appears as if broken, spread out and open from the inside. This concern for complete realism differentiates Cubism from all the other abstract movements derived from it, and separates it from the decorative tendencies of Fauvism. The problem of simultaneity has always preoccupied artists who, in the imitative, visual

phase of painting, from Van Eyck to Manet, have been unable to find any better means than a mirrorlike reflection. For, spatial simultaneity through successive juxtapositions, used by the painters of the Trecento or the Quattrocento, cannot be compared with the unitary, structural principles of Cubism, obtained by the flattening and superimposing of planes, and the polyhedric fragmentation of volumes. This period of extreme analysis and systematic experimentation was not without a certain danger of 'hermetism' which Braque and Picasso proposed to remedy by the use of *papiers collés (*)* and real materials, such as sand, glass, newspaper and cloth, inserted in the canvas to stimulate perception. During this period Cubism was widely publicized, thanks to the publication of the doctrinal work of Gleizes and Metzinger, *Du Cubisme,* in 1912. It also saw its division into many tendencies, of which the principal two were Orphism *(*)* and the Section d'Or *(*),* which preceded the later derivations of Abstraction (*vide* Abstract Art) and Purism *(*).*

In the following year, 1913, Apollinaire published *Les Peintres Cubistes,* in which he spoke already of conceptual painting (*vide* Apollinaire). This term was premature, because it can be applied only to the last, or synthetic, phase of Cubism, which began in 1913, with the very active participation of Gris and Léger (*vide* these names). Although Léger's interest in Cubism dates back to 1910, he did not go through the analytical period, being restrained by his sense of the monumental and his taste for the massive. In 1911 Juan Gris had begun to break down the object methodically in his painting, but reversed his procedure in the summer of 1913, during his stay at Céret with Braque and Picasso. He defined the change in attitude in these words: 'From a cylinder I make a bottle'. The multiple figuration of the same object on a canvas had made it difficult to understand and distorted its rhythm, even though it remained figurative. In synthetic Cubism the break with the naturalist and traditional representation practised since the Renaissance is complete. The new method discarded completely all imitative processes, and used freely invented plastic 'signs' comparable to the metaphors of poets. These signs created a reality through lyrical allusion, rather than representative illusion. Gone was the initial austerity of their palettes. The planes grew broader and more supple, the colours of the spectrum began to appear, form and local colour could at last be harmoniously united without breaking the basic architecture of the picture. Cubism ceased to be an aspect, an empirical technique, and became a conceptual aesthetic philosophy, an objective ordering of the world represented in its essence, and not its appearance. The realist cult of the 'object' (the importance of which has been revealed by psychology and sociology) played, at the beginning of the twentieth century, the same role as the passion for 'subject' did during the Romantic period. In line with the evolution of science and contemporary thought, a new plastic language has been created, whose rigour fosters, without fettering, the *élan* of the individual. The 1914 war dispersed the creators of Cubism, each to follow the course of his own artistic destiny. But the collective exaltation of those heroic years from 1907 to 1914 will never be lost.   J. LE.

GRIS. POEMS IN PROSE. 1915.   *Private Collection.*

D

DADA The Dada Movement developed between 1915 and 1922, between the dispersal of Cubism *(*)*–from which it borrowed, and generalized for its own ends, the technique of *papiers collés (*)*– and the advent of Surrealism *(*)*, which succeeded it and for which it constituted a preparatory though negative phase. Dada made its first appearance almost simultaneously in Zurich, New York and Paris, before reaching Germany and then concentrating in Paris. Switzerland's neutrality during the war had made it a refuge for all kinds of political exiles and agitators. Lenin was there, rubbing shoulders with dissident elements and anarchists from almost every country. Among the latter were the Rumanian poet Tristan Tzara, the German writers Hugo Ball and Richard Hülsenbeck, and the Alsatian painter and sculptor Hans Arp. In February 1916 they founded the Cabaret Voltaire *(*)*, a literary club, exhibition gallery, and theatre hall all in one; the name is a clear indication of its sarcastic and critical intentions. A dictionary, opened at random (this appeal to chance was to become systematic) furnished the name of the movement: Dada. Learned lectures on Klee, or Lao-tse, alternated with scandalizing or mystifying entertainments, designed to undermine by every possible means the traditional bases of culture and social order. Works by Arp, Chirico, Max Ernst, Feininger, Kandinsky, Klee, Kokoschka, Marc, Modigliani and Picasso were exhibited in a very eclectic manner at the Dada gallery in 1917. The typical artist of the movement was Arp, illustrator of Hülsenbeck and Tzara, who, with his coloured papers, his woodcuts and his sculptures, organized the co-called *'formes libres'* (free forms), born of fantasy and the unconscious *(vide* Arp).

The real precursor of the Dada spirit in its destructive sense was the painter Marcel Duchamp, a man of implacable logic and exceptional gifts, who sacrificed his career as an artist to the principles of inversion, negation and anti-aestheticism. He settled in New York in 1915, where his famous 'ready-mades' (mass-produced objects arbitrarily raised to the level of works of art) created a sensation, and became the central figure of the Stieglitz group and the review *291* (Man Ray, Picabia, de Zayas, Arensberg), an anti-artistic movement parallel to the Dada movement of Zurich. Picabia, a painter of Spanish origin, had visited New York in 1915. He went to Barcelona and founded the *391* review there in January 1917. He turned up in Switzerland in 1918 and contacted the Dada group. Two numbers of *Dada*, the review edited by Tzara, were published in 1917. *Dada III*, in which Picabia collaborated, appeared in December 1918, and contained the *Dada Manifesto*, in which the meaning and destructive force of the movement were confirmed. The *Dada Anthology* (number 4-5 of the review) appeared in April 1919 *(vide* Duchamp, Picabia). Tristan Tzara then settled in Paris, and was enthusiastically received by the group of the review *Littérature* (March 1919), run by the poets Breton, Aragon, Soupault, Éluard, Ribemont-Dessaignes and Péret. A Dada salon opened at the Montaigne Gallery on June 6th, 1922, but the Parisian movement was more literary and, after a summer demonstration in the Tyrol, it dissolved in internal disputes in the autumn of 1922 *(vide* also Breton, Tzara).

In Germany, because of the 1918 defeat and the social crises of the time, Dada found fertile soil for expansion. With the more direct participation of artists, the movement took on a more political character. The Berlin group, created by Hülsenbeck in 1917, broke up in 1920, after a large-scale exhibition which was a triumph for Georg Grosz, ferocious caricaturist of the German feudal bourgeoisie and militarism. The Cologne group showed itself still more violent on the social plane, by the publication of the

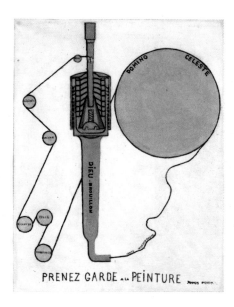

PICABIA. FRESH PAINT. 1917.
Private Collection, Paris.

Electric Fan (a Communist and Dadaist periodical confiscated by the British occupation authorities). On the artistic plane it was, perhaps, the most interesting group, as a result of the activities of Max Ernst who, joined by Hans Arp, began to make his collages, of which the most famous series is entitled *Fatagaga* (short for '*fabrication de tableaux garantis gazométriques*'). The exhibition of April 1920, held at the Winter Café and closed by order of the police, reached a level of scandal and provocation which has never been surpassed. The departure of Max Ernst for Paris in 1921 marked the end of Cologne Dadaism. Mention should also be made of the movement in Hanover, founded by the poet and painter Kurt Schwitters, whose collages entitled *Merz (*)* were formed of unusual materials and all sorts of litter (*vide* Ernst, Grosz, Schwitters).

Dada was less an artistic movement than an intellectual revolt, born of the convulsions of the 1914-1918 war, and too directly bound to its anguish to be anything other than a cry of negation, which inevitably carried within itself the seeds of its own destruction. But it was necessary for the coming of Surrealism, which was to build on its ruins.

Dada had little appeal in England, and, in the U.S.A., existed only briefly in New York. The living members of the original Dada groups, such as Hülsenbeck and Tzara, still pursue old feuds and keep alive controversies which no longer arouse public interest. Hülsenbeck lives in New York and practises as a Jungian psychiatrist under the name of Charles R. Hulbeck. Grosz also lives in America. His current work, though sometimes more spectacular than the old, is considerably less effective. Dada's main contribution to this century was its satirical character, and that, at least, is not quite dead.   J. LE.

DALI Salvador. Spanish painter born in Figueras, Catalonia, in 1904. His father was a notary, a native of the village of Cadaqués. It is the scenery of this village that is Dali's true spiritual home. After a stormy passage through the various schools in Figueras, during which he was given lessons by a drawing teacher named Núñez, Dali went to Madrid, where he entered the School of Fine Arts. With ease and conviction–for, despite his originality, he is methodical and conscientious–he absorbed the academic recipes of the old historical painter Moreno Carbonero, who had been teaching there even in Picasso's time. But, above all, he fed himself on Freud and books on philosophy which, he claimed, were the only ones that could move him, even to tears. Through art reviews he became keenly interested in Cubism, Futurism and, particularly, Metaphysical Painting, which seemed to him the prime ideal. A close friendship bound him to Federico García Lorca, and they spent long hours comparing notes on their respective problems. Lorca drew and painted with an ethereal fantasy; Dali countered its suggestiveness with concrete plastic forms. In his respect for an exact realism, he resorted to *trompe-l'œil* and photography, the extraordinary possibilities of which he was to emphasize much later in such films as *Le Chien Andalou* and *L'Age d'Or*. The paintings which he showed at Dalmau's in Barcelona in 1925, and in Madrid in 1926, at the first exhibition of the Iberian Artists, alongside Ferrant, Palencia, Cossio and Borés, were already founded on strangeness and contrast. After a brief period of Cubist influence, in which he tried to reconcile the teachings of Gris,

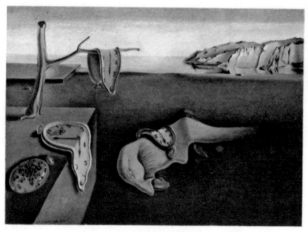

DALI. PERSISTENCE OF MEMORY. 1931.
Museum of Modern Art, New York.

Chirico and Carrà with the best technique of the past, his own universe revealed itself in all its distinctiveness: distant views of seascapes, clear and luminous, seen through deep windows framed in black, with silhouettes of bending women in the foreground. But this poise, so inconsistent with his excitable nature, could not satisfy him. He made a trip to Paris by taxi in order to get acquainted with Picasso, Versailles, and the Grévin Museum (the French Madame Tussaud's). He made contact with Surrealism, finished *Blood is Sweeter than Honey*, published (in Barcelona in 1928) the insulting Groc Manifesto, brought the members of the Parisian Surrealist group to Cadaqués, organized a triumphant exhibition at the Galerie Goemans, in 1929, and married Gala, the wife of the poet Paul Éluard. A newcomer to the group, Dali was full of fight, fanaticism, and conviction. Using a rich philosophical terminology, he elaborated a new method of creation, which he defined as 'paranoiac-critical activity' (cf. his book called *The Visible Woman*, published in 1930). By intensifying the excitability of the mind, he wanted to create a lasting, frenzied pattern by the juxtaposition of chance objects. He knew very well how to use visionary experiences, interpretations of memory, and all the mental distortions that he came across in his systematic, conscious study of psychological derangement and pathological ac-

cidents. By absorbing oneself in the contemplation of something, he maintained, it is possible to enter another plane. The artist, placed before an external object, is led to describe the ascendancy that this object has over him. By painting it, he liberates-at one and the same time-his subsconscious from this hold, and the object from its conventional meaning (*vide* also Surrealism). Dali shows his desire to drain reality, and go beyond it, in one single operation. He may take as the basis of his work elements produced in the most mechanical fashion, such as a snapshot of an expressive face, or the reproduction of a very conventional painting, such as Millet's *Angelus*. Then he lets the image deteriorate by a sort of decomposition, expressed by the softening or the elongation of its substance, or, simpler still, by painting in a few flies or some other real and visible sign of putrefaction. Thus the object is taken far from its original meaning towards a new representation. In his Surrealist work, however, Dali has remained faithful to his initial mythology, pushing to the extreme only the pathological and morbid distortions to which he subjects his materials. When he began to undergo the influence of the Italian Renaissance, in 1937-1938, and to prepare for the return to Classicism which has marked his recent work, he was on much less sure ground. He was disowned by his friends, and the Surrealist leader, the poet André Breton, denounced his technique as ultra-reactionary and academic. However, he has had considerable success with a certain set in the United States, where he went to live in 1940. He has influenced both fashion and advertising. He now gives his models so-called 'atomic' interpretation, and tackles religious themes. When he returned to Spain after the war, at Cadaqués he found nourishment for his basic pictorial realism, and also the elements of a baroque tradition which seems better suited to his temperament than the austerity of a classicism drawn from Raphael. Some of his best known works, which have been most frequently reproduced, are the *Crucifixion* (1951, Glasgow Art Gallery) in which the figure hangs over the world and *The Last Supper* (1955) acquired by the National Gallery of Washington. Salvador Dali the man is even more of an enigma than Dali the painter. Although he has been very lavish with his secrets in his writings (*The Secret Life of Salvador Dali*, 1942, *Fifty Secrets of the Art of Magic*, 1948), in which the parts containing personal revelations are far more extensive than his essays with philosophical pretensions, Dali has assumed so many masks and poses, that it is hard to uncover his true personality. One can, nevertheless, discern elements of authenticity and continuity in his temperament. This applies particularly to the physical presence (which he never denied) of the landscapes of his childhood: the hills of Ampurdan, stretches of sand, and the shores of Cadaqués, bleached white by the sun. This landscape, which Dali, with unaffected

STUART DAVIS. SALT POT. 1931.
Museum of Modern Art, New York.

pride, considers the most beautiful in the world, is in his subconscious mind. It is the common denominator of all his external adventures. In spite of the variety of themes that have been superimposed on it, nothing affects this persistence of memory. The survival of such aspects of his childhood helps to explain and, to a certain degree, gives a human quality to many of Dali's irritating caprices.   J. LA.

DAVIS Stuart (born 1894 in Philadelphia). American painter. His father, a newspaper editor and cartoonist, was a close friend of some of the painters of 'The Eight,' especially Sloan, Shinn and Henri. Davis left high school after a year in 1909 to attend Henri's classes in New York. Under the influence of Lautrec and the populism of the 'Ash Can School,' he sought inspiration in the saloons and dance-halls of New York and New Jersey. He exhibited with 'The Independents' and did satirical illustrations and covers for the leftist review, *The Masses*. But the Armory show in 1913 which he describes as the 'greatest single influence I have experienced in my work' opened his eyes to broader horizons than those of the social realism which prevailed among the artists connected with *The Masses*. In 1915 he and several others resigned from the review. Deeply attached to the landscapes of the New England coast, especially those of Gloucester where he sojourns frequently, he paints landscapes and seascapes in an expressionist technique close to Van Gogh, and later in a concise epigrammatic style strongly influenced by Léger.

His reflections on modernism culminate in 1927-1928 in the famous *Eggbeater* series of abstractions. Here he retreated to his studio and nailed an eggbeater, an electric fan and a rubber glove to a table: they remained his exclusive subject for a year. He writes: 'I had come to feel that what was interesting in a subject or what had really caused our response to it could be best expressed in a picture if the geometrical planes were arranged in a direct relationship to the canvas as a flat surface. I felt that a subject had its emotional reality through our awareness of such planes and their spatial relationships. The result was the elimination of a number of particularized optical truths which I had formerly concerned myself with. In effecting this elimination, however, the subject was not repudiated in favor of some ideal order; but this approach was regarded as a more intense means of equating the sensible material one responds to in various subjects. My aim was not to establish a self-sufficient system to take the place of the immediate and the accidental, but . . . to strip a subject down to the real physical source of its stimulus.'

In 1928 he travelled to Paris where he stayed for more than a year. His views of Paris reintroduce recognizable forms: kiosks, café tables, Paris façades with their lettered signs, as elements in otherwise abstract compositions. But in spite of these particularities, his aim remains the same as in the *Eggbeater* paintings: to portray the concrete essence of a subject with abstract means. Literal references, he feels, do not conflict with the 'structural approach': particular truth does not eliminate general truth, nor vice versa.

These visible 'signposts' remain after his return to America, but after a time they begin to break up into fragments which are organized in monumental compositions of increasing complexity, such as *Swing Landscape* of 1938, whose innumerable brilliant-coloured scraps allude to landscape and urban forms without suggesting them explicitly. Elements of landscape are now reduced to a 'common denominator of colour-shape. Their simultaneous presentation in positional relationship creates a dynamic space extension analogous to the pleasure we feel in brilliant scenes in nature.'

Although his fame was slow in coming, Davis is regarded today as one of the leading living American painters. Europeans cannot always see the true originality of his work, because of its frequent use of the French idiom. But Americans, including the following generation of Abstract Expressionists with whom he has little in common, value it precisely because Davis was the first American to borrow vital discoveries from France and to incorporate them in a style which remains essentially American. As Davis himself explains it: 'Paris school, abstraction, escapism? Nope, just color-space compositions celebrating the resolution in art of stresses set up by some aspects of the American scene.'   J. A.

DEGAS. DANCER ADJUSTING HER SHOE.
Private Collection.

DEGAS Edgar. French painter born in Paris in 1834; died there 1917. He was the son of a banker, Auguste de Gas, and, like Manet, belonged to the upper middle class by birth. His taste for classicism, the correctness with which he conducted himself, seem to be in keeping with his origins, but his exceedingly strong personality and independence of mind threw him into the camp of the revolutionaries. He learned to paint at the École Nationale des Beaux-Arts, under Louis Lamothe, a pupil of Ingres, for whom Degas always had a profound admiration. Whatever the evolution of his genius, he was never critical of his early training. No doubt it was his great respect for human creation that was at the bottom of the misanthropy of which he is often accused, and behind which one can sense a deep tenderness. The evolution of his art explains the very special position that Degas occupied in relation to Impressionism. In his earliest paintings, such as *Spartan Girls and Boys Exercising* (1860), *Semiramis Building a City*

(1861), and the *Misfortunes of the City of Orléans*, for which he made numerous studies, or even (a little later) the *Cotton Market in New Orleans* (1873), which he painted during his stay in the United States, we are indisputably looking at an extremely classical art, with meticulous draughtsmanship. Little by little, without weakening the rigour of his drawing, he allowed colour to become more and more important. Colour was, however, always subordinated to a realism which

DEGAS. AT THE RACES. 1869-1872. *Musée du Louvre.*

would have been dry and narrow had not the genius of Degas brought it a breadth of vision and an originality in composition which saved him from academism, and gave his work a significance far in excess of the place he is given in the Impressionist movement.

Degas certainly belongs to Impressionism be-

cause of his desire to capture the fleeting moment, and his concern for presenting exact reality. His division of colour, however, never went so far as the dispersal stressed by the landscapists. Whereas with the Impressionists, form tended to dissolve in the atmosphere, with Degas it kept its density. In fact, unlike them, Degas wanted to sum up the living world within strictly determined limits: he had no taste for suggesting the rustle of leaves, the shimmer of water, or the changing effects of the sky. When landscape does intrude into his composition—in his racecourse scenes in particular—it never gives the impression of a work executed on the spot; nor does one feel, with him, that Nature was necessary to his inspiration. The picture-

DEGAS. STUDY FOR 'MISFORTUNES OF THE CITY OF ORLÉANS'. 1865. *Louvre.*

DEGAS. ABSINTHE. 1876-1877. *Louvre.*

Cézanne, it will be remembered, wanted to make of Impressionism a solid painting like that of the museums. One might say that Degas dreamed of creating a museum painting as living and modern as that of the Impressionists. Whereas Monet, Sisley and Pissarro sought the maximum possibilities of colour, and Cézanne did the same with respect to volume, Degas cherished an equally tenacious passion for drawing. 'I am a colourist with line', he said. He drew, and colour came only to complete, by its material and fixative quality, what the drawing had caught of the dynamic reality. Drawing was, for him, the result of swift observation. It was necessary to see quickly, and the mind must be able to select; painting was the result of a series of verifications, and did not require the same inventive qualities. Slowly, however, he began to discover the wider limits of colour. He began to seek in it something more than local tone, and the means of characterizing a volume. From then on colour brightened the body surfaces, caught the light on the filmy *tutus* of the dancing girls, and produced some of the most glamorous and fairylike scenes of the close of the nineteenth century. These dancers, these women at their

dealer Ambroise Vollard records this significant remark made by Degas: 'The air which one breathes in a picture is not the same as the air one breathes outside'. He did not seek chance beauty improvised by Nature, he preferred that created by man. He preferred the artificial light of the theatre to sunlight. He was interested in the human presence, and never treated the silhouettes of his figures in the casual manner of the other Impressionists. In that way his art was not a repudiation of the Classicism glorified by Ingres, but actually an extension of that formula enriched by new experiences. All these points, on which he differed with his friends, are not, in fact, sufficient to exclude him from the Impressionist movement–in the first place, because Degas himself decided otherwise (in fact, he participated, from the beginning, in a number of their exhibitions, at a time when this participation meant taking a stand, a declaration of war); but, above all, it should be understood that although he had his differences of opinion with Monet, Sisley and Pissarro, he did not oppose the new school but, with Cézanne, completed it.

DEGAS. STUDY FOR A PORTRAIT OF MANET. 1864. *Metropolitan Museum, New York.*

toilet, are certainly neither intelligent nor beautiful. They are commonplace, often vulgar in their physique and in their poses, but Degas strips them of matter, picking out only the essential rhythms of their movements, making beauty itself spring from the banality or vulgarity of their gestures. He does it so naturally, so completely, that he never gives the impression of resorting to artifice in order to transfigure reality. His was a more complex, intellectual creation than those achieved by most of the other Impressionists.

One thing is certain: if Degas, starting from Classicism, felt isolated in the midst of those who claimed to have broken with the past, he was still more opposed to those who wished to preserve it with a dismal and narrow fidelity. The deep hostility and spirit of revolt that made Degas reject all the academic formulas transmitted by the École des Beaux-Arts, can never be sufficiently stressed. This stubborn search for the new, the hitherto unattempted, was with Degas more a means than an end. He wanted to cast off all that was conventional, trite or commonplace, in order to transcribe reality without having anything impede or distort his vision. Degas is really the first artist in whom indifference to all that was not real was carried to its extreme. His attitude is similar to that of the zoologist, or the physiologist. He outlines a human attitude as a doctor describes a clinical case. It is therefore Naturalism that transformed this traditional artist (as he was at first) into one of the most daring innovators in the transcription of the scenes of modern life. But this search, however persistent, was never provocative. Breaking with the accepted conventions, his *Portrait of the Bellelli Family*, which he painted when he was only twenty-six, contains a real stage setting, which must have surprised his contemporaries somewhat. Degas portrayed M. Bellelli with his back turned, seated in an armchair, an arrangement which was hardly in conformity with custom. In his pictures of this period, no matter how traditional they might be, he seemed to be already avoiding static forms, seeking instead the effect of photographic instantaneity, which was to become characteristic of all his work. His *Cotton Market in New Orleans* (1873) is a synthesis of his art over a period of years: audacity in the placing of the subject,

very important foreground, scrupulously exact draughtsmanship, and a very solid, though somewhat conventional perspective. Without a doubt this very need to represent life led him to doubt his characters at work, such as laundresses, milliners (1882-1884), surprising them in characteristic attitudes. For several years before then dancers had revealed to him the resources of the human body, and shown him what an artist who

DEGAS. CARLO PELLEGRINI. 1876-1877.
Tate Gallery, London.

cared about draughtsmanship could find in the acts of everyday life. It is only natural that the name of Degas should conjure up, for the less informed, dancers in *tutus*, practising their points, tying their shoe ribbons, or revolving about the stage from strange perspectives with oddly foreshortened bodies. For these dancers represent Degas's decisive contribution to the Impressionist movement. They represent the very movement of perpetually changing reality surprised, immobilized–that obsession of the artists of the period. However, the reality seen by Degas is his own: anxious to express the maximum of life, he selected aspects of reality that had never been observed before, and were thus more striking in their truth. His nudes–women at their toilet–reveal attitudes that do not appear very natural, the limbs being contracted in awkward gestures. For the same reason he tried to get from light effects which were contrary to natural lighting; he tried to capture the light of the footlights, which rises from the floor, inverts shadows, transforms faces, and brings gestures out in unusual relief. Degas went beyond this stage in the expression of movement and took up sculpture: his statuettes of horses and dancers became a real arabesque in space, and the analogy of gesture between dancer and horse, the same way of nervously extending the leg, reveals his keen and exacting observation.

If Degas belongs to Impressionism, it is by his mental disposition rather than his technique,

by his clear refusal to accept a conventional world. Study gave him a technique; the spectacle of reality gave him a sense of life. Degas appeared to divine the potentialities of the modern world to a far greater extent than his friends did. It is no mere accident to find in his work a forecast of new ways of disposing figures on the canvas, and unexpected angles of vision which, many years later, photography and the cinema were to use. His views seen from above, his method of depicting the main figure in a portrait off centre, of giving the foreground unexpected importance in relation to the subject as a whole, of putting the emphasis on an inert and accessory detail in order to accentuate, by contrast, the expression of life in face–all these innovations correspond exactly to what the camera gives us today. In *Le Secret Professionnel* Jean Cocteau writes: 'I have seen photographs that Degas enlarged himself, on which he worked directly in pastel, amazed by the arrangement, the foreshortenings and the distortion of the foreground'. But that is reducing too much to chance the part played by the artist, without taking into account the sharpness of his magnificent drawing, which goes far beyond instantaneous photography, no matter how exceptional that may be. These new possibilities interested him only in so far as they enabled him to emphasize the everyday action. Degas always refused to paint from Nature. Although, in his work, he gives an impression of spontaneity, of having captured a gesture or pose at a dress rehearsal in the theatre, or on the race-course, his pictures are all studio productions, the results of long hours of hard work under conditions where, unlike the artist who works from Nature, he is not limited by time. His painstaking drawings were made from memory, or from 'notes'. At a time when some painters were proclaiming their desire to depict their passing impressions, Degas's profound and patient observation produced masterpieces full of the feeling of life.

He brought the same research approach to the problems of technique, and there, too, his classical

DEGAS. RECLINING WOMAN. PASTEL. ABOUT 1880.

sense, far from limiting him, impelled him to seek that mastery of his craft which the painters of the past had had. Though he used the most varied mediums, he found pastel the one that suited him best. Sometimes he used different mediums in the same picture, or else he would superimpose coats of pastel in order to obtain, as in oil-painting, a play of transparencies between the strokes. Towards the end of his life, his sight failing, he developed a preference for working in charcoal, multiplying the sharp, nervous strokes, often enhancing them with pastel. Degas is as indispensable to the history of Impressionism as Renoir, Monet, Cézanne. Even if his work has had less influence than that of Cézanne, it contains enough mystery to enable it to be rediscovered one day for reasons which we do not suspect, and which will, perhaps, be far from those for which we admire him today. R. C.

DELAUNAY Robert. French painter, born in Paris in 1885; died at Montpellier in 1941. As painting was the only thing he really cared for, he gave up his studies early, and entered a school of theatrical design. From 1904 on he devoted himself exclusively to art. His work soon got away from traditional techniques. After a holiday spent in Brittany in 1904, he began to paint in large touches of pure colours similar to those of the Fauves. His self-portraits, with dominant reds and greens, are his first results in this direction. In 1906, when Delaunay was under the influence of Seurat, this technique evolved logically towards the breakdown of colour, not by Pointillist methods but by laying it on in large flat patches. In the composition of *Le Fiacre* he translated the movement by means of a kind of elongated mosaic, but in his *Manège de Cochons* (1906), a theme which he took up again in 1913 and 1922, he affirmed for the first time his preoccupation with circular rhythms. He began to study the theories of Chevreul, and became interested in Cézanne's conception of space. Cubism was just being born. Delaunay scrutinized the works of Braque and Picasso, Negro statues, and the works of art of Egypt and Mesopotamia in the Louvre. He became a great friend of the Douanier Rousseau, from whom, at his request, his mother commissioned *The Snake Charmer*, now in the Louvre. His large

DEGAS. FIGURE STUDY FOR THE PICTURE IN THE LOUVRE, 'BALLET REHEARSAL ON STAGE'. 1874.

studies of foliage and vegetation, painted from Nature, as well as a small panel with a grey atmosphere in which the first of his Eiffel Towers appears, date from 1908. It would seem as though before undertaking his great chromatic adventure Delaunay was gathering (while reducing them to the extreme) the essential elements of his inspiration. In 1909 he painted the Saint-Séverin series: in it light is broken down into the colours of the spectrum, while the architecture is simplified and tends to give the impression of forms turning in space. These fascinating works foreshadowed *The Windows* of 1912.

In 1910 Delaunay married Sonia Terk, whom he had known since 1907, and who worked side by side with him. With his two compositions called *The City*, Delaunay entered Cubism. This time he no longer had recourse to chromatic scales but to the search for values. Working in dominant greys and greens, his touch became finer and more precise. On the other hand, the three large compositions entitled *Eiffel Tower* (1910), now in the Basel Museum, the Guggenheim Museum in New York, and a private collection in Germany, represent a remarkable attempt to increase the height and depth of the canvas in a most audacious fashion, solely through construction and colour. Divergent planes are superimposed, the perspectives multiply and swell as in an accordion, space acquires a new thickness and consistency. In the large composition *The City of Paris* (Musée d'Art Moderne, Paris), painted in three weeks for the Salon des Indépendants of 1912, three large figures of nude women are developed according to the same principle of superimposition. In this major work Delaunay again takes up his prismatic method of composition, though in a more systematic manner, one part of the picture being dominated by a red and yellow light, the other by blue and violet shadow. Writing of it, Apollinaire said: 'It is the most important picture in the Salon'.

This work marks the beginning of what is called Delaunay's constructive period, as opposed to the preceding, so-called destructive period. Setting out to find something which would not be torn, jagged or dramatic, Delaunay composed

his *Windows*. From then on he gave up all images drawn from reality, he abolished objects 'that come to break and corrupt the coloured work' (*vide* illustration, page 9). Apollinaire fully appreciated the import of this transition from the representational to the non-representational: he invented the word Orphism *(*)* to designate all those colourful manifestations which brought a ray of hope into the rigid and cold monotony of Cubism. Delaunay has been accused of having returned to Impressionism and become a decorative painter. In reality, a new art was created, which set forth the formal representation of space and movement.

After *Simultaneous Prismatic Windows*, Delaunay freed himself altogether, and reached pure painting in *The Discs* and *Cosmic Circular Forms*, all dated 1912. Modestly, he did not consider his research–so important for the birth of abstract art–as culmination but, rather, as a necessary transition. 'We are at the ABC of the new painting', he used to say. However, in *Homage to Blériot* (1914), even though his abstract research is predominant, Delaunay found again a certain meaning in representation. The theoretical importance of his discoveries, the shock power of his coloured universe, brought him considerable prestige. His influence extended far beyond Paris. At great friendship sprang up between him and the two young German artists Franz Marc and August Macke. Kandinsky invited him to the two Blaue Reiter *(*)* exhibitions. Klee translated one of his articles. Apollinaire's lecture at the Delaunay exhibition in Berlin, at the Der Sturm Gallery in 1913, made a tremendous impression.

During the 1914-1918 war Delaunay spent a long time in Spain and Portugal. In his Portuguese still-lifes there is some return to the use of subjects, and a predominance of rounded forms. After the war he went back to his old themes, particularly the Eiffel

R. DELAUNAY. RUNNERS. 1926. *S. D. Collection, Paris.*

SONIA DELAUNAY.
COMPOSITION.
1952. *Private Collection.*

Tower which continued to arouse his amazement and then began his dazzling series of the *Runners* (1924-1926). In 1925 he painted his large *City of Paris* for the Mallet-Stevens Pavilion at the Exhibition of Decorative Arts in Paris. Returning to his *Discs* of 1914, he amplified them in his *Unending Rhythms* and *Coloured Rhythms*. About 1930, he began working at his first plaster reliefs. He discovered new cadences and expressed them with an ever renewed joy and youthfulness. The Paris International Exhibition in 1937 gave him the opportunity of realizing his greatest ambition. After two years of intensive preparation, he executed, in a month and a half, ten enormous bas-reliefs in colour for the Hall of Railroads and a gigantic *Rhythm* about a thousand square yards in size for the Hall of the Air, works which, with their enormous dimensions, represent one of the most imposing efforts in modern decoration. Colour had become the subject, and Delaunay achieved abstraction in the fullest sense of the term. In 1938, gravely ill, he painted his last *Rhythms*, and finished writing about his research. These writings are still unpublished. In 1940, fleeing from the German invasion, he took refuge in Auvergne, then in Mougins. He died in Montpellier on October 25th, 1941. J. LA.

DELAUNAY Sonia Terk. French painter, born in Ukraine, 1886. She was brought up in her uncle's house in St Petersburg. She was attracted by mathematics but chose painting. On the insistence of her drawing teacher (who was also an ethnographer), she obtained her parents' permission to go to study in Germany, where she stayed for two years, at Karlsruhe. Then she went to Paris and enrolled at the Académie de la Palette, which was frequented by Ozenfant, and by Segonzac and his friends. Under the influence of the work of Gauguin and Van Gogh, she sought a means of liberation and expression in the intensification of colour (*Philomena, the Seamstress*, and the portraits of little girls she painted in Finland). She made the acquaintance of Wilhelm Uhde, who was on the side of the Fauvist painters (then in their Cézannian period), and exhibited in his gallery. Cubism was soon to begin. She met Robert Delaunay, whose taste for poetry and pictorial ideas she shared, and married him in 1910. Swept along by his dynamism, Sonia elaborated a personal mode of expression, which summarizes her experience with Cubism and Orphism, and used it in designing bookbindings, cushions, rugs and collages made of violently coloured paper and cloth. She covered her walls with abstract compositions, and made herself dresses of 'simultaneous colours'. On the same principle she created pictures which are orchestrations of colours with no representational purpose, which suggest movement and emotion merely by their combinations. In 1913, at the Herbstsalon in Berlin, together with Robert Delaunay, she exhibited some twenty objects and pictures, and the first 'simultaneous book', created to illustrate Blaise Cendrars' poem, *La Prose du Trans-Sibérien et de la petite Jehanne de France.* In 1915 the livid light of Spain awoke in

Sonia Delaunay coloured memories of her native village. In Portugal the beauty of the country and of the national costumes inspired some brilliant compositions (*Market at Minho*) and encouraged her to widen her field of decorative activities. In Madrid, inspired by the Spanish dances, she painted some abstract water-colours in which she studied the relationship of colours in their reciprocal action. She met Diaghilev, who commissioned her to design costumes for the ballet *Cléopâtre*. Robert Delaunay painted the décor. On her return to France in 1920 she decided to apply her ideas to fashion. She revolutionized the art of fabric design, replacing traditional patterns by geometrical motifs, combinations of coloured planes, and scales of tones with exciting contrasts of rhythmic variations. Her fabrics were reproduced and adopted by the leading couturiers, and exerted a great influence over many aspects of our life (the theatre, the cinema). This occupied so much of her time and energy,

ROBERT DELAUNAY. ÉQUIPE DE CARDIFF. 1913. DRAWING. INDIAN INK.

that Sonia was obliged, in the end, to give up her commercial obligations in order to be able to devote herself to painting. The practical application of her ideas shows their importance and, particularly, their architectural value. Sonia Delaunay's discoveries were shown at their best in the vast compositions in the Hall of the Air and the Hall of Railroads at the Paris International Exhibition in 1937. After their flight before the invading Germans in 1940, and the illness and death of Robert Delaunay in 1941, a new period opened for Sonia, a period of meditation and research. In 1942, in Grasse, in the south of France, where she met Sophie Taeuber-Arp and Magnelli, she painted a series of harmonious and subtle gouaches. After the war she helped to found the Salon des Réalités Nouvelles (an idea put forward by Robert Delaunay in 1930), where, for the first time, abstract paintings from all over the world could be seen together. In 1953 an important retrospective exhibition of her work, held at the Bing Gallery, showed the evolution of an art which, for all its ascetism, has never sacrificed richness or intensity.   J. LA.

DELVAUX Paul. Belgian painter born in Antheit, Belgium, in 1897. This painter was a long time finding his way. He was alternately a Neo-Impressionist and an Expressionist until about the year 1935. Then, the combined influence of Giorgio de Chirico and René Magritte drew him into the Surrealist movement. His aim, from then on, was no longer to interpret faithfully the exterior world, but to explore the intimate and secret domain of his inner life. Objective reality ceased to interest him, except as a frame for his dreams. In his depiction of these dreams, one encounters strange combinations of people and places. From their contrasts and affinities, a disquieting poetry is born. Temples, moonlit towns, streets and public squares, empty rooms: these are settings for the same type of woman, young and beautiful, sometimes nude, sometimes dressed in lace, in foliage or in long robes with heavy folds. The painter is obsessed by this person. All his work, except for a few compositions with skeletons, reflects his need to come closer to an ideal being who, as the result of a paradoxical reversal of situations, seems to pursue him, instead of

DELVAUX. HANDS. 1941. *Private Collection.*

After studies at the Pennsylvania Academy of Fine Arts, he visited Europe in 1907 and again in 1912, when he remained for two years, studying at the Académie Colarossi, the Académie Moderne and the Académie Julian. His early work was influenced by the Fauves, especially Matisse, by Cézanne and by John Marin. In his early watercolour landscapes of 1912 to 1915 he combines Cubist analysis with the Expressionists' free brushwork and space-defining colour. Back in New York, his contacts with the Stieglitz 'stable' of which he becomes a member and with Duchamp influence him profoundly. He begins to work in several

being joined by him. Surrealism *(*)*, as a movement, envisaged the freeing of man through an appeal to his instincts and his subconscious. Each of its painters used different means of expression and different techniques. Delvaux's style much more realistic than that of Max Ernst or Joan Miró, is closer to that of Chirico. But whereas Chirico's manner is dry, ascetically bare, deliberately barren, Delvaux is a lyrical artist who has inherited from his Flemish ancestors a taste for harmonious forms. He paints meticulously, but the excess of detail, the literary content of the overworked backgrounds, sometimes divide the attention instead of concentrating it on the principal subject of the picture. Delvaux's palette, sombre at the beginning, has grown progressively brighter until it is now brilliant. Several journeys to Italy have strengthened his taste for bright colours. Some handsome water-colours round off his work, which can be described as classical in method and Surrealist in spirit. C. S.

DEMUTH Charles (1883-1935). American painter; born and died in Lancaster, Pennsylvania. His parents, well-to-do and cultivated, encouraged his artistic vocation.

styles, each associated with a different kind of subject matter. His flower studies are watercolours (the medium most characteristic of him) in which mild influences of Cézanne and perhaps of Redon are transformed into something quite personal: delicate, oblique, sophisticated with a hint of mystery also. These qualities are predominant also in Demuth's illustrations and his studies of circus and cabaret performers —his most important works despite their seemingly fragile and ephemeral character. Chief among the illustrations are those for Zola's *Nana* and *L'Assommoir*, Wedekind's *Die Erdgeist* and for Henry James' *The Turn of the Screw* and *The Beast in the Jungle*. The thin, flowing washes of colour and the scribbled pencil drawing convey the characters as transparent phantoms of the author's imagination. A kind of expressionism called for by the subject (Lulu, Nana) is diverted from its course by the deft handling and a *je ne sais quoi* of tender irony. Again, Demuth's circus types and scenes of *low life*, though inspired in part by Lautrec, are equivocal, viewed through a screen which surrounds them with an aura of mystery. Finally, the curious studies of colonial architecture and of modern factories, are close in their prismatic technique to Feininger and to Sheeler's 'immaculate' urban landscapes, though once more the directness is muted by irony, ambiguity and fantasy.

Demuth visited Paris again, in 1921. Always in fragile health (he had been lame from childhood as the result of an accident) he was found in the following year to be suffering from diabetes. During the remaining years of his life he travelled little, except for summers in Provincetown, and he died in Lancaster in 1935.

DEMUTH. ACROBATS. 1919. WATER-COLOUR.
Museum of Modern Art, New York.

Elegant, frivolous, witty, dandified, he supplied American art with the one thing it needed: an aesthete. He is perhaps the living example of Bernard Shaw's remark that America passed from barbarism to decadence without going through any of the intervening stages. Scarcely has an independent American art arisen when Demuth appears to bring it his curiously attractive blend of *weltschmerz* and light-hearted so-

phistication. He is another proof of the many-sided vigour of American art during the two decades following the Armory show.   J. A.

DENIS Maurice. French painter born in Granville in 1870, died in Saint-Germain-en-Laye in 1943. Maurice Denis was the originator of the famous definition used whenever anyone wants to explain contemporary art: 'Remember that a picture–before being a horse, a nude, or some sort of anecdote–is essentially a flat surface covered with colours assembled in a certain order'. That text dates from 1890. Maurice Denis was then not yet twenty, but he showed already an unusual lucidity in such matters. Through Sérusier, who came back from Brittany in 1888, he had just been introduced to the message of Gauguin, whose ideas on Symbolism, and its offshoot Synthesism, were taking shape. In fact, it was the group at the Académie Julian *(*)*, in which, around Sérusier and Maurice Denis, were to be found Bonnard, Vuillard, K.-X. Roussel, René Piot and Ranson, that began the reaction against Impressionism, which these young artists nevertheless admired. All the philosophical theories, all the ideological formulations, led to a new aesthetic doctrine (*vide* Nabis) which rejected the technique of the older generation. As against the improvisation of Monet and Sisley, and the dispersal of form, Gauguin put forward an art into which went a good deal of thinking, a choice, harmonies in which what the painter wanted counted more than the observation of Nature. Gauguin wanted the reconstruction of form by colour applied over large areas, and also strong, precise drawing, sometimes even going to the extent of a thick outline around the figures or subjects. Before adopting this formula, Maurice Denis had tried to paint the vibration of light by the use of small touches and the division of colour in accordance with the principles of Seurat. But, whatever the importance he attached to technical problems, his keenness for ideas inevitably led him to treat, in his pictures, subjects with a much more complex significance than simple landscapes or still-lifes. If, then, Symbolism was an intellectual and poetic concept which demanded that a picture should not be merely the material representation of the external world but should also express and suggest certain thoughts or states of mind, then the birth of Synthesism was inevitable. The desire to spiritualize painting sprang from a need for synthesis, a very controlled art, the opposite of Impressionist spontaneity, which is analytic. The introduction of philosophical and poetic elements into painting was bound to satisfy Maurice Denis, who remains one of the most important theorists of the time, through his two basic works, *Theories* and *New Theories*. His work as a painter is an exact reflection of the state of mind which, little by little, led him to devote himself almost exclusively to religious art. He is – with Georges Desvallières – one of its most able renovators.

Nevertheless, there is a strange contradiction between Maurice Denis's work and his ideas. After having been one of the first to stress the idea that a work of art ought to find its justification in itself, the subject being only of

DENIS. THE MUSES. 1893.
Musée d'Art Moderne, Paris.

secondary importance, Maurice Denis is also the man who has given the subject back its primary importance; for, in religious art, the representation of the Nativity or of the Crucifixion is the picture's main *raison d'être*.

Maurice Denis travelled widely in Belgium, Spain, Germany, Switzerland, Algeria, the United States and Canada. Greece and Palestine impressed him strongly. But it was Italy that influenced his work most decisively: Rome gave him classicism; Siena his harmony of colours; Florence his simplicity of design; and Assisi the purity of his landscapes. For his art, like his faith, was nourished by his love for the loftiest embodiments of the mind and of beauty. He executed numerous mural decorations, especially for churches, and his predilection for static forms and almost immobile figures is particularly suited to this type of work. Through his calm drawing, his range of light colours, his delicate harmonies of blue and rose, he gives the impression of a serenity which is rather exceptional in the painting of his time. And that might, perhaps, be his main fault. At times one would like to sense more unrest in his work, a humanity less satisfied in its beatitude, a calm less manifest and less complete. In his writings one gets the distinct feeling that this calm is actually tremendous self-control, and that Maurice Denis the man, with his restlessness and his doubts, deliberately imposed on himself the solution of life to which Maurice Denis the artist bowed.   R. C.

DE NITTIS Giuseppe (1846-1884). Italian painter; born in Barletta, died at Saint-Germain-en-Laye. His family was well-to-do and he was taught painting by G. B. Calò. He attended the Institute of Arts in Naples and then followed Cecioni at the 'School of Resina', a sort of branch of the Macchiaioli (*). De Nittis did not actually meet these until later in Florence, where he joined in the discussions at the Café Michelangiolo. During this Florentine period, which continued until 1860, De Nittis stood out as one of the most remarkable of the Macchiaioli. He visited Paris for the first time from 1867 to 1870, then returned to live there in 1872, toning down his Tuscan style a little to suit the tastes of an elegant and sophisticated public. He painted scenes of Parisian life and often achieved an exceptional refinement of subject and colour and a subtly poetic atmosphere. He died when he was thirty-eight.   D. F.

DE PISIS Filippo (1898-1956). Born at Ferrara; died at Milan. Pseudonym of Luigi Tibertelli. A critic confronted with his work might get the superficial impression that he has never had any problems or submitted to any discipline. He lived in Paris from 1925 to 1939, but without arousing much interest, his preoccupations having nothing in common with those of the other artists of his age. He seemed to be living in reverse, anxious, as he was to revert to the Venetian origins of Impressionism, to throw a bridge across from Paris to Venice and thus hide the poverty of Italian painting of the previous century. In an epoch of serious and laborious researches, his apparent facility is disconcerting. And yet, just as certain pictures by Picasso would not have been disowned by Ingres or Raphael, a snowy landscape by De Pisis would not have displeased Pissarro, Marquet, or Utrillo. As Delacroix wanted to, he really paints a man as he falls from a window and before his body crashes to the pavement. That is why the execution may appear sketchy, almost stenographic. He is clearly not a creator of forms but a painter of sensations, of unexpected encounters. Chance plays a great part in his work. It is uneven: every painting by De Pisis is an adventure, but not every adventure is felicitous. Nevertheless, there are many successful pictures among them, which justify the popularity he enjoys among Italian collectors. Writer and poet, De Pisis was one of the most original personalities in contemporary Italy. He is considered the greatest Italian landscapist of the century, but his love of Nature is hardly ever founded on direct sensation. He might, perhaps, have been indifferent to Nature, had it not inspired so many masterpieces. Reminiscence stimulates his imagination, and his most beautiful landscapes, like *Notre-Dame de Paris*, *Trafalgar Square* or *Saint Mark's*, are those which, for centuries, have inspired the most mediocre but also the greatest artists.   S. L.

DERAIN André (1880-1954). French painter born in Chatou; died in Chambourcy. Intelligent and studious, he had a fine academic record. Then he suddenly decided to devote himself to painting. He became friendly with Vlaminck *(*)* and from 1900 shared a studio with him at Chatou. He painted with Matisse at Collioure during the summer of 1905, frequented the Bateau-Lavoir *(*)* in the Rue Ravignan in Paris at the same time as Braque and Picasso. About the same time he made the acquaintance of Guillaume Apollinaire. Therefore none of the new ideas and new currents of sensibility that traversed the early years of the century were foreign to him. Derain was one of the first to discover Negro art, to feel the zest of popular imagery and the richness of folklore, to admire the beauty of the Sienese primitives and the painters of the École d'Avignon. But, first of all, he was an exponent of Fauvism *(*)*. Like his friend Vlaminck, he employed the segmented touch, the swift curve, and garish colours. But his touch was less brutal, his curves more sustained, his colours more harmonious. The dominant tones in his palette were green, blue, and the whole range of violets from pink

DERAIN. THE BARGES. 1904. *B. J. Fisz Collection, Paris.*

insatiable curiosity and, possibly, by lack of confidence in himself, he began to examine the masters of the past and delve into problems of technique. In fact, Derain was always concerned with problems of *métier*, and it began to assume a preponderant importance in his work. Setting aside the dictates of the mind in order to triumph over some technical obstacle, the artist accomplished many a *tour de force* without, however, calming his restlessness. He went to the Louvre to copy the great Italians. Then, having been won over to Cézanne, he participated in the elaboration of Cubism, but refused to adhere to the movement. He was a man who lived with History, although he seemed to live with his time. He proceeded to study the secrets of the Old Masters, drawing from tradition the nourishment that his proud will demanded. Towards 1911 he became interested in the French and Italian primitives, who knew how to combine

through purple. In his canvases there is none of that harsh, careless workmanship which indicates violence of instinct, but harmonies of proportions and tones, a sign of careful thought and reflection and, even then, of virtuosity for virtuosity's sake. He knew all the glamour of colour, and yet continued to pay careful attention to form and construction. That is why he executed some of the best Fauvist paintings: *Westminster Bridge* (see illustration, page 124), *A Corner of Hyde Park* (1906), his landscapes of Collioure and of l'Estaque, and *Woman in Deck Chair*. More eager than exacting, he wanted to include in a picture all the gains of modern painting, the discoveries of Impressionism, of Gauguin, of Van Gogh, and the influences of his friends Matisse and Vlaminck. It was this ambition that led him to paint *The Bathers* (1907), a work that seems to be a summary of the achievements of a quarter of a century. But, driven by an

DERAIN. COLLIOURE. 1905. *Private Collection, U.S.A.*

DERAIN. THE WINDOW. 1913. *Kunstmuseum, Basel.*

intellectual tension with grace of feeling. He admired the Gothic painters, but also the Douanier Rousseau, the Ferrara painters, and the old French folk-artists. From 1920 on he applied himself to the schools of the Quattrocento, Piero della Francesca, Raphael, the Bolognese painters and, still later, the art of Pompei. From then on he became a Realist and (to his credit, let it be said), a sincere and convinced Realist. Although he had been a Fauve, he had the originality to treat the problem of colour as secondary, and concentrate primarily on structure, in order to satisfy the demands of his own mind. At a time when form was being dissolved in the shimmering light of the Impressionists, or broken down under the analytic efforts of the Cubists, Derain wanted to grasp it by the simplest and most direct means. Nature then became his inspiration, and the Old Masters of the museums his models. His landscapes, his still-lifes and his portraits were composed with clear, precise draughtsmanship and rather dull, muffled colours. It is difficult to sort out in them the numerous influences to which he voluntarily submitted–those of Caravaggio, the Caracci, Corot, Cézanne and Renoir–for he amalgamated them with infinite skill. Surrounded by colleagues who were all for mobility, intensity and sensory excitement, Derain advocated order,

sobriety and reason. Methodical, if not dogmatic, curious but versatile, at times more concerned with surprising than persuading–he revived in French painting the old classical spirit, and with indisputable authority. His work may look like a product of the brain, like a technical exercise. He has crammed too many recollections into it, accumulated too many thoughts. Furthermore, the emotional quality of his work runs the risk of being smothered under the weight of intellectual constraints, although moments of softness and abandon come to remedy the essentially cerebral dryness of his style. But when his hand lets itself go there is such fantasy, such easy grace ! Certain critics, thinking of his early promise, have accused him of lack of faith, of apostasy. Others have regarded him as 'the greatest living French painter'. A return to the use of a subject, to chiaroscuro, to modelling; a return to academic ideas of resemblance, imitation and finish; a return to the human, not through the quivering thickness of flesh but through the severe discipline of museums; discoveries instead of inventions; cautiousness rather than wisdom; an extreme virtuosity, yet restless and morose: such appears to be Derain's art. All the same, Derain is not a dry, academic painter. And he is more than just a talented painter. This is what Apollinaire said of him in 1916: 'Derain has passionately studied the masters. The copies he has made show how anxious he was to get to know them. At the same time, with unparalleled courage, ignoring all the audacities of contemporary art, he found in freshness and simplicity the principles and the rules of art.' Will posterity confirm this opinion ? One way or the other, the fact remains that he has no influence today on the young French painters. But even if one rejects his later paintings, it would be unjust to forget the good canvases he painted at Vers, Martigues and Albano, his still-lifes of 1912 and 1913, his astonishing illustrations for Apollinaire's *L'Enchanteur Pourrissant* (1909) and Rabelais's *Pantagruel* (1946), as well as the décors and costumes that he designed for the Ballets Russes *(*)*. No other painter has shown, at one and the same time, so much doubt and so much mastery. No other painter has so conveyed the feeling of wanting to dominate his century and, at the same time, reject it.   F. E.

DESNOYER François. French painter born in Montauban in 1894. Cubism and Fauvism had already begun when Desnoyer was old enough to interest himself in painting. It was no longer tempting to adopt one or the other. Besides, a lucid and independent mind like his could not choose one trend to the exclusion of the other. Recognizing the importance of the contributions made by the new schools, Desnoyer took from each what best suited his temperament. He took over the rigid construction and geometrical framework of Cubism, and the intensity of colour of Fauvism. From this duality Desnoyer built up a stable and solid art. Everything in him lends itself to a double interpretation: he is a mild giant, and a placid southerner; his art has the freshness of spontaneous impressions, and the sureness of well-thought-out work. Desnoyer's originality lies in his having found unity in these apparent contradictions, of having created a healthy language for himself, in which everything is in place, without affectation. His personality is so much in evidence that it always dominates the subject. A landscape of Venice, Albi or Sète, a nude or a still-life, is first and foremost a picture by Desnoyer, with his particular harmonies and structure; that is to say, a combination of vividly coloured planes, sonorous contrasts, clean-cut drawing with a rhythm provided by the play of straight lines; a work in which one feels the will but not the effort, a balance between reason and instinct, leaving no room for misunderstandings, just as there is no room for shadows in these compositions in which everything has the right resonance.   R. C.

DIX Otto (born in 1891 at Gera, Thuringia). German painter. He was the son of a railway worker and attended the Art School, first at Dresden (1910-1914), then at Düsseldorf (before 1925), after receiving instruction from a painter-decorator. He was receptive to the influences of the time and went through a Dadaist phase before adopting a naturalistic manner about 1920. It remained a characteristic of his style, which enabled him to express all the disillusion and bitterness that social conditions after the war roused in him. His sympathy for the working class appears in a symbolic manner in pictures like *The Workman* (1921) in which the atmosphere of emptiness and desolation is reminiscent of Chirico. In spite of its realism, his painting, even the portraits, cannot possibly be described as objective; his moral purpose makes it symbolic and subjective. In 1927, he was appointed to a teaching post at the Dresden Academy, but was dismissed in 1933 as a 'decadent artist'. He has been living at Hemmenhofen on Lake Constance since the end of the Second World War, where he has devoted himself to painting religious subjects (*Saul and David*, 1945; *Crucifixion*, 1946).   E. R.

DESNOYER. THE PORT OF MARSEILLES. 1940.
Musée d' Art Moderne, Paris.

DOESBURG Theo van (1883-1931). Dutch painter; born in Utrecht, Holland; died in Davos, Switzerland. Van Doesburg–his real name was Küpper–at first planned a theatrical career. He wrote fables, plays and articles. In 1913 he published a collection of poems and began his research on the unification of painting and architecture. When still very young, he had begun painting and had exhibited for the first time at The Hague in 1908. In 1915

VAN DOESBURG. COMPOSITION VI. 1917.
Private Collection, Meudon.

he published a laudatory article on Mondrian, whose acquaintance he made later. From then on his painting veered towards abstraction. The transformation that Mondrian had undergone slowly from 1911 to 1914 (successive abstractions on the themes of the tree, scaffolding, etc.), Van Doesburg accomplished much more quickly from 1916 to 1917 (themes of a cow grazing, still-life, and cardplayers). In 1917, with Mondrian, Huszar, Van der Leck, Vantongerloo and several avant-garde Dutch architects, he founded the review *De Stijl (*)*, which, in the years following, exerted great influence upon the evolution of arts, particularly in Germany. In 1921 he left Holland for a crowded lecture tour through Central Europe. He caused much excitement, especially at the Bauhaus *(*)* in Weimar, where in 1924 he published *Fundamentals of the New Art*. After an exhibition of the *De Stijl* group in Paris in 1923 at Léonce Rosenberg's Galerie de l'Effort Moderne, Van Doesburg abandoned the rigorous principles formulated by Mondrian and set out in a new direction, which he would later (1926) call Elementarism *(*)*. In 1927 he executed the decoration of several rooms of the 'Aubette' dance hall in Strasbourg, where Arp and Sophie Taeuber were also at work. This was his greatest work, unfortunately since destroyed. His last years were, like the others, full of feverish activity. In 1930, with the assistance of the painters Hélion, Carlsund and Tutundjian, he published the only issue of the magazine *Art Concret (*)*. He died suddenly at Davos, in March 1931, during a treatment for hay fever.

More keen than profound, Van Doesburg was first of all an agitator and then a creator. He divined everything, understood at once, assaulted the obstacle with no concern for prudence. In this he was the exact opposite of Mondrian, who proceeded slowly, always in search of a deeper understanding of what he had already explored for a long time. Van Doesburg's nature was more aggressive than constructive. In his review he sometimes insulted those whom he had praised the day before (Lissitzky, Malevitch). But this did not prevent his mind from being fertile and sometimes clairvoyant. In Holland, as early as 1916, he published pamphlets on art and also an essay called *Classic, Baroque, Modern*, published at Paris in 1921. But

VAN DONGEN. RECLIN-
ING NUDE. 1904-1905.
Private Collection.

he was above all a brilliant showman, the fiery propagandist of Neo-Plasticism at the side of Mondrian. His chief claim to fame rests in his having divined Mondrian's value. Without the wholehearted support of Van Doesburg, who put *De Stijl* at his full disposal, Mondrian would probably never have codified Neo-Plasticism *(*)* in the memorable articles he produced from 1917 to 1920.   M. S.

DONGEN Cornelius T. M., called Kees van. Dutch painter, born 1877 at Delf-shaven, Van Dongen astonished his family by his precocious gifts. When still an adolescent, he drew and painted realistic works, and was soon influenced by the French Impressionists. In 1897, seven years after the death of his countryman Vincent van Gogh, he settled in Paris. To make a living, he practised all professions–house-painter, porter at the *Halles*, newsboy, com-missionnaire and fair-ground wrestler–and did sketches on café terraces. Like Steinlen, Jacques Villon and Vallotton, he contributed to satirical papers. He mingled in Montmartre life and acquired a simpler, more nervous, more concise line. Druet became interested in him in 1903, Vollard exhibited his work in 1904 and Berthe Weill in 1905. About the same time, he moved into the Bateau-Lavoir *(*)* in Montmartre. In 1906 he rallied enthusiastically to Fauvism *(*)*, predisposed by a latent expressionism and gifts as a colourist. He was faithful to Fauvism for a long time, through temperament and taste. He

attracted attention by his long and flexible arabesques, his clear and intense colour, his rich and oily paint. He juxtaposed tones in wide parallel strips, without much concern for depth. At this time he was already making brilliant use of a manner so cursory and elliptical that it would not have escaped unbearable dryness but for his vigorous sensualism. None of the other Fauves attained such richness, such fantasy, with means so direct, so concentrated, so simple. Before canvases like *Woman in a Hat* (1908) or *The Fellahin* (1912, Musée d'Art Moderne, Paris) one marvels at the effects he obtained by placing pure white and an ultramarine blue side by side, a vermilion in the light and an acid green in the shadows, by opposing a golden yellow to a bright red or black background. He was too devoid of intellectualism, too eager to experience sensations to care about drawing and composition. But what dexterity, what a sharp savour, what insolent ease in the works he executed from 1905 to 1913 ! What sureness of the eye, what life in every form, in every stroke, every passage painted for its own sake ! At the end of the First World War, he had al-ready become the fashionable portraitist, the painter in demand, taken up by an aristocratic and dubious society, in which the Maharajah rubbed elbows with the hired dancer, the banker threatened with bankruptcy, the *nouveau riche*, the authentic Marquise, the parvenu actress. All the leading figures of this troubled period wanted their portrait signed by the former porter at the *Halles* whom they had consecrated as the painter of society. And each of them wanted his own portrait done exactly like Van Dongen's others. Yet while he made some concessions to them, he did not humour them. He did not flatter them with his brush, did not even conceal the contempt he felt for them, did not hide their physical and moral flaws. However, to comply with their wish, he had to practise his art according to an invariable formula. It is thus that he created a sort of feminine type, the Theodora of the drawing-room, the Messalina of the boudoir, the princess

VAN DONGEN. THE ENCLOSURE.
Doctor Roudinesco Collection, Paris.

of the international set, with an exaggeratedly thin body, her pallor broken only by a gash of lipstick, half-clad in transparent tulle and adorned with glittering jewels. His vision remained nevertheless that of a painter, of an incomparable colourist. If he attenuated the virulence of his tones in time, sought more to please by using greys, modulations, shading, and to reassure by accentuating naturalistic illusion, he was none the less capable, when working only for himself, through pride and conviction, of producing works of fascinating free-

dom and mastery. Although he has left pitiless interpretations of Anatole France, the politician Rappaport and Boni de Castellane, for example, which condemn a period and a class, he also did some portraits of little girls in all their appealing grace and innocence, which he painted with tact and sincerity.

It is nevertheless in landscape that Kees Van Dongen has best fulfilled himself, no doubt because before nature he was himself again and painted for pleasure, without calculation. Then he quite naturally gave up artifice and the display of virtuosity. He showed tact, discretion, vigour, sacrificing the accessory, reducing form to the essential, employing a few tones, but the most direct and telling. His views of Paris and Versailles and the seascapes at Deauville are most expressive in their shorthand treatment, but these qualities have become more and more rare. In spite of a vigorous old age, Van Dongen no longer avoids facility, flabbiness, insipidity. Submitted too long to the vanities of the world, his will for expression has given way to a will to please. His sensuality, his pessimism, his dexterity, his impertinent boldness, his improviser's verve, all seem to have disappeared from his later work.   F. E.

DOVE Arthur G. (1880-1946). American painter; born in Canandaigua, N.Y. His father, a successful building contractor, sent him to Hobart and Cornell University and insisted on an extra year of law studies in the hope of discouraging his artistic career. Later he refused to help him financially, saying, 'I won't encourage this madness.' Though Dove's work was appreciated by critics from the beginning, he did not taste real success until several months before his death, and spent most of his life in straitened financial circumstances. Passionately fond of the water, he had no other home during the 20's than his boat, the *Mona*, where he lived with his wife, the painter Helen Torr.

Dove began after college as an illustrator for magazines like *Scribner's* and *The Saturday Evening Post*, and by 1907 had saved $4,000 with which he came to France where he spent eighteen months, meeting American artists: Alfred Maurer, Arthur Carles and Jo Davidson; with Maurer he set about 'simplifying Impressionism'. He soon went to stay in Cagnes, for he could not live without the country; there he produced Cézanne influenced landscapes and still-lifes like *The Lobster*, shown in the 1909 Salon d'Automne.

Dove's true personality did not emerge until he had returned to New York and met Stieglitz *(*)* in whose '291' he was to show frequently. In 1910 he painted six abstractions; the following year he showed chez Stieglitz a series of ten abstract pastels which he called *The Ten Commandments*.

The critic Frederick Wight says in his book on Dove that he 'deserves to be ranked with the dissimilar Kandinsky among the earliest abstract expressionists'. One cannot help thinking of Kandinsky's first abstractions, which were contemporary with Dove's, but the dissimilarity exists. Whereas in early Kandinsky shreds of the visible world remain as a kind of last vestige before the artist launches into the unknown, Dove is concerned with arriving at a deeper and truer image of that world. He attempts this through a methodical process of elimination and selection far removed from Kandinsky's romanticism, in order to discover the exact colour and shape (motif) which will spell out the hidden essence of the object to the viewer.

He writes: 'The first step was to choose from nature a motif in colour and with that motif to paint from nature, the forms still being objective. The second step was to apply this same principle to form, the actual dependence upon the subject (representation) disappearing, and the means of expression purely subjective . . .' Or again: 'There was a long period of searching for something in colour which I called a "condition of light." It applied to all objects in nature, flowers, trees, people, apples, cows . . . To understand that clearly, go to nature, or to the Museum of Natural History and see the butterflies. Each has its own orange, blue, black, white, yellow, brown, green and black, all carefully chosen to fit the character of the life going on in that individual entity.' Once Dove had developed his art it changed little, though the paintings of his last years, when he was ill and beset by financial worries, are often sombre, peopled by tense, hieratic shapes, as in *Long Island* (1940), *Parabola* (1943); *That Red One* (1944) and *High Noon* (1944). They are among the profoundest state-

ments from this lonely and curious genius, who even in America is far from having the place he deserves.   J. A.

DUBOIS-PILLET

Albert (1846-1890). French painter; born in Paris, died at Puy-en-Velay. In spite of a precocious gift for drawing, he entered Saint-Cyr. He was a second-lieutenant in the infantry during the 1870-1871 campaign and an officer in the Republican Guard afterwards, but he did not neglect his real vocation. In 1877 and 1879 he succeeded in getting his work accepted by the jury of the official Salon, but from 1880 to 1884 the same jury was adamant in refusing it. This was how a soldier came to be among the handful of rebels who, in 1884, founded the Société des Artistes Indépendants and with the slogan: No jury, no rewards, brought a new salon into existence that would be open to everybody. It even seems that it was Dubois-Pillet who drew up the rules and

DOVE. UNTITLED. 1942.
Metropolitan Museum, New York.

undertook the work of organisation. He was elected vice-president of the new society. At the first Salon des Indépendants, he exhibited a picture, *The Dead Child*, which impressed Zola and which he later described and attributed to Claude Lantier, the hero of his novel, *L'Œuvre*, published in 1886.

It was during the meetings that led up to the founding of the Indépendants that Dubois-Pillet met Seurat and Signac, whose works were to rouse the greatest interest in the first salons of the society. But it was not till 1887 that he adopted—and he was one of the first to do so—their Divisionist technique and exercised his talents in trying to perfect the theory and practice of his young friends (he was about fifteen years their senior). His particular innovation was to apply the meticulous technique of Divisionism to portraiture. However, it is above all in landscape that his delicacy, decorative sense and his subdued colouring can be best appreciated. All his leisure was spent painting and he regularly took part in the exhibitions of the Indépendants. One of his friends called him that 'stimulating painter of twilight, morning and spring in Paris'. He was made commanding officer of the gendarmerie company of the Haute-Loire and was 'exiled' to Puy, where he painted a series of fine, rather restrained landscapes before he died from meningitis.　J. R.

DUCHAMP Marcel. French painter and theorist, born in Blainville, near Rouen, in 1887. His father was a notary, and had six children, of whom four are well-known artists: in addition to Marcel Duchamp, the painters Jacques Villon and Suzanne Duchamp, and the sculptor Raymond Duchamp-Villon. Marcel Duchamp was first a librarian at the Sainte-Geneviève library in Paris, a post which hardly interfered with his liberty at all. 'Comfortably seated, he let his thoughts dwell on anything he liked, and was pleased to give information or advice to anyone who came and asked for it politely.' About 1908-1910 he had painted a few canvases in the style of the great Impressionists, 'just to find out for himself how they did it'. In 1911 his own genius asserted itself in his *A Propos de Petite Sœur*. His breakdown of forms grew more marked until, in 1912, he finished up by producing a number of decisive works, including the famous *Nude Descending a Staircase*. When this canvas was shown at the Armory Show *(*)* in New York in 1913, it made Duchamp famous overnight. The conservatives thought the picture an abomination, a nameless horror, while those who were looking for something new called it the 'light at the end of the tunnel'. One critic described the canvas as 'an explosion in a shingle factory'. It was a series of five schematized human forms, overlapping one another, descending a winding staircase, with a marvellous rhythm and precision. Duchamp was offered several commissions at the time, but he replied: 'No, thanks. I prefer my liberty.' He earned his bread and beer by giving French lessons to New York artists (and anyone else who felt so inclined at two dollars an hour (the current price). He became acquainted with Francis Picabia, and they

DUBOIS-PILLET. THE SEINE AT PARIS. ABOUT 1888.
Arthur G. Altschul Collection, New York.

were for a time insepar-
able. The friendship was
a great source of pleasure
to both of them. They
were two of the people
responsible for the Dada
movement and the Dada
spirit. Between 1915 and
1923, taking it very easy,
he executed his major
work, more than three
yards high; the first picture to be made on a sheet
of transparent glass, with
fragments of cut-out and
painted tin fixed to the
glass with a permanent
varnish. 'Canvases', he
said, 'have dusty be-
hinds.' This work was *The
Bride Stripped Bare by Her Bachelors*. This is a
mystical-mechanical epic of Desire. The bride-
fiancée hangs from the sky, with her antennae,
and communicates with the massed group of
her bachelors: nine of them, red, erect in their
uniforms or liveries: the priest, the cuirassier
the gendarme, the policeman, the bar boy, the
department-store delivery man, the undertaker,
the valet and the station-master. They receive
the bride's essence and set in motion a dramatic-
mechanical and interstellar ballet on 'human love
seen by one from another planet, who can't
make head or tail of it,' as André Breton, the
Surrealist poet, said, not without humour.
Little by little, the hermetic quality, precision
and splendour of this singular work brought
Duchamp world-wide, acclaim, which left him
quite unmoved. All he wanted was to play chess.
He did not want to paint, anyhow.

His maxim was never to repeat himself. He
alone among the great painters succeeded in
carrying it out–by the simple expedient of just
ceasing to paint, all of a sudden. His twenty
canvases and glass panels, sold to intimate
friends of his (now dead), were bequeathed by
them, in accordance with his wish, to a single
museum, that of Philadelphia, where nearly all
his works are concentrated. He is the father of
the 'ready-mades': mass-produced objects ready
for use which, with a little inspired alteration,
can be transformed into works of art. The most

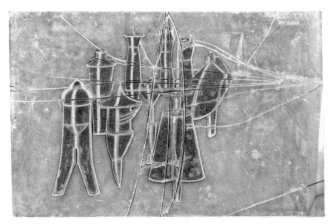

DUCHAMP. STUDY FOR 'BRIDE STRIPPED BARE BY HER BACHELORS'. 1915.
H.-P. Roché Collection, Paris.

famous among those are: the big bottle-drier, the
fountain urinal which he signed 'Mutt' and
exhibited in New York in 1916, and the reproduction of the Mona Lisa, 'L.H.O.O.Q.' (1919),
which he decorated with a becoming moustache.
He was intimately bound up with Surrealism *(*)*.
He invented the ceiling made of coal-sacks for
the International Surrealist Exhibition in Paris in
1938 as well as the Rain Hall and the pink breast
in foam rubber, labelled 'Please Touch', which
adorned the cover of the de luxe catalogue of the
1947 exhibition. He made a kind of portable
museum (three hundred of them) for his friends.
It was a valise containing reproductions of all
his principal works, and a little phial with fifty
cubic centimetres of Paris air, a souvenir for an
exile. One phial broke, and Duchamp had
another specially sent to New York, containing
genuine Paris air. Preferring a young and growing civilization to those that are too ripe or too
cocksure, he has been living in New York for
years now. His example of art for oneself, and
of disinterestedness, has slowly had its effect.
He has become a world legend. His name evokes
independence, boldness, and total success in his
own domain.   H.-P. R.

DUFRESNE Charles. French painter born at
Millemont, in the Seine-et-Oise,
in 1876, died at La Seyne, in the Var, in 1938.
At a very early age he was sent to work for an

DUFY. THE THICKET. 1930. *Musée d'Art Moderne, Paris.*

and the exaltation of the object. Dufresne also had the courage to attempt religious themes and, among the painters of his generation, seems to have been the one most capable of giving the subject its full value. That is why he was able to exercise such great influence over the young painters whom he taught for several years at the Scandinavian Academy. Together with a few friends, he founded the Salon des Tuileries in 1923; in 1924 he decorated with tapestries a collection of furniture by the decorators Sue and Mare, which was one of the

industrial engraver, and attended evening classes in drawing. Despite the opposition of his family, he succeeded in gaining admission to the École Nationale des Beaux-Arts, in the medal-engraving section. His first important canvases date from 1908, after a long stay in Italy. In 1910 he won the Prix de l'Afrique du Nord, and spent two years at the Villa Abd el Tif in Algiers. This contact with an Oriental civilization, even though a declining one, had a decisive influence on the evolution of his art. Dufresne had a gifted imagination. Like Delacroix, for whom he had the greatest admiration, he found his purity of form and violence of colour beneath Mediterranean skies. Later, in his studio crammed with curios brought back from his travels, he reconstructed an exotic and fabulous world of vivid intensity. He was not interested in historical reconstructions. On the contrary, he wanted to give back to the modern world the colour of life, and integrate this colour in large, sweeping rhythms, thus reacting in his own way against the fragmentation of themes

attractions of the Exposition des Arts Décoratifs of 1925. He executed décors for the Paris Opera (*Antar*), and sketches for tapestries (*La Plage ou les Plaisirs de l'Été*). Finally, in 1937, he painted two panels (*Le Théâtre de Molière*) for the Chaillot Theatre in Paris, and some vast murals for the great amphitheatre of the École de Pharmacie, which he completed only a few days before his death. In these he showed his taste for broad swaths of colour, sweeping movements of figures, a measured lyricism full of passion, and an understanding of texture, which is to be found even in the smallest of his rough sketches.   J. LA.

DUFRESNE. LION HUNT. 1932. *Lew Fox Collection, Chicago.*

DUFY Raoul. French painter born in Havre in 1877; died at Forcalquier in 1953. At fourteen Dufy worked as a clerk in a coffee-

DUFY. JULY 14TH AT LE HAVRE. 1907.

importing firm in his native town. Beginning in 1892, he attended evening classes at the municipal art school after work. In 1900 he went to study in Paris, in Léon Bonnat's class at the École Nationale des Beaux-Arts. Dufy seldom went to the Louvre, maintaining that the great Masters frightened him (although he loved the works of Claude Lorrain). What really interested him was the work of Van Gogh and the Impressionists, which he saw at the Galleries of Vollard and Durand-Ruel. He exhibited in Berthe Weill's gallery. In 1905 Dufy chanced to see a canvas by Matisse, *Luxe, Calme et Volupté*. It was a revelation to him. 'When I saw this picture', he said, 'I understood at once the new reasons for painting'. Dufy then decided to change his style: no more beaches in the manner of Boudin or

Sisley, but streets bedecked with flags and very colourful open-air dances, like the paintings of the Fauves, who made the Salon d'Automne of that year so memorable. His art had greater affinities with Marquet, his friend, with whom he worked in 1906 at Sainte-Adresse, Trouville and Le Havre, than with Matisse. Back in Paris, he held his first one-man exhibition at Berthe Weill's gallery. He soon abandoned Fauvism; living with Braque, in 1908, at L'Estaque he developed a more restrained colour range and a stricter spatial composition that showed the influence of Cézanne. In the hope of earning a living, he learned wood engraving and illustrated Apollinaire's *Bestiaire*, when he met Paul Poiret, the couturier who assured his economic independence by giving him works as a dyer and painter on fabrics. He also worked for Bianchini-Ferrier, the silk manufacturer. In 1920 he stayed at Vence in the South of France, where he painted many landscapes. Then he went on a journey to Sicily and Morocco, and brought back with him a collection of paintings and water-colours. Fame began to come his way, and the first monographs on him were published. At the International Exhibition of Decorative Art in 1925, he exhibited a series of fourteen printed hangings in Paul Poiret's barges and at the Georges Bernheim Gallery he exhibited decorated ceramics for indoor gardens. In 1927, he went to the South of France (Nice, Hyères, Cannes) where his changed style was characterized by its freedom of form and colour. Back in Paris, he painted a series of nudes (1928-1930) in his studio in the impasse de Guelma. He executed an enormous decorative work (about 11 yards high and 65 yards long) for the Palais de l'Électricité at the Paris International Exhibition in 1937. About this time Dufy was beginning to feel the first attacks of arthritis, which was later to cause him much suffering. When the war began in 1939 he finished the panel of the Monkey House at the Paris Zoo and that of the Seine, which decorates the smoking-room of the Palais de Chaillot. Fleeing before the German advance, he took refuge in Nice, then Céret and finally at Perpignan, where he stayed till 1949. During these years, he worked at the cartoons for a series of high-warp tapestries, which were exhibited at the Galerie Louis Carré in 1948. In 1950, he went to Boston for cortisone treatment. In America this charming and cheerful man was welcomed wherever he went. The American scene captured his fancy (he had been there previously, in 1937), and he gave the Americans some interesting and curious observations on their country and their culture, both verbally and in paint. He painted racetracks, views of the Charles River (Boston), and the crowds and skyscrapers of Times Square, which enthralled him. In Arizona he drew rodeos and dramatic sunsets. 'The trouble with the American artist,' he said, 'is that he does not see what is around him until he sees it in a picture.' He advised them to throw away their cameras and then paint. On his return to France he settled down in his country house at Forcalquier, where he died on March 23rd, 1953.

Dufy was a painter of joy–the joy of seeing, imagining and creating, without ever repudiating the reality of the world around us. He did not mind admitting that there was representation in his painting. 'My clients buy my subjects from me', he said jokingly. 'The rest is just thrown in.' From the visible world Dufy chose a few themes which pleased him, and he made successive variations of them up to the time of his death: streets

DUFY. CONSOLE WITH YELLOW VIOLIN.
Private Collection.

gaily hung with bunting, the beaches of Normandy, regattas, homages to Mozart and Claude Lorrain, the Bois de Boulogne, race-tracks, garden parties, the farms and forests of Normandy and the South, brass bands and orchestras, fields of corn, work in the fields. The painter would pick out and accentuate a few precise details, such as a palm tree, a balustrade, the hull of a ship, the curve of a shell, a violin bow. Such elements as these became his trade-mark. Dufy summed up all these themes on the cottons he decorated for Poiret, and used them on tiles decorating the walls of his indoor gardens. He spread them over his panel *Electricity*, and his other masterpiece, *Itinerary from Paris to Sainte-Adresse and to the Sea*, in the home of Doctor Viard. There, in the limited space of the picture, Dufy, cleverly immobilizing everything that changes, succeeds in giving us the illusion of passing time. Far from weakening one another, Dufy's variations give one another value. They are the 'states of soul' of a particularly receptive painter, who started seeking afresh in every picture. There is no repetition in his stages of progress. He said: 'When you have succeeded in something or other, quickly turn your back on it, and enter on a new adventure'.

Another of Dufy's points of originality, the most outstanding perhaps, is his prodigious draughtsmanship, the importance of which has not always been recognized. Dufy put infinite imagination and cunning into his drawings, using the whites of his paper with unequalled skill and knowledge. In fact, in his sketches of race-tracks one is astonished to find that what pleases so much is what has been left out. A few chairs, a few spots for the spectators watching the jockeys parade, suffice to suggest a crowd. Dufy's calligraphy, in graphite, India ink, oil or water-colour, with its precise, rapid, staccato signs, has often been compared to shorthand. But shorthand signs are fixed, stereotyped. There is nothing like that about Dufy's 'handwriting', which, although is does show a few more or less fixed signs in the manner of the Japanese artists, has nevertheless been perpetually enriched and modified by constant observation of the visible world. There is nothing more amazing than a drawing by Dufy. The painter has succeeded in tracing in it the very dynamism of his intimate self. Through this multiplicity of

DUFY. A FINE SUNDAY. 1943. *Louis Carré Collection, Paris.*

squares, rectangles, triangles, ovals, ideograms of every sort, the charm of a vision is composed and presented. Everything, even the formless, has a contour, a rhythm. Everything is art, nothing is really Nature. By the direct use of line and colour, the painter transmits to us his state of mind, his feeling–with the result that the objects he depicts speak only through the man who created them, with a pleasure the like of which cannot be found in any painter since Renoir.

And now, his colours. These have, especially in his water-colours, the resonance of primordial freshness. How can one describe Dufy's blue, his subtle red, the serene glow of his greens? Every painter has his dominant colour. Dufy's is blue, the only colour that keeps its individuality through all its nuances. Nobody knew its innumerable variations better than Dufy: vibrant blue, the blue of the sky broken by drifting white clouds, the fascinating blue of a creek at midday, the blue of the sea, ultramarine, the cerulean blue of a fair girl's eyes.

Later, he tried to restrain his palette. He began

a series of yellow consoles, red violins, black cargo-boats, where the fundamental colour, skilfully modulated, is broken only by a few tones. 'What tempts me now', said Dufy (and this only a short time before his death), 'is to take up the problem of colour again outside the law of complementaries. I would like to try to contrast or combine colours which do not go together; that is to say, which our usual attitude to colour harmony makes us reject.' All that, coming after such considerable achievements, does not fit in with the 'petit maître', elegant and charming, that some people thought Dufy to be; he was a difficult painter on the whole. Dufy could do well only what he did happily, without reworking. But how much reflection 'between the acts' before he took up his brush again! He would forget what he knew, and awake each morning like a child before the great secret of life and the universe.

Toning down a once proverbial desire to please, his illness intensified his vision and made him concentrate his entire being on his creative work. He lived only through and for his art, but without becoming a slave to it. For him painting was one of the superior activities, a means of communicating with others, of bringing them sustenance. Dufy knew how to do everything, and do it artistically. He liked to stress how important technique could be in the work of a painter. But, at the same time, he would state that the artist should get beyond technique, in the sense that he should cease to be preoccupied with it. In that, and only that, he belonged to the Renaissance. He did not work according to classical perspective. He rejected the laws of chiaroscuro, as well as everything based on the physical lighting of the object. He organized and illumined his canvas according to his own conception of light. He had conceived a theory of white shadows (neutrals) and coloured lights. Dufy was never satisfied with what he knew. Up to the last he could be seen throwing himself with extraordinary youthfulness into the quest for new ways of expression. For instance, he tried to convey, by using black, the effect of being dazzled by looking straight into the sun.

Dufy did not give a thought to fame, but at the end of his life he was overwhelmed by the indications of his triumph that came to him from practically all over the world. He lived to see the great retrospective exhibition of his works held in Geneva in 1952. The posthumous Paris exhibition, in the summer of 1954, showed the importance and fecundity of his work.   P. C.

DUNOYER DE SEGONZAC André. French

painter, born at Boussy-Saint-Antoine, Seine-et-Oise, in 1884. Dunoyer de Segonzac seems to have been untouched by the intellectual, technical and emotional restlessness of his time. Refusing to yield to any external pressure, hostile to fashion and theories at the risk of appearing out of date, he thought only of serving those talents that he had already revealed in 1907, in his drawings of nudes and his landscapes. A friend of La Fresnaye, Boussingault, Jean Marchand, and Luc-Albert Moreau, he reacted with them against the disintegration brought about by Impressionism and the excesses of the Fauves, by limiting himself to an austere palette dominated by ochres, earth colour, cadmiums and ultramarines. But the painter soon learnt that to use too many successive coats, meant risking the loss of one of the most powerful attractions of oil-painting: transparency. From 1919 on, his landscapes, his nudes and his still-lifes are more relaxed. The lesson of Corot began to be added to that of Courbet. Making long stays at Saint-Tropez and in the Ile-de-France, Segonzac, whose cult of the great forces of Nature goes back to his childhood, fled from all dissonance and all that might disperse and compromise the over-all stability of a picture. He holds that all good painting needs, over and above the state of grace in which the artist ought to be, the quality of certain harmonies, and not contrasts and violence. One is

DUFY. ORCHESTRA. 1936.

DUFY. YACHTS AT DEAUVILLE. *Doctor Roudinesco Collection, Paris.*

is primarily a great draughtsman? Just as he identifies himself with his characters when he depicts boxing matches (*Boxing*), a nude, soldiers at the front (*Wooden Crosses*), Grock or Isadora Duncan, he *is* that pear tree resisting the wind, that poplar pulsating in all its leaves. He is that field of tenacious vines, clinging to the slopes, that sun armed with rays, those ripples through which the sky and the water show their density. In his water-colours, as in his engravings, the more line dominates colour the more resonance colour has. Drama without emphasis, a quiet, deep vehemence, sometimes big scars, evoke the conflicts and

struck by the unity of his work, whether it be his drawings, water-colours, oils or engravings: the same conception binds the masterpieces of his youth, such as *The Drinkers* (1910), to the etchings illustrating the *Georgics* (1947). Is it a belittling of Dunoyer de Segonzac to say that he

varying moods of Nature. Drawing which keeps guard like a conscience forbids any slackness of form, any overflowing of colour. On his return from the 1914-1918 war Segonzac, after a brief initiation by his friend Laboureur, began to draw as freely on copperplate as on a sheet of

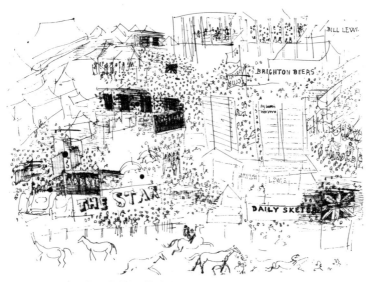

DUFY. EPSOM RACECOURSE. 1934. INK DRAWING.

paper. Far from losing the joyous quality of his work in his engravings, the artist instinctively discovered his methods and the means of condensing his inspiration on a small surface. A catalogue of his engravings would today list over two thousand works. Several of them are in series, such as *Le Morin* (1923), *Beaches* (1935), *From Joinville to Bougival* (1936), and, together with his illustrations, constitute the most brilliant work on copperplate that has come from any painter since Pissarro. CL. R.-M.

DURAND-RUEL Paul (1831-1922). The influence of the great picture dealers on the development of painting in the nineteenth and twentieth centuries has been considerable, probably owing to the fact that at the beginning they acted, more often than not, out of disinterested enthusiasm. Durand-Ruel's gallery was first at 1 rue de la Paix, then in 1867 he moved it to 16 rue Laffitte. He was first a friend of Corot, Millet, Théodore Rousseau, Daubigny and Boudin, and gave them both moral and material support, sharing their enthusiasms and their disappointments, and disposing of their canvases for them, often with reluctance. He was most heroic in his backing of the Impressionists in 1870. In 1871 he fled to London, and there made the acquaintance of Monet and Pissarro. On his return to Paris in 1872 he bought twenty-three canvases from Manet for 35,000 francs. For more than ten years Durand-Ruel did his utmost to popularize the Impressionist works, which no one wanted and everyone condemned. But he was convinced that 'a true picture-dealer should also be an enlightened art-lover, who is ready to sacrifice, if need be, his passing interests to his artistic convictions and prefers to fight against speculators rather than be associated with their doings.' That is how Manet, Renoir, Monet, Sisley, Cézanne, Degas and Pissarro became his friends. He was really a philanthropist, and narrowly escaped bankruptcy before he succeeded in interesting America in the new school in 1886. In the history of Impressionism his name is linked particularly with the second exhibition of the group, which he arranged in his premises at No. 11 Rue Le Peletier in 1876, as a protest against the pigheadedness of the official Salon, which refused

DUNOYER DE SEGONZAC. LA QUEUE-EN-BRIE. 1931. *Musée d'Art Moderne, Paris.*

to accept the adherents of the new school. It was because of this exhibition (which came up against the most violent hostility) that Duranty (*) wrote his famous book in support of *The New Painting*. The stubborn refusal of French collectors to accept the Impressionists made Durand-Ruel decide to open galleries in London, Brussels, Vienna, and finally in New York in 1887. In spite of all this, when Fénéon congratulated him on his eventual success, Durand-Ruel replied: 'It is the collectors that we have to thank for that'. Renoir has left a fine portrait of this great collector and picture-dealer, dated 1910. Today, Durand-Ruel's gallery has been moved to the avenue de Friedland and is run by his grandsons M. R.

DURANTY Louis-Émile (1833-1880). This little-known novelist of the French realist school was one of the most ardent supporters of Impressionism right from the start. In his impassioned articles in the *Gazette des Beaux-Arts* he traced the relationship between the Impressionists and the Venetians and Constable. In 1876 he published his book *The New Painting: Concerning a group of artists exhibiting at the Durand-Ruel Gallery*, in which he developed some very accurate views. Taking to task the very official École Nationale des Beaux-Arts for inspiring in its young pupils 'a strange system of painting bounded in the South by Algeria, in the East by mythology, in the West by history, and the North by archaeology', he hailed the works of the Impressionists, all of them inspired (so he wrote) by things of their time. After paying tribute to Courbet, Corot, Boudin, and, in particular, Manet, whom he regarded as the initiators of the new painting, he extolled the great work begun by Monet, Degas, Pissarro, Sisley and Berthe Morisot. He expressed the hope that he wall separating the studio from everyday life had at last been broken down, and that the picture would be a window opened out onto Nature and modern life, seized in their dynamism and the inexhaustible diversity of their character. He was the friend of many painters and writers, and was included by Fantin-Latour in his painting *Homage to Delacroix*, together with Manet and Baudelaire. There is a well-known portrait of him painted in tempera by Degas.

DURET Théodore (1838-1927). French writer and art critic, a contemporary of the Impressionists and one of their first supporters. However, in his *The French Painters*, published in 1867, Duret, not being sufficiently informed, strongly criticized Manet, who had already painted *The Fifer* and *Le Déjeuner sur l'Herbe*. The matter was evidently soon straightened out, as Manet painted his portrait (now in the Petit Palais, Paris) the following year. After having generously assisted Renoir, Duret became his friend and one of his most ardent supporters. Meanwhile, in 1873, he went to Japan and came back full of enthusiasm for Japanese art. 'The Japanese', he wrote, 'were the first and most perfect Impressionists.' In 1878 he published his *Impressionist Painters*, this time praising them unreservedly. The book included monographs on Monet, Sisley, Pissarro, Renoir and Berthe Morisot. Manet was presented as the initiator of the movement. In a revised edition which appeared in 1906 the author added studies of Cézanne and Guillaumin. His catalogue *Manet and His Work* was not published until 1902. In 1894 Duret was obliged to sell his collection, comprising, among others, six Manets, six Monets, four Pissarros, three Renoirs, three Sisleys, three Cézannes and eight Degas.

E

ELEMENTARISM An offshoot of Neo-Plasticism *(*)* started by Theo Van Doesburg. In 1924 Van Doesburg, while still advocating the right angle, gave up the horizontal-vertical position of this angle and so came into conflict with the conception of Neo-Plasticism formulated by Mondrian. In 1926, in his review *De Stijl (*)*, Van Doesburg wrote an article in the form of a manifesto, in the course of which he said: 'Elementarism is partly a reaction against the too dogmatic application of Neo-Plasticism, and partly a consequence of Neo-Plasticism itself. What it seeks, above all, is a strict rectification of the Neo-Plastic ideas.' He then went on to explain what he meant by 'rectification'. As against the homogeneous construction of Mondrian's Neo-Plasticism, he proposed a heterogeneous form of expression, deliberately unstable, with inclined planes. He tried, in this way, to increase the dynamic effect, and renew the element of surprise. The painters Cesar Domela and Vordemberge-Gildewart, previously disciples of Mondrian, followed Van Doesburg. M. S.

ENSOR James. Belgian painter of English and Flemish parentage, born in Ostend, 1860; died there, 1949. Except for a stay in Brussels, Ensor never left his native town, thus showing his indifference to the schools, aesthetic doctrines, and artists of his day. All the same, his early works show certain influences, such as Degas, Manet, Renoir, the Symbolists, and particularly Turner. To his father, who was of British origin, he possibly owed his fidelity to the real, even in the realm of the imagination, and that truculent vitality which seem derived from his more northern ancestry. In any event, it is this combination that characterizes Ensor's expressionism and clearly differentiates it from the popular and rustic tendencies of a Van den

ENSOR. THE INTRIGUE. 1890. *Museum of Fine Arts, Antwerp.*

Berghe, a Gustave de Smet, or a Permeke. *Lamps* (1880), *The Rover* (1883), are of clearly Flemish inspiration; *The Living Room* (1881) would not have been disowned by the Parisian *intimistes*. *Carnival on the Beach* (1887) has the characteristic Ensor flavour, his ardour, his predilection for the fantastic, his lyricism, his creamy medium which diffuses a pallid light crossed by glittering flashes of clear yellows and vermilions. In 1888 he painted his most important and best-known canvas, *Entrance of Christ into Brussels*, about three yards by four, a work which is at the same time burlesque and grandiose, a saraband of baroque forms and strident colours, a disordered, tumultuous, vulgar but thoroughly alive composition. In a flaming riot of reds, blues and yellows (these yellows are now dull), one can see yelling crowds, processions of masqueraders, surges of hilarious faces, streamers flapping in the wind, and brass bands parading. The work teems with grimacing faces, monstrous legions, exaggerated gestures, and rattling bones, confirming his lineal descent from Breughel and Hieronymus Bosch. He had a taste for farce, for extravagance and caricature, and to this he sacrificed cohesion,

construction, purity of form and accurate tonal harmonies. However, Ensor is a true painter. No matter how dissonant his colours may be, they have a density, a brilliance, a distinctiveness, which the other Belgian painters certainly lack. When he wanted to, he could show that he was an informed and original draughtsman, particularly in some of his admirable etchings and drypoints: *The Cathedral, Fantastic Ball, Kermesse at the Mill, Death Pursuing the Humans*. The best of his work was accomplished between 1888 and 1892. For this artist, who lived to the age of eighty-nine, had said everything he had to say in five years, at the end of the last century. Decline set in immediately. Old age left him still clownish, but without any creative strength. He expended his imagination on his eccentric subjects and themes rather than on the search for a personal art.   F. E.

ERNST Max. A painter of the *École de Paris*, born in Brühl, near Cologne, in 1891. He studied philosophy at the University of Bonn from 1909 to 1911. He became interested in the latest works of Picasso and Chirico, also in those of August Macke, and in the Expressionist trend among the young German painters. Dadaism, however, had a much more determining influence on him. In 1914 he made the acquaintance of Hans Arp, who, three years later, became one of the founders of the first Dada group in Zurich. After the war Ernst, together with Baargeld, founded the Dadaist group of Cologne (*vide* Dada) and, with Arp and Baargeld, published the review, *Die Schammade*. In 1922 he came at last to Paris, and became one of the active figures of the Surrealist group, joining up with the poets André Breton, Paul Éluard, Louis Aragon, Philippe Soupault, Robert Desnos, Benjamin Péret, Arp, Chirico, and René Crevel, all of whom are represented in one of his canvases, in the company of Raphael and Dostoevski (1922). Owing to certain techniques which he discovered or revived, Ernst became the Surrealist painter who fitted in best with the activities of his poet and writer friends. He found a pictorial equivalent for automatic writing (so much in vogue for the creation of a poem) in the process of *'frottage'*: black lead was rubbed onto paper held against an object, producing the

effect of the weave of a piece of cloth, the grain-
ing of wood, or the veining of a leaf. These
impressions, skilfully done and exploited, formed mysterious works suggesting strange landscapes and animals, and vast expanses of imagi-

ERNST. PAIRED DIAMONDS. 1926.
FROM THE 'HISTOIRE NATURELLE'.

nary country (*cf.* his *Natural History*, published
by Jeanne Bucher in 1926). Ernst also used the
process of 'collage', which the Cubists had used
to integrate elements of purely plastic value into
their work (*vide* Papiers collés). But Ernst looked
for disparate elements of an anecdotal and descriptive nature, in the illustrations of such
varied forms of writing as tales of adventure,
love stories, technical treatises. Their juxtaposition in the same work increased (often
humorously) their powers of evocation. A meaning which is always fantastic and sometimes

horrible, sentimental, and pathetic, reveals itself
behind his most innocent compositions (*cf. La
Femme 100 Têtes*, engravings with captions,
published in 1929 by the Éditions du Carrefour,
and *Une Semaine de Bonté*, a collage-novel,
published by Jeanne Bucher in 1934). Yet these
divertissements are characterized by a juxtaposition that is a little too mechanical. Each of his
works has been produced with a precise aim in
view: to induce a kind of confusion in the
spectator in order to make him sensitive to the
appeal of the bizarre and the fortuitous. Purely
plastic preoccupations became secondary, if
they were not sacrificed altogether. After 1936,
with the *Nymphe Echo* and *Villes Entières* and
particularly after the years he spent in the United
States from 1941 to 1949, his works freed
themselves more and more from this tendency.
The artist created a world which was quite his
own, without diminishing its poetic power. He
remembered his '*frottages*' and created a strange
chaos of forms which seem like an abbreviation
of the cosmic evolution: madrepores and
strange minerals, plants that change into insects,
human eyes and animal muzzles on the surface of
petrified silhouettes. All the kingdoms–animal,
vegetable and mineral–meet in confusion on a
planet in effervescence. These forms are freely
created by the painter, in accordance with the
requirements of his picture. Their perfect plastic
coherence makes them seem intensely alive. They
constitute one of Surrealism's *(*)* greatest
successes in its exploration of unknown worlds
born of dreams and imagination.   J. I.A.

ESPRIT NOUVEAU, L'   The title of a
review found-
ed in 1920 by Ozenfant and Jeanneret (Le Corbusier), which for twenty years reflected the new
trends in intellectual activity in the period following the First World War. The collaborators of
the *Esprit Nouveau* felt that a great epoch had just
begun, and that all forms of human activity were
at last going to be governed by one single principle. The aim of their efforts was the triumph of
the spirit of construction and synthesis, which
they considered was as necessary in the sphere of
art and letters as in that of philosophy and the
applied sciences. 'The constructive spirit', they
said, 'is as necessary for the creation of a picture

or a poem as it is for the building of a bridge.' The review, which had many distinguished contributors in all fields of creative activity, had a significant influence on modern thought.

EVENEPOEL Henri (1872-1899). Belgian painter; born at Nice, died in Paris. Although Evenepoel's parents were Belgian and although he began his artistic training at Brussels, in 1892, he settled in Paris and it was there he spent almost all the rest of his short life. There he continued his training at the École des Beaux-Arts in Gustave Moreau's studio, where he met and soon made friends with Marquet and Matisse. He developed earlier than his friends and, before they had worked out their personal idioms, he had ended his career and left a considerable body of work. He painted scenes of Parisian life reminiscent of Forain and Lautrec (*Café d'Harcourt in the Latin Quarter ; Fête at the Invalides*), but his best works were his portraits. His debt to Manet, whom he admired greatly, is evident in them. Although this influence is apparent in the bold brush work and a tendency for the sitter to stand out clearly from the background, he was more concerned than Manet with the character of his models; he delineated their state of mind as well as their features. His favourite models were his cousin, Louise, and her three children, people whom he respected and loved. His colours were very personal too; their tones were restrained, but had individuality and subtlety. A few months visit to Algeria in 1897 lightened and warmed his palette. Generally, however, it was nearer the colouring of the Nabis than the tone range adopted a little later by his friend, Matisse. His gentle, melancholy temperament inclined him less towards the unequivocal statement of pure tones than the delicacy and unusualness of muted harmonies.   J.-E. M.

EXPRESSIONISM Impressionism, Fauvism, Cubism, Futurism, Surrealism–titles adopted by the artists themselves or given them by their opponents–apply to contemporary and clearly defined groups or movements. Expressionism, on the other hand, denotes a permanent tendency in art, characteristic of the Nordic countries, which becomes accentuated in times of social stress or spirituel disturbance. Expressionism has found particularly fertile soil for expansion in our turbulent age. Although the idea always existed, the term for it is a recent invention of German aesthetics, popularized by Herwarth Walden, publisher of the avant-garde review *Der Sturm*, in Berlin, who classified under the heading of Expressionism–as opposed to Impressionism–all the revolutionary manifestations between 1910 and 1920, including Cubism

EVENEPOEL. THE SPANIARD AT PARIS. 1899.
Museum of Fine Arts, Ghent.

and the abstract trends. This broad definition, as confused as it is exaggerated, is to be found in the writings of nearly all those who concerned themselves with Expressionism, prior to Sheldon Cheney, who takes it to signify modern art as a whole and at its best. As against that, a large number of critics, fascinated by the *École de Paris* and its technical advances, deny, or fail to recognize, the emotional value of Expressionism. There are two conflicting viewpoints–the one putting the accent on plastic *form* and its autonomy, the other on psychological *force* and its impetus–bringing up again the traditional duality of Classicism and Romanticism, of being and becoming, of the Latin and German temperaments. Expressionism constitutes the present phase of Romanticism, in a tragic mode, bound to the anguish of our times, and to the resurgence of the Slavic and Nordic spirit. Unlike the painters of the *École de Paris*, who wanted to create an international language, Expressionism favoured individual and ethnic distinctions. Although every case in Expressionism is a particular one and cannot be covered by any overall formula, it is, nevertheless, possible to indicate briefly the successive phases it has passed through and its areas of expansion.

As a reaction against Impressionism (*) and the objective tendency of Cézanne and Seurat, which Cubism (*) continued, the first Expressionist movement, with Symbolist and Modernstyle influences, came into being in 1885 and lasted until 1900. The leading figures in it were Van Gogh, Toulouse-Lautrec, Ensor, Munch and Hodler. Their subjectivism expressed itself in obsessional and dramatic themes, and not only through their intensity of colour but also through the monumentality of their forms and the violence and sharpness of their drawing, which explains the return to the expressive line and simplified engraving and illustration techniques.

Van Gogh, setting an example with his way

NOLDE. YOUNG COUPLE. LITHOGRAPH. 1913.

of life as well as his work, was the founder and hero of modern Expressionism. Often in his letters, notably on the subject of his portraits, he explains what he is trying to do, afraid all the time lest his deliberate exaggeration be taken for caricature. Caricature is, in fact, a popular and spontaneous form of Expressionism, but with Van Gogh it acquires a very special value, attaining religious grandeur through its style.

His essentially Nordic message, in the humanist train of Rembrandt, has hardly been heeded in France. Lautrec created the modern poster, and realized the synthesis of contrary elements of illustration and decoration. Hodler, Munch and Ensor figured in the second wave of Expressionism, which arose (about 1905) in Germany with the creation of the Brücke (*), and in France with the decisive contribution of Rouault, of Picasso of the blue and Negro periods and, in some respects, of Matisse and Fau-

KOKOSCHKA. PEN-AND-INK SKETCH. 1919.

vism (Derain and Vlaminck). The Belgian Ensor vacillated between Impressionism and an expressive symbolism which he resuscitated from Bosch. The Swiss Hodler often indulged in an allegorical and irritatingly exaggerated realism. Munch, a compatriot of Ibsen, touched by the morbid side of Kierkegaard's philosophy, was the central figure of Nordic Expressionism, and left his mark on it both in Germany and Scandinavia. His influence in those countries is eminently comparable, though in an opposite direction, with that of Cézanne in France. His first exhibition in Berlin in 1892 caused a scandal, but shook Germany out of its academic and nonrealist torpor, so out of keeping with its temperament. He brought that country back to its true tradition, that of Grünewald and Gothic Expressionism. The Secession movement reached Munich, Vienna, Berlin (*vide* Van Gogh, Toulouse-Lautrec, Ensor, Hodler, Munch, Rouault; Sturm and Secession).

Expressionism in its dual aspect-social and physical-took firm root in the Brücke group, nurtured by Munch, Van Gogh and Negro sculpture (the most Expressionist of all the arts), and in a general way permeated the various currents in Germany on the eve of the war up to the Blaue Reiter *(*)* of Munich. The creative fever became dramatically intensified, but without being able to assimilate the constructive lesson of Cubism. There are some outstanding names in the movement: Nolde and Kirchner, specifically Germanic temperaments openly at war with the art of Paris ; Kokoschka in Vienna, who, at the very moment when Freud, in the same city, was elaborating psychoanalysis, executed a striking series of portraits which resemble flights into the subconscious.

Suddenly the Jewish and Slav soul, dormant for centuries, manifested itself in painting, its expressionist tendency bringing a new ferment into art. From far away in distance and in time came men like Soutine, Pascin, Chagall, full of nostalgia and anguish, brimming over with tenderness. They settled in Paris before 1914. Expressionism penetrated to the United States about 1908 through Max Weber, also of Russian origin (*vide* Nolde, Kirchner Kokoschka, Soutine, Pascin, Chagall, Weber).

After the extraordinary outbreak at the beginning of the century, the interim period between the two wars stabilized itself in a sort of neoclassicism, interrupted by only one revolutionary movement, Surrealism *(*)*. But the great masters of Expressionism, Munch, Ensor, Rouault, Nolde, Soutine, Kokoschka and Weber, continued on their own, each perfecting his own work, while national forms of Expressionism developed in other countries, notably in Belgium, with the School of Laethem-Saint-Martin (Permeke, de Smet, Van den Berghe), solidly bound to the Flemish soil; in Latin America, fertilized by the spirit of the old Indian races –Brazil (Segall, Portinari) and, particularly, Mexico (Rivera, Orozco, Siqueiros, Tamayo) in the monumental and popular form of the fresco. Defeated Germany tried desperately to react

MUNCH. KARL-JOHANS GATE. 1892.
Rasmus Meyer Collection, Bergen.

KIRCHNER. WANNSEE STATION. 1914.

against its instinctive Romanticism, but the so-called New Objectivism group (*Die Neue Sachlichkeit*), graced with the presence of artists like Dix, Grosz and Beckmann, dominated the last phase of Expressionism with its trenchant realism and social violence. Expressionism was expelled by the Nazis. Beckmann took refuge in Holland, where Expressionism evolved in a parallel manner (Sluyters, Charley, Toorop). Expressionism gave us Gromaire in France, Auberjonois in Switzerland, Solana in Spain, Rossi in Italy, and, after the 1929 crisis, gained many recruits in the United States, notably Rattner and Knaths. The Civil War in Spain, and the Second World War, moved Picasso to a new Expressionist style of hitherto unheard of violence, of which the masterpiece is *Guernica*. This brought in its wake a general revival of Expressionism, in Europe (1935-1950), in Latin America, and especially in the United States, as a result of the direct influence of Beckmann and the Germanic tendencies (*vide* Laethem-Saint-Martin, Permeke, Smet, Van den Berghe, Segall, Portinari, Rivera, Orozco, Siqueiros, Tamayo, Beckmann, Grosz, Sluyters, Toorop, Gromaire, Solana and Picasso). J. LE.

F

FANTIN-LATOUR Théodore. French painter born in Grenoble in 1836; died at Buré in the Orne in 1904. Although he was a friend of the Impressionists, being about the same age as Manet (born 1832), Degas (born 1834) and Monet (born 1840), his work is not Impressionist, either in spirit or in form. He was more like a late Romantic, inclined to serve his imagination rather than to depict reality, even a poetic reality such as Monet's. The exact representation of ordinary landscapes and their changing lights did not interest him. He painted fairies gambolling in clouds, or in rivers, or–when music, which he loved passionately, invoked them–in airy farandoles. He also painted flowers in great quantities, because those were the paintings that his clientèle bought. Between 1864 and 1896 he painted flowers almost exclusively. His gift of transfiguration was so natural that he invested each canvas with that secret life, that sweetness, which makes his work as a whole so ineffably appealing. Can he be described as a Realist because he painted some fine portraits and knew how to catch a likeness ? We are, in fact, indebted to him for some group portraits of his friends: leading musicians, writers and painters of his time, among them Baudelaire, Rimbaud, Zola, Manet, Monet, Renoir and Whistler. These are photographic documents (not unlike the early paintings of guild groups) which will hold infinite interest for later generations, and testify to Fantin-Latour's sentiments and good taste. But there again, what he sought, even in those portraits with their striking likenesses, was to gratify his own sympathies rather than to preserve any one particular moment, or any one particular aspect of these people. Fantin-Latour did not adhere to any of the revolutionary theories and techniques of his friends and of his time. This was not due to cautiousness on his part. He was by nature discreet and peaceful, and he wanted his art to be the same. Unattached to any school, Fantin-

FANTIN-LATOUR. FLOWERS. *Musée du Louvre.*

Latour propounded nothing and invented even less. He created a world of his own and gave it material form without seeking originality and without acknowledging any dominant influence–unless, perhaps, that of Delacroix, adapted to his own more modest capabilities.   R. C.

FATTORI Giovanni (1825-1908). Italian painter; born at Livorno, died in Florence. Fattori dominates the 19th century in Italy. He trained as a painter in Florence from 1846 to 1848, the year in which he took part in the first war of independence. In 1855, he joined the Macchiaioli (*) movement and his rather academic style became increasingly freer and more spirited in its expression. He turned from large paintings of battles (*The Italian Camp* *after the Battle of Magenta,* for example, which won the Ricasoli award in 1861) to scenes of military life, brushed with a power and vigour that were unusual for the period, and landscapes of the Tuscan Maremma where he arranged his light horsemen, bulls and herdsmen with incomparable judgement. In 1875, he went to Paris and greatly admired the Impressionists without, however, abandoning his own manner (the Macchiaioli, anyway, had discussed the Parisian movement at length and it is possible to detect in their work a distinct wish to retain their independence). Fattori was appointed to teach painting at the Academy of Art in Florence. When he died there in 1908, he left an impressive number of paintings, rough sketches, drawings and etchings.

Fattori's work has a vigorous character that is peculiarly Italian. In an age of sentimentality and almost morbid vapidness, his painting pulses with health and energy. He paid little respect to the conventions and, in his best works, could treat a considerable subject with freedom of brushwork allied to strict composition. There is a poetry in the realism of his vision and, although his colouring is restrained, there is subtlety in its deliberately muted tones. Fattori was one of the first to frequent the Café Michelangiolo *(*),* but without any particular zest for the discussions on theory, in fact, almost keeping himself apart, but through force of circumstance, he became the leader of the Macchiaioli. However, far from being a mere formula the use of spots of colour (the *macchie* of the Macchiaioli) suited his artistic sensibility; with them the could

VLAMINCK. PORTRAIT OF DERAIN.

give vitality and drama to vast spaces and communicate fleeting and ephemeral emotion through his treatment of the painted surface. Hasty sketches and small paintings had never before had such power and suggestive force. Monumental yet intimate would sum up a work that has the strength and honesty of a peasant and was carried forward with the steady, sure pace of a countryman. D. F.

FAUVISM Fauvism, based on the exaltation of pure colour, was the first art revolution of the twentieth century. It was not a school, complete with programme and theory, but the result of the temporary conjunction of a

GIOVANNI FATTORI. THE ROTUNDA OF PALMIERI. 1866.

number of painters, actuated by the same motives and brought together through the kind of chance meetings that so often create highly productive movements. In the famous Salon d'Automne of 1905 twelve colourists, grouped around Matisse and conscious of the similarity of their views, exhibited together. The explosive forces of their work provoked a scandal. They came together again for the Salon des Indépendants of 1906. Louis Vauxcelles, the art critic, noticing a small bronze in the Florentine manner by the sculptor Marque in the middle of the hall full of the riotous colours of those who were still called the 'Incoherents' or 'Invertebrates', exclaimed: '*Donatello parmi les Fauves!*' (Donatello among the wild beasts). The name *Fauves* caught on, and by the time of the Salon d'Automne of the same year it was in general use. The history of Fauvism is a brief one, beginning in 1905 and reaching its full development in 1907. It may be useful to go over briefly the succession of exchanges and contacts that assisted in its creation and crystallized around the dominant personality of Matisse, the oldest in experience and undisputed leader of the movement. Three main groups of different origin (joined by Van Dongen, an independent) came under his sway, and rallied to his principles during those heroic years: the group of the Atelier Gustave Moreau and the Académie Carrière (Marquet, Manguin, Camoin, Puy), the Chatou group (Derain, Vlaminck) and, lastly, the Havre group (Friesz, Dufy, Braque).

Matisse entered the École Nationale des Beaux-Arts in 1895 as a pupil of Gustave Moreau. Rouault was already there. Marquet joined them soon, and Camoin in 1897. Moreau's enthusiastic and liberal teaching permitted the strong temperaments of the Fauves-to-be, who had become close friends, to develop without restraint. 'I am the bridge', he told them, 'over which some of you will pass.' When he died, his pupils dispersed. Matisse, who already had considerable authority over his comrades, spent a year in Toulouse and in Corsica, and brought back from these two places, in 1899, a series of small landscapes violently sketched in pure tones with a Pointillist technique. On his return to Paris he rented a studio at No. 9 Quai Saint-Michel, in the same building as his close friend

VLAMINCK. RED TREES. 1906. *Musée d'Art Moderne, Paris.*

Marquet, and stayed there until 1907–that is to say, for the whole period of Fauvism. He painted figures in pure blue, still-lifes radiant with scarlet and orange, with the same audacious treatment as his Southern landscapes. In his researches he was closely followed by Marquet and, though more warily, by Manguin and Camoin. In 1899, at the Académie Carrière, he met Jean Puy, Laprade, Chabaud and Derain. Over all of them, and Derain in particular, he exercised a strong influence. He exhibited at the Salon des Indépendants in 1901, together with Marquet. 'We were the only two painters to express ourselves in pure tones', Marquet later said, adding: 'Already in 1898 Matisse and I were working in what was to be called the Fauve manner.' Derain and the self-taught Vlaminck, who shared a studio at Chatou, outside Paris, tried similar experiments, in an even more violent manner.

MARQUET. THE PORT
OF MARSEILLES. DRAW-
ING. *Private Collection.*

It was in the midst of the famous Van Gogh retrospective, held at the Galerie Bernheim-Jeune in 1901, that Derain introduced his friend Vlaminck to Matisse. The years 1899-1901 marked, therefore, the first Fauve 'push', one part of it led by Matisse and Marquet, under the structural influence of Cézanne, the other by Vlaminck and Derain, under the Expressionist influence of Van Gogh. This period was different from the period of happy, free expansion, between 1905 and 1907, dominated by the decorative influence of Gauguin.

In 1902-1903 Matisse and Marquet painted interiors and views of Paris, going back to the sombre workmanship of the early Manets. Derain went on military service, and Vlaminck, on his own, surrendered himself to his passion for colour. A small gallery run by Berthe Weill (*) gave some preliminary exhibitions of the works of the future Fauves from 1902 to 1904: Matisse, Marquet, Manguin, Flandrin, Camoin; then the childhood friends from Ha-

vre, Friesz and Dufy; and later, Van Dongen, a Montmartre bohemian of Dutch origin. They exhibited again as a group at the Salon des Indépendants of 1903 (Matisse, Marquet, Puy, Manguin, Camoin, Friesz and Dufy), still without attracting public attention. Matisse had his first one-man show in the shop of the art dealer Ambroise Vollard, in June 1904, and spent the rest of the summer at Saint-Tropez,

DERAIN. WESTMINSTER BRIDGE. 1906. *Private Collection, Paris.*

on the Riviera, painting in the company of Signac and, particularly, Cross, whose Pointillist technique he adopted, intensifying it force and luminosity. At the Salon d'Automne he showed thirteen pictures done in this manner, which were a revelation to Friesz. In the Salon des Indépendants of 1905, where Matisse exhibited his *Luxe, Calme et Volupté*, it was Dufy's turn to experience a decisive shock when he saw 'this miracle of the imagination at play in drawing and in colour'. He and Friesz abandoned Impressionism, the tradition in which they were trained, to follow the 'pictorial mechanics' of Matisse. Derain came back from military service, and there were very active exchanges between Matisse and the reconstituted Chatou group, which manipulated colours like 'sticks of dynamite'. During the summer Derain joined Matisse at Collioure, and from the stimulating contact between these two lucid and lively natures there, beneath the brilliant southern skies, the first real Fauvist canvases were born. They were to create a sensation at the historic Salon d'Automne of 1905, together with those of Marquet, Manguin, Puy, Valtat, Vlaminck, Friesz and Rouault, the latter exhibiting with his friends but remaining on the fringe of the movement with his sombre colours and moral passion. The year 1905 also saw the formation of a parallel movement in Germany, the Brücke *(*)*, which, however, soon turned to Expressionism.

The Salon des Indépendants of 1906, in which Braque (the last of the three men from Havre to be won over) participated, and the Salon d'Automne of the same year (the Gauguin retrospective), when Van Dongen came to complete the group, mark the peak of Fauvism. Its principles can be summed up in a few words: uniformity of light, space-construction by colour, illumination of the flat surface without illusionist modelling or chiaroscuro, purity and simplification of means, absolute correspondence between expression (emotive suggestion) and decoration (internal organization) by composition. 'Composition', said Matisse, 'is the art of arranging in a decorative manner the diverse elements through which the painter expresses his feelings.' Form and content coincide, and are modified by mutual reaction, for 'expression comes from the coloured surface which the observer takes in as a whole'. In short, it is dynamic sensualism ('the

MATISSE. LE LUXE. 1907.
Musée d'Art Moderne, Paris.

shock to the senses of what the eye beholds') disciplined by synthesis ('condensation of sensations'), and subject to the economy of the picture ('whatever is useless is consequently harmful'). This unity of transposition distinguishes the Fauves from their immediate successors, who superimposed colour on a conventional framework, and from the Expressionists with their illustrative tendency. No doubt such a balance between order and passion, fire and restraint, could not be maintained at such a high level for long. At the end of 1907 the collective paroxysm of Fauvism had already given way to incipient Cubism, which Matisse and Derain, as well as Braque, helped to create. Each went his own way; some, misunderstanding the message of Cézanne, went back to a sort of neo-classicism, while Matisse alone (perhaps Dufy too, though in a different mood) kept to the end the eternal youth of Fauvism. But for all of them this heroic exaltation remained, to quote Derain, the 'trial

FEININGER.
SCHOONER AT SEA.
*Doetsch-Benziger
Collection, Basel.*

by fire' which has purified painting, and revealed the best in themselves to a number of highly gifted temperaments (*vide* Braque, Camoin, Derain, Van Dongen, Dufy, Friesz, Laprade, Manguin, Marquet, Matisse, Puy, Rouault, Valtat, Vlaminck). J. LE.

FEININGER Lyonel (1871-1956). American painter; born and died at New York. His parents, German immigrants, were both musicians. Having shown early a marked talent for music, he went to Germany to study, but in 1887 decided to devote himself to art instead. Towards 1912 the influence of Cubism helped him to find his own manner. Feininger was one of the first artists to be invited by Gropius, founder of the Bauhaus *(*)* in 1919, to teach with him in Weimar. Although he did not teach there for long, he stayed on at the Bauhaus until it was disbanded by the Nazis in 1933, and his art, as well as his personality, contributed largely to the formation of its spiritual climate. Feininger left Germany in 1937, for political reasons, and settled in New York. From Cubism he learnt the transposition of forms and volumes into simple planes limited by straight lines, very rarely by curves. These planes were segmented. The structure of his pictures, after 1912, is akin to that of the Cubism of the *Section d'Or* in Paris, but subsequently became more and more complex and crystalline, until it attained an almost non-representational autonomy, between 1915 and 1919. After 1919, influenced by the architectural

spirit of the Bauhaus, the ordering of his planes became clearer: they are joined in an order without heaviness, and are organized into architectural visions in which the aspect of the medieval streets of the towns and villages around Weimar is marvellously transposed. But Feininger does not think and construct in terms of architecture, as Walter Gropius has justly said. In fact, the constituent elements of his pictures are, in the transparent fluidity of their colours, rays of light which, by their interpenetrations, create that atmosphere of purity and unreality which is so characteristic of Feininger's art. A romantic nostalgia, his German heritage, thus finds definite form in precise constructions of a delicate sensibility. Like the American painter John Marin (to whom he is akin), Feininger had, since childhood, a passion for boats and the sea. As with Marin, water-colours occupy an important place in his work, particularly since his return to the United States. His language then became even more precise, more musical, and his colour denser. His work was always the slow and methodical ripening of a theme–architecture in Manhattan, or a view of the ocean–which the painter never relinquished until it had been fully realized in the full expanse of the picture. F. M.

FÉNÉON Félix (1861-1944). French writer and art critic. He was a friend of Seurat and Signac, and became the spokesman of Neo-Impressionism *(*)* setting out its basic principles in a kind of pamphlet under the title of *The*

Impressionists in 1866, which was a great success. Using the scientific theories of Chevreul, Sutter, Charles Henry and O. N. Rood, Fénéon explained the Neo-Impressionist methods, and did so with a warmth and conviction that earned him considerable support. Although he railed against Gauguin, and criticized (though not without respect) Monet, Degas and Renoir for not having systematically applied the principle of division of colour, he adopted a milder attitude toward Pissarro, who had allowed himself to be for a while attracted by Divisionism, and championed Seurat, Signac, Cross and their friends unreservedly. The same year, 1866, Fénéon contributed an article on Seurat and Divisionism in *Vogue*, a Symbolist review. It was, however, in *Art Moderne*, a Belgian periodical whose correspondent he was in Paris that he published some of his most important articles from 1886 to 1890. Afterwards, he became one of the regular contributors to the *Revue Blanche (*)*, founded by the Natanson brothers in 1891. In 1900, he organized an outstanding restrospective exhibition of Seurat's works on the premises of the review. Furthermore, faithful to his friend's memory, he took it upon himself, after Seurat's death, to compile a thorough and precise catalogue of his works.

Although he loved order and logic, he was never at any time insensitive to the painting of young artists, such as Vuillard or Bonnard, whom he got to know in 1891, and with great perspicacity he supported the Nabi *(*)* movement from its inception. He was an ardent admirer of Toulouse-Lautrec, who depicted his curious silhouette in *The Dance of La Goulue and the Almehs*, which he executed in 1895 for the dancer's booth at the Foire du Trône. There are numerous portraits of Fénéon, but the most symbolical is the one Signac left, with a title that must have enchanted Fénéon himself, *Sur l'émail, d'un fond rythmique de mesures et d'angles, de tons et de teintes,*

portrait de M. Félix Fénéon en 1890. (On enamel, with a rhythmic background of measurements and angles, tones and tints, portrait of Mr Félix Fénéon in 1890.)   M. R.

FINCH Willy (1854-1930). Born at Brussels; died at Helsinki. His parents were English, but he trained in Belgium and at Paris. He was a friend of Theo van Rysselberghe and in 1884 became an active member of the Société des Vingt *(*)* and shared in the artistic revival, which marked the Symbolist period in Belgium. About 1890, he came in touch with Seurat and Neo-Impressionism, which had a great importance in his life. When he was invited to Helsinki in 1897 to run a ceramic factory, he gave up painting for the time being and turned all his attention to decorative art. It was to revolutionise Finnish ceramics. When he began painting again in 1905, he described the landscape of the Finnish archipelago in the luminous colours of Neo-Impressionism. It was something entirely new and his Divisionist technique, which was a radical break with the severe and sombre art of the Finnish School, caused a sensation. Before that, he had been responsible for organizing with his friend, the painter, Magnus Enckell, a large Impressionist and Neo-Impressionist exhibition at Hel-

SIGNAC. PORTRAIT OF FÉLIX FÉNÉON. 1890.

FREUNDLICH

sinki (1904). Again with Enckell and Sigurd Frosterus, the leading Finnish art critic, he founded the Septem group in 1912, which attacked provincialism and tried to forge closer links with France. Finch was a refined and sensitive artist and his works show a sound technique.   B. L.

FREUNDLICH Otto (1878-1943). Born at Stolp, Pomerania; died in the Lublin-Maidanek concentration camp in Poland, where he was deported by the Nazis. He used to draw a great deal during his childhood. When he left school, he worked as a business employee in Hamburg. At the age of twenty-five, he returned to his studies and followed courses in art history at the Universities of Berlin and Munich. It was at Florence in 1905 that he produced his first painting and sculpture. Art nouveau, which was sweeping Munich at the time, influenced his allegories, but after 1908 he gave up its flowing ornamentation for a style of painting which was built up of pure colour with clearly defined outlines. He went to Paris in 1909 and lived in the Bateau-Lavoir. He was a neighbour of Picasso and Herbin and made friends with Delaunay, Kandinsky, Juan Gris, Max Jacob and Braque. From 1910 to 1913, Freundlich took part in various exhibitions: Paris, with the Cubists; Amsterdam; Berlin, with the New Secession; Cologne, at the large, international exhibition of the Sonderbund, in 1912. He returned to Germany in 1914 and stayed there for ten years. He was called up to serve as a nurse at Cologne during the war, then he went to Berlin where he contributed towards the review, *Action,* and the activities of the Novembergruppe. His first stained-glass and mosaics in which he experimented with new materials, date from this period and also the beginnings of completely non-figurative painting (1919). He returned to Paris in 1924, exhibited successively at the Salon des Indépendants and the Salon des Surindépendants, became a member of the Cercle et Carré *(*)* then of the Abstraction-Création *(*)* groups. In 1930, he married the artist, Jeanne Kosnik-Kloss. When Hitler condemned 'degenerate art' at Berlin, one of Freundlich's sculptures, *The New Man,* was chosen for the cover illustra-

tion to the catalogue of the exhibition organized by the Nazis. A considerable amount of his work was then destroyed, including several figurative paintings and most of the mosaics. But Freundlich persevered and showed an unwavering strength of character in the difficult path he had chosen for himself and for which he had sacrificed everything. He continued to send work to the great exhibitions of abstract art and in 1938 his friends gave an enthusiastic celebration for his sixtieth birthday at Jeanne Bucher's gallery, where an exhibition of his paintings, gouaches and the most important of his sculptures was being held. He was interned when war was declared, released in 1940, interned a second time and again released. He was living in the Pyrenees under police supervision when he was arrested on the 21st February, 1943, at Saint-Martin de Fenouillet, imprisoned at Drancy, then deported to the Lublin-Maidanek concentration camp, where he died on March 9th.

Otto Freundlich was unassuming and humble, but his whole being was gathered into an unshakable will to create, which produced an unusual work that escaped from the frigidity of geometry by the intensity of light and the power of its vibrant colour. His paintings are like large sheets of bright colour, broken down by subtle variations of tone and composition by flat rectangles. In his mosaics he found a modern solution to the technical problems of mural decoration and gave it a universal significance without losing any of its individuality. There was nothing weak about his art; it was built up in strong, contradictory rhythms that possessed a monumental quality. Freundlich described his essential aims which show a thorough understanding of himself and the fundamentals of his art: 'When the artist has the power to detach himself gradually but definitely from generally accepted forms and truths, he is fulfilling the desire for a new reality. Every artistic creation has a purpose; a narrow purpose when it safeguards the artist: a wider purpose when the artist relinquishes his private life and his creations become the signs of shifting boundaries. This shifting of boundaries—social, political and spiritual—takes place at the beginning of every great period of history. Ours will achieve for the first time the union of man with the whole earth and through this our nostalgia and longing for the *unattainable* will change into something else, which is certainly far greater, although it is everywhere within our reach.'   R.-J. M.

FRIESZ Othon. French painter born in Havre in 1879; died in Paris, 1949. As a student at the school of fine arts in his home town he was guided in his early efforts by Charles Lhuillier, an obscure artist with a passion for the masters of French painting: Poussin, Chardin, Corot. The future Fauve never forgot what he had learnt from his kindly old teacher. In the latter part of his life, after having weathered the storms of the new century, Friesz returned to the spirit of this teaching, and began to listen

FREUNDLICH. COMPOSITION. 1930.
Private Collection, Paris.

rediscovered the virtues of logical composition, simple tones, and thick volumes. Trips to Portugal, Italy and Bavaria helped to accentuate his reconversion to Humanism and tradition. But the vigour, the robustness, the sensuality, which had given such emphasis to the work of his youth, still showed in his landscapes, in his still-lifes, in the female figures which he grouped round a fountain, or on the banks of a river, beneath the shade of big gnarled trees. In 1912 he opened a studio and taught until 1914. On the outbreak of the First World War he was mobilized, returning to live in Paris in 1919. After that he rarely left, except for brief stays in Toulon or in the Jura. From then on, far from the revolutionary movements agitating modern art, Friesz went on producing rather than creating, resorting to the cheap devices, easy effects and outworn rules of his craft. The one-time Fauve had given up adventure. The son of a sea captain had cast anchor in the pool of stale ideas. And when, in January 1949, he died, he left a body of to the voice of reason, rather than that of instinct. But what a strong and impetuous instinct that was ! In 1898 Friesz went to Paris, to the École Nationale des Beaux-Arts. He was not at ease there. He soon left, in rebellion against the official instruction. He joined up with some good friends of his, to fight against prejudice and raise the banner of a living art. He exhibited at the Salon des Indépendants in 1903, and at the Salon d'Automne in 1904. One of the most enthusiastic and brawny of the Fauves (*vide* Fauvism), intoxicated with colour, a devotee of the arabesque, hostile by nature to affectation and preciosity, Friesz painted (up to 1907) his series of Flanders, La Ciotat, and *Bathers*, and his admirable *Portrait of the Poet Fernand Fleuret.* Then he went back to Normandy–and tradition. In 1908 the Fauves had already dispersed. Alone with himself, Friez work in which the

FRIESZ. PORTRAIT OF FERNAND FLEURET. 1907.
Musée d'Art Moderne, Paris.

most brilliant promise was followed by skilful evasions. He boasted of having been one of the first to kill Fauvism, but it was his own art that he had destroyed.   F. E.

FRY Roger Eliot (1866-1934). Eminent English art critic, little known as a painter; born and died in London. Fry studied Natural Sciences (taking a first-class degree) at King's College, Cambridge, but gave up this field for art. He went to Rome in 1891, where he was profoundly influenced by Raphael and Michelangelo, and then to the Académie Julian, Paris, in 1892. He again visited Italy in 1894, and wrote essays on Bellini and Giotto. In 1905 he published a critical edition of Sir Joshua Reynolds's *Discourses*. Unable to find a suitable position in England, he accepted that of Director of the Metropolitan Museum of Art in New York in 1905. (He returned to London five years later.) He wrote a study of Cézanne, published in 1906, and became interested in the work of Gauguin, Matisse, Van Gogh and Maillol. It was Roger Fry (together with Clive Bell) who aroused an interest among the English-speaking peoples in what he aptly named 'post-Impressionism', with his two Grafton Gallery Shows in 1910 and 1912, the equivalent of the American Armory Show of 1913. In 1933 he was appointed Slade Professor of Fine Art at Cambridge, and died the following year.

Fry had a vast enthusiasm for, and an intellectual understanding of art, but little creative ability. As a painter he was soon forgotten. In his views on art he was elastic and always open to new ideas. His many short studies and articles on the subject of art and artists are of great interest. His honesty and lack of conservatism won him lasting respect as a sensitive, perceptive and helpful critic.   M. M.

FUTURISM February 20th, 1909, the Italian poet, Filippo Tommaso Marinetti, published the Manifesto of Futurist Poetry in the *Figaro*. The text, with its lively controversial and prophetic tone, aimed at a complete break with the fossilised forms of tradition and heralded the arrival of a poetry that was more in keeping with the machine age, its speed and the 'masses effervescing with work, pleasure and revolt'. Speed, Marinetti proclaimed, was our God and the new canon of beauty; a racing car was more beautiful than the Victory of Samothrace. This was the essence of a concept that was fundamental to Futurism. Marinetti concluded with these words: 'Time and space died yesterday. We are already living in the absolute, for we have already created eternal, omnipresent speed' (*vide* Marinetti). In the early part of 1910 three Italian painters, Carlo Carrà, Umberto Boccioni and Luigi Russolo, met Marinetti in Milan and, after lenghty discussions on the state of Italian art at the time, decided to issue a call to the young artists in the form of a manifesto. This was how the Manifesto of the Futurist Painters came to be written. Carlo Carrà, in his *Memoirs*, writes that 'when distributed a few days later in thousands of copies, this appeal to fearless and open rebellion . . . had the effect of an electric charge'. The manifesto, dated February 11th, also bore the signatures of Giacomo Balla, who was living in Rome, and Gino Severini, who had been living in Paris for several years. A public lecture was given about it at Turin on

March 8th, 1910, in the Politeama Chiarella Theatre.

The first turbulent manifesto, which was in general terms, was followed on April 11th by a Technical Manifesto of Futurist Painting, bearing the same signatures as the first. It stated the necessity of discovering 'the perpetuation of dynamic sensation as such', discussed the multiplication of things in movement and the interpenetration of bodies, the purity of original sensations and finally the virtues of Neo-Impressionist technique. The signatories of this document went to Paris soon afterwards, where they could see the paintings of Picasso and Braque. They had actually intended to hold an exhibition, but Severini managed to persuade them that they must do some more work before confronting the Parisian critics. The exhibition finally took place in February, 1912, at the Galerie Bernheim-Jeune. The preface to the catalogue, signed by the five Italian founders of the movement, insisted on the clear distinction between their own point of view and that of their 'Fauve and Cubist friends', and reaffirmed the total character of a revolution aimed at transforming life and manners. They found Cubism too static, too gallery-conscious, too alien from the dynamic exacerbation of the

modern world. All this was already evident from all the paintings in exhibition, although the paths of the different personalities in the group diverged later on. While Severini brought to Futurism the pure colours of Seurat, Carrà, on the other hand, adopted the grey tonalities of the Cubists. Boccioni, the theoretician of the movement, never lost sight of the 'realism' of Picasso, visible even in his Cubist compositions. Russolo, by sheer poetic intuition, was already foreshadowing the advent of Surrealism.

From the first exhibition Severini emerged triumphant. In the following year, 1913, Giacomo Balla painted a series of masterpieces, suggested to him, it is true, by three of Severini's canvases entitled *Spherical Expansion in Space*. While the technical means of his companions was still uncertain, Balla was the only painter of the group to succeed in giving plastic expression to the desire for power proclaimed by Futurism. Boccioni, in his picture *Elasticity* and his sculptures, achieved results which were no less miraculous (*vide* Balla, Boccioni, Carrà, Severini).

It is clear that Futurism was more than just an impetuous rush towards the spirit of modernism, more than just a doctrine. In linking art with life, and conceiving of life as force, the Futurists posed the problem of art in a way which was

BOCCIONI. THOSE WHO GO AWAY. 1911.

quite new at the time: philosophically, as well as scientifically. Among their happier intuitions are the ideas of 'simultaneity' and 'space'. While the simultaneity of which the French poet and critic Apollinaire (*) spoke in 1913 concerned only vision and the laws of optics according to the latest scientific discoveries, the simultaneity postulated by the Futurists is essentially psychic, and is concerned with memories, associations, and all the diverse emotions which assail an artist at the moment of creating. On the subject of space, Boccioni ventured to speak of a fourth dimension, but that was neither a sufficient nor a particularly Futurist definition. The Futurists touched on the real problem when they announced that 'henceforth the spectator will be placed in the heart of the picture', which implies an absolutely original conception of space. Italian Futurism (to which Apollinaire lent his support for a short while) had numerous faithful supporters and emulators. Apollinaire went so far as to propose that all avant-garde tendencies be labelled 'Futurist', but Marinetti turned the suggestion down. Since Futurism set out to embrace all the activities of the mind, it also invaded the sphere of poetry, drama and even music with Russolo's 'noise-instruments' and concerts with the 'Rumorharmonium'. In Italy, the centre of the movement was the Florentine review, La Voce (1908-1916), whose bookshop held, in December 1913, a Futurist exhibition of works of the five founders of the movement and also Ardengo Soffici. The same year, Soffici and Papini founded the review, Lacerba, while the group was increased by additional members, including Mario Sironi, Ottone Rosaï and Enrico Prampolini. The movement became whole-heartedly involved in the First World War. The disappearance of Boccioni, a leading personality of the group, and the increasing number of members led to the final disintegration of Futurism (vide Prampolini, Soffici and Sironi). Although its theories are often confused, Futurism is none the less one of the principal manifestations of the crisis that European culture passed through at the beginning of the century in its search for a more authentic expression of contemporary man.   s. l.

G

GACHET Dr Paul (1828-1909). Born in Lille; died in Auvers. His innate taste for painting and abiding friendship for painters, rather than the collector's urge, prompted Dr Gachet to gather around him at his home in Auvers-sur-Oise the greatest painters of his time. Not only Cézanne and Van Gogh but Pissarro, Renoir, Monet and Guillaumin were frequent visitors at the doctor's home. He became fond of them all, and their friendship went far beyond the usual relations between artist and collector. In fact, Cézanne stayed in Auvers for two years, from 1873 to 1874; moreover–and this is of capital importance in his life–it was at Auvers that he abandoned his romantic style and turned towards the new vision of reality that was to characterize his work and revolutionize modern painting. It was during his conversations with the doctor, and in the company of Pissarro, that Cézanne made in a few hours the disordered version of his *Modern Olympia*, at the same time that he was painting, in quite another vein, the celebrated *House of the Hanged Man* (*see* picture, page 60).

The relations between Doctor Gachet and Van Gogh were particularly close. After leaving the asylum at Saint-Rémy, Vincent, on the advice of Pissarro, went to stay at Auvers on May 16th, 1890, and saw much of the doctor, who was the artists' physician as well as their benefactor. Their friendship was to be short and tragic, for it ended, on the 27th of July with Van Gogh's suicide. Dr Gachet had tried, with the utmost skill and discretion, to persuade Vincent that he was not so ill as he thought. He gave him a measure of confidence in his abilities, and patiently endured his rebuffs and violence. In his calmer moments Vincent showed a tender affection for the doctor and his wife. In June he painted a picture of *Mademoiselle Gachet at the Piano* and the celebrated portrait of the doctor wearing his famous white cap. When Van Gogh shot himself near the heart on the evening of July 27th, Doctor Gachet tended him for two days in a desperate effort to save him. Gachet has left us two moving mementoes of Van Gogh on his death-bed–a charcoal drawing and an etching.

Dr Gachet was himself a competent artist with a strong predilection for engraving. There is a drawing in existence by Cézanne in which the artist is shown being given a lesson in engraving by the doctor. At his death his collection of Impressionist pictures was kept intact. The most important paintings such as Renoir's *Portrait of a Model*, Monet's *Chrysanthemums*, Cézanne's *Modern Olympia* and *The House of Dr Gachet*, Pissarro's *Road to Louveciennes*, Sisley's *Saint Martin's Canal*, and Van Gogh's pictures *The Doctor's Portrait*, *Self-portrait* on a turquoise background, and *Auvers Church* were left by Dr Gachet's son Paul to the Louvre.   M. R.

Dʳ GACHET. VAN GOGH ON HIS DEATH-BED.

GAUGUIN. THE YELLOW CHRIST. 1889.
Albright Art Gallery, Buffalo.

GAUGUIN Paul. French painter born in Paris in 1848; died in Fatu-Iwa, one of the Marquesas Islands, in 1903. A knowledge of the circumstances of his birth, marriage and belated career as a painter is indispensable to a proper understanding of Gauguin and his work. Paul Gauguin was born in the Rue Notre-Dame-de-Lorette in Paris, the son of Clovis Gauguin, a republican journalist from Orléans, and Aline Chazal, daughter of the painter and lithographer André Chazal, and Flora Tristan Moscoso, an eccentric writer and militant socialist. Through his maternal grandmother Flora Tristan, Paul was related to the Borgias of Aragon, who had given several viceroys to Peru. It was therefore quite natural for Clovis Gauguin to think of Peru as a refuge when Louis Napoleon's *coup d'état* forced him to leave France in 1851. He died on the journey. The family continued on its way and went to live in Lima. Aline Gauguin was a loving mother, simple and sweet. (In 1892 Gauguin painted a portrait of her from a photograph and his recollections of her.) After four years in Peru she decided to return to France with her children. Paul was then seven years old.

Aline was made welcome in Orléans by Isidore Gauguin, her brother-in-law. Little Paul was sent to a religious school in the town. At the age of seventeen he joined the Navy, just as Baudelaire and Manet had done before him, and visited Rio de Janeiro, Bahia, Sweden and Denmark. After the death of his mother, he gave up the sea and went to work for a Paris Exchange broker. He remained there for twelve years. An intelligent, punctual and methodical clerk, he soon attained an enviable position in the firm. He made money, spent it wisely, and lived in comfort. Eventually he married a young, beautiful Danish girl, Mette Sophie Gad (1873). Evidently Mette, a healthy, practical, steady and not unintelligent woman, thought she was marrying a distinguished man with a brilliant future, capable of bringing her happiness and security. What she wanted, above all, was the peace and pleasure she derived from running her home and supervising the upbringing of her five children. It was not to work out that way. Gauguin struck up a friendship with Schuffenecker, also in the brokerage business, who painted in his leisure time. It was he who introduced Gauguin to painting (1874). His period of apprenticeship was brief and he contributed to the Impressionist exhibitions of 1880, 1881 and 1882. Answering the irresistible call of his vocation, Gauguin gave up his work

GAUGUIN. WOMAN OF TAHITI. 1892.
The Art Institute, Chicago.

in 1883 in order to devote himself entirely to painting. Mette was thunderstruck and frightened. From then on, incapable of understanding her husband, or really loving him, she never ceased to give vent to her resentment and deep humiliation, and heap endless acrimonious reproaches, grievances and complaints on his head. Paul Gauguin was free to paint, but he was to suffer till the end of his life. Sick of her husband's 'foolishness', feeling insecure and fearful for the future, Mette decided to take the children and go to live with her parents in Copenhagen. Gauguin went with them. He felt as much a stranger among the Danes as he was to feel at home, later on, among the Polynesians. He took his favourite son, Clovis, and went back to Paris, promising to send for the others as soon as he could (1885). Then began one of the most unhappy periods of his life. Without money, without any hope of making any, he could not even provide for his son. But his passion for painting sustained and stimulated him. He was convinced of his power, his mission, and his genius.

In 1886 he went to live in Pont-Aven, a charming village in Brittany, but stayed for only a few months. Brittany did not give him the stimulus he had hoped for. Old visions, long dormant, reawakened in him. A year later he embarked for Panama with his friend Charles Laval. A typhus epidemic drove them away. They left for Martinique, where the revelation that Gauguin had so long awaited came to him: lush vegetation, ever-clear skies, lavish Nature, and a simple, happy existence. For lack of funds he had to drag himself away from this tropical paradise and return to France (December 1887).

Gauguin was then a man of forty, vigorous, domineering, with a noble and haughty bearing. His features are well known, thanks to his numerous self-portraits: the narrow, prominent forehead, the blue, deep-set eyes, the hooked nose and determined chin, the thick neck that suggests heaviness and arrogant power. However difficult his character, however uncompromising his opinions, he could be extremely charming and friendly when he was not contradicted or when those he talked with inspired his confidence.

His was a strong personality, irritating and engaging, in which the rustic was mixed with the aristocratic, at heart generous and good, despite the legend built up and maintained by the spiteful letters his wife wrote to friends she had left in France. For this husband whom she angrily accused, of 'monstrous egotism', this 'unnatural father', never ceased to love his wife and to suffer because he was separated from his children. To get some idea of his real feelings, his humility, tenderness and shyness, one must read his letters. But he was an

GAUGUIN. WOMEN ON THE BEACH. 1891.   *Musée du Louvre.*

artist, a man apart, resolved to pursue his destined course regardless of what it might cost him. His social duty counted for nothing in the face of his artistic duty. And, as a result, he made himself suffer as cruelly as those he loved.

Why these various stays in Brittany, Panama and Martinique? As his friend Daniel de Monfreid put it: 'He went to find, in what he believed to be a country of ancient customs, an environment, an atmosphere different from our over-civilized one'. In the Antilles he found the answer to his quest: a paradise setting with clear-cut lines and hard, strong colour contrasts. Gauguin broke with Impressionism, which had hitherto influenced his painting (1887). On his return to France he expressed his disapproval of Monet's and Pissarro's naturalist fiction. He formulated and preached 'Synthesism'. It may well be that the aesthetic principles designated under this name were inspired by Émile Bernard, as Bernard claimed. But that does not matter, for it was Gauguin who first enunciated this new theory and practised it with supreme mastery. Massive, simplified forms, flat colours, cloisonnism (*), shadowless drawing, abstraction of design and colour, free treatment of Nature–such were the principal articles of the credo that Gauguin formulated in 1888 during

GAUGUIN. VAHINI WITH GARDENIA. 1891.
Glyptothek, Copenhagen.

his second stay at Pont-Aven, and completed in the same year at Arles (where Van Gogh (*) revealed Japanese art to him), and at Pont-Aven and Le Pouldu (from April 1889 to November 1890). It was at this time that he painted the *Vision after the Sermon* (1888) and *The Yellow Christ* (1889). He also tried mural painting, sculpture, engraving and ceramics.

His ancestry, his childhood memories, the impressions he brought back from Martinique, his three stays in Brittany–all these gave him the incentive to renew an art that had been corrupted by the Impressionists. Eight painters grouped themselves around him, and constituted the School of Pont-Aven. Led by Sérusier, the Nabis (*) came and joined them. Fêted in Paris by the independent critics, by writers such as Stéphane Mallarmé, the poet, and Octave Mirbeau, the novelist, Gauguin might well have been content with such a strong position. But in the midst of his court he began to feel more and more alone. Brittany had nothing more to offer him, and France was too small for him and his dream. On the 23rd of February, 1891, he put thirty of his paintings up at auction, and with the proceeds embarked for Tahiti on the 4th of April.

At Papeete he found Europe again, with its vices, its stupidity and its frivolity. He went to live in Mataiéa, in a straw hut, among the peaceful, ingenuous population. He joined in all their rites and games, determined to destroy whatever trace of 'civilization' still remained in him. When his money ran out, and his debtors in Paris ignored his requests for payment, he was left without food, without clothes, and completely debilitated by a year of fierce, feverish work. He decided to return to France. *Women on the Beach, Vahini with Gardenia, Otahi, I raro te oviri* (Minneapolis), *When will you marry ?, Arearea* (Louvre), are a few of the many canvases he painted during this period. When he returned to France, in April 1893, sick, and at the end of his resources, he found a small legacy awaiting him, left by his uncle, Isidore Gauguin. He had several months of happiness. Dividing his time between Pont-Aven, Le Pouldu and Paris, he soon disposed of all his money. In his studio in the Rue Vercingétorix he gave a number of noisy parties, presided over by Annah, the Javanese girl, a monkey and a parrot. The free-spending, easy-going days soon came to an end. An exhibition of his Tahitian works at the Durand-Ruel Gallery on the 4th of November, 1893, held at the suggestion of Degas, was a fiasco from the financial point of view. But his new painting, mysterious and barbaric, aroused the enthusiasm of Bonnard, Vuillard and all the Nabis. After a series of misfortunes (including a last, painful interview with his wife in Copenhagen, and the flight of Annah, who ransacked his studio), Gauguin decided to return to the South Seas. A second auction to finance

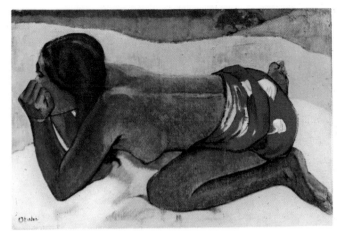

GAUGUIN. OTAHI. 1893. *Private Collection, Paris.*

him was a complete failure. He set out nevertheless, for Tahiti, and arrived there in July, 1895. He settled in the north of the island, and set to work immediately. And that is how the legend began, so common today, so unusual then: the legend of the European casting off civilization, alone and naked before the splendour of Nature. In October Gauguin began to have severe physical suffering. Whenever it abated, he applied himself to his work with renewed ardour and frenzy. The year 1897 was one of great sorrow for him: his beloved daughter, Aline, died; his correspondence with Mette came to an end; he was in hospital for a time. But it was also the year of his masterpieces *Whence Come We? What Are We? Whiter Do We Go?* (Museum of Fine Arts, Boston), *Nevermore* (Courtauld Institute, London). His manuscript *Noa Noa* appeared in the *Revue Blanche (*)*. The following year, after an attempt to commit suicide, he went to work as clerk and draughtsman in the Department of Public Works. Sick at heart, suffering from the effects of syphilis, he nevertheless had the courage to paint, draw, sculpt, engrave and write. He got himself into trouble defending natives from rough handling by the whites. He was even sentenced to three months' imprisonment and a fine of a thousand francs. Finally, worn out by privations, almost unable to move, he died on the 6th of May, 1903, after executing some of his finest canvases: *Barbaric*

GAUGUIN. RIDERS ON THE BEACH. 1902.   *Folkwang Museum, Essen.*

Tales, Horsemen on the Beach and *The Gold of their Bodies* (Louvre). The last thing he painted was a Brittany snow scene.

What Gauguin went to find in the South Seas was original purity, innocence, a way of forgetting oneself, natural man saved from the artificialities of civilization, and the universality and permanence of art. In his desire to reach the source of inspiration he reached the very sources of communication. He attained the solemn grandeur of ancient and primitive art through the immobility of his figures, the impassivity of their features, the serene gravity of their attitudes. That is why he is as close to Cretan and Egyptian art as he is to that of his contemporaries.

A creator who wanted to dominate his aesthetic adventure by the intellect, he succeeded in finding the appropriate means for realizing his conceptions. It was in order to give his compositions a monumental and, consequently, decorative character that he deliberately rejected modelling, form values, linear perspective, recession of planes, and secondary details, and neglected movement, relief, and the sensuality of expression. His South Sea canvases inspire a feeling of awe toward life, bitter regret for lost love and liberty, and a fear of the unknown, through the quiet cadence of their lines, their broad, flat areas of colour, and their grave, transfixed sumptuousness. Gauguin excelled in the art of composition. More than that, he invented a composition as different from that of the classical masters as theirs was from the composition characteristic of the Middle Ages. It is true that other precursors have, like him, felt the need to go back to the beginnings of the world, and find again purity of style. But no one was more courageously resolved to do it than Gauguin. 'Barbarism', he said, 'is for me a rejuvenation.' In his search he renewed pictorial art, and gave modern painting a meaning. His companions at Pont-Aven and the Nabis submitted to his leadership, and the *Fauves* were his direct heirs. Gauguin was also the one who inspired the present interest in ancient civilizations. His sculptures prepared the ground for the acceptance of Negro and Melanesian fetishes.

It was he who made possible many of the gains and discoveries of contemporary art. Of all the great innovators of the nineteenth century, it is Gauguin whom many non-representational artists of today regard as their precursor.

Like Cézanne, Gauguin lived a spiritual adventure; but, like Van Gogh, he lived a searingly temporal one too.   F. E.

GLEIZES Albert (1881-1953). Born in Paris, died in Avignon; descended from a family that was half southern French and half Flemish, Gleizes was both painter and writer; his life was inextricably linked with the evolution of Cubism, and he was the exponent of its theory. He began to paint in 1901, in the Impressionist style. In 1906, however, he began to seek 'a simplification of colour, in accordance with his desire to simplify form', and thus turned naturally toward Cubism. In 1910 he exhibited at the Salon des Indépendants (*The Tree*) and at the Salon d'Automne, and in 1911 he was one of the exhibitors in the famous Cubist Room at the Salon des Indépendants. At the Salon d'Automne in the same year his *Portrait of Nayral* had a *succès de scandale*. In 1912 Gleizes published, together with Metzinger, the book *On Cubism*. This was the most important work up to then on the theory of the new movement (*see* Cubism). He exhibited in Moscow and Barcelona, at the Armory Show (*) in New York in 1913, and at the first Autumn Salon in Berlin. After being called up in 1914, he painted several pictures on military themes. When he was discharged he went to America, and during his stay there, in 1917, he had a religious revelation. Upon his return to France he continued his experiments in technique, and in 1923 set them down in a book, *Painting and Its Laws*, which was a study of the objective laws of art based on the religious experience of the Middle Ages. He proclaimed the impending return of the Christian era, and endeavoured to develop an objective technique that would be easily transmissible, so that painters should have the means of praising God. To this end he worked out a scientific discipline ordered by a whole philosophical framework. In the logical course of his research he came across Romanesque art, about which he wrote works full of insight, and he endeavoured to put artistic creation at the service of the highest ambitions of Catholicism. In 1932 he published *L'Homocentrisme ou Retour à l'Homme Chrétien* (*Homocentricity, or Return to Christian Man*) and *Form and History*, a vast work in which he set himself the task of showing the superiority of an art based on religious thought and expressing movement and life by means of symbolic rhythms. While remaining faithful to the spirit of Cubism, Gleizes applied himself to defining quasi-impersonal modes of expression which constituted the language of a new type of mural painting. He returned to his former themes, transposing them in this spirit, and he was not afraid to present a modern version of the compositions dear to the Middle Ages–a majestic Christ or Virgin, popes and emperors. From 1939 on Gleizes lived in retirement at Saint-Rémy-de-Provence, continuing to exert a marked influence, by his writings and lectures as well as by his paintings and his example, on many groups of young artists and artisans in the Rhône Valley. His last important work was the illustration of the *Pensées* of Pascal, consisting of fifty-seven original etchings.   J. LA.

GLEIZES. WOMAN WITH GLOVE. 1920.
Private Collection, Paris.

GOERG Édouard (born in Sydney, Australia, in 1893). Goerg, who was of French and Irish parentage, soon left Australia and spent several years in England; then, at the age of seven, he moved to France. In 1912 he enrolled for a year's study at the Académie Ranson (*), where Maurice Denis was teaching. Goerg's predilection for Goya, Daumier and Rouault indicates that his art was inspired by realism, but he was to accentuate the sentimental note. 'What I love in art is man . . . I well know that a painting has its laws, that it is a plane surface, a combination of volumes . . . but I say that that is not enough.' In that remark Goerg seemed to be condemning genuine plastic emotion and to be preferring the anecdotal. His work fell into a sort of naturalism, a characteristic aspect of which was the representation of nude young girls barely out of adolescence, accompanied by men in evening clothes, all enveloped in shadowy atmosphere relieved by conventional gleams of light. Goerg has illustrated a number of literary works (the *Tales* of Hoffmann and Baudelaire's *Les Fleurs du Mal*) with engravings and lithographs in which his understanding of contrasts has enabled him to accentuate the dramatic elements very skilfully, with a certain stress on the macabre. M. R.

GOERG. IMAGINARY PORTRAIT. 1929.
Private Collection, Paris.

GOGH Vincent van (1853 - 1890). Dutch painter; born at Groot-Zundert, in North Brabant; died at Auvers-sur-Oise. If, in December 1885, Van Gogh had not experienced a near-blinding revelation as a result of which he produced the masterpieces of the five last years of his life, he would no doubt be hailed today as a great painter of labour and poverty, of workmen and peasants overwhelmed by weariness, the first of the Dutch Expressionists. He became a painter in order to solve an inner conflict by which he was torn, to take revenge in the domain of art for the failures he had experienced in his life. He was of a Protestant family, a family of clergymen. But two of his uncles were art dealers, a fact that allowed him to start out in The Hague as a salesman in a gallery recently sold by one of them to the firm of Goupil (*) of Paris. Vincent was sixteen then. Four years later, he was sent by his firm to London, to work in the English branch. In London he fell in love with his landlady's daughter. He asked her hand. He was turned down.

Unstable by temperament, acutely nervous, too sincere, he was deeply dejected by this first failure. He left London and went to work at Goupil's head office in Paris, in 1875. He was immediately borne away upon the current of ideas of which Paris was then the centre. He read all the books within his reach, visited museums, underwent the influence of humanitarian writers and of painters concerned with the sufferings of the humble. The Bible became the chief stimulus of this self-taught son of a clergyman. He was dismissed by Goupil in 1876, and went back to England. He worked at a small school at Ramsgate, and then at another, where he did some preaching. He applied for a job as an evangelist among the miners. 'I feel drawn to religion. I want to comfort the humble.' His application was rejected. At Christmas of the same year he returned to Etten, to his parents, but soon there was conflict. From January 21st to April 30th, 1877, he was a clerk in a bookshop in Dordrecht. But he was unable to adjust himself to a practical and regular existence. Therefore, increasingly tormented by his religious calling, he went to Amsterdam to prepare for the entrance examination to the Theological College. After fourteen months of

VAN GOGH. SELF-PORTRAIT. 1886-1888.

of the darkest periods of his life, months of poverty, moral distress, anguish, roving on the roads. To his brother Theo, who was about to enter Goupil's in Paris, he wrote a poignant letter, in which he announced his decision to devote himself to painting. In October 1880, he was in Brussels, where he studied drawing and made copies from Millet. From April to December 1881, he stayed at Etten with his parents. He experienced another sentimental disappointment there. Turned down by his cousin, Kee, he went away and settled in The Hague. The painter Mauve, another cousin of his, took him in cordially and gave him useful advice. In January 1882, he met in the street a prostitute named Christine, who was ugly, drunk and pregnant. He took her with him. To this woman he gave all the love of which he was capable. The episode lasted twenty months, until he realized definitely that he was no better at individual love than at the love of humanity and the love of God. From then on his humiliated pride took refuge in art. With his artistic apostolate his misfortunes grew. He quarrelled with his father, who disapproved of his artistic career. He fell out with Mauve and Israels, the teachers of The Hague School, whose teaching had finally become unbearable to him. Then, in December 1883, he

desperately hard work, he had to give up and return to his family. His exasperated father ended by entering him at the Evangelical school at Brussels. In December 1878, Vincent left for the Borinage in Belgium without waiting to be given an appointment. He undertook to bring the miners of this forsaken region back to Christ. He adopted their own poverty, slept on a board in a wooden hut, shared their sufferings, attended the sick, showed the exalted zeal of an apostle, but without success. He was then an ill-clothed, gawky, red-haired fellow, with abrupt gestures and too-bright eyes. His spirit of sacrifice seemed astonishing, his excessive asceticism alarming. Men pursued him with sarcasm, children feared him, and as for women-who could love this terrible man ? His superiors got rid of him in July 1879. Then began one

VAN GOGH. SHOES.

V. W. Van Gogh Collection.

VAN GOGH. MOORED BOATS. AUGUST 1888. *Folkwang Museum, Essen.*

Lautrec and Émile Bernard, who was eighteen then and with whom he kept up a regular correspondence. He worked desperately. He painted streets of Paris, portraits, flowers. He exhibited a few canvases at Père Tanguy's *(*)* among others by Monet, Guillaumin and Signac. His brother, who was then the manager of the Goupil Gallery, encouraged and backed him. Obsessed by Japanese prints, he copied *The Bridge under Rain* and *The Tree* of Hiroshige. His palette lightened; he even borrowed the Impressionist pointillist technique, as in the *Portrait of Père Tanguy* (1887, Musée Rodin) or in *View from the Artist's Room, rue Lepic*

returned to his father's house, this time at Nuenen, and courageously gave himself up to painting. He did studies of the heath, cottages, weavers, peasants, executed in the rough, black dismal manner of *The Loom* (1884) and *The Potato-Eaters* (V. W. Van Gogh Collection, Laren), his first large picture. His native tendency, the influence of his environment, the contagion of example-all incited him to persevere in this gloomy realism. How, then, can the radiant masterpieces that were to follow be explained ?

In November 1885, he was in Antwerp. His father had just died. His brother Theo, with whom he had been in correspondence for five years, had sent him some money. He had discovered Rubens and the joy of life, and also Japanese fabrics, whose colours delighted him. He bought some, decorated his room with them, spent hours contemplating and studying them. He glimpsed an outlet for his still obscure desires, a new world of light, consolation, balance. He decided all of a sudden in February 1887 to leave for Paris. Theo received and sheltered him affectionately. He was dazzled by Impressionist pictures. He met Pissarro, Degas, Gauguin, Signac. In June 1886, he enrolled at the École Nationale des Beaux-Arts in the Cormon studio, where he made friends with Toulouse-

(1887). In the pictures of Pissarro, Monet, Guillaumin, he rediscovered the light handling and the fresh tones of the Japanese. But French Impressionism had caused a decisive shock to

VAN GOGH. SCHOOLBOY. 1888-1889. *São Paulo Museum.*

his thinking mind. He felt such a need to emulate the Impressionists that he did some two hundred pictures during the twenty months of his stay in Paris. This prolific and sometimes uncontrolled production includes outdoor scenes, such as *Fête at Montmartre* (1886), *Restaurant la Sirène* (1887), *Little Gardens on Montmartre* (1887), still-lifes such as *The Yellow Books* (*Parisian Novels*) and a series of twenty-three self-portraits, including the one at his easel (1888), which in a way marks the end of this period. The winter of 1887 was an unhappy one for him. The grey sky, the gloomy streets, the sadness of the capital became unbearable to him. The Parisian painters could not give him more than he had taken from them. The rejuvenation he had received from their contact was already exhausted. He needed light, heat, to warm his frozen soul and awaken his eagerness for work. Upon the advice of Toulouse-Lautrec, he went to Arles, on February 20th, 1888. In Provence everything delighted him, the orchards in bloom, the beautiful women of Arles, the Zouaves of the garrison, the drinkers of absinthe. He exclaimed with rapture, 'This is the Orient !' He was thirty-five and felt happy. With ease and enthusiasm he drew with a reed, painted well-balanced canvases, firmly arranged, almost serene. At last he had found clear-cut contours, light without shadow, pure colour, dazzling, crackling vermilion red, Prussian blue, emerald green, sacred yellow, the emblem of the sun. He shed the finery of Impressionism, gave up the divided stroke, fragmented design, subtle modulations. Vigorous, precise, incisive, his line captured the inner structure of objects. He painted nearly two hundred pictures in fifteen months, executing three, four and sometimes up to five versions of some of them: *The Drawbridge at*

LETTER FROM VAN GOGH ADRESSED TO ÉMILE BERNARD. FROM ARLES. 1888.

Arles, The Plain of la Crau, Sunflowers, Café at Night, L'Arlésienne (Mme Ginoux), The Postman Roulin, his wife and their son, *Armand Roulin.* From a short stay at Saintes-Maries-de-la-Mer he brought back drawings and canvases, notably his *Barges on the Beach* (Laren) and a *Seascape* (Moscow). He left an admirable representation of his *Bedroom in Arles* (October 1888), of which he later made, at Saint-Rémy, one replica from memory.

However, his material existence was most precarious. He did not have enough to eat. He sold nothing. He suffered from hallucinations and crises, from which he emerged dazed. The idea

VAN GOGH. HOUSE IN PROVENCE. 1888. PEN DRAWING.

of death haunted him. As if he had a presentiment of his approaching end, he hurried, worked furiously, in a state of exaltation that saved him from despair. His mind was on fire. His pictures dripped with golden light. He was 'in the centre of the universal fusion' that transmuted his colours and consumed his brain. Crises grew more

VAN GOGH. PORTRAIT OF ARMAND ROULIN. 1888.
Folkwang Museum, Essen.

numerous. He played with a project for an artists' colony that he would have called 'The Studio of the South', where groups of men would work at projects in common. Late in October 1888, Gauguin responded to his appeal. Vincent was quite cheered up. But in stormy discussions the relationship between these two opposed natures soon deteriorated. On Christmas night, during a futile quarrel, Van Gogh threw his glass in Gauguin's face. The next day, Gauguin, walking in the street, heard hurried steps behind him. He turned and saw Van Gogh with a razor in his hand. Under Gauguin's steady gaze Van Gogh stopped, then fled to his room, cut off an ear with a stroke of the razor, wrapped it in a handkerchief and went to offer it as a present to a girl in a brothel. After two weeks in a hospital he came back to paint the extraordinary *Man with an Ear Cut Off* (January 1889). Meanwhile his hallucinations returned. Neighbours raised a petition for his internment. His unattractive appearance, his touchy character, his whims had alienated people. He had never analyzed his illness more clearly, endured men's hostility with so much resignation, or spoken of his art with more common sense and lucidity, but now he was considered mad. He was sent back to the hospital. In Paris, Theo, who was going to be married, became alarmed and sent the painter Signac to see him. Signac spent the day of March 24th with Vincent, who kept on painting, reading, writing, in spite of his crises. When he felt too ill, he asked to be interned at the asylum of Saint-Rémy-de-Provence, on May 3rd, 1889.

The Arles period was over, the most fruitful if not the most original of his career. During the year he remained at the asylum he produced another hundred and fifty pictures, and hundreds of drawings, working as one possessed, interrupted in his labour by three long crises, followed by painful prostrations. He painted *Yellow Wheat, Starry Night, Asylum Grounds in Autumn*, a few portraits including that of the *Chief Superintendent of the Asylum*, delirious landscapes, surging mountains, whirling suns, cypresses and olive trees twisted by heat. His colour no longer had the sonority of the preceding period; the yellows had become coppered; the blues darkened, the vermilions browned. In compensation, rhythm became more intense: whirling arabesques, dismantled forms, perspective fleeing toward the horizon in a desperate riot of lines and colours. What he represented then on his canvases he seems to have seen through a vertigo of the imagination. The fire lit by his hand was communicated to his brain. A feeling of failure overwhelmed him. Could his works be inferior to those of the masters whom he admired ? This thought frightened him. In February 1890, he learned of the birth of Theo's son, called Vincent after himself. The generous Theo, so indulgent a brother, at whose expense he, the failure as an artist, the painter incapable of selling a single canvas, had been living so long ! Yet, in the *Mercure de France* the critic Aurier had just published the first article devoted to his work. This tribute brought him little comfort. He felt ill, exhausted. Vigilant as ever, Theo asked Doctor Gachet *(*)* to take Vincent under his care at Auvers-sur-Oise. It was thus that Van Gogh came to Paris, on May 16th,

1890, and settled soon at Auvers. Doctor Gachet attended him, showed him an affectionate friendship, served as a model for him. For Vincent had resumed painting. He did his last self-portrait, now in the Louvre, *The Church of Auvers*, also in the Louvre, *The Town Hall of Auvers*, the *Portrait of Mlle Ravoux*, that of *Doctor Gachet* (Louvre), and other works, for which he had at his disposal only a technique which had already begun to disintegrate. He feared a new attack of his illness. An unspeakable

VAN GOGH. YELLOW WHEAT. 1889.   *Tate Gallery, London.*

sadness invaded him. Go on working when the hand refuses to obey, when the enemy within will now always be the stronger ? What was the use of trying ? That last Sunday in July, Vincent slipped out of the Pension Ravoux, where he was staying. He made for the fields of ripe corn, where a few days before he had painted the famous *Wheat Field with Crows*. The village was deserted. He stopped in front of a farm. Nobody there. He entered the courtyard, hid behind a dunghill and shot himself in the chest with a pistol. He had the strength to return to the inn, go up to his room and get into bed like a wounded animal. He died two days later, in the presence of Theo, who had hastened to his bedside. He was thirty-seven years and four months old

VAN GOGH. THE PLAIN AT AUVERS-SUR-OISE. 1890. *XIXth Century Gallery, Vienna.*

Unbalanced, painful, tragic, such was certainly his life. That he suffered from neurosis and epilepsy is equally true. Like Rousseau, like Baudelaire, Van Gogh felt very vividly that his life was a failure and suffered deeply from it. He was perpetually anguished, and against his anguish he tried various means of defence: religion, humanitarianism, art. He gave himself to painting with all the more passion as he saw himself threatened by an implacable disease. Lifted out of himself by art, he was able to overcome his physical failings, or at least not to think of them too much. This unstable, high-strung, obsessed man, in unceasing conflict with society and himself, created a body of work outstanding in its concerted perfection of ends and means. However impetuously inspired and executed it may be, this art is certainly not that of a madman. Although he put all of himself into his painting, Vincent never abandoned his very obvious concern for balance, order and reason. His shortcomings are more than offset by an activity which drew from his very failures enough vigour to fight against his weakness and live in his work. He might have sunk into mental chaos; instead, he triumphed through discipline, work and meditation. In the midst of his greatest discouragements, he retained his love of simplicity and harmony, sought a reconciliation of form and colour, an abstract, coherent transposition of the world. He gave himself an infallible system of principles and rules to reach the artistic ideal that he had glimpsed in his moments of acute insight. Each of his works was the fruit of a thought, a decision, a wish for serenity rather than for strangeness. What did he want? 'Something peaceful and pleasant, realistic and yet painted with emotion; something brief, synthetic, simplified and concentrated, full of calm and of pure harmony, comforting like music.' He tamed his exaltations and his impulses by the laws he had established for himself. Far, then, from being the painting of a madman, Van Gogh's is that of a thoroughly conscious artist and at the same time of a robust man, a dedicated creator. If anything, he saw too clearly. He sought always elements of a beauty of which he could find only an insufficient amount. 'There is an art in the future, and it will be so beautiful, so young ! . . .' What bitterness in this cry of hope ! He hoped for, prepared, made possible a golden age of painting, knowing nevertheless that he would not see it. More assured of his victories than of profits, it was reserved to him, the discoverer and the pioneer, only to bequeath the means of success to those who came after him. In a way he triumphed over his illness, for his suicide prevented his madness. But he did not create the new art of which he had a presentiment and which he announced with moving certainty in his letters, because the moment for it had perhaps not yet come.

The sureness of his hand equalled that of his will. There is no groping, no working over, nor

VAN GOGH. WHEAT FIELD WITH CROWS. 1890.   V. W. Van Gogh Collection.

the slightest alteration in his landscapes or his portraits, which were almost always undertaken directly on canvas, in the manner of the Japanese. 'It is not only by yielding to one's impulses', he wrote, 'that one achieves greatness, but also by patiently filing away the steel wall that separates what one feels from what one is capable of doing.' So Van Gogh expressed the inner duel that eventually exhausted his strength. But if the man died prematurely, the work remains, and contemporary painting was, in a great measure, born of it. Van Gogh appeared when the Naturalist fiction was casting its last glow with Impressionism, at a time when academic conventions were collapsing, when tradition was dying of old age. With Cézanne and Gauguin, he questioned the technique of painting and in doing so prepared for the art of the twentieth century. He used the picture not to imitate appearances or humour the tastes of a cultivated society, but to re-create the world according to his own intelligence and sensibility. While Cézanne was concerned with a new conception of space and Gauguin with composition, Van Gogh emancipated colour, carrying it to its maximum intensity and expressiveness. In his canvases colour reinforces drawing, accentuates form, creates rhythm, defines proportions and depth. It even acquires the value of a sign, addressing itself to the soul as well as to the eye: 'colour not locally true,' he said, 'from the realistic point of view of *trompe-l'œil*, but sugges-

tive of some emotion'. He used it raw, dry, aggressive, in abrupt harmonies, now strident, now muted, without shades, without semitones, with cruel frankness. 'I have tried to express with red and green the terrible human passions', he also wrote. But he always refrained from sacrificing colour to form. And it is right that today his drawings should be admired as much as his pictures. He has left a great number of them, and all of them are surprising in their simplicity and acuteness of expression, their assurance and swiftness of line, the variety of the graphic means which the artist used to transcribe on paper the quivering elements of his vision. And this vision was thoroughly his own, of undeniable depth and originality. He has had no direct descendants, although his influence has been felt by all modern painting: Fauves like Vlaminck, Derain, Dufy, Friesz; the Expressionists, in particular Soutine. But Van Gogh was also a poet, a mystic, a thinker. No artist today raises more passionate an interest than he: his painting, his drawings, his correspondence. For Van Gogh lived in advance the drama of our time, a time that 'now liberates and now enslaves'. Nowhere is the study of the artist's correspondence more vital than in the case of Van Gogh. His letters to Theo, in addition to the intrinsic interest they have as deeply moving human documents, are indispensable to a thorough understanding of his concepts and intentions. (*The Complete Letters*, Thames & Hudson, 1958.)   F. E.

GONTCHAROVA Nathalie (1881-1962). Born in Russia, in the Toula region; died at Paris. She was brought up in the country in the calm and traditional ways of an old, aristocratic family. She was descended from Pushkin through her great grand-mother and her father was an architect. Drawing, as well as botany and zoology, interested her when she was very young. She went to school in Moscow in 1891, then began studying for a history degree, but never sat for it. She joined the School of Painting, Sculpture and Architecture in 1898, attended Troubetzkoi's classes in sculpture and was awarded a medal and a diploma at the end. She began exhibiting in 1900 and was represented in the huge collection of Russian art organized by Frantz Jourdain and Serge Diaghilev at the Autumn Exhibition of 1906. By 1904, she had given up sculpture and taken up painting. Lévitan helped her in this. She visited England, Spain, Switzerland, Italy and Greece. On her return to Russia, she met Larionov, became his companion and shared his theories on Rayonism. She exhibited on her own or with him in several shows: the Venice Biennale; the Sturm Gallery, Berlin;

Munich with the Blaue Reiter in 1912. Although her painting began by a formalisation of shape, first of lines only, then of volumes that ended in a sort of prismatic Cubism (1908), it possessed from the beginning the brilliant colours of popular art and a rhythmic expression, which culminated in Rayonism *(*)* in 1910. Until 1914—the date of her arrival in Paris with Larionov, where they exhibited at Paul Guillaume's gallery and were introduced to the public by Apollinaire—Gontcharova produced her best paintings, which were among the first non-figurative compositions. Appearances gradually disappeared into the stridences of pure colour as her style developed from the architectural *Forests* to the *Cats* (1910) and the whiplash dynamics of *Electricity* (1911). But Gontcharova did not stop at Rayonism; she anticipated Russian Futurism by introducing letters and numbers into her painting and gave free rein to her imagination in tragic visions of cities and streets, which later inspired the sets for Robert Wiene's film, *The Cabinet of Dr. Caligari* (1920), which were designed by three artists of the Der Sturm group: Herman Warm, Walter Röhrig and Walter Reinmann. In 1914, through their friend, Serge Prokofiev, Larionov and Gontcharova began to work for Diaghilev's Ballets Russes *(*)*, which offered them a new form of expression. Gontcharova interpreted the popular sources of her art into a modern idiom for the décor of the *Coq d'Or* (1914); she discovered a new conception of theatrical space, which simplified to an extreme degree for *Les Noces* (1923) with music by Stravinsky. Like Larionov, she did not content herself with designing sets and costumes, but gave her advice on choreography and even wrote the plots of several ballets. She differed from her companion, however, in that she never gave up painting and, right to the end of her life, she was painting still-lifes, the series of the *Spaniards*, a whole group of abstract compositions, which were like sheaves of light, derived from the Rayonism of her youth. R.-J. M.

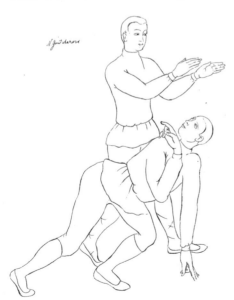

GONTCHAROVA. STUDY FOR 'LES NOCES'. 1923.

GORKY Arshile, derived from his real name, Vosdanig Adoian (1904-1948). Born at Hajotz Dzore, Turkish Armenia; died in Sherman, United States. He occupies an unusual place

GONTCHAROVA. THE CATS. 1910.   *Private Collection, U.S.A.*

of experiencing European art. It was ironic that Gorky died the same year that the New York School began to win recognition for iself, a year after Pollock painted his *Cathedral*.

Gorky's childhood left a permanent, nostalgic mark on his painting. He lived in the mountain forests of his native country until 1914, when his mother died and his family lost all its possessions. Then followed the emigration to Russia, where from 1916 to 1918 he studied at the Polytechnic Institute of Tiflis. In 1920, he took refuge in the United States and changed his name. There he led the precarious existence of a self-taught man, haunting the museums and from time to time attending the art schools: evening classes at the Rhode Island School of Design, the New School of Design of Boston in 1923 and 1924, the National Academy of Design of New York in 1925. From 1926 to 1931, he taught at the New York School of Design, then at the Grand Central School of Art. Like most American artists of his generation (Baziotes, Guston, de Kooning, Pollock, Rothko, Tworkov), he worked during the Depression at the WPA Federal Art Project and his mature work dates from this period. The great frescoes for the airports of Newark and New Jersey, and for the Pavilion of Aviation at the New York Exhibition in 1939 belong to these years.

When he painted *The Artist and his Mother* in 1926, Gorky was still influenced by Picasso's pre-Cubist period. He then went through a Cubist phase himself, followed by the influence of Kandinsky's first abstract paintings. In the evolution towards his own style, meeting the Surrealists, particularly Matta, in 1939, was decisive. Nevertheless, as André Breton realized, his artistic procedure was the opposite to that of the Surrealists. His point of departure was always the observation of nature, but the

in contemporary art. While his own work is a late phase of Surrealism, profoundly original in its abstraction and peculiar sensibility, recondite and difficult, the part Arshile Gorky played in the birth of the New York School of Abstract Expressionism has a considerable importance. One of its most distinguished adherents, W. de Kooning, wrote in 1949: 'I am glad that it is almost impossible to escape from his powerful influence. As long as I remain affected by it, I shall feel sure that I am on the right path.' It is in fact owing to Gorky's receptiveness that American painters of Pollock's generation were indirectly subjected to a number of very different European influences : not only Cézanne, or above all Picasso and Miró, but also Kandinsky from whom he sometimes derived his colours and rhythms, and Matisse whose unconstraint he shared. Gorky was rather slow in conquering his 'legitimate strangeness' and his perviousness to the formal ideas of others and his ability to assimilate them constituted a sort of reactive or catalyst for the New York artists in whose work there is no apparent trace

process of abstraction and dislocation led him paradoxically to the creation of a subjective and symbolical world. His space has often been compared to Matta's multiple perspectives. Both men are primarily draughtsmen, who have a predilection for curving lines and a certain evanescence of form. But Matta is a visionary of the external world, while Gorky's gaze is ultimately set on exploring the world of the mind. His paintings are built up both by the interpenetration of lines and forms and the colour, which is always decided by the dominant colour of the background on which a few brilliant splashes act like a source of light. The bright colours, used about 1944, when *The River is the Cockscomb* was painted, were distinctly subdued in the series of masterpieces, produced in 1947-1948, just before his suicide: *Dark Green Painting*, *Agony* (Museum of Modern Art, New York), *The Betrothal II*. An exhibition, covering all Arshile Gorky's work, was shown for the first time in Europe at the Venice Biennale of 1962.   F. C.

GOUPIL (Gallery). In the years around 1850 the Goupil Gallery, then located in the Rue Caulaincourt, was a small shop which sold principally engravings of the works of such painters as Horace Vernet, Paul Delaroche and Ary Scheffer. In 1877, with the third Impressionist exhibition, Goupil became interested in the new movement and from then on the growth of the gallery was rapid. Van Gogh worked in the branch in The Hague in 1869 and was later transferred to the Brussels shop, where he was replaced by his brother Theo prior to his transfer to the London branch. In 1875 Vincent worked for a while at the Paris head-

quarters, from which he was dismissed the following year. Later, he sent some of his paintings to his brother, Theo, still employed by Goupil, who tried to place them with the Gallery, but they were rejected as 'horrors'. In 1893 Toulouse-Lautrec exhibited a group of his Montmartre canvases at the London shop. Another Goupil related to the founder of the firm, was the author of a book on painting which was instrumental in Matisse's choice of career.

GRIS Juan (1887-1927). Born in Madrid; died at Boulogne-sur-Seine, near Paris. José Victoriano González, known as Juan Gris, was born of a Castilian father and an Andalusian mother. According to his sister Antonieta, his vocation was evident in early childhood, at the age of six or seven. Nevertheless, he received a general education and then enrolled at the School of Arts and Crafts in Madrid. His preliminary education was essentially scientific, and this is seen in his writings and pictorial theories. When financial ruin struck his family, he made a living by selling drawings to humorous papers in Madrid. It was not long before he devoted himself entirely to painting, entering the studio of an old academic painter, Moreno Carbonero, who,

GORKY. AGONY. 1947. *Museum of Modern Art, New York.*

he said, 'made him disgusted with good painting'. He lived among painters and writers, and took the name Juan Gris. At that time the more advanced artistic circles in Spain were becoming initiated into 'Modern-style', under the influence of German publications and reviews.

At the age of nineteen Gris decided to go to Paris, paying for the journey by selling all his possessions. Since he left without doing his military service, he was never able to obtain a passport, and this prevented him from ever travelling out of France. He asked for French nationality, but he died without obtaining it. Attracted by the rising fame of Picasso, he settled at the Bateau-Lavoir (*), 13 Rue Ravignan, where he lived precariously by making satirical drawings for newspapers and magazines. But he worked mostly for himself, and when he decided, after four or five years of endeavour, to exhibit his work, he gave up his old livelihood for ever. His first buyer was the dealer Clovis Sagot, and he first exhibited at the Salon des Indépendants of 1912, to which he sent a *Hommage à Picasso*. In the same year he showed his works in Barcelona, Rouen, and the exhibition of the *Section d'Or (*)* in Paris. Kahnweiler who had known him since 1907, became his dealer. He also became his best friend, and the book which he wrote about him in 1946 was the first definitive work published about him. Gertrude Stein, Léonce Rosenberg and Alfred Flechtheim acquired his works. These were still painted in the style of analytical Cubism. Cubism, reacting against imitation, had recourse at first to the analysis of objects, which it tried to grasp not merely in their changing appearances but in their successive aspects, in all their facets, even in cross-section, the result on the canvas being a juxtaposition of planes and lines that was often complicated but was particularly expressive. Gris's first works, especially his portraits, are always intelligible and well balanced. The Cubists very soon tried to introduce elements taken from everyday life into their compositions, to serve as guide-posts and explanations for the public: for instance, *trompe-l'œil* wood and marble, printed letters, and actual pieces of newspaper. Juan Gris used these ingenuous and empirical methods with great distinction, but he started a reform that was more profound and coherent, a truly scientific doctrine of modern

GRIS. STILL-LIFE WITH DIE. 1922.
Musée d'Art Moderne, Paris.

painting. He played a decisive role in what has been called synthetic Cubism (*).

In the summer of 1913 Gris stayed at Céret with Picasso, who encouraged him, and with Manolo, with whom he had endless arguments on theory. From then on he strove to make Cubism clearer, more precisely defined, more irrefutable. The war found him again at Céret, in 1914, with Matisse and Marquet. On his return to Paris he set to work at once, helped by Léonce Rosenberg the art dealer, who held an exhibition for him in 1919. At the Salon des Indépendants of 1920 he participated in the last exhibition of the united Cubist group, which was to break up soon after that. He was not very successful, and he saw himself disparaged, even by his friends, although he always showed them the greatest kindness. It disturbed him to see the meaning of Cubism distorted–its

GRIS. THE SCOTSWOMAN. 1918.
Private Collection, Paris.

impetus had been broken perhaps by the war—and he decided to pursue alone his search for a 'grand style' suited to his time. Possessed by a sort of craving for knowledge, in which he seemed to seek compensation for the ineptitude against which he raged, Juan Gris would have been one of the universal men of the Renaissance had he lived at that time.

What was synthetic Cubism, according to Juan Gris ? A certain discrepancy already existed between the structure and composition of the picture and its colours, for the latter were sometimes indicated only by a smudge. Thus, in the *papiers collés*, the details could be interchanged without any damage to the solidly established structure. This was the starting-point of Juan Gris's method. Kahnweiler has reported a talk on this subject in 1920: 'I begin', declared Gris, 'by organizing my picture; then I characterize the objects.' Another of his declarations—often quoted and generally misinterpreted—states, even more precisely, that he went from the general to the particular, starting from an abstrac-

tion and arriving at a real fact. Yet the context is very clear. He began by saying: 'I work with the elements of the mind; with the aid of the imagination, I try to make concrete what is abstract'. And he continued: 'I want to arrive at a new set of characteristics, to create specific individuals by starting from a general type . . . From a bottle, Cézanne made a cylinder, but I make a bottle from a cylinder—a certain type of bottle.' Because he spoke of the mathematical structure of a picture, it is assumed that he had a theoretical and abstract mentality which arbitrarily reversed all the normal processes of artistic creation, excluding from them every human element. It is sufficient to look at Gris's work to dismiss these legends and hasty interpretations. The basis of the new work is a sort generalized drawing, charged with memories, concepts, ideas, all long meditated upon by the artist before they took form.

He chose consciously the geometrical architecture that emerges therefrom. Then, with his imagination and reason, he strove to make this construction objective, so that it should be communicated, and comprehensible, to the spectator. This process could justly be compared with the creative work of musicians and writers. It is not surprising, then, that Gris should appear a true classicist whose pure, noble, and austere art is fixed in the essential, from which everything peripheral has been excluded. At the end of his life Gris, a great admirer of the seventeenth century and particularly of Philippe de Champaigne, turned to the art of Pompeii, the Fontainebleau school and the work of David. His style is the result of a remarkable effort. He used a process of reversal of forms which almost recalls the repetitions of rhyme and gives a curious undulation to his lines, creating the impression of volume. His art is a logical, complex, coherent system.

In 1920 Gris fell seriously ill with pleurisy and went to Touraine for a few months, then spent the winter in Bandol, on the Côte d'Azur. Diaghilev, who was at that time in Monte Carlo, suggested that he do the décor and costumes for a Spanish ballet, but this project did not materialize. Gris spent the following winter at Céret and returned to Paris in the spring, apparently restored to health. He settled in Boulogne, just outside Paris. Musicians, painters, poets and critics came to see him on Sundays, and the evenings were gay, for Gris loved dancing. The week spent in calm, reflective work. Diaghilev, returning to his old project, commissioned Gris in 1923 to design the décor and costumes for a Louis XIV ballet, *Les Tentations de la Bergère*, then the stage set for *La Fête Merveilleuse* which he was presenting in the Gallery of Mirrors in the Palace of Versailles, and a décor fort *L'Éducation Manquée* by Chabrier. But the feverish, disordered atmosphere of the ballet, and the intrigues and jealousies that abounded there, exasperated him so that he refused to repeat the experience. On May 15th, 1924, Gris read to the philosophical and scientific study group at the Sorbonne his paper on *Les Possibilités de la Peinture*, which was published in French, German and Spanish, and had tremendous repercussions. Gris had even greater success in 1925, when he painted his serenest and most perfect works. But his health was gravely undermined. He spent his winters in the south–in Toulon in 1925, in Hyères in 1926. The climate at the latter place did not suit him, so that his health grew steadily worse, and he was brought back to Paris, where he died on May 11th, 1927.   J. LA.

GROMAIRE Marcel. Gromaire was born in 1892 in Novelles-sur-Sambre, of a French father and a Flemish mother. From 1909, while he was studying law, he used to visit the various academies of Montparnasse (Colarossi, Ranson Palette), but they left him dissatisfied and still trying to find his own individual idiom. The only master he recognized at that time was Matisse, whom he had often met and whose skilful draughtsmanship greatly impressed him. In 1911, he exhibited his work for the first time at the Salon des Indépendants. He was attracted to the countries of Northern Europe and by 1913, when he began his military service, he had visited Belgium, Holland, Germany and England. During the war, in 1916, he was wounded on the Somme. An opponent of theories, Gromaire has remained outside all schools. Nevertheless, his art has generally followed the lines of an expressionism that is far removed from the pathological form this movement has taken in Scandinavia and Germany; his is an expressionism that reflects the inspiration of the Romanesque and Gothic primitives.

Gromaire has generally taken the subjects of his significant compositions from the life of the peasant or workman. Although any strictly naturalistic expression is foreign to his canvases, the most moving of them show a very great decorative talent. And if he has often borrowed from Cézanne or Seurat, it is because he has tried primarily to make his art conform to strict rules of composition. Whether he paints smugglers or fishermen, beer-drinkers or card-players, Gromaire subjects his themes

GRIS. THE ALBUM. 1926.   *H. Rupf Collection, Bern.*

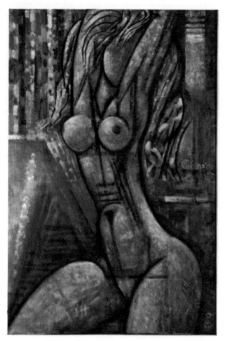

GROMAIRE. BLOND NUDE. 1957.
Private Collection, Paris.

nating, and more recently reds and grey-blues. In his latest works, particularly since his visit to the U.S.A. in 1950, Gromaire seems to have freed himself from any remaining traces of stylization, and to be taking new liberties with a reality that is more and more detached. M. R.

GROSZ George (1893-1959). German painter; born in Berlin. After studying at the Academies of Dresden and Berlin, Grosz drew for humorous reviews. Although he had already begun to paint before 1914, it is his drawing that is of chief interest. Grosz was haunted by actuality. At first, in 1916, it was the evil, absurd face of war; then, after 1918, the buffoonery of the post-war years that were depicted in his incisive drawing with its savagely aggressive social satire. He was trying to make his art a weapon in the struggle against the ruling classes, and he simplified his drawing for political action. A number of lithographs reveal his acrid, fanatically topical art. Whereas in 1918 Grosz was a member of the Dada *(*)* group of Berlin, which had a very pronounced political character, in 1925 he turned towards the realism of the *Neue Sachlichkeit*. In 1932 he was invited to

to exacting graphic formulas. Nothing is more significant in this respect than his canvas entitled *War*, which he exhibited àt the Salon des Indépendants in 1925 and which caused a sensation. In this, excluding the picturesque and scorning the anecdotal, he gives himself up to the vision of a monumental universe that is rigorously exact. In this sense his art approaches that of the fresco, and it is not surprising that Gromaire, with Lurçat, is among the contemporary revivers of tapestry (*The Four Elements, The Four Seasons*). One of the most important reforms he introduced at Aubusson, as at the Gobelins, was to banish the use of a large number of colours and to keep their register strictly limited; for instance, the huge panel of *Flanders* only contains twelve colours. A similar concern to discipline his natural feelings and make their expression a development of tradition, made him choose for his work colours that were sober, rugged, dramatic and powerful with browns, ochres, greys and greens predomi-

GROSZ. THE ENTRÉE. 1929.
Private Collection, New York.

teach at a New York art school, the Art Students' League, where he stayed until his return to Germany in 1959, shortly before his death. In America a romantic and idyllic note has appeared in his painting, but his satire is still alive. He first directed it against the materialism of the middle classes; since the last war it has been on a broader, humanitarian basis, in visions of nightmares, like the fantastic series of *The Stick Men*.   F. M.

GRUBER Francis. French painter, born in Nancy in 1912; died in Paris, 1948. Gruber's health was so delicate that he was incapable of sustained study. At a very early age he showed unusually precocious gifts for drawing and painting. He was guided by Bissière and Braque, who had neighbouring studios, and in 1928 he entered the Académie Scandinave, where he became the favourite pupil of Friesz and Dufresne. He was so successful at the Salons d'Automne and Salons des Tuileries that by the time he was eighteen he was one of the 'characters' of Montparnasse. His truculence and verve were as apparent in his *kermesse* paintings–he was a great admirer of Breughel, Bosch, Grünewald and Dürer–as in his voluble speech and his irregular existence. He was, however, an ardent and punctilious worker, with a passion for technique. Moreover, he had the courage to paint on the grand scale. There is not one of his works, from the vast mural composition he did for the Lycée Lakanal (*Homage to Le Nôtre*, 1936) to the least of his still-lifes, which is not monumental in conception. His scenes from everyday life, studio settings, or groupings of familiar objects, are peopled with a whole mythology of figures, symbols and monsters, representing the palpable background of life, be it morbid or exalting. Each picture is the expression of a state of mind in which the painter's reasons for living, his obsessions, even the necessity for his death and destruction, are at stake. He dreamed of finding a great technique that would make art intelligible to all. In his last years of serious illness, his work became more and more austere and abstract. The greater his body's struggle against the tuberculosis that was draining its strength, the more his painting freed itself from the morbid and hallucinatory. His

very last paintings attained a purity that indicated his approaching end. They were angular nudes shut up in a closed, stifling world that was reduced to the red hangings, the grey walls and the floor of a studio, or large canvases inspired by the movement of trees, with elongated young bodies in the midst of imaginary forests.   J. I.A.

GUILLAUMIN Armand (1841-1927). French painter; born and died in Paris. Although he exhibited with the Impressionists from 1874 on, and was a close friend

GRUBER. MODEL IN THE STUDIO. 1945.

of Monet, Pissarro and Cézanne–the latter copied one of his landscapes–and the teacher of Signac, Guillaumin was able to withstand all influences. Barge-filled quays and landscapes of the Creuse Valley are frankly depicted by this Parisian who, whenever he touched the soil, seemed to recover the ruggedness of his peasant ancestors, whose stature and direct gaze he inherited. It can easily be imagined that his occasional abuse of reds, violets and mauves, and his raucous tone, which only just avoided commonness, as well as the absence of certain transitions in colour, shocked the public of 1874. With these reservations, how can one fail to admire the authentic and joyous

GUILLAUMIN. QUAY ALONG THE SEINE. 1887.   *De Ruaz Gallery, Paris.*

nineteenth century were so straightforward, so free from sentimentality, or so frankly earthy. While his work is uneven, and certain views of Agay and Le Trayas are rather harsh, some of his Sédelle valleys and impressions of autumn seem to foreshadow Cézanne. The tone of his portraits in pastel and still-lifes is that of a virile painter who stands high above the secondary Impressionists with whom he has too often been confused. Moreover, towards the end of his life his art came singularly close to that of the Fauves.   CL. R.-M.

lyricism that accompanies the river in its course, and gilds the woods with the autumn sun ? Few of the landscape painters at the end of the

H

HARTLEY Marsden (1877-1943). American painter; born in Lewiston, Maine, died in Ellsworth, Maine. Studied first at the Cleveland School of Art, then in New York at the Chase School (1898) and the National School of Design (1901). In 1909, at Stieglitz '291' Gallery, he had his first show, of *black landscapes* in which Ryder was a strong influence. In 1912 Stieglitz and Arthur B. Davies helped to send him to Europe. In Paris he met Gertrude Stein and admired the work of the Cubists, but he soon pushed on to Munich where the painting of Marc and Kandinsky was destined to have a much greater effect on his work. In 1914 he embarked on a series of abstractions which owed little to Paris—teeming with boldly outlined forms, violent in colour, aggressively painted, they created a strong impression in Berlin where they were exhibited. Hartley remained in Berlin and Dresden during the first years of the war, then returned to America where he shortly abandoned abstraction and began to evolve a figurative style of his own, borrowing a tendency toward abstraction and an idiomatic treatment of volumes from the Cubists and the strong emotive colour of the Expressionists in simplified interpretations of the violent scenery of New Mexico or the New England coast. The colour, often mixed with black or white, is cold and harsh even at its brightest; the austere beauty of the landscape speaks of confinement and relentless pressure, and, as Milton W. Brown

points out, has roots in 'the Puritan mysticism of Hawthorne and the Gothic mysticism of Poe'. One thinks also of contemporary European Expressionism, especially the winter landscapes of Munch or Kirchner's alpine scenes, on looking at such works as *The Dark Mountain* or *Maine Landscape, Autumn*, with its tiny houses crushed under the inhuman weight of the mountains overhead.

Hartley continued to travel widely and, as it were, restlessly; during the twenties he visited Berlin and Paris again, and also London, Mexico, and the Midi where he felt the influence of Cézanne and brought a new discipline into his painting. But the more dramatic austerity of New England remained however the focal point in his life as in his work: during the last ten years of his life he spent half the year in Maine and the rest in New York.

Hartley was a rather uneven painter who seems never to have completely decided among the

HARTLEY. MOUNT KATAHDIN IN AUTUMN. 1939-1940.
University of Nebraska.

various currents which mingle in his painting: at times the conflicting claims of French formalism and German emotionalism cancel each other out. At his best, however, as in *The Wave* or *New Mexico Recollections*, they fuse in an image of nature which is at once both representative and symbolic, and speaks with a strange, moody power. As the critic Frederick Wight says, 'He knew how to profit by the paradox that old Europe was developing a crude new way of seeing that could be applied to a raw new continent.'   J. A.

HECKEL Erich (born in Döbeln, Saxony, in 1883). German painter, one of the founders of the Brücke *(*)*. The style of that movement is reflected in his painting, with its angular, pointed forms, influenced by wood-engraving, at which he was a master.

But these forms, in his case, convey intensity of feeling rather than an emphasis on structure. He is attracted by the invalid's quiet sadness, by a Dostoevskian anxiety (*Two Men at a Table*, painting 1912, woodcut 1913), by the enchanting transparency of light (*Translucence*, 1913). His wartime landscapes show the elements in conflict. Since 1920 the expressive force of his plastic language has diminished, and Heckel, drawing closer to Nature, has set himself to revealing the rhythmic grandeur of certain landscapes in Germany and Italy. The lyrical tenderness of his art is evident in his choice of colours, in the mat shades of his palette.   F. M.

HERBIN Auguste (1882-1960). French painter; born at Quiévy, died in Paris. He was a student at the École des Beaux-Arts at Lille and went to Paris in 1901. This northerner made several visits to paint in Bruges and the Dutch ports, but his art was transformed by the peculiar quality of the southern light, which he discovered in Corsica in 1907, just as Matisse and Léger did. There his forms acquired a concentration that stripped them of inessentials and brought them closer to their essence. His style acquired a symbolical quality. Herbin occupied an unusual position in contemporary ideological movements, which he skirted without becoming involved. His landscapes and portraits of 1907 depended primarily for their

HERBIN. VEIN. 1953.

effect on colour, which was really fiery rather than 'fauve'. Their angular construction tended to be geometric and to lay importance on surface relationships. Herbin, whose studio was in the Bateau-Lavoir, figured as a precursor of later painting at the Salon des Indépendants in 1906 and 1909, but he soon stopped exhibiting there and did not take part in any of the first startling revelations of Cubism. He was meanwhile actively pursuing experiments of his own that took the form of investigating colour values in his large, vividly painted still-lifes and prominently structured landscapes. His work was exhibited in 1912 and 1914 at the Galerie Clovis Sagot.

The gradual process of simplifying and modifying forms continued until they were reduced to outlines or to characteristic symbols. In 1917 they became abstract compositions with fine, hard-edged indentations and there is no doubt that these and the similar experiments of Juan Gris were the most interesting formal developments that came from Cubism. He lived at Céret in 1918 and 1919. Great circular rhythms vitalised his paintings with sharply defined, central points. Even when Herbin

transposed them into three-dimensional pyramids or complex constructions in polychrome
wood, which were like intricate totems or
endless columns, his work had to be viewed
from the front and appreciated as an arrangement
of surface relationships.

There was no reversal of this development
when from 1922 to 1926 Herbin returned
to representational painting. He applied his
rhythmic movements and curves to the southern
landscape of Vaison-la-Romaine, where he was
then living, which was dominated by buildings
and rocks, to huge symbolic figures and to
large still-lifes in flat areas of paint. These
subjects suggested a number of forms from
which he drew out their latent rhythms. Soon
these alone remained as embryonic forces in a
state of becoming that developed independently,
revealing further significances in the process.
After 1927, Herbin's painting became completely
abstract. In 1931, he and Vantongerloo founded the Abstraction-Création (*) group. His
colours, freed from all representational reference, became sources of energy in which tension, contrasts and harmonies were combined in
carefully calculated variations. The forms were
derived from plane geometry, circles, triangles,
squares, rectangles or rhomboids, their colours
imparting an added fascination to them. They
became concrete presences, although not objective, which Herbin considered superior to
reality, movers of the instincts and signs of an
ideal beauty. With this latest phase, Herbin,
who had been interested since 1924 in Goethe's
scientific writings, had actually evolved an
exceptionally precise grammar of painting and
explained its laws in a theoretical work, *L' Art
non figuratif non objectif*, published in Paris by the
Galerie Lydia Conti in 1949.

The idea that colours have a psychological
significance had never been so clearly stated.
The aim of this curious work by a man, who had
thought so deeply and devoted his energy to
promoting his ideas, was to show how colours
correspond to vowels, consonants and musical
notes. Herbin had a vital personality; he was
enthusiastic, gay, disinterested and single-
minded. His was absolute painting and, like
all pure things, it possesses an incantatory magic
through the splendid variations of his last
constructions.   J. LA.

HILL Carl (1849-1911). Born and died at
Lund, Sweden. After training at the
Academy of Fine Arts at Stockholm, he went to
Paris in 1873. The following year, he went to
Barbizon with the Hungarians, Paál and Mun-
kácsy, and the German, Liebermann. The
landscapes of 1874-1875 bear a strong resemblance to Paál's paintings in particular. When
he left Barbizon for Montigny, he gave up his
dark, romantic style to paint landscapes in the
Impressionist manner. The Impressionists noticed this and invited him to contribute to the
third exhibition of their group, but this could
not be arranged. In the end, his art grew more
and more audacious until it evolved in the
course of 1877-1878 towards Expressionism.
Although his work was refused for the Salon, he
said : 'When the demon of art possesses me, I am
indifferent to everything that hinders my
freedom.' And in fact, he felt that he was free.
He wrote to his family that his painting 'was
becoming so audacious, original, new, fresh,
unbridled and at the same time bridled by a real
feeling for nature,' but, he added, 'you have to
be a painter and a painter of the highest degree
to absorb it. As an experience, it is difficult,

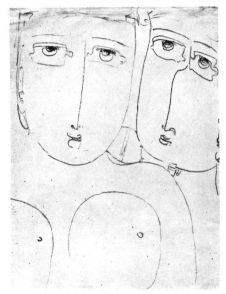

HILL. TWO 'PERSIAN HEADS.
National Museum, Stockholm.

in fact, to imagine anything more unpleasant than this.' Hill was painting then with all the frenzy of despair and was wearing down his mental powers. After an accident, he began to suffer from mental illness in 1878. What he had painted the previous year was so strange that his shocked Swedish friends burnt nearly all of it. The few paintings that escaped destruction are actually among the greatest works of Swedish art. During the thirty-five years of mental illness he spent at Lund, his mother and sisters looked after him. He continued to work and did pencil or ink drawings nearly every day. Sometimes he painted too. His art shows signs of his illness, but his genius remained unimpaired. His best works are strikingly expressive and their visionary qualities make them comparable to the major works of Swedish Expressionism. In some of his compositions he appears as a precursor of Surrealism.   B. L.

HIRSHFIELD Morris (1872-1946). American painter, born in a small town in Poland near the German frontier. Died in New York. As a child he sculpted and painted a large ornamental stand showing two lions holding between them the Ten Command-ments for the Cantor's prayer box in his village synagogue. He came to New York at the age of eighteen, worked in the garment district, eventually founding a clothing business and later a highly successful women's slipper factory which he called the 'E. Z. Walk Company.' As a result of an illness he had to give up work for a long period, during which his business went so badly that he was obliged to retire. Only then, in the middle thirties, did he return to painting. His hallucinatory naive canvases were discovered in 1939 by Sidney Janis who included him in the exhibition 'Contemporary Unknown American Painters' at the Museum of Modern Art of New York.

Hirshfield's figures, rigid and hieratic, have a dreamlike intensity. His first painting, *Beach Girl* (1937) was painted on an old canvas which he had acquired: he used a face from the previous painting for his figure, who stands in a naively abstracted landscape of sea, sand and sky. Hirshfield worked slowly and painfully at his canvases, painting hair for example strand by strand, accumulating infinitesimal brush strokes for textural effects. His experience working with textiles no doubt accounts for the herringbone and tweed-like patterns which abound in his work.

Other remarkable paintings by Morris Hirshfield include *Angora Cat*, *Lion*, *Tiger*, and *Nude at the Window*. Each of these depicts in a minimal, quasi-symbolic decor (for example the urn-like window niche containing the figure in *Nude at the Window*), an oniric image which take possession of the spectator. Hirshfield's work is among the powerful naive expression in American painting.   J. A.

HIRSHFIELD. THE LION.   *Sidney Janis Collection, New York.*

HODLER. MONT BLANC. 1918.

At the age of nineteen Hodler entered the École des Beaux-Arts at Geneva, where he studied hard under Barthélemy Menn, a pupil of Ingres and friend of Corot. Hodler made his début with *The Schoolboy* (1875), a portrait in the manner of Holbein, which he painted at Langenthal during his holidays. While he was making portraits of labourers and artisans at work, such as cobblers, locksmiths, carpenters and watchmak-

HODLER Ferdinand (1853-1918) (born in Gürzelen, Canton of Berne, died in Geneva). Swiss painter. After a great success, a sort of European triumph, his fame has declined steadily since his death. At present this self-taught painter is overestimated by some, given insufficient recognition by others, no doubt because of the duality of a talent which turned from an all-pervading gentleness to hardness. It is a strange fact that the Impressionist movement raged for over a quarter of a century without having the slightest effect on the man or leaving the faintest trace in his work. Hodler jumped straight from the gentle painting of Corot–as it was taken over by the Barbizon painters–to the pedantic harshness of the Munich school. How can such a surprising break be explained ? One must bear in mind the ideas and feelings that were then common among the Swiss. For them there were two schools of painting, the French and the German–Paris and Munich. As for Impressionism, they dreaded its fluidity, the subordination of line to colour; they were afraid of its daring ventures in colour. They thought the antidote was to be found among the professors across the Rhine, who, by stressing draughtsmanship, were producing Denners rather than Dürers.

ers, he was at the same time painting in a very sober style on large, simple planes, landscapes that were luminous, limpid, perhaps a bit too precise yet never hard. But then came the break. In 1891 Hodler exhibited *Night* at the Société Nationale du Champ-de-Mars. The following year, in his *Disillusioned Souls*, which was the principal attraction of the Salon de la Rose-Croix, he showed himself to be infected with the disease that was then befogging the minds of so many of the vanguard: Symbolism. To a rather rough-hewn man, initiation into Symbolism could be disastrous. That is what happened to Hodler, who, thoroughly at home in depicting everyday life, now set himself to painting *The Elect* (1894), a little boy kneeling before a miniature garden and dreaming, under the protection of angels, clad in nightgowns and ranged in a semircircle, and *Eurythmics*, 1895. This rather ludicrous mythology, although it did not exactly ruin him, did at least give him a taste for grandiloquence, as practised by the Germanic artists. From that time on his work consisted of a succession of large pictures on historical subjects, ranging from *The Retreat from Marignan* (1899) and *The Truth* (1903) to *Departure of the Jena Volunteers* (1908). Toward the end of his life Hodler painted lakes and landscapes in which the colours were more

from the Swiss collector, Theodor Reinhart, enabled him to stay a long time in Italy (1903-1908), where he painted large compositions with monumental figures, which continued the tradition of Hans von Marées. In 1908, he went to Paris, where he obviously learned much from Cézanne's work. He settled in Berlin in 1913, and, during a visit to Tessin in 1920, he painted a number of landscapes. His fiftieth birthday in 1928 was celebrated by a large retrospective exhibition of his work at the Berlin Secession. In 1934, he was awarded the first prize of the Carnegie Institute of Art at Pittsburgh, U.S.A. In 1943, his Berlin studio was destroyed in a bombardment and a large part of his works were lost. He had been made director of the Berlin Art School at the end of the war and in 1950 was elected president of the Deutscher Künstlerbund (Association of German Artists).

Hofer's painting had certain well defined psychological qualities and his maturity was characterised by a very marked tendency towards melancholy. His figures were set apart from the world of men and things, completely isolated by alien mental attitudes of their own. His pessimism, which sprang from an erotic and romantic temperament, represented a more restrained and more lyrical form of Expressionism than that of the Brücke painters.   E. R.

tastefully distributed. What was it that he lacked for creating work of a pronounced character? Somewhat like the Norwegian Edvard Munch, Hodler was exposed to conflicting influences and therefore produced work of uneven quality. And although he was a forerunner, in certain directions, of tendencies which were to appear after him, he was not capable of stamping his art with that profound spiritual life which communicates emotion. Reared in the hard school of Nature and poverty, Hodler was first and foremost a master of his craft. Perhaps the artisan in him was stronger than the artist. Some of his canvases have, none the less, a powerful significance. A sure draughtsmanship that is expressive and extraordinarily precise gives them lasting value. P. C.

HOFER Karl (1878-1955). German painter; born at Karlsruhe; died in Berlin. From 1896 to 1900, he trained at the Karlsruhe Academy of Arts and was profoundly influenced by Böcklin and Hans Thoma, who was teaching there at the time. Financial help

HOFMANN Hans (born 1880, in Weissenberg, Bavaria). As a young man he studied physics and mathematics and was an inventor: his inventions include a signaling device for ships and a freezing unit to preserve food on military manœuvres. In 1904 he went to Paris thanks to the patronage of the Berlin collector Philip Freudenberg, and remained there until 1914. In 1915 he opened an art school in Munich. During the twenties he spent summers with his students in Ragusa (Yugoslavia), Capri and St. Tropez. In 1930-1931 he taught in California during the summers, and in 1932 migrated definitively to America where he opened a school in New York and a summer school in Provincetown, Massachusetts. In 1947 he held the first of his annual one-man shows at the Kootz Gallery in New York. In 1957-1958 an important touring exhibition of his work was organized by the Whitney Museum; in 1962 a touring retrospective of some sixty paintings was arranged by the Germanic Museum in Nuremberg. Meanwhile Hofmann had in 1957 closed his schools, after forty-two years of teaching, in order at last to devote himself wholly to painting. Though Hofmann is a painter of major importance, it is only in recent years that the public has begun to appreciate the significance of his work. He first became famous as a teacher, and it is still under this aspect that he is chiefly known. His teaching in many ways paralleled the work of the originators of abstract expressionism (Pollock, Kline, de Kooning, etc.) although none of them actually studied with him. At the same time many of the new generation of figurative painters in New York (Larry Rivers, Jane Freilicher, Nell Blaine, Fay Lansner among others) are products of Hofmann's academy.

In spite of the profound effect of Hofmann's teaching on American painting, it is difficult to summarize his lessons or explain why they had such a revolutionary effect. He initiated his students in the work of the great modern artists, interpreting them according to his own theories of depth in the canvas, to be achieved through color rather than perspective, as in Cézanne; and his famous 'push-pull' theory of opposing forces. Hofmann has said: 'I found my own way to present the object in pictorial giving, not perspective giving . . . A picture must be made, dictated, through the inherent laws of the surface. I invented what I call 'push and pull,' force and counterforce . . . The highest three-dimensionality is two-dimensionality, which no layman can ever understand. Depth is nothing less than suggested volume. I have students who come to me painting in dimensional rhythms, an empty affair.'

But, as Harold Rosenberg points out, the depth which Hofmann's pupils absorbed was not merely pictorial but psychological as well. 'The message of this man,' he writes, 'was above all enthusiasm for the artist as a type and for art as a way of living. This his students could grasp (whatever they missed of his thought) merely by being near him and by watching, as the disciple of the Hassidic Maggid said, how he tied and untied his shoelaces.'

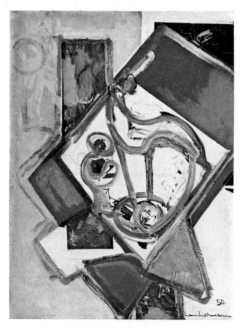

HOFMANN. FRUIT-BOWL. 1950.
Roy R. Neuberger Collection, New York.

Hofmann's own painting is the living example of his teaching. In the pre-war days in Paris he had been influenced in turn by Cézanne, the Fauves and the Cubists; after opening his school in Munich he painted little, concentrating on drawing in order to 'sweat out Cubism'. Around 1936 he began to paint more frequently, at first attempting to keep his work from his students so as not to influence them; in the end it has probably been the example of his painting as much as his ideas which have attracted and inspired other artists. Hofmann's painting is characterized by vibrant planes of colour in dynamic relationships, by signs of surging, heaving activity and violent attractions or repulsions along the forms, and above all by a kind of abstract *joie de vivre*, a feeling of boundless energy and faith in unlimited pictorial possibilities. In his words, 'Pictorial life is created reality. Colour (in nature as well as in the picture) is an agent to give the highest aesthetic enjoyment.'   J. A.

IMPRESSIONISM From April 15th to May 15th, 1874, a group of independent young French painters who had formed a *société anonyme* that included Monet, Renoir, Pissarro, Sisley, Cézanne, Degas, Guillaumin and Berthe Morisot, held an exhibition, apart from the official Salon, at the studio of the photographer Nadar *(*)*. The exhibition caused an uproar, and a journalist named Leroy, writing in the satirical magazine *Le Charivari* of April 25th, jeeringly called the exhibitors 'impressionists', after a canvas by Monet entitled *Impression, Sunrise*. This name, accepted by the painters themselves, became very popular and was universally adopted. The meaning of the term, however, remained vague. The spontaneous Impressionism of the artists was super-seded by the doctrinaire Impressionism of the critics, who turned a living ideal into a set system. Then successive reactions against Impressionism set its limits even more rigidly and distorted its scope. It is therefore quite difficult to recapture its actual climate and to mark out correctly the range of the movement which brought about a renewal not only of vision but of the whole of modern sensibility, and which united so many dissimilar artists. Each of them fulfilled himself according to his own genius, sustained in his freedom by the very principles which constituted Impressionism.

The Impressionist painters were born between 1830 and 1841–Pissarro, the eldest, in 1830, Manet in 1832, Degas in 1834, Cézanne and Sisley in 1839, Monet in 1840, Renoir, Bazille,

MONET. IMPRESSION, SUNRISE. 1872. *Musée Marmottan, Paris.*

164

Guillaumin and Berthe Morisot in 1841. These young innovators, from different environments, came together in Paris about 1860. Pissarro, Cézanne and Guillaumin met at the Académie Suisse (*); Monet, Renoir, Bazille and Sisley at the Atelier Gleyre (*). They soon escaped, however, to the Forest of Fontainebleau, where they began to paint in the naturalistic, compact manner of the Barbizon school. From there they went to

BOUDIN. COMMERCIAL DOCK. LE HAVRE. *Le Havre Museum.*

the Seine estuary and the Channel beaches, which were to become, between 1860 and 1870, the cradle of Impressionism. It was in that light-and-water-saturated air that Monet, in contact with the two innovators, Boudin (1824-1898) and Jongkind (1819-1891), evolved a style of painting that became more and more fluid, ethereal and highly coloured. Pissarro and Sisley remained close to Corot. Cézanne and Degas, the one still under the sway of Romanticism, the other still dominated by Classicism, had no part in this pre-Impressionist phase. Manet, through the modernity of his subjects and his *succès de scandale* in 1863 at the Salon des Refusés, became, perhaps in spite of himself, the standard-bearer of the young school that met at the Café Guerbois (*). In 1869 Monet and Renoir, whose figures and open-air compositions had been inspired by Courbet, painted, at Bougival, a small village on the Seine, the picturesque wharf of the *Grenouillère*, a restless confusion of boats and gaily coloured dresses, while through the foliage a thousand reflections of sunlight broke upon the moving surface of the river. It was in their endeavour to convey the dynamism and the joy of that spectacle, which constantly stimulated them, that they spontaneously discovered what were to become

the technical principles of Impressionism: division of tone and shimmering spots of colour. A new vision was born, derived not from a theory but from on-the-spot observation of the reflection of sunlight along the banks of the Seine. Certainly their style had not yet attained unity, and it was not to become a truly conscious one until 1873, but the freshness of these first achievements was never to be surpassed.

The Franco-German war of 1870 dispersed the group just when their experiments were taking shape. Manet, Renoir, Degas and Bazille were called up and went to war; Bazille was killed in the battle of Beaune-la-Rolande. Monet, Pissarro and Sisley took refuge in London, where Daubigny introduced them to Durand-Ruel (*), the dealer who was to become their chief defender. Their discovery of Turner and Constable hastened the evolution of their technique. In 1872 Monet at Argenteuil, near Paris, and Pissarro at Pontoise (Seine-et-Oise) began painting the new type of open-air landscape. Monet's work, on the grand, universal scale, dominated by the spell of water and by the phantasms of light, attracted Renoir, Sisley and Manet; Pissarro's, bucolic and earthy, with more stress on structural values, influenced Cézanne and Guillaumin. In 1873, with the conversion of Manet, Cézanne and, to a

SISLEY. REGATTA NEAR LONDON. 1874. *Musée du Louvre*.

limited extent, Degas, to light-coloured painting, the Impressionist style spread and became more generally understood. The small brush strokes already used for reproducing reflections in water were now applied to trees, houses, sky, hills, all the elements of the landscape. The colours became systematically lighter and the shadows themselves were coloured. The transitional greys and browns used by Corot gave way to the pure colours of the spectrum, harmonized or contrasted according to the law of complementary colours. Coherence of vision brought in its wake unity of technique, the exaltation and vibration of light as the dominant principle, and consequently the abandonment of contour, of modelling, of chiaroscuro, and of over-precise details, the over-all composition retaining the vigour of a sketch, with the incomplete, unfinished look that so shocked contemporaries. The critic Armand Silvestre made a fine distinction between the three painters: 'Monet, the most skilful and the most daring; Sisley, the most harmonious and the most timid; Pissarro, the most true and the most naïve'. Renoir led his figures into the sunlight. In 1874, with the exception of Manet, who remained faithful to the official Salon, the group as a whole faced the public, under a barrage of insults and taunts. Seven joint exhibitions followed, at intervals, until 1886. In 1876 Duranty (*), the writer and art critic, published *The New Painting*–a signifi-

cant title–and shrewdly analysed the orientation of the young painters: 'Going from intuition to intuition, they have gradually come to the decomposition of sunlight into its rays, its elements, and to reconstructing its unity by the general harmony of the iridescent colours which they spread on their canvases'. The year 1877 was perhaps the peak year of Impressionism, the

PISSARRO. PORTRAIT OF CÉZANNE. ETCHING.

moment of its most homogeneous and complete unfolding. On the occasion of the third exhibition, and at the suggestion of Renoir, Georges Rivière published a little periodical entitled *The Impressionist*, in which he commented intelligently and warmly on his friends' efforts: 'Treating a subject for its colours and not for the subject itself', he summarized, 'is what distinguishes Impressionists from other painters', thus emphasizing the victory of pictorial autonomy. The traditional representation of the 'subject', determined by mythology or history or bourgeois convention, was replaced by contemplation of the 'motif', a tree, a thatched hut, a horizon, detached from space and time, a universal source of values; the painting corresponded to its content, without any literary overtones. In 1878 there appeared a brochure, *The Impressionist Painters*, by the writer and art critic Théodore Duret *(*)*; this work, together with Duranty's, constituted the first study of the movement as a whole. The defection of Monet, Renoir and Sisley in 1880, at the time of the group's fifth exhibition, revealed a profound crisis, both personal and aesthetic.

After a heroic decade of enduring contempt, and producing masterpieces, Impressionism, at the very moment that it began to gain recognition, ceased to exist as a spontaneous ideal. Each of its founders, having reached maturity, thenceforth went his own way, while retaining allegiance to the common cult that had brought them all together—that of Nature and of liberty.

The death of Manet in 1883—by then a new generation has arisen (Seurat, Van Gogh, Gauguin and Lautrec), nourished on Impressionism but reacting against it—coincided with the complete breaking up of the original group, despite the efforts of Durand-Ruel. Geographical dispersion (Pissarro at Éragny, Monet at Giverny, Sisley at Saint-Mammès, Cézanne at Aix-en-Provence, Renoir alternately travelling and staying in Paris before finally settling in Provence) was accompanied by a divergence in their aesthetic principles. At that time, as Lionello Venturi puts it, 'Monet tended toward a symbolism of colour and light, Pissarro was attracted to pointillism, Renoir wished to assimilate elements of academic form, Cézanne concentrated on problems of construction, and Sisley took satisfaction in style'. Renoir and Cézanne, carried along by their genius, fulfilled themselves without faltering, in a continuous upward surge. Monet, Sisley and Pissarro, however, the three landscape painters most closely linked to Impressionism, and the most confused, had many vicissitudes, producing uneasy and uneven work, sometimes merely decorative, without being able to recapture the fine equilibrium and spontaneity of their beginnings. Certainly they were still achieving much, but a spirit of system and literary or scientific influences often restricted the freedom of their intuition. After 1895 Pissarro regained an astonishing creative vigour, and his last masterpieces, like those of Monet,

MONET. BRIDGE AT ARGENTEUIL. 1874.   *Musée du Louvre.*

RENOIR. THE SWING. 1876. *Musée du Louvre.*

desire to free their own personalities for a dynamic contact with Nature and life, and to shatter–following Manet's lead–all official conventions, all academic fetters. 'The effect of sincerity', said Manet, 'is to give one's work the character of a protest, the painter being concerned only with conveying his impression. He simply seeks to be himself and no one else.' In point of fact, the Impressionist painter, guided solely by his intuition, could only rely on his own sincerity, and each of his paintings, being an act of 'creation', was a reaffirmation and rediscovery of painting. The world did not exist once and for all in a set form, but every glance rediscovered it in its renewed freshness, and the least of its aspects was part of its moving beauty. Such liberty could not but shock the people of that time, whose vision had been petrified by the École des Beaux-Arts (itself an expression of social petrifaction). To us, however, the Impressionist experiment appears to have fitted naturally into the pictorial tradition which has come down to us from the Renaissance, while pursuing more and more faithfully the optical expression of reality. Under the dominant influence of Courbet, the Impressionists started out in a more or less realistic tradition, which they intensified to the point where it was overthrown, and replaced by the flight from reality of modern painting. Although the visible world that they offer us appears more real, or is perhaps a better likeness, than the objective data of Realism, it is important to realize that the two attitudes are much more in opposition to each other than they are a continuation of each other. The realistic painter still rests his work on an intellectual basis and adapts his emotions to his knowledge–that is, he fits them into traditional frames: respect for contour, the rules of anatomy and perspective, the primacy of chiaroscuro. Opposed to this realistic intellectualism is the sensualism of Impressionism; the unity of its style is founded on personal intuition, on an emotional choice unfettered by any theoretical data. The external universe loses its constraining power and, entirely transposed into anti-naturalist pure

Renoir and Cézanne, still derived from Impressionism in the broad sense of the term, by reason of their cosmic sweep, vibration of light, and direct emotion before Nature.

Thus Impressionism was not a set group with a congealed programme or a master-disciple relationship; it was a privileged correspondence of taste, a living experience, a moment of brotherhood, shared by young artists indifferent to ideas but rich in sensations, who suddenly discovered the world and found it vast enough for each of them to draw upon it without constraint. And because painting for them was something spontaneous, not derived from a theory, they revolted against its traditional 'laws'. If almost all the artists of the avant-garde, different as they were in temperament, joined together, between 1860 and 1870, to contribute to the formation of what was to be called Impressionism, it was not as a result of their gradual submission to some uniform principle or technical prescription, but because of their impatient

colours, becomes for the artist a 'theme' in the musical sense of the word, on which he can make variations to his heart's content. Delacroix comes to mind, but the freedom of Impressionism is both richer and more rigorous than that of Romanticism. Romanticism was, in fact, tinged with too much torment and day-dreaming, too many external elements that were often artificial, too many fantastic and literary suggestions. Impressionism delivered painting from the literary passion of Romanticism and from the social rhetoric of Realism, and restored its purity. Having won its autonomy, at the price of heroic struggles, Impressionism expresses none the less the moral vision of its period–straightforwardness, sincerity, an impetus towards individual liberty and social equality, poetry revealed in the most rustic themes, in humble, everyday life. This was the universal fraternity of light, as opposed to the 'select', the exceptional, the 'finished', as opposed to the hierarchical canons and false elegance of the *Salon officiel*.

It is obvious that Impressionism, even in its most homogeneous period, from 1870 to 1880, showed a variety of tendencies. After that date, with the coming of a new generation, other tendencies sprang up–Neo-Impressionism, Symbolism, Expressionism–that reacted violently against it, even though they derived from it. Nevertheless, in spite of the complexity of temperaments and movements, a vast spiritual unity, from 1860 to 1900, marks the whole of a period which may still justly be called Impressionist, when painting, thanks to an unparalleled constellation of geniuses, acquired full autonomy, at the same time bearing witness, in the most sensitive and truthful manner, to the life of the period and to its deepest aspirations.   J. LE.

PISSARRO. RED ROOFS. 1877.   *Musée du Louvre.*

J

JAWLENSKY Alexej von (1864-1941). Russian painter; born at Souslovo near Tver; died at Wiesbaden. Giving up his career as an officer in the Imperial Guard to become a painter, Jawlensky studied from 1889 on in Moscow at the Academy and with Répine, and beginning in 1896, in Munich at Anton Azbe's school, where he met Kandinsky. From 1902 on he worked alone. With Kandinsky, Kubin, Gabriele Münter and others he founded the New Association of Munich Artists in 1909. Though he did not join in the Blaue Reiter (*) exhibitions, he was in close agreement with the aims of that movement. During the war Jawlensky lived in Switzerland (Saint-Prex, Zurich, Ascona) and, in 1921, settled at Wiesbaden. In 1924, with Kandinsky, Klee and Feininger, he formed the Four Blues Group, which exhibited in Germany and America. At Munich he was influenced by Western art. Cézanne and Van Gogh impressed him and spurred him on in his search for a greater, simpler and more expressive form. A stay, in 1905, in Brittany and Provence liberated his gifts as a colourist, and his meeting with Matisse helped him to find his way. So the composition of his pictures of 1909, with their large flat masses of pure, bright colour, is related to Matisse's work. But whereas Matisse's line is dynamic and active, Jawlensky's passively outlines the masses of colour with a rich, sensual building up of the *matière*. In his frank, exuberant art the colours seem to sing with an earthy force and expressive primitive violence which recall Russian folk art. Jawlensky painted some landscapes but, more often, heads and half-length figures whose powerful vitality, in the work he did between 1911 and 1914, is concentrated in an even simpler and more monumental form. During the First World War Jawlensky's art underwent a great transformation. The road which led from his pre-war painting to the *Variations* on a landscape of Saint-Prex, in colours now more delicate, and

JAWLENSKY. GIRL IN BLUE APRON. 1909.
Private Collection.

from there to *Mystic Heads* (1917), to *Visions of the Saviour* (1919) and the *Abstract Heads* of later years, was that of spirituality. The human face became the only theme which interested him, and its essential architecture–the cross of the nose and the arch of the eyebrows, the mouth, the oval of the chin, the forehead–determined the symbolic composition of the picture, a new form of iconography stamped with a profound, mystical religious sense. 'Art is nostalgia for God', Jawlensky often said. Enclosed within the linear structure which it stresses, colour now burned with a rarer and more secret flame. Light and transparent until 1935, it darkened in his last works as the painter, in his life, as well as in his art, found once more the way to the faith of his childhood.   F. M.

JEANNERET (*see* Le Corbusier).

JOHN Augustus Edwin (born in Wales in 1878). Augustus John studied at the Slade School from 1894 until 1898. When he left he was acclaimed the best draughtsman in England. He has remained first and foremost a draughtsman, and for many years his best painting drew its strength from its drawing. John was a true bohemian, living with gypsies and learning their language and tramping through Wales and France. Yet there are two aspects to his character: one of them has been grasped by Wyndham Lewis, who has written of John's 'fits of seeing' and has described him as 'a great man of action into whose hand the fairies stuck a brush instead of a sword'. The other aspect has rarely been touched upon but is manifest in several of his landscapes and his *In Memoriam Amedeo Modigliani*. John has fits of seeing, he is a visionary like El Greco (and, perhaps, Modigliani, whom he admired and who was also influenced by El Greco), and yet he is an intellectual who has absorbed the influences of Cézanne, Puvis de Chavannes and the *Fauves*. He can organize words almost as well as the materials of his art, as his autobiography clearly shows. His greatest portraits (Lady Ottoline Morrell, Madame Suggia, W. B. Yeats, Viscount d'Abernon, among others) show a visionary power allied to great intellectual force; his landscapes and studies for large compositions show more of his intellectual nature. When these qualities are not satisfactorily balanced, his work suffers and becomes mannered. Yet when he is successful, few other painters of modern times give such

a sensation of pure ecstasy and joy and effortless achievement. Long after his personality and wit have ceased to have a direct effect on the public, his art will exercise its great appeal, and his portraits, his gypsy types, his women and his landscapes will outlast the mannered and popular work of some of his more fashionable contemporaries.   M. M.

JONGKIND Johann (1819-1891). Dutch painter, born at Latrop, Holland; died at Grenoble. For a long time Jongkind was considered with Boudin as a precursor of Impressionism. It is clear that in his watercolours, and still more in his drawings, before Sisley and Monet, he knew how to translate the fluid atmosphere and distant horizons, the movement of trees and the glittering changeableness of water. But it is also true that his merits did not limit him to the role of forerunner. He has his own distinct value, as have his works, and the best of them give him a place among the great painters of the nineteenth century. His vision is acute, his drawing trembles with life, and the least of his sketches, done with a few strokes of the pencil, is intensely alive. Should we see in his Dutch origin the reasons for his exclusive

JONGKIND. DUTCH LANDSCAPE. 1872.   *Private Collection, Paris.*

taste for landscapes, for broad horizons where stretches of earth and sea are separated from sky by only a lightly curved, uncertain, extremely fine line: great flat landscapes, formed of horizontal lines, in which the masts of ships and the sails of windmills balance in contrast? Jongkind's art is, above all, an art of atmosphere; it does not pretend, as Impressionist painting did, to the pretext of scientific discoveries to justify an aesthetic doctrine. Jongkind simply set down the appearances of the moment. New as his technique and his vision were to his time, it is not exact to make everything begin with him and not to relate him to the past. There is a definite relationship with certain Dutch artists like Ruysdael and Van Goyen, but Jongkind seems to have a freshness of feeling and interpretation whose spontaneity recalls some of the drawings of Saint-Aubin. In a sense, then, he sould be thought of as climaxing a certain tradition. If the whole of his work is considered, his painting, however, calls for some reservations, for a good many of the canvases were executed for commercial reasons and ill reflect his qualities. His night scenes, with light falling among the boats can, in most cases, be discarded in any search for the artist's true sensibility. Though freely and admirably expressed in the water-colours, it is sometimes less in evidence and less natural in the oils, yet even in this domain one must recognize certain masterly and subtle successes. There were strange contradictions in his destiny, an incomprehensible contrast between his serene, luminous art and his life, which was often miserable. Though his life was unstable and sordid, in Paris he had several faithful friends: the painters Isabey, Sano, Cals and, later, a Dutch teacher of drawing, Mme Fesser, whose life he shared and with whom he succeeded for a while in leading a fairly calm existence, at times in Normandy and more frequently in the Dauphiné or in Provence. With her Jongkind settled, in 1878, at the Côte-Saint-André between Lyons and Grenoble. When he left this district it was to be taken to the lunatic asylum at Grenoble, where he died.   R. C.

JOSEPHSON. PEN AND INK DRAWING.
National Museum, Stockholm.

JOSEPHSON Ernst (1851-1906). Swedish painter; born and died at Stockholm. He came from a well-to-do Jewish family. He trained at the Stockholm Academy of Fine Arts and went abroad in 1876. He was strongly attached to traditional art and the most important part of his training consisted in copying the old masters, Titian, Velasquez and Rembrandt, in museums. In 1879, he got to know Impressionism better in Paris. In 1881, he went to Spain where his nostalgia for northern scenery found a relief in his first sketches for the 'Näcken', one of the first expressions of Symbolism at the end of the century. (A Näcken is a character from Scandinavian mythology, a water spirit, who plays the violin in the midst of torrents to lure men into drowning themselves.) Theo van Gogh bought one of these sketches. It roused a keen interest in Vincent, who commented on it in one of his letters from Nuenen. Josephson was the leader of the independent artists in opposition to the Swedish Academy of Fine Arts and he presided in 1886 at the foundation of the association

'Konstnätsförbundet'. But the intrigues of artistic circles exhausted him and hardship and failure ruined his health, so he decided to leave Sweden and retire to the island of Bréhat, off Brittany. There in 1888, after a spirit séance, he became mentally deranged, ten years after Carl Hill. While he was acting as a medium, Josephson did some strange drawings in the name of the greatest masters of the past. Although it is undeniable that they have a certain affinity with the work of the artists he invoked, there is every reason to think that this affinity is due to the intensity with which he had assimilated their different styles when he was studying in museums in the '70's. Gradually, however, the drawings and paintings lost their derivative character and an extremely personal manner took its place. Then he did those painfully expressive drawings in which the lines are pure and precise and yet the proportions of the human body are often deformed. On his return to Sweden, Josephson was cured, at least partially, and he was able to appreciate both the aesthetic and psychological qualities of the drawings, produced during his period of illness. He came to the conclusion that their style was a more genuine expression of his personality than the 'healthy' painting of his youth, and he continued to cultivate this style consciously until about 1890, when he gave up all artistic activity. These last works have influenced modern Swedish painting considerably. B. L.

JUGENDSTIL The term *Jugendstil*, derived from the Munich review *Jugend* (Youth), founded in January 1896, designates in the German-speaking countries, in which it was particularly developed, the movement known in England under the name of Art Nouveau; sometimes it is just called 1900 Style, because of its extreme vogue in Europe about that time. It was a sort of essentially decorative baroque and romantic resurgence, characterized by an exuberance of decoration based on plants and undulating forms, and was related more to fashion and taste than to art itself. Its historical importance and implications have been too lightly dismissed in the reaction against it. Even though the decorative arts and architecture were affected most of all, its effect

on painting and the graphic arts was greater than many care to admit. The expressive or decorative line, with its sinuous contours, clearly appears in the last canvases of Van Gogh and of Seurat; is found in the wood engravings of Gauguin and Vallotton; marks the entire work of Lautrec, and the early work of Munch, Hodler and Kokoschka, for example.

The artistic atmosphere of the end of the century was very complex, and it is difficult to isolate the specifically 1900 Style (which really first appeared in 1880 and did not really end till 1925). Symbol (*vide* Symbolism), décor and expression are the bywords of the Post-Impressionist generation, which returned to the practice of drawing, or engraving in all its forms, and which took up eagerly the new techniques of illustration. The earliest example is the title page of a book published in 1883, which was designed by the young architect and decorator, Arthur Mackmurdo (1851-1942) and was made up of strongly stylised animal and plant motifs. The leading figure of Art Nouveau in England was the amazing young mannerist Aubrey Beardsley (1872-1898), illustrator of the *Yellow Book*. His success in Paris coincided with the prestige of Jacques-Émile Blanche and the rediscovery of Botticelli. In France Art Nouveau played an important role in the renaissance of the minor arts, thanks to the school of Nancy, directed by Emile Gallé (1846-1904), and which also included, besides decorators, a few painters of talent (Sellier, Friant, Victor Prouvé).

The Art Nouveau elements which can be detected in the last works of Seurat (*Le Chahut* and, above all, *Le Cirque*) and of Van Gogh (Saint-Rémy and Auvers-sur-Oise periods) are developed in the engravings and decorative compositions of Gauguin and the Nabis *(*)*, and also affect certain canvases of Matisse and the Fauves. It is in the poster, the dynamic creation of the period, that the most significant and highest expression must be sought, carried to the point of perfection by Lautrec and his emulators, Steinlen (1859-1923), Chéret (1836-1930) and Cappiello (1875-1942). In 1896, in the Rue de Provence, the dealer Bing opened his Galerie de l'Art Nouveau and soon exhibited the work of the Norwegian painter Edvard Munch. Munch frequented Mallarmé, designed the production of *Peer Gynt* for the Théâtre de l'Œuvre, and surrounded his pictures and drawings with allegorical and decorative borders in the spirit of Jugendstil. In Belgium, the most interesting and dynamic personality was Henri van de Velde (1863-1957), a Neo-Impressionist painter who gave up painting about 1890, to devote himself to architecture and to the applied arts, decoration, wall papers, book binding, furniture, textiles, and clothes. The social implications of Art Nouveau were more marked in Belgium than in France and he was surrounded by ardent adherents of Art Nouveau among the architects, like Paul Hankar, Victor Horta, Gustave Serrurier and by painters like Adolphe Crespin, Henri Evenepoel, who was also an outstanding poster designer, Theo van Rysselberghe, and William Finch. The most active centres of the movement were Barcelona, Munich and Vienna.

Barcelona, the centre of the Spanish cultural revival, where the fantastic architecture of Gaudi (1852-1926) was being created, with its ornamentation of plant forms, was deeply penetrated by Nordic and Germanic influences. There was a group of artists who were enthusiastic about the new forms : Santiago Rusiñol, Ramón Casas, Opisso, Sebastian Juñyer, Isidro Nonell (1873-1911). It was in this 'modernist' atmosphere that the genius of Picasso was being formed. His first drawings appeared in *Joventut* and *Arte Joven*, periodicals which were inspired by the Munich review *Jugend*. His first journey to Paris took place in 1900 and his 'blue period' showed him still under the influence of Lautrec and Steinlen.

In Germany, whose two artistic capitals were Munich and Berlin, the *Jugendstil* helped to break the fetters of traditionalism and encouraged new trends. The Secession group in Munich was created in 1892 with Franz Stuck, Trübner and Uhde, spurred by memories of Böcklin (1827-1901), who had lived in Munich eleven years before settling in Florence. It was presided over in 1897 by Max Klinger (1857-1920), whose engravings the French symbolist poet Laforgue found enchanting. In January 1896 Georg Hirth began publishing the *Jugend* review with the collaboration of the best German artists. In 1899 Erler, Jank and Putz formed the *Die Scholle* group (The Land), which had some influence on

Kandinsky, when he came to Munich in 1896, before he opened his own art school. The influence of the Jugendstil was also felt by the future members of the Brücke *(*)*. In 1899 the Berlin Secession group was founded under the presidency of Max Liebermann. From 1895 to 1900 the review *Pan* put out by Bierbaum and Meier-Graefe, published drawings by Beardsley, wood engravings of Vallotton, etchings of Munch, and lithographs of Lautrec.

But it was in the cosmopolitan and fastidious Vienna of the end of the century that the Jugendstil found its supreme expression. Its uncontested leader was Gustav Klimt (1862-1918), who executed the decoration of the University (1900-1903), and who remained, till 1905, president of the Secession, whence the name of Style of the Secession, which is still given to the Viennese version of Jugendstil. In January 1898 appeared *Ver Sacrum*, the Secession review. The group's exhibitions (notably that of Hodler in 1904) had a great success, and their headquarters, specially constructed in the taste of the day by Josef M. Olbrich, was opened on November 12th, 1898. The poets and musicians Hugo von Hofmannsthal, Peter Altenberg and Gustav Mahler were all part of this atmosphere of culture and aestheticism, which was evident also in the furniture, the jewellery and the objets d'art of the Wiener Werkstätte (Viennese Studio), created in 1903. Here, too, grew up the young Kokoschka a fellow-pupil of Egon Schiele (1890-1918), at the School of Decorative Arts, friend and protégé of the celebrated architect Adolf Loos. In 1908 Kokoschka exhibited the illustrations for his book *Die Träumenden Knaben* (The Boy Dreamers) in which can be recognized the double influence of Klimt, to whom the work is dedicated, and of Hodler, and which constitutes, by its refined sensibility of line and the decorative use of colour, perhaps the masterpiece of the Jugendstil. There was also the exhibition at Paris, organized by the Council of Europe in 1960-1961, 'The Sources of the XX Century', where considerable prominence was given to the various aspects of the '1900 Style' and its extension all over Europe. (See articles on Beardsley, Evenepoel, Finch, Hodler, Klimt, Kokoschka, Munch, Rysselberghe, Steinlen, Van de Velde and the Secession).   J. LE.

K

KAHNWEILER Daniel Henry (born in 1884 in Mannheim, Germany). When he was eighteen he went to Paris and spent three years there before arriving in London, where his uncle began to train him for a career in banking. But his passion for art history and painting soon made him neglect his work at the stockbroker's with whom he had been placed, in favour of long hours in museums. It was not long before he threw over his banking career. On his return to Paris in 1907, when Fauvism was triumphing at the Salon des Indépendants, he opened a picture gallery which rapidly became famous. The first painters who interested him were Derain, Vlaminck, Van Dongen, then Braque, Picasso, Léger and Juan Gris. In 1908 he exhibited Braque's first Cubist canvases after they had been refused at the Salon d'Automne. He not only materially supported the Cubist painters but also took up his pen in their defence. In 1909 he began his series of art books with Apollinaire's *L'Enchanteur Pourrissant*, with woodcuts by Derain, then *Saint Matorel* by Max Jacob, with etchings by Picasso. During the 1914-1918 war Kahnweiler retired to Switzerland. In his absence, his belongings were confiscated and his collection dispersed after the Armistice at an absurdly low price, despite the efforts of his painter friends. After his return in February 1920, he opened almost immediately a new gallery at 29 bis rue d'Astorg, in partnership with his friend, André Simon. The same year, he published three works, one after the other, which he had written during his exile in Switzerland: one by Vlaminck, another by Derain, and one in German, *Der Weg zum Kubismus*. Kahnweiler's house in Boulogne became an artistic centre frequented by avantgarde writers and painters. New artists were shown at his gallery: with the sculptors Manolo and Henri Laurens there were Masson, Beaudin,

PICASSO. PORTRAIT OF D.-H. KAHNWEILER. 1957.

Suzanne Roger, Roux, Yves Rouvre and Kermadec. During the Second World War Kahnweiler sought refuge in the unoccupied zone of France, after placing the management of his gallery in the hands of his sister-in-law, Louise Leiris. During the years 1939-1944 Kahnweiler wrote his book on Juan Gris, the standard work on the artist, his life, work and writings, which was published in 1946. In it he showed that knowledge, insight and faith which, throughout his career, he has put at the service of a cause of which he has been one of the most lucid and ardent defenders.

His publishing ventures, which he began so brilliantly with Apollinaire and Max Jacob, have continued through his career and up to the

KANDINSKY. IMPROVISATION 30 (CANNONS). 1913.
Art Institute, Chicago.

Academy under Franz Stuck. In 1901, he founded the Phalanx group, became its president and opened his own school of painting and drawing. After visits to Holland in 1904, Kairwan in Tunisia in 1905 and Italy at the beginning of 1906, he went to live at Sèvres, near Paris in June 1906 and spent a year there. He began exhibiting at the Salon d'Automne in 1904 and the Salon des Indépendants in 1907. His Impressionist period, characterized by long strokes of colour laid on with a palette knife, and a concern for construction, was succeeded by a lively kind of Fauvism, which was better adapted to dream landscapes or imaginative themes than to realistic description. On his return to Munich at the end of 1907, after stays in Berlin and Dresden, where he exhibited at the Brücke *(*)*, Kandinsky founded the New

present time include almost forty works, most of them illustrated by the painters of his gallery. In 1957, the gallery was moved to the rue de Monceau.   M. R.

KANDINSKY Wassily (1866-1944). Born in Moscow, died in Neuilly-sur-Seine. His father was Siberian, born near the Chinese border. He began his studies in Odessa and then studied law and political economy in Moscow. In 1889 he was a member of a mission charged with studying legal customs of the peasant communities in a northern province. The decorative richness of the interior of the village houses was a revelation to him. It was in 1895, when he visited an exhibition of the French Impressionists at Moscow, that he discovered Monet and fully realized for the first time, as he stood in front of one of his *Haystacks*, what a modern 'picture' really meant. The following year, he gave up his legal career to take up painting full-time and, with this in view, went to Munich at the end of the year. There, he worked first at Azbe's, then after 1900 at the

Association of Munich Artists in 1909. In 1910 he painted his first entirely non-representational works and wrote his treatise *Concerning the Spiritual in Art*, which was published in 1912. He met Franz Marc, August Macke and Paul Klee. With Marc, he was responsible for the publication of the Blaue Reiter *(*)* year book, which gave its name to the movement whose two exhibitions, in December 1911 and 1912, are landmarks in modern German painting. The appearance in 1910 of Kandinsky's first non-figurative work, *Abstract Water Colour (see* illustration, page 2), was the result of a long evolution whose stages he traced in his book *Glimpses of the Past*. 'I felt more and more strongly', he wrote, 'that it is the inner desire of the subject which determines its its form . . . The separation between the domain of art and the domain of Nature grew wider for me, until I could consider them as absolutely distinct, one from the other.' And he concludes: 'I knew then that objects harmed my painting'. In the two so-called 'dramatic' periods, between 1910 and 1920, Kandinsky painted pictures characterized by their disordered, violent lines, and very vivid colours. But this

KANDINSKY

chaos gave way to order in response to an inner necessity; it was not a matter of the liberation of automatism but of a concerted attempt to express cosmic forces which transcend the powers of the individual..

Kandinsky had his first retrospective exhibition in Berlin at the Der Sturm Gallery in 1912 (an album was published in 1913), and he retired to Switzerland at the outbreak of war. On his return to Moscow after the Revolution he occupied several important official posts at the Commissariat for Popular Culture and at the State Studios. He organized twenty-two museums and directed the Museum of Pictorial Culture. In 1921 he founded the Academy of Artistic Sciences and was elected its vice-president. In December 1921 he returned to Germany and, in 1922, became a teacher at the Bauhaus (*) in Weimar. He met Klee, Jawlensky and Feininger again, and with them formed the Four Blues group. The Bauhaus moved to Dessau in 1925. Kandinsky did important work there: teaching, various publications (the most important was *Point and Line in*

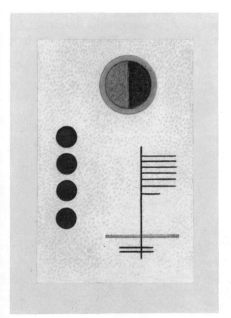

KANDINSKY. UNBIEGSAM (INFLEXIBLE). 1929.

Relation to Surface, 1926, in a series of books published by the Bauhaus), finally the production and décor for Mussorgsky's *Pictures from an Exhibition* for the theatre in the town. In 1929, his first one-man exhibition in France was held at the Galerie Zack. In 1931, at the request of Christian Zervos, he published *Reflections on Abstract Art* in the Cahiers d'Art. The same year, he visited the Middle East. In 1933 the Bauhaus, which had moved to Berlin, was closed by the Nazis. Kandinsky's canvases were confiscated and sold as examples of degenerate art. He then came to Paris, where he lived until his death.

From 1920 to 1924 the so-called 'architectural' period maintained the dynamism of the 'dramatic' periods, but more precise forms began to emerge: dots, bundles of straight or broken lines, segments of circles, rectangles and lenticular forms. Circular, concentric or overlapping outlines characterize the so-called 'circular' period (1925-1928), the other elements being more particularly used in the following period, called 'romantic or concrete'. The plastic signs to which the painter clung were employed for their own sake, quite apart from any reference to the material world. When Uccello put a diagonal in his picture, it had to be a lance. Kandinsky confined himself to the line itself, to its orientation and its relationship to the other elements of the composition. In this way he effected a liberation of form within a picture, which recalls what the Fauves did for colour when they freed it from any localization implied by the object represented. Kandinsky abandoned all reference to the real world and did not even make allusions of the kind found in Paul Klee's work. He deliberately tried to create purely unreal figures, detached from all representation. No doubt it was difficult for him to cut himself off from all memories, impressions or obsessions. However, he did attain that state in his last years; he seemed to move in an unknown world to which he had gained entrance by a combination of poetic intuition and a spirit of scientific deduction. That was the result of long research. In fact, when he began his abstract adventure in 1910 it was with a very romantic and lyrical enthusiasm. This Russian, half-Asiatic by ancestry, impregnated with Oriental arts and Slavic mysticism, had a supremely spiritual ambition. If he laboured to study scientifically the mechanics of painting and

KANDINSKY. DRAWING. 1923.

with his friends, especially from 1907 to 1909, he gave to this technique a still more systematic character. The painters sought to express plastically the immediacy of life in a music-hall, a brothel or a circus. Kirchner, above all, was haunted by the concentrated energy of athletes' bodies and by the animal freedom, the tremulous eroticism of nude women. In 1911 the members of the Brücke left Dresden for Berlin. From that moment Kirchner's painting–in portraits and street scenes–conveyed the acid flavour of the intense, artificial life of Berlin at the time. The plastic structure of his canvases became more solid, more dynamic, Kirchner having learnt from the new Cubist movement the concentration of spatial aspects and their translation by angular forms. Through this technique, he tried to express the immediate presence of the human being with his vital energy, though at the same time he tried to give it transcendental significance. The passersby in his street scenes, the *cocottes* and dandies in the electric atmosphere of his pictures look

to rediscover quasi-mathematical laws for the use and meaning of colours, it was because, like Seurat, he counted on finding in this way meanings which had been unknown till then. It was as a conscious act that he invented forms which had no precedent. These elements group and arrange themselves according to a rather mysterious and yet convincing order, one in which the artist had no need of dimension to attain the monumental.   J. LA.

KIRCHNER Ernst Ludwig (1880-1938). German painter born in Aschaffenburg; died in Davos, Switzerland. Kirchner was the dominant personality of the group of young artists who, in Dresden in 1905, joined together to found the Brücke *(*)* movement. The example of Munch as well as the discovery, in 1904, of Polynesian and Negro art, helped him to grow out of his first works and led him to simplify form and colour. Working together

KIRCHNER. THE AMSELFLUH. 1923.

like half-closed gigantic fans. By this transformation he intensifies their power to communicate their solitude in the cold, crowded coexistence of city life. 1913 saw the break up of the Brücke group. During the war, in 1916, unable to bear the hardships of military life, Kirchner fell ill: he had to leave Germany in 1917 to rest in Switzerland, at Kreuzlingen, then in the district around Davos, where he stayed until his suicide in 1938. Thus, at first against his will, he encountered a reality which moved him deeply—mountain scenery. In the life of the peasant bound to the grandiose rhythm in his surroundings, he found the image of man at peace with the forces of Nature. In his pictures the scenes of peasant life sometimes take on a monumental character. This theme is developed in great allegorical compositions after 1926. In the following years, inspired by the simultaneous representation in Picasso's work, Kirchner found new ways of solving his problems. Nevertheless, of all the work painted at Frauenkirch, it is the landscapes which are the most interesting. A mountain landscape as conceived by Kirchner is at the same time a representation and a symbolic reality. The village in the depths of the valley, the steep slopes, the ridges and summits, have at once a mystical and a symbolic quality.

Ernst Ludwig Kirchner was not only a painter. His sculptures in different materials and, above all, his immense output of drawings and engravings, are no less important (*see* drawings, pages 50 and 120). Above all, Kirchner was a great master of the woodcut, and his illustrations for *Peter Schlemihl* by Chamisso (1916) and for *Umbra Vitae* by the expressionist poet Georg Heym (1924), rank among the best work in modern engraving.   F. M.

KISLING Moise (1891-1953). Born in Cracow, Poland; died at Sanary, Var. Kisling's art presents rather clearly the characteristics of what is called the *École de Paris*, in the sense that he tried to associate the ideas of French art with those of his ethnic temperament. As a boy he was so gifted a draughtsman that his family wished to make him an engineer. But at fifteen he entered the Academy at Cracow, where his teacher was Pankiewicz, who opposed the Munich style of art then in fashion in Poland and

KISLING. PORTRAIT OF A BOY. 1937.
Private Collection, Paris.

initiated Kisling into the art of the Impressionists he had known personally. On the advice of his teacher, Kisling went to Paris in 1910 and settled at Montparnasse, where his witty joviality, charming, sensitive nature, along with his talent, made him one of the most picturesque and likeable figures of the quarter. At the time of the 1914-1918 war he joined the Foreign Legion, was wounded in 1914, and then invalided out. He was one of Modigliani's closest friends and helped him till the very last. His art always reflected a dynamism of coloured form, which he inherited from his Slav origins. Under the influence of the French sense of proportion, particularly that of Derain, he tried for a time to repress his sensual exuberance. Despite the apparent gaiety of his character, Kisling often painted female nudes and young boys' faces which show something of Modigliani's melancholy. This melancholy, often obscured by passages of bravura, is completely dispelled from his portraits of actresses and fashionable women, in which his *brio* and verve are magnified to enhance the effect of his brilliant colouring.   M. R.

KLEE Paul (1879-1940). Swiss painter, born at Münchenbuchsee, near Bern; died at Muralto-Locarno, in the Canton of Tessin. No other painter of the last half-century, formed far from the Nabis, Fauves and Cubists, and owing nothing at all to the École de Paris, has exercised such a widespread influence. Even more than the variations of Picasso, whose genius recapitulates the history of forms, Klee's art opens on the future. His work is not easy to understand. There are no clichés to be found there nor anything that has been seen already–nothing, at least, that has already been fully expressed. At first glance his compositions seem hermetic and the drawing childish. But when they are

founders of the Blaue Reiter (*), and he exhibited with them. After a visit to Paris in the spring of 1912, he set off, in April 1912, with his friends, Macke and Moilliet, to Tunisia, where they visited the site of Carthage and stayed at Tunis, the port of Hamammet and Kairwan, the city of a hundred mosques. This journey was decisive in his evolution. Up to the age of thirty-five Klee was essentially a draughtsman and had painted only water-colours. In his Journal he wrote these particularly significant words, which testify to the new era opening in his life as well as in his art: 'Colour and I are one; I am a painter'. From 1920 on he taught at the Bauhaus (*), first in Weimar and then in Dessau. December 1928 he embarked for Egypt. Although he only stayed for a month, it had the same importance for the last period of his work as the visit to Tunisia for his middle period. In 1931, he resigned from the Bauhaus and accepted a post at the Dusseldorf Academy. Resolutely hostile to Hitlerism, he left Germany in 1933, settling in Switzerland, where he worked till his death.

KLEE. ANIMALS IN THE UNDERBRUSH. 1938.

Klee drew a great deal. That is one of the secrets of the profoundness of his art. The notes he took

looked at more closely, a hidden world reveals itself by stages. From the hidden mysteries of this art there suddenly appears a dream world, peopled by apparitions which seem to light up, one after the other.

Although he was born in Switzerland, the son of a music teacher of Bavarian origin and a mother from Basel, it was in Germany that he made his career. After briefly hesitating between music and painting, he decided for the latter. He studied at Munich at the Academy of Fine Arts under Franz Stuck. After visits to Italy and Paris, Klee settled in Munich, where he married a pianist. Between 1908 and 1910 he discovered Cézanne, Van Gogh and Matisse. He was a friend of Kandinsky and Franz Marc, the

from Nature, before his subject, are full of shrewd insights. Their suggestive filigree is as personal as his non-figurative drawings, in which he creates his own world by twisting lines that sometimes recall honeycombs. Here and there he can be seen attempting a hieroglyphic, an indication of synthesized power, signs which are never static–hence this writing, which is so strange at first, labyrinthine, but in which new meanings keep appearing. These drawings have a rhythm based on associations, contrasts, balancings and interruptions. In them are found what might be called directional arrows (arrows frequently appear in Klee's work, in which every line points to the inner life of man and the elements). Houses huddled together in a village, vegetation springing upwards, the wake of fish in the water, flames dancing, the rise and fall of waves, the formation of crystals, roads and encounters, comings and goings–Klee gives form to everything which perpetually puzzles mankind, and the succeeds in suggesting its perpetual activity. By his blue foregrounds and grey backgrounds he gives space and vibrancy to his coloured planes. Klee owes to Cézanne his conviction that Nature does not lie in its superficial appearance but in its depth, so that, on the surface, colours are the expression of this internal force. Colour is not just incidental for him; it is an integral part of the organization of the picture. Who can resist those shades of blue contrasted with vermilions verging on orange and mauve, those golden browns, yellows, the pale violet punctuated with bistre ? Sometimes Klee uses a Fauve palette, but not stridently. With his quiet reds and greens he evokes the tender radiance of the moon which, 'itself like a dream of the sun, reigns over the world of dreams'. His colour has the extraordinary gift of associating planes and giving rise to rhythms in the drawing. By modulating the extreme values of chessboard white and black and superimposing his shining spectrum on them, he creates the effect of distance and evokes the sense of movement.

Klee was in everything he did, not just superficially but by a projection of his physical being in a profound way. He actually becomes the amœba trembling in the depths of the water, the crumbling mountain peak, the plant growing towards its fulfilment. He was completely at one with Nature. He had the power of giving substance to shadow and of giving form to everything that was fleeting or evanescent, be it a flower, foam or smoke. He was perhaps the only artist of our time who, without resorting to Impressionism, could paint the ceaseless movement of the

heavens as seen by a child lying in the grass and dazzled by the beauty of a fine summer's day.

Towards 1924 Klee set down his reflections on art in the form of notes, which were published in the following year by the Bauhaus under the title *Pedagogical Sketchbook*. His aesthetic system was only fragmentarily expounded there. His theories, which he employed in his lectures, were far from being the codification of a method; on the contrary, they forbade his having a pre-established vision and led him to seek new means of expression. When he set to work, Klee gained power from them to throw himself freely into the improvisation of his fantasies. Far from becoming a manufactured product, work was a process of rebirth for him. He knew well enough that the creation of a painting was not a logical matter. 'One comes to know a thing', he said, 'by its root. Thus one learns the prehistory of the visible. But that is not yet art at the highest level. On the highest level, mystery begins.' Klee arrived at this conclusion: 'Nothing can replace intuition'. Even though his draughtsmanship was extremely deliberate, Klee was fortunately able to forget all about method while he was creating. No doubt certain paintings do point to the pedagogue–he taught for over twenty years–but his

KLEE. LANDSCAPE WITH YELLOW BIRDS. 1923.
Doetsch-Benziger Collection, Basel.

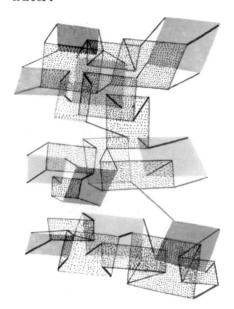

KLEE. FLOATING CITY. 1930.
Private Collection, Bern.

planes and colours which, in turn, give rise to new perceptions. Nobody was quicker to seize more competent to suggest the primal movement of life. In the very act of creation Klee seized upon this life-force. He wrote: 'As a child plays at being a grown-up, so the painter imitates the play of those forces which created and still are creating the world'. Klee's ideas on the origin of these forces were somewhat tinged with Eastern mysticism. He delighted in the idea of metamorphosis. Almost all of his work was done on very small canvases and papers. What they lack in show, they gain in depth.

His work is strictly individual, but never set apart by egocentricity nor arrogantly superhuman. Klee's painting plumbs the most secret depths of the human soul and opens on mysterious paths. And yet it never loses its purpose, and its language always remains that of visual possibilities.   P. C.

poetic inspiration spreads everywhere. 'To make memories abstract', was his purpose. No other painter in the last thirty years has so subtly touched the emotions or diffused such bewitching and rare poetic feeling. Werner Haftmann, his biographer, has said: 'He was the primitive of a new sensibility'.

Why does his work give such a sensation of music and poetry? Klee did not deliberately strive to transpose these feelings from one medium into another. That would have been a sign of weakness, an underestimation of the resources of drawing and colour. It is simply that, with an artists of Klee's importance, everything flows from visual expression and everything is suggested by it. Every impression takes form, instinctively, in lines,

KLIMT Gustav (1862-1918). Austrian painter; born and died in Vienna. After training at the School of Decorative Art in Vienna, in 1883 he founded with his brother an independent studio, which specialised in mural painting. Between 1898 and 1903, he was president of the Vienna Secession and contributed allegorical illustrations to the periodical, *Ver Sacrum*. His painting was decorative and linear and the subjects, often symbolical, femi-

KLEE. FAMILY WALK. 1930. DRAWING.

nine and decadent, were typical of the 'fin de siècle' style. In 1902, he did an allegorical frieze for the Secession building, which caused a considerable stir among the young painters. Its monumental paintings, *Philosophy, Medicine, Jurisprudence*, intended for the ceiling of the University of Vienna, were violently criticised by the public and the university authorities. After this set-back, Klimt retired from public life and spent most of his time on portraiture. His style in which the third dimension had been eliminated and colour had ceased to be anything but decorative, became increasingly ornamental and, turning quite naturally to the applied arts, he joined the Wiener Werkstätten (Vienna Workshops), founded in 1902 by Joseph Hoffmann. Because of the very personal character of his style, Klimt did not have any direct followers, but he was much admired by E. Schiele and Oscar Kokoschka who found a spiritual affinity with his symbolism. E. R.

KLINE Franz (1910-1962). American painter; born at Wilkes-Barre, Pennsylvania; died in New York. After Girard College, Philadelphia, Boston University and the Heatherley Art School, London, Franz Kline settled in New York in 1938. The long formative years began with painting landscapes, studio interiors, street portraits. He was quite unknown from 1940 to 1945 and earned a living selling humorous drawings and decorating bars and cabarets in New York. Although these panels were only intended to create an 'atmosphere' with their conventional subjects, their impressionistic handling of colour reappears with poignant effect in the synagogue scenes (1944) and in simple flower paintings. Throughout this period, the portrait of his wife often appeared in his painting, particularly in his drawing. It is not so much their precision that distinguishes his pen and ink drawings as their sense of space, but while he was producing these, he continued to work industriously at paintings of street scenes in a heavy naturalistic style. From 1945 to 1950, Kline endeavoured to gain a more immediate sense of the reality of things. There followed a rejection of naturalism and the gradual development of his forms from the pressure of their inner force, which is

apparent in the portraits of Nijinsky. The studio walls were treated as areas of plane colours, the rocking-chair became an ornamental arabesque and the figure of his wife, still present, tended to dissolve into light and space. After 1948, he produced more townscapes: composite views of streets and iron bridges, crowded, colourful impressions of Chinatown, in fact, a whole new interpretation of New York was coming into existence. About 1949, Kline formalised the objects in his still-lifes, while the style of his drawings already seemed to be escaping from its subjects. He spent more and more time drawing with brush and pen with the obvious purpose of giving clearer definition to his linear conceptions. Suddenly, the representational reference became more cursory,

KLIMT. THE KISS. 1909. CARTOON FOR A MOSAIC. *Musée des Beaux-Arts, Strasbourg.*

the linear rhythm became more pronounced, driven by a quickened movement into large, abrupt strokes. Appearance exploded and his creative gesture appeared in all its power, but still inspired by reality, its impulse expressed the shapes and cadences of the world.

Just like his friends, Jackson Pollock and Willem de Kooning, whose work influenced Kline until his own became freer, this change led to his use of large size canvases. Kline very rarely used medium sized canvases after this. He passed without any transition from cursory sketches, savage collages of torn and crumpled paper and the unpremeditated idea to a surface whose size compelled him to cover it with a gesture in proportion. His point of departure then was pen drawings, flashed out over the paper in the heat of action, from ideas that rushed impetuously up from his visual memory. Its forms clashed with each other and in the confusion merged with forms from the past: engines, cars, landscapes, faces, iron bridges, ports and motorways. Across the expanse of the canvas, the gesture became a sign. It was black so that it should be more arresting and there should be no distraction from colour. In a single movement, it displaced volume, affronted the whiteness of the canvas and swept recklessly across it. The whiteness resisted and

broke into fragments. Impulsive, frenzied and violent, his gestures nonetheless showed a complete discipline and a powerful decisiveness that could control all stresses. He never calculated his aesthetic effects: it was enough if they were simply effective. He projected and expressed himself in the very act of creation and, in so doing, asserted his powerful, trenchant personality. It was no longer writing or calligraphic rhythm, but an architectonic, elemental gesture, which was sometimes contradictory in its aggressiveness, but always convincing by its imperious necessity. It was, in fact, more than a sign—it did not originate in any convention and lacked any distinctive structure or any imaginative artifice—because its genesis was entirely natural, born from a premeditated action in so far as it was the gesture of a man. After he had reached this point of extreme tension between a solid blackness and lacerated white, Kline returned to colour about 1957, without however giving up the fury of his projection onto canvas or its unmeasured passion. Even in his use of colour, it was not a bodily struggle like Pollock's painting, but the unremitting conflict of man with nature, a determined investment, a physical act in which the painter revealed himself without any constraint.

Franz Kline taught at Black Mountain College (1952), the Pratt Institute of Brooklyn (1953), the Philadelphia Museum School (1954). Since 1950, he has taken part in several international exhibitions and the Venice Biennale (1960). Its downright vehemence has made his work some of the most significant of American contemporary painting; it possesses the breadth of Walt Whitman's poetry. It is self-consciously gauche and hasty and preserves the urgency of creation and an instinctive sense of the hugeness and speed of our civilisation. Far from dislocating the world, it prizes the musculature of concrete and steel and lays bare with a savage pride the

KLINE. HIGH STREET. PAINTING. 1950.

KLINE. GREEN VERTICAL. 1958.
Sidney Janis Gallery, New York.

dazzling traces of the hand of man, which patiently fashioned it. Kline died at fifty-two, when he had only given us an intense prefiguration of his future vision in these brilliant examples of his work.   R.-J. M.

KOKOSCHKA Oskar. Austrian painter; born in 1886 in Pöchlarn. Kokoschka studied in Vienna, beginning in 1904. Vienna at that time was the capital of an immense, dying empire and the centre of great intellectual activity. The artistic movement most in evidence was the Jugendstil *(*)*, marked by the affected, decorative art of Klimt. After being part of that movement, which inspired his book *The Boy Dreamers*, Kokoschka soon showed his independence. His painting, as well as the expressionist dramas he wrote, astonished and deeply shocked the public. Official disapproval even led to his exclusion from the School of Applied Arts. The distinguished architect, Adolf Loos, became his friend and protector and defended him against these attacks. He went to

Berlin in 1910, made the acquaintance of Herwarth Walden, the editor of *Der Sturm (*)* and became one of its principal illustrators. Dividing his time between Berlin and Vienna, he painted some portraits, particularly of writers and actors, which are psychological documents of haunting accuracy. The colours are very gloomy–blacks and browns, sometimes shot with blue, sometimes touched with highlights of red. Nervous and feverish, the drawing does not trace in a normally reassuring fashion the external aspect of his sitters so much as the strange lines of their inner personality.

Kokoschka seems to have a gift of second sight that has allowed him to portray physical transformations which later actually show themselves in the model. He is haunted by his subjects. The problems of form have only a secondary importance for him. The interest of his paintings resides essentially in their visionary character. The psychological preoccupations which one notices in his early pictures transform themselves little by little into a more general passion for all the human realities. Kokoschka's conception is dramatic, and his work carries an echo of that tradition of dynamic and visionary baroque painting which was still strong in Austria before 1914. His major work before the 1914-1918 war was *The Tempest* (1914), in which two lovers, transposed as myth, become all the forces of Nature unleashed.

Seriously wounded in 1915, Kokoschka had to wait for years before he was completely recovered. He settled in Dresden and, in 1919, became a teacher at the Academy. He was then influenced by the Brücke *(*)*, particularly in his use of colour. After his gloomy portraits and the cold blue night of *The Tempest*, his Dresden paintings astonish by their frank colouring, even though colour is not always perfectly integrated into the structure. It was only much later that he solved this problem by using a dramatic Impressionism of feverish brush strokes. In 1924 Kokoschka suddenly decided to leave Austria, and for seven years he travelled through Europe, North Africa and Asia Minor. With the same passion he had shown in his portraits of men he now painted sites, mountains and, above all, cities. He generally chose a very elevated or distant viewpoint from which the principal features of his subject could be seen in a broad, rhythmic-

al pattern. In this manner he portrayed Paris, Aigues-Mortes, Lyons, Marseilles, Jerusalem, Toledo, London, Amsterdam and Prague. In the visionary synthesis of the picture these cities appear to be living beings, with their legends, their stories and their secrets. In 1931 Kokoschka again settled in Vienna, but in 1934, after Doll-fuss was assassinated by the Nazis, he left for Prague, and from there, in 1935, went to London. During these years, and also during the war, the ideological struggle gained mastery over his painting, and he composed a number of large allegorical and historical pictures (*Loreley*, *Anschluss*). After the war, painting gained the upper hand in his landscapes, streaming with colour, of the Valais and of Italy, and in a series of portraits. In the following year, he twice made use of classical themes: in 1950, when he was commissioned to decorate a large ceiling in London, he chose the myth of Prometheus for an allegory of our civilisation; again in 1954, he painted a huge triptych, *Thermopylae*. The unflag-ging vigour of his work and the variety of his subjects have made Kokoschka one of those artists who have done much to enlarge the scope of European Expressionism.   F. M.

KUPKA Frantisek (1871-1957). Czech paint-er; born at Dobruska, Bohemia, died at Puteaux, near Paris. Kupka studied at the School of Fine Arts in Prague. To support himself, he gave lessons in religion and worked as a medium at spiritistic séances. He was immers-ed in the thought of the French eighteenth century, and so was overwhelmed by an exhibi-tion of the Impressionists in a Prague gallery. In 1892 he studied in Vienna and, in 1895, in Paris, where he has lived ever since. He studi-ed from Nature and greatly admired Rodin and Toulouse-Lautrec. He undertook some im-portant illustrative work: *Lysistrata*, *Prometheus* of Aeschylus and *Les Érinnyes* of Leconte de Lisle. He learnt Hebrew when commissioned by Élie Faure to make drawings for a new transla-tion of the *Song of Songs*. His studio had the calm atmosphere of a religious workshop. From 1906 on his painting changed profoundly; his technic-al development served an imagination which saw beyond appearances. In his landscapes Kupka sought the distortions of bodies in water and expressed them in cold, strident colours. He gave them a life of their own, independent of the subject and freed of the demands of reality. In a portrait of 1907 a yellow tone dominates the expression and even features. The large *Nude* painted in 1909 and exhibited in the Salon d'Automne of 1910 marks a decisive stage: the body is cut up into severely constructed and brightly coloured zones of purple, orange, yellow, rose and dark green. A bridge had been thrown between a methodical Fauvism and a Cubism which was soon to rediscover the use of colour. A portrait of Kupka's wife is invaded by lines and only the face survives among the clean-cut verticals and diagonals. But this rather hybrid combination of contrasting elements is soon left behind and an interest in construction predominates: the image springs up amid the interplay of complementary planes, as if through a series of screens.

In 1911-1912 Kupka painted the first totally abstract work: *Fugue in Red and Blue*, in which concentric rhythms in blue, red, green and black are ranged on a white ground. He super-imposed coloured masses, chromatic blocks which seem to emerge from one another (as in *Vertical Planes*, exhibited at the Salon des Indé-pendants in 1913), and from which shoot out isolated lines which sometimes recall graphic motifs.

Kupka joined with his neighbour Jacques Villon in the meetings of the *Section d'Or (*)*, in which a whole group of young Cubists were seeking the ideal proportions of a new painting. He was mentioned by Apollinaire as being among the Orphist painters *(*)* and the creators of the art of the future. In 1913 the *New York Times* devoted an article to him in which he was quoted as saying: 'To people who claim that

one cannot create forms or colours, I will reply that man has created the Ionic column and the Doric column and that architecture has con-stantly created forms with well-proportioned and fully justified modifications . . . Man expresses his thoughts in words . . . Why not create in painting and sculpture, independently of the forms and colours which surround him ?' A little later, in the preface to an album of abstract woodcuts, he wrote: ' The work of art, being in itself abstract reality, needs to be made up of invented elements'.

During the 1914-1918 war Kupka joined an infantry company before becoming an officer in the Czech Legion. The French poet Blaise Cen-drars, his comrade in battle, has described their experiences in *La Main Coupée*. After the war Kupka continued his experiments, his expedi-tions to the extreme limits of knowledge. In 1924 he exhibited his *Diagrams* and *Whirling Ara-besques*. But his contemporaries did not appreciate him, and this pioneer of non-objective art saw himself almost ignored. Uncompromisingly, he continued with his work and attained a purity and balance which evoke a sort of philosophical architecture. In 1936, in a large exhibition at the Musée du Jeu de Paume in Paris, he arranged a vast panorama of his creations, in five sections: *Circulars, Verticals, Verti-cals and Diagonals, Trian-gulars, Diagonals*. But it was not until after the recent war that his work received the recognition it merits: first in Czecho-slovakia, where an impor-tant retrospective exhibi-tion was organized in 1946 for his seventy-fifth birth-day, and from which fifty pictures were bought to form a Kupka Museum; then in Paris and New York, where it was re-cognized, because of its unity and logical deve-lopment, as one of the key sources of Abstract Art *(*)*.   J. LA.

KUPKA. BLUE AND RED VERTICAL PLANES. 1913.
Galerie Louis Carré, Paris.

KUTTER Joseph (1894-1941). Born and died in Luxemburg. His formative period was spent in Germany, particularly Munich, but he produced his best painting in his native city, where he returned to live in 1924. His asperity, melancholy seriousness and search for a forceful manner that would make an immediate impact connect him without any doubt with Expressionism. Yet, he diverged from German Expressionism, just as he was momentarily influenced by Vlaminck and Permeke and left them. Far from distinguishing himself by a taste for crudity, vehemence and debauchery, he was distinguished by the restraint of his manner. His art is full of strength, but there is nothing chaotic about it. A generous personality is revealed in it, but he refused to be kept within the bounds of a style with clearly defined characteristics. This is well illustrated by his *Man with a Cut Finger* of 1930 (Musée d'Art Moderne, Paris), which is a fine piece of painting in spite of its subject, a moving work with its firm, geometric form, the warm, vibrant colour and its free, but well knit composition. Up to the time of painting the *Clowns* (1936-1938) when he was suffering from a painful heart disease and laid himself bare in such a disturbing way, he never ceased to be preoccupied with the problems of painting. He was never content to find relief in anguished cries, but composed a song that is as touching in its beauty as its pathos.

His landscapes are no less striking than his figure painting, because the subject is always completely transformed by his state of mind.

KUTTER, CLOWN. *Private Collection.*

Even those that were inspired by the South of France have something harsh and dramatic about them and several of his German and Dutch landscapes have a desolate and tormented atmosphere. In spite of this, the richness of his harmonies increased through his career; the range of his colours was restrained, but not ascetic. Warm or vivid hues vibrate in contrast to the dark tones in the shadowed depths of his painting, and, as Kutter grew older, his palette became brighter and more intense.   J.-E. M.

L

LAETHEM-SAINT-MARTIN The school of Laethem-Saint-Martin was founded in the last years of the nineteenth century, when Valerius de Saedeler settled there, a few miles from Ghent, in a bend of the River Lys. The exceptional beauty of this district began to attract a number of Flemish artists, who formed a group around Saedeler—Gustave van de Woestijne, Albert Servaes and the sculptor Georges Minne, among them. Laethem had already known an extremely gifted primitive painter named van den Abeele, a local government employee who at the age of forty had begun to paint modest but penetrating works inspired by local scenes and customs. Valerius de Saedeler, a great admirer of Breughel and the Flemish Primitives, particularly excelled in the treatment of snow seen through the black branches of dead trees. Servaes united Flemish realism with such personal power and originality that the clergy banned his religiously inspired works from the churches, including a *Stations of the Cross* in charcoal for the Carmelites at Luythagen, Antwerp, which had caused a scandal.

A few years later a second group of painters formed at Laethem, including Albert Saverys, Constant Permeke, Gustave and Leon de Smet, Frits van den Berghe, Edgar Gevaert, Huber Malfait, Jules de Sutter, Piet Lippens, and several others (*vide* van den Berghe, Permeke, Smet). The artists met on familiar terms in the modest tavern they had chosen as their meeting-place. They were rather strongly opposed to the idea of Impressionism. Their villagers and peasant types were painted in a kind of healthy expressionism in a clearly Flemish tradition. They sought to express a full sense of life. A certain *joie de vivre*, a robustness of form, transfigured a reality which was no longer seen in the manner laid down by the old academic canons. The

Laethem-Saint-Martin school was violently attacked by the Academy. But its final success confirmed its interest and its value, and the influence it has had on Belgian painting in general has been its surest justification. M. R.

LA FRESNAYE Roger de (1885-1925). French painter; born in Le Mans; died in Grasse. Descended from an old Norman family, Roger de la Fresnaye was reared in the best French tradition. His precocious childhood drawings show surprising precision, purity and directness. In 1903 he

LA FRESNAYE. STILL-LIFE. 1918.

LA FRESNAYE. SEATED MAN. 1914.   *Private Collection, Paris.*

fitted together to give solidity and density to the objects. His palette was reduced to ochres, browns, muted blues and greens. More preoccupied with volume than with space, he sought above all for right proportions. In the landscapes he executed in 1911, at La Ferté-sous-Jouarre and Meulan, in *Man Drinking and Singing* (1910), *Cuirassier* (1910) and *Joan of Arc* (1912), those works in which, through Cézanne, La Fresnaye reached back to Géricault and Poussin, he succeeded in interpreting Nature by means of a strictly intellectual discipline. Energy under control, a direct and somewhat lofty tone, much nobility, despite a certain youthful sharpness—these are the characteristics of La Fresnaye's painting at this time.

enrolled at the Académie Julian and followed the courses at the École Nationale des Beaux-Arts until he was tired of the pettiness of the teaching there. He then entered the Académie Ranson, where Maurice Denis and Sérusier were teaching. These two artists taught that painting, far from being a mere copy of reality, was an absolute and convincing ensemble of forms and colours, that art was the concrete image of the inner life, the fruit of intelligence and discipline, that it was consequently natural to modify Nature and to obtain a new reality by deliberate distortion. Such was the theory of the Nabis *(*)*. Nothing could have better suited La Fresnaye's own inclinations. He submitted to the influence of Sérusier, Maurice Denis and Gauguin for several years. A mixture of irony and tenderness, of mannerism and austerity, even a certain literary quality, give his first canvases, particularly his *Self-Portrait* (Museum of Modern Art, Paris), a definitely Nabist accent. Unlimited possibilities were soon revealed to La Fresnaye by Cézanne. The *Ève*, which he executed in 1910, was already more plastic than the works of the Nabis. However, he took only the construction of forms from Cézanne: cubes, cones, cylinders,

As an admirer of Paul Cézanne, he could not ignore Cubism, and from 1913 on La Fresnaye joined Braque in this movement. More intellectual than Braque, he saw Cubism only as a method; less baroque than Picasso, he sought a classical basis in Cubism. La Fresnaye soon tried to check the splitting-up of form and the multiplication of planes which were the consequences of analysis. Probably he was the first to introduce the synthesis lately extolled by Gauguin into the Cubist experiment, to eliminate details and fussiness of every kind. In this spirit he painted *Seated Man* (1913), *The Conquest of the Air* (1913), *Married Life* (1913), and the beautiful series of *Still-Lifes with Square-Rule, Diabolo, Bottle of Turpentine* and *Bottle of Port Wine*. In each of these works line and colour are so closely bound together, so marvellously combined that the composition has not a single flaw. From then on La

LA FRESNAYE. PORTRAIT WITH A PIPE. 1918.

Fresnaye was obliged to work. Confined to his sickbed, incapable of sustained physical or intellectual effort, cut off from all contact with Paris artists, even obliged to abandon oil-painting, La Fresnaye could put only meagre means at the service of his talent. The few paintings he was able to turn out were inevitably marked by these conditions, but his drawings retained the same qualities of purity, sharpness of insight, and that characteristic aristocratic distinction of his, with occasional touches of preciosity. On December 29th, 1924, he wrote to one of his correspondents: 'In thinking of the common difficulties we have known for twenty years, of all those I have gone through, and of all that I should wish to do if I were in good health, I cannot help sighing when I consider the time and energy lost through lack of a guide or authority'. An admirer of Cézanne, a satellite of Cubism, he put grace and sobriety, boldness and moderation into his compositions. But unfortunately he never let himself be content with a single god. He worshipped Gauguin, Géricault, Ingres,

Fresnaye heightened his tones, brightened his reds and blues (he who had used such austere colouring during his Cézanne period) while the other Cubists were impoverishing their palettes. La Fresnaye made only a brief foray into Cubism before the First World War interrupted his work. He had never been very strong. But when war came, he enlisted, asked to be sent to the front, and distinguished himself there by his courage and self-effacement. When the troops were resting, he drew or painted water-colours. He came down with fever and was evacuated to a temporary hospital in Tours. Then began that doleful, restless sickbed life, which he bore without complaint, and in spite of which he continued his work. But his energy was sapped. In 1919, ill with tuberculosis, he settled in Grasse with his friend Gampert, a painter and engraver. He executed several portraits of Gampert, drawings, water-colours and gouaches. Stoically, he watched his strength and genius decline. He died on November 27th, 1925.

By 1918 La Fresnaye had said everything he had to say. His work of the following seven years –his last–was not without its importance, but one must remember the conditions in which La

LA FRESNAYE. PORTRAIT OF J.-L. GAMPERT. 1920.
Musée d'Art Moderne, Paris.

LA FRESNAYE. STUDY. 1914.

completely changed world in which the triumphant Cubist movement was imposing a new vision, a new order which had all the appearances of disorder. Amid such an abundance of new roads and stupendous promises, La Patellière's work invited repose and meditation, and proved that there could be several solutions to the problems of the time. Today we see that his art, beneath its apparent calm, sought to resolve the same problems, and that the means he employed were not so very different from those which then appeared revolutionary. Like the Cubists, La Patellière returned to strictly constructed compositions, seeking a distribution of objects in three-dimensional space which still retained unity of surface, refusing the

and the Florentines of the Quattrocento. With his complex nature and whimsical mind, he often achieved real style, but he did not always maintain it. Despite his adventurous spirit, he was really a classic, but today, whether because of his premature death or for some deeper reason, his work seems incoherent and incomplete.

One cannot help wondering where his talents would have led him after 1918 if his strength had remained unimpaired. 'The more I live', he wrote, 'the more I believe that painting is not a question of intelligence; it is almost a physical discharge'. These are the bitter words of a sick man who cannot develop his capabilities and is aware of his plight. His masterpieces such as *Portrait of Guynemer* (1921-1923) and *The Countryside at Hauteville* show that he possessed the artistic resources of a great painter. But for the onset of his illness he would no doubt have forged a coherent and original style of his own, and ceased to be an inspired eclectic.   F. E.

LA PATELLIÈRE Amédée Dubois de (1890-1932). French painter; born near Nantes; died in Paris. La Patellière belonged to the generation of painters which, after the 1914-1918 war, found itself in a

LA PATELLIÈRE. STUDIO WINDOW. 1929.
Musée d'Art Moderne, Paris.

picturesque, using light to give rhythm to his compositions and not to transform the colours, limiting himself to simpler forms and to a range of sober tones dominated by browns. This is equally true of the Cubists. However, in his strict observance of these principles, La Patellière wished to keep in close touch with Nature, with the inner reality of things, and so was able to use the poetic feeling which springs from a reverence for Nature; thus his work has a quiet poetry which harks back to the peasant inspiration of the Le Nain brothers. Through the sense of mystery which arises from this sentimental aspect of his work, La Patellière's contribution to modern painting deviates from more modern formulas, particularly those of Cubism; no doubt that is why he has been given a place rather outside contemporary painting, a solitary place, despite the admiration given him by the other artists who were his friends.

On the other hand, because his powerful personality did not exercise all the influence which might have been expected of it, because he died too soon, without revealing his full potentialities, and, finally, because his return to tradition was not a return to inertia, ignorance and mediocrity, but a quiet and deeply positive attitude, La Patellière's art has a value which extends beyond the modest place he is given at the moment.   R. C.

LAPRADE Pierre (1875-1923). French painter; born in Narbonne; died in Fontenay-aux-Roses. Seven or eight years younger than Bonnard and Vuillard, Pierre Laprade is one of the most tender of modern 'intimists'. Dividing his life between his little house in Fontenay-aux-Roses and his studio in Paris, he lived without ambition or need. Like Corot, he loved to wander through the French provinces; there was not a cathedral whose bells he had not heard. Italy was his second home, and he brought back rich harvests of water-colours from there, like Claude Lorrain mixing French harmony and a sense of balance with classical memories.

He excelled in suggesting a poetic atmosphere by using the most familiar elements–a window opening on a town or on the sea,

LAPRADE. THE MUSICIANS. 1907.
Private Collection, Paris.

garden terraces, Chartres Cathedral rising above harvest fields, Florence dreaming beside the Arno, or a young woman resting in a hammock as unsubstantial as a dream. It was not so much the actual forms as the colouring of the atmosphere in which they were bathed that he loved to paint. A kind of sad enchantment envelops all reality: ears of corn or yellow roses among blue pottery or among old books and masks, dusty puppets and pierrots, parks full of soft light. From youth Laprade used water-colour with mastery. At first his paintings were in monochrome, but they soon grew more colourful without losing those silvery tones with which his brush so successfully created the iridescent atmosphere of his dreams. This friend of poets was born to illustrate such works as the *Fêtes Galantes* of Verlaine. His delicate line is never insistent, sometimes even appearing uncertain; it does not so much describe an object or a particular landscape as a sentimental moment enveloped with deep or light greens with rose tints or blues dancing among the tender whites and yellows.   CL. R.-M.

LARIONOV Michel (born in 1881 at Tiraspol, near Odessa). Russian painter. He took an interest in painting when he was twelve years old. His family went to Moscow in 1891. In 1898, he joined the School of Painting, Sculpture and Architecture of Moscow and from that moment he took an active part in various artistic movements. At the end of his training with the award of a medal and a diploma, he painted at first in a

LARIONOV. DIAGHILEV AND APOLLINAIRE AT A REHEARSAL OF THE 'BALLETS RUSSES'. 1917.

traditional manner, then in 1909 at the Society of Free Aesthetic, he exhibited a painting influenced by Cubism, *The Glass,* which was one of the first steps towards non-representational painting. The following year at the Kraft Studio, he exhibited, beside Nathalie Gontcharova's *Cats,* a painting called *The Boulevard* and talked for the first time about Rayonism (*).

In a manifesto, which he wrote in 1912 and which was not published till a year later in Moscow, when Rayonism had already passed its peak, Larionov clearly stated his ideas: 'We must find a point of departure where painting, while preserving the stimulus of real life, can realise itself completely and the forms it uses are impregnated with the creative spirit and a broader vision. Painting should accept colour as its guiding principle, just as music has its real life in sound . . . Here begins the creation of new forms, whose significance and expression depend solely on the degree of intensity of the tonality and the position it occupies in relation to other tonalities.' Larionov also gave demonstrations at the Kraft Studio of the different resonances of the same colour. He was friendly with Malevitch and taught Tatlin, whose portrait he did in the Rayonist technique. The brief history of Rayonism, which is considered one of the first forms of non-representational painting, is practically limited to the work of Larionov and Gontcharova. According to some critics, it was influenced by Marinetti as a result of his first lecturing tour in Russia in 1910. The two Russian artists denied this and Michel Seuphor remarked that they 'rejected outright the literary allusions dear to the Futurists' so that they could engage in pure abstraction, which is the real distinction between them. Their painting, in fact, depends on the emotive values of colours by playing on the bright and less bright, parallel or intersecting, 'rays' of light. Larionov, however, still continued to paint figurative subjects, soldiers, flowers, or peasants, which are sometimes covered with inscriptions to emphasise their naïve and unusual forms.

After exhibiting in 1912 at Munich with the Blaue Reiter group, Larionov moved to Paris in 1914, so that he could be at the centre of the artistic life of the period. As soon as he arrived, he exhibited with Nathalie Gontcharova, his companion, at Paul Guillaume's gallery. Apollinaire wrote in the preface to the catalogue that 'the refinement of Rayonism is the barest and latest expression of present Russian culture.' The same year, he also met Serge de Diaghilev and practically gave up painting to work with him in the Russian Ballet (*). He not only designed décors, which were often distinguished —*Soleil et Nuit* (1915), *Contes Russes* (1917), *Chout* (1921), *Renard* (1922)—but also made his contribution to the choreography and even the aesthetic principles of the ballet, which marked it with their austere influence. Besides a re-

LAURENCIN. PORTRAIT. 1913.
J. Paulhan Collection, Paris.

Laurencin's art of this period that 'it dances like Salome between that of Picasso, the new John the Baptist, who cleanses the arts in a baptism of light, and that of Rousseau, the Herod of the sentiment, magnificent and puerile old man, that love led to the very edge of intellectualism'. Her art has never changed its character and throughout her career she has sought the same dream of gentleness in the pathetic faces of women, filmy veils, feathers and flowers and delicate colours. Perhaps the only exception is Poe's *The Raven*, which she illustrated for Apollinaire with red and black lines and dots and which has remained unpublished. In the thirty works she later decorated with lithographs or water-colours, she returned to figurative representation. Among these were *La Tentative Amoureuse* by André Gide and *Alice in Wonderland*. She designed the décor of *Les Biches* by Francis Poulenc for Diaghilev's Russian Ballet in 1924, and the décors of *A quoi rêvent les jeunes filles* by Musset for the Comédie Française in 1928. She read widely, and her best friends were the books which lined the walls of her apartment; sometimes, too, their authors, for

trospective exhibition of Rayonism at the Galerie des Deux-Iles, Paris, in 1948, about forty works of the artist, dated from 1903 to 1915, were on show at the Galerie de l'Institut in 1956. R.-J. M.

LAURENCIN Marie (1885-1957). French painter; born and died at Paris. She attended the Lycée Lamartine until she was twenty. Of average ability, she received some rather discouraging advice from her drawing teacher: 'You would be better off learning to play the mandolin'. Nevertheless, she began to attend drawing classes at a municipal night school. Then she met Clovis Sagot, a small art dealer, who spoke to Picasso and Apollinaire about her; soon after, Gertrude Stein bought one of her canvases. She used to go to the Bateau-Lavoir *(*)*, where painters and poets congregated. Though she took part in the feverish discussions which gave rise to Cubism, she was hardly influenced by this movement: in the group portraits she painted of Apollinaire and his friends there is that great simplicity and stylization of bodies and faces from which she never departed. Apollinaire wrote of Marie

LAURENCIN. THE SPANISH WOMEN.
Etching.

Marie Laurencin always preferred the company of writers to that of painters. She described herself in these terms: 'Loves luxury. Very proud of having been born in Paris. Likes neither long speeches nor reproaches nor advice, nor even compliments. Eats quickly, walks quickly, lives quickly. Paints very slowly.' M. GR.

LEBOURG Albert (1849-1928). French painter; born in Montfort-sur-Risle (Eure); died in Rouen. Lebourg is one of those artists exactly described by the epithet 'minor master', with all that this expression conveys in the way of talent, refinement and reserve. He did not play the revolutionary role of the great Impressionists, but he fully understood their poetic quality and the benefits they brought, especially to landscape painting. In his taste for landscapes seen through the rain and monochrome skies, he follows in the tradition of Boudin and Jongkind. His origins and also his education–he was a pupil at the Rouen Art School–explain the harmony between his sensibility and the landscapes of the Seine valley. Between 1872 and 1877, during his stay in Algiers, he undertook, in the Monet tradition, to paint series of pictures exploiting the same theme (*Arab Fountain, Moorish Café*). Lebourg, however, remained on the margin of true Impressionism and did not draw from these series any of the extreme conclusions reached by Monet at that same time. His Impressionism is never provocative; it is, rather, a discreet harmony of half-tones with the vibration of light-filled atmosphere. In him Paris found one of its most sympathetic interpreters, because he knew how to remain scrupulously exact without being banal. He was the echo, in a minor key, of the great Impressionists; but however discreet his canvases might be, they were never impersonal. Subtle harmonies are to be found there; above all, a great freshness through the use of light colours, more often complementary than contrasting. By his work Lebourg proved the error of academicism in refusing the new benefits of Impressionism and becoming obstinately static. He demonstrated what a non-revolutionary conception of art rejuvenated by new ideas might have become.

R. C.

LE CORBUSIER (real name Édouard Jeanneret). Swiss painter and architect; born in 1887 at La Chaux-de-Fonds. We are not concerned here with the work of this original architect but with his important contribution to the ideas which have renewed contemporary painting. For five years, until he was eighteen, Le Corbusier was apprenticed to an engraver and was the pupil of L'Éplattenier at the art school in La Chaux-de-Fonds. When he began his architectural studies in 1905 he did not completely give up the graphic arts, and he was keenly interested in the first Cubist experiments. As an architect he did not feel that the new aesthetic doctrine agreed sufficiently with a discipline which had to be respected and cultivated if the picture was not to debased to the level of a decorative ornament. Thus arose his idea of demanding from painting a total submission to the architectural setting destined to contain it. It was still understood, however, that the picture remained, above all,

LEBOURG. APSE OF NOTRE-DAME. 1899.
Lorenceau Collection, Paris.

'a machine to work upon the emotions', and the work of art 'a game'. The paintings and drawings dated 1918-1919, still signed with the name of Jeanneret, already appeared as imperious calls to a new order founded entirely on numbers and geometry. When he founded *L'Esprit Nouveau (*)* in 1920 with Ozenfant, and gave birth to what was called Purism *(*)*, it was essentially with the intention of preserving Cubism from the decorative tendency which threatened to engulf it. Nevertheless, Le Corbusier did not outlaw lyricism or attempt to repress the mysterious, intimate demands of sensibility. Beginning in 1929, the human face appeared in his painting alongside the still-life, the only genre he had practised till then. From then on he seemed to let his plastic imagination go adventuring, in compositions in which nudes adopted violently dramatic attitudes. Le Corbusier saved from his old Purist discipline only an absolute rejection of bewitching arabesques or facile arrangements of tones which were more particularly suited to easel painting. His work gained frescolike characteristics and began to show a development of audacious and striking shapes specially adapted to mural painting. In 1936 he executed tapestry designs for the Aubusson workshops; in them he showed a tumultuous imagination always restrained by the notion of a plan which, he felt, helped 'to avoid waste'. In short, the profoundly human side of Le Corbusier as an architect is strengthened by his feeling as a painter. If he subjects his aesthetic emotions to rules, they are not those of mathematical canons but of norms proper to a feeling human being.   M. R.

LE CORBUSIER. STILL-LIFE. 1920.
R. *La Roche Collection, Paris.*

LEGA Silvestro (1826-1895). Italian painter; born at Modigliano, in the Romagna, died in Florence. He was a typical personality of Italian art in the last century. He studied painting at Florence, where he came in contact with the 'purist' school of Mussini which, like the Nazarenes and Pre-Raphaelites, preached a return to the Italian masters of the Trecento and Quattrocento. The charming genre paintings of his first phase (*Little Girls Playing at Grown-Ups, The Lesson,* etc.) are in an academic manner from which he soon freed himself, certainly by the time he retired to Pergentina, a suburb of Florence. There with Abbati, Sernesi, Telemaco Signorini, and Bozzani, he founded the so-called School of Pergentina, which tried to introduce more poetry and suppleness into the theories of the Macchiaioli *(*)*. Works such as *The Visit, Afternoon, La Signora Bandini and her Daughters at Poggio Caiano* suggest with great felicity the remote, almost musical charm of quiet, provincial life.

D. F.

LÉGER Fernand (1881-1955). French painter; born at Argentan, died at Gif-sur-Yvette, Seine-et-Oise. Though he was of peasant stock and left the soil to follow his irresistible vocation, nobody remained more faithful to his humble origins than this robust, simple, generous man, this artist gifted with powerful instinct and unfailing good sense. In 1897 he

LÉGER. JULY 14TH. 1914.

the mechanical aspect of which had a profound effect on him. Between 1912 and 1914 Léger had painted objects reduced to their geometrical form–cones, cylinders, polyhedrons *(Contrasts in Forms)*; the dynamic phase of his work began about 1917. He renewed his inspiration and choice of subjects from what he saw about him. While his friends–such as Braque, Picasso and Gris–chose such familiar objects as playing-cards, a packet of tobacco, newspapers and drinking-glasses as themes for creation, Léger used objects invented and constructed by industrial civilization: railway wheels, cogs and tugs. He introduced human figures, workers, acrobats, Negro chauffeurs and signalmen into his mechanical universe. He painted *Discs* (1918), *The Town* (1919, Philadelphia Museum). Broad planes and large areas of colour create rhythm and space in these pictures, which have the impersonal precision of machines. But these various elements are not arranged in a naturalist manner: that is to say, in combining them Léger had no intention of reproducing some aspect of reality. His works are images proceeding from direct experience, immediate sensation, stark, evident, familiar, banal reality, which we see every day without really seeing it because the

became an apprentice in an architect's office in Caen. He went to Paris in 1900, did his military service at Versailles, and after a short spell in the École Nationale des Beaux-Arts, settled at La Ruche in 1908. He was first influenced by Cézanne. He met Picasso and Braque in 1910. In 1911, he exhibited his *Nudes in the Forest* at the Salon des Indépendants. He joined Delaunay, Gleizes, Metzinger, Marie Laurencin and Kupka when they met at Jacques Villon's in Puteaux, which led to the founding of the Salon de la Section d'Or *(*)*. In 1912, he exhibited his *Woman in Blue* at the Salon d'Automne, now at the Basel Kunstmuseum. He was called up in 1914 and fought at the front, and made drawings of soldiers and weapons of war,

LÉGER. THE FINE TEAM. INK. 1944.

veil of fiction intervenes between it and us. Up to 1921 the people he fits into his composition only form accessory elements—simple fragments of architecture, cogs of machines, machines themselves—and, are, therefore, devoid of humanity, physiognomy and name. From 1920 on, however, the human figure begins to dominate in his pictures, but it still appears as an automaton or puppet. Léger seemed to renounce movement in favour of a static art. His immobile forms, his machines are masses in repose. Up to 1924 he constructed a monumental art, peopled with proletarian gods, with a mythology both strange and common, unusual and concrete, majestic yet vulgar. Such famous canvases as the *Mechanic* (1920) or the *Dinner* (1921, Museum of Modern Art, New York) belong to this period.

In the years that followed, his desire for stability and purity was accentuated, he returned to still-life, executed mural, decorative, frankly abstract paintings which permitted him to liberate colour from form, to discover the value of coloured surfaces in modern construction. The problem that absorbed Léger more than anything else was how to create space with colour. He was already feeling towards it in the *Woman in Blue* (1912) and was clearly aware of it in *The Town* (1919). He finally mastered it and the full richness of its solution can be measured, when later on he decorated the hall of the International Exhibition of the Arts at Brussels (*The Sports,* 1935) or the Palais de la Découverte at Paris (*Le Transport des Forces,* 1937). It would not be an exaggeration to say that, from that moment, all Léger's work was conceived in relation to a wall Whether the wall was real or imaginary is irrelevant: what matters is that mural painting is an integral part of social life and the aspirations of human beings.

The décors and costumes he did in 1921 and 1922 for the Ballets Suédois *(*)* (*Skating Rink* and *Création du Monde*) and the film, *Le Ballet Mécanique* in 1924 illustrate the new preoccupations of the artist: how the requirements of visual art could be satisfied by colour values, how stability and movement could be realised in the same picture and how all these could be finally synthesised. In his direct, brutal manner, Léger tore quite different, natural objects from their natural surroundings and juxtaposed them

in an artificial space: a compass and a flower, a leaf from a tree and a human profile, the body of a woman and a bunch of keys (*Still-life with Pipe,* 1928; *The Gioconda with Keys,* 1930). At the same time, he did studies of tree trunks and leaves and painted the *Three Musicians* in a more realistic style. The *Objects in Space* led logically to *Figures in Space: Adam and Eve* (1934), *Two Sisters* (1935) and the monumental *Composition with Two Parrots* (1939, Musée d'Art Moderne, Paris), which he had been preparing since 1933 with some admirable studies.

His escape from the advancing Germans led him to Marseilles where the sight of the dockers, swimming in the port, inspired the series of the *Swimmers* (1941-1946), figures set in a space, that were more supple and less stiff. He was profoundly influenced by American civilisation, when he took refuge in the United States in November, 1940. The *Swimmers* were followed by the *Dancers* (1942) and the *Acrobats* (1943-1948) in which he tangled bodies and limbs in every direction, suggested volume by a few

LÉGER. COMPOSITION. 1920.
Louis Carré Collection, Paris.

shadows, fashioned the forms into broad rhythms and dissociated the areas of colour from outline, a new technique that he always used. At the same time, he produced some wonderful still-lifes in which plant motifs and mechanical components were juxtaposed and superimposed. On his return to France in December 1945, he painted a masterpiece, *Adieu, New York* (1946), as a gesture of gratitude to the country that had welcomed him. In 1947, he painted some portraits, notably that of Paul Eluard whose features are succinctly indicated by large, black lines, standing out over bands of bright colour. His figures, which had before been interlinked in mid-air, were now firmly planted on the ground and immobilised in an entirely classical composition. It was not without reason that he called the first important painting of the *Leisure* series, *Hommage à Louis David* (1944-1949, Musée d'Art Moderne, Paris). His interest grew in the theme of popular amusements and he used the same classical grouping for the *Cyclists* (1943-1951), the campers in the *Parties de Campagne* (1952-1954) and the clowns and acrobats of *Grande Parade* (1954, Solomon Guggenheim Museum, New York) a painting about 129 sq. ft. whose

decorative character is emphasised by the complete separation of outlines and areas of colour. His series of the *Builders* (1950) showed an unfortunate flirtation with a crude naturalism and the conventions of a popular ideology. However, Léger recovered from this and, although some of his last works show a certain triviality and heaviness of treatment, his water-colour landscapes of Normandy (1950), the *Two Women with Flowers* (1954), the circus scenes and nearly the whole series of *Leisure* show that his imaginative power and all his creative resources remained with him to the end.

There is further evidence of this in his bold experiments with techniques other than painting: the décors and costumes for *Le Pas d'Acier*, a ballet by Prokofiev (1948), the chapel at Assy (1946), the Bastogne memorial (1950), stained-glass windows for the churches at Audincourt (1951) and Courfaivre (1954) and the University of Caracas (1954), the decoration for the large hall of the UN Building at Manhattan (1952) and the hospital at Saint-Lô (1954-1956). Léger also did illustrations, tapestries, polychrome sculptures and ceramics (1950-1955) which were made at Biot, where the museum, bearing his

LÉGER. WOMEN WITH BOUQUET. 1921.

name, was later built. All the time he was occupied with this work, he was thinking about the conditions of community life, its turmoil, speed and the tensions set up in the human masses by modern civilisation. His thoughts were always on the public buildings, houses and décor which constitute the new space in which we move. Léger offered abundant interpretations of this new space, all based on the principle of contrast. Contrast of motif: a flower and a mechanical component, a banal utensil and a woman bather. Contrast of form: a ladder and a wheel, a disk, and a draught-board. Contrast in colour: blue and green, yellow and vermilion, heightened to their most vivid hues and in utter disregard for the rules of complementaries. Contrast in rhythm: a plank and a rotating propeller, the circle of a circus ring and the straight line of a tight-rope. The most incongruous objects, the most static with the most dynamic forms found themselves in aggressive combinations in the same painting, but without breaking the laws of pictorial logic. It was his instinct for placing, with a complete rightness, the most unexpected, vulgar and ridiculous things, as well as the most delicate, graceful and subtle objects that gave each work its sincerity and absolute value.

Léger was a man of his times. He spoke the living language of his age, the language of a creator who was strong enough and sufficiently sure of himself to ignore models and references. He never went into a museum. He never copied an old master, even when he was a student. Everything he created, form, space and light, was original. His justification was in the future, not in the past. He deliberately chose to be ignorant of his predecessors. He was happy in the streets, fields and factories, everywhere he could feel the brotherly presence of men. It is because he was so completely of his age and country that his work is timeless and universal. Themes, forms, colours, composition—he drew on his own resources for them all. He never left anything to improvisation, caprice or chance: everything he did was deliberate, intentional, calculated. In its honesty, imperturbality and sanity, his art belongs to the great creative periods of art. His *Swimmers* could very well mix with the dancers on the tomb of Tarquinia. His *Adams* and *Eves* can be easily imagined on the

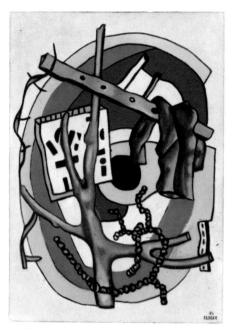

LÉGER. COMPOSITION WITH BRANCH. 1946.

tympanum of a Romanesque church, his *Mechanics* besides Uccello's warriors. Yet there is not a trace of archaism in his work, no literary appeal, not a hint of romanticism, no concession to nostalgia, nor empty rhetoric. The American critic, Sweeney, has called him the 'Primitive of modern times'. Léger is also its 'Classic'. F. E.

LEGUEULT Raymond. French painter; born in 1898 in Paris. For years Legueult has belonged to that group of artists called 'painters of poetic reality', each of them being inspired by the same desire to preserve, in a rather conservative way, the direct inspiration of Nature filtered through his individual personality. Legueult has shown himself especially attracted by colour, which transforms all his compositions into an extremely subtle play of rainbowlike iridescence in which the volumes of forms count less than the areas they offer for the use of colour. His art is not much concerned with the space and volume of objects but is completely captivating in its delicacy and

LEGUEULT. THE BLUE DRESS. 1952.
A. Margulies Collection, London.

grace. He joined the École des Arts Décoratifs in 1914, and was called up in 1917. After the war, a travelling scholarship enabled him to go to Spain, where he discovered Velasquez and Goya. When he was only twenty-seven years old, in 1925, he was appointed to a teaching post in the École des Arts Décoratifs. Soon afterwards, he collaborated with his friend, Maurice Brianchon, and designed the décors and costumes for *Grisélidis* and *La Naissance de la Lyre* at the Paris Opéra. Notable among his works are the decoration for the reception room of the Collège de Jeunes Filles at Fontainebleau (1937) and the cartoon for the tapestry, *The Studio* (1941). Not only in the drawings or the composition or the settings in which he places his people, but in the subtlety of the relationship between tones, his art

gives the impression of certain Oriental painting. He introduces us to as poetry in which fantasy has the freshness and unexpectedness of a spring morning. The forms dilute themselves in this magical world in which everything has an equal density and, as in Bonnard's canvases, one has the impression of confusion, but little by little details appear to recompose the forms and thus to give to the poetry the added value of secret language.   R. C.

LÉPINE Stanislas (1835-1892). French painter; born in Caen; died in Paris. It would not be exact to place Lépine among the innovators of his time, and one can hardly compare him with the masters of Impressionism, even if one admits his gift for finding an inspiration of refined poetry in the representation of Nature, in changing skies and landscapes glittering with light. It would also be unjust to see him merely as a respectful follower of a careful academic tradition. Actually, Lépine is one of those artists indispensable in explaining the transitions of art. The history of art is not just a series of violent reactions, as one is tempted to believe in viewing the works of the great artists alone. It is the minor masters who discreetly stake out the progress of ideas so that developments result from forward steps and not contradictions. It is the minor masters, from Daubigny to Lépine, who make the history of French nineteenth-century landscape painting a logical process, far removed from revolt dominated by Corot and Courbet, long before anyone

LÉPINE. PLACE DE LA CONCORDE.   *Arthur Sachs Collection, Paris.*

knew the more violent audacities of the Impressionists. The Impressionists needed to lean on the achievements of more modest figures such as Lépine and Lebourg, and perhaps the refined, quiet art of such painters was the most effective way of preparing the ground for public acceptance of the great masters. Lépine's art, however, was not just that of an intermediary. He has his own charm. His numerous views of Paris remain among the memories which can best evoke the atmosphere of the city at that period. They are valuable witnesses of the time, the more so because the artist never sacrificed anything to anecdotal details. Perhaps Lépine was one of those last artists to know how to make a landscape intimate, how to fix the secret soul of a city, a street or a river. His life was as discreet as his art, and practically nothing is known of him except that he died in such poverty that his friends had to make a collection to pay for his funeral. R. C.

LEWIS Wyndham (1884-1957). His parents were English. He was born on a yacht off the coast of Nova Scotia and his birth was registered at Amherst. He died in London. After studying at the Slade School *(*)* he travelled widely in Europe, returning to London in 1909. Here he threw himself into the polemical battle for modern art with unparelleled exuberance. 'In art I was a *condottiere*', he was to write. Around him formed a circle of friends that included Ezra Pound, Jacob Epstein, T. E. Hulme, Richard Aldington, Gaudier-Brzeska, and it was these names that were to be associated with the Vorticist movement which Lewis founded in 1914. Vorticism derived in part from Cubism, in part from Futurism. More than anything, however, the movement was a weapon, dynamic and aggressive, explosive as the title of its review *Blast (*)*, and it set itself to hustle Britain into step with the European avant-garde. Wrote Lewis later: 'Really all this organized disturbance was Art behaving as if it were Politics. But I swear I did not know it'.

The war failed to inhibit his activities. 1914-1915 saw the completion of his first major novel *Tarr*, the publication of a folio of twenty drawings entitled *Timon of Athens*, his first portrait of Ezra Pound, the first Vorticist exhibition and

LEWIS. THE SURRENDER OF BARCELONA.

the second number of *Blast*. In 1917 he was seconded as an official war artist to Canadian Corps H.Q. at Vimy Ridge; in 1918 appeared *Time and Western Man*; in 1919 he held his first one-man show at the Goupil Galleries. For some years from this period, date a great number of those incisive, marvellously constructed pencil portraits which show his powers of visual analysis at their most lucid. In 1924 appeared another review *The Tyro*, and in 1930 perhaps his best-known book *The Apes of God*. All his life in fact, Lewis alternated between painting and writing, continued to wield a savagely satirical pen–as a novelist, as critic and as pamphleteer. In his books he lashed out at the grotesque incomprehension of actuality evidenced by a society based on outmoded values; as a critic he was remarkable, penetrating and accurate in his analysis of contemporary art.

It must be faced that Lewis was equally at home with the brush or the pen, but he was not therefore to be grouped with those English painter-writers whose background is chiefly literary and whose painting is more or less a side

LHOTE. RUGBY. 1917.   *Musée d'Art Moderne, Paris.*

LHOTE André (1885-1962).
French painter; Born at Bordeaux, died at Paris. He exhibited in the Salon des Indépendants beginning in 1906 and the Salon d'Automne in 1907. With such surprising work as *The Widow*, he could not be disregarded. He was fortunate enough to be appreciated at once by the critics and poets. Generally it is difficult to forgive a painter who writes or a writer who paints. Lhote is the exception, however. As an art critic–he contributed to the *Nouvelle Revue Française* until 1940–and as a writer of such books as *Treatise on Landscape* (1938), *Painting First* (1942), *Treatise on the Figure* (1950) and *Masterpieces of Egyptian Painting* (1954), Lhote has raised outstanding questions, analysed the aims of art and explained matters of technique which no writer before him had even dared to touch. He has exercised a lasting influence on the younger generation, not only by his writings but also by his example, by the teaching he has done in the school he founded in 1922, and by the advice he has never withheld from the young people who have asked him for it. André Lhote joined in the first Cubist activities without becoming lost in that movement. His cult of Cézanne, his admiration for Picasso, have not prevented him from expressing himself, from unequivocally becoming a painter devoted to analysis and construction.

A picture such as *Rugby* (1917) is a good example of his method and ideas: the geometrical transcription of figures or objects, the clear articulation of planes through contour and colour, subtle composition, emphasis on movement and intelligibility of style. His logical, austere technique was also applied to the large decorations for the Exposition Universelle of 1937 and the municipality of Bordeaux (1957). Always searching for perfection, Lhote tried to put everything into his pictures: form, light, space, intelligence and sensibility, energy and stability. He attempted the absolute. And every one of his works seems like a demonstration rather than an outpouring. His is an integral, supple, reflective art which offers all the genres

issue. Lewis was a born painter, whose dominant characteristic, both in his nonfigurative works and in his portraits and other more naturalistic compositions, is an innate sense of construction. Most of his works are built on a vertical axis with a precise framework, somewhat metallic; occasionally they seem cold at first glance, but they are generally redeemed by their qualities of strength, dignity, and clarity. After 1914 his work was hardly ever entirely abstract. A painting by Lewis may strike one as pre-eminently a kind of geometrical or rhythmical speculation; yet it will invariably have, in addition to its sculptural qualities, a totemic character which makes of it a sort of magical object with a soul and a life of its own, as in the case of *The Contemplator* or of his drawings for *The Enemy*. *Sunset in the Atlas*, on the other hand, Cubist in structure but fluid in atmosphere, sums up rather well the characteristics of the Vorticist movement. Two paintings in the Tate Gallery are representative of his art: *Red Scene*, a composition of sombre, flat tones and a masterly geometric construction, and his *Portrait of Edith Sitwell* (1921), vertical, metallic, powerful. His *T. S. Eliot* has the same characteristics. Lewis must indeed be regarded as one of the foremost portraitists of the present century.   F. MC E.

and all the themes. Lhote, until his death, was still as lucid, charming, active and keen as in his youth. He was indifferent to nothing connected with the art of forms–surely the explanation of his influence on contemporary painting.

F. E.

LIEBERMANN

Max (1847-1935). German painter; born and died in Berlin. Liebermann's studies in Berlin and Weimar were completed from 1873 onwards by long periods of study in Paris and at Barbizon. After that, he worked in Munich and in 1884 settled in Berlin, where he remained until his death. Every summer, from 1879 until the First World War, he spent several months in Holland. Liebermann's painting continued the Berlin tradition, the tradition which had culminated in Menzel. However, he was the first in Germany to feel the influence of the great currents of foreign painting, from Naturalism to Impressionism. His early canvases were genre scenes. But the example of Courbet and, above all, of Millet, helped him, from the time of his first stay in Paris, to find a personal language which was colder and less sentimental in its realism than that of the French masters. *Plucking the Geese* of 1873, his first large canvas, created a scandal; he was accused of making himself the apostle of ugliness. Liebermann took a great step forward

several years later, when he came into contact with Dutch art. From then on he saw men and objects in an atmosphere impregnated with dampness and light, just as the great Dutch masters had painted, in particular Frans Hals. His works of this period–scenes from orphanages or old people's homes–and those which follow, are more monumental in their construction. In them Millet's influence predominates, and they are technically more finished. Their principal quality, nevertheless, remains a rather cold cautiousness, and they have that sobriety in the evocation of Nature which seems to correspond to the puritanism of the Berlin tradition. In 1873, during his stay in Paris, Liebermann had not recognized the importance of the Impressionists. It was only after 1890 that he discovered Manet and submitted to his influence. His palette became lighter, his painting gained in light and movement. His landscapes, his street scenes (especially those of the Jewish quarter of Amsterdam) and beach scenes acquired a new unity of tone and colour. But with Liebermann, Impressionism was only a process by which light was added to naturalism without totally transforming it. A few years later, Degas' influence appeared in the drawing, which became more dynamic and nervous, and in the bolder arrangement of his figures. In the last thirty years of his life Liebermann evolved a discreetly refined work in which, alongside views of his garden at Wannsee, portraits and self-portraits occupy a prominent place. Liebermann's work is of capital importance for Germany. Through it and through the struggle of Liebermann and other pioneers for the recognition of French art, German art came in contact with the main currents of European painting. F. M.

LISSITZKY

El (1890-1941). Russian painter; born in Smolensk; died in Moscow. He studied engineering at the Darmstadt technical school from 1909 to 1914. He then returned to Russia, where he was influenced by Malevitch and the Constructivists. In 1919 he began a series of drawings and paintings to which he gave the generic name *Proun*, a term he applied to all his work thereafter. In 1921 he was named professor at the Moscow Academy, but because of the growing hostility of the

LOEVENSTEIN. HARMONY IN BLUE. 1938.
B. Jaskarzec Collection, Paris.

children. Lissitzky's very personal art *(Proun)* is based on a composite conception of space, of three-dimensional forms mingled with flat forms. No other Russian artist among those who were active in Central or Western Europe exercised such a radical influence on the course of art. This influence was felt, first of all, at the Bauhaus *(*)*, through the teaching of Moholy-Nagy, who was named professor there in 1923.　　M. S.

LOEVENSTEIN Fedor (1901-1946). Born in Munich. His origins were Czechoslovakian. He studied painting first at Berlin, then at Dresden, before going to Paris in 1923. His promising talents singled him out immediately and he was represented several times at the Salon d'Automne. In 1938, he exhibited with Estève, Pellan and Szobel at the Galerie L'Équipe. The following year he exhibited a collection of his works at the same place. They were lost in 1940, when the artist sent them to a New York gallery that was going to put on a one-man show of his work. After the war years, which were particularly painful for him, Loevenstein had the joy of seeing his paintings, which had escaped confiscation, assembled in a gallery of the boulevard Raspail. That was the end of his career. A few months afterwards, he died. His work, so prematurely cut short, reveals a strong personality. After the bitter comicality of *Harlequin* and *Pierrot* (1936) and the pathos of a painting like *The Fall* (1938), all veiled in silvery mist, Loevenstein went on to compositions that are pure painting, imaginary constructions, waves of light in which abstraction assumes a strictly painterly idiom which has a dream-like fantasy combined with a surprising control. Twelve paintings, about twenty wonderfully imaginative watercolours, are all that remain of this melancholy, touching artist.　　F. E.

Government towards new art, he left his homeland in that same year for Germany. There he met Moholy-Nagy, with whom he became friendly, and on whom his influence became important. In 1922, in Berlin, he made the acquaintance of Theo van Doesburg, who published in Holland several months later a very curious *Story of Two Squares*, a set of six drawings that Lissitzky had composed in Russia in 1920. He worked with Hans Richter and published with him, in 1922 and 1923, the review *G* *(Gestaltung)*. Then he went to Switzerland, where he created the group and review *ABC*. In 1925, in collaboration with Hans Arp, he published *The Isms of Art*. From 1925 to 1928 he was in Hannover at the invitation of the Kaestnergesellschaft. It was at this period that he did the interior decoration of the Modern Room at the Landesmuseum, later destroyed by the Nazis. He then returned to Moscow, where he occupied himself mainly with organizing exhibitions of international art and publishing books for

LONDON GROUP 'The London Group', wrote Roger Fry, 'has done for post-Impressionism in England what the New English Art Clib did, in a previous generation for Impressionism'. To a greater extent than the NEAC however–indeed, more than any other British exhibiting society–the London Group has contrived to avoid that hardening of the critical arteries which comes to affect most such societies with the passing of the years; of all those in Britain it remains the most broadly representative of all that is best in non-academic painting and sculpture. Founded in 1914, its origins lie a decade further back. When Sickert *(*)* returned to London in 1905 he at once became the centre of a group of painters–most notably Lucien Pissarro, Harold Gilman, Charles Ginner and Spencer Gore–who looked to Gauguin and the other post-Impressionists rather than to the watered-down Impressionism of the NEAC. These artists met regularly at Sickert's studio at 19 Fitzroy Street; they stood for urban and 'low life' subject-matter, for a light palette and a high colour key, and opposed the jury system of exhibition selection. The Allied Artists Association, which also subscribed to the latter viewpoint, held a first exhibition in 1908 at which over 3,000 works were shown. Considering this scale of operations so vast as to defeat its own objects, the Fitzroy painters finally founded, in 1911 (the year following Fry's first post-Impressionist exhibition), the Camden Town Group, which held its first showing at the Carfax Gallery under the presidency of Gore. Among the original sixteen members, besides Sickert, Pissarro, Gilman, Ginner and Gore, were W. Baynes, R. Bevan, J. D. Innes, A. John *(*)*, H. Lamb and J. B. Manson. In 1914, under the presidency of Gilman, the Group amalgamated with several smaller groups–notably the Vorticists–to form the London Group (the name was suggested by Epstein), showing as such in the same year at the Goupil Gallery. Among the new members were D. Bomberg, Sylvia Gosse, W. Lewis *(*)*, J. Nash, C. R. W. Nevinson and E. Wadsworth; other names which became associated with the London Group within the next few years were those of V. Bell, D. Grant, M. Gertler, B. Meninsky and P. Nash *(*)*. Today the membership stands at about ninety, and embraces painters and sculptors of every creed from the most realistic to the completely non-figurative, quality and integrity being the Group's only concern. Participation in its annual exhibitions is open to non-members and it is thus to the London Group that many young artists look for their first showing.   M. M.

LUCE Maximilien (1858-1941). French painter; born and died in Paris. Luce was only a minor artist, but his simple, sincere nature was satisfied with such a role, for he had an inborn disdain for honours, and his only desire was to paint. He sought neither to innovate nor to dazzle but, with the conscientiousness of an artisan, devoted his long, retired life to painting. 'It was no easy task', wrote his friend George Besson, 'to make a name at twenty at the moment when Monet was painting his *Gare Saint-Lazare* and Renoir his *Moulin de la Galette*, or to hope for notoriety at thirty with only the will to do good work to pit against Gauguin's genius for the picturesque, or at seventy, with only disdain for M. Dali's bluff.' However, Luce was not entirely indifferent to the artistic trends of his day, and he joined the group around Signac and Seurat for a few years, until finally his poetic sensibility could no longer submit to the inflexibility of their system. On abandoning Divisionism he came under the influence of his friend Camille Pissarro, and his work tended towards Impressionism: fixing the fugitive effects of Nature in subtle, delicate tones, he produced paintings which were both poetic and poverful.

In his youth Luce was an anarchist, and in 1894 was implicated in the celebrated '*Procès des Trente*'. Acquitted at the trial, he left prison and continued all his life to paint steadily, taking part in no group activities and never abandoning his independence of mind and pride in his working-class birth. Apart from his landscapes, some of Luce's best paintings represent the humble, arduous life of the people: labourers, dockers or masons at their daily work. His art, which has its own highly individual side, has its place between that of Pissarro and Bonnard.

When Signac resigned from the presidency of the *Société des Artistes Indépendants* in 1934, Luce was elected to succeed him–the only worldly honour he ever accepted.   J. R.

LURÇAT Jean (Born 1892, at Bruyères in the Vosges). The success of his tapestries has too often made us forget that Lurçat began as a painter and still is one. After studying medicine for a short while at Nancy, he wanted to become a painter and trained under Victor Prouvé in the same town. Towards the end of

LURÇAT. BLACK TABLE. 1953. TAPESTRY.

(1944), 18 lithographs, one for each of the poems; André Richaud's *The Creation of the World* (1949); J. H. Fabre's *The Marvellous World of Insects* (1950); *Le Bestiaire Fabuleux* (1951), poems by La Tour du Pin, and Supervielle's *The Fable of the World* (1959).

Lurçat has been tireless in his efforts to revive French tapestry, particularly in giving an unrivalled reputation to to the Aubusson workshops. Through him and the young artists he trained, an art, which had almost died out, has once again become one of the finest in the world. His first tapestries, on canvas, date from 1915. He has designed about a tousand cartoons for tapestries. Among the best known and most accessible to the public are those at the Palais Royal at The Hague (1936); the Musée du Vin at Beaune (1947); The *Apocalypse* in the church at Assy (1948), placed at the end of the choir and measuring about 603 sq. ft.; those in the Palais de l'Europe at Strasbourg (1951-1954); *Homage to the Dead of the Resistance and the Deportation* (1954) in the Musée d'Art Moderne, Paris. From 1957 to 1960 he worked at a series of panels that together made up a hanging about 5,382 sq. ft., called the *Song of the World*. Lurçat's work is surrealist. He communicates the character of a particular landscape by using a startling symbolism for the state of mind it rouses in him. His expression of its harshness is almost ascetic, a bare synthesis of a subjective experience. In several tapestries, he has turned to a sort of sur-real expressionism, dominated by the motif of the sun, where the cock, announcing the dawn, is associated through its violent colours with the browns and greens of the earth. He may not be more a poet than painter, but he is certainly a visionary. M. Gi.

1912, he went to Paris. At first he was an independent painter, then he was strongly influenced by Cubism from 1920 to 1923. The aesthetic discipline of that influence gave no idea of what his painting would be like after 1925. Two long visits, one to Spain in 1923, the other to the Sahara, then to Greece and Asia Minor in 1924 determined his very personal vision of the world. What struck him so much in the Sahara, Spain and Smyrna was the landscapes like deserts, harsh, dry, burned, stony, and their bare or ruined public buildings: a surrealist tragedy, not inhuman, but overwhelming for the humanity lost in it, a self-sufficient humanity that seemed a part of the hostile land or simply indifferent to it. In 1930, a visit to Arcachon transferred this tragic vision from the earth to the naked immensities of the sea, with its lonely dramas of shipwrecks and struggles with death. To this period belongs the series of pictures with poles and sails. Lurçat went to New York in 1928. The same year appeared his paintings with figures, which are rare in his works, but the Stedelijk Museum, Amsterdam, possesses fourteen. Besides oil painting, he also produced gouaches and coloured lithographs. His outstanding illustrations were done for Ch.-A. Cingria's *Limbo* (1930); his own *Animal Geography*

M

MACCHIAIOLI This name was given to the most important of the 19th century movements that endeavoured to inject new life into Italian painting. It means 'Splashers'. It started in Florence between 1850 and 1855 out of the enthusiastic discussions of a group of artists, who used to meet in the Café Michelangiolo (*), gathered momentum between 1855 and 1860 and culminated with an exhibition, held at Florence in 1861. It was a sort of focus for the ideas and aspirations that were stirring the peninsula at that time. 'Friends would go to Venice or Rome and return,' wrote Signorini, 'and the acquaintances they made across Italy came in their turn to us, so that the Café Michelangiolo presented an impressive scene . . . Americans, English and French were to be found there.' The leading promoters of the movement were Giovanni Fattore, Telemaco Signorini, then later on, Silvestro Lega, Adriano Cecioni (who, with Signorini, was the theorist of the group) and Diego Martelli, an intelligent and enthusiastic Maecenas. Cecioni's writings are evidence that the discussion eventually centred on their common rejection of traditional painting. They talked about destroying the 'religious respect for aesthetic conventions' and the 'academic cult of form.' Art, once again according to Cecioni, is not concerned with form, but in the way it renders *impressions,* or immediate perceptions of reality, by means of 'macchie' (splashes) of bright and dark colours. This was the solution they found to the problem of form, by considering it in terms of colour values and their relations. It was a very similar theory, although the result was different, to the one that the French Impressionists were to advance later. It was not chance that the Macchiaioli were the first in Italy to grasp the significance of Impressionism. In fact, in 1886 Diego Martelli gave a lecture on Manet, Renoir, Degas, Pissarro and Cézanne to the Philological Circle of Leghorn. It would be true to say that between 1860 and 1890, the period when their endeavours to make a fresh start in painting were most widely appreciated (and to the original names should now be added those of Nino Costa and Giovanni Boldini) the Macchiaioli made a whole-hearted and consciously enthusiastic contribution to the revolution that the Impressionists had brought about.   D. F.

MACDONALD-WRIGHT Stanton (born 1890 in Charlottesville, Virginia). American painter. He began to study art at the age of seven. In 1907 he made his first trip to France, living principally in Paris and Cassis. After his encounter with Morgan Russell in Paris he discovered Cézanne and began to experiment with colour in relation to space. With Russell he devised a style of painting which they called 'Synchromism,' based on the principles of Cézanne. Increasingly abstract, their work attempted to create form in space through the feeling of volume given by the optically receding or advancing qualities of warm or cool colours. Macdonald-Wright wrote in the catalogue of the 1913 Synchromist exhibition at Bernheim-Jeune: 'Every colour has its own position in emotional space and possesses a well-defined character. I conceive of space itself as endowed with plastic meaning, expressed through color. Since form is not the volume of each object seen separately, I organized my canvas as a whole, as much in depth as on the surface . . . With us the quality of depth provokes a subjective emotion.' In fact, Synchromism owed not a little to Delaunay's Orphism which was the Synchromists' *bête noire:* in the Bernheim-Jeune manifesto they challenged Delaunay to hang his best work with theirs so that the public might judge the respective merits of the two movements. Synchromism created considerable interest and there were exhibitions also in Munich

MACDONALD-WRIGHT. SYNCHROMY. 1914.
Private Collection, U. S. A.

Los Angeles in 1956 was enthusiastically received, and Macdonald-Wright's second artistic career had begun.

In 1944, looking back on Synchromism, he had written with a note of regret: 'I still feel that a related colour design is the characteristic expression of our age.' Whether or not one agrees, and whatever one may think of his aesthetic reasoning, it is impossible not to be impressed by the vigour with which it is set forth in his painting. The tumultuous, kaleidoscopic effect of the shifting forms and chromatic contrasts has the vehemence of Expressionism channeled and strengthened by the lucid control of Cubism. The acute contrasts in depth do in fact create emotional excitement of a kind often lacking in comparable French painting of the period. With Russell, Bruce, Carles and Covert, Macdonald-Wright is one of a small group of highly original American artists who flourished around the time of the first World War and whose achievement has for various reasons remained little known.   J. A.

and New York. But it was short-lived and without lasting repercussions. Still, some critics, such as Milton W. Brown in his 'American Painting from the Armory Show to the Depression,' regard it as 'the most advanced and radical manifestation of abstract art in those years,' and it is also the first movement in American art to receive international attention.

Russell soon returned to figurative painting (he remained in France throughout the two wars, living obscurely in the provinces) and Macdonald-Wright returned to America where the lack of enthusiasm for modern art caused him too to turn away from abstraction in 1920 to embark on a life of varied activity which took him successively to California and the Far East. He was head of a WPA art project for a time, professor of oriental art at the University of California, and lectured on modern art in Japan where he also mastered Chinese and Japanese and became interested in Zen Buddhism. In 1953 he returned to America and seemed to undergo an artistic metamorphosis. He took up Synchromism again; a show of his new work in

MACKE August (1887-1914). German painter; born at Meschede in the Ruhr; died at Perthes, in Champagne, during the war. After a childhood spent in Cologne and Bonn, Macke studied at the Academy of Düsseldorf. During visits to Paris after 1907, he came in contact with French painting: the Impressionists, then the Fauves, and later Cubism. In 1909-1910 he met Franz Marc and Kandinsky in Munich, and in 1911 the took part in the preparation of the Blaue Reiter *(*)* almanac. Breaking off a stay at Hilterfingen by the Lake of Thun in the spring of 1914, he went on a trip to Tunisia along with Klee and the Swiss painter Moillet. A few weeks after his return to Bonn, he left for the war and was killed shortly afterwards.

Because Macke was associated with the Blaue Reiter, it is tempting to consider his work only in relation to that movement. But his position was quite different from that of Kandinsky or Franz Marc. Whereas Marc turned towards direct expression of a spiritual reality, Macke always remained deeply concerned with visual experience. His sensitivity allowed him to benefit more than any other German painter from the lesson of French painting. It is possible that the spirit of the Rhineland, where he spent nearly all his life, made this contact easier for him. As early as 1910 his painting, which had undergone the influence of Impressionism and then of Cézanne, developed a broader, freer rhythm inspired by the works of Matisse. In fact, the painting of his friends of the Blaue Reiter confused him more than it helped him find his way. It was the influence of Cubism, to some extent of Futurism, and, above all, of Delaunay, that helped him as early as 1908 to find his own idiom. He was enthusiastic about Delaunay's *The Windows* (reproduced on page 9), and paid a visit to the painter in Paris; the latter came to see him in Bonn with the poet Guillaume Apollinaire. While the influence of Cubism simplified Macke's form, Futurism suggested a means for more complete representation of life. This representation he meant to accomplish by the use of light and colour in 'simultaneous contrast', after the example set by Delaunay. In this way his painting found its own form. In just about a year, at Bonn and Hilterfingen, in Tunisia, and again at Bonn, a body of work of luminous colour and perfect grace and distinction was born. Some small abtract compositions, in 1913-1914, reveal Delaunay's influence, but, unlike the abstractions of Franz Marc, Macke's did not indicate the general direction of his work. Macke's painting, on the whole, remained representational: strollers by a lake, children, girls under trees, women before a milliner's display—such are the subjects he preferred. The figures are quiet in the midst of motion, or as they wait, and the moment becomes fixed in a hazy space created by pure and luminous colours. From the Tunisian trip Macke brought back, in addition, watercolours of crystalline structure, which communicate the enchantment of African light.   F. M.

MAGNELLI Alberto. Italian painter; born in 1888 in Florence. After having studied in technical schools, Magnelli devoted himself to painting, away from all academies and professors. In 1913 he associated with the Futurists Boccioni, Carrà, Marinetti, Papini and Soffici, but without belonging to their movement, and his own experimentation stemmed from other preoccupations. During a stay in Paris, from February to June 1914, he made friends with the poets Apollinaire and Max Jacob, and the painter Fernand Léger. He painted a series of large still-lifes and compositions of very simplified human figures in Florence.

This synthesis of severe forms led him, in 1915, to his first complete abstractions, in which bright colours were applied flat. After this period of extreme severity, he returned in 1918 to a semi-representational way of painting, very violent both in colour and in form. He then painted several series of figures and landscapes, extremely architectural in composition and clear and sober in colour. But, about 1933, he turned towards a new form of abstraction, which had been developing for a long time. This began by what is known as his 'stones period', because the forms suggest fragments of stones, before it became uncompromising

MACKE. GIRLS UNDER TREES. 1914.
Private Collection, Austria.

abstraction, resting upon no theory but still based upon imagined figures. During the Second World War he stayed at Grasse, in the south of France, together with Arp, Sophie Taeuber-Arp and Sonia Delaunay.

Magnelli's art strives to rediscover the pure and archetypal forms which lie behind superficial sense impressions. If he brings to mind the ideal abstraction of mathematical figures, he always provides sensory and plastic equivalents, for he does not think that a picture can be only a blueprint. In him there is a creative will as far removed as possible from the fortuitous, and a health and natural strength that prevent even his most enigmatic forms from ever being meaningless or literary.   J. LA.

interested in the world about him and its objects. He wanted to reveal their existence by means of a representation that was realistic but poetic nevertheless, making painting both a way to knowledge and a means of moral liberation. From 1924 to 1936 he applied himself to producing surprise effects by bringing together incongruous objects, creating new ones, and transforming familiar ones. By means of exchange or opposition, he enlightened us about them: stone-burned, the sky was wooden or cracked, the bells of horses became dangerous flowers. Some ten years before, Chirico had already made use of unexpected combinations of elements unrelated to one another, to create an atmosphere of mystery and bewilderment. Magritte's dryness, his precision, and his will to paint 'anti-painting' sometimes recall the style of Chirico. From 1936 to 1940, expanding his field of investigation, Magritte no longer juxtaposed dissimilar objects, but instead explored the affinity that the object, isolated, could have with itself. The question was to discover the relation of the encompassing and the encompassed–the relation of the tree and the leaf, the landscape and the picture, the shoes and the feet, the sky and the bird. This problem, solved a hundred times with astonishing imagination, made Magritte a

MAGNELLI. DISTURBING VISION. 1947.

MAGRITTE René. Belgian painter; born in 1898 at Lessines, in Belgium. In 1925, after a short glance in the direction of Futurism and Cubism, Magritte joined the ranks of the Surrealists. He lived for five years in Paris, where he made friends with the poet Paul Éluard. While most Surrealist painters were making use of automatism, paranoia or the exploration of dreams, on the basis of the 'purely interior' standard that their leader, André Breton, suggested to them, Magritte was more

wonderful inventor of images. Each of his canvases, admirably painted, was a discovery in which intelligence and sensitivity mingled. At the same time his tonality lightened. It passed from brown to green, from grey to blue. This metamorphosis announced other research in a sphere where colour would play a role of primary importance. Although very much questioned, the Impressionist period of Magritte, which dates from the Second World War, should not be a surprise. Painting being for him only a means of deepening his knowledge of the world, every technique, even an old one, was useful in so far as it made us reconsider object from an angle and in a light that the painter could dictate at will. On the other hand, it is regrettable that this flood of colours was accompanied by only a few discoveries about the object itself. The aspect of the canvases changed; the content became less rich. Towards 1946, in the final *volte-face* of an amazingly independent man, Magritte returned to his former manner. His ideas are without doubt less numerous and his hand less sure, but *Scheherazade*, a woman's face outlined with pearls, is an enchanting find. Above all, he repainted two celebrated pictures, the *Madame Récamier* of Gérard and *The Balcony* of Manet, replacing the figures with coffins. Recreating masterpieces or remaking objects is the same process. In both cases the aim has been to teach us to see. Magritte is a great visionary. C. S.

MAGRITTE. SUMMER STEPS. 1937.
Private Collection.

MALEVITCH Casimir (1878-1935). Russian painter; born in Kiev; died in Leningrad. Malevitch was first influenced by the Post-Impressionists and the Fauves. Later he made friends with Larionov and the more advanced Russian poets. The latter, in 1915, helped edit his Suprematist manifesto (*vide* Suprematism). As a member of the Jack of Diamonds group in 1911, he exhibited works of Cubist inspiration; and he became the leader of the Russian Cubist movement, to which his wife Udalzova belonged as well. In 1912, he began to paint in the manner of Léger, although he emphasized straight lines and clean geometrical figures slightly more (*The Scissors-Grinder, Woman Carrying Water*). This step brought him to the threshold of complete abstraction, and in Moscow at the end of 1913 he exhibited a black square on a white background, making a great sensation. The square, whose area was painsta-

kingly filled in with black pencil, was the first element of Suprematism. It was soon joined by the circle, the cross, and the triangle. During the next few years, with these basic shapes, Malevitch painted a number of compositions, most of them quite simple, the shapes themselves being created by clear colours upon a white background. The acme of simplicity and delicacy was reached in 1919, when he painted his *White Square on a White Background*, exhibited in Moscow in the same year (now in the Museum of Modern Art, New York). He was then appointed professor at the first National School of Applied Art in Moscow. A few years later, when modern art fell into disrepute with the Soviet Government, he was transferred to Leningrad, where he could nevertheless keep on teaching until his death. Until the end he was surrounded by the discreet admiration of a number of friends, but it is not known whether he continued to paint after the opportunity to exhibit was over. He was granted permission, however, to go to Germany in 1926, in order to prepare his book *Die Gegenstandslose Welt* (The World of Non-Representation), an elaboration of the Suprematist manifesto of 1915, for publication at the Bauhaus (*). Along with Mondrian and Kandinsky, Malevitch is one of the pioneers and most important representatives of Abstract Art (*). As in the case of Mondrian, the starting point for his discovery of abstraction was Cubism; but what Mondrian gained as the result of a slow and gradual evolution, Malevitch grasped in a sort of sudden revelation that led him immediately to the most absolute result–the famous black square on a white background–which he afterwards devoted years to achieving dialectically.   M. S.

MANET Édouard (1823-1883). French painter; born and died in Paris. Manet belonged to the upper middle class, and his existence was bound to that class; he remained attached to the privileges it enjoys, wished to receive the honours and recognition it confers, and at the same time gave rise during his lifetime to the most violent scandals and unwittingly produced through his painting a complete revolution. He brought a taste for liberty that did correspond to the aspirations of the time but was not yet admitted in its consequences. Academic art was still dominated by what was

MALEVITCH. SUPREMATIST COMPOSITION. 1914-1916. *Private Collection, Stuttgart.*

thought to be a tradition but in fact consisted of no more than the impoverished remnants of superannuated formulae. At the beginning Manet probably had no intention of playing the part of a revolutionary leader. He had very prudently begun by setting out upon a more conventional career. Yielding to family insistence, he started out in 1848 as a student pilot on a training ship, and made the voyage to South America. When he returned, he failed his examination at the Naval School and at last succeeded in persuading his father to let him become a painter. In January 1850, he joined the studio of Thomas Couture. His independence brought him into immediate conflict with his teacher. He did not, however, approach the profession with preconceived ideas, sure of inventing a personal technique. He frequented the Louvre very assiduously, his lessons left him unsatisfied, and the example of masterpieces convinced him that he had more to learn from the masters and from Nature. His character as a painter therefore derived from his stays in Fontainebleau and from his admiration for Tintoretto, Titian and Velasquez. In his first works, already stamped by these influences, an inclination can be discerned for clear colours, a free touch, and large, vibrant flat areas. His visits to Holland, Germany and Italy reinforced this tendency, in which he was reviving the freedom and dash of Frans Hals and the Venetians of the Renaissance. His *Portrait of a Spanish Musician* won an 'honourable mention' at the Salon of 1861 and, because of the subject, also earned the praises of Théophile Gautier. The following year, a show given by a troupe of Spanish singers and dancers made him all the more enthusiastic about Spain and inspired a whole series of paintings. The famous *Lola of Valencia*, which Baudelaire called a 'jewel in pink and black', was one of them. The affinities between Manet's art and Spanish painting were once thought so obvious that a critic described Manet as a 'Parisian Spaniard', and Courbet, on the occasion of the 1865 Salon, where *Olympia* was exhibited, said: 'This young fellow had better not try to pull Velasquez over our eyes'. However, it was not until that year that Manet finally went to Spain to see the masters by whom he was supposed to have been influenced. His admiration for Velasquez was strengthened and he discovered Goya.

From the beginning, then, Manet was astonishing and bewildering. The first violent reactions of the public dated from 1863, when he exhibited *Le Déjeuner sur l'Herbe* at the famous *Salon des Refusés*. The scandalousness attributed to this picture is difficult to understand today. It seemed indecent because it represented a naked woman sitting on the grass between some young men in contemporary dress. At the time nudes were tolerated only in allegorical scenes, when the figures were supposed

MANET. LE DÉJEUNER SUR L'HERBE. 1863. *Louvre.*

to represent gods. Actually it is very likely that the technique was even more shocking than the subject. With its freshness and vivacity of colour and its broad execution, the canvas seemed to have been painted on the very spot rather than in the studio. All this indicated on the part of the young artist an inexcusably warped character, an audacity which made him exceed the limits of decency. The rejection of convention, the boldness of the elements employed had at the time an aggressive character, which, in drawing the opprobrium of the righteous bourgeoisie down upon him, made Manet the leader of the young painters. His attitude became even more apparent at the Salon of 1865, where he exhibited *Olympia*. Zola found it the pictorial counterpart of the theories he was himself beginning to elaborate. He felt in the work, in its reaction against accepted standards, a frankness and certainty revealing an art already liberated and sure of itself, leaving all hesitations and gropings behind it. The public was offended by the presence of a black cat at the foot of the bed, and the Negress offering a bouquet of flowers seemed out of place. The critics, for their part, deplored the lack of shading, the brutality

of the drawing, and the crudity of the light, when they did not go so far as to insult. Jules Claretie, very categorical in his denunciations, typified the attitude adopted by the antagonists: 'What is this odalisque with the yellow belly, some indecent model picked up God knows where, presuming to represent Olympia ? Olympia ? What Olympia ? A prostitute, beyond a doubt. M. Manet will never be reproached for idealizing the foolish virgins–he'll drag them all through the mud, more likely.' The model Claretie so grossly insulted was the pretty Victorine Meurend, the central figure of *Le Déjeuner sur l'Herbe* before she became *Olympia* and who was to be *The Fifer* the following year. Today *Olympia* seems to us one of the finest achievements of modern art. In it one admires the unexpectedness of the pose, the firmness and purity of outline, the sincerity of the expression, and the consummate mastery of the composition. Enclosed in its abstract but still living whiteness, seldom has a woman's body known such nudity.

The painters a few years younger than Manet who were soon to create Impressionism did not underestimate the importance of these experiments. They recognized in Manet a percursor

MANET. THE FIFER. 1866.   *Louvre.*

behind whom they could gather to renew painting more drastically than the art of a Courbet or a
Corot had undertaken to do, much as they
admired those painters. Manet benefited in turn
from the good feeling of the younger men:
having set them the example of his mastery and
youthful boldness, he found them, with their
glorification of light colour, a stimulus and a
new source of inspiration. Although he did not
participate in the Impressionist exhibitions
organized after 1874, he felt the appeal of this
renovation, as his lightened palette testifies.
However, he did not become devoted to landscape for its own sake: his outdoor scenes always
contained figures, which were the occasion for
him to arrange, among the blue and grey reflections with which he surrounded them, dark
colours that were set off by the contrast. While
he shared with the Impressionists the desire to
express sense impressions in all their immediacy,

he never resorted to the systematic breakdown of
colour. Unlike his young friends, he had no
horror of black–quite the opposite. Black was to
him, as to Frans Hals, a real colour, which he
often used, and which gave an extraordinary
brightness to many of his compositions. Neither
was he haunted by plastic problems like Cézanne,
or obsessed with drawing like Degas. Manet did
not attempt to set up a system: less a thereti-
cian than a painter, instinctively inspired and
gifted, he wanted, above all, to re-create on
canvas the vividness and intensity of what he
experienced. No doubt he was always surprised
by the scorn he encountered in academic circles.
For a long time he persisted in exhibiting at the
Salon and ended by being awarded a secondary
medal that put him out of the running. But this
was in 1881, and his career was already fulfilled–
so much so, in fact, that the next year he was
made Chevalier of the Legion of Honour
(through the intervention of Antonin Proust,
his fellow student at the Collège Rollin, who had
by then become Minister of Fine Arts).

The art of Manet is an introduction to the
future, in its freedom of handling and the importance accorded to colour. Even when he applied
the pigments flat and refused to tone them down,
his colour retained spatiality, and this was probably his most characteristic contribution to the
art of his time. The importance he gave to colour
made him sometimes summarize the surface of a
volume in a few essential planes and sometimes,
on the contrary, adopt broad, uniformly coloured surfaces, as in *The Fifer*. It was in connection
with this canvas that Daumier accused him of
wanting to reduce painting to the 'faces on playing cards'. This was a failure to recognize the
boldness of Manet's experiment; for thus to
plant a figure in vivid and brilliantly coloured
dress against the emptiness of a monochrome
background suggested by Velasquez without
allowing such extreme simplification to end in
a total lack of life, called for the very surest kind
of hand. Although every shadow has disappeared and become concentrated in the vibrancy of
outline round the form, is it astonishing that this
mysterious process has not allowed either the
fluidity of outline or solidity of form to diminish.
The art of Manet, in spite of all innovations in
technique, is nevertheless bound to tradition,
because of the influences it has felt, and especially

because of the over-all concept of a picture that it presupposes. Like the very greatest artists, Manet was able to take a hackneyed theme and give it such life that it seemed new. Without proof, an unsuspecting person would not think of Rubens behind *Le Déjeuner sur l'Herbe* or Titian behind *Olympia*, and yet the relationship is indisputable. *La Pêche (Fishing)* mixes elements found in two works of Rubens: *The Rainbow* and *The Park of the Castle of Steen*; also from Rubens comes *The Nymph Surprised*, a reversed fragment from *Susanna at the Bath*. *The Dead Toreador* is a replica of *The Dead Warrior* of Velasquez, and *The Execution of Maximilian* a pendant to Goya's *The Second of May*. These are neither imitations nor plagiarism, but real creations starting from an external and independent reality, whether it be an object, a person, or another picture. No matter what theme he selected, Manet fits it to the measure of his own personality. There is no less intensity or life in the canvases inspired by classic works than there is in *The Bar at the Folies-Bergère*, the subject of which was taken from an episode in contemporary life; and this composition conforms to laws no less severe than the others do. Throughout all his changes Manet preserved a surprising unity. No doubt the ability of some men to invent a new vision, so unexpected that it comes as a surprise, and yet so perfectly in accord with still unformulated

MANET. PORTRAIT OF IRMA BRUNNER. 1882. PASTEL. *Louvre.*

aspirations, that its style immediately compels recognition, is a sign of genius. Works like these are of lasting value; when they can no longer surprise they become classics, for the feeling of life they diffuse bears witness to their truth.

Free as it may seem, the art of Manet is not improvised; his compositions are not the product of chance but are rigorously and purposefully constructed. He was not so entirely detached from the subject as might be believed, at least not so detached as his successors. He was easily tempted by large historical compositions, not only in his youth, as the works discussed above reveal, but also when he was in complete control of his powers: *The*

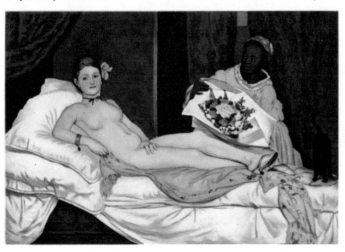

MANET. OLYMPIA. 1863.   *Louvre.*

Execution of Maximilian furnishes an example. In 1879 he even proposed to the Prefect of the Seine to decorate the Hôtel de Ville with compositions depicting Paris life: the markets, the railways, the bridges and the race-track. Finally, in 1881, he produced a picture on the escape of Henri de Rochefort from the Noumea penitentiary, which illustrated an event hardly seven years old. One can conclude that he did not have the reticence about anecdote, or even the distaste for it, that began with Impressionism, and was to become one of the principles of modern art.

The interest he took in human subjects made him one of the best portraitists of the nineteenth century. The numerous portraits he did of Berthe Morisot, particularly the one with the black hat, and those of Proust, Clemenceau, Théodore Duret, Zola, Irma Brunner and Méry Laurent, not to mention one of the finest, that of Stéphane Mallarmé, should not be forgotten. Towards the end of his life, when he began to feel the onset of paralysis, he took up pastels, easier to handle, and produced portraits of Parisian celebrities that are among his finest accomplishments. The natural elegance of his work permitted him to be a precise and exact observer, who never fell into the slightest

vulgarity. Although he always remained on the fringe of the Impressionist group and did not give up work in the studio for outdoor painting, as later artists did, Manet deserves the position of leader that is usually granted him in the history of Impressionism, for he was the first, and for years the only, painter to fight for a new art that sought a renewal of inspiration and technique in direct observation of Nature and contemporary life.

R. C.

MANGUIN Henri Charles (1874-1949). French painter; born in Paris; died at Saint-Tropez. Manguin's work can best be described as joyful painting: what it expresses is neither a burst of self-astonished happiness nor the exuberant joy of a moment or of a sequence of exceptional moments but a tranquil fulfilment conveying a feeling of duration. Bright but not violent tones, coloured harmonies without contrasts, everything blends in a serenity attained freely and effortlessly. To Fauvism (*), in which he ranks just below the great leaders, Manguin brought a vividness free from anxiety. One has only to analyse the means employed to see that this state of mind is apparent in every technical detail: the drawing is firm, without ever being

MANET. THE BAR AT THE FOLIES-BERGÈRE. 1882. *Courtauld Institut, London.*

stiff or brutal, the straight line is virtually proscribed, and every theme is resolved into flowing arabesques. The angles of the volumes soften, the object is not sharply isolated, everything harmonizes and interconnects, and the colour suggests and outlines the forms, whose relief calls for another set of colours rather than any real shadow. Certain nudes or still lifes are related to those of Matisse, but with less austerity and severity. Manguin never gives the impression of a will bent upon reaching a difficult goal. His charm is largely due to an air of facility, which one soon realizes to be the result of a thorough craftsmanship that allows extreme flexibility. Manguin's great merit is that he did not attempt to exceed his limits. In a period when a young artist was easily tempted to try to outdo his fellows, he was able to preserve enough calm to keep to the work that suited him; in a region where Nature offered the appeal of extreme colour (Manguin lived a great deal in the south of France), he could retain sufficient control to obey the dictates of his own taste. Thus his paintings still appear the harmonious result of the artist's expressing himself without reticence. Manguin belonged to the group of painters who, before the First World War, gave the Salon d'Automne in particular such a distinctive character, countering the austerity of Cubism with the vision of a joyously coloured world. R. C.

MARC Franz (1880-1916). German painter; born at Ried in Bavaria; killed at Verdun. Marc was the son of a Munich painter. In 1900 he decided to become a painter also and enrolled in the Academy. But his attainment of a style that was truly his own was to be long and arduous. He experienced years of deep depression. As early as 1903 a stay in Paris brought him in contact with Impressionism. The *Jugendstil (*)*, the most advanced movement in Munich, helped him state more clearly the problems of form. On a second visit to Paris, in 1909, he was strongly impressed by Van Gogh. In 1910 he met Macke, who was to remain his best friend, and a little later Kandinsky, with whom he was to fight for the new painting and publish the *Blaue Reiter (*)* almanac. In 1911 he came into his own. Between then and 1914, when he left for the war, he produced his best work.

Although problems of form occupied him, they were subordinated to his desire to express himself. He felt an almost religious need, as did

MANGUIN. JULY 14TH AT SAINT-TROPEZ. 1905.
Lucile Manguin Collection, Paris.

Kandinsky, to find through the work of art an objective and spiritual reality beyond the deceptive illusions of Nature. He freed himself only slowly from the wholly subjective sentimentality of his early work. His first step in this direction consisted in the choice of his subject-animals; beings involved in the universal harmony, capable of bringing the painter to a more objective realization of the world. Marc studied them for years before acquiring a thorough knowledge of their movements. This knowledge enabled him to find the essential form (*Wesensform*) in which all their tenderness, innocence and nobility could be contained. Thus *The Blue Horse* in its youthful vigour, *The Roe* cowering in a hollow of the wood, the beautiful and dangerous *Tiger* become, like *The Dog before the World*, the centre of a universe peculiar to themselves, and thereby they take on the force of symbols, the symbols of communion and peace.

After Pointillist experiments, Marc, having come in contact with Kandinsky and his friends,

MARC. TYROL. 1913-1914. *Bavarian State Museum, Munich.*

used colour in a free and expressive manner that recalled the Fauves. But for Marc nearly as much as for Macke the most important influence was Delaunay. In 1913 the coloured forms in his pictures, animals in their setting, began to interpenetrate, the colours brightened and grew more transparent, the forms more crystalline. To create new forms was to live. All living things drew closer and entered into the primal harmony. The large pictures of 1913 attain a mythic force which recalls the painting of the Douanier Rousseau, for whom Marc had a profound admiration. *The Destinies of the Animals* and *The Tower of the Blue Horses* are among the most important works of this period. However, the forces conflicting in the cosmic struggle of the large landscape *The Tyrol*, begun in 1913 and taken up again in 1914 had no further need of animal form to achieve expression. From then on Marc's course led towards an abstractionism bordering upon the play of the pure forces in a still undivided Nature. In the short time that remained before the war he finished a series of abstract compositions, profoundly lyrical (*Broken Forms, Serene Forms*).   F. M.

MARCOUSSIS Louis (1883-1941). His real name was Louis Markous, transformed into Marcoussis–after a village near Monthléry, outside Paris-by the poet Guillaume Apollinaire. He was born in Warsaw and died at Cusset, in the Allier, in central France. After his arrival in Paris in 1903 he exhibited at the Salon des Indépendants and the Salon d'Automne. Until 1907 he painted in the Impressionist style. In 1910, he met Apollinaire and Braque, who introduced him to Picasso and after that he took part in the experiments of the first Cubist painters and in 1912 was active with the *Section d'Or (*)* group. Even though he gave a vigorous structure to his landscapes and still-lifes, his style retained a poetic lightness, evident in subtle passages of colour and in an elliptical and sensitive line. From 1919 to 1928, he tried to avoid anything that might approach facility by using the technique of painting on glass, a process that does not allow for second thoughts or any unskilfulness. The result was about a hundred 'object-paintings' which, although they have a certain preciousness, are among the best of his works. His art, based upon a graceful balance, always evokes a season, the charm of a faintly seen light, a real and emotionally experienced atmosphere of tender, restrained lyricism. This obedience to the beauties of Nature and this understanding of the aerial density of space came only as the result of an inspired search for the secret rhythms that animate the universe.

Marcoussis presents a curious mixture of sensitivity, reason and submission to the supernatural, to signs and messages. The poet Max Jacob, one of his oldest friends, has told of Marcoussis' superstitions, his continual interpretation of events, the protection he invoked of 'benevolent' monuments, his communion with the dark forces of the earth and his sense of portents. Indeed, towards the end of his life Marcoussis devoted his final collection of drypoints to the theme of *Soothsayers*. In his painting, which always resembles a poetic or musical interpretation, he avoided the stylizations into which so many post-Cubist painters lapsed. He never strayed from the natural order, even when he strove to incorporate into it the notion of a beyond; but neither was he ever content with realistic description: until the end his severe landscapes and sober still-lifes revealed a vision of constantly renewed freshness.   J. LA.

opened his own office. In 1899, relinquishing that career, he enrolled at the Pennsylvania Academy of the Fine Arts in Philadelphia. Here he profited from the reaching of Thomas T. Anschutz and Henry Breckenridge before shifting to the Art Students' League in New York and then to France, the land of his paternal ancestors. After some study in various Parisian *ateliers* he applied himself to the craft of etching, which he learned largely by consulting the prints of Rembrandt and Whistler, whose stroke and shading appealed to his nature. He exhibited ten etchings in the Salon d'Automne of 1910. Then, after nearly six years of residence in France, he returned to the United States, exhibiting annually at '291' and participating, in 1913, in the New York Armory Show, which included such other innovators as Arthur Dove, Hartley and Weber. In 1936 the Museum of Modern Art in New York organized an important retrospective of his work, and in 1950 the Venice Biennale devoted two of its rooms to a fairly comprehensive showing of it. Marin's painting reveals a play of colours not dissimilar to that of the Fauves, though actually their work had touched him but little. Majestic and violent spectacles kindled him, and he resorted for motifs to the lines and volumes of skyscrapers and bridges, and the

MARIN John (1870-1953. American painter; born in Rutherford, New Jersey. Inevitably the name of John Marin is linked to the vanguard in American painting that developed once Alfred Stieglitz (*) had established his '291' gallery in New York in 1907. Also associated with this project were such rebels and forerunners as Marsden Hartley, Max Weber and Alfred Maurer, who likewise broke with the academic and sought new freedom. After some uncertainty, Marin had become an apprentice architect and then, in the mid-90s, he

MARCOUSSIS. THE PORT OF KÉRITY. 1927.
Musée d'Art Moderne, Paris.

more tumultuous aspects of sea and mountain. Great magnitude, in short, could compel him, though he strove endlessly for force and high expression, as well as for intensity of colour, which he would heighten by outbursts of lyricism sometimes almost ecstatic. He concerned himself somewhat less with the resolution of more strictly plastic problems, his object being to liberate the emotions he experienced before Nature and his other motifs. Yet, whatever his propensity for idealization, he never narrowed himself to a literal depiction of what gripped him. He endeavoured rather to transpose all such matter into some more tuneful substance, scoring it meanwhile with stenographic notations which he did not hesitate to push to the very limit of abstraction.   J. M.

MARINETTI Filippo Tommaso (1876-1944). Italian poet; born in Alexandria, Egypt; studied in Paris. Although he made a name by writing a play in French, *King Bombance*, which was produced at the Théâtre de l'Œuvre in 1909, his real title to fame is to have invented the word 'Futurism' for that movement, whose first manifesto he published in

the newspaper *Le Figaro* on February 20th, 1909. In it he wrote: 'Until now literature has glorified pensive immobility, ecstasy and sleep; we want to exalt aggressive movement, feverish insomnia, the quickstep, the somersault, the slap in the face and the punch'. But this was still only literature, and it was not until Marinetti met the Italian painters Carlo Carrà, Umberto Boccioni and Luigi Russolo in Milan that painting in turn became involved in the movement.

MARINOT Maurice (1889-1960). French painter; born and died at Troyes. He went to Paris in 1901 to train as a painter at the École des Beaux-Arts in Cormon's studio. Influenced by the works of the Impressionists, Gauguin and Cézanne, which he saw in exhibitions at Paris, his paintings between 1905 and about 1909 have a certain affinity with the Fauves, although he did not know them personally. Between 1905 and 1913, he exhibited regularly at the Salon des Indépendants and the Salon d'Automne. About 1911-1912, he went back to Troyes and began to learn glass-making. He spent all his time on it until 1937, when he took up painting again

MARIN. MAINE ISLANDS. WATER-COLOUR. 1922.
Phillips Collection, Washington.

222

MARQUET. COLONIAL ARMY SERGEANT. 1907.
Private Collection, New York.

A year later he painted landscapes and nudes that already showed his originality and independence. At the Salon des Indépendants in 1901, the Salon d'Automne, 1903, and the Berthe Weill Gallery his canvases hung next to those of Matisse. For this reason he has been considered one of the original Fauves. But he was really not allied to any group, although he was one of the young rebels who, at the turn of the century, made the last assault on the Impressionist stronghold. His alleged Fauvism was no more than the effect of an attack of fever transmitted by a band of boisterous artists, for never, even when he painted the *Fair at Le Havre* (1905) or the *Beach at Sainte-Adresse* (1906), the *Sergeant of the Colonial Troops* (1907), did Marquet regard colour as an end in itself or as a means of relieving emotions. Between 1909 and 1910 he worked occasionally at the Académie Ranson, where he met Jourdain and Manguin. In 1912 he accompanied Matisse on his trip to Morocco. The fever having abated, and each Fauve retired to his cage, Marquet followed his own inclina-

because the state of his health no longer allowed him to blow glass. In 1944, his studio was burnt down during the fighting that preceded the liberation of Troyes. Although his achievement in painting is modest, it deserves to be known. It is easily recognisable by Marinot's fondness for certain fresh red tones and a turquoise blue that appear in his glass. His glass work has made him one of the outstanding designers of our time. It was his work that made artists and the public alike appreciate the beauties inherent in glass, when it is treated, not for its brilliance and transparency, but for its mass and thickness. By doing this, he gave it back the dignity of a natural element.

MARQUET Albert (1875 - 1947). French painter; born in Bordeaux; died in Paris. Arriving in Paris as a young man, Marquet, like his friend Matisse was, from 1896, on, a pupil of Gustave Moreau. His beginnings were particularly difficult. To make a living he worked with Matisse on the Modern Style decoration of the Universal Exhibition of 1900.

MARQUET. WOMAN WITH A PARASOL. 1901.

MARQUET. QUAI CONTI. 1947.

ponderable, alert, so nervous is the execution, so quick the decision, so direct the painter's vision. A few horizontals, colour applied in thin layers, skilful composition, a refreshing spontaneity, a sure craftsmanship, along with taste, elegance, will and a quick intelligence–all these things are sufficient explanation for this landscapist's renown. Marquet gave the landscape and the seascape that intelligibility, simplicity and poise which the Impressionist works of a Monet or a Pissarro so lacked. It is gratifying, moreover, that he did not fall into the trap of facile picturesqueness and insipid sentimentality. Marquet's judgement was, in fact, as sure as his eye. One will remember his contempt for lyrical effusions, the concision of his style, and the sobriety of his means, although some will less readily accept another aspect of his classicism, a sometimes excessively bridled imagination and a temperament that modesty often restrained to the extreme. Marquet, in fact, had no other ambition than to set forth a faithful image of Nature. It was before Nature and in the midst of it that he felt happy. He experienced an ever-renewed pleasure in reproducing it. In this way he forgot man, who eventually disappeared from his work. At the beginning he showed promise of becoming a great portraitist and a great figure painter. One is inclined today to see in him only a specialist of harbours, beaches and bridges. Rather indifferent to humanity, whom he regarded without indulgence, he devoted all available emotion to Nature. At most he allowed himself to reduce it on his canvas to a simplified image. No daring transpositions, no marked distortions, but always the natural light, local tone, free-and-easy perspective characterize his landscapes; and it was always to his astonishing

tions. He who had painted portraits and nudes of such firm design and vigorous touch devoted himself entirely to landscape: the Seine, its quays and tugboats; the harbours of Fécamp, Honfleur, Algiers and Naples, of Hamburg and Stockholm; repeating untiringly the same themes and the same subjects: the Pont Neuf in various seasons, the Pont Neuf at dawn, at midday, at night, always the same Pont Neuf, but never the same picture. He did not make the slightest attempt to humour his public; the man who had refused the Legion of Honour, membership in the Institut de France and every other official recognition, who lived in simple, dignified solitude, working for his own pleasure, unconcerned with critics, art dealers and collectors, was above making any concession. A master draughtsman, Marquet reduced drawing to quick notations, concentrated it to the extreme and subordinated it to plain and limpid colour, seemingly monotonous, but varied in gradations. A picture by Marquet asserts itself by its harmony, its balance, its solidity and its stability, but has nothing that is heavy or strident. Masses, compact forms, a dense atmosphere, an almost solid light: all this appears nevertheless clear, im-

dexterity that he resorted rather than to the daring of speculation and instinct. A realistic painter, Marquet can no longer be regarded as a Fauve, even a repentant one. His credo was that of Poussin, of Corot, of Courbet. He was a master of line. His hasty pencil sketches, his drawings, which recall the strength of suggestion of the Japanese compel admiration. 'He is our Hokusai', Matisse said of him. It is perhaps into this minor part of his work that Marquet put the best of himself, his rigour, his fine sensitivity and the sharpness of his mind.   F. E.

MASSON André (born in 1896 at Balagny, France). After beginning his training at the Académie des Beaux-Arts in Brussels, he went to Paris in 1912 and entered the École des Beaux-Arts to learn mural painting. He owed as much to the work of thinkers and writers: Heraclitus, Nietzsche, Rimbaud, Lautréamont and Sade, as to the great painters: Poussin, Delacroix, Mantegna, Uccello, and later on El Greco and Piranesi. His meeting with Kahnweiler in 1922 enabled him to give all his time to painting. His work was influenced by Cubism and Juan Gris. In 1923, he painted his first uncompromisingly symbolical picture, *The Four Elements* which, when it was exhibited at the Galerie Simon the following year, attracted the attention of André Breton just before he published his first *Surrealist Manifesto*. He was then living at 45, rue Blomet, and with a group of friends among whom was Miró in the studio next door, Michel Leiris, Antonin Artaud, Georges Limbour, Roland Tual, he was drawn into the Surrealist movement and took an active part in it until 1929. He was particularly sensitive to the fundamental drama of existence and the interdependence that exists between all the particles of the universe, so that he always placed the individual in a carefully related setting, while he searched in his inner being for what made it move, act, love and suffer. His *Fights Between Fish* anticipate his later paintings of the struggles of human beings; their naked, overt cruelty is like the contortions of human love that are erotic without being obscene. For Masson, the earth only exists in state of fusion, its substances in a process of decomposition or consumption. Even when he surrendered

himself to automatic writing (*v.* Surrealism), the significant forms show that his hand had retained its accustomed exploration and fashioning of the material, so that from the background of sand, which he used in muted colours of brown and delicate green, the sinuous, incisive line stands out in variations of upstrokes and downstrokes.

Masson found Spain a land after his own heart. After visiting Andalousia, he stayed a long time at Tossa, in Catalonia, from 1934 to 1936, painting insects and bull-fights. When the Civil War broke out, his works were a testimony to his rejection of oppression (he was once again to make the same rejection in distressing, personal circumstances during the Algerian war). In connection with this, Breton spoke about his *œuvre d'art-événement* with its power of revelation.

In 1941, Masson at first took refuge in Martinique, then in North America, where he stayed until 1945. He found a new source of inspira-

MASSON. AMPHORA. 1925.
Louise Leiris Gallery, Paris.

MATISSE. WOMAN IN A BLOUSE, DREAMING. 1936. INDIAN INK.

finished his secondary studies he was employed as a clerk in a solicitor's office at Saint-Quentin. His interest in art was awakened in 1890 during an illness, when he read a treatise on painting by Goupil. At this time he painted his first picture, a still-life with a tobacco jar. He took evening courses at the Quentin-Latour Municipal School and finally obtained his father's permission to go to work in Paris, first at the Académie Julian (*) and then at the École des Beaux-Arts, where he enrolled in the studio of Gustave Moreau. There he made the acquaintance of Rouault, Camoin and, especially, Marquet, with whom he was to remain particularly friendly. His teacher urged him to study both Nature and the masters. Acting on this advice, he made many drawings from Nature and haunted the Louvre, where he executed numerous copies from Philippe de Champaigne, Poussin and Chardin. At this time his art was extremely conservative and tradition-al: an example can be found at the Museum of Modern Art in Paris in the *Breton Weaver* of 1896. In this painting, greys, so frequent in French painting from Louis Le Nain to Corot, are used

tion in Negro and Red Indian myths and the violence of his expression and brushwork in-fluenced the development of young American painting. When he returned to France, he settled in Aix-en-Provence (1947-1956) and once again found an inexhaustible source of inspir-ation in nature and the elements. His art lost the harshness that had sometimes grated and acquired directness of expression through a more flexible idiom. The infinite variety of the visible world came as a magic revelation to him. Retrospective exhibitions of paintings and drawings (Masson's illustrative work is considerable) were followed by an exhibition of the large paintings of 1960 and 1961 at the Galerie Louise Leiris, whose concentrated style was a culmination of preceding manners and a paean to the forces of nature and their symbolism.   J. LA.

MATISSE Henri (1869-1954). French paint-er; born at Le Cateau, in the north of France; died in Cimiez near Nice. Matisse's father was a grain merchant and his mother an amateur painter of some talent. After having

MATISSE. WOMAN WITH A GREEN HAT. 1905. *Private Collection, San Francisco.*

with extreme subtlety, and re-create beautifully the dark, soft atmosphere of the room in which the craftsman is at work. It was natural, then, that Matisse should participate in the very official Salon of the National Society of Fine Arts, where he exhibited canvases such as *La Desserte* (*The Sideboard*) of 1897. Meanwhile, when he was in Brittany, he met John Russell, a friend of Monet's, who introduced him to the work of the Impressionists. This discovery was the beginning of his adventurous and triumphant career. The influence is apparent in the seascapes he painted in 1897 at Belle-Isle in Brittany, where Monet had already worked, as well as in the landscapes executed in Corsica the following year and on the French Riviera. His palette grew brighter and more varied, the drawing became less conventional and revealed a more definite personality; an effort to portray the brilliance of light was evident. But he had already parted ways with the Impressionists: whereas they intended to transcribe the atmosphere that envelops objects, softens forms and veils colours, he chose to express a light that heightens tones, asserts contours and clarifies forms by simplifying them. The fact that he preferred the landscapes of Southern regions, more highly coloured, more regular, more constructed, to those of the Ile-de-France and Normandy, is in itself significant. Little wonder, then, that he should have undergone successively the influence of various painters who, while connected with Impressionism, had tried to go beyond it: Cézanne, on the one hand, and the Neo-Impressionists on the other. The influence of Cézanne, one of whose *Bathers* he purchased and later gave to the Petit Palais, is apparent in a series of pictures, especially still-lifes and nudes (*Models in the Studio* sequence, 1900; *Carmelina*, 1903). Here the colour is intense but rather dark, the drawing vigorous, the form built up with broadly simplified planes. On the other hand, he drew his inspiration from the Neo-Impressionists in various Parisian landscapes and in a few compositions which he painted according to the Divisionist technique. It is characteristic that Signac should have bought one of these, *Luxe, calme et volupté* (1905). In fact Matisse had just spent the summer of 1907 at Saint-Tropez with Signac and Cross.

Fortified by his experiments and research,

MATISSE. OPEN WINDOW. COLLIOURE. 1905.
Private Collection, New York.

which showed his methodical but wilful genius, he was ready for the peremptory assertion of his personality and art that would be shown in his Fauvist manner, about 1905-1908. In contrast to Vlaminck, Fauvism (*) for Matisse was less a question of heightened sensation than an attempt to reduce the whole art of painting to colour and a few other fundamental elements, chiefly line and rhythm, the necessary and sufficient resources with which the painter can realize himself. 'You are going to simplify painting', Gustave Moreau had predicted to him, and in fact Matisse jettisoned all the impedimenta which since the sixteenth century had encumbered its course, to rediscover the ease and mobility of the traveller without luggage, ready for any adventure. No more 'passages', those pictorial equivalents of the transitions that poets and novelists were giving up at the same time: colours were laid on straight one against the other, and frequently collided, if the combination served to heighten them; but if this was to be avoided, a thick black line around the forms separated them or the white of the canvas was left visible. 'Values' were also abandoned: instead of diversifying the tones by a minute mixture of light and shadow, Matisse unified

MATISSE. GOLDFISH. 1914.
Private Collection, New York.

them and spread out in large sheets, finding other means to express light and model form. These, or rather *this*, other means was colour and relations of colours. In fact, by choosing his tones and establishing relations between them, the painter transcribed the colour of the object (itself a synthesis of the local tone in combination with light), the form of the object, the luminosity of space and depth. Refusing the techniques of *trompe-l'œil* and perspective–for he did not want to hollow out the picture and conceal its nature as a plane surface–he resorted to oppositions of tones: behind the coloured figures, for example, he spread out zones of various colours which, in their relation to one another and to the figures themselves, give an impression of space, a space full of light, without hiding the fact that the picture is a plane without depths. This was a rediscovery (unpremeditated, in fact, not an imitation) of the solution of the Romanesque painters; the stripes of various colours that can be seen, for example, in the frescoes of the Oberzell and the Niederzell on Lake Constance find their equivalent in those which Matisse introduced into his picture *Luxe* (1907), the only difference being that he used them with a representational intent, making

them suggest the beach, the sea, the mountains, the sky. Rhythm and the arabesque, towards which his line often tended, were, along with colour, Matisse's fundamental resources during his Fauvist period. That time witnessed an abundant flowering of masterpieces, such as the *Open Window* (1905), the *Young Sailor* (1906), *Still-life with a Red Carpet* (1906, Musée de Grenoble), *La Joie de Vivre* (1906), *Margot* (1907), *La Desserte, Harmonie Rouge* (1908), *Dance* and *Music* of 1909-1910 (now in the Museum of Western Art at Moscow), which was commissioned by the great collector, Stchoukine, and the *Red Studio* (1911).

But the influence of Cézanne was beginning to be felt more and more strongly by young painters: first Derain, then Dufy, Vlaminck and Friesz developed a feeling for construction; Braque went as far as Cubism, soon followed by Picasso and then Léger, Gris, Lhote and La Fresnaye. Matisse, who had been in touch with Picasso, was not the last to give up Fauvism (a trip to Morocco in 1911-1912 particularly accelerating his evolution) to practise a kind of painting that was, if not Cubist, at least so Cézannesque that it sometimes verged on Cubism. *The Three Sisters*

MATISSE. NUDE. INK. 1936.

MATISSE. RED STUDIO. 1911.   *Museum of Modern Art, New York.*

(1916), of the Paul Guillaume collection, *Les Demoiselles à la Rivière* (1916-1917), the *Moroccans on the Terrace* (1916, Museum of Modern Art, New York) the *Piano Lesson* (Museum of Modern Art, New York) and finally the series of *Studios on the Quai Saint-Michel*, of which the Museum of Modern Art in Paris possesses one of the finest examples (*The Painter and His Model*, 1917), reveal the painter given over to an austere chromatism in which blacks, greys, ochres, and forms harder and stricter than those of the Fauvist manner predominate. The sinuous arabesques have given way to straight lines that break into segments and assemble in right or acute angles. The rhythms are jerky, syncopated, and elliptical. The transcription of Nature is still bolder and the interpretation of space more radical. The art of Matisse adopted a slightly contorted look, revealing an inner tension in the painter, the tension that brings about new investigations and the need to transcend oneself.

Every period of tension is necessarily followed by a period of release. A sequence of favourable circumstances, just after the First World War, brought about this release in the art of Matisse:

the euphoria of victory, the discovery of Mediterranean nature (he then established himself at Nice, which became his adopted home), and finally success. For about ten years he had undoubtedly taken on the appearance of the head of a school and had seen a flock of pupils, particularly foreigners, hurrying to the Academy that he had founded in Paris at the former Couvent des Oiseaux. But it was a success felt only by the few. After 1919, however, he won international and universal renown. It is not difficult to understand, therefore, why he should have drifted towards a more amiable art, especially since the same development can be observed at that time in nearly all the painters, from Dufy and Derain to Braque and Picasso. A return to bright colours, less intense and bold than in the days of Fauvism, but fresher and sprucer, in which reds play a leading part; a return to a flowing line of enveloping flexibility, an introduction of very light modelling in the figure, which does not break the unity of the surface; a recourse, to obtain a decorative effect, to certain artifices, such as the representation of hangings with large designs, of tiles, flowered textiles, and Oriental

MATISSE. GIRL IN A WHITE DRESS. 1941. *Private Collection, Paris.*

The synthesis of the complementary tendencies of his genius thus achieved was afterwards evident in all his works, particularly after the execution of a vast decoration on the theme of *The Dance* at the Barnes Foundation in Merion, Pennsylvania (1931-1933), had obliged him to summon up all his resources and take his bearings. For him this was an opportunity to set out again more resolutely than ever. He demanded more of colour than he ever had in the past, either by risking tonal harmonies of unheard-of violence (*The Rumanian Blouse*, 1940) or by establishing a chromatic unity, often red, across his whole canvas, as in the *Still-Life with a Magnolia* of 1941, or in *The Large Interior in Red* of the Museum of Modern Art in Paris (1948), or even in a successful attempt to make black a colour radiating light and almost insupportably intense (*Bed Jacket on a Black Background*, 1939). The drawing became both more flexible and more rigorous and synthetic, more abstract and suggestive and, finally, so bold that it shrank before no interpretation of Nature and the human figure (*Asia*, 1944; *The English Girl*, 1947). The form, flat once more, had none the less great power and this power is due as much to the line surrounding the form and the tones that suggest its mass as to the rythms that animate it with a candid and imposing simplicity (*Jeune Fille en robe blanche*, 1941). The universe of Matisse, composed invariably of young and beautiful women, exotic plants, flowers and fruits, birds, luxurious objects, idleness and sun, testifies to an ever bolder daring of imitation, the fruit of liberty acquired by the painter through mastery of his art and his constant efforts to renew, surpass and enrich himself, always by simplifying himself more radically. If the starting-point for this final synthesis was the decoration of the Barnes Foundation, its climax was the chapel of the Convent of Dominican Nuns at Vence, finished in 1951. There Matisse not only said his last word as a painter, a painter

rugs in the background: it is by these various characteristics that the manner in which Matisse worked between 1919 and 1927 can be defined. His favourite theme was the *Odalisque*. Two words describe the works of this period adequately: ease and grace – ease at having mastered the craft to the point of such assurance that he could be allowed to rest, and grace in the creation of a universe of children, young women, precious fabrics, flowers, leisure, luxury, and light. Matisse enjoyed his success for a while and, as a result, was able to create abundantly, without effort, without anxiety. But he soon grew tired of this oasis of facility and, as early as 1928, he resumed his investigations and again moved towards grandeur and strength. In the *Decorative Figure on an Ornamental Background* of 1927-1928 (Museum of Modern Art, Paris) one sees straight lines meeting at right angles, lines broken into short segments, a hard and powerful form whose bold synthesis bears witness to daring invention, majestic construction (echoed the same year in *The Green Buffet*) and the clearly stated will to make things severe, grandiose, and new. But this time Matisse did not renounce the characteristics of his former manner: richness of the palette, suppleness of arabesques, decorative sumptuousness, and glorification of the sweetness of life.

who renounced colour to content himself with white and an ochre verging on black, but also brought to a conclusion the investigations that he had pursued for a long time in the other arts.

One cannot pass over in silence Matisse's activity in fields other than painting: as an engraver he executed a great number of plates and about ten books, notably Mallarmé's *Poems* (1932), Montherlant's *Pasiphaé* (1944), *Letters to a Portuguese Nun* (1946), *Les Fleurs du Mal* (1947), Ronsard's *Amours* (1948) and the *Poems* of Charles d'Orléans (1950). As a sculptor Matisse has to his credit an imposing number of works, which constitute one of the most important monuments of contemporary sculpture, both on account of their intrinsic beauty and because of the lesson of invention and renewal that they provide. Finally, a special place belongs to the cut-outs, which occupied the artist a great deal in his last years, and with which he created

MATISSE. PLUM TREE BRANCH ON A GREEN BACKGROUND. 1948. *Private Collection, New York.*

masterpieces like *The Negro Boxer* (1947) and *The Sadness of the King* (1952, Musée d'Art Moderne, Paris). Never, indeed, had he manifested such imagination of design; the scissors seem to have allowed him to bestow upon colour an inventive composition that surpassed in daring the chromatism of his former work. A triumph of arabesque and pure colour, his *papiers collés (*)* are perhaps the supreme expression of his genius, while at the same time they represent his discovery of a new domain: there is, in fact, nothing in common between those he did and what the Cubists had produced in 1911-1914.

Important because of the diversity of his work and the new horizons he opened to art, Matisse is no less so because of the example of his powerful personality. In complete opposition to Picasso, he remained close to the tradition of French art and the French spirit, to the line of lucid and determined artists who created with 'clear and distinct' ideas deliberate, conscious and long-thought-out works. It is not surprising, then, that a man of his stamp should have written some of the most pertinent observations on painting–and notably on his own–that have

MATISSE. SAINT DOMINIC. 1947-1951. *Vence Chapel.*

come from the pen of an artist (cf. his *Notes of a Painter* published in the *Grande Revue*, December 25th, 1908). What characterizes his art is first an admirable logic, as witnessed the care he always took to use his most varied tools and techniques in conformity with the requirements of their nature. If he drew with the pen, it being the nature of the pen to trace a precise and clean line, he made use of the line and the line only to express everything–contour, form, light, even matter. If, on the other hand, he used charcoal, whose property is to crumble, and thus to permit the indication of values and shades, he executed drawings in which form grew exclusively out of the play of blacks, greys, and whites. Matisse was logical, lucid and determined. Nothing in his art was left to chance. He wrote: 'Composition should in itself be a form of expression and

MATISSE. THE YOUNG ENGLISH GIRL. 1947.
Private Collection.

be modified by the surface area to be covered. If I take a piece of paper of a particular size, I do a drawing on it that is necessarily related to its size. I do not repeat the same drawing on another sheet with different proportions... An artist who wants to transfer a composition from one canvas to another and larger canvas, should replan it and change its appearance to preserve its character, and not simply place it on the rectangle.' Matisse made no brush stroke or pencil line that was not actuated by reflection. But nothing could be freer or more natural than his art, and these qualities it owes to his method of work. Having prepared for his important works by a great number of drawings, sketches, and studies, he often executed the final work in a single session, so as to preserve all the life of a sketch. Thus the movement of passion joined the equilibrium of thought to make this refined art a creation of inexhaustible richness and salutary complexity. Essentially modern, although rooted in the oldest French tradition, an echo of our present experiments and the fruit of an ancient culture as well as of a spirit that has survived, unchanged, alterations in aesthetics and civilization, the art of Matisse, a bridge between yesterday and tomorrow, constitutes one of the most important expressions of the painting of today, and will doubtless dominate and fertilize that of tomorrow. B. D.

MERZ Invented by the German painter Kurt Schwitters *(*)* in 1919, this term seems to derive from a part of the word *kommerziell*, torn from a newspaper, which appeared glued in one of his first *Merzbilder* or *collages*. From 1923 to 1932 Schwitters published a magazine under the name *Merz*, with the co-operation of Arp, Lissitzky, Mondrian, Van Doesburg, and many others. Nothing could better describe what Schwitters meant by *Merz* than the definition of the word *Nature* that he copied from a German dictionary, to have it printed in large red letters on the cover of an issue of his magazine (April-July, 1924): 'Nature, from the Latin *nasci,* means to become, to come from; that is to say, all that through its own force develops, forms and moves'. The same issue further reads: 'The modern world is the other half of nature, the half that comes from man'. Thus Schwitters took all the cast-off things of everyday life and made them into abstract works, which had no other purpose than to continue Nature through man, but which are moving in their humility, in all the human delicacy they contain and unknowingly communicate. Schwitters' *collages* and compositions (*Merzbilder* or Merz-Pictures) are among the most curious and rare productions of the Dada *(*)* movement. M. S.

METAPHYSICAL PAINTING *See* Peinture métaphysique.

METZINGER Jean (1883-1957). Born at Nantes. He began to paint at fifteen. The emotion he experienced before a picture by Ingres was at the root of his desire to paint. While continuing his studies, he achieved success in local exhibitions, and this incited him to devote himself entirely to painting and settle in Paris. He attended various academies, where the instruction disappointed him because it made painting dependent upon imitation of Nature or of the old masters. For Metzinger there could be no real relationship between the object that the picture constitutes and the other object it represents; the picture had no other value than the particular pleasure produced by its combination of forms and colours. In his search for the laws that govern these relations

MATISSE. NEGRO BOXER. CUTOUT. 1947.
Musée d'Art Moderne, Paris.

and control their effectiveness, Metzinger was first influenced by the Neo-Impressionists and then by the Fauves, who were occupied with the chemistry of colour and attempted to influence the aspect of the pictorial image. But desiring a more coherent construction, he endeavoured to discover the structure of objects. He joined the young painters who, from 1908 onwards, were working along similar lines in the wake of Picasso and Braque. At first Cubism was their common need to emerge from the old ambiguity and restore primal purity to artistic creation. Metzinger took part in the famous Salon des Indépendants of 1911 and in the meetings and exhibitions of the *Section d'Or (*)*. With Gleizes, in 1912, he published *On Cubism*, the first theoretical work on the movement to

MATISSE. STILL-LIFE. 1941. INDIAN INK.

METZINGER. STILL-LIFE. 1917.

be written by painters who participated in it. He took care, however, to avoid a purely abstract manner, endeavouring to express the general harmony of the model by emphasizing characteristic details. He helped to create one of the styles of the period, in which objects rendered by their surfaces are surrounded by a kind of halo that becomes a plane in itself. His work, which he continued on the same principles until his death, aided by a very sure technique, maintained remarkable unity and was an example of what a sensitive human artist was able to draw from the Cubist experiment.   J. LA.

MIRÓ Joan (born in 1893 at Barcelona). Miró is a native of a province that, more than any other part of Spain, has always been the favoured spot of arts and artists. After having served as a bridge between East and West, Catalonia was the cradle of the Romanesque Style. Workshops of illuminators and famous fresco painters flourished there in the Middle Ages, and finally modern art recruited some of its boldest pioneers there. From Catalonia came Miró and Dali in particular, two of the chief creators of the Surrealist movement. At

fourteen Miro entered the School of Fine Arts of Barcelona. Later he attended courses at the Gali Academy. In 1915 he felt official teaching did more harm than good, and he decided to work alone. He had the good fortune to be taken up by Dalmau, the perspicacious manager of an important art gallery in Barcelona. It was Dalmau who, in 1918, organized the first exhibition of his protégé. Some works like the *Portrait of Ricart* (1917) were influenced by Van Gogh and the Fauves. After a short stay in Paris (1919) when he made friends with Picasso, his painting caught the beneficial germ of Cubism, although it remained definitely representational, if not imitative. The drawing was dry, planes sharply evident, the colours light without intensity. In 1921 the critic Maurice Raynal presented at La Licorne Gallery in Paris, which no longer exists, an important group of Miró's canvases. Connoisseurs did not fail to observe the incompatibility of Cubism with the temperament of the Catalan painter, with his instinct, his native ingenuousness, his fundamental anti-intellectualism, and his already asserted passion for colour. It was not among painters or through study of the works of the masters that he came to recognize his calling but by associating with poets and the young rebels who were preparing to set off the bomb of Surrealism. He first made the acquaintance in 1922 of Michel Leiris, Roland Tual, Georges Limbour and Antonin Artaud, then in 1924 he met Breton, Éluard and Aragon. No one was, in fact, less suited to speculation and less willing to tolerate restraint and discipline than Miró.

An anarchist by birth, naturally hostile to any tradition or cult, either of Nature or of museums, his enthusiastic enlistment in a movement that proclaimed the bankruptcy of the intellect, contempt for reality, and the sovereignty of intuition can be easily understood. For two years, dividing his time between Barcelona and Paris, he continued to execute landscapes and representational still-lifes (*The Farm* (1922), *The Ear of Corn* (1923)). In 1924 he finished his first definitely subjective and unrealistic picture, *Turned Soil*. At the same time he signed the first *Manifesto of Surrealism* published by André Breton. In November 1925 he participated in the first exhibition of the Surrealist group at the Galerie Pierre. In collaboration with Max Ernst, he designed the settings and costumes of *Romeo and Juliet* for the *Ballets Russes (*)* of Diaghilev. From this period dates *Harlequin's Fair* (1925), in the Albright Art Gallery of Buffalo.

His works were already very characteristic of his art as we admire it today. All of Miró is in them, with his schematic forms, his powerful, heavy 'spots', his patiently prepared grounds, and also his fantasy, his humour, his freshness of emotion, his innate affinity for the craftsmen of the African jungles or the American prairie. These are complex works, overburdened but already containing the repertoire of signs that Miró had only to amplify, particularize and accentuate in order to achieve the paradoxical mastery that makes the value and originality of his current work. In 1928 he visited Holland. He exhibited for the first time in the United States at the Valentine Galleries in New York. The same year he showed his *papiers collés (*)* at the Galerie Goemans, Brussels. In 1932 the Ballets de Monte Carlo commissioned the settings and costumes for *Jeux d'Enfants* from him. He executed a large mural decoration for the Paris Exhibition of 1937. In 1940, obliged to leave France, he returned to Catalonia and soon settled at Palma in Majorca. Withdrawn from the tumult of arms, he continued to paint, took up litography and, in collaboration with Artigas, ceramics (1944). In 1947, he went to the United States for the first time, where he was commissioned to decorate the Gourmets restaurant in Cincinnati with a mural painting. After his return to Europe in 1948, he divided his time between Paris and Barcelona. His reputation was growing and his activities were becoming more widespread. He experimented in techniques, other than painting, with equal

success. Important commissions were given to him: a mural painting for Harvard in 1950 and seven years later two walls in ceramic for the UNESCO building at Paris. Since the war, the Galerie Maeght has held several exhibitions of his recent paintings, ceramics, tapestries and polychrome wood. In 1956, he finally made his home at Palma in Majorca. In the space of a few years, in spite of the unusualness of his art, he has become world famous. He was given the official honour of a retrospective exhibition at the Musée National d'Art Moderne at Paris in 1962.

His career, clearly enough, offers nothing to captivate amateurs of the picturesque and unforeseen. Besides, he has not made the least attempt to ornament it or bestow the romantic touch of which the public is so fond. It offers neither comment nor confidence: Miró is a silent man. Even though his work is dirgged into the limelight by his admirers, he himself remains in the background, reserved, unobtrusive and unnoticed. No one has solicited or intrigued less

MIRÓ. SNOB EVENING AT THE PRINCESS'S. 1944.

to assert himself and to make himself known. But no one has ever asserted himself and become known in less time. How can this be explained, if not by the fact that his painting came to fill a gap, to satisfy a need and to offer something that other painters, even the greatest among them, have denied?

What is there in a picture by Miró that casts such an irresistible spell over the spectator? Is it form? There are no forms, only elements, embryos of forms, rudimentary figures like the *graffiti* that children scratch on walls, signs that recall those engraved in caves by prehistoric man. Is it colour? With Miró, to be sure, the lyricism of colour recovers 'its significance at the point where the Fauves and Matisse had left it', as Maurice Raynal has said. Observe, however, how restricted Miró's palette is: a few elementary

MIRÓ. FRAGMENT OF A TRIPTYCH. 1939.
Private Collection, Paris.

colours, blue, vermilion, yellow, green, black, used sparingly but with assurance and infallible accuracy. Nor is it composition. Miró seems to throw lines and spots nonchalantly on to his canvas, unconcerned with their interrelations, or the requirements of space and depth. Blood-red or electric-blue crescents, black masses softly spread, cells holding their nuclei like targets, childish silhouettes daubed with artificial carelessness, hairy placentas entangled in their cords: a whole world, unexpected, whimsical, droll, larvae, madrepores, spasmodic amœbas, long and sinuous filaments, vagrant lines ending in a kind of cup-and-ball or kite. It is a dreamworld transcribed by a master technician. One can understand, therefore, why André Breton could write in 1928: 'Miró is probably the most Surrealistic of us all'. Miró is a Surrealist quite naturally, without recourse to artifice or attitudinizing, with sincerity and humility. He is, in fact, the only Surrealist painter with no contempt for the resources of his art or the constraints of his profession. Although there is neither subject nor object, neither volume nor logical construction in his painting, it is undoubtedly plastic. And because of its plasticity it has survived the breakdown of Surrealism (*). But this is not enough to explain the fascination it exercises. Tired of studio experiments, aesthetic demonstrations and rhetoric, we find in Miró's work a fresh spring water to dispel our fever and clear our head. Here at last is a painter who poses no problems, for he is aware of none; who resorts to the conveniences of tradition no more than to the calculated extravagance of the professional avant-garde; who refuses the legacy of his predecessors and does not try to outdo anyone. He does not reinvent painting, he invents it, like primitive man or a child. He does not speak any of the idioms current in our time, but the time is nevertheless grateful to him for speaking a language it has forgotten but still longs for. A poetry of the unutterable, of the unreal, of germinations and beginnings, is the secret of his power. He will never be the head of a school or the advocate of a trend. Unclassifiable, unassimilable, inimitable, in complete simplicity, complete innocence, he holds a place apart in contemporary art. It is not the highest place, but it is the least disputed. F. E.

MODERN-STYLE A term for the movement that developed about 1895-1910, called *Jugendstil* in Germany and, in general, *Art nouveau* or *Style 1900* (vide *Jugendstil*).

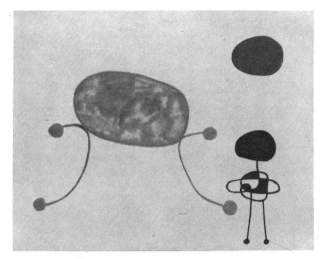

MIRÓ. PERSON LOOKING AT THE SUN. 1942.
Private Collection, Basel.

MODERSOHN-BECKER Paula (1876-1907). German painter; born at Dresden, died in Worpswede, near Bremen. After training as a teacher at the insistence of her parents, she decided to become a painter and, when she was twenty years old, joined the Berlin Art School. The following year, in 1897, she made her first acquaintance with the colony of artists at Worpswede, who were painting in the lyrical manner of Böcklin's landscapes. In the autumn of 1898, she finally went to live with them and became one of Mackensen's students. However, she very soon reacted against the decorative naturalism of her teacher, which she thought too representational, and searched instinctively for a more subjective, more severe conception of art in which illusionist space would be eliminated. Her first visit to Paris in 1900 gave her a chance of seeing for the first time at Vollard's, some paintings of Cézanne. She assimilated his strict construction, the high viewpoints that drew the subjects nearer the picture surface and the arrangement of planes by successive steps, but she did not follow Cézanne's method of creating space by colour alone, in fact her paintings remained more analytical.

Returning to Worpswede, she married one of the painters of the group, Otto Modersohn. In her determined search for a personal idiom, she returned to Paris three more times, in 1903, 1905 and 1906 and each visit gave her an opportunity to extend and deepen her understanding of the leading modern painters. There were two decisive events on her last visit: her meeting with the sculptor, Bernhard Hoetger, who was the first person to give her art an unreserved admiration, and the great retrospective exhibition of Gauguin's work at the Salon d'Automne, which confirmed her own method of composition by large, flat areas of colour, surrounded by a strong line. Gauguin's example also encouraged her in the last year of her life—she died a year later—to begin the large compositions in a monumental, archaic manner with simplified lines and deeper colours, which made her reputation.

It is to her credit that she studied and assimilated the lessons of the French Post-Impressionists before they were widely known in Germany. This attitude was encouraged by the advice of Rainer-Maria Rilke, who stayed in 1902 at Worpswede, with his wife, Clara Westhoff, who was a sculptor and Rodin's pupil. Paula Modersohn-Becker's reputation, however, was slow to establish itself. The only exhibition of her work, during her lifetime, which was held at the Kunsthalle at Bremen in 1899, was a failure. Although she is now considered a precursor of Expressionism, she certainly does not illustrate what are known as Germanic tendencies: a love of excess, a febrile creativeness and obsessive themes. She followed instead the example of Cézanne and Gauguin in her completely objective approach to her art in which she rejected the popular individualism of the day so that she could emphasise the unchanging essence and universality of human beings and things. She died when she was hardly thirty-one, three weeks after the birth of a little girl. It was at her death that Rainer-Maria Rilke wrote his *Requiem for a Friend.* She was a very gifted woman with the unerring instinct of a true artist. She left a valuable collection of letters and a diary which reveals her strength of mind and her simplicity and generosity.   E. R.

MODIGLIANI Amedeo (1884-1920). Italian painter; born in Leghorn; died in Paris. The widow of a ruined banker, his mother recognized her son's calling early and never opposed it. She acquainted him with all the Italian museums and sent him to work at academies in Florence and Venice. Finally, in 1907, he arrived in Paris. Handsome, aristocratic in appearance, but already a prey to tuberculosis, he soon became one of the eccentric young men of Montmartre, where he lived for six years, taciturn, prodigal, moving incessantly from lodging to lodging, wandering from café to café, but also participating in aesthetic battles, drawing, sculpting, painting pictures. He took part in the discussions at the Bateau-Lavoir *(*).* His tall, languid figure could be seen in the same places that had been frequented by Toulouse-Lautrec, whose work he admired at the

time. The offspring of the upper middle class, he showed humanitarian tendencies. His love of the humble people, the pity he had for the outcasts of fortune, he expressed in his actions, his work and his choice of models: the daughter of his concierge, sickly children, girls of the lower classes. In 1909, he left Montmartre for a studio in the Cité Falguière, where he made friends with the sculptor, Brancusi, who was his neighbour. Like so many other painters, he, too, discovered Cézanne at the large retrospective at the Bernheim gallery, in 1910, and then Negro sculpture, which thereafter exercised a profound influence on his drawing. From his contact with Brancusi he felt a need to carve stone himself. He is the maker of statues that were, unfortunately, never finished. To be sure, plastic art was less his medium than drawing. He was a familiar figure in Montparnasse, at that time, a prowler, miserable, full of alcohol, drugs and talent, wasting his gifts as he did his money. He never, in fact, had enough money to live. He used to sell his admirable drawings for a few *sous,* drawings jotted down with a disconcerting sureness, and his portraits and nudes for a few francs. He was frequently to be seen on the terrace of the *Rotonde,* or the *Dôme,* drawing portraits with an acute, rapid stroke, and then offering them to his chance models in exchange for a drink. Then he worked in the studio of Kisling. Soutine and Pascin were his friends. He drifted from café to café and from attic to attic, occasionally finding a haven or a compassionate soul. An English woman poet, Beatrice Hastings, supported him for some time; Zborowski sheltered him later and denied himself necessities in order that his protégé might paint. He met a young girl, Jeanne Hébuterne, married her and fathered a child. Consumed by fever, overwhelmed by tuberculosis, he entered a hospital, where he died on the 25th of January, 1920, in his thirty-sixth year, murmuring

MODERSOHN-BECKER. NUDE GIRL WITH FLOWERS. 1907.
Private Collection, Wuppertal.

'Cara, Cara Italia !'. On the day of his funeral, which was organized by André Salmon and Kisling, and made something of a sensation, his wife jumped from a fifth floor and was killed.

The compatriot of Duccio, Castagno and Botticelli, Modigliani was, above all, a linearist, a draughtsman and a mannerist. Colour adds nothing to drawing in his pictures, although it is applied with accuracy and is both resonant and enjoyable. Nevertheless, Modigliani, loyal in this respect to the Tuscan tradition, expressed himself entirely through drawing, in the flexible, subtle, melodious line which for a time was perhaps excessively prized. Elegant and frail, supple to the point of preciosity, with what indulgence it curves in upon the oval of a face, turns round a shoulder, excessively lengthens a neck, accentuates a hip ! And how it dominates the form and suffices for volume and space ! Modigliani answered in his own way the question raised by the Cubists. The Cubists tried to render the object in its totality by multiplication of the points of view. Modigliani was aware of the experiments of Picasso and Braque, but he was neither a constructor nor a synthesist. His intelli-

MODIGLIANI. LITTLE GIRL IN BLUE.
Private Collection, Paris.

gence was not adapted to organization and reflection. He was therefore prudent enough to refuse to join the Cubist band. He resorted to distortion rather than to invention and to techniques rather than to a coherent system. Although, like the Cubists, he was indifferent to light, atmosphere and *sfumato*, and aspired to express tactile values and the solidity of volumes, he had at his disposal only limited means: simply and solely line. He paid tribute to modern art by adopting its canon of abstraction and inflicting upon forms the elongation, distortion, contraction, disruption of axes and overlapping of planes that constitute his 'expressionism'. Observe the bent heads, sloping shoulders, swan necks, interminable arms, and the disproportion between torso, legs and head, and, in the head itself, the nose thinned to the extreme, the almond-shaped eyes, close-set and hollowed out, the thin and pinched mouth; observe further the

MODIGLIANI. PORTRAIT OF SOUTINE.

MODIGLIANI. PORTRAIT OF ZBOROWSKI.
Private Collection, Paris.

of whose painters, foreigners, are characterized by the fact that their works betray a certain sickness of life. Modigliani, however, who suffered more than anyone, made it a point of honour to hide his pain. His laconic style did not always succeed in repressing an irremediable pessimism. But an innate pride, nobility and dignity preserved him from excessive lyricism as well as from shoddy craftsmanship. An anxious, tense intellectualism, which he shared with numerous other Jewish artists of his day, gave his work a disillusioned tone. Rather than a new idiom, Modigliani contributed to his time a new sensation. He had in him something dark, irrational and complicated that his drawings and paintings put within the reach of a generation eager for vivid sensations and acrid pleasures.   F. E.

nudes with frail limbs, high waist, and sinuous arabesques: everything contributes to the impression of delicate and precious distinction, rare and somewhat unhealthy, of a *morbidezza* that would not have been disowned by Botticelli. Modigliani can therefore not be regarded as one of the founders of contemporary painting. He found a style, both graphic and decorative, an idiom that was on the whole rather restricted, but self-sufficient and not without effect. The curves, spirals, elongations, the austerity in the midst of gentleness, nonchalance in the midst of fragility, purity in the midst of the suggestive, the Italianism adapted to satisfy the modern mind, the mannerism saved by a proud gravity, and finally the Expressionism held in check by a certain sense of dignity and aristocratic reserve: these are sufficient reasons to admire Modigliani but also to wish him no descendants. Modigliani belonged to the *École de Paris*, the largest number

MOHOLY-NAGY Ladislaus (1895-1946). Born at Bacsbarsod in Hungary; died in Chigaco. Inducted into the Austro-Hungarian army in 1914, he was severely wounded on the Russian front in 1917. During his convalescence at Odessa, then at Szeged, he began drawing portraits and landscapes in a very personal, undulating style that he did not resume later. Upon his discharge from the army, he returned to Budapest, where he obtained the degree of Doctor of Law (1918). He met Lissitzky in Düsseldorf in 1921 and produced his first abstract paintings, which were exhibited in Der Sturm Gallery in Berlin. In Vienna in 1922, in collaboration with the Hungarian poet Lajos Kassak, he published a kind of anthology of the new art: *Buch Neuer Künstler*. In 1923 he met Walter Gropius, who, impressed by his personality and enthusiasm, appointed him a professor at the Bauhaus *(*)*. His activity in this famous school of fine and applied arts was very important from 1923 to 1928. In particular, he edited the collection of *Bauhausbücher* there, publishing several of his own works, which show the novelty of his ideas and experiments with materials and various techniques. While continuing to paint, he was chiefly known at the time for his photograms and photomontages. Under the pressure of political developments in Germany, he left the Bauhaus and travelled throughout Europe (Hungary, Switzerland, Finland, Norway, France, Greece, Italy). He was in Amsterdam in 1934, in London in 1935. It is there that he published several volumes of documentary photographs and began the series of his painting-sculptures or painting-objects which hecalled 'space modulators'. In 1937 he went to the United States, where he founded an autonomous school, the School of Design, which met with great success. At the same time he developed his experiments with space (sculptures in plexiglass in combination with other materials) but also continued to paint. In 1946 he published *The New Vision* in New York. He died of leukemia the same year. In 1947 a posthumous work called *Vision in Motion* was published in Chicago, condensing in non-technical form the sum of his experiences and concepts of art. Moholy-Nagy is the most authentic type of the experimental artist.

His works must be considered as pure experimentation; otherwise one could easily be indifferent to his plexiglass sculptures or studies of transparency of colours. In transferring his investigations to new spheres, Moholy did not always avoid dispersion, but he feared nothing more than petrification in a closed theory. His plastic works seldom achieve greatness, but his didactic works contain an inexhaustible wealth of ideas, documents, examples and original propositions of interest to all students of modern art and everyone engaged in independent research.   M. S.

MOILLIET Louis (born in 1880 at Berne) Swiss painter. When he was a boy, he knew Paul Klee and they used to play music together and draw in the country on Sundays. From 1900 to 1903, Moilliet trained under Mackensen at Worpswede and Olde at Weimar. After 1904, he worked under Kalckreuth at the Stuttgart Academy. Then he lived for a time in Rome, Provence, Sicily, Tunisia and Corsica. He did his first oil paintings in 1910. The following year, he met August Macke and found Klee again at Munich. He introduced him to Kandinsky through whom he came into touch with the artists of the Blauc Reiter (*) group. Moilliet was represented at the first exhibition of the Sturm (*) group at Berlin. His visit to Tunisia in 1914 with his

friends, Klee and Macke, brought a change of style in his work, particularly noticeable in his water-colours. His frequent travels, especially those he made later to Morocco, Algeria, Spain and the Balearic Islands, always inspired his painting, but those of 1914 marked a break for Moilliet and his companions with a particular way of seeing the world. While the basis of his painting had almost always been a composite vision of reality, with a colouring very similar to Delaunay's, Moilliet was able with water-colour to seize a fleeting, luminous impression and to evoke, for example, a whole landscape through the subtle interplay of allusion and transparent colour, in an idiom similar to Matisse's water-colours of 1905 from Collioure, without however, equalling them. Although he cannot equal Klee's imaginative originality either or Macke's natural brightness, he did at least find a sincere means of expression in the simple harmonies of water-colour. From 1930 until the war, he also did stained-glass and murals, without any human figures, which are characterised by a rather rigid line, as can be

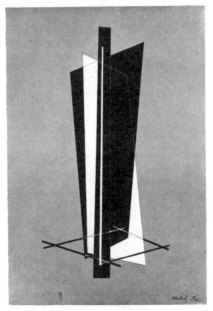

MOHOLY-NAGY. CONSTRUCTION. 1922-1923. *Jeanne Coppel Collection, Paris.*

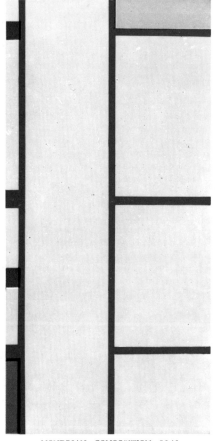

MONDRIAN. COMPOSITION. 1942.
The Miller Company Collection, U.S.A.

and, after getting two certificates to teach drawing in state schools, he joined the Amsterdam Academy (1892), where he was a hard working student and highly esteemed by his masters. There followed a difficult period, when he painted a great deal, sold little and earned his living by making copies in museums or scientific drawings. He also gave private lessons and paid a few brief visits to England, Belgium and Spain, which he found disappointing. His favourite subject remained the Dutch countryside. He painted principally in the environs of Amsterdam and often returned to the same subjects; the farm of Duivendrecht, for instance, was painted several times from the same point of view. His colouring was often delicate, although subdued grey and green predominated. The style was direct and the construction confident. A long stay, about 1903, among the Catholic peasants of North Brabant, seemed to open new horizons for the painter. He was extremely interested in religious questions and read books published by the Theosophical Society, which he joined a few years later. At that time, his favourite subjects were isolated houses and the recesses of woods in purple and grey, which sometimes had a mystical feeling about them. His first visit to Dombourg, on the Island of Walcheren, in the summer of 1908, brought a complete change in his manner. He met there the painter, Toorop, whose Divisionism influenced him for a time. His palette became lighter; purple gradually disappeared and was replaced by pale blues, white, pinks and gold (the series of the *Dunes* and the *Towers of Westkapelle,* 1908-1911). Some friends advised him to go to Paris. The Dutch painter, Kickert, lent him his studio in Montparnasse and Mondrian left at the end of December, 1911. He was immediately influenced by Cubism and painted the series of *Trees,* a succession of abstractions on the same theme that have remained unique in the painting of this century. In other paintings he tried to go the very heart of Cubism and, as he experimented in one direction and then in another, he came upon an undiscovered region of painting where everything was transformed into a rhythmic orchestration of lines and colours without any reference to objective reality. These lines were gradually reduced to simple horizontals and

seen in the churches of Bremgarten, Lucerne and Winterthur. He is one of the last survivors of the Blaue Reiter group and lives a retired life at La Tour-de-Peilz, near Vevey, on the lake of Geneva.   R.-J. M.

MONDRIAN Pieter Cornelis, called Piet (1872-1944). Dutch painter; born at Amsfoot, Holland, died in New York. His family were strict Calvinists. His father, who was a teacher, wanted him to follow his profession too, but in the end his son refused

verticals, while the colours were generally restricted to the three primary colours of red, yellow and blue, relieved by black and white, sometimes grey.

Fifteen days before the First World War broke out, he had to return to Holland because his father was ill. He was caught in Amsterdam when war was declared and could not return to Paris until after the Armistice was signed. During those four and a half years, he lived at Dombourg, Scheveningen, Amsterdam and the village of Laren, where he made the acquaintance of the painter, Van der Leck, which was a great encouragement to him. He continued his experiments in abstraction (the subjects of the *Sea* and the *Façades of Cathedrals*) which in 1915, developed into the same pure rhythm of horizontal and vertical lines (paintings and drawings that Alfred Barr later called the series of *More and Less*) which were the immediate prelude to what the painter was to call Neo-Plasticism or pure plasticism. It was in the same year, 1915, that he made the acquaintance of Theo van Doesburg, a dynamic and enterprising man, painter, poet and journalist, who was the first to spread his ideas and help him to found the review, *De Stijl (*)* whose first number appeared in October, 1917. Mondrian, during this period, spent more time on his writing than on his painting. He published long theoretical essays in *De Stijl,* some of which were in dialogue form. One of them, *Natural Reality and Abstract Reality* is one of the basic documents of Abstract Art *(*)*. Returning to Paris at the beginning of 1919, Mondrian continued his long exploration of the Neo-Plastic, horizontal-vertical theme, which only ended with his death, twenty-five years later. The backgrounds of these paintings were grey at first, then a very pale blue, but after 1922 they all became and remained white. Some compositions were often repeated with slight variations (the series of paintings of squares between 1929 and 1932). Red

was his favourite colour. Some works of this middle period consist of a red rectangle that sometimes covers two thirds of the painted surface. He exhibited very little, only sold to very rare collectors and lived simply in a studio, quite near Montparnasse station, which he arranged and decorated according to Neo-Plastic principles. He lived a silent existence there, almost a recluse, but his remarkable audacity made his name known through the world. The importance of his work was appreciated far beyond the frontiers of his own country. It was during this phase that his ideas influenced Léger and Baumeister and his first followers appeared among young painters. In 1925, the Bauhaus *(*)* published his book, *Neue Gestaltung,* and enlarged German translation of a booklet that had been published in Paris in 1920 by the Galerie l'Effort Moderne, under the title, *Le Néo-Plasticisme (*).*

In 1926 he wrote: 'We need a new aesthetic based on the pure relationships of lines and pure colours, because only the pure relationships of pure constructive elements can achieve a pure beauty. Today, pure beauty is not only a necessity for us, it is the only means to a pure

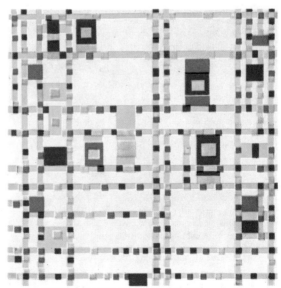

MONDRIAN. BROADWAY BOOGIE-WOOGIE. 1942-1943.
Museum of Modern Art, New York.

manifestation of the universal force that is in everything. It is identical with what was known in the past under the name of *divinity* and is indispensable to us, poor mortals, in the search for an equilibrium in our lives, because things are essentially opposed to us and external matter is hostile . . . Since denaturalisation is one of the milestones of human progress, it has consequently a primary importance in Neo-Plastic art. The power of Neo-Plastic painting lies in having shown the necessity of this denaturalisation in painterly terms. It has denaturalised the constructive elements and their composition at the same time. For this reason it is true abstract painting because to denaturalise is to abstract. To denaturalise is to deepen.", By 1924, he had stopped contributing to *De Stijl* because of Van Doesburg's attitude, which he considered heretical (see *Elementarism*), but he wrote articles for various French reviews, notably *La Vie des Lettres et des Arts* and *Cahiers d'Art*. In 1930, he joined the Cercle et Carré *(*)* and the following year the Abstraction-Création *(*)* movements.

The significance of Mondrian's art consists primarily in his search for purity of form through reducing its means of expression to a simple statement of relationship, the essential relationship being created by two straight lines meeting at right angles. Not only curved lines and spatial illusion, but also any indication of brushwork and any treatment reminiscent of Impressionist technique were rejected. The result was a sort of mystical pursuit of the absolute, which swept away the world of appearances. Since the picture surface is a plane, the painting on it should also be a strict plane and as a result becomes the means of communicating a conception, bound neither to time nor space, but concerned only with relationship. However, Mondrian always tried to express this relationship dynamically, in other words, by an asymmetrical equilibrium.

Although he was poor, sometimes almost destitute, his studio became a sort of place of pilgrimage for avant-garde intellectuals and artists from all over the world. Among his visitors were Moholy-Nagy, Marinetti, Gropius, Gabo, Pevsner, Arp, Baumeister, Schwitters and the American, Katherine Dreier, who began in 1926 to introduce his work to the American public though the travelling exhibitions of the Société Anonyme *(*)*, which she directed with the help of Marcel Duchamp and Man Ray. In the catalogue to an exhibition at the Brooklyn Museum, she had the courage to write: 'Holland has produced three great painters who, while they were a logical expression of the spirit of their country, rose above it through the strength of their personalities. The first was Rembrandt, the second Van Gogh and the third is Mondrian.' Another distinguished visitor was Ben Nicholson, who later gave this vivid description of his experience: '–the thing I remembered most was the feeling of light in his room and the pauses and silences during and after he'd been talking. The feeling in his studio must have been not unlike the feeling in one of those hermoits' caves where lions used to go to have thorns taken out of their paws.'

In 1936, the expropriation of the old house where he lived forced him to remove. He never got used to his new home in the boulevard

MONET. HÔTEL DE LA PLAGE. 1870.
Private Collection, Paris.

Raspail where he could not recreate the unusual atmosphere of the rue du Départ. So, when he felt that war was imminent and that Paris would be in an exposed position, he did not hesitate in September 1938 to leave for London, where he found Gabo, Ben Nicholson and other friends. But he only stayed there two years, working in a Hampstead studio where he was nearly bombed during the Blitz. September 1940 he left for New York. He arrived there exhausted and almost penniless. After recovering in the country, he began working in New York itself, encouraged by the kindly interest of numerous friends and admirers. Paintings, begun in London and even Paris two or three years before, were finished in New York by the unexpected addition of coloured squares or lines that relieved the effect of the black lines which, in some works towards the end of his Parisian period, increased until they were almost oppressive. The last two years of his life brought him more satisfaction than fifty years of ceaseless toil. A modest degree of material comfort led to a more relaxed feeling in his works. He no longer used black. *New York City* consists only of yellow, red and blue lines. In *Broadway Boogie-Woogie,* the lines are broken up into little rectangles as if by a gay pizzicato. Finally in the unfinished *Victory Boogie-Woogie,* his joy is expressed by a symphony in which control and freedom, restraint and exaltation combine in a perfect unity, still governed by the Neo-Plastic, horizontal-vertical principle.

During these last two years, the painter took part in all the important exhibitions in New York. With the help of Charmion von Wiegand, he produced English versions of the principal articles he had already written and wrote fresh ones, including a very significant autobiographical essay. When died on February 1st, 1944, his funeral was attended by artists and intellectuals of all nationalities, who were refugees in New York. The leading American newspapers were full of eulogistic articles. Retrospective exhibitions were held soon afterwards at the Museum of Modern Art, New York, in 1945; the Stedelijk Museum, Amsterdam, in 1946; the Kunstmuseum, Basel, in 1947; the Venice Biennale, in 1956.

Mondrian's importance for the painting of this century is considerable, not only for his

MONET. ROUEN CATHEDRAL. 1894.
Musée du Louvre, Paris.

gradual evolution from naturalism to the most extreme form of abstraction, but also for the quality that characterised that evolution. Each step was characteristic of the whole man. There was not a moment of indifference in the development of his paintings: his entire responsibility as a painter was involved in it and compromise was unknown to him. On the most arid heights of abstraction, something still vibrates behind the painting that gives it warmth and humanity and makes it inimitable.   M. S.

MONET Claude (1840-1926). French painter; born in Paris; died at Giverny. Claude Monet is the most Impressionist of Impressionists, and his work is the symbol of the movement. It is appropriate that one of his pictures, exhibited in 1874 and called *Impression, Sunrise* (reproduced on page 164), should have led a Parisian columnist to baptize the new movement. The title of the picture was in itself significant. It revealed the artist's will to tran-

MONEΓ. BRIDGE AT
ARGENTEUIL. 1874.
Nene Staatsgalerie,
Munich.

scribe his own feeling rather than to represent a particular landscape; and such an act was revolutionary in its time. This was the point at which modern art broke with that of preceding centuries. It is likely that the persons concerned did not fully appreciate the radical change that their new attitude constituted; they did not foresee its consequences, but kept enough faith to continue their efforts in spite of the greatest difficulties. In his youth Monet had met Boudin at Le Havre and then made friends with Pissarro at the Académie Suisse (*), where the two of them worked. A few years later he entered the Atelier Gleyre (*), where he met Renoir, Bazille and Sisley. Thus, Fate brought together fortuitously the men who would soon shatter the formulae in which official art was imprisoned. For several years, however, they were not so uncompromising as is thought today. Monet sent works to the Salon that were not always refused. The first painting he sent, in 1865, was accepted, and even enjoyed some success. Furthermore, he was admitted several times in later years, although of course with more difficulty. In addition to his landscapes, Monet executed a few figure studies at this time, first a large composition, Le Déjeuner sur l'Herbe, which he destroyed after it had been criticized by Courbet (an admirable sketch for it survives in the Frankfurt Museum), then Portrait of Camille, which attracted much attention at the Salon of 1866, Women in the Garden, in the Louvre, and Lunch in an Interior. These canvases, together with a few portraits executed at various periods, are almost the only works in which he gave himself over to the representation of the human figure. This indifference may seem surprising and be regarded as a sign of insensitivity, but a more accurate interpretation suggests that for an artist as scrupulous as Monet–and scrupulousness is characteristic of the Impressionists –the portrait added psychological problems to purely pictorial ones, and that he preferred the more neutral theme of the landscape. Pictorial problems were important enough in themselves for Monet not to want to complicate them still more. He then went through one of the darkest periods of his life. His circumstances became increasingly difficult. His goods were distrained and he saw two hundred of his paintings sold by auction in lots of 50 frs. each. He was twenty-seven years old. In despair, he tried to commit suicide, but his faithful friend, Bazille, helped him to get over his difficulties and failures. Even the work he sent to the Salon of 1869 was refused. The same year, he went with Renoir to Bougival, where together they painted the baths of La Grenouillère. When war broke out, Monet left for Trouville, then for London, where he found Pissarro again, admired Turner's paintings with him and made the acquaintance of Durand-Ruel. Returning to France in 1872, he went to live at Argenteuil, where he made a studio-boat for himself from which he could study at leisure the play of light on water. A suggestion that Bazille had once made came back to him and he invited his friends to form a group and exhibit their work together. They did so in 1874 at Nadar's, but the exhibition–now famous in the history of art–only caused derision and the most malicious comments. To the stiff and static art, manufactured in studios, that was then in favour, Monet opposed a fluidity captured from Nature: not only the fluidity of movement but also that, much more subtle, of environment and atmosphere. Had he been content to seek lifelike postures for figures, like those revealed in a candid photograph, his theories would no doubt have been accepted, but what he wanted to paint was the glow of light, the shimmering of water, the transparency of the atmosphere, the scintillation of foliage. His idea of the instantaneous concerned not forms in motion but an arrest of time: a landscape is not the same at dawn and at twilight, in autumn and in spring. He wanted to paint the sun, the cold, the wind, the mist. These ideas were new and came as a revelation. Oscar Wilde later remarked of him that Nature certainly imitates art, since although nobody before Claude Monet had ever discovered that fog becomes iridescent around the London bridges, nobody could afterwards see London fog without thinking of him. Thereafter Monet confined himself almost exclusively to landscapes, and mostly to those in which water adds an element of movement. Channel ports, the banks of the Seine, England, Holland, and Venice furnished him with inexhaustible themes until his death.

Today it is difficult to understand that this art, full of freshness and youth, sensitive to the charm of all seasons, luminous as a song of joy, could have raised storms and brought many years of poverty to its apostle. But his tenacity succeeded in convincing the unbelievers and, about 1880, Monet began to see hostility subside. Calm entered his life little by little and, later, comfort and even wealth with the fame that crowned his old age. However, the crown was not untarnished, for if Alfred Sisley had died too young to see the beginnings of his success, Monet lived to witness the new assaults that triumphant Impressionism was to undergo, this time not from official or academic artists but from the members of the new generation who, making use of the freedom won for them by the Impressionists, rejected them to explore other paths towards other feats of daring, other concepts, even other repudiations. The Impressionist technique, carried to the point Monet finally reached, can undoubtedly be criticized for giving less importance to forms than to the atmosphere enveloping them. But an artist cannot be denied the right to think his thought through to the end. Monet was not afraid to seek out this finality. Already in the series of *Cathedral of Rouen* one finds no concern for suggesting effects of mass, but only a desire to observe light in all its intensities. It was

MONET. WATER LILIES AT GIVERNY.

mainly at Giverny, in the garden that he arranged himself, that Monet achieved his dream in a magic art free of any concern for stable form. His garlands of wistarias, reflected in the shifting mirror of the lake, his sheets of water lilies floating on the changing water, provided him with a whole dazzling play of coloured mirages that were their own justification, like certain variations in music, whose theme is nothing more than a pretext and a place to start. The whole development of Monet's work was toward a complete liberation that allowed him, near the end of his life, to arrive at an art as independent of reality as that of the most abstract painters of today. The astonishing mural ensemble inspired by *Water Lilies*, which occupies two rooms in the Musée de l'Orangerie in Paris, demonstrates the attainment of a poetical world rid of all concern with form, a world in which the evocation of reality is no more than a vague pretext. A curious magic emanates from it, but also the certainty that a point has been reached that cannot be passed, a point where the artist, at the height of his powers, has discovered a purity beyond which he cannot go without dissolution.

This extreme experiment could not have been attained if Monet had not previously undertaken many times to paint the same landscape seen at different hours, in different seasons, under different lights, with the sole purpose of extracting new effects from the same subject. The views of *The Gare Saint-Lazare* (1876-1877), of *Rouen Cathedral* (1892-1894) and of the garden at Giverny (1905-1908) are among the most celebrated, but there are other sequences, *The Ice Breaking* (1880), *Haystacks* (1891), *Poplars on the Bank of the Epte*, and the views of London and Venice, that deserve being equally known. Those fortunate enough to have seen several canvases on the same theme, assembled and exhibited by the artist at the Durand-Ruel Gallery, realized the interest and appeal of such a grouping. In them Monet demonstrated that no absolute colour exists in Nature, only light; and that since the appearance of all objects changes perpetually, the art of the painter should consist in choosing one moment in preference to any other, in order to fix its individuality in a definitive image. The demonstration is convincing, although Impressionism would have been justified even without it.

It is easy to understand why this art, which at the beginning won the support and encouragement of Naturalists in literature, who regarded it as an illustration of their theories of objective reality, was later disowned by the same writers. It was, in fact, not so much a Naturalist expression that Monet sought as a poetry of suggestions in which imprecision and the absence of clear figures leave a large place for dreaming and a constantly renewed play of colour. Monet's art, as it appears to us today, claims no ancestry in the past, even though some of the painters of the eighteenth century seem to have been its forerunners. One predecessor of Monet can be found in the English painter Turner, although his is an art of pure imagination and magic. The art of Monet, in fact, remains closer to Nature; and if a divergence seems occasionally to exist, the explanation is that the painter's eye has succeeded in catching what previously seemed impossible to seize. He is quite distinct from some of the other painters classified as Impressionists. He has almost nothing in common with the rigorous draughtsmanship of Degas, except when Degas, in later years, indulged, in his pastels and particularly for his dancers, in similar iridescences; his construction was entirely different from Cézanne's, and he had real kinship only with Sisley and Pissarro, although he has more assurance than they. Jongkind and Boudin paved the way for him and succeeded in transcribing similar wet atmospheres in their own manner, but without achieving the poetical quality that remains the unique achievement of Monet.   R. C.

MONTICELLI Adolphe (1824-1886). French painter; born and died in Marseilles. The offspring of an old Piedmontese family, Monticelli was, as a painter, the direct heir of the great Venetians. In 1846 he left Marseilles for Paris, studied there for three years, went back and then returned to the capital in 1863, where he lived until the war of 1870. Then he returned to his native city, on foot, and did not leave it again until his death. His last ten years were the most fruitful and original period of his career, a period of exaltation and certainty, of lucid entrancement, although it is the least known. Up to 1870 Monticelli was influenced by the art of museums and of his illustrious contemporaries, by that of Watteau, Veronese, Rembrandt, and also of Diaz, Delacroix, Courbet. Personal as it may be, his painting was then precious, brilliant and mannered. This is the painting that would tempt forgers: *The Courts of Love* and *Scenes of the Park* and *Scenes of the Opera*, of which there are innumerable imitations. After 1870 he did not give up scenes of the park and the opera, but from then on it was in his dreams that he saw the masquerades, balls and *fêtes galantes* and pursued their scintillating illusions. He also painted flowers, portraits and travelling shows. He had conquered his idiom and he enriched it with all the technical means his instinct suggested: thick layers of paint, varnish, mixtures of tones, shading, glaze. In this oily, kneaded, tormented mixture forms seem to bog down, colours to vanish. And then, as the attention persists, the forms reassemble, and the colours emit vivid glows. Golden yellows, midnight blues, reddish shadows, sumptuous blacks sprinkled with touches of emerald and a few drops of vermilion: everything that would be a thick pudding with others is, with him, an alchemist's secret. 'Monticelli taught me chromatism', Van Gogh said later, with gratitude. In preparing his mixtures and reactions, Monticelli was aware of the wonders time would work with them; he knew that one tone would dim, another intensify; that the years would bring out an unnoticed form and an unsuspected contour; that his work would live and relive, changing, multiple, giving off here a nugget, there a gem, hitherto buried in the affectionately mixed paste. 'I paint for fifty years hence', he prophesied. He worked with frenzy, executing landscapes that dripped with light and

MONTICELLI. THE ACROBATS' PARADE. 1877.
Grobet-Labadié Museum, Marseilles.

were saturated with warmth; portraits, flowers, fruit, whose shifting splendours hide none of the admirable draughtsmanship, figures and objects cast in a kind of lava of melted gold and silver. The trees devoured by slow combustion are almost the same ones that Van Gogh was to set on fire. These woods along a rough slope of hills in Provence seem to reappear in the canvases of Soutine, but devastated by a violent tornado.

Monticelli announced modern Expressionism, and he can also be regarded as a precursor of Impressionism. Were not air, light and atmosphere his chief preoccupations ? Nevertheless, instead of reproducing natural light and its fugitive variations, he put an invented light, a pictorial light, into his works. And this light is not only a personal, absolute medium, it is also a sign of spiritual elevation. He said of his discovery: 'I am the luminous centre; it is I who light'. That part of his production is open to criticism, there is no doubt. However, it cannot be denied that Monticelli was one of the great French painters of the nineteenth century. Delacroix singled him out. Cézanne was fond of him. We know from letters how much Van Gogh admired him. There are more powerful painters, of harder and more sonorous metal. But no one attempted this learned and bold painting before him.

A belated and fertile genius–he accumulated over eight hundred pictures in less than ten years–Monticelli seems an innovator in direct line of the baroque artists who, from the Romantic Delacroix to the Expressionist Van Gogh, practised what can be called a painting of temperament.   F. E.

MOORE Henry (born in 1894 in Castleford, Yorkshire). After studying at the Leeds School of Art and, later, at the Royal College of Art in London, Moore won a sholarship which enabled him to travel in France and Italy. He has been a member of the London Group and of the Seven and Five Group, and has exhibited at home and abroad with the Surrealists. During the Second World War he made a remarkable series of drawings of London Underground stations in their function as air-raid shelters. In 1934, in a manifesto published by Sir Herbert Read, Moore defined his position in the following terms: 'Beauty, in the later Greek or Renaissance sense, is not the aim of my sculpture. Between beauty of expression and power of expression there is a difference of function. The first aims at pleasing the senses, the second has a spiritual vitality which for me is more moving and goes deeper than the senses'. In response to this conviction, Moore has attempted to give his sculpture a power based on his working out of the sculptural problem rather than on the subject portrayed, while, technically, his purpose has been to form a bridge with the great archaic traditions of Mexico, Egypt and even pre-history. He has sought to attain these ends through respect for his material, feeling that stone, wood or metal–hard and compact as they are–should not be made to lose their identity by attempts to make them look like flesh. In all his work from 1930 onwards there is a growing sense of the material being pushed from within by its own inner energy, an aspect perhaps of Moore's increasing preoccupation with the opening-up of the sculptural mass. 'A hole', he has said, 'can itself have as much shape-meaning as solid mass. Sculpture in air is possible, where the stone contains only the hole which is the intended and considered form.' From this conception of truth to material, of the outer forms and surfaces of sculpture resulting from the pent-up energy within, of the penetration of the sculptural mass, have sprung Moore's most typical sculptures. Tunnelled and eroded like some ancient landscapes in miniature, his biomorphic forms are related to that same vision which has led Paul Nash and Graham Sutherland to create 'object-personages' – double-image metaphors for landscape–in paint. Moore has acknowledged his particular debt to the organic processes of nature as exemplified in the forms of pebble and rock, shell and tree and bone. He has said. 'I would rather have a piece of my sculpture put in a landscape, almost any landscape, than in, or on, the most beautiful building I know'.

In idiom, Moore

MOORE. LYING FIGURE. STUDY FOR A SCULPTURE IN WOOD.
Sir Kenneth Clark Collection.

has ranged from the sweetly formalized naturalism of the *Madonna and Child* commissioned for St Matthew's, Northampton, to completely non-figurative exercises in spatial relationships. Best-known are his long series of reclining figures, but among his more notable commissions since the war have been the *Three Standing Figures* in Battersea Park, London; the abstract screen for the roof of the *Time-Life* building in London; and the *King and Queen* group at Middelheim, Antwerp. Moore's central position between realism and abstraction, and the slow working out of his thoughts over a long period, have combined to give great stability to his development. He has worked with stone, wood and bronze with equal ease, and has also experimented with cement and terracotta. His sketches and drawings form a considerable body of work by themselves and are important in their own right: they include not only preparatory studies for his sculptures, but works of independent values in which Moore elaborates new forms and techniques. He has executed commissions for public monuments and buildings, schools and parks in Britain and other countries; in 1948 he won the International Sculpture Prize at the Venice Biennale and five years later the equivalent prize at the São Paulo Biennal. F. MC. E.

MORANDI. STILL LIFE. 1918.   *Jucker Collection, Milan.*

MORANDI Giorgio. Italian painter; born in 1890 in Bologna. Morandi's first landscape dates from 1911. He is one of the few Italian artists never to have been to Paris, although he underwent the Parisian influence in his first works. An aloof and lonely artist, he was to complete successfully the metaphysical cycle of Italian painting in 1918 and 1919, far from Ferrara where Chirico and Carrà had just painted their most famous works. As Chirico put it, Morandi 'sanctifies' Metaphysical Painting *(*)* by reducing it to a kind of linear magic. The intelligence and sensitivity with which he re-creates objects are more an engraver's than a painter's. Although he has painted a few beautiful landscapes, only a very few figures studies by him are known, among which is one self-portrait. His universe is the very humble world of still life. He gave up spheres, regular shapes and metaphysical polyhedrons, and a few familiar objects sufficed him: cups and salad-bowls, long-necked bottles that he imprisoned in a very chaste line to produce a strange and rarefied atmosphere. Later, having gradually softened the rigour of his contour, he succeeded, halfway between Cubism and Impressionism, in finding his own personality in a delicate compromise between form and colour. Like Léger, he is capable of creating an atmosphere with three tones; but while the three tones of Léger have become more and more vivid and dazzling over the course of years, Morandi's modulations have been further toned down, as if he wanted to reduce painting to the semitones of etching. His tonal 'intimism' had great influence upon the Roman School (Scipione, Mafai, Cagli, Capogrossi), which was the most valid artistic expression on the peninsula under Fascism. The work of Morandi is perhaps the best that contemporary taste has produced in Italy. S. L.

MOREAU Gustave (1826-1898). French painter; born and died in Paris. Gustave Moreau plays, in the history of contemporary art, only an episodic part. He has the merit of having been, at the École Nationale des Beaux-Arts, the teacher of Rouault, Matisse, Marquet and Jean Puy–the group of young men from whom Fauvism would spring. One is grateful to him for having preserved the personality of his pupils and thus prepared the blossoming of an essential movement in contemporary art. But there would be some injustice in seeing him merely as a teacher. We should like to see him placed at the source of Surrealism, for more than any other painter he possessed the secret of an unexpected magic. He knew that the object contains a mystery and can express a whole unknown world beyond appearances, and that forms and colours are a language. He may be reproached for a somewhat artificial fantasy and an excessively literary mythology, but in this field, too, he is a forerunner of the Surrealists.

Excluded from modern painting, in this way he has his justification as a precursor. He was not only concerned with the plastic problems that form the basis of contemporary art, he was also the master of an extremely elaborate technique. He wanted to introduce a notion of magic into painting, a part of the incomprehensible and unconscious world in which everything could become a symbol. Considered in this light, the art of Gustave Moreau acquires a significant value. There was religious feeling in his mind, less involved with the Catholic faith than attracted by a curious pantheism. He made his fabulous heroes–the Sphinx, the Chimera, Salome–live in a glitter of gems, in the glow of sumptuous clothes and strange lights. His admiration for Delacroix and especially for Chassériau could not save him from certain excesses and bondage to a pseudo-poetry whose artificiality is transparent today. What appears to us the bric-à-brac of cheap fantasy is none the less the work of a thoroughly sincere artist quite free from morbid obsessions.   R. C.

MOREAU. THE APPARITION. 1876. WATER-COLOUR.
Cabinet des Dessins, Louvre.

MORISOT Berthe (1841-1895). French painter; born in Bourges, where her father was a high government official. Berthe Morisot was brought up in cultivated but traditional middle-class surroundings. Nothing in those surroundings would have led one to predict that from the very outset she would be drawn towards the best artists of her time. Her temperament asserted itself at once in the reticence with which she met the mediocre teaching of her first instructor, Chocarne, in the profit she was able to draw from that of the second, Guichard; and further in the desire she expressed to work with Corot. It was under his guidance that she painted from 1862 to 1868. She assimilated his lessons perfectly, and to them she owed a great deal. Their influence is apparent until about 1874: *The Harbour of Lorient* (1869), *On the Balcony* (1872), *The Butterfly Chase*, *At Maurecourt* (1874). But attracted by the art of Manet, she made his acquaintance in 1868, and his influence, in addition to that of Corot, was especially apparent in the years 1875-1876: *Woman at the Mirror*, *Le Déjeuner sur l'Herbe*. However, having joined the Impressionist group at its beginning, she drew Manet towards light colours and outdoor painting. It was between 1877 and 1879 that she forged her own style, which began to crystallize during this period (*Young Woman Powdering Her Face*, 1877; *Behind the Blind*, 1878; *Summer Day*, 1879). She did not resort to the systematic divided stroke but to large strokes very freely applied in all directions, which gave her canvases an aspect characteristic of herself alone. The familiar interior or open-air scenes she painted are bathed in radiant and iridescent light, in which silvery tones mingle in harmonies of a rarely achieved delicacy and sensitivity. Extremely characteristic of her genius, these paintings are feasts of light, of aerial mobility and lightness, of a spontaneous freshness, constantly renewed from 1879 to 1889 (*Eugène Manet and his Daughter at Bougival*, 1881; *The Veranda*, 1882; *The Garden*, 1883; *On the Lake*, 1884; *Reading*, 1888). This very free, personal manner seemed particularly to suit her temperament, which found in it a medium made to order. However, towards 1889 she became disturbed by the danger inherent in the Impressionist vision, which was too exclusively attached to the atmospheric aspect of the world and she sought greater unity and respect for form. She assumed a long and flexible stroke that followed the form without encircling it, but shaped its mass and luminosity: *The Mandolin* (1889), *Young Girl Asleep* (1892), *Young Girl with a Fan* (1893), *The Two Sisters* (1894). This is her final manner, for she died early in 1895. Without separating it from the rest, the important place that water-colour occupied in her work should be stressed, as this medium corresponded particularly well to her nature as a painter and is one of which she made masterful use. A few simple, limpid spots, applied with extreme audacity, were all she needed to express herself completely. Specifically a painter,

Berthe Morisot was responsive, above all, to the play of light upon the world which surrounded her; she drew her emotions from it, and in its pictorial interpretation she expressed her nature as a woman and an artist. She allowed no ideology or spirit of system to impair the spontaneity of her art, at whose service she put only purely plastic means. She excluded brutality, preferring delicacy, and she found her most favourable climate in the intimate atmosphere of family scenes animated by the simple gestures of life, from which she could extract poetry.   D. R.

MOSES Grandma (1860-1961). American painter; born Anna Mary Robertson, in Washington County, N.Y., died in Hoosick Falls, N.Y. Her parents were farmers of Scotch-Irish descent. At twelve she left home to earn her living as 'hired girl.' In 1887 she married Thomas Moses and moved to Virginia; in 1905 the couple sold their farm there and moved back to upstate New York to a dairy farm near the hamlet of Eagle Bridge, where Grandma Moses lived until her death at the age of 101. Though her first large picture was painted in 1918 and a number of embroider-

MORISOT. AT MAURECOURT. 1874.   *Private Collection, Paris.*

GRANDMA MOSES.
HALLOWEEN. 1955.
*Grandma Moses
Properties, Inc.,
New York.*

ed worsted pictures succeeded it, she did not take up painting seriously until the thirties when her hands 'were getting tired and lame and I could not sew as I used to.'

She recorded scenes of her childhood and vanishing American occupations such as *Catching the Turkey for Thanksgiving* and *Sugaring Off* (boiling down maple syrup for the sugar) in a naïve style remarkable for its pristine colours, its decided drawing, for the depth and sweep in her landscapes, but especially for her imperturbable innocence and for the romance with which she invested humble scenes of American provincial life. In 1938 her first exhibition of paintings in the window of a pharmacy in Hoosick Falls was discovered and acquired by a collector; in 1939 three of these were exhibited in the Museum of Modern Art in New York. In 1940, at the age of eighty, she had her first one-man show in New York, at the Galerie St. Etienne. Her paintings became immensely popular, especially after they were first reproduced on Christmas cards in 1946. She became a national figure: in 1949 she was received at the White House by President Truman; in 1960 Governor Rockefeller proclaimed her birthday, September 7th, as 'Grandma Moses Day' in New York State. At her death she was able to look back on her life 'like a good day's work. It was

done and I feel satisfied with it. I was happy' and contented, I knew nothing better and made the best out of what life offered. And life is what we make it, always has been, always will be.' It is, no doubt, as much for her translation into painting of these sentiments, so rarely encountered in modern art, as for the quality of her work, that she enjoys a special place not only in the heart of the public but among artists as well. Jean Cassou puts it well in his preface to the catalogue of her Paris exhibition (1962): 'Les cubistes . . . avaient auprès d'eux le Douanier Rousseau . . . Les États-Unis sont aujourd'hui à l'avant-garde des plus hardies recherches artistiques: mais ils ont aussi leurs forces originelles, leurs eaux vives. L'adorable Grandma Moses . . . nous donne à entendre qu'il y a encore un peu de paradis en ce monde.' J. A.

MÜLLER Otto (1874-1930). German painter; born at Liebau, Silesia, died in Breslau. He was adopted by the sister of Robert Hauptmann, father of the dramatist, Gerhart Hauptmann. It has been suggested that the interest he took in gypsies, whom he often chose as the subject of his paintings, was because he was a gypsy child himself. After learning lithography in a commercial studio, he trained at the Dresden Academy from 1895 to 1898. At Berlin, where he settled in 1908, he made friends with Lehmbruck, the sculptor, and Erich Heckel. He belonged to the Brücke *(*)* group from 1910 to 1912 and accompanied Kirchner on a visit to Bohemia. He was appointed to a teaching post at the Breslau Academy in 1919 and taught there until his death. Müller's style differed appreciably from that of the other Brücke painters; its effect was never violent or aggressive. The main source of his inspiration was Egyptian painting, which gave him a taste for simple forms. Nudes were a specially frequent subject in his paintings, placed here and there in paradisiacal landscapes, and painted in green and yellow tones and always with strongly emphasised outlines. The imaginative quality and decorative element in his art invite certain comparisons with Gauguin.   E. R.

MUNCH Edvard (1863-1944). Norwegian painter; born at Loyten; died at Ekely, near Oslo. He was only a child when his mother and then two of his sisters died. His father, who was a doctor in a poor district, often used to take him on his visits. He joined the Oslo School of Arts and Crafts in 1878 and also attended the classes of the painter, Christian Krohg, from 1881. In 1885, he went to Paris for three weeks for the first time. The year after his return to Norway, he joined the Christiana's Bohemia group, which was led by the anarchist writer and poet, Hans Jäger. After a second visit to Paris in 1890, he went to Berlin, where the Association of Berlin Artists invited him to exhibit a considerable collection of his works (1892). These caused a scandal, the exhibition was closed and his name was publicised in the press. During the three years he spent in Berlin, he made friends with Strindberg, Stanislas Przybyszewski and Julius Meier-Graefe, who all gave him their support. Back again in Paris in 1896, he joined the circle of writers and artists connected with Mallarmé and the *Mercure de France*. He was also in touch with the Nabis, exhibited at the Galerie de l'Art Nouveau, designed the programme for *Peer Gynt* at the Théâtre de l'Œuvre and exhibited his *Frieze of Life* at the Salon des Indépendants in 1897.

From 1898 to 1908, he lived in Germany and made brief visits to France, Italy and Norway. He began to suffer from mental disorders in 1908 and went to Dr. Jacobsen's clinic in Copenhagen for treatment. When he was cured, he returned to live permanently in Norway, working in the country in the jealously guarded solitude of his properties at Kragerö, then Ramme and finally at Ekely, where he died.

In Munch's painting there appears the ancient face of the Nordic world, a world animated by forces which still remain extremely close to their source. The unreality of dream mingles with the reality of an imposing and awesome Nature. Like the Scandinavian writers of the same period, he saw the life of man first on the psychological plane. But transposing this frequently too literary vision, Munch conferred a mythic power upon it through his art. Thus he created real symbols that far surpassed the allegories of a Boecklin or a Hodler. Plastic problems were only secondary and remained subordinate to the requirements of expression. His work underwent the influence of Im-

MULLER. NUDE GIRLS.
Wallraf-Richartz Museum, Cologne.

pressionist painting chiefly after his second stay in 1890 at Paris, when he discovered Van Gogh, Gauguin, Seurat and Toulouse-Lautrec. His colours became more clear and expression was concentrated in large forms with simple and rounded contours. The expressive density of the pictures of this period seems due to the painter's obsession with certain subjects: death, which had made an impression on him when he was still a child, painful loneliness, melancholy terror before the immensity of Nature and especially love, which appeared to him a terrible and threatening power. For him, woman personified the Vampire who, in the world of Strindberg, triumphs over man. The principal pictures after 1890 belong to an ensemble he called *The Frieze of Life*. This frieze was meant to be 'a poem of life, love and death', in which the suffering and

MUNCH. GIRLS ON THE BRIDGE. ABOUT 1899.
National Gallery, Oslo.

joy of each man would meet. *The Dance of Life* (1899-1900) is in the centre of the frieze. There the painful loneliness is overcome, and man's destiny, in its misery as in its joy, is intimately linked with the great forces of Nature. Munch's

landscapes express, without allegory, a similar understanding. Dark blue trees of simple, dense forms stand out against snow with the power of primitive signs; a naked peninsula, green and ochre, a gigantic paw of earth, crawls towards the water of the fjord and, in the starlit night, the spell is at last complete. The picture of *Girls on the Bridge* about 1899 is in the same spirit. For the University of Oslo, in 1909-1911, Munch painted mural decorations, in which a huge sun, the symbol of force and light, stands out in the centre. These murals belong to the second period of his work, which is characterized by an increasingly greater freedom and light, revealed in other decorations that he undertook in 1921-1922 for the dining hall of a factory. From then on colours became bright, almost 'Fauvist'. Munch was increasingly liberated from his obsession with the terrible forces of Nature, and the mystery of life, round which his work continued to be organized, seemed to become a mystery in broad daylight. This is particularly clear in the poignant series of self-portraits done in his last years. Many of his pictures exist in several versions. This is partially due to his habit of making a replica for himself of each canvas that was sold.

The great themes of Munch's painting occur again in his engraved work, which is particularly important. Both in black-and-white and in the simplified colouring of lithography and woodcuts Munch frequently achieved a concision that gave the image a strength sometimes surpassing that of his painting. Munch's art, with that of Van Gogh and Ensor, was the first great manifestation of Expressionism (*) on a European level. He can indeed be reproached with being dominated by preoccupations that go beyond the limits of painting.

However, he was filled with a desire to make a synthesis of modern form and symbolic expression; and his influence was felt in the development of art wherever such a synthesis was being sought after. In Germany, for example, the Expressionism of the Brücke (*) arose out of contact with Munch's work.   F. M.

N

NABIS (The). It was in the last days of September 1888 that Sérusier had his decisive encounter with Gauguin at Pont-Aven(*), and upon his return could show his fellow-painters at the Académie Julian (*) the famous landscape that he had painted in the Bois d'Amour in juxtaposed pure tones, at the suggestion of Gauguin and that, for this reason deserved to be considered a 'talisman'. The exhibition of the Impressionist and Synthesist Group (Gauguin, Bernard, Laval) at the Café Volpini early in 1889 completed the revelation. Converted to the new gospel were Bonnard, Ibels (1867-1936), Ranson and Maurice Denis, who were soon joined by a number of fugitives from the École des Beaux-Arts : Vuillard, Roussel, Piot (1869-1934) and, a little later, Verkade, Vallotton, the sculptors Lacombe and Maillol, and the latter's friend, the Hungarian painter Rippl-Ronai.

The Nabis, so baptized by the poet Cazalis with a Hebrew term meaning 'prophets', met every month for dinner at *l'Os à Moelle*, in the Passage Brady in Paris, and every week in the studio of Ranson, who found a picturesque nickname for each of them: Bonnard, 'The Nipponizing Nabi'; Verkade, 'The Nabi Obelisk'; Vuillard, 'The Zouave'. They also assembled at the art dealer Père Tanguy's (*), in the rue Clauzel, where they discovered Cézanne and Van Gogh; at their own art dealer Le Barc de Bouteville's, who devoted several exhibitions to them from 1891 to 1897; or at the Théâtre de l'Œuvre, founded by their friend Lugné-Poë, for whom they designed settings, and on the premises of the *Revue Blanche (*)*, which was also frequented by Lautrec, whose friendship they made along with the acquaintance of all the celebrities of Symbolism in literature. To these numerous contacts and to the momentarily dominating influence of Gauguin were added that of Puvis de Chavannes, Odilon Redon, folk images and Japanese etching and, to a lesser extent, of Gustave Moreau and the English Pre-Raphaelites. The Nabis' doctrine was summed up, according to Maurice Denis, in the Theory of the Two Distortions: 'The Objective Distortion, based upon a purely aesthetic and decorative concept, upon technical principles of colour and composition, and the Subjective Distortion, which brought into play the artist's own perception . . .' They applied these principles not only to easel painting, 'a plane surface covered with colours brought together in a certain order', but also to a series of decorative techniques whose spirit they revolutionized, such

BONNARD. POSTER FOR THE 'REVUE BLANCHE'. 1894.

RANSON. WOMEN IN WHITE. CIRCA 1890.
Tapestry Cartoon.

as painting on cardboard, tempera, stained glass, lithography, posters, theatre settings, and book illustration. The variety of their experiments and increasing exchanges between the worlds of art and entertainment characterize the end of the century, which bore the Nabi stamp in all fields (cf. the articles on Bonnard, Denis, Sérusier, Vallotton and Vuillard).

Bonnard, Vuillard, Denis and Lugné-Poë, the latter three schoolmates at the Lycée Condorcet, shared a studio for a time in 1890, in the Place Pigalle. Then Denis, Sérusier and Verkade–the latter became a monk at the famous Benedictine monastery of Beuron in 1893–drew together in a certain neo-classical mysticism vaguely derived from Pont-Aven, while Bonnard and Vuillard, the sensitive Intimists, by far the most gifted of the group, unamenable to the theories of Sérusier, soon separated from Gauguin and formed with Roussel an actual group within the group. During this period Vallotton practised chiefly

wood-engraving in black-and-withe. He made the doctrine and the art of his friends known in Switzerland, but after 1900 his tense, severe style developed into an extreme realism close to German expressionism. The Nabis exhibited together for the last time at the Durand-Ruel Gallery in 1899, in tribute to Odilon Redon, but by then each of them had already gone his own way. In 1908 Paul Ranson opened an Academy *(*)*, which his premature death the following year prevented him from managing long, but which was maintained by his widow with the assistance of the former Nabis, especially Maurice Denis and Sérusier, both of whom were the authors of the group's doctrinal books, Denis of *Theories* (1913) and *New Theories* (1922), and Sérusier of *An ABC of Painting* (1921). J. LE.

NADAR Pseudonym of the pioneer French photographer Felix Tournachon (1836-1910). A friend of painters and writers, he left portraits of both, and these portraits make him a true precursor of modern art. Recalling his own difficult beginnings, as well as those of his friends, Claude Monet once said: 'Nadar, the great Nadar, as good as gold, lent us the place...' It is not the least of his glories that the famous photographer lent his studios to the future Impressionists, who organized there (from April 15th to May 15th, 1874) the first of eight exhibitions of the 'Painters, Sculptors and Engravers Company'. It was at this event that the word *Impressionism* was spoken for the first time by a critic who had burst out laughing in front of Monet's canvas *Impression, Sunrise* (reproduced on page 164). Entrance was 1 franc and the catalogue 50 centimes. The entire avantgarde was represented, all the painters rejected by the official Salon. In addition to Boudin, Lépine and some others, who had been invited at the suggestion of Degas, and who were to serve as a sort of guarantee, the future Impressionists, Cézanne included, were present in full strength. Manet alone was absent. Besides the picture previously mentioned, Monet exhibited the *Boulevard des Capucines* and *Boats Leaving the Harbour of Le Havre.* Renoir was represented by, among others, *La Loge*, Berthe Morisot by *The Cradle*, and Cézanne by his *Modern Olympia*, and particularly *The House of the Hanged*

Man. Pissarro, Sisley and Guillaumin were present. It was, with Press and public alike, an unprecedented scandal, but 'the good Nadar' was exaltant, although he had certainly not suspected the historical importance of his generous gesture. All his life Nadar had the luck and the intelligence to do the right thing. His name will always be inseparable from those of the great artists of his time, of whom he has left unsurpassable portraits. Other than his own *Baudelaire*, no painted portrait has exceeded in psychological interest his feverish *Delacroix*, his disquieting *Constantin Guys*, his Assyrian *Courbet* or his majestic *Monet*. With the same felicity he brought out the cautious finesse of Manet, the sensitive good nature of Corot and the moving melancholy of Daumier. In his attentive search for expression, Nadar always obeyed a strict discipline, which contributed in great measure to the perfection of his results. Thanks to him, photography sometimes equalled painting in the psychological interpretation of characters and faces.   M. R.

NASH. PAINTING. 1936. *Private Collection.*

NASH Paul (1889-1946). Born in London; died in Boscombe. Studied at the Slade School, then joined the London Group and the New English Art Club. In 1933 he was one of the founding members of the group of painters, sculptors and architects called 'Unit One'. Nash was an official war artist in both world wars, and during the period between his stark, angular records of the Western Front and his more visionary records of the Battle of Britain, his gentle yet disturbing romanticism made him a dominant figure in British painting. Although Nash underwent a number of influences–first Cézanne, later Surrealism and Rossetti –he remained essentially true to his origins, and his concept of art was profoundly marked by a Nordic and Celtic strain. He felt that his destiny was to find his way back to the sources of English art. Technically his roots may be found in Cotman and Turner: his colours were the soft colours of the moisture-laden atmosphere of England and even his oils maintain a fluidity and lyricism which relate him to the best traditions of the English water-colourists. Poetically his roots were in the work of Blake: he had the same tireless imagination, tinged with mysticism, which drove him constantly to search in new directions. His painting suggested a sort of druidical rite inspired by his contact with Nature and its overtones of history and memory. When he erected sinister, obsessive monoliths in a moon-bathed desert landscape, he was only responding to the call of a magic symbolism which can be found at the origin of all primitive arts. He was acutely aware of analogies and correspondences. The sea of German aircraft destroyed in the Battle of Britain suggested to him the waves of a sea of death, and he called it *Totesmeer*. For him the tree trunks in *Monster Field* blasted by lightning had entered another existence. 'We are not studying two fallen trees that look like animals', he wrote, 'but two monster objects outside the plan of natural phenomena.' The association of, or 'encounter' between, objects in different elements fascinated him, and several of his last paintings are built around the mutually echoing forms of sun and sunflower. In any landscape Nash sought the active element, the drama–but it was always a drama of the inner eye. The most striking image in the Bible, he once said, is the sentence 'Why leap ye, ye high hills ?' because it ascribes a power of movement to inanimate things. It is just this same animistic-force upon which Graham Sutherland *(*)* and Henry Moore *(*)* have since drawn. nash is represented in numerous British museums; in addition to his painting he carried out a good deal of book illustration, some textile and poster design, and some theatre décor.   F. MC E.

NEO-IMPRESSIONISM

A movement whose members were Seurat, Signac and the group of painters who followed their principles, the scientific study of colour and the systematic division of tone as they had been practised instinctively by the Impressionists. The term is supposed to have been created by the painters themselves, in homage to their elders, or by their friend and interpreter Félix Fénéon *(*)*, who used it for the first time in the Brussels magazine *L'Art Moderne*, in the issue of September 19th, 1886. It was taken up by Arsène Alexandre, who is usually credited with originating it, in his review in *Événement*, December 10th, 1886, of Fénéon's famous pamphlet *The Impressionists in 1886*. The term was definitely consecrated by Fénéon in May 1887 in the decisive essay in *L'Art Moderne* on 'Neo-Impressionism', in which he set forth with accuracy and rigour both the aesthetic and technical tenets of the movement.

The dispersion of the Impressionist group in 1880 was accompanied by a tightening of method and a return to classical discipline. In the same year, in the magazine *Art*, David Sutter published an important series of articles on *The Phenomena of Vision*, defined in 167 rules that seem to forecast the Neo-Impressionist programme, and ending with a statement of the validity of the link between art and science. Rules, he declared, do not hinder spontaneity of invention or execution, despite their absolute character; science liberates from all uncertainty, allows free movement in a very wide area; it is thus unfair both to art and to science to think that the one necessarily excludes the other. Psychology and physiology of vision, problems of optics, and analysis of light and colour were the order of the day. Recent experiments by the physicists Helmholtz (1878) and O. N. Rood (1881) completed the previous discoveries of Chevreul, whose work, *The Law of Simultaneous Contrast*, published in 1839, was reprinted at the expense of the State in 1889 for the centenary of the birth of the scientist, who was still alive. In this atmosphere of theoretical fervour Georges Seurat (1859-1891) was reaching artistic maturity. His experimental works of 1882 were already characterized by little spots of colour and long even strokes of vibrant luminosity. In the spring of 1884, along with the artists refused by the official Salon, he founded the Salon des Indépendants, to which he sent his first large composition, *La Baignade*. Also among the numerous exhibitors–without knowing each other as yet–were Paul Signac, Henri-Edmond Cross, Charles Angrand and Albert Dubois-Pillet, who were similarly oriented. He made friends with them, and in June constituted, on the basis of regular by-laws and under the presidency of Odilon Redon, the Société des Artistes Indépendants, within which they became the most active group. Their aim was

SIGNAC. BEACHED SAILS. 1902.

SEURAT. SUNDAY IN SUMMER AT THE GRANDE JATTE. 1884-1886. *Art Institute, Chicago.*

to rationalize the expression of light with pure colours and to substitute a scientific method for the empirical one of the Impressionists. At the first show of the new Société des Indépendants, in December, Seurat again exhibited his *La Baignade*, based on 'contrasts of shades', which, in a still flexible handling, achieved his purpose: to reconcile the eternal and the fugitive, architecture and light, figure and landscape, Impressionist vibration and classical stability. Signac, four years younger, dynamic and pugnacious, himself given to the same investigations, was enthralled by this canvas and became an eager proselyte. In 1885, at Guillaumin's, he met Pissarro, whom he introduced to Seurat, and who enthusiastically took up the new discipline, which met his need for order and structure; Pissarro interested his eldest son Lucien and the latter's fellow student Louis Hayet in the movement. Between 1884 and 1886 Seurat executed his second large composition, *A Sunday at the Grande Jatte*, based upon 'contrasts of tones', in accordance with his now fully established technique, the methodical fragmentation of stroke that he called 'Divisionism' and carried as far as 'Pointillism'.

'To divide,' explained Signac, the theoretician of the group, 'means to secure all the benefits of luminosity, colouring and HARMONY: (1) by optical fusion of pigments pure in themselves (ALL THE SHADES OF THE SPECTRUM AND ALL THEIR TONES); (2) by separating various elements (local colour, colour of lighting, their reactions); (3) by balance of these elements and their proportion (according to the laws of CONTRAST, GRADUATION AND IRRADIATION); (4) by the choice of a stroke proportionate to the size of the picture.'

In March 1886 the art dealer Durand-Ruel went to New York with three hundred Impressionist canvases, to which he added works by Signac and Seurat, including *La Baignade*. The same year the *Grande Jatte* was the chief attraction at the eighth and last Impressionist exhibition, May 15th-June 15th, which marked the breakup of the original group, impending since 1880, and the official appearance of Neo-Impressionists' or, in Pissaro's terms, the separation of 'Romantic Impressionists' and 'Scientific Impressionists'. Monet, Renoir and Sisley withdrew. Degas accepted the participation of Seurat, Signac and Lucien and Camille Pissarro exhibiting in the same room, but asked that the word 'Impressionist' be eliminated from the poster, and rejected the works by Angrand and Dubois-Pillet as inadequate. At this time Fénéon made the personal acquaintance of Seurat and his friends. He was to remain their faithful advocate and official interpreter. He devoted a series of masterly articles to them in avant-garde magazines, articles which were collected in a booklet at the end of the year. The Neo-Impressionists made an appearance as a group at the second Salon des Indépendants at the Tuileries (August 21st-September 21st, 1886), where Seurat showed his *Grande Jatte* again. Pissarro exhibited at Nantes in November and succeeded in getting Seurat and Signac accepted with him. These three painters were invited to exhibit in Brussels by 'the Société des Vingt *(*)*, an independent group courageously led by Octave Maus. Signac and Seurat were present at the opening in February 1887. Though admired by Verhaeren, the *Grande Jatte* attained only a *succès d'estime*, but it won several Belgian artists over to Divisionism, among them Henry van de Velde and Theo van Rysselberghe. In France new Divisionists appeared: H. Petitjean, Maximilien Luce, and, a little later, Lucie Cousturier, to mention only the more important. The movement also spread to Italy, with Segantini, Previati, and Morbelli, who appeared for the first time in Milan in 1891. Finally, three of the principal artists of the late nineteenth century, without belonging to Neo-Impressionism, underwent Seurat's influence and practised Divisionism for a time: Gauguin in 1886, Lautrec in 1887 and Van Gogh during almost his entire Parisian period (1886-1888), when his relations with Signac and Seurat were particularly fruitful.

The methodical enterprise of Seurat culminated in two great compositions: *Le Chahut* (1890) and *The Circus* (1891), based upon 'contrasts of lines', in which his will for style turned to stylization and touched Modern Style. He died at thirty-two on March 29th, 1891, exhausted by work but having delivered his message. Pissarro, who was asked to assume leadership of the movement, refused, chiefly because he had just given up Divisionism to return to the freer handling of his initial manner. Only Lucie Cousturier, Cross and Signac, who in 1889 published the doctrinal work that has since become a classic, *From Eugène Delacroix to Neo-Impressionism*, attempted to remain true to the spirit of the method that had been for some no more than a recipe, but though which the architectonic genius of Seurat had been able to crystallize its fervour. In 1899, and even more in 1904, the Fauvism of Matisse was prepared by a Pointillist stage, through contact with Signac and Cross, at whose side he worked in the summer at Saint-Tropez, and the large Seurat retrospective at the Salon des Indépendants in 1905 brought on Cubism (cf. the articles on Cross, Dubois-Pillet, Fénéon, Luce, Pissarro, Seurat, Signac and van de Velde).   J. LE.

NEO-PLASTICISM The doctrine of pure plastic art derived by Mondrian *(*)* from Cubism, and consisting in the exclusive use of the right angle in a horizontal-vertical position and of three primary colours in conjunction with the three 'non-colours', white, black and grey. Mondrian's development of the concept of Neo-Plasticism was the result of five years of research and active meditation, brush or pen in hand (1912-1917). Theo van Doesburg *(*)* was his first follower (1916). From their meeting in Amsterdam was born the magazine *De Stijl* (1917-1928), in which Mondrian could express his ideas at leisure, and which was, until 1924, the organ of radical Neo-Plasticism produced with the collaboration of the painter Huszar and of the painter and sculptor Vantongerloo (*vide Stijl*). Later, Mondrian continued alone but untiringly until his death to apply the law of Neo-Plasticism, so that his name is almost synonymous with the term. Besides writing numerous articles in *De Stijl*, he developed his ideas in a booklet, *Neo-Plasticism*, which appeared at the *Effort Moderne* Gallery of Léonce Rosenberg in Paris in 1920. A German version of this essay appeared in 1925, in the series of books published by the Bauhaus, under the title *Neue Gestaltung*. Finally, as *Plastic Art and Pure Plastic Art*, Mondrian's essays in English were published in New York in 1945.   M. S.

NICHOLSON Ben, born in 1894 at Denham, Buckinghamshire, son of the painter Sir William Nicholson (1872-1949). He studied at the Slade School, then in Tours, Milan, and Pasadena, California. In 1933-1934 in Paris he exhibited with the Abstraction-Creation group and during the inter-war period was one of the foremost links between Great

NICHOLSON. STILL-LIFE. 1948.
Private Collection.

Britain and the modern movement in Europe. He is considered the leading English non-figurative painter. The creator of abstract compositions –sometimes treated plastically as bas-reliefs–and of highly stylized landscapes and still-lifes, Nicholson seeks above all to express static, architectural themes of great simplicity of form. His art is a kind of exact, refined geometry, controlled always by exquisite judgement and heightened by a range of colours that is best described as chaste. The same objects borrowed from everyday life–a pitcher, a table, a glass–serve as the basis for an infinite number of variations which, through subtle modulations, result in an increasingly complex series of linear rhythms and constructions. Within the fastidious limits imposed by his intellect and his sensibility, Nicholson has been drawn, now towards the classical, now towards the romantic ideal. He started from a basis of clear-cut reality and gradually, after a period of increased schematization, reached in his white plaster reliefs of around 1935 a culmination in the organization of static relationships. His evolution did not stop there, however, with these pure distillations of the circle and the rectangle, but has come full cycle to a renewed, even more purified concept of reality. In this more recent work are resolved the

two sides of his nature, represented by his respect for Mondrian and his admiration for Alfred Wallis, the old Cornish primitive. Nicholson has written '. . . so far from "abstract" art being the withdrawal of the artist from reality (into an "ivory tower") it has brought art once again into common everyday life . . .', and '. . . the problems dealt with in "abstract" are art related to the interplay of forces and therefore, . . . any solution reached has a bearing on all interplay between forces: it is related to Arsenal *v* Tottenham Hotspur quite as much as to the stars in their courses.' Nicholson's contribution to the abstract movement is a highly individual one. In spite of the severity of his style and the rigour of his geometrical conception, his work retains an intensely English character. A certain gentleness and discreet lyricism relate him to the English water-colourists, as do the lightness of his touch and the transparency of his colour. He is represented in museums all over the world. In 1952 he was awarded the first prize for painting at the 39th International Exhibition at the Carnegie Institute, Pittsburgh.   F. MC E.

NOLDE Emil (1867-1956). German painter; born at Schleswig, died at Seebüll, near the Danish frontier. His real name was Emil Hansen and he was born of a Danish-Frisian family. About 1904 he changed his name to that of his native village and from then on signed his canvases Nolde. A teacher of drawing, he devoted himself entirely to painting from 1898 on. He studied in Munich, Paris and Copenhagen. In 1904, after Impressionist beginnings, his touch became stronger and more free, and colour played a more active part in his work. In addition to landscapes of his native region, its sea, swamps, and gardens, fantastic and grotesque figures began to appear in his canvases. From 1906 to 1907 he participated in the Brücke *(*)*, but later, being of an unsociable and solitary nature, he remained outside all groups. In 1908 his art attained its most monumental form, and colour charged with expression burst out in unrestrained force. As early as 1909 he produced large religious compositions: *The Last Supper*, *Whitsun*, *The Life of Christ* (1912), an altar piece in nine parts; also figures from a personal mythology, such as *The Warrior and His Wife*

(1912). At the same time, masks, primitive statuettes and exotic textiles appeared in his still-lifes. In 1913-1914 he was a member of an ethnological expedition that travelled to Russia, China, Japan and reached Polynesia. What he discovered in the latter area was not so much the more authentic life that Gauguin had sought as an elemental demoniac essence in the attitudes of the primitive beings that he studied with keen interest. Later, Nolde was bitterly attacked by the Nazis, who went so far as to forbid him to paint As a water-colourist and.

NOLDE. MARSH LANDSCAPE. 1916. *Kunstmuseum, Basel.*

engraver he did important work (etchings, lithographs, woodcuts, from 1905 to 1922), which is among the most exciting in contemporary German art. A demon chained to earth, Nolde seems to have shaped the landscapes, flowers and the savages or girls he represents with their luxuriance of flesh from the very earth itself. And the colours he generously spreads out on his canvas are opaque and dazzling, like earth on fire. Colour does not represent, st *is* the magic presence of things and men on the canvas, and thus their primitive being is unmasked before the spectator with a sudden shock. Mystical in his way, Nolde discovered a religiosity in the very heart of the most primitive sensuality.   F. M.

NOUVELLE ATHÈNES

About 1877 the Impressionist painters dispersed. Starting from this period, certain painters, whose names remain none the less linked with Impressionism, began to frequent the Café de la Nouvelle Athènes, in the Place Pigalle. From then, the writers predominated and included Duranty, Armand Silvestre, Burty, Paul Alexis, Zola's friend, and George Moore, the novelist, who gave a vivid description of the evenings in his *Memoirs.* The only painter who went there fairly regularly was Renoir, who was still living in Paris, Monet and Sisley only put in rare appearances, while Cézanne only went there when his friend, the musician Cabaner, a rather eccentric character, succeeded in taking him along. The only regulars among any eminent artists were Manet and Degas. They were even more out of touch with their Impressionist friends for having kept rather detached from the movement before and they ended by being the only members of the group to frequent the café. It is said that, in one of the rooms of the Nouvelle Athènes, the painter and engraver, Marcellin Desboutin, sat with the actress, Ellen Andrée, for Degas' picture, The *Absinth Drinker* (*vide* p. 86), and that Manet did his sketch of George Moore, sitting at a table in an easy, elegant attitude.

O

OROZCO José Clemente (1883-1949). Born in Zapotlan, in the state of Jalisco; died in Mexico City. Along with Diego Rivera, Orozco can be considered one of the initiators of the Mexican painting of today. Less influenced than Rivera by European painting, probably closer to Aztec tradition, Orozco appraised perfectly the requirements made by the immensity of the American continent. He did not accept the limits suggested to European artists by the will inherited from the ancient Greeks to reduce plastic arts to human scale. As he worked out cartoons for his frescoes, Orozco no doubt thought more of skyscrapers than of houses and monuments in Mexico, although the Maya or Aztec pyramids could have justified his choice. His resolution to put his art at the service of his political opinions was certainly more decisive. Every work was to illustrate a grievance of contemporary man. The tendency led him to give to his work the character of an appeal, a message, and therefore to arrive eventually at a poster style. In this field Orozco's virtuosity is incomparable. His art not only solicits, grips the attention of the passer-by, but also attempts to make him react, and succeeds in doing so. Aesthetically, this will of the painter has not failed to create serious misunderstandings. It is, nevertheless, true that the work of Orozco has enabled contemporary painters, Mexican in particular, to escape from affectation, free themselves of their repressions and broaden their vision. In some respects Orozco was a renovator. He showed that modern painting could be directed towards a field deliberately neglected by the painters of the late nineteenth century, who had forgotten the example and lesson of Delacroix. The dramatic violence and anguished, dark vision of his art are the expression of a people who revolted after years of suppression. The age-old song of humanity can be heard in his drawings, engravings, easel painting and particularly in his vast murals; there the poet and the soldier, the prostitute, and the widow, the peasant and his master, the slave and the free man, all find a place. A Promethean breath gives life to everything and leaves its powerful mark everywhere. Notable among his mural paintings are the Palace of Fine Arts in Mexico City (1934), the six mobile panels for the

OROZCO. ZAPATISTAS. 1931. *Museum of Modern Art, New York.*

Museum of Modern Art, New York (1940), the Hall of the Reform in the National History Museum, Chapultepec (1948) and the dome of the Hospicio Cabanas, at Guadalajara (1937-1939), which is certainly his masterpiece. In spite of the definitely local, deeply Mexican character of his painting, Orozco has been recognized by many inhabitants of the Western Hemisphere as one of the first painters to have expressed the spirit of a new civilization. It is, moreover, indisputable that not only the dimensions of his work but even the very light in his painting correspond to those of the cities of the New World. No wonder, therefore, that European artists, borne upon frequently contrary currents, find it so difficult to accept the genius of Orozco. None the less, this painter offers them one of the most precious means for escaping the impasse to which a number of them have come. The influence of Orozco is at present undergoing an eclipse, for today his art appears to be too faithful to a certain period in the history of his country. But is it likely that justice will be done in the future to the powerful and incontestable personality of this artist.   PH. S.

ORPHISM A word used, from 1912 on, by the poet Guillaume Apollinaire, particularly in the lecture he gave in Berlin at the time of Delaunay's exhibition at the Der Sturm Gallery, to designate the movement in the new painting of the time, which proclaimed the primacy of pure colour in pictorial construction. Realizing the extent to which these manifestations of vitality reflected a will to escape the severe harmonies of Picasso and Braque, Apollinaire prophesied the disruption of Cubism; then, invoking the name of Orpheus, under whose patronage he had just placed the poems of his *Bestiary*, or *Cortège of Orpheus*, he compared the experiments of Delaunay, Kupka and the young painters surrounding them to the poetic and musical games whose fancy delighted him. According to Apollinaire, Delaunay believed that when a primary colour does not determine its complementary, it shatters in the atmosphere and produces simultaneously all the colours of the spectrum. After having stressed his attachment to the pure colours of Ingres and praised Seurat's major creation, the contrast of colours, Delaunay claimed that behind all pure expression in modern painting there would thereafter be Simultaneous Contrast, the sole means of securing dynamism of colours and their arrangement in the picture. This exaltation of the dynamic mission of colour brought forth an entirely new art, with its own laws of creation, capable of emerging from any objective, visual representation of Nature.   J. LA.

OUDOT Roland. French painter; born in 1897 in Paris. Oudot belongs to the group of artists who, without trying to shock, have asserted themselves between the two wars and been given the name of 'painters of poetic reality'. They are generally considered as the final product of Impressionism. This has meant giving Impressionism and its consequences an interpretation that the movement certainly did not have at the beginning; and it is not because these painters have taken the landscape as an essential theme that they should

DELAUNAY. PARIS. 1937. AIR, IRON AND WATER.

OUDOT. PEN-AND-INK SKETCH. 1954.

to systematic formulae. He is one of those who remain true to a very classical conception of art, in which an always controlled emotion admits of no facility. Nature remains his inspiration under all circumstances, but it is Nature conceived anew, seen through a tense, penetrating sensitivity that is never lacking.   R. C.

OZENFANT Amédée. French painter; born in 1886 at Saint-Quentin. After studying the classics in Spain, Ozenfant returned to Saint-Quentin, where he attended an art school. He was given the La Tour pastels to copy and noticed with surprise that in his big box of clear colours none was suitable; he ascertained, for example, that 'sky blues or the flesh tones are neutrals transfigured by tones even more neutral'. The painter was to remember this lesson when he taught his disciples, 'Painting starts where reality ends, where illusion begins'. From 1915 to 1917 Ozenfant laid down the principles of Purism in his magazine *L'Élan*. In 1917 he met Charles-Édouard Jeanneret, the future Le Corbusier, and made him part of the movement. In 1919 they published together *After Cubism*, a manifesto of Purism (*). Ozenfant's work then consisted of compositions of simplified forms, organized according to a set of strict rules, strictly followed in order to avoid 'facility' and force the imagination to exert itself fully. While Juan Gris at the same period was proceeding from the abstract to the concrete, Ozenfant started from real or possible objects and moved toward abstraction, eliminating everything variable or accidental from each object, to retain only constants. The Purist rules of organization have often been compared to those imposed upon the fugue by J. S. Bach, and it is quite natural that certain paintings by Ozenfant bear the name of *Chord* or *Fugue*. From 1920 to 1925 Ozenfant and Jeanneret published their magazine *Esprit Nouveau* (*), which enabled the boldest and most diverse tendencies in contemporary art to express themselves. From 1925 to 1928 the whole activity of Ozenfant tended toward the renewal of mural painting; the central work of this period is the vast composition in the Paris Museum of Modern Art, *The Four Races*. In 1928 he published *Art* (I: *The Balance Sheet of Modern Art*; II: *The Structure of a New Spirit*), which is

be credited with Impressionist descent; Oudot's art has, in fact, a fixity that contradicts the mobility of Impressionism. His large blue skies, his dominant greys, his slate tones are the opposite of scintillating light; he seeks stability rather than instantaneity. After having very strongly felt, until about 1920, the influence of Cézanne, Oudot turned toward Fauvism and Cubism, but without allowing himself to be diverted from close contact with Nature. At first interested by the landscapes of the Ile-de-France, he has recently taken up those of Provence, whose austerity suits his temperament. His dominant grey is far from being monotonous; it gives a mineral resonance ot his very intense reds and hard blues, which are softened by the contact. Even though his landscapes maintain an austerity from which man is nearly always absent, Oudot introduces into his compositions a note of calm fantasy, of sober and reserved elegance. His compositions attest a rigorous sense of balance, and a nice disposition of elements allows him to adjust his style to the requirements of mural composition without recourse

OZENFANT. STILL-LIFE. 1925.
R. La Roche Collection. Paris.

now a classic and has been reprinted many times in several languages. In 1931 he began a vast composition called *Life*, in which over a hundred figures handled in the Purist manner lyrically sing human solidarity, and he worked on it for seven years. This work now belongs to the Museum of Modern Art in Paris. From 1935 to 1938 he published *Journey Through Life*, his diary for the years 1931-1934, in which he recorded all events, whether general or personal, in so far as they influenced the work in progress, *Life*. Since 1938 Ozenfant has been living in New York, where he founded the Ozenfant School of Fine Arts. Developing his theory of 'Pre-Forms', he has endeavoured to show that great works of art, like all truths, exist necessarily, potentially, in humanity's subsconscious before being revealed by an 'inventor'. While his work before the important composition *Life* was dominated by a will for economy, to say as much as possible with a minimum of means, since 1950 the artist seems to have set himself the goal of 'giving as much as possible to be seen'; in fact, his recent works appear quite simple from a distance, but on closer inspection, series of details are revealed. E. L.

P

PAPIERS COLLÉS This is a technique
as old as Time. But what was originally
only a children's game has become a
genuine and undeniable art form in this
century. What is its origin, and who
was its inventor ? While collages appeared in the work of both Picasso and
Braque at the end of 1912, it is apparently the latter who first had the
idea and was the first to apply it. His
Still-life with a Fruit-dish of 1912 was
historically the first *papier collé*. In fact,
by introducing, in 1911, a typeset
phrase into his picture *The Portuguese*,
Braque discovered a new plastic element, which, in a way, was a preparation for the arrival of *papier collé*. At
this time Cubism was already loosening
its ties with reality and drifting toward

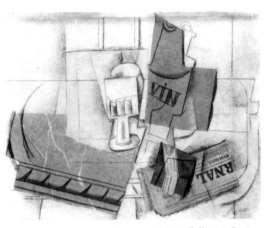

PICASSO. PAPIER COLLÉ. 1914. *Private Collection, Paris.*

abstraction. The subject tended to be eliminated;
the picture was not so firmly constructed. The
question was less one of representing the object
in its concrete totality than of considering it as
an ensemble of pure signs, of exclusively graphic
or pictorial effect, as an intellectual and often
hermetic creation. Thus at the time when Synthetic Cubism was being substituted for Analytic
Cubism, it is not surprising that painters in
general, and Braque in particular, should have
sensed the dangers of an art divorced from the
world of appearances. It must not be forgotten,
moreover, that Braque had never ceased being a
craftsman, and a craftsman in the French tradition. Consequently, typographical characters
and, after this, imitation wood and marble, the
trompe-l'œil effects that he had seen used and had
used himself during his childhood in his father's
workshop, appeared in his work as reminders of

external reality. From *trompe-l'œil* painting to the
use of the very materials reproduced was only
one step, and one which was soon taken by both
Braque and Picasso. Evolving Cubism lent itself
to the new technique: there were no more intricate architectures, entangled lines, minute
strokes or monochrome colour, but only plane
surfaces, large flat areas, lighter and more vivid
tones. Braque glued pieces of printed or decorative papers packing paper or of newspaper to
cardboard or canvas, and then applied either ink
or pencil lines or touches of gouache or oil
paint to them (see *Aria de Bach* reproduced on
page 43). Picasso's procedure was not much
different in his *Cane Chair* (1912) or *The Bottle of
Suze* (1912). Soon both incorporated into their
pictures sand, pieces of cloth or wood, odd
objects like playing-cards, boxes of matches or
wrappers from tobacco packages. While Picasso

GRIS. BREAKFAST. PAPIER COLLÉ. 1914.
Museum of Modern Art, New York.

mark the high point of the Cubist *papiers collés*. But the experiments that Jean Arp, another sculptor, made at the same time revealed entirely different preoccupations. Arp, a deliberate and reflective artist, concerned, above all, with sobriety, if not austerity, of expression, cut out from paper with great precision plain forms that he had only to glue upon a ground to obtain simple and straightforward rhythms.

Italian Futurists, in turn, experimented in the technique practised by the French Cubists: Balla, Boccioni, Carrà, Prampolini, Severini. The Dadaists made use of it also, but in a spirit that was different from, if not opposed to, that of the inventors. Whereas the latter desired to accentuate the plastic value of the image, the boisterous followers of Dada used the same technique to destroy the traditional concept of a picture, to exhibit in the most extravagant juxtapositions their contempt for logic and reason. In the collages of a Max Ernst or a Schwitters, for example, with their incongruous contrasts and their challenging metaphysical and literary allusions, it would be fruitless to look for a new dialectic of form, colour and space. Nevertheless, the humour and fantasy of these artists could not fail to influence the Surrealists Miró, Tanguy and Magritte about 1928. Russian Constructivists, Germans from the Bauhaus (*) and Neo-Plasticists, also made uses of the collage technique. Today, among non-representational painters, there are an enormous number of interesting experiments going on. The term, collage has acquired a so much wider and more generalised meaning that it is now no longer distinct from the term, painting, and has sometimes replaced it. There are countless artists who add plaster, grit, cement and tar to traditional mediums, who attach sheet-iron, nails, scrap iron or bronze, sacking, bits of glass and gold leaf to their canvas or hardboard and who combine crumpled or cut out paper, animal and plant remains with their paint. Neo-realism's consumption of torn posters, fragments of lace, display accessories and everyday utensils must be considerable and it is all attached to a support, at times with a sense of humour, but only too often without any regard for order or taste. Matisse's experiments should not be underrated; for there is no doubt that they are the most important since the Cubist *papiers collés*. It was, in fact, Matisse

sought unexpected effects of contrast, Braque succeeded in revealing the relations between the concrete elements employed and forms mentally conceived, to achieve an intimate poetry of exquisite appeal. The common, inert, dead substances had only to be incorporated by human ingenuity into a picture to take on artistic life. Picasso has always remained faithful to this new form of expression and, unlike Braque, has returned to it from time to time all through his career. Thus, in 1937-1938, he put the finishing touch to the largest *papier collé* in existence, 15 ft. by 9 ½ft., *Women at their Toilette*.

As early as 1913 Juan Gris made harmoniously rhythmic collages of selected materials, juxtaposed with the melancholy, somewhat haughty lyricism peculiar to him: pages of books, musical staves, decorative flowered papers, old-fashioned engravings. But while Picasso and Braque applied the *papier collé* technique to drawing as well as painting, Gris used it exclusively for painting. Between 1914 and 1918 the French sculptor Laurens executed numerous compositions which

who revived collage as an idiom and endowed it with an inimitable vocabulary, syntax and style. The *papier collé* was the happy culmination of his art and life. Barred by illness and age from easel painting, he gave up the brush for the scissors and paint for coloured paper during his last ten years. Cut and glued paper came to be his sole medium. He mastered it so completely, made it a tool so obedient to his will, so suited to his gifts, that his *papiers collés* illuminate his entire past and justify all his previous experiments. His constant effort, continued during half a century, to increase the emotional value of the arabesque and the sonority of tone, to create an increasingly acute feeling of pictorial space, could not fail to lead to the cut and glued coloured papers to which his book, *Jazz*, introduced us in 1947. There is indeed little difference between his pencil drawings and the designs he made with scissors; indeed he said himself 'scissors can achieve more sensitivity than the pencil'. As he preferred to apply colour on his canvases flat, he had prepared himself for a long time to substitute paper for paint. Moreover, by cutting out sheets of coloured paper with scissors he could simultaneously associate line with colour and contour with surface. This was the most unexpected, although quite predictable, consequence of the new experiment for Matisse's art: in resorting to new tools and consequently new principles, in submitting to a craftsman's discipline, he was forced to give to form the same opportunity he had previously given to colour. This is why, completing the Cubist experiment, Matisse was able to make *papiers collés* an autonomous medium, an idiom as authentic, as alive as the weaving, enamel and stained glass of the past. Thanks to him, *papier collé* has become a completely convincing and irreplaceable form of art, and it may stand as the modern equivalent of medieval illumination. His technique has been effectively used by painters like Gischia and Lanskoy and professional designers of posters and other forms of advertising.

F. E.

PARIS (School of). 'L'École de Paris' was the name given to a group formed after the First World War by a number of foreign painters, brought to Paris by similar needs and united by similar affinities. Since then the name

MATISSE. SORROW OF THE KING. 1952. COLLAGE OF PAPER PAINTED WITH GOUACHE. *Musée d'Art Moderne, Paris.*

has acquired a looser meaning. Originally, the School of Paris consisted of Modigliani, Pascin, Chagall, Kisling, Soutine (q.v.): an Italian, a Bulgarian, a Russian, a Pole and a Lithuanian. To these can be added the names of Leopold Gottlieb, Eugene Zak, Krémegne, three Poles; Mintchine, a Ukrainian; Max Band, a Lithuanian. All these painters were of foreign birth, and however diverse their ideas, temperaments, ways of life, they were brought together by common bonds of age and race. They belonged to the same generation, all having been born between 1884 and 1900, and they were all Jews. These uprooted ones liked France and drew from French sensibility, thought, and art the elements they needed to bring their gifts to fulfilment. But as painters they did not succeed in making themselves French. Contemporary with the Cubists, they did not espouse their theories nor follow their example. They always remained lyricists, romantics, expressionists and passionate individualists. Looking out upon the world through tormented souls, they rendered it with a subtle and disenchanted grace like Modigliani, or, in a burst of desperation, like Soutine. Whatever their individual style, all shared the same disquiet, the same moral suffering under different forms. These Expressionists were very different from the French, German, Scandinavian or Flemish Expressionists. It is possible, therefore, to speak of a school, but to speak of a School of

PASCIN. GINETTE AND MIREILLE. 1929.
Petit Palais, Paris.

Paris is less accurate. Besides, these three words have acquired an increasingly wide meaning.

For many the 'School of Paris' tends to include all the immigrant painters who have settled in the shadow of the Eiffel Tower since the beginning of the century: Picasso, Juan Gris, Van Dongen and Foujita as much as Chagall, Kisling and Pascin. For several years opinion outside France has tended to identify the School of Paris with all the innovating activity of modern painters who work in Paris, the artistic movement that develops and feeds on all the contributions and personalities attracted by the universal prestige of French painting.

In short, for most people today the School of Paris is synonymous with the vanguard of contemporary painting.   F. E.

MODIGLIANI. PORTRAIT OF KISLING.

PASCIN Pseudonym of Julius Pincas (1885-1930), a painter born in Vidin in Bulgaria; died in Paris. The son of a Spanish-Jewish father and a half-Serbian, half-Italian mother, Pascin did his early work in Vienna, Berlin, and Munich, where he collaborated while still very young on the satirical paper *Simplicissimus*. He came to Paris for the first time in 1905. Adopted very soon America, he became the perfect example of 'internationalism', as Pierre Mac Orlan has written. Having hob-nobbed in all cafés of the old and new worlds with painters of every school, he was fond of camping in Paris, in the midst of the greatest disorder, among dusty sofas on which he made his models sit or lie, suggesting to them the least chaste poses. Although success came to him, he was found hanged in his studio on June 20th, 1930, the opening day of his exhibition at the Georges Petit Gallery. Like Toulouse-Lautrec, Pascin asserts himself above all as a great draughtsman even in his paintings, most of which were done after 1920. Colour often enhances only slightly, with exquisite restraint and delicacy, meanings that have already been brought out by the drawing. The life of the various planes is suggested with an authority and a charm that recall the great masters of the eighteenth century, whom he particularly liked. A supernatural atmosphere bathes his prostitutes, with their short legs and vague eyes. Alone or in pairs, they look like prostrate or passive little girls killing time. Sometimes there is a sort of mystical note in this acute and tender eroticism, occasionally mixed with Biblical reminiscences

PECHSTEIN. THE ARTIST'S WIFE. 1910.
Wallraf-Richartz Museum, Cologne.

(*The Prodigal Son, Salome, The Judgment of Solomon*). From this voluptuous art emanates a kind of irremediable despair.

Pascin drew everywhere, and with passion. A line, at once fine and heavy, often impressed through sheets of carbon paper, nervously accentuates rhythms and contours. Modelling is achieved by shading light greys with a finger as voluptuous as Renoir's. The heightenings in water-colour are hardly felt. Illustrations of books and sketches brought back from Tunisia and Florida reveal Pascin, whose portraits have such subtlety, as one of the best witnesses of life between the two wars.   CL. R.-M.

PASMORE Victor (born in 1908 at Chelsham, Surrey). English painter. He was educated at Harrow, but although he had already shown a remarkable talent for painting, the premature death of his father forced him to begin earning his living without training at an art school. He worked for the LCC as a clerk at County Hall, London, from 1927 to 1938. During this period, he painted in his spare time and attended evening classes at the Central School. From 1930 he exhibited regularly with the London Artists' Association, later known as the London Group. In 1937, he was one of the group of artists who founded the Euston Road School, which closed when war broke out. At this time, Degas, particularly his portraits, Bonnard and Vuillard were the most important influences on him. His impressionistic paintings of everyday occupations, still-lifes and portraits were built up of luminous, carefully modulated tones in which green, yellow and rose predominated. Space was suggested by tone-colour alone and outlines were dissolved in the atmospheric effect of light (*Lamplight*, 1941, Tate Gallery and the *Dressing Table*, 1941). Between 1943 and 1947, the *Thames at Chiswick* and *Hammersmith Gardens* series showed a gradual development towards the complete abstraction that first appeared in two paintings at the London Group exhibition, 1948. Certain landscape features in the *Thames at Chiswick* (1946-1947) appear as almost isolated rectangular forms in the hazy landscape and in some areas the colour is applied in an adaptation of pointillist technique; in *River Scene* (1946-1947) the whole emphasis is on the formalised curves of tree trunks and branches. From abstract elements in landscapes such as these, Pasmore went on to pure abstractions in collages and oil paintings, built up of rectangles and triangles. He explained how he had been led to them by studying the writings of the Impressionists.

Several of his paintings at this point, particularly those on the *Curvilinear Motif* and the *Spiral Motif*, like the *Coast of the Inland Sea* (1950, Tate Gallery), had their starting point in purely abstract form, but were strongly suggestive of landscape, hill shapes, the sea and rocks. It was because these associations had become so strong that he felt a need to break away completely. The relief constructions, simple spatial arrangements of horizontal or vertical blocks of painted wood attached to perspex, were the result. His collaboration with architects was both a result and an encouragement of this development, notably in planning the new area of Peterlee, begun in 1955. There, in order to design a well proportioned architectural whole in harmony with the landscape, the first housing layouts were formed with wooden blocks on the workshop floor and not on paper.   B. W.

PECHSTEIN Max (1881 - 1955). German painter; born at Eckersbach, near Zwickau, died in Berlin. His career began in 1896, when he was apprenticed to a decorative painter. In 1900, he joined the Dresden School of Applied Arts and, after 1902, the Academy of Fine Arts. After meeting Heckel and Kirchner in 1906, he became a member of the Brücke *(*)*. The easy appeal of a simplified style won him an immediate popularity and he became one of the best known painters of German Expressionism. He won the Prix de Rome in 1907, made friends with Van Dongen in Paris on his way to Italy and exhibited at the Salon des Indépendants in 1908. He was the only one of the Brücke painters to visit Paris and the impressions it made on him are reflected in his paintings from 1908 to 1913 in which the influences of Van Gogh, Gauguin and Cézanne appear. If Kirchner is to be believed, he also became 'an imitator of Matisse.' This opinion demands qualification; for the obvious way in which Pechstein reveals his sources is an indication of his naïve acceptance of their influences rather than his gift of imitation. Anyway, his 'imitations' of French painters in their turn influenced

CHIRICO. ENIGMA OF THE TIME. 1911.   *Mattioli Collection, Milan.*

his friends, who could learn from a sort of demonstration of the new tendencies in Parisian art. When his works were refused at the Berlin Secession in 1910, he helped to found the New Berlin Secession, which chose him as their president. He was elected a member of the Prussian Academy of Arts in 1922, but he was struck off the role by the Nazis in 1933 as a representative of 'degenerate art'. From 1945 until his death, he taught at the Berlin School of Fine Arts.

He acquired a personal style by studying exotic art (in 1913-1914 he paid a visit to the Pellew Islands, then a German colony, for this purpose). It is characterised by

PASMORE. BEACH IN CORNWALL. 1950. PEN AND INK.
The Arts Council Collection, London.

an almost brutal simplification, a natural boldness of composition, a boldness that reappears in his use of hot colouring, generally lacking any variety of tones or subtlety. But a sturdy, joyful sensuality redeems these defects and gives the same vitality to his landscapes and flower paintings as it does to his nudes. Although he always drew his inspiration from nature, later on his style became far too academic and lost the vigorous qualities it possessed in his youth.   E. R.

PEINTURE MÉTAPHYSIQUE (Metaphysical Painting). It is Giorgio de Chirico who must be credited with the invention of Metaphysical Painting. It was born in Paris between 1910 and 1915 and was, above all, a reaction against the Futurist dynamism. It revived a longing for antiquity, exalted the dream, discovered the mystery of apparitions. 'Around me', Giorgio de Chirico wrote, 'the international gang of "modern" painters was making a foolish commotion in the midst of worn-out formulae and sterile systems. I alone, in my dismal studio of the rue Campagne-Première, was beginning to glimpse the first traces of an art more complete, more pro-

found, more intricate and more *metaphysical*'. During his stay in Munich, Chirico had read Nietzsche, Schopenhauer, Weininger. Otto Weininger had said 'the arc of a circle, as an ornament, can be beautiful; it is capable of completion: it still leaves room for imagination'. In Turin, before the eighteenth-century porticoes and arcades, Chirico must have thought of Weininger. And Schopenhauer had urged his countrymen not to put statues of their famous men on columns or high pedestals, but instead on low stands, 'as it is done in Italy, where marble men seem to be on the level of the passers-by and to walk among them'. Metaphysical painting would be lacking an essential element of its aesthetic doctrine of the 'mannequins' that populated Chirico's canvases were not there. The idea of 'mannequins' was suggested to him by a poem of his brother Alberto, a painter, poet and musician known as Alberto Savinio. The objectives of Metaphysical Painting could not be better described than in this sentence by Chirico himself: 'We who know the signs of the metaphysical alphabet know what joys and sorrows are present in a portico, on a street corner, within the walls of a room, or inside a box'. To Cubism Chirico owed 'at least the suggestion of chromatic composition, which became freer, more rhythmical, more dancing about 1913' (Giorgio Castelfranco, in *Pittura Moderna*).

Although Metaphysical Painting was born in Paris, it was in Italy, at Ferrara, during the First World War, that it became not a movement, like Futurism, but a 'school', which could have adopted the mannequin as an emblem. Chirico and Savinio had been called up and assigned to the Ferrara depot. Chirico's *Metaphysical Interiors*, which were painted in this city, were suggested to him by certain shops in the ghetto, 'in which one could see cakes and biscuits of extremely metaphysical and odd shapes' (*vide* Chirico).

The first to undergo Chirico's influence was the painter Carlo Carrà, who was also an infantry soldier and a former Futurist. With less fantasy, Carrà painted the same objects as Chirico: mannequins, copper fishes, biscuits; he placed them in a three-dimensional space, transporting them from the oleograph that inspired Chirico to the ideal climate of Giotto, for both form and colour. With Carrà objects are no longer metaphysical signs, as in the works of Chirico. For him the painters' imagination must express itself 'through lines and colours', through the relation 'it discovers between light and shadow, the full and the void'. In short, Carrà employed the language of a painter not of a poet, as Chirico did. His paintings exercise a less fascinating but more profound magic than Chirico's, which were to influence the Surrealists (*vide* Surrealism) so strongly. Alberto Savinio, the theoretician of Metaphysical Painting, maintained that it was 'total representation of spiritual necessities within plastic limits–power to express the spectral side of things–irony'. Surprisingly enough, it was Carlo Carrà who fulfilled the third condition, irony, perhaps unconsciously, by clothing the pensive mannequins of Chirico in tunics with folds and putting tennis rackets and balls in their hands (*vide* Carrà).

'We metaphysical painters have sanctified reality', contended Chirico. For us the painter who seems to have actually sanctified reality is Giorgio Morandi: 'closing the triangle of Metaphysical Painting', he brought it to its purest expression. With three tones and a few very simple lines, Giorgio Morandi creates mystery, as Chirico himself admitted when he wrote in *Valori Plastici*, the magazine of Metaphysical art

published by Mario Broglio, 'He sees with the eyes of a man who believes; and the inner framework of things that are dead for us, because motionless, appears to him under its most comforting aspect, under its *eternal aspect*' (*vide* Morandi). Metaphysical Painting did not survive the First World War, which confronted artists with new problems, but it has proved to be one of the key periods of twentieth-century painting.

Its collapse may be said to be due to over-elaboration of design and obscurity of intention. Lines and perspectives multiply in all directions, weird figures stripped of life and sexuality are no more than mannequins. The movement played itself out and was attacked by its own creator, Chirico, who from 1930 onwards has denied his former pictures and has painted in an orthodox style which bears no relation to his earlier experiments; Morandi now prefers the world of Nature.   S. L.

PERMEKE Constant (1886-1951). Belgian painter; born in Antwerp; died at Jabbeke, near Bruges. Permeke attended courses at the Academies of Bruges and Ghent before settling in Laethem-Saint-Martin (*), the cradle of Flemish Expressionism, in 1909. He

PERMEKE. THE FIANCÉS. 1923.
Musée des Beaux-Arts, Brussels.

CHIRICO. ENIGMA OF AN AUTUMN EVENING. 1910.

human, the vigour of muscles, the vitality of the people, everyday toil, all that man receives from the soil: the strength of instinct, generosity of the heart, humble and patient devotion. And this with the resources of the earth, the colours of earth. Passionately devoted to the plastic, he was quite naturally led to sculpture, beginning in 1936. But his modelling is no more than the solid, massive, summary forms contained in his canvases transposed into clay. Permeke was the faithful interpreter of his race, his native country, in a period of artistic renewal. He was a Flemish painter with absolute sincerity. He was an Expressionist painter without preciosity, without mannerism, with great naturalness. This is why his proletarian giants, his colossal effigies, his huge constructions, achieve a virile, wholehearted grandeur. One therefore pardons him his total lack of finesse, elegance, charm. He was a proud workman of painting, one of the very few Expressionists to have spared us a display of their sufferings or their despair.   F. E.

belonged to the second Laethem group with Servaes, Frits van den Berghe and the Smet brothers. Severely wounded at Antwerp in 1914, he was evacuated to England. He returned to Belgium after the hostilities. He worked successively in Antwerp, Ostend and finally at Jabbeke, where he spent the last twenty-five years of his life. At first influenced by Impressionism (*Winter in Flanders*, 1912), his work drifted toward the baroque as early as 1913, the baroque peculiar to a generation of Belgian artists, among whom Permeke was the central figure. His English landscapes, seascapes of Ostend, harbour scenes, fishermen's homes, studies of peasants, views of Flanders, nudes, all bear the stamp of his plebeian temperament, rough, jovial and powerful. No one has represented Flemish Expressionism better than Permeke: by his physical health, his muscularity, his dynamism, as well as by his elemental, monumental vision of Nature and man. There is nothing artificial, studied or cerebral in canvases such as *The Caravan*, *The Harvester*, *Green Seascape* and many others, in which the artist placed rough, full forms, titanic figures, encircling them with a thick stroke, colouring them on a very sober scale of heavy, dark tones. Indifferent to light, he wanted to exalt the human and, in the

PETTORUTI Emilio (born in 1895 at Buenos Aires). His parents were Italians who emigrated to Argentina. He went to Florence in 1913 to study Renaissance painting, but it was Futurism that fascinated him and Cubism that soon after absorbed all his attention. He took part in several international exhibitions, notably one in 1923 at the Berlin gallery, Der Sturm, of work by Villon, Gleizes, Marcoussis, Klee, Archipenko and Zadkine. In 1924, Pettoruti met Juan Gris whose work he felt had affinities with his own. He was on the point of signing a contract with Léonce Rosenberg, when he was summoned back to Buenos Aires by his family. He intended to spend six months there, but stayed for thirty years.

PETTORUTI. SPRINGING LIGHT. 1916.

which he aimed above all at purity of line, stability of form and the investigation of colour values. He steadily pursued his experiments until their logical conclusion eliminated all natural references. The Papiers collés of 1917, followed by the superb Still-lifes and the great Harlequins, showed him to be one of the most skilful and sensitive of the Cubists. His particular contribution to the movement was his conception of space and light. The Cubists had not been concerned with the effects of light, but he added them to the Cubist analysis of form. It was a subjective, artificial light produced by contrasting areas of flat colour and the use of chiaroscuro. There would be a gap in the history of Cubism and of non-figurative art of which he was one of the earliest exponents, if his contribution to them went unrecorded. In the completely non-representational composition of the last dozen or so years, Pettoruti shows the same severe, reflective qualities and the same rejection of emotional extravagance and facile expression that has always characterised his work.   F. E.

His activities brought modern art to Latin America and were responsible for an important movement to bring fresh life to its art. At the same time he acquired a reputation that spread all over the countries of the new continent. He influenced several artists through his teaching and example. In 1930, he was appointed director of the Museum of La Plata, but was dismissed by the dictator, Perón, in 1947 and returned to Europe. He settled in Paris in 1953 where he was awarded the Guggenheim Prize three years later.

After 1916, Pettoruti gave up the Futurist analysis of movement for a further exploration of the Cubist experiment in

PEYRONNET Dominique (1872 - 1943). French painter ; born in Talence, a suburb of Bordeaux; died in Paris. Peyronnet, a printer, came to painting rather late and brought to it his craftsman's conscience, his

PEYRONNET. MEDITERRANEAN. 1942.   *Private Collection, Paris.*

love of precision, of work well done, of a well-learned trade. He was almost fifty when he began to paint, with the patient honesty he had acquired in printing coloured pictures. He judged his achievements with as calm a certainty as when he made an exact adjustment on his machine. He did not fear to tackle the greatest subjects in Nature; the sea was his favourite theme, and he did not hesitate to think that no one could represent certain subjects better than he. It is true that this pride was genuinely naïve; it is also true that he painted with a concern for never falsifying reality, and thus he succeeded in extracting from familiar subjects a secret life that certainly does not have the grandeur present in the works of Rousseau, but is not devoid of mystery. His art is somewhat frigid, but never dry. In his very special way of isolating every object, making it a whole in itself, he recalls the Gothic Primitives. In his faithfulness to his subject there is a fervour, put to the service of Nature, that exalts reality and doubles its intensity. Thus he has created an immobile world in limpid air, whose poetry is outside all the present problems of painting. R. C.

PICABIA Francis (1879-1953). Picabia was born and died in Paris. His father was Cuban, his mother French. He spent his life changing residences, friendships, ideas and styles, fighting for a cause and then against it, in favour of a new one that he abandoned in turn. An anarchist by atavism and temperament, a prolix and subversive artist, making fun of everything and of himself, fond of disparaging ideas, institutions, men, sceptical to the point of dogmatism, a lover of freedom to the point of libertarianism, much less concerned with making a career than with creating a scandal, Picabia nevertheless left his stamp on his time as an artist and, even more, as an individual. A pupil of the École Nationale des Beaux-Arts, he painted definitely Impressionist pictures until 1908, and then compositions influenced by Cubism. In 1911 he joined the *Section d'Or (*)* group but left it the following year, to come over to an Orphic concept of painting. The same year he painted one of his canvases, *Procession in Seville*. In 1915 he came into contact with Marcel Duchamp in New York and, in co-operation with him, laid the foundations of the Dadaist

rebellion. Picabia was in Barcelona in 1916 and founded there the magazine *39*, which sparkled with his verve and sharp irony. The magazine appeared until 1924, irregularly to be sure, in Barcelona, then in New York, Zurich and, finally, Paris. In 1918 he joined forces with the Dada group *(*)* in Switzerland. Returning to Montparnasse, he served as a link between the German Dadaists in Zurich and the French Dadaists. 'It was from this moment', noted Ribemont-Dessaignes, who became the historian of Dadaism, 'that Dada was really born.' Picabia took part in the sensational events that scandalized the Parisian public and composed his famous 'ironical machines', which stood as a manifesto and a challenge. The baroque, the droll, the preposterous were the means he used to destroy traditional dogmas, laws and accepted formulae, the established order. He signed a tract of February 5th, 1920, as 'The Joker', and baptized one of his pamphlets *The Unique Eunuch*. In 1921 he quarrelled with his friends, to follow the poet André Breton when the latter founded the Surrealist movement. For the Ballets Suédois *(*)* he created the settings and costumes of the ballet *Relâche* (1924), and exhibited with Miró, André Masson, Max Ernst, and Dali. Suddenly, he

OPTOPHONE

PICABIA. OPTOPHONE. *H.-P. Roché Coll., Paris.*

PICASSO. THE FRUGAL MEAL. 1904.
ETCHING.

edness, and his independence. But if he exercised an influence, it was, above all, as an animator and an inspirer. Besides, he never wanted any other title to fame.   F. E.

PICASSO Pablo (born 1881, in Malaga). Spanish painter. Although he has participated in all the adventures of French painting for half a century, Picasso has remained inalienably Spanish. The sumptuous, tragic and ponderous Spanish legacy he carries within himself, in his thought and his mood, and he squanders it without ever exhausting it. However, to find in his work, his vocabulary, his syntax and his themes solely this composite and sumptuous Spain, nourished on the myths and forms of Oriental civilizations, barbarian contributions, Greek and Gothic reminiscences, would be a vast oversimplification. In the formation of his genius it was the Spain of Góngora and Goya, of the baroque architect Gaudi, of catalan anarchism and insurrectionism, a very

turned his back on Surrealism and reverted to representational art. During the war, he retired to the French Riviera and condescended to paint academic nudes for Algerian clients. In 1945, he took up abstract painting again, which he had been one of the very first to practise, as early as 1909 (*Rubber*). These erratic shifts reveal a man curious but unstable, enthusiastic but ineffective. Pursuing his researches in all directions, he indulged in the most gratuitous experiments, contradictions and provocations, cultivating, not without humour, a rhetoric of the absurd, more as a poet than as a painter. However, his gifts as a painter are incontestable, as are his high standards. Did he not destroy a portion of his work more than once ? But his love for jest and his desire to astonish never left him even with age. In 1949, under the name of 'sur-irrealist' paintings, he exhibited purely abstract compositions which he entitled: *You'll Never Sell It, Upside-Down, I Don't Want to Paint Any More, What Do You Call That ?* He was then seventy, but still as aggressive and spontaneous as a student. This is why he was surrounded by young men full of admiration for his disinterest-

PICASSO. THE HARLEQUIN'S FAMILY. 1905.
Lewisohn Collection, New York.

special Spain, ardent, subversive, violent, passionate, that played the most important part. Be this as it may, no living foreign artist working in France has allowed himself to be less absorbed by the customs and spirit of France; no one has more asserted his loyalty to his origin. For everything is contradiction in Picasso, his life, his character, his work.

He was born of a Castilian father, José Ruiz Blasco, who was a teacher of drawing, and an Andalusian mother of Majorcan origin, Maria Picasso. At an age when most children are still playing with marbles, he had already painted pictures worthy of figuring in a museum. In 1900 he came to Paris. He admired the pictures of Van Gogh and the Montmartre scenes of Toulouse-Lautrec. The latter's influence is noticeable in the paintings he executed at the time, and also in those of the 'Blue Period' (1901-1904). Poor and sick people, outcasts of life, were the objects of his attention. These themes, dear to Spain–poverty, solitude, sadness–he took up, but in a spirit influenced by

PICASSO. MA JOLIE. 1913.
Private Collection, Paris.

French art and with means refined by contact with Montmartre draughtsmen. He drew single or grouped figures with increasing precision, but he elongated or narrowed them to stress their tragic expression; he painted them almost in monochrome, in a blue tonality, the blue of mystery and night. Picasso was then twenty-three, but already his name was known far beyond the narrow circle of friends who surrounded him. His output was as exceptional in quality as it was prolific and included these well known works : *La Vie* (1903), *Poor People on the Seashore* (1903), *Célestine* (1903), *Woman with a Crow* (1904), *The Two Sisters* (1904), *Acrobat with a Ball* (1904). He established himself in the Bateau-Lavoir *(*)*, 13 rue Ravignan, in Montmartre, as early as 1904, and his studio became a meeting-place where artists and writers worked out the principles of a new aesthetic doctrine. The poets Apollinaire, Max Jacob, André Salmon, Pierre Reverdy, the painters André Derain, Van Dongen and Juan Gris frequented this place or even lived there. After 1907 Georges Braque, introduced to Picasso by Apollinaire, could also be met there. Fernande

PICASSO. WOMAN IN AN ARMCHAIR. 1918.

PICASSO. THE VIOLIN. 1913.
H. Rupf Collection, Bern.

Olivier has left the following striking portrait of Picasso at this time: 'Short, dark, stocky, disturbed, disturbing, with dark, deep, piercing, strange, almost immobile eyes. Awkward movements, a woman's hands, badly dressed, unkempt. A thick lock of hair, black and shiny, gashed the intelligent forehead. Half Bohemian, half workman in dress, he had long hair that swept the collar of his worn coat.'

With his 'Rose Period' (1905-1906) Picasso seemed to soften, even to mellow. Nudes, itinerant players, harlequins, circus scenes offered him the opportunity of lightening his technique, making his line more supple, accentuating distortions. His works recalled those of the Japanese painters of phan-

toms. They are characterized by a morbid feeling, something elusive and floating, a rather troubled charm, finally by almost flat forms, sparingly coloured: *The Family of Harlequin* (1905), *Acrobats with a Dog* (1905), *The Jugglers* (1905), *La Toilette* (1906). But he was not long in reacting. Probably under the influence of Negro and Iberian sculpture, he executed statues, drawings, pictures in which his plastic preoccupations stand out. How could he not be won over by the monstrous distortions of the African fetishes that were then being revealed to Europe? Distortions? Were they not rather invented forms, volumes charged with emotional power?

Be this as it may, Picasso fell under the spell of these primitive works; he certainly admired their sensitivity, rawness, luxuriant vocabulary, and bold abstraction. And when, in 1907, in his dilapidated studio in the Bateau-Lavoir, he showed his disconcerted friends the *Demoiselles d'Avignon* (reproduced on page 77), a page of history had been turned. The composition of this famous canvas lacks unity, the colour is hard and dry, the figures gesticulate, have no relief. But the lines, the angles, the slope of the planes, announced a new direction in modern painting. The Cubist revolution was not far off. The *Demoiselles d'Avignon* is not only a picture, it is also an event, a date, a starting-point, as much as

PICASSO. DRAWING IN INDIA INK. 1923.

were in other times the *Mystic Lamb* of the Van Eycks, the *Battles* of Uccello, *Dante's Barque* of Delacroix.

Fauvism was already drawing its last breath. In it the century had sown its wild oats, but had pulled itself together rather quickly, and the artist, sobered, had begun thinking. Confined in his studio, he attentively observed the objects that surrounded him, the table, the decanter, the glass, the package of tobacco, the newspaper. He observed them with so penetrating an eye that they appeared unknown to him. He entered into them as the novelist enters into his characters. He settled into them with the aid of a sympathy that was neither love nor passion but total consent and total respect. Thereupon things revealed to him their form, their structure, their top, their inside, their underside. When he represented them with his new vision, Cubism *(*)* was born. Gauguin was deserted for Cézanne. The real was rediscovered and essentially, in the real, volume and space. A prey to his contradictions, Picasso saw in this transcendence of realism a means of resolving them. He countered the sensualism of the Fauves by an intellectualism that writers were undertaking to explain and encourage at the same moment. As early as 1908 he assumed leadership of the movement with Braque. The question for them was to introduce the illusion of volume on a plane surface without resorting to modelling, chiaroscuro, linear perspective and other outmoded conventions. They succeeded in doing so through the breakdown of planes and representation of the object under several angles simultaneously. From then on they painted not what they saw but what they represented to themselves through analysis. In 1911 Cubism ceased to be analytic; it renounced contemplation of Nature and drifted toward an authoritarian conceptualism. At last tamed and dismantled, the object was subordinated to forms imagined *a priori*.

While their companions went off in other directions, Picasso and Braque exploited their discoveries. The Cubist adventure was like a dazzling conquest of unknown lands, each painting was a step forward from the last and anticipated the next. His new manner enabled Picasso between 1908 and 1915 to produce works with a hitherto unsuspected logic of composition. The portraits of *Vollard* and *Kahnweiler*

PICASSO. HARLEQUIN. 1915.
Museum of Modern Art, New York.

(1910), the *Aficionado* (1912), the *Card Players* (1914) and the *Harlequin* (1915) illustrate well the distance he had travelled. The same audacity in the process of abstraction and possibly even greater freedom are noticeable in the still-lifes in which the motif of the guitar and violin constantly reappeared. From that point, he created objects and created them freely. He accounted for reality, but by destroying it and substituting for it a subjective reality, autonommous, absolute. The picture became for him an object in itself. Indifferent to light, he concentrated all his faculties upon the transposed expression of forms, in order that the forms might suggest to the spectator images different from their counterparts in the world of appearances. But there came a moment when Cubism lost through its own excesses the strength it had drawn from the excesses of Fauvism. It was a prisoner of still life, of a closed room. It had not opened the door upon life. Impersonality of handling, poverty of colour, bleak and dreary materials. On the other hand, it had restored to drawing and form a necessary and sometimes tyrannical predominance. As a result, painting had returned to linear purity, geometry, exactness of proportions, rigour of composition. However, Picasso soon saw the limitations of the doctrine he had been the first to set forth and illustrate. And he who had been its most ardent instigator became its least faithful practitioner. No sooner did he see that he was followed than he took another path. The painter of angles, cubes, geometrical architectures, applied himself to the study of the old masters. This was the period when he worked for the Ballets Russes *(*)* and executed settings and costumes for *Parade* (1917) and *The Three-Cornered Hat*

Picasso had practised the technique of the *papier collé (*)* a few years before. Nevertheless, he who had gathered together on his canvases pieces of newspaper and boxes of matches and indulged in *trompe-l'œil* for love of realism, could not fail to be led to paint like Ingres in moments of relaxation. On the other hand, a man so torn by different, if not opposing, needs, so sensitive to the currents of his time, so given to every kind of daring, could not remain indifferent to the explorations of Surrealism *(*)*. Besides, in this insurrectional movement there was a taste for challenge and a will for destruction that could not fail to stimulate his fundamental nihilism. But Surrealist art resorted to means so poor, so worn, so unplastic that Picasso neglected them deliberately. He retained from the experience only the ferment capable of renewing his inspiration. After a short Romantic period, during which he painted various portraits of his son

and bull-fights in the spirit of Goya (1923), he tried to make explicit his dreams and impulses. While his countrymen Dali and Miró were obeying the metaphysical-literary derectives of the Surrealist poet AndréBreton, Picasso let crop up in his pictures the madrepores and larvae that stir in the depths of the unconscious (1928-1932). Fantastic forms, without significance, swarmed under his brush. These forms are strongly schematized, feebly coloured, with very dense volumes, that stand out, absurd and comic, in a space without depth (*Standing Swimmer*,

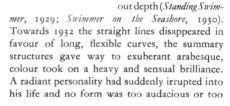

PICASSO. FAUN UNCOVERING A WOMAN. 1936. AQUATINT.

(1919). He resumed his old themes, acrobats, harlequins, dancers. Then, influenced by Greco-Roman art, he begot a race of giants, of heavy women, drawn and modelled in an entirely classical way. Until 1925 his production was characterized by calm, balance and an exceptional health. One would not believe the same

mer, 1929; *Swimmer on the Seashore*, 1930). Towards 1932 the straight lines disappeared in favour of long, flexible curves, the summary structures gave way to exuberant arabesque, colour took on a heavy and sensual brilliance. A radiant personality had suddenly irrupted into his life and no form was too audacious or too

PICASSO. STILL LIFE WITH ANTIQUE HEAD. 1925. *Musée d'Art Moderne, Paris.*

fantastic to express his passion (*The Dream*, 1932; *Young Woman with a Mirror*, 1932). In 1936 the latent expressionism of Picasso reappeared, exasperated by the tragedy that was drenching his motherland with blood. The line twisted or swelled, the colour heightened, the emotion burst out and, at the climax of a pathetic crescendo, reached its paroxysm in *Guernica*. This large composition in black and white is certainly one of his masterpieces, if not his masterpiece. For while he expressed in it the horrors of war in apocalyptic images, for his purpose he called only upon form and contrasts of shadow and light. Instead of describing, as did Goya or Delacroix, for example, a certain military episode or scene of slaughter, Picasso succeeded, for the first time in the history of Western painting, in terrifying the spectator merely by a plastic transcription of an actual event and convicting him of guilt by combining, with shrewdness and passion, specifically pictorial values. The tragic and the burlesque, sarcasm and pity, imprecation and irony, the palpitation of life and the immobility of death, a tumult of thoughts and emotions spring from this agonizing picture with an intensity that is at the limit of human endurance. After this, Picasso explored

courses he had already followed, carrying his investigations ever farther, now casting anchor in the peaceful river of Humanism, now venturing in full sail among Romantic storms. The same year in which he finished *Guernica*, he also painted the series of *Weeping Women* and began the *Seated Women* (1937-1944) series. Sometimes pleasing, more often hideous, with dislocated limbs and atrociously tortured anatomies, they were aggressions against the human figure and, in their own way, were a witness to the dark tragedy that humanity was suffering at the time. The war did not interrupt the frenzied tempo of his work, in fact, he painted some of his least questionable successess: *L'Aubade* (1942), *Still-life with a Bull's Skull* (1942), *Reclining Nude* (1942), *The Tomato Plant* (1944), which was a triumph of equilibrium and contained energy. The *Charnel House* (1945) in contrast is a dramatic composition. He produced numerous lithographs during the same period and worked nearly every day at the Mourlot workshops. In July 1946, he left Paris and divided his time between Golfe-Juan and the Musée d'Antibes, where he was provided with a studio. He painted an impressive number of works there in four months, which he donated to the museum. They are based on the ancient myths and magic beliefs brought in former times to the western shores of the Mediterranean by Greek sailors. In 1948, he went to live in Vallauris, where he devoted himself to ceramics with such enthusiasm that he brought new life to a declining art. The birth of his son, Claude, in 1947, and his daughter, Paloma, in 1949, inspired the paintings of motherhood and portraits of his children that are full of tenderness. He painted, engraved, sculptured and made pottery, all at the same time. Decorative painting attracted him and in 1952 he began and completed the two large panels of *War and Peace* for a disued chapel in Vallauris. Six years later, he painted a mural for the UNESCO building in Paris. While continuing his sculpture and lithography, from time to time he painted landscapes, still-lifes and portraits (*Portrait of Hélène Parmelin*, 1952; *Portraits of Sylvette*, 1954; *Portrait of Jacqueline*, 1954) and all this with his usual impetuosity and an unusual love of life. And whatever his subjects, his motifs, he always metamorphoses them, gives them a life similar to his own, an ill-restrained violence, a desperate note, something wild, troubled, disquieting. He is curious and unsatisfied, irritating and fascinating, generous and avaricious with his feelings, laden with fame and wealth, continuing nevertheless to work like a slave, the slave of his impatient

genius, but also the master of his forces, of his faculties, prodigiously active, never at rest, knowing no weariness, always seeking in the world an ever-elusive joy and meeting only with anguish, doubt, fury. The age he seems to be is not his real age. He works, conceives, feels, hates and loves as at twenty. It is therefore difficult to study his production without studying his life, so inextricably are the two mixed. All the facts, all the events in which he has been an actor or a witness are registered in his various works. He has nourished his art with his loves, his contempts, his torments, his whims, revolts, his presumptions, not without complacency, not without trickery, with a sometimes embarrassing insistence. An heir of the Humanist tradition, an individualist by temperament, an anarchist by race, his actions and reactions are always unpredictable, sudden and brutal. An unbeliever, he believes only in himself. A revolutionary, he baffles his followers. Always the contradiction.

There is neither unity nor continuity nor stability in his work, as there is none in his life. Inconstant, multiple, fiery and irascible, amiable or insolent, sincere or affected, charming or uncivil, he can be one or another according to his mood or the moment, and yet remain unfailingly true to a single passion: freedom. He wants to be entirely free, free to remake the world to his liking, free to exercise his omnipotence–no rules, no conventions, no prejudice. From Naturalism to Expressionism, from Expressionism to Classicism–from Classicism to Romanticism, then to Realism and to Abstraction, to revert to Naturalism and resume his indefatigable quest, grace alternating with horror, elegance with the monstrous, he goes to and fro, he begins again, remaining an inveterate baroque in spite of his incarnations. When he wants to be classical, he startles less and does not move. He is too individualistic, too anxious to surprise and hurt, too hostile to all restraint and to any serene vision of the universe, to put up with limitations, discipline, humilities.

PICASSO. CANDLESTICK, JUG AND ENAMEL SAUCEPAN. 1945. *Musée d'Art Moderne, Paris.*

PICASSO. GUERNICA. MAY 1937. *On loan at the Museum of Modern Art, New York.*

Freedom alone suits him, absolute freedom, even if it has to take on the forms of the bizarre, of chaos, of the hideous. Picasso is a baroque by atavism, by principle, by inclination. And as one gets used to everything, to the exceptional, to extravagance, to strangeness, even to horror, he is naturally led to outdo his previous violence; hence his immoderateness and his recklessness, but hence also the percussive force of each of his creations, his violent drawing, aggressive forms, hurried and tense composition. In this he has no rival. It is by virtue of this that he dazzles, upsets, intoxicates and convinces. Electricity runs along his line; there is dynamite in the hollow of his objects.

Prodigious as his vitality may be, Picasso does not express happiness, hope, or joy of living, but mostly an incurable disquiet, the drama of man at grips with Nature, of man in revolt against his destiny–his own drama. When he is playful or facetious, when he wants to please or to charm, it is rare that the mask succeeds in concealing entirely the wan face of Death. His laugh is more like a sneer, his exultations sound like blasphemies, his banter like sarcasm. Wisdom, renunciation, serenity, naturalness, he has none of these in him. It is with his resources alone that he wants to substitute for the world of permanence his personal and therefore fragile, ever-threatened world. Picasso is an individual who strives to extend the borders of his empire in order to go farther, ever farther; who tends to absorb everything, no doubt because he needs to be absorbed himself. Is there today an artist more profoundly an innovator, more determined to reject the fictions and forms of the past? Picasso is, in fact, the last representative, the most passionate, the most terrible, of the Greco-Latin tradition. He is the prodigal descendant of Goya, Velasquez, Michelangelo, Uccello. One will, then, perhaps understand why this paradox should have resounded with such painful echoes in a body of work with which no other can be compared. The works of the last years have been grouped around a few subjects, generally taken from celebrated pictures. Just as he had given his own interpretation in 1950 of Greco's *The Painter* and Courbet's *Les Demoiselles des Bords de la Seine*, in 1955 he did fifteen paintings after Delacroix's *Women of Algiers*. After the series of the *Studios*, painted in Cannes, 1955-1956, Velasquez's *Las Meninas* inspired about fifty audacious variations. In 1958, he began working at lino-cuts, and during the next two years, printed a dazzling series of forty-five plates in which bucolic subjects and bull-fights predominated. At the same time, he painted about a hundred water-colours, which can be grouped under the title of *Romancero du Picador*. At the château of Vauvenargues, which he had just bought, he painted landscapes, still-lifes, silhouettes and heads of women between 1959 and 1961. Between February 1960 and August 1961, it was Manet's *Déjeuner sur l'Herbe* that

PICASSO. PENCIL DRAWING, ANTIBES. 1946.

Window (1924), *Still-life with Antique Head* (1925), *Still-life with an Enamel Saucepan* (1945, Musée d'Art Moderne, Paris) and the great paintings of the Musée d'Antibes. Never has technique been for him an end in itself, despite his fabulous dexterity. But never has such dexterity stopped him from exploring new paths, nor has his boldness ever given way to virtuosity. He does not scorn effect, but to obtain it he commits himself entirely, with his sincerity and his guile, his resolution and his uncertainty, his confessions and his malice, his discoveries and his artifices—all of him.

His finds have often been taken up by the new generation. It is certainly easy to discern here and there in contemporary painting a sign, a form, a technique that bears his stamp. But these are superficial borrowings, fragmented and unassimilated imitations. For art, like

provided his inexhaustible imagination with the theme for twenty-seven pictures. When in 1961, his friends and admirers flocked to Mougins, where he was then living, to celebrate his eightieth birthday, they found him as active and youthful as ever. His output is huge It has to be accepted as it is, with its failings, its lightning-flashes, its imperfections, its grandeurs. In it one can count many sketches, experiments without conclusion, but also ardent confessions, incontestable successes. It is not a question of masterpieces; Picasso has never been concerned with producing eternal masterpieces. As a result, he has always appeared indifferent to the materials he employed. He draws and paints on anything: a paper tablecloth, cardboard, wood or plywood, fibrocement. He does not concern himself with the preparation of his canvases, the quality of his colours, the improvement of his tools. As a sculptor he uses earth, wood, cloth, broken pieces of hardware, which he often covers with wide strokes of the brush. But the waste of his abundant production can be forgotten for his having been capable of creating works like *Woman in Green* (1909), *The Accordeon Player* (1911), *Ma Jolie* (1913), *Three Musicians* (1921), those fine examples of Cubism; *Guernica* (1937), *War and Peace* (1952), fine flowers of Expressionism; *Mandoline and Guitar, or the Open*

PICASSO. SPHINX. 1953.   *Private Collection.*

PICASSO. THE DINING-ROOM. VAUNEVARGUES. 1959-1960.

Picasso's individuality, is autonomous, incommunicable, intransmissible, a closed world. 'I do not search, I find', he once announced. His person cannot serve as a model, his life as an example, or his work as a lesson. Picassos are not born in every century. And who does not feel that without him our century would have been flatter, duller, less worth living in ?

We must be grateful for his boldness and inventiveness, and the shocks he administers to sluggish ways of thinking and seeing. He is the most original creative genius of our time. F. E.

PICKETT Joseph (1848 - 1918). American painter; born and died in New Hope, Pennsylvania. Pickett was a storekeeper who produced several remarkable naive landscapes in the back room of his grocery store. He was discovered only after his death by Holger Cahill who included two of his paintings in a show of 'American Primitives' at the Newark Museum in 1930. No letters or photographs of Pickett are known to exist, and the few biographical details we possess were gleaned from neighbours who remembered him. He seems to have been of an inventive and mildly eccentric

turn of mind, 'handy' with tools, and with the oldfashioned manners and flowing moustaches of a 'Kentucky colonel'. Besides his general store he also owned a shooting gallery decorated with landscapes painted by himself. At the age of forty-five he married and 'settled down;' he began to paint only at sixty-five, perhaps as a compensation for the quiet life he was then leading.

The handful of paintings that exist by him have been called by Dorothy C. Miller 'among the most remarkable landscapes ever produced in America'. Of these the best known is *Manchester Valley* in the Museum of Modern Art, New York. There is something inexplicably awe-inspiring about this scene with its furiously cascading perspectives, its rigid and geometrical houses with their inexorable rows of windows In defiance of all the laws of perspective Pickett makes the school building in the background several times larger than the factories in the foreground: Sidney Janis says that 'Formal perspective gives way to a personal perspective and objects of greater importance to the artist are given greater scale regardless of distance'. He worked on each of his paintings for years adding more pigment until he got the raised surfaces he desired, and simulating the textures of the objets he painted by adding substances such as sand and shells to the paint. One neighbor reported that Pickett used sometimes to ask her if she thought the flag in *Manchester Valley* was heavily enough painted; despite her affirmative reply he would keep adding more pigment. Unlike many American primitives, Pickett avoids the anecdotal and the whimsical: the scenes he depicts are recognizably American but their true locale is outside of time and space. Solemn, strange, organized according to its own handmade logic, Pickett's work is a perfect example of what Uhde calls 'la peinture du cœur sacré'. J. A.

PIPER John (born in 1903 at Epsom). Studied at the Royal College of Art and the Slade School. Attached to the Army as a painter during the Scond World War, he executed a series of paintings of streets, houses and monuments demolished by bombardments, notably the House of Commons and the City of Bath. Piper came to painting rather late, and began as a landscapist, painting the picturesque southern coast of England. About 1933, as a result of his conctacts with certain painters of the École de Paris–Braque, Helion and Arp, among others–his style changed, and he turned to two-dimensional abstract compositions based most frequently upon vertical arrangements of flat colour. His scale of values was again revised, however, and in the late 'thirties he began working in a more realistic vein, which nevertheless retained from his earlier discipline an austere sense of composition and was often superimposed upon an essentially abstract - expressionist colour scheme. Now

began that long series of dramatic, even melodramatic, portraits of castles and great houses under lowering skies that is most readily associated with his name. In these architectural themes Piper's sense of topography and history–perhaps too his long interest in medieval stained glass–have found their fullest scope: his crumbling patinated façades, painted in rich, warm tones with all the variety of texture that oil paint is capable of, are imbued with true poetic feeling. Increasingly with the years, Piper has felt himself drawn to the traditions of English eighteenth and early nineteenth century Romantic landscape painting; he has returned to the selfsame scenes beloved of Richard Wilson and James Ward–to the frowning crags and fearful sublimities of the Welsh mountains and Gordale Scar–and has depicted them with an ever-greater 'rough and scumble' in his handling. That one who sees landscape so greatly in terms of the theatre backcloth, should have found himself directly engaged in décor is scarcely surprising. Piper has become well known for his work as a theatre and ballet designer (*Job*, by Ninette de Valois, 1948); *Harlequin in April*, by John Cranko, 1951); in particular his name is associated with the operas of Benjamin Britten, for which he has produced settings of striking

PICKETT. MANCHESTER VALLEY. 1914-1918.
Museum of Modern Art, New York.

290

PIPER. ST. MARY LE PORT. *Tate Gallery, London.*

and affecting power. He has also undertaken a good deal of graphic work, and has written with sympathy about the visual arts.   F. MC E.

PISSARRO Camille (1830-1903). Born at Saint-Thomas in the West Indies (then a Danish possession); died in Paris. 'Of all painters', said Cézanne, 'Pissarro was nearest to Nature'. His entire life was devoted to observing the changing effects of Nature, which he succeeded in capturing in innumerable oil paintings, water-colours, drawings and engravings. He never tired of studying the same village church, the same fields in different seasons, a market place, the Paris boulevards, and he infused a rare poetic quality into these subjects. He had a long struggle with his parents—a French father and a Creole mother—before obtaining their consent to leave the West Indies to study art in Paris, and had reached the age of twenty-five when finally he arrived in France. His first enthusiasm was for Corot, and he started work under his supervision—with permission to style himself 'pupil of Corot'. But his aged tutor disapproved when in 1865 Pissarro joined up with Monet, Renoir and other young artists grouped around Manet, though Daubigny and Courbet (whose influence is evident in some of

Pissarro's early work) accepted the newcomers with goodwill. In 1870 Monet and Pissarro fled to London to escape the Prussian occupation, and there found Daubigny, who gave them valuable help and advice and introduced them to the young French art dealer Durand-Ruel (*), whose name has since become firmly linked with that of the Impressionists. Durand-Ruel bought Pissarro's work first in London and then on a larger scale in Paris; little by little he became the regular dealer of Monet, Pissarro and all their friends, sharing their setbacks as well as their painfully slow climb to fame. In England Pissarro studied Turner and Constable. On his return to France he found his house looted and his canvases (nearly a thousand) destroyed. But his joy at being back in France lent him courage, and he settled in Pontoise, where Cézanne came to work with him (1872-1874) and profit from his advice. Pissarro made regular trips to Paris, thus keeping in touch with his friends. With them, in 1874, he countered the official Salon's systematic refusal to hang their work by organizing the first independent picture exhibition. A hostile critic writing about this exhibition, in the *Charivari* of April 25th, first applied the word 'Impressionists' to their work. The following eight exhibitions organized by the Impressionists between 1874 and 1886—which met mainly with ridicule and insults—were due in large part to Pissarro's indefatigable initiative and his gift for reconciling adverse factions. He was the only member of the group to exhibit at each show, and he was alone in offering his friendship to the younger painters of promise. In 1879 he interested himself in Gauguin and introduced him to the group. Later he joined up with Seurat and Signac in their efforts to reconcile art with science, and he insisted on their being included in the final exhibition of 1886.

Pissarro, senior by two years to Manet and by ten to Monet, was the eldest of the group. Without exception, all the painters and writers included in his circle felt a profound esteem for this kind and gentle man, who united an innate goodness with an indomitable fighting spirit. A convinced atheist, Pissarro was also a socialist tinged with anarchist ideas, and he considered the artistic struggle as inseparable from the question of the artist's role in modern society. But however radical his views, they were free from

PISSARRO. ENTRANCE TO A VILLAGE. 1872.   *Musée du Louvre.*

ception of Nature is expressed in hardy strokes of the palette knife and his colours are often as dramatically sombre as those in Cézanne's first paintings. Little by little his colours grew lighter and he stressed the solidity of masses in subtle but opaque shades, greys often dominating. 'As early as 1865', Cézanne tells us, 'he eliminated black, bistre, sienna browns and ochres'. It was just before the 1870 war that he took the decisive step towards light colouring and the analysis of shadow, and the study of English landscape painters during his exile in London encouraged him to pursue this course and confirmed his conclusions. The outcome was the series of intensely vital, lyrical canvases painted between 1870 and 1880–his truly 'Impressionist' period of open-air painting and discoveries in the use of colour. Light itself became a 'subject'–the principal element in his picture. The artist was attracted by golden and silver effects, vast stretches of green, delicate foliage, trees in flower, corn-fields, streams and mottled skies. He studied all these first around Pontoise, then at Osny and Éragny-sur-Epte near Gisors, where he settled in 1885. With these lighter colours he worked in small commalike brush strokes, which enabled him to depict the brilliance of light without breaking up the forms on which it shone. By 1884 Pissarro began to feel dissatisfaction with this technique, finding it too crude, and it is not surprising to find him attracted in the following years to Divisionism (*see* Neo-Impressionism) in an attempt to reconcile Seurat's rigid theories with his own poetic temperament. This effort was doomed to failure; in 1890 Pissarro began to realize, as he put it, 'the impossibility of following my sensations, and consequently of expressing life and movement and rendering Nature's marvellous but

hate and imbued with a disinterested integrity which commanded general respect even among those less socially conscious than he. Everyone knew of his personal difficulties, his continual fight to provide for his family of six children, and they could not but admire the composure and complete lack of bitterness with which he discussed the essential artistic or political problems of his day. Pissarro never ceased to advocate humility before Nature, though he refrained from imposing his ideas on others. The advice he gave to Cézanne and Gauguin must have been similar to that given to his children, to whom he wrote in one of his admirable letters: 'Beware of trusting to my judgment! I am so anxious to see you succeed that I don't hide my opinions from you; but only accept what corresponds to your own feeling and way of understanding. What I most fear is that you should resemble me too much. So go ahead, and work!' To this respect for the individual he added a rare gift for pedagogy. 'He was so wonderful a teacher', said Mary Cassatt, 'that he could have taught a stone to draw correctly'.

Pissarro's artistic development can be divided into various phases. His early work shows the influence of Corot and Courbet: a poetic con-

fugitive effects, of giving individuality to my drawing'; so he abandoned the Pointillist technique 'to retrieve with difficulty and by hard work what I had lost, without losing whatever I may have found'. Pissarro spent the last years of his life in the search for a new liberty of expression. His efforts were astonishingly fruitful and in his view of Rouen and Paris he succeeded in uniting exquisite sensibility with a superbly vigorous technique. Profiting from his Impressionist and Divisionist experiments, his art became powerful yet subtle, firm of line and rich in colouring. Though mainly a landscape artist, Pissarro also painted portraits, still-lifes and nudes. 'If we examine Pissarro's art as a whole', wrote Gauguin in 1902, 'in spite of a certain unevenness, we find not only a tremendous artistic will which is never belied, but also an essentially intuitive, pure-bred art. He took from everyone, you say ? Why not ? Everyone, though denying him, took from him too'.   J. R.

POINTILLISM   This term, or 'Divisionism', refers to the technique perfected and carried to its extreme con-

sequences by the advocates of Neo-Impressionism (*). It consisted in juxtaposing small strokes of pure colours on the canvas.

POLLOCK   Paul Jackson (1912-1956). American painter; born at Cody, Wyoming, died in East Hampton. With Jackson Pollock the painting of the United States freed itself for the first time from European dominance and took a leading part in the history of western art. He has become a symbol of American painting, with its violence and huge scale, a representative figure as Melville is for the novel, Whitman for poetry and Wright for architecture, whose works like his are stamped by the immensities of the American spaces and their brash statement of human problems. Pollock, too, was the embodiment of what the American critic, Harold Rosenberg, called *action painting:* painting produced by rapid gestures on a canvas, placed flat on the floor of the studio, with unprecedented techniques such as 'dripping,' which replaced the limited area of the easel canvas by the new space filled by the human body in movement. He has given his own explanation of his working methods: 'My painting does not come from the easel. I hardly ever stretch my canvas before painting. I prefer to tack the unstretched canvas to the hard wall or floor. I need the resistance of a hard surface. On the floor I am more at ease. I feel nearer, more a part of the painting, since this way I can walk round it, work from the four sides and literally be *in* the painting . . . I continue to get further away from the usual painter's tools such as easel, palette, brushes,

PISSARRO. AVENUE DE L'OPÉRA.   *Belgrade Museum.*

etc. I prefer sticks, trowels, knives and dripping fluid paint or a heavy impasto with sand, broken glass and other foreign matter added'.

Pollock's break with tradition and fresh start have been interpreted as simply giving free play to chance and instinct or an apology for amateurism. On the contrary, it is easy to show the strict cohesion of his work, which was the result of an exceptional craftsmanship, virtuosity and self-discipline. It is just as necessary to refute the legend of alcoholism. Pollock never worked except when he was sober. His bouts of alcoholism coincided with periods of depression during which he was incapable of painting, particularly in the last three years of his life that were practically unproductive.

The origins of Pollock's parents were three quarters Irish and a quarter Scottish. His father, LeRoy McCoy, took the name of his adoptive family. Pollock owed his intimate knowledge of the American soil to his father, who was a farmer in Wyoming, Arizona, and then California. In fact for two seasons, in 1927 and 1929, he helped his father in surveying and geological work. But his artistic vocation made him join the Manual Art School of Los Angeles in 1925. He read a great deal there, painted and sculptured, but was expelled after two years because of his rebellious spirit. In 1929, his brother, Charles (Pollock was the youngest of five boys), encouraged him to go to New York, where he studied at the Art Students' League under Thomas Hart Benton, a violent, genre painter, who became his friend, but whose realism and method of working from Nature did not influence him. 1930, on the other hand, was important for his discovery of Red Indian art (a technique of painting pictogram imagery on sand that haunted him until his death) and

the Mexican mural painters (Rivera, Orozco and Siqueiros). Sketch-books survive from this period of drawings after the European masters, Michelangelo, Tintoretto and El Greco, which show a taste for drama and movement and a considerable mastery of classical draughtsmanship.

In 1936, he began to paint semi-abstract works, characterised by a violent expressionism and forms that reappeared in works at the end of his life (*Moon Vibration*, 1953; *Frieze*, 1953). In 1938, he joined the Federal Arts Project and familiarised himself fresco painting. His first important works date from 1940. Highly coloured, difficult to understand, very often on sexual or mythological themes, it is possible to detect the influences of Picasso and even the Surrealists in them. In spite of this *Male and Female* (1942), *Pasiphae* (1943), *Guardians of the Secret* (1943), *Totem I* and *II* (1944) possess a violence, a kind of dislocation and conception of space that is peculiarly their own. Peggy Guggenheim organised Pollock's first one-man exhibition in 1943 and contracted him to her gallery, Art of this Century, until 1947. This is the moment to clarify the ambiguity that the Surrealists have allowed to confuse their connection with Pollock, Max Ernst even going so far as to claim priority in using the 'drip' technique, which consists in painting with pier-

POLLOCK. PAINTING. 1949.   *Marinotti Collection, Milan.*

ced tins through which the paint flows. In fact, Pollock worked out a method of controlled automatism to produce a manual dexterity that would not hinder the immediacy and speed of free expression. 'Dripping' was his chosen form of calligraphy. For the Surrealists, on the other hand, automatism was not connected with any kind of technique: it was a haphazard, uncontrollable method of investigation, just as Max Ernst's 'drippings' were a game of chance.

After years of exercises and experiments in which he had been encouraged since 1944 by his wife, Lee Krasner, the artist, Pollock succeeded in mastering his calligraphy in 1947. From then until 1950, stretches a series of masterpieces in which violence alternates with tenderness, brilliant with more subdued harmonies: *Cathedral* (1947), *Number One* (1948), *Summer Time* (1948), *Number One* (1949), *Lavender Mist* (1950), *Autumn Rhythm* (1950), etc. The whole picture area became a space for the coursing of a net work of lines whose varying thickness immediately suggests the rhythm of their duration. Its scale is vast, but each element is an integral part of the whole where it is organic, never decorative. This phase ended with *Number 29*, painted on glass with shells, pebbles and bits of metal grating, which was both an end and a begining. Pollock's skill was recorded in 1950 in a short film by the photographer, Hans Namuth.

From 1950 to 1952, he gave up using colour for black and white painting. After reverting to rhythms similar to those in previous paintings (*Number Thirty-two*, 1950), he returned to an expressionism that was at the same time more controlled and more frenzied than that of the first years of the 1940's (*Echo*, 1951; *Number Five*, 1952; *Number Seven*, 1952). But in 1952, Jackson Pollock began again on large coloured canvases with *Convergence* (1952) and *Blue Poles* (1953). Nevertheless, he was trying to find a new path, which he opened with *Deep* (1953), a black hole on a white background and a few paintings, like *Ocean Greyness* (1953), where

POLLOCK. PAINTING NO. 12. 1952.
Nelson A. Rockefeller Collection, New York.

there was a touching return to the circular forms that obsessed him in the beginning and had already risen again in some of the black and white paintings. However, the creative process would no longer respond to his will. In 1956, he was killed in a motor accident, which was really the culmination of long months of anguish and inaction.

The work he left is among the most important, if not the greatest of the twentieth century. He has created an entirely new conception of space, satisfied our longing for cosmic rhythms and taken upon himself the tragic predicament of the West by using the human body as the measure of the immeasurable.   F. C.

PONT-AVEN (School of). Pont-Aven is a picturesque little town in Brittany, frequented since 1873 by artists drawn there both by the archaic charm of the country and the celebrated inn of Marie-Jeanne Gloanec. It won fame through Gauguin's visits and gave its name to the school of painting created around him, the principles of which were revealed to him in Brittany. 'When my clogs strike this granite ground', he used to say, 'I hear the low, dull, powerful sound that I seek in painting'. However, his first lonely stay, from June to November 1886, was merely an introduction without immediate importance. In Concarneau, in August, his friend Schuffenecker met a young painter and poet of eighteen, Émile Bernard (1868-1941), precocious, open, cultiveted, full of mystical ardour and passion for the country that he explored on foot in every direction. Schuffenecker introduced him to Gauguin; but the latter's rather cold reception cut the meeting short. Gauguin's second stay in Pont-Aven, from February to October 1888, was to be decisive. He took lodgings at the Gloanec boarding-house, where he was immediately recognized as leader. Around him, in the small room of the inn, an increasing number of disciples drawn by his personality and new ideas grouped themselves: the faithful Charles Laval (1862-1894), his companion on the trip to Martinique the preceding year; Henri de Chamaillard (1865-1930), Moret, Maxime Maufra, Jourdan, Grouchi-Taylor; the Swiss Cuno Amiet; the American O'Connor; and others. The big room was reserved for students at the Beaux-Arts and orthodox painters, among whom a certain G. de Maupassant, supposed to be the father of the writer, was the most hostile to the innovators. Early in August, Émile Bernard, this time cordially greeted by Gauguin, with whom he was to have fruitful exchanges and whose technical evolution he advanced, arrived from Saint-Brieuc with his sister Madeleine, who was to become the 'mystic muse' of Pont-Aven. Under the stimulus of Bernard, Gauguin executed *The Vision after the Sermon*, which marked the beginning of his new manner, characterized by Cloisonnism and Synthesism. Cloisonnism (inspired by cloisonné enamels) consisted in surrounding vast plain surfaces of pure colour, juxtaposed without transition, with sinuous, heavy arabesques. The new use of pure colour–to which, he said, everything had to be sacrificed–without the nuances of light peculiar to the Impressionists, led to glorification of the decorative plane surface, the lifting of the horizon, and the suppression of naturalistic perspective and space. Thus it is that in this picture the meadow, daringly rendered in red, invades the entire sky, while the

figures stand out flatly like Chinese silhouettes. Synthesism was the direct consequence of this process of simplification and resulted from the need to work no longer from the subject but from memory, no longer 'before the thing' but 'entertaining it in the imagination', which eliminates details and retains only the essential form, the 'idea'. Synthesism and Cloisonnism constituted the aesthetic framework of Symbolism (*) in painting. Émile Bernard, with great acrimony, was to claim credit later for inspiring the movement; but this periodically revived quarrel is absurd, for if Bernard seems indeed to have been the precursor for certain technical processes he evolved together with Anquetin as early as 1887–processes which were, anyway, in the air (because of the influence of Japanese prints, stained glass, folk images, primitive art)– Gauguin's genius alone was able to draw masterpieces and an original vision from these techniques. At the end of September Sérusier, then a pupil at the Académie Julian, staying at Pont-Aven among traditional painters, was introduced to Gauguin through Bernard and painted under his direction the famous landscape of the *Bois d'Amour*, a small board covered with 'pure colours assembled in a certain order', which he brought back triumphantly to his comrades, the future Nabis (*), as the 'talisman' of the new doctrine. This was for them a decisive revelation, reinforced by the first public show of the Pont-Aven Group, held early in 1889 at the Café Volpini in the Place du Champ-de-Mars in Paris on the grounds of the Universal Exhibition: it bore the name 'Exhibition of Painting of the Impressionist and Synthesist Group' and comprised, together with seventeen canvases by Gauguin and twenty-three by Bernard, works of Laval, Anquetin, Schuffenecker, Fauché, G. Daniel, L. Roy, all framed with white laths that made a sensation.

In the meantime, Gauguin stayed two months (November to December, 1888), with Van Gogh at Arles, a visit that was tragically interrupted by the drama of the amputated ear. In April 1889 he returned to Pont-Aven, but soon exasperated by the throng of painters and tourists, he moved to a neighbouring and quieter hamlet, Le Pouldu, in October, and took lodgings in an isolated seaside inn kept by Mlle Marie Henry, called 'Marie the Doll'. He

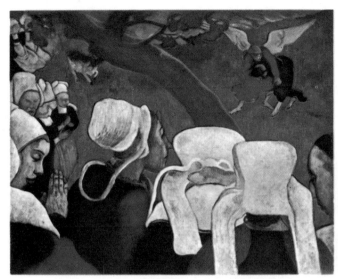

GAUGUIN. THE VISION AFTER THE SERMON. 1888.
National Gallery of Scotland, Edinburgh.

to Maurice Denis, 'stirred up as many ideas as that of Fontainebleau', and renewed the aesthetic current of the end of the century, the gathering of the artists who formed it was due only to the prestige of Gauguin and hardly survived his departure. Only Charles Filliger and Armand Sequin, whom Gauguin was to encounter again during his final stay at Pont-Aven in April to December 1894, between his two trips to Tahiti, remained obstinately faithful to the Breton land and to the principles of Pont-Aven and Le Pouldu. J. LE.

stayed there from October 2nd, 1889, to November 7th, 1890, with the Dutchman Meyer de Haan, his admirer, patron and most gifted disciple. Charles Filliger, another person of unusual temperament, joined him in July 1890. Laval, Sérusier and Seguin spent part of the summer there in shifts. Moret, Maufra, de Chamaillard and Jourdan, who remained faithful to Pont-Aven, came often as neighbours. The small inn was entirely decorated, from window-panes to ceiling, with paintings, frescoes, drawings, ceramics, lithographs and sculptures and adorned with inscriptions like *Honni soit qui mal y pense* or *I Like Onions Fried in Oil*. The front door was ornamented with the famous canvas jokingly imitated from Courbet, *Bonjour, M. Gauguin,* and on the communal tobacco jar one could read the rallying cry *Long Live Synthesis !* It was in this 'retreat' of Le Pouldu that Gauguin, now master of his style, had his longest, happiest and most fruitful stay in Brittany, surrounded by his most fervent disciples; and had he not, as can be seen, taken with some irony his role as leader of the group, it would no doubt be more correct to speak of a School of Le Pouldu rather than of Pont-Aven.

While 'the School of Pont-Aven', according

PORTINARI Candido (1903-1962). Brazilian painter; born at Brodowski, in the state of São Paulo, died at Rio de Janeiro. It may seem surprising that the climate, the vitality, the exuberant landscapes of Brazil should not have induced a more widespread urge to paint. One artist, however, has recaptured the intensity of the twilights of Rio de Janeiro: Portinari.

After having been an attentive pupil at the School of Fine Arts in the Brazilian capital, he came to Paris. It is clear that he felt out of his element there, and Pascin alone seems to have exercised a lasting influence upon his vision. On his return to Brazil, Portinari drifted away very soon from everything the had learned at school and came under the spell of the atmosphere of the Rio suburbs, a city of contrasts, where light struggles day and night with shadow, where the sky threatens to conquer the eath at any moment. He forgot Paris and its mirages to fall in love with the tones that make mountain slopes iridescent and with the clouds that crowd in on the bay of Rio. Turning his back on the excessive lyricism of Brazilian cities, he caught the fascinating mystery of the existence of those who were called by Franklin D. Roosevelt the forgotten men. They taught him, with music on their lips, what is most authentic and intense in the atmosphere of the tropics. Thus, capable of resisting the excesses of the Brazilian climate, Portinari assented to being a painter of semitones, of subtle colours; and he makes us discover the magic of twilight, reminding us that this hour preceding sleep and dreams is the one which men of all times and all places have both dreaded and preferred. And this paradox can furnish us an explanation of the strong spell cast by Por-

composure or his virtuosity, or the fact that he was able to meet the challenge and impose his personality when the conditions he faced might have stifled him.   PH. S.

POUGNY Jean (1894-1956). Born near Leningrad; died at Paris. When this son and grandson of musicians arrived in Paris in 1923, he had already faced all the aesthetic problems of his time. Between 1912 and 1920, he had been an active member of the main Russian avant-garde movements. He was associated with Malevitch and Tatlin and was represented with them at the exhibition, 'Tramways V', at Leningrad (1905). After Cubism, he turned to Suprematism and then Constructivism. In 1920, he went to Berlin, where he exhibited at Herwarth Walden's Der Sturm gallery. After that, his abstract phase ended and from 1925 his art developed towards figuration, an entirely subjective figuration, depending on a kind of intuition that transformed every object. His art made an easy appeal,

PORTINARI. COFFEE PORTERS.   *Private Collection, New York.*

tinari's art. Allied both with Europe, in its most artificial aspects, and with prehistory, this art has victoriously passed the test of the American Continent, and the painter has successfully replied to the requests of the architects who urged him to paint frescoes on the scale of ambitious and oversized buildings. Notable among his principal mural paintings are those at the New Ministry of Education at São Paulo (1936), the frescoes in the Library of Congress at Washington (1942), the decoration of various churches, particularly those at Minas Gerais (1944), designed by Oscar Niemeyer, and the two large panels of *War* and *Peace* (1953-1955), presented by Brazil the UN. One does not know what to admire most in his works, his

particularly in the fascination of its detail. His canvases, all small in size, are as intimate and tender as melodies. Interior scenes and views of beaches assert themselves with moving precision at first sight; but when one looks for motifs or examines the execution in detail, they escape analysis and seem based on a secret technique which is difficult to define. The drawings is imprecise, line absent, the touches of colour shapeless, but the relations are so right, the juxtapositions so live that the subject falls together without the aid of logic or the laws of probability. It is an art that seems totally improvised, but that none the less never conveys a feeling of dispersion or carelessness. Pougny has sometimes been compared to Vuillard, but the comparison is justified only by his mat finish and the muted harmony of tones, discreetly blended with greys to set off the freshness of the modulations in yellow, green and red. There is no attempt to represent reality in this minute art but only to suggest the feeling left by the figure or the landscape. In fact, in recent years no painter has expressed atmosphere better than he, not the luminous atmosphere of the Impressionists but a sentimental atmosphere. The sincerity of this art and the simplicity of the means employed, allowed Pougny to discover very early the formula that suited him and achieve his perfection.   R. C.

PRAMPOLINI Enrico (1894-1956). Italian painter; born in Modena, died at Rome. In 1912, when he was eighteen years old, Prampolini took part in the exhibitions of the Futurist group. There had already appeared in his work and more markedly a few years later from 1915 to 1924, the influence of Cubism and Constructivism along with Futurism. His feeling for building in space and his taste for new materials, which was noticeable in his famous *polimaterici*, gradually drew him away from Futurism and nearer the new French school, particularly Severini and his friends of the Section d'Or. His need for solid pictorial construction is all the more evident in that from Italy he could follow at leisure the avant-garde movements and realise a satisfying synthesis of the various artistic tendencies. A brief 'mechanical' phase, succeeding this first period, gave him experience in theatrical and ballet production. He directed several productions in Italy, Germany and Paris, where every year after 1925 he paid long visits. When he returned to Futurism in 1928, he used it as a vehicle for what he called a 'cosmic idealism'. It was now no longer the turmoil of streets, nor the emotions and state of mind of man that

POUGNY.
CANNES BEACH.
1950.

inspired his painting, but the atmosphere and the movements of stars in space (aeropittura). They are obviously concerned with abstract movements, flight interpreted in the idiom of painting, which place him among the pioneers of non-figurative art, although when opportunity offered he was sympathetic with the Surrealist doctrines that were being developed in the cafés of the day. As a matter of fact, he was incapable of ridding himself completely of the idea of man whose agony never ceased to haunt him. About 1935, he joined the Abstraction-Création (*) movement and once again used plastic materials in his pictures, which helped him to go beyond 'the frontiers of reality'. These works were conceived as 'organisms', as he called them, brilliantly coloured and yet at the same time possessing elegance and restraint. Although a great variety of materials were used in 1935, it had not yet reached the point of the neo-realist macadam and existentialist garbage of 1960. The horrors of war caused a fresh digression in Prampolini's development; he discovered Picasso, the Picasso of *Guernica* and of the realist sculptures on which he wrote a little book. But after 1945, he reverted to his previous manner. His last abstract works from which every trace of humanity had finally disappeared place him without any doubt among those rare innovators whose discoveries have nothing in common with the ephemeral 'formulas' of the great majority of abstract artists of the years 1950-1960. Pierre Courthion wrote of him: 'In the spiritual testament of his works, while creating a rhythmic play of coloured planes, which form a sort of symphony in space, the painter also relies on exceptionally rare tones, peculiar to him: yellows associated with browns, blacks with blues, each in carefully calculated proportions.' In the spring of 1956, a French jury awarted Prampolini the Prix de Paris; but on

June 17th of the same year, he died suddenly from heart failure at Rome where he had been living since 1938.   s. l.

PRENDERGAST Maurice (1859 - 1924). American painter; born in St. John's, Newfoundland, died in New York. His parents moved to Boston when he was two years old. (Some authorities think he may have been born in Boston in 1861.) In 1886, he went to Paris where he spent three years, studying at the Académie Julian and the Académie Colarossi, drawing from life in the morning and sketching along the boulevards in the afternoon. In 1898 he visited Europe with the help of Mrs. Montgomery Sears of Boston and this time travelled in Italy, settling for several months in Venice where he studied the work of Carpaccio and painted scenes of Venetian street life. In 1901 he received his first official recognition in the form of a bronze medal for watercolour from the Pan American Exposition in Buffalo. In 1905 he had a one-man show at the Kimball Gallery in Boston and another at the Macbeth Gallery in New York. Impressed by his Venetian pictures, Robert Henri invited him to exhibit in the famous show of 'The Eight' at the Macbeth Gallery in 1908. In 1912 he again visited Europe with his brother Charles, who was a wood-carver and famous as frame-maker, a craft which Maurice also exercised to make a living. In 1914 the brothers were at last able to move New York, which they found far more congenial than Boston. Here for the last ten years of his life Prendergast lived and worked in a studio on Washington Square, happy in the opportunities for contacts with his fellow artists that life in the city afforded. Nonetheless, recognition was slow in coming: not until 1923, shortly be his death, did it really arrive in the form of a $2,000 prize from the Corcoran Biennial. This scandalously late recognition of one of America's most original painters is, in the words of Suzanne La Follette, 'a severe judgment of American taste during his time'.

Having absorbed Impressionism, Prendergast began to evolve a style which would suggest the Nabis if it were not for something strangely childlike and romantic in his character (children

PRAMPOLINI. COMPOSITION. 1955.
Jonas-Cassuto Collection, Milan.

at play, in parks or along the seashore, were one of his favourite subjects). He applied the unmixed colours to the canvas with a palette knife, building up a mosaic-like surface, a kind of screen in which related tones and touches reply to each other in a complicated counterpoint. Leslie Katz chatacterizes his work well when he writes: 'All space is occupied and meaningful. Each shape is like a piece in a completed jigsaw puzzle. People occupy the spaces left for them—so do trees and shadows. All objects are reconciled in a formal structure, at once flat and multi-dimensional . . . His personal visions, his mystic constructions are inspired demands upon reality'.   j. a.

PRIMITIVES OF TODAY Outside all the great artistic and cultural currents of the last centuries, there has developed a craftsman's painting-decoration of furniture, shop signs, ex-voto offerings and the art of country portraitists–characterized by the supreme importance given to minute enumeration of things, beings, and facts, at the expense of a true representation in pictorial space, which as a result obeys only partially the laws of perspective. These 'naïve' methods have been revived by painters of a new kind, the Primitives of today, who appeared when craft painting came to an end. Far from the teachings of the Fine Arts, and from all contact with contemporary art, these painters have acted upon a genuine vocation. Of folk origin, they remained–because of the circumstances of their life and the frequently belated flowering of their art–outside the artistic and spiritual culture of their time. But this isolation, which deprived them of all cultural exchanges, enabled them, on the other hand, to preserve their primitive vision of the world intact and to express it fully in their painting. This vision is that of the man of the street (hence the phrase 'popular masters of reality' sometimes used in reference to these artists): pathetic subjects, allegory, official 'views' often taken from post-cards, occupy a large place in it; but–more important–their vision was strangely close to the one that man could have formed of the world before entering upon the age of individualism. In France the most outstanding of these 'Neo-Primitives' are the Douanier Rousseau, Vivin, Séraphine, Peyronnet, Bauchant and Bombois. Their work achieves effortlessly the pure miracle of primal poetry, the expression of an intimate and ancient communion between man and the world. Their painting, done with humility and sometimes with real piety, retains extraordinary purity and serenity. In its deeply original character, its often rigorous and logical development (especially in Rousseau and Vivin), it differs both from that practised by earlier naïve craftsmen and from children's or madmen's praintings, although it shares with them certain manners of representation and

a primitive vision of things. It is wrong to consider these primitives as 'Sunday painters': by virtue of the technique they invented instinctively, they are real 'professionals' of painting.

The discovery of the naïve painters, and especially of the Neo-Primitives, was made by artists, poets and a few collectors. The importance of the Douanier Rousseau was recognized about 1905 by Apollinaire, Jarry, Picasso and Robert Delaunay, and also by the German critic Wilhelm Uhde, who discovered Séraphine in 1912. Le Corbusier and Ozenfant chiefly defended Bauchant. The public's taste for the art of these new primitives, although often attracted by the sentimental or picturesque side of their life and works, continued to increase after the great group exhibitions that took place in Paris in 1927 (exhibition of Georges Courteline's collection at the Galerie Bernheim-Jeune), then in 1932 and 1937. The exhibitions at Zurich (1937), New York (1938), Berne (1949) should also be mentioned, which introduced to the public a number of other primitives besides those that have already been mentioned. Every country could now claim its own primitives and a brief list should include the Poles, Teofil Ociepka and Nikifor; the Yugoslav, Ivan Generalić; the Englishman, Alfred Wallis; the Belgian, Léon Greffe; the Swiss, Adolf Dietrich; the Italian, Metelli; the Germans, Paps and Joachim Ringelnatz; the

PRENDERGAST. CENTRAL PARK. 1901.
Whitney Museum, New York.

Spaniard, Miguel Vivancos; the Georgian, Pirosmani; the Greek, Theophilos, whom Le Corbusier was the first to discover in 1936, and the Israeli, Shalom. In the USA, artists like Grandma Moses, Morris Hirshfield, Israel Litwak and Joseph Pickett have become celebrated and known to a large public. In France since the war well known names are Jean Eve, Émile Blondel, Jules Lefranc, Louis Déchelette, Gertrude O'Brady, André Demonchy and Aristide Caillaud. These painters seem to find their place in the history of modern art quite naturally: thus the Douanier Rousseau, the humble creator of a magnificent succession of pictures in which man's imagination and the world's reality miraculously coincide, appears as one of the great forerunners at the source of modern art; he takes his place not far from Cézanne, Gauguin and Van Gogh, his contemporaries. Similarly, one could no doubt detect today profound correspondences between the instinctive or conscious experiments of contemporary painting and the individual adventure of the primitives of today (cf. the articles on Apollinaire, Bauchant, Bombois, Hirshfield, Moses, Peyronnet, Pickett, Rousseau, Séraphine, Uhde and Vivin). F. M.

PUVIS DE CHAVANNES

Pierre (1824-1898). French painter; born in Lyons; died in Paris. It is no longer customary to consider Puvis de Chavannes among the important painters of modern art. However, in his time he was, like the greatest, rejected by the jury of the Salon, and misunderstood by critics. He sided with the most original artists, and was considered in his way as a reformer, a painter whose art brought something new; and if he finally enjoyed official honour, it was without making the slightest

PUVIS DE CHAVANNES. THE POOR FISHERMAN. 1881.   *Musée du Louvre.*

concession, and with the approval of those who were considered revolutionaries. In fact, he escaped all classification and influence of schools; he cannot be situated within Impressionism or any of the currents that derived from it, but neither can he be regarded as a champion of the academic. It is true that this audacities seem timid to us today and are surpassed by the violence with which contemporary art has evolved. At the end of the nineteenth century, when the art of the Impressionists began to dominate, and easel painting gradually became the only medium Puvis de Chavannes wanted to defend the principles of mural painting. He knew that rhythms are not only valid for the exteriorization of feelings but can also be put to the service of necessities outside oneself without losing their value. He was, with Gauguin, perhaps the only painter of the time to have a presentiment of the grandeur of mural painting; and Gauguin was never indifferent to his art. But whereas Gauguin meant to glorify the real, seeking intensity of colours and a harsh nobility of basic forms in the exotic, Puvis de Chavannes desired something similar, at the other pole of refinement, in a calm poetry inspired by history and the legends of Western civilization. What Gauguin thought of obtaining through violence, Puvis de Chavannes wanted to find in tenderness. Thus the two are both profoundly opposed and very closely related, if only by their simplification of modelling in the representation of the human body, the calm and tranquil gravity of their figures, their disposition of figures in the foreground against a backdrop of landscape which covers a great part of the picture and, lifting the horizon very high, leaves little room for the sky. The marked taste of Puvis for fragile elegance can no doubt be regretted, but his large compositions cannot be denied plastic qualities that raise him as a painter far above the pseudo-classicism to which some attempt to confine him today. And the long, slightly too linear silhouette of his figures has not only plastic value. The artist meant to include a number of other meanings in it. He had a liking for symbols and varied imagery, through which his austere and tender poetry could be expressed. To be more precise, with Puvis de Chavannes symbol is not a secret vocabulary and a language for the initiated, but an effort to endow form and gesture with the maximum of human significance. In this respect his picture *The Poor Fisherman* is typical.   R. C.

PUY Jean (1876-1960). French painter; born and died at Roanne. It is customary to classify Jean Puy with the Fauves, and it is fitting to respect this custom, as he belonged to the group that created a scandal at the Salon d'Automne in 1905. Jean Puy painted in bright colours even before 1905; canvases of his exist dated 1902 and 1903, of such daring and frankness in drawing and colour that it is possible to trace Fauvism *(*)* back to that period. Puy's association with Matisse and Derain dates from about 1900, when he was attending courses at the Académie Carrière *(*)*. Fauvism had no name then,

PUY. NUDE. 1920. *Lorenceau Collection.*

but it already existed. In spite of this, is Jean Puy exactly a Fauve ? It seems that he did not arrive at this style or conform to its successive evolutions to obey theories or a system evolved in studio discussions. His work is dominated much more by instinct than by reasoning, the instinct of a painter who experiences a sensuous joy in spreading out and harmonizing colours, in making a form emerge. Sensuousness inspires his nudes, full of robust vitality; a sensuousness based on the hearty appetite, apparent in the still-lifes, a sensuousness that commands simplified forms, dictates relations of clear tones in landscapes, animates and transfigures his snow studies. But this instinctive expansiveness never leads to lack of restraint. In his abandon, Jean Puy retains distinction, a natural characteristic with him, that proves his art more controlled than it seems. Nevertheless, if it preserves something spontaneous in all its aspects, it does so because it has never lost contact with Nature. Whatever the subject of the canvas, Puys always conveys an impression of remaining attached to immediate sensation. However, he adopts neither the small stroke nor the division of tones of the Impressionnists. He employs mostly a broad, open technique.   R. C.

R

RANSON Paul (1864-1909). Born at Limoges; died at Paris. He was a student at the Académie Julian (*) in 1888 and became a member of the Nabis (*), who used to meet every Saturday at his studio in the boulevard Montparnasse. He was a painter and has also left some tapestry cartoons, but he is better known as the founder of the academy that bears his name (*vide* Académie Ranson).

RAY Man (born 1890 in Philadelphia). As a young man he studied architecture and engineering and worked as a mechanical draughtsman. He was inspired by the Armory Show in 1913, after which his own painting grew more abstract but in a satirical style prefiguring Dada. Married to a Frenchwoman, he met French artists who came to New York, among them Duchamp, Picabia, Varèse. With the first two he founded the New York Dada movement during the first World War, and in 1920 he, Duchamp and Katherine Dreier founded the Société Anonyme (*). In 1921 he went to Paris, and on his first day there met Breton, Aragon, Soupault and Éluard who immediately accepted him in the burgeoning Surrealist movement. In order to support himself he took up photography, first photographing his friends' painting and then doing portraits which quickly became fashionable and assured him a livelihood. He remained in Paris until 1940 when he returned to America, living in California until his return to Paris in 1951.

His work presents a number of difficult-to-relate aspects, and in fact he has never been concerned to paint in a style of his own, but rather 'to paint as much as possible unlike other painters. Above all to paint unlike myself, so that each succeeding work, or series of works, shall be entirely different from preceding works'.

From early Cézanne-inspired paintings he progressed rapidly to big, open Dada works like *The Rope Dancer Accompanies Herself with Her Shadows* (1916), a sequence of jagged planes in bold colours, refreshingly devoid of any kind of significance. He began to experiment with airbrush in attempt to produce paintings which would resemble photographs, and in a further attempt 'to create great confusion between the two arts' invented 'rayographs'—pictures made by placing objects against photographically sensitive paper. His Surrealist paintings effectively exploit grotesque juxtapositions of unlikely objects, as in the famous *Observatory Time* which places an immense pair of lips in a sunset sky. Recently he has done abstractions of an extreme, mocking simplicity. Man Ray's refusal to 'be serious' or follow a programme in his work is exemplary: he speaks for the Surrealist generation and its heirs when he says: 'This work cannot be considered experimental. The pursuit of pleasure, my guiding motive, is not a science. Or, a I have previously stated, the desire not the necessity is the stimulant'.   J. A.

RAYONISM This movement, which Michel Larionov began in 1911-1912 at Moscow (*Lucism* in Russian) seems to have partly originated in Futurism, although Larionov has denied this. However, the manifesto of this movement was not published until 1913. In it one reads that a Rayonist canvas must give the impression of gliding out of time and space to convey a feeling of a fourth dimension, and that to achieve this end the painter must resort to parallel or crossed beams of colour. The canvases of Larionov and Gontcharova are among the first really abstract works painted in this century, without any reminiscences of traditional visual reality. (*Vide* Larionov and Gontcharova).   M. S.

REALISM Current confusion between Naturalism and Realism aside, there can be a realism on the level of appearances, as in Impressionism, or a realism on the conceptual plane, as in Cubism. Every great artist creates his own 'reality'–external and internal–which he must transcribe in an autonomous and personal idiom, although two fundamental attitudes are to be distinguished: one that leans toward representation of reality, the other toward suggestive expression of it through metaphor or abstraction. Modern art has resolutely adopted the latter course, so frequently described as non-realistic. After the revolutionary audacities of the beginning of the century and its extraordinary creative outburst, a period of release and reaction occurred at the close of the First World War. This was only a matter of returning to order, to Nature, to traditional realism. The best representatives of this tendency, whose force was felt by all artists for a time, are Dunoyer de Segonzac, Jean Marchand, Luc-Albert Moreau, André Mare, Yves Alix, Boussaingault and La Patellière. Sincere and honest artists of considerable talent, some of them former participants in the exhibition of the *Section d'Or (*)*, they retained of Cézanne only his simplified arrangement of volumes and made up for their lack of plastic invention by masterful craftsmanship and a somewhat ostentatious sensuousness of texture. Sound in its principles but sterile, their attitude revealed a legitimate distrust of intellectualist excesses and a profound longing for good workmanship (*vide* Dunoyer de Segonzac, Boussaingault, La Patellière). A similar phenomenon occurred again in 1945, when the 'painters of poetic reality' (*vide* Brianchon, Legueult, Oudot) formed a group around Brianchon, this time under the banner of Bonnard rather than of Cézanne. J. LE.

REDON Odilon (1840-1916). Born in Bordeaux; died in Paris. Born in the same year as Monet, Redon belonged to the Impressionists' generation but preferred to make his way alone rather than join their movement, which he found too limited in scope. From the start he insisted on the role of imagination in art, and as early as 1868, when Courbet and Naturalism were at their height, he gave his opinion clearly on the subject: 'There are those who want to confine the art of painting to reproducing only what they see. Whoever remains within the narrow limits restricts himself to an inferior ideal. The great painters of the past have proved that the artist, once he has mastered his medium and found in Nature his means of expression, is genuinely free to take his subjects from history or the poets, or to seek it in his imagination'. And he declared that 'while I recognize the necessity of the thing *seen* as a base, true art is in reality *felt*'. These early convictions remained his creed all his life. He loved Nature and studied her closely, but his precise drawings led him to develop a personal style appropriate to the strange world of his dreams. Little by little the reality seen blended in his vision and work with the reality felt. Redon himself explained this double inspiration in a letter to a friend: 'I have always felt the necessity for copying small, fortuitous, individual objects from Nature. Only

MAN RAY. THE ROPE DANCER ACCOMPANIES HERSELF WITH HER SHADOWS. 1916. *Museum of Modern Art, New York.*

REDON. ANEMONES. 1908.
Private Collection, Paris.

after an effort of will faithfully to reproduce a blade of grass, a stone, a branch, part of an old wall, am I fired with the urge to create something imaginary. Nature thus accepted and transformed, becomes my inspirational source. My best works have been the outcome of this approach'. Redon always insisted that his imagination had its roots in the observation of Nature and that his fantastic creations, demoniacal visions in black and white, belonged to a world never wholly divorced from reality. In his own words: 'My originality consists in making incredible beings live according to credible laws, in placing the logic of the possible at the service of the invisible'. Thus Redon succeeded in translating that disturbing dream world which for him partook of reality into a purely plastic language of mysterious lines, subtle contrasts and harmonious colours. He was not interested in probing its meaning; his one aim was to express himself in luxuriant, vigorous colours or in delicate contrasts of black and white.

Redon worked for many years without attracting any attention, or even trying to make a name

for himself. His first album of lithographs (*In a Dream*)–a medium he was to choose for some of his most original and important work–was not published until 1879, when he was nearly forty, and his first small exhibitions in 1881 and 1882 passed almost unnoticed. But as Symbolism in literature developed and reached its peak in 1886, Mallarmé, a close friend of Redon's, and the other poets of the movement were quick to recognize affinities between the painter's work and their own trend. Mallarmé, in a letter to Redon, expressed the pleasure a study of his lithographs gave him: 'The impression received never diminishes, so powerful is your sincerity of vision as well as your capacity for transmitting it to others'. But if it was Symbolism that created the climate necessary for an appreciation of Redon's work, it was not only men of letters who admired his work. The new generation of painters soon came to accept him as of importance to them; Gauguin was proud to be known as his friend, Émile Bernard was unsparing in his admiration, and did all he could to make his work known, while the young *Nabis*–Bonnard, Vuillard and Maurice Denis–came to him for advice. Henri Marisse, attracted by the intense colours introduced by Redon into his painting about 1890, called on the artist to express his admiration. But Redon's role as precursor was not widely acknowledged until after his death when the Surrealists broke in on the world with their fantastic art–often far more literary and intellectual than that of their great predecessor.

Redon's art is not easily accessible; as with Delacroix and Goya– whom he admired without imitating–there is an 'obvious' side to his work which is easy to grasp but also a 'hidden' side an inherent poetry, a masterly control, and a true harmony only visible to the initiated.   J. R.

REICHEL Hans (1892 - 1958). German painter; born at Würzburg, Bavaria, died at Paris. Reichel was only four years old when his father, a paper manufacturer, committed suicide. All his affection was then turned to his mother, who was an excellent musician, and encouraged in him an early love of poetry and art. When she married again to a Dr. Lichtenstein, he followed her to Munich, but bourgeois life was already distasteful to him.

He was sent to a boarding-school in Wasserburg to teach him a lesson. There he lived an introverted life and felt the first stirrings of his artistic personality in the romantic country of the River Inn. His parents were not satisfied with his academic progress and objected, in vain, to his working for a travel agency. After learning by heart a book on Egypt, Reichel acted as a guide to a group of tourists in 1911. He never forgot what he saw of Egyptian art. When he returned, he decided to live on his work as an artist. He was twenty-two, when the First World War broke out, and he pretended to be mad to escape being called up. He was rejected for the army and got married against the advice of his family. The young couple went to live in Munich at the Werneck-Schlossen, where he painted and she played the violin. One evening in 1919, at the café Stephanie where Reichel used to go, he met Paul Klee in the midst of the avant-garde crowd of the day. They immediately became friends and kept in close touch with each other until 1928. This frendship was probably decisive for Reichel's work, which we know nothing about before 1919. All we know is that, when he was still a school-boy, he bought a huge paint-box that he kept till his death. On the other hand, we can be certain it was music that fostered this fruitful friendship between Klee and Reichel.

Klee's father used to teach singing, his mother was a musician, he himself played the violion and his wife was a pianist. For Klee and Reichel music and poetry were an essential source of inspiration; it had induced them to paint, informed their vision and guided their work. They considered Bach and Mozart as stimulating as Hölderlin and Novalis and Brassaï has quite rightly spoken of the 'picture-poems that they put into painting.' Although he discovered an inspiration for his painting through Klee, he made other important friends also: Rilke and Kandinsky. Private concerts gave him a chance to listen to Bartok, Stravinsky and Schoenberg, but at Weimar the spirit of the Bauhaus left him untouched. He was travelling in the Ticino when he met a former pupil, married to an American, who died soon afterwards. He stayed in Italy, Algeria, Paris and again in Munich where he felt a stranger. Then, still absorbed in his own private world, he returned to Paris (1928), where he remained. During the day, he was solitary and unapproachable, because he needed peace for his painting, but he made up for this at night, when he joined in the wild life of Montparnasse with his friends; Lawrence Durrell, Brassaï, Van de Velde, Henry Miller. He worked under Bissière at the Académie Ranson. Jeanne Bucher exhibited his work several times, although it did not rouse much interest. He was interned in 1939 in the camp at Gurs, where he met Lucie Schimek, who became his wife and shared his life and his dreams to the end.

There is no doubt that Klee fascinated Hans Reichel, his work more than his personality, his experimental approach rather than his theories. They were both visionaries; Klee through the diversity and multiplicity of his imaginative constructions: Reichel in the patient, devoted exploration of a strange, unique country, through an almost exclusive use of watercolour, which did not strain his resources. Their art differ-

REDON. SAILING BOATS IN VENICE. 1906. *Private Collection, Paris.*

307

REICHEL. WATER-COLOUR. 1954.
Galerie Jeanne Bucher, Paris.

ed radically; Klee's was essentially intellectual even in his most impulsive phases, while Reichel's was sensuous, fed by the great currents of German romanticism and above all Hölderlin and Novalis. Reichel's world is under a perpetual spell, where the nature of life and dream is so exactly realised and so deeply merged that there is no longer any distinction between them. He thoroughly understood that the use of water-colour is a constant unforseeable adventure of mind and hand; and that he should always be ready to catch the signs of the universe and release them instantly on to the receptive paper. The elements and the seasons are at the very heart of creation. Plants, trees, forests and stones, sea and sky seem to rise to the surface, emerge from silence, through his transparent colours. Animals and vegetables are joined and become one, unless their traces leave some strange resonance in the purely imaginary space. 'I do not think that the nightingale would say in the evening, when she has been singing: I have been working. My little water-colours are no

more a labour than that. They are songs, prayers, little melodies in colour, which have given joy to many people—no more, no less'. These words of Hans Reichel, who had a profound understanding of nature, clearly describe the truly Franciscan spirit of all his creations. His last water-colours show a marked change in the development of his work. Even the fragile suggestions of appearances are lost, spaces acquire an extreme clarity and indescribable shapes evanesce. Poetry resumes its place again over dream-like imagery. Light has absorbed all colour.   R.-J. M.

RENOIR Auguste (1841-1919). French painter; born in Limoges; died at Cagnes in the south of France. Beyond Impressionism, of which he was one of the chief initiators, Renoir joins the line of artists who, from Titian and Tintoretto to Rubens, from Fragonard to Delacroix and Courbet, have seen in painting a kind of pagan and sensual celebration of the glory of woman. The son of a tailor, Renoir began his artistic life as an apprentice, prudently painting small bouquets of flowers on porcelain plates, and then decorating, with the same care, fans and shades for missionaries. However, he had greater hopes. Having saved some money, he gave up being a workman to become a pupil and enrolled, in 1862, at the Atelier Gleyre (*), where he met Monet, Bazille and Sisley; the nucleus of the future Impressionists was thus constituted. The following year, leaving the Atelier, he went with his new friends to the forest of Fontainebleau to paint from Nature. He was at this time under the influence of Courbet, and this influence can be discerned as much in a work like *The Sisley Family* (1868) as in the *Bather with Griffon* (1870): there is the same feeling for texture, the same sensuousness in the volumes, the same frankness. However, association with Claude Monet led him, in certain canvases, to practise the division of the coloured stroke that was to be one of the achievements of Impressionism, and to this we owe the two astonishing versions of *La Grenouillère*, dated 1869. In 1870 Renoir was mobilized; he met his comrades again after the war and participated in the famous exhibition of 1874 at the photographer Nadar's (*), where Impressionism was

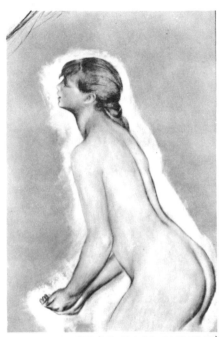

RENOIR. STUDY FOR 'LES GRANDES BAIGNEUSES'.
Art Institute, Chicago.

his friends were chiefly attracted by landscape, his own preference was for group studies and portraits. Having sung the joy of the popular country cafés with music and dancing, he devoted himself to producing some of the most sumptuous images of Parisian society that have been left to us by his period: for example, the portraits of the *Henriot Family* (1876), of *Madame Charpentier and Her Daughter* (1878), of *Jeanne Samary* (1877). A painter of manners, Renoir apparently could not do without the human presence to give measure to his work and express the kind of feeling he wanted to put into it. Whereas Cézanne tended to reduce everything to the impersonal level of the object and to exercise the same calm impartiality for a face as for an apple, Renoir seemed, quite to the contrary, to bring everything into accord with his vision of man. In his work a flower, a fruit are coloured, savoury and palpitating with life, like a human body beneath whose skin one can tell that blood circulates. Cézanne looked and reasoned; Renoir saw and felt. The same opposition is evident in their colour, in the red, or warm, dominants of Renoir, and the blue or green, cold dominants of Cézanne.

But Renoir's Impressionist period proper was

born. Renoir, who exhibited *La Loge*, was one of the painters who incurred the most acid criticism. This was, however, the period during which he produced works of such disconcerting beauty as *The Moulin de la Galette* (1876), *The Swing* (reproduced on page 168), or *Road Climbing Through the Grass* (1876). He was reproached, among other things, with covering his figures with mould when he painted sun filtering through foliage. Now that we are accustomed to coloured shadow and purple tonalities, it is difficult to imagine what a great innovation a canvas like the *Moulin de la Galette* was. The chief characteristic of Renoir's Impressionist period is that he succeeded in adding a sentimental atmosphere to the representation of Nature and seemed to be just as charmed by a tender interlacing of his figures as by the play of foliage or of water. Although he never yielded entirely to anecdote, it is evident that the subject of the canvas remained infinitely more important for him than for any other painter of the new school. While

RENOIR. THE END OF THE LUNCHEON. 1879.
Staedelsches Kunstinstitut, Frankfort.

RENOIR. THE PATH UP THROUGH THE FIELD. ABOUT 1876. *Louvre, Paris.*

approaching its end, and the *Lunch of the Boat Party*, which he conceived during the summer of 1880, while frequenting the café of Mère Fournaise on the island of Croissy, near Paris, was one of the last canvases in which he was to express and sum up the ideal of his youth in a particularly demonstrative synthesis. He was forty and felt the need for renewal. Nothing troubled him more than the facility, the systematic spirit into which Impressionism threatened to lapse. Renoir, like Cézanne a few years earlier, gained a fresh grip by returning to the classical tradition. He left for Italy in the autumn of 1881. After a stay in Venice, he went on to Rome, where he paused long before the frescoes of Raphael at the Villa Farnese, and then proceeded to Naples, where he discovered Pompeian painting. Of this period he would later say, 'A break occurred then in my work. I had gone to the limit of Impressionism and was arriving at the conclusion that I could neither paint nor draw. In short, I was deadlocked'. Under the influence of Raphael he was henceforth to adopt a much smoother manner. Reacting against the disper-

sion and scattering of colour in juxtaposed strokes, he gave a deliberate and rather surprising dryness to forms, which he encircled with a pure and precise line. For what had won him over in Italy, especially in Raphael's work, was the quality of the drawing, which, under a seeming coldness, lingers over the modelling of forms with a keenness and a concentration in which the roles played by the senses and the mind are difficult to separate. Remembering that drawing represents the intellectual element in painting and colour the sensory, it is not a little surprising to see a painter like Renoir adopt such a manner for a time. He who had previously required colour to suggest form, to be its own design, would now imprison it in the severe frame of an increasingly minute and precise painting. This period, which has been called 'Ingresque'–Renoir called it more justly his 'harsh manner'–was characterized by a partiality for cold tones and acid colours, for a smooth, dull surface. A transitory stage in his work, it was nevertheless decisive in so far as it represented an admirable effort of discipline and corresponded to one of those critical moments in the life of an artist when he questions everything and thinks out his art again from its very fundamentals. From this discipline, so contrary to his nature, Renoir was able to extract the best results in numerous canvases about 1885, notably in *Les Grandes Baigneuses* and *The Braid*. However, he did not long endure this constraint, under which his genius was visibly not developing normally, and reverted soon to his characteristic coloured texture. He returned to it with greater vigour than at the time of Impressionism His experience left him with more self-confidence but, above all, with the capacity to be no longer strictly dominated by reality and to impose upon the subject treated the will of his creative genius

With his last 'manner' one witnesses an unprecedented flowering. In a rediscovered unity of colour and line, volume and light, Renoir would untiringly sing woman's body, the centre of the universe, an ever-renewed creation of our desire. Nudes filled his landscapes to the point of occupying the whole canvas, and red, infinitely modulated, became the dominant colour in which all the others were consumed, in the same way that woman in her eternal youth would

be born again every time in Gabrielle, his faithful servant and favourite model. The compositions of this period are unusual in that under the appearance of total freedom they retain infinitely more will than those of Monet or Sisley, but more spontaneity and naturalness than those of Degas. Here Renoir has given the full measure of himself. These canvases achieved recognition very slowly, and even today many collectors consider them inferior to his earlier ones. It is certain that the big nudes that make up the essential part of his production after 1900 represent, when compared to works like *La Loge* or the *Moulin de la Galette*, an art much more difficult to accept, for, liberated of all constraint, the new manner proved capable of transcribing Renoirs' feeling with a boldness that was not yet discernible at the time of Impressionism. The choice of themes is in itself significant. Renoir was not afraid of giving up what had made his success; when his personality was beginning to assert itself in society portraits, he rejected this theme to tackle either group studies, nudes or still-life, with which he could not be sure of conquering a new public. This attitude resulted more from his character than from an aesthetic doc-

RENOIR. BALL AT THE MOULIN DE LA GALETTE. 1876.   *Louvre, Paris.*

RENOIR. Mme HENRIOT.
Private Collection, U.S.A.

Renoir's is a happy art, for as a man he was without bitterness and without jealousy. His work obeyed an inner logic; it was in harmony with a perfectly balanced life able to accept itself at every moment of its development, even the most painful, when illness had deformed his limbs and in order to continue painting he was forced to have his brush tied to his wrist. The impecunious young man he had been at the beginning, who had lived in Montmartre and met the young women of the quarter, nice working girls, models, with light heads and susceptible hearts, was to be received later in families of the Parisian *haute bourgeoisie*. But, in both cases, whether he painted the ball at the *Moulin de la Galette*, *The Swing*, *Lunch of the Boating Party*, or executed portraits he had been commissioned to do, it was first his own sensibility that be expressed, more than just the depiction of the sentimental atmosphere of his works, and,

trine. 'For me', he liked to say, 'a picture must be a pleasant thing, joyous and pretty–yes, pretty ! There are too many unpleasant things in life for us to fabricate still more'.

It was inevitable that the physical pleasure in form and texture that Renoir felt to an intense degree and that made him, in his own words, 'pet a picture, stroke it with the hand', should draw him toward sculpture. This he undertook at a time when, unfortunately, physical disability no longer allowed him much suppleness. He secured the assistance of a young sculptor to work under his constant direction. The only sculpture entirely from his own hand is the portrait of his son Coco, which was executed about 1907-1908. Later works were done by the sculptor Richard Guino, but Renoir's authorship of them cannot be denied; not only do they reveal a close relationship of form and spirit with his painting, but also what Richard Guino executed out of Renoir's presence cannot compare with them. The large *Venus* and the large *Kneeling Washerwoman* (1917) are masterful works that can take their place among the masterpieces of contemporary sculpture.

RENOIR. GIRL WITH HAT AND VEIL.
PASTEL. 1876-1879.

needless to say, it was to himself above all that he meant to be true. Thus his emotions as a painter were in harmony with his feeling as a man and, as a result, an exemplary unity was established between his works, in spite of their differences. Neither was there a sharp break when he gave up too specific subjects almost entirely and preferred to paint bathing women with naked torsos in the innumerable portraits of Gabrielle, this being his own way of creating pure painting. For here again it is clear that love of painting and admiration for woman were indissolubly linked in him and were only the double aspect of his single passion for a clear and healthy life. R. C.

RETH Alfred (born in 1884 at Budapest). He went to Paris in 1905, obtained French nationality and has lived there ever since. He began painting in the studio of J.-F. Blanche, who gave every encouragement to his experiments in linear construction. He became friendly with the orientalist, Jean Buhot, and was so fascinated by the great cycles of Hindu art that they became as important to him as Negro art for most of the Cubists. In 1909, he worked at Varengeville on several variations of different themes. From his observations of nature, he discovered a universal proportion of seven straight lines to one curved line and applied this rule to his interpretation of a subject.

He first exhibited at the Salon d'Automne of 1910 and then with great success, according to Maurice Raynal and Jacques Villon, in the Cubist rooms at the Salon des Indépendants in 1911 and 1912. He was honoured with a large exhibition (80 paintings and drawings) at the Der Sturm Gallery in Berlin in 1913 and held his first one-man exhibition at Paris in 1914 at the Galerie Berthe Weill. The numerous and important works of this period represent a coherent attempt not only to give a geometric analysis of reality, but also to represent the 'relationship of masses', which exist between planes and to express movement and space through this. Reth sought for a serial development of the image and in 1914 he designed a roll, nearly twenty feet long, for Lugné-Poë, depicting the Seine from Robinson to Saint-Cloud.

Reth contributed six old paintings to the retrospective exhibition of Cubist work at the Salon des Indépendants in 1926, but at that time he was engaged on more decorative and abstract experiments. Great rhythms covered the surface of his paintings and his work pointed the way to fresh and unexpected solutions to technical problems. He made systematic use, already anticipated in 1914, of unpromising, utilitarian substances: sand, coal, clinkers,

RENOIR. BATHING. PASTEL. 1890.

mosaic stones, pebbles, plaster, egg shells, which he juxtaposed or mixed with colour and soon used on their own. After he had constructed *Forms in Space* (1935-1939) in wood or metal, he made their counterparts on panels, alternating the built-up portions, which formed the structure of the composition, with planes of pure colour. Reth had been one of the foundation members of the Abstraction-Création (*) movement in 1932 and the Salon des Réalités Nouvelles in 1946. An exhibition, organised in 1948 by Léon Degand at the Galerie Denise René, was a forceful reminder of how important his ideas had been. It was followed by several other exhibitions at Lyons, Paris, Stockholm and London. J. LA.

REVUE BLANCHE (La). This was the first literary review to seek from painters a collaboration that was not occasional but that, on the contrary, based on very subtle affinities, was to be maintained during the twelve years that the magazine existed –a long time for an avant-garde review, and perhaps unequalled. The *Revue Blanche* was founded by the brothers Alexandre and Thadée Natanson in October 1891. Among the contributors who were interested in the plastic arts were, along with Thadée Natanson himself, Octave Mirbeau, Jules Renard, Alfred Jarry, Tristan Bernard, Félix Fénéon, Félicien Fagus and Guillaume Apollinaire. Regular meetings took place on the premises of the magazine, attended by Toulouse-Lautrec, Sérusier, Bonnard, Vuillard, Ranson, Roussel, Maurice Denis, Steinlen, Vallotton and others. It was during these gatherings, often tumultuous and generally conducted by Sérusier, that a number of new artistic theories first were aired. The participants would be first Synthesist, then Neo-Impressionist or 'Neo-Traditionalist', and also Mystic. However, on the whole the tone of the *Revue Blanche* reflected a taste for detailed observation, but was always careful to avoid the excesses and facility of Naturalism. One of the issues that created a scandal was that of May 1900, in which Thadée Natanson, attacking the official Salon des Artistes Français, opposed to it the work of the painters grouped about the magazine, 'intelligent painters' as he said. These words, which the author had chosen for the title of his article, resounded like a challenge and took on the aspect of a manifesto. In 1901 Fagus, in the first article devoted to this artist in France, discovered the Picasso of the 'Blue Period'. Bonnard composed a series of lithographs in colour for the magazine in 1893, and in 1894 his celebrated poster (reproduced on page 257). Vallotton adorned the review with portraits of writers and artists, frontispieces or drawings, for which Jules Renard sometimes wrote commentaries. As early as 1896, when Bonnard exhibited for the first time at the Durand-Ruel Gallery, Thadée Natanson published an excellent study of him, and articles on Lautrec in 1893 and 1901. Fénéon became the interpreter of Neo-Impressionism *(*)* and of the Nabis *(*)*, and he organized on the premises of the magazine itself an important retrospective exhibition of Seurat in 1900. The first exhibition of Vuillard also took place at the office of the *Revue Blanche* in 1891; and it published the famous manuscript of Gauguin, *Noa Noa*, in 1897. It was in the issue of April 15th, 1903, that Fagus announced the end of this publication which, in its boldness and its fidelity to its initial views, had reflected an artistic period whose originality and interest could not fail to make history. M. R.

RIVERA Diego (1886-1951). Born at Guanajuato; died at Mexico City. After taking courses at the School of Fine Arts in Mexico City, Rivera freed himself of Spanish academicism (which no longer was related to Velasquez or Goya and was still strong in Mexico) by living in Paris and becoming one of the Montparnasse painters who have been grouped under the name of School of Paris. A friend of Modigliani, recognized by Guillaume Apollinaire, Rivera adopted, contrary to most of the painters of the period, an attitude of reserve,

BONNARD. LITHOGRAPH FOR THE 'REVUE BLANCHE'.

almost that of an observer. He followed attentively, but without participating in it, the evolution of the painters of the Bateau-Lavoir *(*)*–Picasso, Braque and Juan Gris. However, he benefited from their research. But he clearly did not feel at ease in Parisian circles. He returned to Mexico and set out to discover his country. Profoundly influenced by the ancient art of the Mayas and Aztecs, he was also moved by the revolutionary spirit that was still strong throughout Mexico. These two appeals were so powerful that his formerly reserved personality underwent a real metamorphosis. He rejected the influences that he had accepted only with the tip of his brush during his stay in Paris, and succeeded in becoming a revolutionary painter by adopting the traditions of a remote past. He waged an active campaign in Mexico City which led to the creation of a purely Mexican school of painting. With the assistance of the authorities, who gave him important commissions and supported his efforts, he worked out vast frescoes for public buildings, inspired by the political and social history of Mexico, particularly the history of popular uprisings. In fact, he painted the first modern Mexican mural, that in the Bolivar Amphitheatre in the University (1922). The attempt was decisive both for himself and for other Mexican painters. For the impulse had been given and the Mexican school created. From then on every fresco was a manifesto and a challenge. The outstanding works in this immense output, which covered thirty-five years, are the decorations for the Secretariat of Public Education (1923-1928), the National Palace of Mexico City (1930-1935 and 1944) and the mosaics in coloured stones for the stadiums of the University City (1952). His masterpiece is in the chapel of the National School of Agriculture, Chapingo (1926-1927) on whose walls he painted a sort of paean to life. Can one maintain that this painting, which accepted European methods, techniques and procedures, was actually a modern expression of the prodigious art of the ancestors whose tradition it claimed to continue? Perhaps not. What is more evident is that, thanks to Rivera, Mexican art has proved one of the most dynamic movements in the painting of our time. One of the aspects of Rivera's art that should not be underestimated remains to be mentioned: what may

RIVERA. ARUMS.

be called its will to be a folk image. The colours as well as subjects of the frescoes are popular in intent. Rivera desires to meet the needs and strivings of the masses and does not care much for the élite. Certainly he prefers to address himself to the greatest number, but nevertheless he takes care to create a style.   PH. S.

ROSSI Gino (1884-1947). Born and died at Venice, this exceptionally talented Italian painter explored a solitary way of his own in contemporary art, over a period of about ten years, which were left him to devote to his painting from war, poverty, illness and insanity. He was brought up in comfortable surroundings and given a good education. He felt the urge to paint after seeing the work of Gauguin, Van Gogh and the Cubists at Paris in 1907. After he had sacrificed everything to his passion, he was forced to earn a living as a pedlar. In 1924, he was taken into an asylum where he remained until his death. A year later in 1948, a posthumous, retrospective exhibition of about fifty of his works—landscapes, figures and still-lifes painted between 1908 and 1923—was organised by his friend, Nino Barbantini. It was a revelation of Rossi's importance in the history of Italian painting. There is sample of this in paintings such as *Young Girl with a Flower* (1909) or the *Fisherman in a Green Béret* (1913), which shows the influence of Gauguin's Pont-Aven period; consummate Cubist compositions like *Still-life with a Violin* (1922) and *Still-life with a Revolver* (1922); and a *Village on a Hill* (1923) with its completely Cézannesque structure. His destiny, unfortunately, prevented him from enjoying the rewards of a conscious and systematic experimenting in which there was an undeniable originality.   D. F.

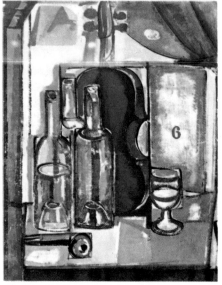

ROSSI. STILL-LIFE WITH A VIOLIN. 1922.

ROUAULT Georges (1871-1958). French painter; born and died in Paris. His father was a cabinet-maker; his aunts did china painting. At fourteen he was apprenticed to a stained-glass painter. He worked on the restoration of medieval windows. From this work he retained a taste for iridescences and colours encircled with a vigorous black line. It developed in him, moreover, a craftsman's integrity, examples of which he had already seen among his family. Of the masters of his time, Rouault possesses the soundest craftsmanship in the traditional sense, both in draughtsmanship and the conventional techniques that once ruled official art, and in the preparation of colours. During his apprenticeship he

attended courses at the Paris School of Decorative Arts. In 1891 he entered the École Nationale des Beaux-Arts, where his teacher was Gustave Moreau. The latter was a man of great culture and extremely broad minded. His work, unfortunately spoiled by excessively literary preoccupations, was related to the Symbolist movement and devoted to the evocation of a legendary and hieratic past, smothered in precious fabrics and jewels. The solid technical foundation he gave his pupils respected the originality of each, More than a teacher, he was a real friend to Rouault, whom he encouraged and to whom he gave self-confidence. But Rouault did not find himself immediately. His master had predicted a difficult career for him, perceiving his taste for rich and powerful pictorial material at the expense of linear precision. These tendencies existed even in Rouault's first works, where he treated religious subjects in a still traditional style. In 1893 he painted *Samson Turning the Millstone*; in 1895 *Christ Dead Mourned by the Holy Women*, both for the Prix de Rome, which he did not win. Here certain figures recall those of Leonardo da Vinci and of some of his disciples, Solario or Ambrogio da Predis. An admiration for Rembrandt is apparent in *Christ and the Disciples of Emmaus*. After a period of material difficulties and moral crisis, following the death of Gustave Moreau in 1898, and coinciding with an estrangement from his family, Rouault participated in the foundation of the Salon d'Automne in 1903. At that time he was already painting the landscapes of suburbs and bleak countrysides that are found throughout his work–the earliest of these is *The Work Yard* of 1897. In 1904 and 1905 he exhibited works in which other themes appeared, themes that he has also taken up incessantly: prostitutes, clowns, pierrots. These canvases were done in a very dark tonality that disconcerted the public. The Catholic novelist Léon Bloy inspired certain subjects Rouault treated in 1905, like *Monsieur et Madame Poulot*, the strange couple of *The Poor Woman*. Bloy hardly understood the real problems of painting, and his nature made friendship difficult; however, the influence of his vehement oracular manner was evident. Rouault put extraordinary violence into the tribunal scenes, prostitutes and clowns he represented. Bestiality and stupidity are displayed on the faces that dark zones delineate cruelly with their black lines, accentuating the grotesqueness of the moral misery and physical ugliness. The horror of this fallen humanity fascinated Rouault; but he painted it with a kind of sensitive irony, dispensing light touches of bright colours, pinks, celestial blues, ardent reds.

In 1907 he worked at ceramics and met Odilon Redon, who was then making his most poetical transcriptions of coloured reveries. Rouault continued to treat social themes: peasants, workmen, individuals isolated or placed in their family surroundings; his characters transcend their station and become mythical figures. Rouault renewed his technique completely, reducing his drawing to essentials that took on a life of their own, giving up shadows, elaborate gradations, successive perspectives and planes, to portray the model directly in its hallucinating truth, created with colours chosen only for their greater expressive value. To reach the essential more directly he had only to block in a figure with large, rough strokes of colour that stand out against the shadow. His works contained the germ of tremendous power. They were starting a life that would be continued in all the painter's future creations. His first one-

ROUAULT. AT THE MIRROR. 1906.
Musée d'Art Moderne, Paris.

man exhibition was held at the Galerie Druet in 1910. In 1917 Ambroise Vollard *(*)* became his dealer. The artist undertook for him, until 1927, a whole series of etchings to illustrate various works: *The Reincarnations of Père Ubu* (1932), *Le Cirque de l'Étoile Filante* (1938) and *Les Fleurs du Mal* of Baudelaire, a project that was abandoned but for which a number of plates were engraved, and finally *Miserere*, published only in 1948. In these plates, which are of exceptional dimensions, form is simplified to the extreme; all the sometimes caricatural picturesqueness of the previous works has disappeared in favour of a vehement expressionism of silhouette and a dramatic opposition of whites and blacks. Form is not only accentuated by dark zones but often uniformly encircled with a vigorous line that recalls the leading of stained glass. After a mechanical transfer to the copperplate of a composition drawn in India ink, Rouault undertook his work as engraver, with all possible tools: an etcher's needle, a roller, a file, a scraper, sandpaper, which he used according to his inspiration, discovering new techniques like the application of acid with wide strokes of the brush.

ROUAULT. THE APPRENTICE. 1925.
Musée d'Art Moderne, Paris.

Unsatisfied, he took up the subject indefinitely, producing up to twelve or fifteen successive states. The plates are accompanied by titles or captions of a rare power of visual evocation. They are not the prodigious philosophical and moral epitomes of Goya, but rather incantations or magic formulas suggested by the requirements of a mysterious inner rhythm. One finds in these etchings the gallery of figures invented by Rouault to represent human misery and the appetites of the flesh: crooked judges, kings and those in high positions wearing frightening masks, so-called women of pleasure, the clown with a pointed hat topping his sad face. There are landscapes in which lines converge toward a powerful light, peaceful countrysides devastated by ruin and fire, empty streets expressing the solitude of cities. However, the artist has moments of poignant gentleness when he paints certain women's or children's face–in the most grimacing Daumiers, too, there are miraculous faces of young girls–or when he tells of the sufferings of Christ and of the Virgin to redeem human sins. Upon this gigantic enterprise, in

ROUAULT. THE HOLY FACE.
Frigerio Collection, Paris.

which the painter mixed acid-like pigments, did violence to metal and put his powerful stamp upon everything, the technique of black and white imposes it harsh and strange discipline. Features stand out, hard, absolute. There is no complacency in the satire, nothing flabby or inflated in the rendering of the horrible. The effect achieved is of a richness, a depth that makes Rouault the greatest visionary of modern times.

In spite of his activity as an engraver, in which should be included the execution of settings for Diaghilev (*Le Fils prodigue*, 1929) and various literary texts, Rouault has pursued his work as a painter. It was especially after 1932 that the main part of his production again came to be in this field. Clowns and judges continued to supply him with themes, but he no longer kept the violence of his first works: anger had given way to pity. Wide, immense eyes, in the midst of livid faces, seemed to transcribe an inner emptiness or the vision of a beyond. Religious subjects grew more numerous and were integrated into the suburban landscapes; imprecise silhouettes stood out against towers and houses whose doors and windows suggested mouths and empty eyes. Scenes were bathed in a strange light, both warm and almost nocturnal, that seemed to radiate from within the forms. All these canvases Rouault kept taking up again, reworking them, never satisfied and never ready to part with them. From 1937 on he hardly ever signed his works and no longer dated them. In 1947 a suit was brought by him against the heirs of Ambroise Vollard. After a verdict that set a precedent, he was allowed to keep all the works still in his studio that he considered unfinished. He burned 315 of them, which he thought too far from the perfection he had glimpsed, and undertook a definitive perfecting of his work within self-assigned limits. It is in the large religious paintings, which compel everyone's esteem, that this great work reaches its peak, solitary but none the less entirely turned towards love for one's fellow man, passionate with fury but also with affection and pity. Rouault has drawn up an indictment of humanity that can be compared with the most terrible, those of Goya and Daumier. Then, by a sort of generosity, he has transcended the misery to reach the eternal myths. He paints the flaws of societies, the decrepitude of the institutions that men of all

ROUAULT. CHRISTIAN NOCTURNE. 1952.
Musée d'Art Moderne, Paris.

times have established; but he fulfils himself in a burning communion with the holy figures and the saints.   J. LA.

ROUSSEAU Henri, called the Douanier (1844-1910). French painter; born at Laval in Mayenne; died in Paris. At nineteen he enrolled in the Army and was assigned to the 52nd Infantry Regimental Band, where he played the saxophone. After he left the Army, settled in Paris and married, in 1869, and entered the customs service as a clerk: hence his name. He allowed people to think that he had participated in the Mexican campaign, but there is no evidence to support this idea. When he was about forty he began painting steadily. He did not, however, retire from the customs service until 1893. In 1886, introduced by Signac and Luce, he exhibited at the Societé des Artistes Indépendants, to which he sent work regularly

from then until 1898, and again from 1901 to 1910. Beginning in 1905, he exhibited also at the Salon d'Automne. He associated with Gauguin, Odilon Redon and Seurat. Through the poet Alfred Jarry, also of the town of Laval, he made the acquaintance of Rémy de Gourmont, who, in the magazine *L'Ymagier*, published *War*, a lithograph based upon Rousseau's picture, exhibited the previous year. Having lost his wife, Rousseau remarried in September 1899 upon the completion of a drama in five acts, *The Revenge of a Russian Orphan*, which was unsuccessfully produced at the Théâtre du Châtelet in Paris. In 1903 his second wife died. He lived in the rue Pernel, in the Plaisance quarter of Paris, and, to make a living, he gave lessons in painting, diction and harmony. He made portraits of neighbouring shopkeepers, and when he drew them he took their measurements, like a tailor. In 1906, he met Apollinaire, who introduced him to Delaunay. It was Delaunay's mother who commissioned the *Snake Charmer* from him. In 1907, he made the acquaintance of Wilhelm Uhde *(*)*, who wrote the first monograph on him (Paris, 1911). The following year

ROUAULT. SELF-PORTRAIT.
LITHOGRAPH.

319

ROUSSEAU. PÈRE JUNIET'S CART. 1908. *Private Collection, Paris.*

his friends organized a banquet in his honour at Picasso's studio in the Bateau-Lavoir *(*)*. In 1909 he painted Apollinaire's portrait, called *The Poet and his Muse*, which he exhibited at the Salon des Indépendants. He also left a replica, now in Moscow. Wilhelm Uhde, Ambroise Vollard and Brummer were his first buyers. Baroness Oettingen (Roch Grey), Ardengo Soffici, the sculptor Hoetzer and Robert Delaunay bought pictures from him. He exhibited, in 1910, *The Dream* at the Salon des Indépendants. But he was driven by the desire to marry again. Turned down by the woman he wanted to marry at any cost and whom he had pressed with increasingly urgent proposals, his spirit broke. He was admitted to the Necker hospital, where he died on September 2nd, 1910. Seven people, among them Paul Signac, followed the hearse. He was buried in a common grave at the Bagneux cemetery outside Paris. The painter Delaunay and the caster Queval, owner of the house in which Rouseau lived, put up the money to buy a thirty-year concession at the cemetery, and the Douanier's remains were transferred to a decent burying-ground. Here, with a medallion by Armand Queval, was set a tombstone on which Apollinaire wrote in pencil the famous poemepitaph that Brancusi and Ortiz de Zarate engraved in the stone the next year, following the poet's handwriting precisely. In 1947, his

PHOTOGRAPH OF THE JUNIET FAMILY AND THE CART.

ashes were laid in a public garden in Laval. Rousseau's attention was drawn only by the freshness of things. For him dream was never severed from reality. The most everyday events were bathed in enchantment. In Plaisance concierges saw him pass by in his big art student's hat, violin-case or paint-box under his arm. In his tiny studio he lived on the hundred francs of his monthly pension, which he stretched out as he could. There he occasionally gave his *soirées*. The studio contained a table in unstained wood, three chairs, a chest for wood, and a makeshift bed concealed behind a curtain. He interrupted his painting from time to time to eat bread soaked in wine or milk. He led the life of a forgotten man, a rather miserable one. He said he had 'suffered much in the heart'. But he was rich, alive with a world of colours and forms, a world impatient to be born, and which found its most appropriate idiom in painting. This idiom, springing from the very surge of life, from the beat of the heart, has its miraculous expression in his painting. He never had to make an effort to convey a sudden emotion. There is nothing reheated in his work. He gave himself totally, without a struggle. 'It is not I who paint,' he said to a friend, 'but someone else who holds my hand.' How did this essentially plebeian art achieve such distinction? Most of what we know of folk art has a direct but often monotonous savour. There is nothing of the kind here. Rousseau had found instinctively the quality of the style that strikes us in those whom we call Primitives. From all the Douanier painted emerges a unique form, a unique harmony of colours, a unique way of treating the detail of the foliage of trees and of subordinating even the tiniest fragments to the monumentality of the whole. A primitive intuition led him to paint weddings, family reunions, the old dreams of the Dream Book. He had the childlike gift of believing in the magic reality of his creations. Those who knew him assure us that he experienced sudden terrors while painting his tiger hunts. Rousseau's production extends over a period of twenty-five years. But works of his exist done before 1886, the year of his first appearance at the Salon des Indépendants. We know that in 1884 he was issued a copyist's card for the Louvre. What old masters could he have interpreted? We do not know. Of his work we know only a

part. Besides the 140 or so paintings exhibited at the Salon des Indépendants and the Salon d'Automne and the works recognized today, many canvases were destroyed through ignorance or ruined through neglect (they were in the possession of concierges or at the houses of workmen, who often took no care of them). Without expecting numerous discoveries, it may be hoped that other Rousseaus will still be found. The themes he treated can be grouped into six categories:

(1) Scenes referring to the life of the Douanier or of his relatives, of people whom he knew: self-portraits, ceremonies, weddings, baptisms, family reunions (self-portraits, 1888-1890; *To Welcome the Baby*, 1903; *A Wedding in the Country*, 1905; *The Cart of Père Juniet*, 1908).

(2) Landscapes of Paris and its suburbs, with strollers and fishermen, which often give off something euphoric (*View of the Foot Bridge of Passy*, 1895; *In the Parc Montsouris*, 1895; *The Chair Factory in Alfortville*, 1897; *The Alley in Saint-Cloud*, 1903; *Malakoff*, 1905; *View of the Isle Saint-Louis from the Quai Henri IV*, 1909).

(3) Exotic scenes: evocations of the virgin forest, big game hunts, bloody fights (*Sleeping

ROUSSEAU. PORTRAIT OF PIERRE LOTI. 1891.
Kunsthaus, Zurich.

Gypsy, 1897; *The Negro Assailed by a Leopard*, 1904; *The Lion Devouring the Antelope*, 1905; *Practical Jokers*, *The Apes*, 1906; *The Monkeys in the Orange Grove*, 1907; *The Snake Charmer*, 1907; *The Flamingoes*, 1907; *Exotic Landscape*, 1908).

(4) Military, patriotic or sports scenes (*The Centenary of Independence*, 1892; *The Gunners*, about 1893; *War*, 1894; *The Republic*, 1904; *The Representatives of Foreign Powers, presenting their respects to the Republic as a Sign of Peace*, exhibited in 1907; *The Football Players*, 1908).

(5) Allegorical scenes (*Present and Past*, about 1907; *The Muse and the Poet*, 1909; *The Dream*, 1910).

(6) Bouquets of wild and garden flowers.

How did Rousseau work ? 'As an embroideress embroiders', say those who knew him. If the man sometimes had the excessive simplicity of naïve persons, the artist was rather ingenuous. He painted with a natural and graceful frankness, adding freedom to his native gifts. Thus his technique had nothing summary to it. He could render details without impairing the unity of the whole in his small canvases. Works of greater dimensions he treated differently, with large planes of even colours. Whence came the monumentality that his landscapes almost always

possess ? From his way of presenting the plant world. Like Poussin, the Douanier enlarged greenery and branches, whose leaves he shows us as if through a magnifying-glass, taking care to distinguish every species. His palette of deep blacks, the colour of slate, is cut by yellows, browns, purplish greens; it has the delicate, almost acid, tones of the Christmas rose. Rousseau drew little, but with an extraordinary sense of plastic values. Usually he described contours directly with the brush, and in colour, but without harshness. Before painting with the very precise density that characterizes him, he sometimes made sketches that approach, though rather distantly, the Impressionist manner. This naïve and gentle man, something of a mythomaniac, ridiculed, scolded by his wife, bullied by his daughter, knew nevertheless that only the fittest survive, that Nature is a jungle full of ferocity, that the child is not always good. But, with his whole being, he sided with the underdog, the defenceless animal, the victim. In his paintig the quality of universal commiseration almost always impregnates the fruits of observation. Beyond reality, this ingenuous man opened paths invisible to the naked eye and had a presentiment of encounters that escape logic.

There exist innocent beings to whom it is

ROUSSEAU. SLEEPING GYPSY. 1897.   *Museum of Modern Art, New York.*

given to see farther than others who are of more complex organization but conform to the common measure. Nothing discourages these ingenuous ones. In them hope springs eternal. Some day, they know, it will be 'different'. The little painter, the 'angel' of the Plaisance quarter, belongs to their family. Rousseau put up with poverty, but without too much resignation. He acknowledged it. He courageously claimed his place, his right to woman and to art, to freedom and Sunday calm. No doubt at the bottom of his heart he vaguely felt joy in having freed himself from the slavery of assigned work. With the resources granted him, the degree of intelligence

ROUSSEAU. THE SNAKE-CHARMER. 1907. *Louvre, Paris.*

fallen to his lot, this child, who had been given more love than knowledge, was conscious of his humble victory as a man who remained true to his first dreams. Hence the kindness of heart and mind that his painting often conveys. At the threshold of our century this 'simpleton' came as a pioneer. At a moment when humanity is wondering whether mechanical distortion has not stifled its creative capacity, the work of the Douanier Rousseau, an antidote to our technical civilization, is still as fresh as prophecy.   P. C.

ROY Pierre (1880-1950). French painter, born in Nantes; died in Milan. The offspring of a middle-class family, related to that of Jules Verne, he was deeply impressed as a child by Verne's stories, which were told to him by the writer's brother. His repressed ambition was to become a sailor. Instead, his secondary studies finished, he entered an architect's office. From this period, which did not last long, he retained a taste for precise, neat draughtsmanship, plans, worked and inalterable materials: stone, wood, rope, metal. Paris attracted him. He first enrolled at the École Nationale des Beaux-Arts and then attended the Académie Julian (*) and the École

des Arts Décoratifs. About 1910 he came in touch with the Fauves and the group of writers surrounding them: Salmon, Max Jacob, and especially Apollinaire. He wrote and illustrated with coloured woodcuts the volume *Comptines*, which was not published until 1926. An heir of the Neo-Impressionists, he changed his manner after the First World War. In 1920 he made friends with the future Surrealists and participated in their first two exhibitions (Pierre Loeb Gallery, 1925; Surrealist Gallery, 1926). Launched and in demand in the United States, he visited America every year and organized large exhibitions. In 1939 he went as far as the Hawaiian Islands and brought back in his work an element of sensitive exoticism and, in comparison with his pictures of the 1925-1935 period, a shade of affectation, except in his portraits, which remained realistic and vigorous. As a decorator he worked for the Ballets Suédois (*) of Rolf de Maré (*Coppélia*, 1938) and for the Champs-Élysées Ballets (*Jeu de Cartes*, 1945); and as an illustrator he produced a series of lithographs for *The Child of the High Sea* of Jules Supervielle (1946). It was on his way to an exhibition in Bergamo, where he was showing some of his work, that he died suddenly in Milan on September 26th,

ROY. L'ÉTÉ DE LA
SAINT-MICHEL.
CIRCA 1932. *Musée
d'Art Moderne, Paris.*

1950. Curious about everything, a fine scholar, a sure, keen critic, he brought to everything the rigour that made him both solitary and classic. In spite of inevitable affinities, his work remains isolated in its time. Its distinctive features are minute care, refinement, finish, realism to the point of *trompe-l'œil*, a rendering of materials comparable to that of the old Flemish and Dutch masters, and–in deliberate contrast–the unusual, the startling in composition. He took pleasure in assembling heterogeneous objects–pieces of reed or wood, even logs, hair, ribbons, birds' eggs, artificial flowers, small pebles, seeds, cardboard castles, shells, wool and silk, wicker baskets, and sometimes simple machines (the wheel, for example, the central motif of several of his pictures)–somewhat in the way that children in their games make up displays or counters, his set purpose being to suggest through transposition of meaning and unexpected juxtapositions, both a new significance and a sort of strange poetry, revealing a thirst for escape and an inner freedom compatable to that of writers and poets.   M. P.

RUSSELL Morgan (1886 - 1953). Born in New York of French and English parents; died in Broomall, Pennsylvania. After studies with Robert Henri he came to France at the age of nineteen, where he met Matisse, Apollinaire, Modigliani (who painted his portrait) and Leo Stein, who encouraged him and helped him financially. But his most decisive meeting was with Stanton Macdonald-Wright *(*)* with whom he founded the movement known as 'Synchromism.' Russell's *Synchromie en Vert* at the Salon des Indépendants in 1913 was the first Synchromist work to be shown; Synchromist exhibitions followed in the same year in Munich, New York, and Paris. In 1916 Russell went to New York for a month to participate in the Forum Exhibition at the Anderson Galleries. Back in France he shortly lost interest in Synchromism, adopting a classical and it must be said conventional figurative style. Occasionally, however, he reverted to abstraction—a canvas in the collection of Michel Seuphor dating from 1925 is in the best Synchromist tradition. Except for several winters in Rome and a trip to California in 1931 where he showed his work at the Palace of the Legion of Honor in San Francisco, he remained in France from 1916 to 1946, mostly on his small property at Aigremont in Burgundy, where he led a solitary existence following the death of his first wife. In 1946 he returned to America with his second wife, a niece of Claude Monet. Deeply religious, he painted a number of large-scale Biblical works in a severe classical style during his last years, and spoke of his early abstractions as belonging to his 'kindergarten period.'

It is the Synchromist works, however, which merit his inclusion here. Russell's work, while closely related to that of Macdonald-Wright, is less suave and harmonious, more abrupt and inhabited by a rude strength, 'avec des détails crus et cruels' (Michel Seuphor). Rough-hewn geometrical shapes, often trapezoidal, are crammed and crumpled into a kinetic image which contrasts with the lyrical undulations of form in the work of his colleague. Writing on his work in the catalogue of the 1913 Synchromist exhibition at the Galerie Bernheim-Jeune, Russell said: 'I have used light as a series of related chromatic undulations and have studied more profoundly the harmonic rapports between colours . . . As is evident, I give up the heritage of old drawing habits. Instead I run the happy risk of falling on some of the correspondences that exist between reality and our colour sensations. It is from an ensemble of colours equilibrating around a generative colour that form should gush out. From this point of view my art is related to the very mechanisms of natural vision.' J. A.

RUSSIAN BALLET (*see* Ballets Russes).

RYDER Albert Pinkham (1847-1917). American painter; born in New Bedford Massachusetts,a died in Elmhurst, New York. He was brought up near the sea in the famous whaling port of New Bedford. About 1870 his parents moved to New York where a brother of Albert had become a successful restaurant proprietor. He was refused admission to the National Academy of Design, but after informal study with the painter William E. Marshall who had befriended him he was finally admitted. He exhibited first at the National Academy in 1873, and later with the rival Society of American Artists, of which he was a founder. After 1880 he exhibited less frequently. He travelled briefly to Europe with two friends in 1877, visiting England, France, Holland, Italy, Spain and Tangier, but the art of the past seems to have made little impression on him. In 1887 and 1896 he crossed the Atlantic on the ship of his friend Captain Robinson, chiefly for the sea voyage; both times he remained for a short time in London before returning him to New York. His work became increasingly popular, but after 1900 Ryder began to live a hermetic existence in a small and filthy flat on West 15th Street. His behaviour became more eccentric. Sometimes he would spend whole evenings walking about the city looking

at effects of moonlight, or gazing out of his windows at the trees in his garden, of which he said, 'I would not exchange these two windows for a palace with less a vision than this old garden with its whispering leafage.' His eyesight, which had always been poor, declined, and so, after 1900, did the quality of his work. He would work on his paintings for years, refusing to part with them. Unfortunately his technical knowledge of oil painting was slight: he often washed his paintings or painted over them while they were still wet, and as a result most of the approximately 150 paintings he left have suffered irreparable damage.

Moody, romantic, a hermit in the modern metropolis, Ryder occupies a position in American painting similar to that of Poe or Melville in literature. He painted dreamlike scenes of dark boats adrift in moonlit seas (*Toilers of the Sea*) or forest landscapes filled with unearthly light (*The Forest of Arden, Siegfried and the Rhine Maidens*). Details disappear under the accumulations of murky pigment, but the sharply outlined masses are charged with energy. At times his imagery recalls Redon as in *The Race Track* (1895) which shows a scythe-bearing skeleton on horseback. But it is difficult to compare him with other painters, and he in fact cared little for the painting of others, looking to his inner world for inspiration. He is, in the words of Alexander Elliott, 'the greatest lyrical painter that America has produced,' Jackson Pollock, writing in 1944, said 'Ryder is the only American painter who interests me.' It is no doubt his independence of tradition and his concentration on a subjective, esoteric vision which accounts for the renewed esteem of Ryder among American avant-garde painters since the war. J. A.

RYSSELBERGHE Theo van (1862 - 1926). Belgian painter; born in Ghent, died at Saint-Clair, France. Even when he was a child, his father, a contractor, and his brothers, who were architects, encouraged his artistic gifts. His family sent him first to the Ghent Academy, then to the Brussels Academy. His first paintings were grisailles, then he discovered the effects of light after visits to Spain and Morocco, but the revelation of the way he really wanted to paint only came when he saw Seurat's *La Grande Jatte* on a visit to Paris. He gave up the classical manner he had adopted up to that point and followed Seurat's theories, which he thoroughly assimilated. He felt the need of a discipline, chose the Neo-Impressionist technique and was the only painter to apply it to portraiture (*Portrait of Octave Maus,* 1885; *Portrait of Mme Charles Maus,* 1890;

He was the principal founder of the Société des Vingt (*) and later on of La Libre Esthétique group. He took part in all their exhibitions and, from 1885, joined the great Brussels movement that included Van de Velde, Verhaeren, Hankar, Serrurier, Horta and that aimed at a socially conscious art. This movement soon became identified with the revolution that had begun about 1895 in every sphere of society by Art Nouveau, which Henry van de Velde was sweeping along into a real crusade for the renewal of the applied arts. During this period, Van Rysselberghe illustrated the books of his friend, Verhaeren, designed typographical ornaments, vignettes, several posters, furniture and jewellery. In 1898 he went to live in Paris, frequented the literary circles of the capital, made friends with Maeterlinck and Félix Fénéon and joined in the battle of the Symbolist school with Verhaeren, who was one of its most active members. He has left us a picture of these literary gatherings in *The Reading* (Musée des Beaux-Arts, Ghent, 1903), a realistic 'portrait of the poets' in which Le Dantec, Viélé-Griffin, Charles Cross, Fénéon, Gide, Henri Ghéon and Maeterlinck can be recognised in a group round Verhaeren. Eventually Van Rysselberghe

VAN RYSSELBERGHE. MARIA SETHE.
Musée des Beaux-Arts, Antwerp.

settled in Provence. There he became more sensitive to the relief of landscape and tried to give greater emphasis to form by using a stronger brushwork. He escaped from the dogmatic spirit of Neo-Impressionism and could express the feminity of a woman's body, bathed by the light of the sea.   R.-J. M.

S

SAVINIO Alberto (1891 - 1952). Born at Athens; died in Rome. Italian painter, polemist, writer and musician, a restless, eccentric personality makes itself felt in his work. He was born of Italian parents and was the brother of the painter, Giorgio de Chirico. At first he devoted himself to musical composition, at Athens, then Munich until 1915. Then he turned his attention to literature and finally in 1927 to painting. Savinio pursued the ideal of unified aesthetic and always refused 'to be confined in a single art,' or to separate the strands of a poetry that permeated every thing. He poured the torrent of his images into a painting that sometimes suffered too much from literary and musical references. Nevertheless, the metaphysical atmosphere of some of his works or the projection of a dream world in constructions like *Sodom* (1929), remain among the most characteristic productions of Italian Surrealism.   D. F.

SCHLEMMER Oskar (1888-1943. German painter; born in Stuttgart; died in Baden-Baden. After studying at the Stuttgart Academy with Adolf Hoelzel, Schlemmer came into contact with modern French and German painting in 1911, in Berlin. After the war, in 1920, he entered the Bauhaus (*), where he was chief of the sculpture and theatre sections. In 1929 he taught in Breslau and in 1932-1933 in Berlin, until his dismissal by the Nazis. Then he retired to Eichberg in Southern Germany, where he led a difficult life, exposed to attacks of the Nazi authorities. If at first the influence of Cézanne drew him near to Cubism, the example of Marées and Seurat soon became more important. Schlemmer's idiom was reduced to a geometry of straight lines and curves as early as 1915. By creating reliefs after the war in mortar and later in wire, he enriched his positions with spatial values. These reliefs organized and invigorated architectural space. At the same time he created ballets, and devoted himself to theatrical production. In a renewal of the theatrical idiom he sought elements of a synthesis of the arts, in which the human figure, the measure of a humanized universe, would recover its primal purity. During Schlemmer's years at the Bauhaus, his painting grew in scope; later (in Breslau) stressed diagonals enriched the dynamism of his composition: the picture *The Staircase at the Bauhaus* (1932)

SCHLEMMER. FIVE WOMEN AND A PASSER-BY. WATER-COLOUR. 1925.

327

stands as a synthesis of his research during this period. He felt the influence of his friend the Swiss painter, Otto Meyer-Amden, a promoter of whose work he became, chiefly after Meyer-Amden's death in 1933. At Eichberg, Schlemmer's colour darkened and figures emerged from a background in which the strokes of the brush were more visible. From then on a more accentuated mystical meaning appeared in his work, as in the abstract compositions he called *Symbolics* (1936) and the series of *Windows* (1942), in which the human figure reappeared, but more remote than before and seen from outside, as though dematerialized by the windowpane.

A contemporary of Paul Klee and Kandinsky at the Bauhaus, Schlemmer was a painter of integrity and refinement. His early death, hastened by his maltreatment at the hands of the Nazis, robbed the world of a fine artist.   E. M.

SCHMIDT-ROTTLUFF Karl. German painter; born in 1884 at Chemnitz-Rottluff. Schmidt-Rottluff was one of the founders of Die Brücke *(*)* together with Kirchner and Heckel. The development of his painting during the years 1905-1910 (Dresden period) was closely linked with the formation of the first Brücke style, born of work done in common. Lithography, to which he introduced his friends, and especially woodcuts, influenced his painting, in which simple forms, applied flat and in pure colours with red predominating, are united in a vigorous rhythm. Schmidt-Rottluff was of a more robust character than Kirchner or Heckel, and within the group his works stand out by reason of their architectural quality. He had a more elemental, more earthy force, which made him a link between them and Nolde. After 1910, in Berlin, the differences between his art and that of his friends became more marked. This was partially due to his practice of producing the illusion of space by perspective, unlike Kirchner in particular. During the very steady development of his painting, Schmidt-Rottluff has obstinately sought a synthesis between this perspective and a powerful and solid organization of surface. Throughout his life he has executed numerous large water colours, but his most valuable production is his woodcuts, and in particular those of the Brücke period. Here blacks and whites, in masses, points and ridges, meet violently; the expression is simple yet powerful.   F. M.

SCHWITTERS Kurt (1887-1948). German painter; born in Hanover; died at Ambleside, England. After his studies at the Royal Gymnasium in Hanover, Schwitters attended the Academy of Dresden for six years. For a long time he painted portraits to make a living and never looked down on this academic work. Mobilized during the First World War, he was so absent-minded a soldier that his superiors finally preferred to limit him to office work. There his mind, Dadaist before the word was coined, found a chosen field in the search for deserters. He succeeded in scrambling the files so thoroughly that in most cases all traces of the fugitives were lost. However, the job was done with such care that he was never suspected. Returning to Hanover after the Armistice, he was first influenced by the work of Kandinsky and Franz Marc, and a little later he began publishing the *Merz (*)* magazine, both Dadaist and Constructivist, of which a score of issues appeared between 1923 and 1932. At the same time, at home, he und-

SCHMIDT-ROTTLUFF. WOODCUT. 1913.

ertook the first *Merzbau*, a sort of column erected in the middle of a room, to which he gave a surprising architectural form and which he decorated or gradually developed with all kinds of odds and ends, many of them picked up in the street. *Merzbau* was to sculpture what *papier collé (*)* is to painting: ready-made elements were superimposed and combined, sometimes alternated, the only concern being for the plastic effect of the whole. Schwitters worked for ten years on the structure, which finally pierced the three floors of the house. Unfortunately it was destroyed during the Second World War. In 1922 he accompanied Van Doesburg on a Dadaist tour through Holland. At the Bauhaus *(*)*, in 1924, he recited for the first time his *Sonata in Primal Sounds*, a work that was not published until 1932. He stayed briefly in Paris in 1927; he collaborated on numerous reviews, notably, after 1919, the famous Berlin magazine *Der Sturm*, to which he contributed a number of poems and stories full of placid humour. At the same time he published *Anna Blume* and wrote fairy tales for a local paper. During all this time he did not give up *collage*. When Nazism came to power in Germany, he settled in Norway. At Lysaker, near Oslo, he began a second *Merzbau*, interrupted when the Nazis invaded Norway a few years later. He went to England, where he was interned for some time as a German citizen. Liberated and finding some support (the Museum of Modern Art of New York made him a grant), he undertook a *Merzbau* for the third time in an isolated farm near Ambleside, in the Lake District. This time it was death that interrupted his work in January 1948.

Schwitters was childhood recaptured. He seemed to play with everything. To compose a poem or a picture, he resorted to the most trivial sentence, the most futile object: a used tramway ticket, a cork, valueless elements that, a scavenger of a new kind, he collected anywhere. Thereupon he transfigured these despised objects and showed that nothing is despicable. The

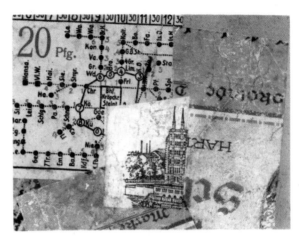

SCHWITTERS. COLLAGE IN BLUE AND WHITE. 1926. *Private Collection.*

tramway ticket glued in a certain way beside other cast-off things was no longer a ticket; it became part of a work whose value is literally inestimable. Touched by the artist's hands, objects suddenly changed their size and atmosphere. The whole animated them, gave them a soul. The artist was a kind of a miracle-worker whose touch transformed everything. Schwitters himself condensed this idea into a seemingly exaggerated phrase: 'Everything the artist spits is art'. It would be difficult to find an apter illustration of this truth than in his own work, for no one has shown better than he that art is indeed anything, if done in a certain way.   M. S.

SECESSION   A programme is implied by the very derivation of this word, which was used to denote various artistic avant-garde movements that sprang up in Germany at the end of the last century and the beginning of our own. Founded in reaction to official art and academic convention, they contributed, admittedly in very varying degrees, to the victory of new tendencies that were gradually appearing everywhere. Consequently, a Seccession was founded in every town where there was a certain amount of artistic activity. The most important were those in Munich, Berlin and Vienne.

The earliest, the Munich group, was founded in 1892 by Stuck, Trübner and Wilhelm Uhde. From 1893, it held important exhibitions, particularly notable for the works of Böcklin, as well as Corot, Courbet, Liebermann and Millet. Although it supported the Impressionist movement, its avant-garde character was less pronounced than that of Berlin Secession. Its foundation in 1899, under the presidency of Max Liebermann, was in fact the result of a long, aesthetic controversy that went back to 1892, the date of an exhibition of the Verein Berliner Künstler (the Association of Berlin Artists) where Eduard Munch had sent fifty-five paintings and was forced to withdraw them at the end of week. This scandal caused a complete split among the artists. Munch and his supporters found allies in the literary circles of the capital where they soon formed strong ties: Bierbaum, editor of the review, *Pan,* Meier-Graefe, the art critic, Prybyszewski, Scheebart and Strindberg. They met in a tavern, 'The Black Pig,' and it was out of their discussions that the Berlin Secession arose. Although the sympathies of the group were distinctly Impressionist, it was not long before the great Neo-Impressionist masters, the Nabis and Fauves were regularly exhibited. In 1902, a brilliant exhibition presented to the public twenty-eight paintings of Munch, including his *Fieze of Life,* Hodler's *William Tell* and three Kandinskys. However in 1910, the Secession jury refused the work of twenty-seven avant-garde artists, notably Emil Nolde's painting, *Pentecost.* A splinter group was inevitably formed and the rejected artists immediately organised themselves into a rival association, called the New Secession, under the presidency of Max Pechstein. Besides Kandinsky, Jawlensky and Kubin, the most important members were the Brücke *(*)* artists. After that, the future of avant-garde art lay elsewhere and the historic rôle of the Berlin Secession came to an end.

The Viennese Secession, founded in 1897 under the presidency of Gustav Klimt, who was its moving spirit, played a decisive part in spreading the Jugendstil. Besides publishing regularly its review, *Ver Sacrum,* it organised various exhibitions which all caused a considerable stir: 1902, Klimt's decorative panels and Max Klinger's *Beethoven;* 1903, French Impressionists and

SEGALL. WIDOW AND CHILD. 1919.

Neo-Impressionists (Seurat's *La Grande Jatte* was a notable exhibit); 1904, Holder's paintings. It was in this distinguished circle where artists, poets, musicians, architects and decorators met each other, that the young Kokoschka was trained and whose exhibition in 1908 caused a scandal that marked the culmination and at the same time the disintegration of the 'new style.' (See also the article on *Jugendstil*).

SECTION D'OR (The Golden Section). The year 1912 marked the passage from Analytic Cubism to Synthetic Cubism and witnessed the movement's widespread propagation. Gleizes and Metzinger published the first doctrinal work devoted to the new movement. In the course of the autumn, the historic exhibition of the *Section d'Or* at the La Boétie Gallery in Paris gathered together in one vast collection all Cubism's adherents—with the sole exception of its two creators, Braque and Picasso, who showed their works only at the Kahnweiler Gallery. The exhibition included not only Juan Gris, Léger, Gleizes, Metzinger

Lhote, Delaunay, Marcoussis and Roger de La Fresnaye, but also Marcel Duchamp, Jacques Villon, Raymond Duchamp-Villon, Dumont, and Agero. Many of these painters retained only the superficial appearance of Cubism, the geometrical fragmentation of the painted surface, and later turned in opposite directions, some going back to traditional formulae, while others were borne away by abstract currents or Dada experiments, but the unity of their search was based on a common admiration for Cézanne and his constructive lesson. The initiative and the title of this exhibition, which created a considerable stir, were due to the painter and engraver Jacques Villon. In his studio at Puteaux, near Paris, a number of artists passionately interested in problems of rhythm and proportion met on Sunday afternoons, among them the two theoreticians of Cubism, Gleizes and Metzinger, Picabia, Léger and La Fresnaye, as well as the poets Paul Fort, Ribemont-Dessaignes and Joachim Gasquet. Villon developed his theory of vision by pyramids, taken from Leonardo da Vinci, and suggested during these meetings the title of 'Section d'Or', borrowed from the treatise of the Bolognese monk Luca Pacioli, *The Divine Proportion*, published in Venice in 1509 and illustrated by Leonardo himself. Formulated by Vitruvius and taken up again during the Renaissance, the golden section or divine proportion (or gate of harmony) is the ideal relation between two magnitudes, expressed numerically as

$$\frac{1}{0,618} = \frac{1,618}{1}$$

and demonstrated in many masterpieces of different arts, applied consciously or, more often, by instinct. 'There is,' Voltaire said, 'a hidden geometry in all the arts that the hand produces.' Although the golden section was not the only constant to which the Cubists referred for the mathematical organization of their canvas, it reflected the profound need for order and measure that they felt more through sensiblity and reason than as a result of calculation. Distorted by the incomprehension or bad faith of critics, the 'Section d'Or' exhibition met with *avant-garde* success in France and abroad, and constituted a general rally under the sign of Cézannian architecture and geometrical discipline. J. L.F.

SEGALL Lasar (1891-1957). Brazilian painter; born at Vilna, Russia, died in São Paulo, Brazil. While he was still a very young, he was attracted by Germany and from 1906 to 1909 trained at the Berlin Academy of Fine Arts, which was very much ruled by academic conventions at that time. He was represented in the exhibitions of the Freie Sezession and was awarded the Liebermann Prize. In 1910, he left Berlin for Dresden and worked at the Academy as a student-teacher. He began to express himself in a freer manner and held his first one-man exhibition. The drama of the Jewish race was the subject of his painting, which was now very much a part of the great revolt of German Expressionism. From 1911 to 1913, he lived in Holland, visited Brazil for the first time and exhibited at São Paulo. War broke out when he was again in Dresden and, as a Russian citizen, was imprisoned at Meissen. He was given permission to live again at Dresden in 1916, where he worked until 1923, taking part in all the exhibitions of the Expressionist movement. He also published an album of five etchings, *Souvenirs of Vilna*, and two books illustrated with lithographs, *Bubu*, and *Die Säufte*.

At the end of 1923, he went back to Brazil and acquired Brazilian nationality. Brazil, with its vast stretches of country and its appealing people, became the crucible for his unquiet, restless nature. Very soon, he was considered, with Portinari and Di Cavalcanti, the most outstanding of the Brazilian painters. In 1926, he exhibited at Berlin, Dresden and, later on, Paris, where he made his first attempts at sculpture (1930). Back again in São Paulo, where he held several exhibitions, with a group of friends he founded SPAM (the Modern Art Society, São Paulo) for which he designed decorations. He also built himself a studio in his own garden (1934). His paintings were shown in Rio, Milan and Rome.

In 1935, there began to appear the great subjects to which Segall gave his whole self. There followed in succession the simple, rustic landscapes of Campos de Jordão, the *Portraits of Lucy*, then the epic groups of *Pogram*, *War*, *Concentration Camp*, *Exodus*, *The Emigrants' Ship*, swarming with humanity from the concentration camps, all in an intensely expressive style in which line was more important than any attempt at the composition of the whole, because the overwhelming effect of his primarily descriptive painting is made through its poignant, detailed imagery. In 1944, the publication of his drawings in *Mangue* were a revelation of the poverty and unhappiness of the slums of Rio. The deliberately naïve clumsiness of his original style, borrowed from hieratic conventions, acquired a fantasy of its own, without, however, escaping from the real world like Chagall. From 1949 until his death, he was engaged on the last cycle of his work, the series of the *Wandering Women* and of the *Forests*. In 1951, two important retrospective exhibitions of his work were held at São Paulo, one of which was included in the first Biennale.   R.-J. M.

SEGANTINI Giovanni (1858-1899). Italian painter; born at Arco, near Trento, died on the Scaf Berg mountain, Switzerland. His mother died when he was six years old and he was brought up in Milan by one of his step-sisters. His poverty-stricken, ill-starred childhood was spent in an attic and his escapades from home were punished with two years in a reformatory. He tried his hand at various trades and finally had the chance to attend the Brera Academy for three years without any benefit other than realising he had an irresistible desire to paint. He was a declared enemy of academic teaching and began to express the passionate love of nature and mountains within him. Between the still-lifes from his first studio in the Via San Marco, Milan, to the large pictures, painted in the open air and the mountain winds, lay the long, hard road of his eventful life, whose changing scene was recorded in his painting. An obscure period of bohemian life at Milan with members of the Scapigliatura movement (1878-1881) was followed by more peaceful years spent on the Brianza hills (1881-1886), then at Savognino among the silent, majestic peaks of the Engadine (1886-1894), the glaciers of the Maloja Pass (1894-1899) and finally he went to live in a retreat on the Scaf Berg mountain, 2,934 feet high, where he died suddenly while at work. All through his romantic life, Giovanni Segantini was helped tirelessly by the Grubicy brothers: Alberto, a

pictured-ealer, and Vittore, a Neo-Impressionist painter who converted Segantini to the new technique.

The positivism of his age and his own pantheistic feeling for nature soon taught Segantini 'to coquer what he saw.' Neo-Impressionism *(*)* of which he was the leading representative in Italy, never meant more for him, to use his own words, 'than a natural search for luminosity'; in fact, he used its technique with the greatest freedöm after the Savognino period. His contribution to Symbolism is more difficult to assess and his work in this style is very unequal. However, the sickly sentimentality of some paintings does not detract from the vigour and power of masterpieces that make Segantini one of the masters of the nineteenth century in Italy, such as *At the Barrier* (Gallery of Modern Art, Rome, 1883), *Spring on the Alps*, or the *Landscapes* of Majola, even to some extent the large triptych, *Life, Nature and Death*, his last work.   D. F.

SÉRAPHINE. COMPOSITION. CIRCA 1930.
Private Collection.

SEGONZAC (*see* Dunoyer de Segonzac).

SÉRAPHINE (1864-1934). Séraphine Louis, sometimes called Séraphine de Senlis, French painter born at Assy in the Oise. After a childhood spent as a shepherdess she came to Senlis, where she worked as a charwoman, forced to do what she called 'black jobs'. Almost nothing is known of her life or of how she began to paint. Later, when she was almost famous, she always guarded the secret of her prodigious enamelled technique. It was Wilhelm Uhde *(*)* who discovered her in 1912. He had rented a small apartment in Senlis for a rest and had hired an old woman to do the housework for him. In a middle-class household nearby he discovered a still-life of apples lying on a table, and was deeply impressed. Enquiring about the artist, he learned that it was the servant Séraphine. The first works of hers that he acquired at this time were confiscated and sold at the beginning of the war, and they have disappeared. It was not until many years later that having established himself in Chantilly, he again saw pictures by Séraphine at an exhibition of regional artists in the town hall of Senlis. Struck by the scope of these new works, he sought out the old woman, who lived shut up in a poor room where a small lamp burned day and night before an image of the Virgin. Séraphine, 'small and withered, with a fanatical look and livid face framed by discoloured locks', devoted herself entirely to painting. With the help of Uhde, who supplied her at last with the vast canvases her overflowing imagination required, she achieved a work of unique spiritual significance within a few years. She painted nothing but flowers, leaves and fruit, but hers bear little relation to their natural counterparts. Descriptive or decorative purposes were completely foreign to her art of mystical effusion, which can be compared only to the most lustrous Persians ceramics. The great stained-glass flames in the churches of Senlis, the only possible sources of inspiration of the pious Séraphine, perhaps gave her the idea for the ascending rhythms that activate her large canvases. The details of these works give access to a strange inner world: leaves, whose centre is a fruit or upon which eyes open and lips appear, fringed with lashes, recall peacock's plumage and the wings of the rarest birds. The precision and

SÉRUSIER. THE SHOWER. *Private Collection, Paris.*

sureness of these imaginary forms should be emphasized, as well as the magic richness of the colours employed and the balance and harmony of the canvases, which are related to no natural order. Despite evidences of certain obsessions—Séraphine died in a lunatic asylum—her works are never repetitions; they are perhaps the most direct attempt at expression of a soul.   J. LA.

SÉRUSIER Paul (1863-1927). French painter; born in Paris; died at Morlaix. Sérusier the theoretician overshadows Sérusier the painter, a victim of his fondness for ideas. Before meeting Gauguin in Brittany, he had already assembled his comrades of the Académie Julian (Maurice Denis, Bonnard, Vuillard, Roussel, Ranson, Piot, Ibels) into a group, in which philosophy and aesthetics were discussed. This was the origin of the Nabi movement, as much a gathering of friends as an aesthetic current. In 1888, when Sérusier brought back from Brittany Gauguin's theories about painting—synthesis and the symbol—he found ready recipients for the message (*vide* Nabis). To the art of the Impressionists, directly inspired by nature, Sérusier opposed the logic of his reasoning and demonstrations; to improvisation and intuition he replied with intelligence. His painting fed upon intentions. The simplicity of his drawing and composition was not naïveté. Unceasing self-control marked all of his work, and his sensibility is evident in it, although restrained, as if hidden behind the screen of austere discipline. One would often wish he had a little less constraint, for intellectual honesty, refined taste and crafsmanship are insufficient for the construction of a masterpiece. Sérusier's ideas are more convincing than his works, but seeing the works one cannot help thinking of what they might have been if their author had not confined his gifts within such rigid barriers. As it is, Sérusier's work is an indispensable link in the chain of contemporary painting. Sérusier the painter explains a 'moment'–incomprehensible without him–in the art of today, and avoids a break in continuity. He reconciles what would be contradictory between the Impressionists, Gauguin, Maurice Denis, Bonnard and Vuillard. Sérusier was born a few years too early His fondness for poetry corresponded to the Symbolist movement. Had he been born some fifteen years later, he would have participated in the enthusiasm of the young when Cubism was born. His taste for deliberate construction, composition within the framework of purely linear design, simple and expressive volumes, would have found in Cubism a most favourable environment, and his wish to take part in the development of a valid system would have been satisfied and have realized itself more amply.   R. C.

SEURAT Georges (1859-1891). Born and died in Paris. Seurat's life can best be summed up by dates corresponding to his paintings rather than to events, for the only remarkable facts of his short life are the large canvases to which he devoted all his time and immense creative powers. They represent progressive stages in a drive which led him to heights reached by only a few. Like Van Gogh and Lautrec, who both died under forty at the end of the nineteenth century, Seurat worked feverishly and unceasingly, as though realizing that he was to be allowed only a few years in which to express himself. After attending a muni-

SEURAT. FISHING FLEET AT PORT-EN-BESSIN. 1888. *Museum of Modern Art, New York.*

SEURAT. THE PAINTER AT WORK. 1882-1883.

cipal drawing school, he endured two years' instruction at the École Nationale des Beaux-Arts before serving a twelve-month term of military training at Brest. Next he spent his time studying such masters as Ingres, Delacroix and Veronese in the Louvre, and reading the works of Charles Blanc, Chevreul, Sutter, Rood and other theoreticians of colour. Blanc's assertion that 'colour, reduced to certain definite rules, can be taught like music' impressed him deeply, and he examined in detail Chevreul's law governing the simultaneous contrast of colours.

In 1882 and 1883 Seurat devoted nearly all his time to drawing, devising a highly individual language in black and white–the language of form rather than line, of skilfully balanced contrasts, of light and shade stripped of any incidental detail. He confined familiar forms within new profiles and raised them to an unforeseeable summit of poetical expression. Rejecting line as a means, he composed in masses. On rough-grained Ingres drawing paper he blocked in black masses in pencil, leaving clear forms to emerge in the intervening white. By shading and perfectly balanced contrasts he revealed unthought-of resemblances. He captured light and

colour and transposed them into velvety blacks and expressive whites, thus creating a new world in which plastic forms emerge from dark shadow, the light parts breathe mystery, and the greys, blending black with white, disclose an intense inner life. Flowing arabesques counterbalance one another, forms melt into or emerge from shadow, light shines forth through the mass of his pencil strokes. It was an entirely new conception of drawing; later Signac described them as: 'drawings dependent on values; mere sketches, yet revealing so fine a perception of contrast and shadow that one could paint from them direct without the model'.

Having thus systematically mastered the problem of black and white, Seurat devoted a year's work to his first great painting, *Une Baignade*, for which he did numerous preparatozy drawings and colour sketches. The picture was refused by the jury of the 1884 Salon, and their particularly uncompromising attitude that year led to the formation of the Société des Artistes Indépendants, which was to organize annual exhibitions without jury or prizes. Seurat collaborated with Signac, Dubois-Pillet and Redon in drawing up the rules of the new Society and

SEURAT. PORTRAIT OF SIGNAC. 1890.
Private Collection, Paris.

the first Salon des Indépendents opened its doors in May 1884. Seurat exhibited his *Baignade*. Signac was immensely struck by it, but while admiring the keenly observed laws of contrast he was astonished by the dull colouring.

It was Signac who now introduced Seurat to the works of the Impressionists, explaining their efforts and pointing out the advantages of pure colour, sunlight and the interplay of colours. With small, short brush strokes to interpret local colour, sunlight and the interplay of colours. Next they adopted a technique in which instead of mixing their colours on the palette they worked in tiny dots of pure colour, to obtain better balance and a closer interpenetration. Seen from a distance these myriad dots revealed the colour intended. From this time on Seurat's art was essentially based on the laws of simultaneous contrast (to which he later added research on the symbolic significance of line direction), the use of small dots in pure colours, and optical blending. In accordance with these theo-

ries he proceeded to paint a series of large compositions and a number of landscapes. He explained to his friend Verhaeren that the spent the summer of each year by the sea or near Paris painting landscapes, to rest his eyesight by contact with nature, whereas in winter he worked indoors on large canvases, trying out and if possible resolving the problems he set himself. In his studio he undertook successively: figures out-of-doors (*Un Dimanche à la Grande Jatte*, 1886) (*see* illustration, page 261); a reunion of people in the open air, the artificial quality of light combined with horizontal forms producing an effect of gloom (*La Parade*, 1887-1888); nude figures in the studio (*Les Poseuses*, 1888); dancing figures under artificial light, with vertical and diagonal lines accentuated to express gaiety (*Le Chahut*, 1889-1891), and the unfinished *Le Cirque* (1890-1891). Just before his death he produced his only portrait–*Jeune Femme se poudrant* (1889-1890)–a painting of his mistress Madeleine Knobloch (his friends knew of this liaison only after his death). Originally this canvas showed the reflection of Seurat's head in the mirror on the wall (his only self-portrait); but one of his friends, ignorant of the intimate relations between artist and model, having remarked that this might lead to dubious jokes on the part of the critic who were nearly all ill-disposed towards Seurat, the painter replaced his image with a pot of flowers.

SEURAT. YOUNG WOMAN POWDERING HERSELF. 1889-1890. *Courtauld Institute, London.*

Indifferent to the heated polemics which followed the exhibition of each of his works, Seurat withdrew more and more into himself, spoke little except when questioned on his theories, confided rarely even in his few intimate friends, and adopted an almost disdainful attitude towards the new recruits attracted to his circle by Signac's tireless propaganda. He showed openly that the enthusiasm of these painters, who adopted his system and profited by his discoveries, clashed with his desire 'to create something new'. However, a limited nucleus of friends gradually formed round Seurat, respecting him as their leader, and the art critic Félix Fénéon wrote articles explaining the theories of those henceforward to be known as the Neo-Impressionists (see Neo-Impressionism, also Fénéon). In the summer of 1890, as though realizing that his days were numbered, Seurat agreed to sum up and commit to writing his theory of the concordance between tone characteristics (dark, light), colours (cold, warm) and lines (rising, descending–gay, sad). He formulated his code in the dry, precise style of a man of science rather than in the idiom of a painter:

'AESTHETIC – Art is harmony. Harmony consists in the analogy of contrary and the analogy of similar elements of *tone*, *colour* and *line*, considered according to their dominants and under the influence of light, in gay, calm or sad combinations. The contraries are:

For *tone*, a more luminous (lighter) for a darker.

For *colour*, the complementaries, that is to say a certain red opposed to its complementary, and so on (red-green; orange-blue; yellow-violet).

For *line*, those forming a right-angle.

Gaiety of *tone* is rendered by the luminous dominant; of *colour* by the warm dominant; of *line* by lines rising from the horizontal. .

Calm of *tone* is the equality of dark and light; of *colour*, equality of warm and cold; calm of *line* is given by the horizontal.

Sadness of *tone* is given by the dark dominant; of *colour* by the cold dominant; of *line* by lines descending from the horizontal.

TECHNIQUE – Taking into account the phenomena produced by the duration of a light-impression on the retina, synthesis necessarily follows as a result. The means of expression is the optical mixing of the tones and colours (local colour and that resulting from illumination: sunlight, lamplight, gaslight, etc.), that is to say the mixing of light and its effects (shadows), in accordance with the laws of contrast, gradation and irradiation.

The frame is in opposite harmony to that of the tones, colours and lines of the painting'.

In March 1891, a few months after having formulated these principles, Seurat was struck

SEURAT. THE CIRCUS. 1890-1891.
Musée du Louvre, Paris.

down by a fatal fever. 'At the time of Seurat's death,' said Signac later, 'the critics acknowledged his talent but considered that he left no body of work behind him ! It seems to me that on the contrary he gave superbly all he had to give. He would certainly have gone on and produced more, but his task was finished. He had investigated and demonstrated all his principles: black and white, harmony of line, composition, contrasts, and colour harmony. What more can be asked of a painter ?'

Seurat would undoubtedly have been delighted by the dry obituary notice in which his loyal friend Félix Fénéon recorded the principal dates of the artist's life: 'Seurat died, on the 29th of March, at the age of thirty-one. He had exhibited: at the Salon in 1883; at the Groupe des Artistes Indépendants in 1884; at the *Société des Artistes Indépendants* in 1884-5, 1886, 1887, 1888, 1889, 1890 and 1891; at the *Blanc et Noir*, Amsterdam, in 1886. His work comprises: 170 small wooden panels, 420 drawings, 6 sketchbooks, and about 60 canvases (figures, seascapes, landscapes) among which five measuring several square metres (*la Baignade, Un Dimanche à la Grande Jatte, Poseuses, Chahut, Cirque*), and, probably, many a masterpiece.'   J. R.

SEVERINI   Gino. Italian painter; born in 1883 in Cortona. In Rome, in 1901 he met Boccioni, the future theoretician of Futurism, and in the following year Balla, who became his first master. In 1906, coming to Paris, he found in Seurat an inspiration and an example. He settled in the studio where later Dufy, Braque, Suzanne Valadon and Utrillo were to work. He painted his most important pictures there, among them *The Boulevard* and *Pan-Pan at the Monico* (1909-1911). In Montmartre he made friends with Picasso, Max Jacob, Pierre Reverdy and Apollinaire, who was a witness at his marriage to the daughter of the poet Paul Fort. In 1910 his name figured among the signers of the Futurist manifesto (*vide* Futurism), and in the following year he brought about a meeting of Boccioni, Carrà and Russolo with Picasso, Braque, Juan Gris and Apollinaire in Paris. He participated in the first Futurist exhibition at the Bernheim-Jeune Gallery. His picture *Pan-Pan at the Monico* is considered the masterpiece of Futurism. Raymond Escholier writes in his book *La Peinture au XXᵉ Siècle* that the Cubists, after having seen these canvases painted with the pure colours of Seurat, gave up chiaroscuro and returned to the colour and bright tones of Neo-Impressionism. In this justly famous picture Severini attempted to introduce a feeling of movement into space by multiplying the frenetic rhythms that isolate form while still pursuing it. Later he felt a need to counter Picasso's frenzied individualism with an art liberated from the tyranny of personality, and his research brought him close to work of La Fresnaye, Léger, Juan Gris, Metzinger and Gleizes. His subsequent works and studies on the *Section d'Or* led him from Cubism to Classicism.

In 1922, in a series of frescoes executed for Montegufoni Castle, near Florence, he painted masks from the Italian *commedia dell'arte*, a motif that can also be found in his canvases. But at this time he was already beginning to be more interested by mural art than by easel painting. Invited to Switzerland, he decorated several churches in Semsales, La Roche, Fribourg and Lausanne with frescoes and mosaics. He also executed mosaics in Italy and then in France. He has published notable works, in both Italian and French, as well as a volume of memoirs.   S. L.

SEVERINI. THE BOULEVARD.   *Estorick Collection, London.*

SHAHN Ben (born in 1898 in Russia). He emigrated with his family to the United States, where he was naturalised and is one of those artists whose works are typical of American realism. A thorough craftsman's training is responsible for his technical virtuosity; his father was a carpenter and he worked with a lithographer to earn enough to study successively at New York University, the City College of New York and the National Academy of Design. After two visits to Europe at the end of the 1920's, he

SHAHN. HANDBALL. 1939. *Museum of Modern Art, New York.*

gave up purely aesthetic experiments and turned to subjects with a social purpose that characterised all his work from that point. His first important works date from 1930 (the series of gouaches on the Sacco and Vanzetti case were painted between 1931 and 1932).

Ben Shahn's favourite medium is tempera, which suits his precise, graphic style. His paintings generally depict people with extremely stylised features and outlines, when they are not actually caricatured. They are set against landscapes, painted in modulated tones and sometimes containing a considerable wealth of detail. A complete absence of perspective, the use of clear, bright colours and the play of contrasting primaries, the meticulous, descriptive detail that is always taken from the concrete reality surrounding the painter, are all reminiscent of some of the Italian Primitives who made a deep impression on Shahn during his visits to Europe. The apparent naïveté, which appears through his very personal combination of realism and abstraction is used for controversial aims and sometimes a rather black humour. Shahn's development has been characterised by an increasing stylisation. Since 1950, he has introduced more or less regular geometrical designs in his compositions that seem to have a satirical value and ironic flavour (*Ave*, 1950, is a notable example). J. A.

SICKERT Walter Richard (1860-1942). English painter; born in Munich of an English mother and a Danish father. His father, O. A. Sickert (1828-1885), who had settled in England in 1868, and his grandfather, Johannes Sickert (1803-1864), where also painters. He studied at the Slade School (*) in London with Alphonse Le Gros and then became a pupil of Whistler. Later he fell under the influence of Degas and became a close friend of his. In 1911 he helped found the Camden Town Club to promote an independent art. With Steer (*), Sickert was the most influential of the English Impressionists. His family originally dissuaded him from becoming a painter, so Sickert spent several years in the theatre-a *milieu* with which he remained in contact all his life. In 1883 he visited Paris, sent by his teacher, Whistler, to deliver to the Salon the famous *The Artist's Mother*, now in the Louvre. About 1900, Sickert settled in France, where he lived for five years. He worked often at Dieppe, drawn there by his admiration for Degas, whom he considered the greatest painter of his day. A bit of a misanthrope, he divided humanity into two categories: patients and nurses. He enjoyed depicting incidents, sometimes sordid, of the everyday life of poor districts. He grew critical of Whistler's surface brilliance and facility and began to work in a slow, thoughtful manner, using a smooth, rich-toned palette. From Whistler he retained sombre shadings and a sober, restrained style. Prudent and cautious, he never let himself be carried away by what he considered the too facile charm of the light palette of the French Impressionists. Sickert owed a good bit of his popularity to his personal dynamism–much as Whistler and Degas did theirs–but he was the undisputed master of that hollow period in English painting between the death of Turner in 1851 and the growth of the new contemporary school. *Ennui* (*c.* 1913), in the Tate Gallery, and *Portrait of Victor Lecour* (1924), in the Manchester City Art Gallery, are among his finest work. F. MC E.

SIGNAC Paul (1863-1935). Born and died in Paris. Signac loved life and was a man of passionate enthusiasms: for painting, science, literature, politics. Jovial and heavily built, he looked more like a Breton sailor than a painter. Vehement and impulsive in his talk, he delighted in probing problems to their depth; his every comment, in which words of kindness mingled with expressions unfit for print, revealed his intelligence, exuberance, conviction

SICKERT. THE BLUE HAT.
Private Collection.

and combative nature, but even his most impetuous outbursts were never tinged by the slightest pettiness or malice. His position was not an easy one, for he was fired with a determination to face all the issues. Yet however violent his opposition might be, it always revealed a generous mind searching for truth, ready to admit different ways of arriving at truth and accepting the validity of research diametrically opposed to his own; but both in art and in life he was the implacable enemy of flattery and pretentiousness, self-seeking and hypocrisy. Signac was in his element when wrestling with problems, whether social or artistic, for they seemed to nourish his vigorous temperament eager for action.

His middle-class family put up no resistance to his early decision to take up painting. At the start he was influenced by Monet–at that time not yet widely appreciated as an artist–and in 1884, at the age of twenty-one, he became one of the founders of the Société des Artistes Indépendants with Georges Seurat and others, and exhibited for the first time in their Salon. Seurat and Signac became intimate friends and were soon to collaborate in formulating the theories of Neo-Impressionism, the most important and revolutionary art movement of the late nineteenth century. They quickly rallied to the cause a small circle of friends of varying degrees of talent, such as Camille Pissarro and his son Lucien, Henri-Edmond Cross, Maximilien Luce, Charles Angrand, Hippolyte Petitjean, Theo van Rysselberghe, Albert Dubois-Pillet and a few others. Signac was the driving force of the group, trying at all costs to attract adherents, untiringly professing his creed in discussions and by letter. After the premature death of Seurat in 1891 he undertook the difficult task of continuing the struggle for their ideals as leader of the group.

Signac had a passion for sailing, which led him to visit and paint nearly all the French ports. He sailed to Holland and Corsica, travelled to the Alps, Italy and Constantinople. For many years his base was Saint-Tropez, which he 'discovered' as he also 'discovered' Port-en-Bessin, Collioure, etc. From all these ports of call he brought back innumerable water colours, in which line and vibrant colour fuse spontaneously to seize the changing aspects of nature. Afterwards, in the studio, he used these quick sketches for the pre-

SIGNAC. THE SAINT-MARTIN CANAL. 1933. *Private Collection, Paris.*

paration and execution of large canvases, in which his aim was to balance the different elements of nature in order to achieve what he called 'the most harmonious, luminous and colourful result possible'. Félix Fénéon, a friend of Signac's from the start, described his painting: 'His colourings spread out in spacious waves, tone down, meet, fuse, and form a polychromatic design similar to a linear arabesque. To express these harmonies and oppositions he uses only pure colours. Arranging these on his palette in the order of the spectrum, the painter mixes only contiguous colours, thus as far as possible obtaining the colours of the prism, adding white to graduate their tone scale. He juxtaposes these dabs of paint on the canvas, their interplay corresponding to local colour, light, and varying shadows. The eye will perceive them mixed optically. The variation of colouring is assured by this juxtaposition of elements, its freshness by their purity and a brilliant lustre by the optical blending, because unlike a mixture of pigments, optical mixing tends to brightness.'

Of insatiable curiosity, Signac threw himself into the study of Chevreul's optical laws and often wrote on behalf of these theories. He wrote *From Eugène Delacroix to Neo-Impressionism* (1899), the vital textbook of the Neo-Impressionist movement, a study on *Jongkind,* a lucid essay on *The Subject in Painting (Encyclopédie*

Française, vol. XVI, chap. 2), an introduction to the catalogue of an exhibition *Seurat and his Friends* (Paris, 1934), as well as a Diary, of which the entries for the years 1894 to 1899 were later published in the *Gazette des Beaux-Arts* (1949-1953). As though these multiple activities were insufficient to occupy his ebullient temperament, Signac accepted the presidency of the Société des Artistes Indépendants in 1908 and for twenty-six years worked untiringly in the service of his friends, encouraging the younger generation (he was one of the first to buy a picture by Matisse) and advocating the principles of his conception of art. His vigorous personality, which always pushed him into the limelight, may have sometimes caused his contemporaries to overlook the fact that this active, dominating man was also a talented painter of great poetic sensibility.   J. R.

SIQUEIROS David Alfaro (born in 1896 at Chihuahua, Mexico). He was only fifteen years old when he took part in the students' strike at the Fine Arts School of Mexico City, one of the aims of which was the abolition of academic teaching. One of the results of this strike was the founding in 1913 of the first open-air school at Santa Anita. The following year, after the discovery of the workers' and students' plot against the government of the usurper, Huerta, and the terrible repression that followed, Siqueiros joined the Mexican revolutionary army and was promoted a captain. In 1919, he exchanged his captain's pay for a student's grant and went to Europe. There he met Diego Rivera at Paris and worked out with him the principles of 'a monumental and heroic art, guided by the great pre-Hispanic traditions of America,' then he returned to Mexico. His first mural painting, The Elements, at the National Preparatory School of Mexico City, was executed in 1922. It coincided with the sudden appearance of a strong movement of mural painting, initiated by Rivera and Orozco. 'What we are concerned in is art that is public by its very nature and is intended for the masses,' Siqueiros wrote later on to distinguish it from easel painting.

Siqueiros was as whole-hearted in his painting as in his activities as trade union and political leader; he took part in mass organisations, led strikes, became secretary-general of the union of Mexican painters, sculptors and engravers (1923) and organised miners' trade unions (1926). He was imprisoned several times for his artistic and militant activities or, forced into exile, worked at Los Angeles, then in Uruguay and Argentina (1932-1933). In 1935, he opened in New York a studio for experimenting in mural painting and, during the Spanish Civil War, was promoted to lieutenant-colonel and took command of several brigades. On his return to Mexico in 1939, he was accused of having taken part in an attempt to assassinate Trotsky and arrested. He again went into exile and painted two vast murals: Death to the Invader, in Chile; Allegory of Racial Equality, in Cuba. As soon as he returned to Mexico, he decorated a large number of public buildings, while continuing to paint a great many easel paintings, in which he tried out new techniques. He travelled tirelessly all over the world as an ambassador for Mexican art, painting, for example, the façade of the Etcheveria Polytechnic School at the revolutionary Cuban government. His imprisonment in August, 1961, interrupted the work on two important frescoes on which he had been working up to twelve hours a day, helped by his team of assistants: The Theatre in Social Life (990 sq. ft.) for the theatre of the National

Association of Mexican Actors and The Mexican Revolution (4,842 sq. ft.) for the Museum of Anthropology and History in the castle of Chapultepec.

All Siqueiros' work has been a continuous experimenting and mastery of the new materials of our age, used in the service of a monumental art. He went far back into the sources of Mexican popular tradition and gave them the unity of national character. From them he developed an epic art that corresponded to a 'collective consciousness' and an ideological realism that possessed an essentially humanistic character. His painting is tempestuous and tragic, with a baroque frenzy of movement and contrasted masses that make a powerful appeal on the wall and still retain the rugged, passionate character of their creator.   R.-J. M.

SIRONI Mario (born in 1885 at Tempio Pausania, Sardinia). Italian painter. He gave up his studies in mathematics and engineering to devote his time to painting and take a direct part in the battles of the Futurist movement. After joining the Academy of Fine Arts in Rome, where he attended classes for figure painting, he made friends with Severini and Boccioni, who persuaded him to attend Balla's studio. His contribution to Futurism showed immediately the originality of his position and his scant concern for the problems of 'spatio-temporal' simultaneity that were worrying his friends. His own aim was to express the condition of contemporary man in an epic manner. He succeeded better than anyone else in giving a consistent, painterly interpretation and an existential grandeur to the tragedy of our times. Although he contributed towards Futurism and Cubism and, later on, the early phase of German Expressionism (he went on to Germany after a visit to Paris), Sironi remained faithful to his own principles, determined and singleminded, as he experienced each movement in turn. It is this consistency, the breadth of an impressive body of work and the emotional impact produced by a perfect harmony of ends and means that have made Sironi one of the outstanding figures of Italian art. His material has often had a sculptural quality; it is built up into the solid angles of buildings or crumbled to nothingness, stretched like metal plates or heaped, layer by layer, like ancient clays eroded by time. His spacious, severe composition achieves grandeur in his mural painting, while his colour has deep tones and muted harmonies, flaming here and there with reds or caught by the livid reflections and yellows of a dull light. From a consideration of this aspect of his work, it is true to say that Sironi represents the complete negation of everything that Impressionism stood for, even in its final developments. *The Lorry* of 1914, the *White Horse* of 1919, the *Townscapes* and the *Town Outskirts*, which reappear again and again in his work after 1920-1922, stand out like solitary affirmations that recall, on another plane, the clamant tones of a Rouault. Even during the period of the Novecento of which he was one of the leaders, Sironi, in spite of some regrettable concessions to rhetoric, retained all his power. There is sufficient proof of this in the reception hall of the V Triennale of Milan, in 1933, where he exhibited a remarkable cycle of frescoes, bas-reliefs in terracotta and *Labour*, one of the most restrained and vigorous of his mural paintings. In the work that followed, academic and archaic elements were mixed in huge compositions and nude studies of Michelangelesque dimensions, but they were redeemed by the strength of the composition and the exceptional qualities of the colouring. These qualities, particularly in the gouaches of the last years, have gained in limpidity and purity.   D. F.

SISLEY Alfred (1839-1899). French painter; born in Paris; died at Moret. Together with Monet, Sisley represents Impressionism *(*)* in its purest form. He was tempted less than anyone by portraits or still-lifes, except at the beginning; he confined himself almost exclusively to landscape, and his work did not undergo any profound change during the

course of his life. His first known pictures, notably those he sent to the 1866 Salon, have been compared, in tonality, to the work of Corot and Courbet; this similarity revealed the nature of his preferences. He was lucky enough not to experience materially difficult beginnings like his Impressionist friends, but when he began to fight for the new painting, he was ruined and felt financial hardship even more than they. While in their worst days Pissarro and Cézanne received forty francs for their pictures, Sisley had more than once to give his away for thirty or even twenty-five. Moreover, he died before he could benefit from the triumph of his ideas and his work. Immediately after his death his talent was recognized, and his paintings soon fetched high prices. Sisley's art consists almost entirely of landscapes, and even for these he confined himself to the valley of the Seine, the Ile-de-France, especially the Fontainebleau region, of which he remains one of the most authentic interpreters. He succeeded admirably, and with as much sensibility as Monet, in transcribing the movement of foliage or the scintillation of light on water; but at the same time he succeeded better than Monet in preserving the structure of the landscape by not reducing it to luminous

SIRONI. LANDSCAPE.   *Private Collection.*

343

effects with unstable colours. Form remained firm in his work, not dissolved in the atmosphere; a tree is a tree, a house a house. There is nothing systematic in his art. He did not adopt the low horizons of Boudin, and while he gave an important place to the sky in certain pictures, this was because, in its movement and colour, it was part of the subject he was representing. In each of his canvases he gives the impression of having achieved as much as was possible. One could not imagine thicker undergrowth than that he painted in the forest of Fontainebleau, scenes of floods more desperate than those he transcribed at Port-Marly, snow scenes more sadly luminous than those of Louveciennes, springtimes clearer than those at Saint-Mammès, although he avoided dramatizing his subjects. His delicate and tender art enabled him to evoke with infinite poetry and grace the peaceful and picturesque life of the town of Moret, where he lived permanently after 1879. Although he experienced a fate similar to that of the other Impressionists, although he had also attended courses at the Atelier Gleyre (*) in his youth, like Bazille, Monet and Renoir, and had fallen back upon the modest generosity of the baker and collector Murer, little has been written about his work and life. This is not because he lacked talent, but rather because his life was neither adventurous nor picturesque, because his art was entirely ruled by sensibility, did not strive to illustrate a rigorously established system and thus does not lend itself to commentary. Neither a few sojourns in England, his wish to be received at the Salon nor poverty shook Sisley's conviction or altered his art. As modest in his ambitions as he was tenacious in his convictions, he remained true to himself and to his friends. R. C.

SLADE SCHOOL Of the three schools which have dominated the teaching of painting and sculpture in England during the past century–the Royal Academy Schools, the Royal College of Art and the Slade– the latter has maintained the most consistently liberal reputation. The history of the recovery of British art from its nadir in the nineteenth century is, in some measure, the history of the students of the Slade. Among those who have passed through the School are D. S. MacColl, Sickert (*), William Rothenstein, Augustus John (*), Gwen John, Ethel Walker, Wyndham Lewis (*), Harold Gilman, Spencer Gore, Mark Gertler, Stanley Spencer, and Paul Nash (*). Felix Slade, who died in 1868, in addition to leaving his own collections to the nation, founded three chairs of Fine Art at the Universities of Oxford, Cambridge and London. His further endowment of six scholarships to University College, London, led to the founding of the School of Art which opened in 1871– one of the first in the world to be established within a university.

Sir Edward Poynter, the first Slade Professor, friend of Courbet and Manet, sounded the note of reform at the outset by introducing students

SISLEY. FLOOD AT PORT-MARLY. 1876.   *Musée du Louvre.*

to the living model without delay and deploring the meretricious finish demanded by the academic conventions of the day. He was succeeded five years later by Alphonse Legros, who had settled in England some years earlier at the suggestion of Whistler *(*)*. Through his contacts with the leading impressionists, Legros brought to the Slade a knowledge of contemporary French painting which was to affect a whole generation of students. The Professorship passed, in 1892, to Frederick Brown, who appointed Henry Tonks and Wilson Steer *(*)* among the teachers; in 1919 to Tonks himself; in 1930 to Randolph Schwabe; in 1949 to William Coldstream.

Today the School has some two hundred whole-time students and thirty part-time. Admission is by competitive examination, and most students follow the three-year course leading to the University of London Diploma in Fine Art. Painting, sculpture, graphic and stage design are taught, and emphasis is given, as it always has been, to the history of art. D. S. MacColl, Roger Fry, Tancred Borenius and R. Wittkower have held lectureships or professorships in the history of art, and the school has close ties with the Courtauld Institute of Art.   M. M.

SLUYTERS Jan (1881-1957). Dutch painter; born at Herlogenbosch, North Brabant, died in Amsterdam. After working at the teachers' training college for a diploma to teach art and at the Academy of Fine Art Amsterdam, he won the Prix de Rome and worked under the influences of Symbolism, Art Nouveau and Burne-Jones. From 1904 to 1906, he travelled in Italy, Spain and France, where he discovered Toulouse-Lautrec. On his return to Amsterdam, Neo-Impressionism attracted him to Van Gogh. Decoration and poster work interested him and, about 1910, his painting owed much to Cézanne. Finally, after a brief Cubist period (1913-1914), he was influenced by Fauvism through the works of Vlaminck and Van Dongen. After that, his painting, with its bright colour range, derived, with more or less of his own individuality, from those numerous painters of the School of Paris, whose style originated in Matisse. He was an eclectic adapter of the Parisian avant-garde with a technical virtuosity that sometimes

DE SMET. LA LOGE.   *Kunstmuseum, Basel.*

showed a certain subtlety, but he did work in a personal manner of his own during a brief stay in Staphorst (1915-1917), which made a profound impression on his painting. He turned his back on the rustic idylls of The Hague painters and tried to paint the tragic reality of the Dutch countryside. The condition of his peasants resemble Van Gogh's *Potato Eaters* and the landscape has a bareness that is moral as much as it is physical. The figures, which are swiftly brushed in, are broken by work and unhappiness. The colour is dull, and sombre, sometimes warmed by the fleeting flash of bright colour. The brutal, popular expressionism of Sluyters, who was at that time in touch with the French painter, Le Fauconnier, influenced the Belgian school of Laethem-Saint-Martin and painters like Gromaire and Yves Alix.   R.-J. M.

SMET Gustav de (1877-1943). Belgian painter; born in Ghent; died at Deurle, With his younger brother Léon, also a painter, he took part in the business of his father, Jules de Smet, a contractor in interior decoration. However, he attended courses at the Academy of Fine Arts, whose discipline delayed the blossoming of his talent for a long time. No sooner had he emerged from adolescence than he established himself in the country, in the region of the Lys, to which he remained faithful until his death. From 1901 on, he could be seen at Laethem-Saint-Martin *(*)* with Permeke *(*)*, Van den Berghe, Servaes and his brother Léon. In 1914 he took refuge in Holland. After the war he did not hasten to return to his country, although he visited there frequently. He exhibited several times in Brussels, founded 'Selection', a studio of artistic renewal, with André de Ridder, and became one of the most determined advocates of modern painting. In 1922, he established himself in a small village near Ghent, and then, in 1927, at Deurle, where he died after a long illness. His youth had been rather uncertain. It was only in his maturity that his expressionism developed a personal note, and only after 1922 that he found his idiom and painted images in which simplification of design and colour, geometrical construction of forms, reddish earth tones, and a disjoined composition combine to give the spectator an impression, not devoid of charm, of some scene of childhood. He painted landscapes, acrobats, life in the fields, peasants and their animals, doleful young women and adorable little girls. In these paintings, the baroque artist disappears behind the compassionate and affectionate man. Much less vigorous, more delicate, less gifted, but more sensitive than Permeke, Gustav de Smet represents the other face of Flemish Expressionism, a gracious melancholy rather than sad Expressionism, less taciturn, often even tender. His technique lacked assurance, or at least dexterity. And if he holds an enviable place in the history of Northern Baroque, it is chiefly due to the peacefulness, gentleness and meditativeness that his work contains. F. E.

SMITH. WOMAN WITH ROSE. 1930. *Private Collection.*

SMITH Sir Matthew (1879-1959). Born at Halifax, England; died at London. After studying at the Manchester School of Art and later, at the Slade School in London, Smith went to Paris in 1910 and has alternated between France and England ever since. He was a member of the London Group. His father, a well-known collector of academic painting, at first encouraged his son's career, but when he saw that he was being drawn to the work of the Impressionists, he attempted to put a stop to it. It was only in 1908, at the age of twenty-nine, that Smith obtained his father's permission to go to France–and even then he was forbidden to go to Paris! Attracted by the Gauguin legend, he went first to paint at Pont-Aven *(*)*. When he finally got to Paris, he enrolled at the academy Matisse had founded in the former Convent of the Birds. Unfortunately it closed a month after Smith's arrival. In 1914, he adopted the Fauvist manner, which he retained throughout his career but which he enriched with more and more brilliant arabesques, using rich, oily colour dominated by his sonorous reds. Sir Matthew Smith occupies an important position in the contemporary English school: as the ambassador of French painting he has aroused among his compatriots an interest in 'pure' painting and has restored to the act itself a dignity which it had not known since Turner's day. In 1950, 26 of Smith's works were shown in the British Pavilion at the Venice Biennale and in 1953, the Tate Gallery held the first complete Matthew Smith retrospective, surveying his career from 1909 on by means of a selection of 81 oils.   F. MC E.

SMITS Jakob (1856-1928). Dutch painter; born at Rotterdam, died at Mol, in the province of Antwerp. Until he was thirty-three, he was incapable of staying in one place. From the Academy at Rotterdam, he went on those of Brussels, Munich, Vienna and Rome. When he returned to Holland, he worked in Amsterdam, Blaricum, Laren in the province Drenthe, in the Kempenland of Limburg and finally at Haarlem, where he became head of the School of Industrial and Decorative Arts. In 1889, however, he discovered the village of Mol, in the Belgian Kempenland and the district, which at that time was poor and deserted, attracted him so much that he settled there for the rest of his life. He acquired Belgian nationality in 1901. His work includes the interiors of country houses, religious scenes and landscapes in which the figures have a human warmth that does not always escape from sentimentality. He also did portraits and these are the best of his works. Those painted before 1910, especially of his second wife, Malvina, are remarkable for their spiritual depth and seriousness and the richness and luminous freshness of their colouring. It is more than just their quivering chiaroscuro that is reminiscent of Rembrandt for whom Smits had a fervent admiration. Later on, his paint, which was already rich, grew thicker until it became heavy, compacted and clotted. It was not because he had lost his ideals or that he no longer valued light; it was simply that he thought a thick, whitish material would be easier to handle from the technical point of view. Actually, he ended by deadening it rather than making it vibrate. Forms in his work were as heavy as the paint. A greater freedom appears in the paintings he did at the end of his life; emphatic lines are replaced by swifter traits and the colours become lighter, but not to the point of losing their sombre, muted tones.   J.-E. M.

SOCIÉTÉ ANONYME In 1920, Duchamp, Man Ray and Katherine S. Dreier decided to found an organization which would awaken the American public to the latest currents in the arts. This was to be accomplished through publications and lectures, and especially through a collection of works of art which would be freely available to institutions who wished to exhibit it. The title was provided by Man Ray, who had been fascinated by the term 'Société Anonyme'— when Duchamp told him it meant 'Incorporated' they decided to name their organization 'Société Anonyme Incorporated.'

The first works in the collection of the Société were six of his own paintings contributed by John Covert, who had just given up a promising career as an abstract painter to go into business. From then on the collection grew rapidly, and when in 1941 its founders decided to donate it to the Yale Art Museum it included works by 169 artists from 23 different countries. Since the collection often borrowed works from private collections for its exhibitions, especially from those of Arthur B. Davies, John Quinn and Miss Dreier herself, there were gaps in it which have since been filled by the Yale Museum, and at present it is one of the most important and representative collections of modern art in the world.

Thanks to the enlightened taste of its founders and also to the proselytizing and financial aid supplied by Miss Dreier, the Société Anonyme really accomplished its aim of educating the public. American taste, among the most reactionary in the world in 1920, is today perhaps the most advanced, and no small credit for this change must go to the countless exhibitions, talks and publications arranged by the Société.   J. A.

SOFFICI Ardengo (born in 1879 at Rignano sull'Arno). Italian painter, polemist and writer, he took an active part in the Italian movements from Futurism (*) to the Novecento (*). He trained at Florence, then went to live at Paris in 1900, where he remained for the next seven years. Returning to Italy, he settled in Florence and, helped by Giovanni Papini and Prezzolini, founded the review, *La*

Voce, which preached a revival of Italian culture and attacked the cult of d'Annunzio as well as various fashionable forms of mysticism. It was in this spirit that Soffici organised at Florence the first exhibition of French Impressionist painters, which was held in 1913 at the bookshop of the review, and an exhibition of the Futurist group, which included works by Boccioni, Balla, Carrà, Russolo and Soffici himself.

The same year, Papini and he founded a new avant-garde review, *Lacerba*, which was Futurist and anti-conventional in aim and which was reponsible for cultural activities of some importance in spite of its rather vague and slightly artificial programme. Ardengo Soffici then produced the best of his painting with his still-lifes, 'Decompositions' and 'Syntheses of Landscapes' in which he applied the lessons of Cézanne and Cubism. His adherence to the new theories was short-lived and in February 1915 he broke with the Futurist movement. After that he reverted to figurative painting and, with an extreme simplification in style, he returned to Fattori and the colouring of a Spadini, returned in fact to the very provincialism he had condemned before with such perspicacity and vigour.   D. F.

SOFFICI. FRUITS AND DRINKS. 1915.

SOIRÉES DE PARIS After the *Revue Blanche* (*) suspended publication in 1903, there remained no magazine entirely devoted to contemporary art. Temporarily, *Soirées de Paris*, on the initiative of Guillaume Apollinaire, attempted to fill this gap. However, *Soirées de Paris* was at first an exclusively literary magazine; it was organized as early as 1911, and the first issue appeared in February 1912. Its founders were Apollinaire, Billy, Dalize, Salmon and Tudesq. The novelist and critic André Billy was the editor. Apollinaire's first article, 'On the Subject in Modern Painting', frightened his comrades somewhat. It was a formal defence of the Cubist doctrine, and they feared that such adventures might jeopardize the magazine's success, which was promising. In fact, *Soirées de Paris* remained strictly literary until November 1913, when Apollinaire took over the editorship with Jean Cérusse (pseudonym of the painter Serge Férat). The magazine set up its offices in the apartment of Baroness Oettingen, Cérusse's sister. Meetings were organized there between men of letters and artists: Picasso, Léger, Kisling, Cendrars, Raynal, Zadkine, Picabia, Archipenko, Dalize, Modigliani, Max Jacob, Severini, Soffici, Chirico, his brother Savinio, who gave memorable piano recitals there, and others, all more or less contributors to the review. From then on *Soirées de Paris* devoted numerous pages to the plastic arts. One issue was entirely devoted to the Douanier Rousseau. Works by Matisse, Picasso, Léger, Vlaminck, Archipenko, Picabia, Marie Laurencin, Gleizes and others were regularly reproduced. Cubism, Futurism, Simultaneism were commented upon. During the two years that the magazine appeared, the general tone of the artistic part was polemical: attacks, retorts, challenging letters followed one another; even duels were provoked but without going farther than an exchange of seconds. With its success, in the spring of 1914 *Soirées de Paris* contemplated publishing art books, which were to be inaugurated by an album of ideograms of Apollinaire, when the order for general mobilization was given, dispersing most of the contributors and thus, abruptly, putting an end to the publication of the magazine. The short life of *Soirées de Paris* did not prevent it from bringing about fruitful exchanges between writers and artists. Full freedom had been granted to the expression of the most diverse tendencies, upon the sole condition of their being disinterested, bold and new. This is why *Soirées de Paris* was soon echoed. Even during the war, those who had not been mobilized gathered together, and new magazines were born, animated by the same spirit: *L'Élan* of Ozenfant (1915), *Nord-Sud* of Reverdy (1917), *SIC* of Pierre Albert-Birot (1917). At the same time a similar effervescence could be witnessed outside France; first in New York, in 1915, in the magazine *291* with Marcel Duchamp and Picabia (*vide* Stieglitz); in Zurich in *Dada (*)* with Tzara and Arp; in Leyden in *De Stijl*, a review of abstract art founded by Van Doesburg in 1917 (*vide Stijl*), all publications more or less directly inspired by the example of *Soirées de Paris*.　　　m. r.

SOLANA José Gutiérrez (1886-1945). Spanish painter; born and died in Madrid. The descendant of an old and half-ruined family of Santander, Solana always worked alone, beginning to paint when he was very young, without going through any recognized school. His painting is no more than the illustration of the secret passions of his life, which was spent almost entirely in the slums and suburbs of Madrid, and in the Cantabrian harbours. In very curious literary works, among them the two volumes of *Scenes and Customs of Madrid* (1912 and 1918), written in a direct and bitter style, he drew up a kind of a balance sheet of his interests: he associated his existence closely with the proletarian districts of the Spanish capital or the wretched villages of Castille that he visited tirelessly in stagecoaches, in ramshackle vehicles of another age, or in dirty third-class railway carriages. In rustic feasts and their coarse masquerades he discovered rites of ancient grandeur. At the Madrid 'flea-market', the *Rastro*, he picked up odd debris of the past and filled his tudio with exotic or bizarre objects, which became for him an inexhaustible source of inspiration. He was particularly fond of dolls and wax figures, whose coloured effigies come mysteriously to life behind shop windows. The Musée Grévin in Paris inspired him to a reconstruction of strange revolutionary scenes (*Charlotte Corday, Madame Roland*). He also excelled at painting groups of friends and representatives of the same trade or the same class; he gave living beings something like the plenitude and indifference of objects; individual qualities were obliterated in favour of collective evocations of unusual power; *The Choristers, The Return of the Indian, The Bishop's Visit, Outcasts of Fortune*.

José Gutiérrez Solana painted with thick pigments, charged with greenish glitters, under a dark light, with sometimes blood-red flashes of lightning that recall the black paintings of Goya. It is an essentially physical painting that reflects the author's fondness for terrible smells and strong flavours. But in his extensive graphic work, scenes reduced to their mere structure retain the same quality of presence. In spite of the fear he inspired, Solana was recognized by his countrymen. He was awarded the chief official distinctions of his country, and large exhibitions abroad confirmed his renown. However, until his death he led a gloomy, retired life in Madrid. Isolated and savage, he expressed the anguish and tragic despair of a great, torn nation. While Spanish writers of

SOLANA. THE MASKS. 1938.　　　*Edgar Neville Collection.*

SOLDATI. COMPOSITION
1950. *Jonas-Cassuto*
Collection, Milan.

the preceding generation–Unamuno, Ganivet, Ortega–analyzed the causes of Spanish decadence to find remedies in them, Solana did not want to give up any part of the legacy with whose miseries he was as well acquainted as anyone, but whose haunting qualities and obsessions he loved because he sensed their hidden meanings.   J. LA.

SOLDATI Atanasio (1896 - 1953). Italian painter; born at Parma, died in Milan. He qualified at Parma in 1920 as an architect. In 1925, he settled in Milan where he taught illustration in the department of book production at the Umanitaria School for eighteen years. He began painting in 1928 and his first works show the influence of Cézanne. He held his first one-man exhibition in 1931, but in 1933 the influence of Kandinsky cost him the support he had won at the beginning. He led a solitary life; his only friends were a few artists and the critic, Carlo Belli, whose tactless support of his work against the official artists of the régime had exposed Soldati to reprisals from the Fascists. It was particularly through his colour that he expressed his feelings and imaginative conceptions. He picked out what was valuable to him from a variety of sources: Kandinsky, De Chirico, Morandi, Klee and, later on, Magnelli. The forms and symbols, which he borrowed, acquired through the individual colouring of his work a fresh significance and intimacy that brought it close to 'the heart of the creative process'. Gillo Dorflès wrote of him that he

resumed in himself the whole prehistory of non-figurative painting. In spite of the high praise that Lionello Venturi paid him at the end of his life, Atanasio Soldati must be considered a minor master, whose work expressed and anticipated the taste of an age; it could not resist unfortunately the violence of Expressionism and action painting, but possesses a grace that makes it still one of the most appealing in modern painting. It is an art that is still cherished by poets and Leonardo Sinisgalli and Alfonso Gatto, two great Italian poets, paid a hommage to him in 1954 that the critics had not the perception to offer him until after his death in 1953.   S. L.

SOUTINE Chaim (1894-1943). Russian painter; born at Smilovich, near Minsk; died in Paris. Although hailed as a master while still very young, Soutine remained all his life isolated and almost ignored, most of his work buried in collections. In 1923, for example, Doctor Barnes bought one hundred of his Céret canvases in a lot. Soutine steadily refused to exhibit, not out of false modesty but because of an insuperable restlessness that made him take up again, and often destroy, all the old works within his reach. Except for his participation in the large exhibition of Independent Art in Paris in 1937, one had to wait virtually until the last few years to see important shows devoted to him. And in the meantime he had died. So it is only now possible–thanks also the accounts published by those who knew him well–to appraise the secret and sensitive personality of this painter.

Chaim Soutine was the tenth in a family of eleven children. His father was a poor tailor. To escape the poverty of the ghetto, Soutine went as a boy to Minsk and then to Vilno, where he enrolled in the School of Fine Arts while working as a photographer's assistant. A doctor impressed by his gifts gave him the chance to go to France. Arriving in Paris in 1911 to enrol at the École Nationale des Beaux-Arts, Soutine was still almost a child. Besides, he kept for a long time the closed face, with eyes that seemed turned inward, that his friend Modigliani rendered in an unforgettable portrait (1917). He carried awkwardly in front of him the beautiful small, pale hands mentioned by Élie Faure, who also described his frightened ingenuousness and the way he seemed to be fleeing under a shower of rain. He was all gentleness, his friend Henri Serouya adds, recalling his candid child's smile, which showed his big white teeth.

He lived in *La Ruche*, the famous phalanstery of the Rue de Dantzig near the Vaugirard slaughter-houses, where Chagall, Lipchitz, Cendrars and Kremégne were already installed. He went through these trying years with the same certainty that had made him thrust his incomprehensible urge to paint upon his family and his scandalized village. His formation was entirely inner, tenacious and obstinate, consisting as much in desultory reading of novelists, poets and philosophers, as in contemplating the works of masters, from Rembrandt to Courbet and Cézanne. He so distrusted his first attempts, which were always secret, that hardly anything is left of them. They constituted much less a technical apprenticeship than the attainment of a state of grace, a moral preparation, a novitiate of which he remained always proud. He needed a chance: he liked the word and believed in what it meant, as do all those who have been miserable. The collector and patron of arts Zborowski, whom he met through Modigliani, gave him this chance in 1919 by sending him to paint in Céret, in the Pyrénées-Orientales. He stayed there for almost three years. During this first respite, at he contact of the dazzling light of the South, the long-awaited transformation was achieved almost at once. Soutine's colours livened little by little, lost their opacity and their resistance as inert material. He succeeded in amalgamating them into his emotions and pas-

sions. It seemed that he wanted to charge them with animal or vegetable substances. To discover these, he raked furiously through living tissue; he broke the lines and reliefs of landscapes as if to extract their essence.

The secret of Soutine was probably that of immense love. He could not bear the incommunicability of beings, which made him suffer cruelly, or the immobility and vacuity of death. When he interrogated inert faces, he did not hesitate to breathe his own life into them. If he examined rotten flesh, a skinned ox, dead poultry, it was to discover the germs of new growth and resurrection in them. Awareness of his imperfection and his own misery created in him the perpetual dissatisfaction that made him resume the same theme unceasingly and destroy pitilessly all that was not up to his standards. But, in the search for the impossible fusion, never achieved in painting, of the life of the world and the inertia of the materials employed, Soutine perhaps came closer to a solution than anyone else. His painting was charged with

SOUTINE. LANDSCAPE. 1939.
M. and Mme Castaing Collection, Lèves.

substances, fermentations, and movements. He worked under a terrible nervous strain: to begin, to prepare to receive the shock and respond to it, he had first to wake up from a sort of somnolence in which he no doubt collected his forces. He frequently experienced periods of complete sterility, and then suddenly he threw himself into action, literally killed himself on the canvas, and could accomplish an enormous amount of work. From his stay in Céret he brought back two hundred canvases. This manner of working explains why he considered all preparation not only useless but even harmful, because it involved the risk of dispersing and shattering his inspiration. He never drew, in the traditional sense of the word; he simply roughed in his elements swiftly with charcoal, making the frame-work and not the delineation of the work to come. These preparatory notes had meaning only for him. This was what he had already done on the walls of his native village, to the horror of his playmates. He could fill in a form, inflect a contour, give it warmth and life only with paint itself. He ground his colours furiously, mixing pastes that he poured out by whole tubes. However, Anne Collié, who knew him well, assures us that he never lost sight of his aim, never put a stroke on canvas without having considered it in relation to the preceding one, in a tension of his whole being that exhausted him. After Céret, he stayed in 1925 at Cagnes, where his intense probing of his figures reached a state of paroxysm. He did numerous portraits and painted the series of *Choirboys* in 1927. In 1929, at Châtel-Guyon, he met M. and Mme Castaing and at last found a home at their Château of Lèves, near Chartres. He made long stays there, frequenting Montparnasse less and less and refusing to take part in any public shows. In 1940 the German occupation brought him painful trials. He took refuge in a small village in Touraine, Champigny-sur-Veude, where he continued to paint admirable landscapes, despite the threats that weighed upon him. At the beginning of August 1943 an intestinal perforation made it urgently necessary that he be moved to Paris. Operated upon too late, he died on the morning of August 9th.   J. LA.

SOUTINE. CHOIRBOY. 1925.
M. and Mme Castaing Collection, Lèves.

SPENCER Niles (1893-1952). American painter; born in Pawtucket, Rhode Island. After studies at the Rhode Island School of Design he went to New York where he studied with George Bellows and Robert Henri. He travelled in France and Italy in 1921-22 and again in 1928-29, and also sojourned frequently in New England, first in Ogunquit, Maine, and later in Provincetown. His work of the twenties is in the prevailing Cubist Realist style, with landscape or urban architecture reduced to its geometrical components. This work is severely judged by Milton W. Brown in his book *American Painting from the Armory Show to the Depression:* 'Here the world is so cleansed of all accidental encumbrances that it becomes a desert of geometry without life or atmosphere, a neat wasteland in which people and their activities are out of place.' But Spencer himself felt that 'the deeper meanings of nature can only be captured through disciplined form and design. The visual recognizability is actually irrelevant.'

Probably Spencer came nearest to realizing this ideal in his last work of the late forties and early fifties—work increasingly two-dimensional and with frequent abstract passages, though always with roots in the man-made geometry of modern urban life. Works like *Two Bridges* (1947), *Erie Underpass* (1949) and *In Fairmont* (1951) live up to his Purist ideal and at the same time have a solemn and sober organic richness which may be the reflection of the artist's belief that 'wherever art ends it begins with nature'. J. A.

SPENCER Stanley (1891-1959). English art has always boasted more idiosyncratic individualists than it has groups and movements. No English painter of recent times has been more idiosyncratic and individualistic than Stanley Spencer, both in his work and as a man. The outward facts of his life may be quickly listed. He received his training at the Slade School; during the First World War he served in Macedonia, where his experiences in the Royal Army Medical Corps formed the basis for a series of mural decorations, conceived in 1923 and executed a decade later for a specially constructed chapel at Burghclere in Berkshire; in the Second World War he was commissioned to record the work of the Glasgow shipyards; in 1954 he visited China. Apart from these excursions, Spencer spent his life in Cookham village, where he was born, finding there in its people and its everyday events the very mainspring of his art: an icono-

graphy of the ordinary which was transmuted by his odd and original vision into images that are entirely extraordinary. Spencer contrived to link a whole private mythology with the burning reality of his religious beliefs, and his efforts to define that vision with the utmost conceptual clarity inevitably recalls Blake's struggle for precision of expression. Though there is little in common between the two artists stylistically, or even in their quintessential purpose, they shared a love of the particular and a contempt for visual ambiguity. This and an unflagging tenacity of purpose, lend to Spencer's efforts to depict the events of the Bible as though they were current events in Cookham, both naivete and power. Though he was utterly unaffected by national or international trends, his natural affinities were with northern expressionism rather than with Mediterranean classicism. Even those landscapes which he painted with photographic accuracy recall the heightened reality of the *Neue Sachlichkeit* painters, or the American 'magic realists,' rather than the English Pre-Raphaelites; while in his religious compositions, often on a considerable scale, the expressionist distortions grew ever more subjective, more odd, even perverse with the passing years. It follows that, in general— the Burghclere wall paintings, his most complete creation, are an exception—his work is not notable for its formal organisation. Nor is any

NILES SPENCER. TWO BRIDGES. 1947.
Roy R. Neuberger Collection, U.S.A.

STANLEY SPENCER. THE PATH, COOKHAM.
Thelma Cazalet-Keir Collection, London.

sensual enjoyment to be derived from his colour or his dry, workaday application of paint—for Spencer, a painting had been completed in all essentials when the cartoon had been drawn; its enlargement and colouring were inescapable but tiresome chores. Such was the conviction behind his vision, however, that, more often than not, its imaginative impact remains intact and surprising. Stanley Spencer received numerous academic and other honours during his lifetime: the CBE in 1950, a knighthood in 1959; he was made a Royal Academician in 1950 (after earlier election as ARA in 1932 and resignation in 1935). His work is represented in the Tate Gallery and very many provincial collections in Britain as well as overseas.   M. M.

SPILLIAERT Léon (1881 - 1946). Belgian painter; born at Ostend, died in Brussels. He was the son of a perfumer and he taught himself to paint. His first works date from 1900 and were influenced by Symbolism. In 1908, he met Verhaeren and became friendly with him. After a few years in Brussels (1917-1921), he returned to Ostend. He was a member first of the Indépendants, then of the Sillon and, in 1920, joined the circle grouped round the review, *Sélection*, where Belgian Expressionism originated. His independent, critical spirit

soon separated him from them, just as later on he kept his distance from the Surrealists, although he contributed for a time to the review, *Variétés*. He illustrated a number of works, notably Maeterlinck's *Serre Chaudes*, Franz Hellens' *La Femme au Prisme* and Lecomte's *La Servante au Miroir*. The sea was a constant subject all through his life; Ostend, with its beaches, its bathers and its pier, was one of the main sources of his inspiration. After moving to Brussels in 1935, forests and trees appeared among his subjects. There is a reflective, disquieting quality in his painting of their bare branches. The best of his work, however, was done before 1920. Like Odilon Redon and the Belgian Symbolists, he left painting in oils for gouaches, water-colour or pastel, even coloured crayons, processes that he knew how to use to their best advantage. He has sometimes been compared to the Nabis, because of his taste for sinuous lines and decorative arabesques. It is certainly true that his elimination of unimportant detail and his organisation of space with a certain distortion of perspective created an emotional tension that charged the most trivial subject with a restless, dream-like suspense. Mme F.-C. Legrand has quite rightly said: 'The memories he recalled were of dreams. He remembered reality as others remember a dream.'

STAËL Nicolas de (1914 - 1955). Russian painter; born at Leningrad, died at Antibes. His father was a Tsarist officer from the Baltic region and his mother was a Slav from the family of the composer, Glazunov. His childhood was passed in the wandering existence of an exiled family. Two years after the October Revolution, his parents left the USSR for Poland, where his father died in 1921 and his mother the following year. A friend took him and his two sisters to Brussels, where an engineer became their guardian. De Staël was a brilliant pupil at a Jesuit school, then at a richly endowed college. He entered the Royal Academy of Fine Arts at Brussels in 1933, where he was awarded a first prize. When he was still a child, his mother encouraged him to draw and he probably painted his first water-colours when he was sixteen. He loved outdoor amusements, particularly touring on a bicycle. He visited Holland, France, Spain and Italy, explored their countryside and visited their museums. On a visit to Paris, he was specially interested in Cézanne, Braque, Matisse and Soutine. He drew in the Louvre and felt life was beginning for him. It was only in 1936, in Morocco, where he was living the people, that he began to paint from life and think seriously about his art. When he returned to Paris, Jeanine Teslar, who was a painter, became his companion. They lived in poverty until the war, when they had to go to Tunisia. He was demobilised from the Foreign Legion in 1940 and went to Nice, where he painted still-lifes and the *Portraits of Jeanine*. Their daughter, Anne, was born in 1942 and Jeanine ruined her health fulfilling the terms of a harsh contract, while de Staël spent a great part of his time in sterile discussions with painters, intellectuals and Surrealists. His painting was cluttered with unreal problems and had lost the strength of his 1939 studies. He missed Paris and in 1943, through the help of Jeanne Bucher he found a place for

himself, his wife and daughter in a decayed, private hotel whose bareness seemed a symbol of the times. Yet it was there that de Staël from the depth of poverty, in all seasons, drew nearer each day and each night to what he had been passionately searching for since his youth, the real source of the work that was about to be created.

Now he knew what he wanted, he worked towards a deeper understanding and sureness of himself. He was quite indifferent to his mediums and painted ceaselessly on table-cloths, sheets, anything that came to hand. He began with a tree in his garden or some familiar object, drew it first in all its simplicity, then refined it before painting it and in so doing, explained himself through it and explained it through himself. This dialectic of line and form, of drawing and colour, very soon led him to realise the possibilities of non-figurative expression. He threw himself into it without any restraint, while still maintaining even at the most intense moment of violent creation, a sense of proportion, which he had always admired in Braque, who was now his friend.

The war ended and the Galerie Jeanne Bucher organised an exhibition of his work which introduced him to the Paris public. De Staël went several times to the cinema to see the same Russian films and, having got used to drawing in the dark, he made charcoal sketches of scenes of massacres, with his eyes fixed on the screen. Two paintings resulted from these sketches. Then the private hotel was sold. He sent his family into the country and spent the summer in a maid's room, struggling in the stifling heat to paint large-sized canvases. In November, he moved into one of the studios of Domenguez. Gradually the galleries and collectors got interested in his work. Jean Bauret, who soon became a friend, showed his faith

SPILLIAERT. PIETA. 1910. DRAWING IN CRAYONS.

STAËL. PARC DES PRINCES. 1952.
Private Collection, Paris.

ter. In 1948, he obtained French nationality.

De Staël's drawing is clarity itself. He not only found it a stimulus, but also a whole field for experiment in itself, where the artist, while unleashing the riot of his intentions, revealed nevertheless the mainspring of his inspiration. His drawing transcribed before painting the profound nature of his expression. Precise and essential without being dry, it often has a greater vitality than his impastations of colour. It achieved a difficult synthesis between the severity of a Cézannian conception and the oriental sensitiveness of composition. It went further than his painting in investigating the object of his experimenting and showed no restraint over the random movements of his hand, so that the sudden emphases in the linear rhythm, its pauses and expansions, possess a more powerful and more direct means of communication. It is a drawing that has broken into fragments through the intensity of its feeling and light. It is among the purest drawing produced by the post-war generation.

From 1948 to 1952, Nicolas de Staël's painting freed itself more and more from the appearances of the outer world, but it was still not 'abstract.' He gave up the harmonious involvement of structures, the display of delicate tones and the criss-cross of lighting and instead simplified his composition by emphasising the main movement that gave it vitality. The greyish wall of his studio, with its pots of paint ranged against it, like thick, shapeless splashes, became a living landscape, an opaque, muted space, which merged with the bluish townscape of the roofs beyond. The sky, heavy with storms, stands up like the wall of the studio, a closed world on which the painter made a reckless, frontal attack. With his roots embedded in reality, he crushed on the colour with a palette knife to smother or kindle the light, painted large areas of vibrant, massive compositions, which were planted without any irrelevant niceties, like boulders on the edge of a field, and vibrated with light, like a freshly plastered façade. The impression made on him by a football match at night and the tension of coloured masses under the search-light beams led to his painting the *Footballers* (1952) series, a monumental building up of materials and colour harmonies. Forms are clearly and

in his painting and encouraged him by buying it. But Jeanine could no longer follow him; the life they had led and illness had exhausted her. She died in 1946, leaving de Staël grief-stricken and terribly alone. He felt her death in his deepest self and reacted by demanding the impossible of painting. He painted as if he were possessed. He was now exhibiting regularly at Jacques Dubourg's gallery and continued with him. In 1947, he took possession of a studio that was large enough for him, married Françoise Chapouton and had two sons and a daugh-

simply defined in them under the action of elementary forces that the painter alternately submitted to and controlled. His vehemence was such that he laid on his colour and his hand revelled in its thickness, as if he were walking in time to a tune. His inspiration became so dynamic that it produced a ceaseless, tempestuous outpouring of appearances. He was consumed with a desire for creation; he was interested in books, tapestry, engraving and sculpture, while he was fashioning all the time a new image of the world: a new landscape, a new sea, new men. About this time, he began to experiment with collages, which were really daring interpretations and equivalents of his own paintings. Flat coloured pieces of paper, clean cut or torn became symbols of reality, as they shot across the space of vast black, blue and red surfaces.

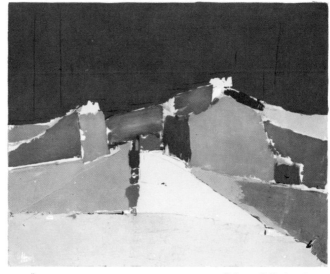

STAËL. AGRIGENTO. 1954.   *Private Collection, Paris.*

The museums were now beginning to buy his paintings and, in 1953, he exhibited at the Knoedler Gallery at New York. Cézanne's *Bathers* made a deeper impression on him than anything else on his visit and he found it unforgettable. When he returned to France, he lived at first in a ruined château in Vaucluse, then at Antibes in a studio, overlooking the sea (1954). He worked frenziedly. It was almost as though he were in a hurry to finish although he once said of his painting: 'It is always imperfect, never perfected—like life.' At this point in his life when he had at last no material worries, outwardly de Staël seemed to have attained peace of mind and a warmer feeling towards the world, but it was only that his strength of will concealed an inner anguish beneath a neutral expression. There were other problems, more insidious and tenacious than material ones, which had been worrying and

exhausting him for a long time. While reality assumed an outward order for him, de Staël resumed his grey, half-toned painting, but with a bareness it had not possessed before. His misty and superficially serene vision of our world, did not mask the inner conflict that was taking possession of the artist and invading his painting. He wanted to grasp the essence of things, but everything escaped him, everything faded away. It was a deadlock. Space, stretched to infinity, seemed at breaking-point and equilibrium about to collapse. Either the resistance of the creation or the resistance of its creator would have to snap. Depressed and incapable of sleeping, de Staël surrendered, defeated by his own nature. One night in March, 1955, at Antibes, he put an end to the struggle and threw himself from the window of his studio.   R.-J. M.

STEER Philip Wilson (1860-1942). English painter born in Birkenhead. After studying at the Gloucester School of Art and then, in Paris, at the Académie Julian and the École des Beaux-Arts, Steer was one of the founders of the New English Art Club. Between

1893 and 1930 he taught painting at the Slade School of Art *(*)* in London. As a landscapist and, occasionally, a portraitist, Steer was a leading figure, along with Sickert, in the English Impressionist movement. Although he was

he played a leading role in the London art world. Philip Wilson Steer was awarded the Order of Merit, the highest distinction available to a British artist. The Tate Gallery has a wide selection of his works from all periods. F. MC E.

STEER. THE BEACH AT WALBERSWICK. *Tate Gallery, London.*

STEIN Leo (1872-1947) and Gertrude (1874-1946). American writers, brother and sister, born in Pittsburgh, Pennsylvania. After completing their university studies, Leo and Gertrude Stein arrived in Paris about 1900 and settled themselves in a *pavillon* at 27 Rue de Fleurus, which shortly became the gathering place for an endless stream of poets, critics and other writers, as well as the leading avant-garde artists. The Steins early indicated a preference for the work of Matisse and Picasso, who were still relatively unknown. Over the years, Leo winnowed out his reflections

strongly influenced by Whistler, Manet, and Monet, his first 'manner' has an authentically poetic quality and a sufficiently individual style so that one of his canvases of the period stands out at once from the work of his predecessors or contemporaries. That style is characterized by a sharp emphasis on line and a nervous construction which might seem, at first glance, to be the result of naïve or facile simplification. Those qualities were, on the contrary, achieved through an accomplished mastery of draughtsmanship and a carefully worked out synthesis. His style developed slowly and became fuller, freer and more sensuous, particularly so in his nudes, where the paint has a heavy, unctuous quality. In his landscapes can be seen the influence of Constable and Gainsborough, and in his figure compositions one sometimes notes motifs drawn from Fragonard and Boucher. Toward the end of his career he worked at a series of paintings thinner in texture and whose lyrical quality recalls Turner. By then he was into his seventies and his sight was failing. Up until then, however,

on art in three volumes, *ABC of Esthetics, Appreciation: Painting, Poetry and Prose* and *Journey into the Self.* What he had to say about art can be distilled into a single proposition–that an aesthetic accomplishment can be fully seized only if one has first learned to behold nature with the eyes of a painter. This contention, which he sustained with reasons of a highly personal character, enabled him to illuminate the basic impulse of an artist even when he did not altogether sympathize with it, and he did not, in fact, invariably cherish the most advanced men. His sister, on the other hand, never altered in her fidelity to Cubism and its exponents–especially to Picasso and Juan Gris. Her most imposing work is a complex and original novel, *The Making of Americans,* and her impish libretto did much to ensure the fame of Virgil Thomson's *Four Saints in Three Acts.* She particularly relished the work of Juan Gris, devoting to him several critiques, notably the one in *Transition,* in 1927. In 1933, in her *Autobiography of Alice B. Toklas* she set forth with warmth and sharpness her account of her many contacts with artists and writers (some of whom subsequently had their complaints to make on her interpretation of history–as did brother Leo). Her name will always be intimately associated with the Cubist adventure and the formation of avant-garde taste in America. As a writer, of course, she has long been accredited as a liberating agent, not only in the United States but also in France, which she did not desert–except for brief visits–even during two world wars.   J. M.

STEINLEN Théophile - Alexandre (1859 - 1923). Swiss painter; born in Lausanne; died in Paris. Among the professional humorists who, like Willette and Forain, influenced him slightly at the time of the *Chat Noir* cabaret, Steinlen, arriving in Paris in 1883 from his Vaudois country, cut a serious figure. He was the friend of all outcasts of fortune and all vagabonds of cities and villages who creep on, thin and bent, under wind and rain, tramps who inspire fear, couples who embrace interminably, nervous dogs and adventurous cats. He took pleasure in illustrating the dreams of a generous generation that believed, with Anatole France, in the coming of 'better times'. His drawing, as enveloping as that of Carrière, seemed to defend and protect. Even in violence and revolt, he preserved a kind of humility and tenderness. In his generosity, he was, like Daumier, the exact opposite of Forain. From even his most cursory works, from his posters and sketches for *Gil Blas* or *L'Assiette au Beurre*, from his illustrations for the *Dans la Rue* of Aristide Bruant, *Les Soliloques du Pauvre* of Jehan Rictus and *La Chanson des Gueux* of Jean Richepin, there rises a continuous and comforting warmth. This great craftsman of drawing saw his work as a journalist less as a livelihood than as a means of defending truth and helping his neighbour. While his painting, which is excessively dark, has not always aged well, and while his colour is sometimes uncertain, his etchings and lithographs–his work in black and white, dominated by chiaroscuro–evoke the life of the streets, the factories, and the mines and suggest hunger, accidents, war and love, with a pathetic quality that transcends anecdote and sentimentality. Although he always treats familiar things, his feeling for the epic, which most of his contemporaries lacked, makes us forget his unevenness–the price of his great abundance–to admire only his active goodness and the soaring of his line.   CL. R.-M.

STELLA Joseph (1879-1946). American painter; born in Muro Lucano, Italy, died in New York. As a youth he came to New York to study medicine, which he abandoned for painting, studying at the New York School of Art and the Art Students' League. He worked as an illustrator for the magazine *The Survey* which sent him to sketch the steel mills of Pittsburgh, and he came away impressed and inspired by the spectacle of the industrial metropolis. On a trip to Europe in 1909-1912 he met the Italian Futurists, and on returning to America he set about translating the new continent into Futurist terms. He attracted great attention with his ambitious *Battle of Lights: Coney Island* which transforms the amusement park into kaleidoscopic pa-

STEINLEN. THE RUE CAULAINCOURT. LITHOGRAPH.

norama of shifting, glittering fragments. He soon developed this Futurist style into a more personal one of his own in the famous painting of Brooklyn Bridge, which he looked on as 'the shrine containing all the efforts of the new civilization of America.' 'Seldom,' writes John I. H. Baur, has a feat of engineering been more romantically celebrated.' Here instead of the hectic dynamism of Futurism, Stella selects certain details of the bridge and the city behind it which he arranges in a more stable composition which still retains the surging movement of his earlier work. This style becomes more schematic while remaining effective in the series of five panels entitled *New York Interpreted* (1920-1922). Unfortunately Stella's later work, up until his death in 1946, often confuses symbolism and sentimentality and seldom reaches the level of these early paintings.   J. A.

STELLA. BROOKLYN BRIDGE, VARIATION 1949.
Whitney Museum, New York.

STIEGLITZ Alfred (1864-1946). Born in Hoboken, New Jersey. Intending to become an engineer, Stieglitz had enrolled at the Berlin Polytechnic in 1881, but there discovered photography to be his vocation. He was awarded a first prize at an international exhibition in 1887. He returned to the U.S. in 1891 and soon after began working for the recognition of his medium as an art. He insisted that photography, no less than painting, must be exacting as to design, composition and values, even though these should be kept pertinent to its own purposes. In collaboration with various associates (chiefly Edward Steichen), he founded, in 1902, 'Photo-Secession', in an attic loft at 291 Fifth Avenue, New York City. The next year (and until 1917) he issued his quarterly *Camera Work*, filling it with discussions on art by such writers as Bernard Shaw, Maeterlinck, H. G. Wells, Galsworthy and Gertrude Stein. Starting in 1906 Stieglitz flung himself with still greater vehemence into another cause, adding to the exhibition of photography examples of modern graphic and plastic art. Drawings by Rodin, which he presented in January 1908, produced a shudder among the New York public, and a Matisse show (the artist's American première), which followed, prompted charges of imbecility. Thereafter, despite its name, *Camera Work* increasingly devoted its pages to plastic art as well as photographic. And, as a further sign of this change, the gallery was called '291', after its address on Fifth Avenue. Despite the splutters of the conventional, Stieglitz inaugurated the following American 'first': Toulouse-Lautrec lithographs (1909), Matisse drawings (1910) and sculpture (1912), Henri Rousseau (1910), Cézanne water-colours (1911), Picasso (1911). Following the 1913 Armory Show in New York, he also presented Picabia (1913), Brancusi (1914), Braque (1914), African Negro Sculpture (1914), Manolo, and others. Aided by Agnes Ernst Meyer he founded in 1915 another periodical, *291*, enlisting as colleagues Marius de Zayas, Picabia, and Marcel Duchamp, and discharging through its pages a series of blasts on 'anti-painting', which almost simultaneously had a counterpart in the Dada movement in Zurich. Stieglitz did not neglect the American moderns then emerging. His shows included John Marin, Alfred Maurer, Hartley, Max Weber, MacDonald-

Wright, Walkowitz, and later, from 1925 to 1929, Dove, Strand, Bluemner, Peggy Bacon, Demuth, his own wife Georgia O'Keeffe and the sculptor Lachaise. Finally, installed from 1930 to 1946 at An American Place, 509 Madison Avenue, he continued his efforts there. Regularly he showed his artists, notably Marin, whose name he fully established by thirty-seven years of almost uninterrupted exhibiting. This roll call, both European and American, demonstrates the nature of Stieglitz's fight for modern art, but it hardly indicates the intelligence, pugnacity and alertness required to subdue a public and press consistently hostile. The issue long remained unsettled. His resources were slight, his proceeds were often barely sufficient to support his artists and meet minimal expenses. Stieglitz could often manage only because of disinterested and voluntary outside support. Yet his intention never wavered. He might well be termed the first campaigner for modern art in the United States.   J. M.

STIJL (De) (Style). A Dutch periodical created by Van Doesburg *(*)* in 1917 for the defence of the Neo-Plastic principle, and whose central figure during the first three years was Piet Mondrian. The other contributors were, besides Van Doesburg himself, the Belgian painter and sculptor Vantongerloo, the painter Vilmos Huszar, the Futurist painter Gino Severini, the Dutch poet Antonie Kok, the architects Wils, van't Hoff and Oud, and, fleetingly, the painter Bart van der Leck. In the second year, the architect Rietveld joined the group and later, in 1921, the film director Hans Richter. In 1923, Van Doesburg, celebrating the fifth anniversary of the review, paid tribute to Mondrian in an editorial: 'Although several artists, in various countries, have worked consciously and unconsciously to evolve a new plastic expression, it was the painter Piet Mondrian who, about 1913, was first to arrive at a realization of the new plastic conception in painting as a logical continuation of Cubism. This accomplishment, which won the approval of the younger generation of artists in Holland, awakened the confidence of the most advanced painters in the possibilities of a new medium. De Stijl hails in Mondrian the father of Neo-Plasticism.' However, in the following year Van Doesburg himself forsook

the severe principles of Neo-Plasticism and published, in 1926, in *De Stijl* itself the manifesto of Elementarism *(*)*. Meanwhile *De Stijl* had opened its columns to Dadaism by publishing a supplement called *Mecano*. New names appeared: Van Eesteren, Kiesler, Arp *(*)*, Antheil, Graeff, Schwitters *(*)*, Ribemont-Dessaignes,

PICABIA. DRAWING FOR THE REVIEW '291'. 1915.

Man Ray, Roehl, Lissitzky *(*)*, Domela, Vordemberge-Gildewart, Pansaers, Kupka *(*)*, Parnak; but Mondrian had stopped contributing (his last article appeared in 1924). *De Stijl* ceased to appear in 1928. However, in 1932, Mme Petro Van Doesburg published a last issue, devoted to the memory of her husband, who had died in 1931. Among the number of avant-garde magazines, frequently short-lived, that appeared throughout Europe between 1920 and 1930, *De Stijl* exercised an unmistakable influence upon art between the two wars (cf. articles on Mondrian and Van Doesburg).   M. S.

STRINDBERG August (1849-1912), Swedish painter; born and died at Stockholm. Strindberg was a self-taught painter. When he was young he admired the

Barbizon School, but he eventually reacted against Impressionism, although he analysed its originality with perception. In the *Son of a Servant* (1886), an autobiographical narrative, he described his aims in these words: 'He had to paint his soul and not depict trees and stones, which have no meaning in themselves and can only acquire form by passing through the mould of the observer, who can perceive and feel. That was why he did not paint outside, but in the house, with the help of his memory and his imagination. Johan always painted the sea with the shore in the foreground, pines twisted by the wind, a few reefs further out, a white beacon, a sea-mark and a buoy. The sky was generally overcast, with a break in the clouds faintly or strongly lighted on the horizon.' During the difficult years of his divorce (1890-1891), he painted with a turbulent realism what he called 'symbolic landscape.' He went to Berlin in 1892 and was friendly with the Norwegians, Munch and Charles Krohg, without, however, being influenced by their work. The problems of his craft fascinated him and, in 1894, he published in French an article, that was surprising for his times (*New Arts or, Chance in Artistic Production*) in which he suggested how chance could be used. They were ideas that certain schools today would not repudiate. He wrote, for instance, about pieces of coal he found in his stove and described them as 'masterpieces of primitive sculpture.' In 1895, Gauguin asked him to write a preface to the catalogue of his exhibition at Paris. Strindberg did not like his painting, but he thought he ought to explain his refusal by analysing it. Gauguin considered this analysis so perceptive that he had it printed at the beginning of the catalogue. Strindberg ended his letter with these words: 'I am beginning to feel an immense desire in myself, too, to become a savage and create a new world.' A few years later, he had faced the great crisis that produced *Inferno*. He was living at the time in Stockholm and working at symbolic dramas, like *The Dream*, but there is no symbolic content in the paintings he was doing at the same time. Their colour range is severe, but made luminous with greys and blacks, massive syntheses of sea, sky and clouds that merge into a single element, that of the painting itself.   B. L.

STURM Der (The Storm). Founded by Herwarth Walden in May, 1910, at Berlin, Der Sturm was not only a periodical, but also an art gallery, a school of painting, a bookshop and a club. Lothar Schreyer, who was his closest associate, summed up the situation perfectly when he said: 'Der Sturm *was* Herwarth Walden.' Walden was born in 1878 at Berlin and was playwright, poet, essayist and musician all at the same time. He was in his own way a genius, and without doubt an exceptional personality, who had an insatiable need for action and struggle. He dominated the whole German artistic scene at the beginning of the century. He composed the music for an opera, *The Four Deaths of Fiametta*, produced at Dresden in 1910, wrote a middle-class tragicomedy, *Instinct*, and a book on the German Expressionist movement, called *The New Painting* (Berlin, 1918). He travelled all over Germany in a constant search for new talent and some of the greatest names in modern art are to be found among his discoveries. It was Walden who enticed the young Kokoschka to Berlin in 1910 by offering him a job as assistant on his review. Two years later, he held Kokoschka's first one-man show at his gallery. As an editor, Walden reproduced in his review the graphic work, drawings and woodcuts, of the leading artists of the Brücke (*) and Blaue Reiter (*) movements. Der Sturm was a free platform, where all forms of avant-garde art could express itself, and not only published the writings of Franz Marc and Kandinsky, but also the Futurist manifestos and articles by Robert Delaunay (translated by Klee) and Léger. The art gallery was just as active and after Kokoschka, Walden held exhibitions of the Italian Futurists and the first French Cubists. Besides this, it is particularly to his credit that he made known the works of Archipenko and Chagall, who had his first one-man show at his gallery in 1914.

However, Walden's biggest enterprise was his organisation of the first Deutsche Herbstsalon (German Autumn Exhibition), which included 366 paintings and sculptures of about ninety artists from fifteen different countries. It was the largest survey of modern art that had ever been seen at that time. The star artist was the Douanier Rousseau with twenty-two paintings on show. Walden's activities did not stop

KOKOSCHKA. HERWARTH WALDEN. 1910.
Charles Clore Collection (on loan to the Tate Gallery).

there, but extended far beyond Germany; he organised travelling exhibitions that went as far as Japan and Canada. In 1914, in the same spirit he embarked on a French edition of his review. During the war, *Der Sturm* continued to appear, although its scope was diminished. It never again recaptured its former public and from a weekly it became a quarterly, which finally died out in 1928. In 1932, Walden emigrated to Russia, where he was reported missing in 1941. E. R.

SUPREMATISM

The name given by Malevitch *(*)* to the geometrical abstractionism he derived from Cubism in 1913. The elements of Suprematism were the rectangle, the circle, the triangle and the cross. Although the first public appearance of Suprematism took place in 1913, when Malevitch exhibited his perfect square, black on a white background, the manifesto of the move-

ment was not published until 1915. It was drawn up with the assistance of the Russian poet Maiakovski and other avant-garde writers. Almost simultaneously Tatlin originated the Constructivist movement and Rodchenko Non-Objectivism, both closely related to Suprematism. Later (about 1920) Constructivism was revived when Gabo and Pevsner published the *Realist Manifesto* in Moscow. When modern movements were banished by the Russian authorities, Gabo left Moscow for Berlin, and Pevsner for Paris. However, it was chiefly through the activity of the painter and draughtsman El Lissitzky *(*)* that Constructivist and Suprematist ideas were introduced (starting in 1922) into Germany, where, in Bauhaus *(*)* circles, they encountered the Neo-Plastic current brought from Holland by Van Doesburg *(*)* during the same period. The Neo-Plasticism *(*)* of Mondrian was plastically more reasoned and consequently more dogmatic than Suprematism. While Neo-Plasticism has more deeply affected the art of our time, it is Malevitch that must be given credit for having gone the farthest in the shortest time, by leaping from Cubism to Suprematism in the space of a few months, starting anew on an entirely different and quite simple basis: the black square on a white background.

All painting that takes as its groundwork exact geometrical forms, without any attempt at representation, necessarily descends, therefore, from Malevitch and the Suprematism of 1913. The movement may have appeared futile at that time, but from it has emerged a whole new sphere of art that is far from being exhausted today. M. S.

SURREALISM

The systematic dismantling of established values at which Dadaism had worked could lead to constructive results only by bringing into play and organizing–and this was the role of Surrealism– the host of obscure impulses which, springing from unexplored realms of the mind, called up concepts hitherto considered so many baseless fancies; although in the past, masters like Leonardo da Vinci, Botticelli, Bosch, Breughel, Arcimboldo, Blake, Grandville or Goya had not been unaware of them and had used them for limited and specific purposes. It was a question of themes supplied by the unconscious, chance,

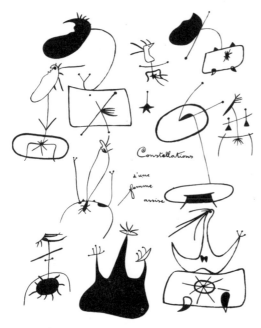

Constellations
d'une
femme
assise

MIRÓ. CONSTELLATION OF A SEATED WOMAN.
1938. INDIAN INK.

relations to be observed between the various aspects of things, the role of Surrealism consisted in discovering new relations between objects unreflectively, this being possible only through the irruption into life of the irrational, the unconscious, the spontaneous, the fortuitous and an automatism outside all systematization and codification. Moreover, the painter could no longer allow himself to be thwarted by traditional plastic means. Aragon 'defied' painting in a very aggressive manner. Surrealists even went so far as to poke fun at the 'old barnstormer Cézanne' with his 'three apples on a plate'. Every artist was to work alone at his own vision of the world, unconcerned with that of the others, even if they were themselves followers of Surrealism. In answer to a test given to them, which consisted in indicating what painter the sight of a piece of pink velvet suggested to them, Surrealists named in turn Manet, Böcklin, Utrillo, Renoir, Watteau, Monet, Jean-Paul Laurens, Gustave Moreau, Delacroix and El Greco. They were no longer striving toward a single truth capable of stirring sensibility before a given object. Surrealism transcended the ocular perception on whose value and legitimacy Cubism had already cast doubts. It joined, but more profoundly, and within a freedom of interpretation sometimes carried as far as anarchy, the religious, mythological, fabulous or magic representations that, from remotest antiquity, have heightened man's awareness by upsetting his sensibility. Surrealism refused to see in art an object of enjoyment, but rather discovered in it a way of deepening that knowledge whose progress it associated with that of science.

madness, dream, hallucination, delirium or humour, psychic states capable of creating in the artist's imagination zones of 'systematic estrangement' that he would then have to identify and populate. Dada had exhausted itself chiefly by making tracery out of the rubble of its demolitions when Surrealism undertook to experiment scientifically with the mysterious materials furnished by the unconscious and at the same time to deliver sensibility from the grip of the conventions that had governed artists of all times. Therefore, when André Breton published his *Manifesto of Surrealism* in 1924, an absolute directive was given to make a clean sweep of rational vision and to substitute for it an irrational and, so to speak, primal knowledge of things. Accordingly, Max Ernst, in his *Treatise on Surrealist Painting* contended that 'any conscious, mental control of reason, taste, will, is out of place in a work that deserves to be described as absolutely Surrealist'. While traditional aesthetic principles were based upon the 'reflective' discovery of

Surrealism revolted against traditional plastic means, but not in the manner of the Dadaists, who denied the very idea of them. For these means Surrealism substituted others that were boldly new. Whether in the technique of collage or in the composition of 'Surrealist objects', its intention was always to bring to the point of paroxysm the association of unlike elements of objects, depriving them of their conventional purpose in order to give them a new one, born of most unexpected and surprising juxtapositions. The most revolutionary ambition of the Surrealists seems to have been revealed by André Breton when he wrote: 'I shall not conceal that for me the strongest Surrealist image is the one that presents the highest degree of the arbitrary, the one that takes the longest to translate into practical language, whether it contains an enormous amount of apparent contradiction, whether one of its terms is curiously concealed, whether, promising to be sensational, it seems to come to a weak conclusion; whether it draws from itself a derisory *formal* justification, whether it is of an hallucinatory nature, whether it lends very naturally the mask of the concrete to the abstract or vice versa, whether it implies the negation of some elementary physical quality, or whether it provokes laughter'. One can wonder now what the Surrealist work of art brought to the general position of the movement. Whether painting, collage or Surrealist object, it appears that the chief contribution of the plastic work is to have opposed the precious immobility of an image fixed in space to the undulating, varying and dynamic quality of Surrealist writing proper and its development in time. By the unexpected, even arbitrary nature of the cut of the object, by its sudden coagulation on the canvas, and by the unreal atmosphere that

emanates from the whole, the works of Surrealist painters have indeed imposed the anguishing mystery of their upsetting fixity. Feelings of unending expectation, anxiety before enigmas, or the strangeness of certain meetings in an unknown past enabled the artists to uncover mysterious impressions charged with the most secret, sometimes the most baffling, but always a deeply human poetry. Their untiring quest for the marvellous took on various aspects, according to each painter's imagination or gift for premonition. Chirico, in his first 'manner', discovered the secret motives of metaphysical anguish, as it could be born in the unexpected encounter of known objects. Hans Arp caused a strange life to spring up in the very heart of objects supposedly inert. Max Ernst, both in his *frottages* and in his paintings, endowed with real existence, elements suggested to him only by hallucination. As for Joan Miró, he created a universe inhabited by signs that his will for metamorphosis charged with symbolic values. And while André Masson enquired into the perpetual struggle between life and death in us and in things, it was beyond the infinity of the sky or in the very depths of the ocean that Yves Tanguy sought to capture the essential mysteries. Dali, behind a front of delirious interpretations, deliberately undertook the disquieting organization of a metaphysical universe. Man Ray, who made use of photography for his rayographs, drew particularly moving poetical suggestions from the fixity of objects. Finally, Magritte discovered 'lyrical facts' hitherto unsuspected in the juxtaposition of familiar objects. In short, the intentions of the Surrealists stemmed for painters as well as for poets from a desire to escape the absurdity of events and the stupidity of the official literary and artistic formulae that weighed heavily upon the future of the intelligence. If, then, the young people of 1924-1930 attempted to destroy adulterated values, imagining that

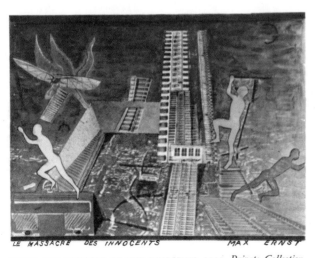

LE MASSACRE DES INNOCENTS   MAX ERNST

ERNST. THE MASSACRE OF THE INNOCENTS. 1921. *Private Collection.*

365

they were starting again from scratch, from the very beginnings of sensibility, there was nothing illegitimate in their action.

One could discuss at length the problem of whether Surrealist thought has only reached an elementary stage and whether certain indispensable changes in it will develop and give it greater depth. It is enough to observe here that, now Surrealism has rid itself of the aggressive attitudes, inevitable in any revolution, it has to be accepted as a discovery that cannot be ignored and that has already decisively influenced the conditions and development of contemporary art.   M. R.

It is beyond the scope of this article to give even a brief account of the history of Surrealism. It must suffice to mention a few important landmarks in its development, which throw an interesting light on the artistic life of the movement. The final disintegration of the Dada movement came in about 1922 and the history of Surrealism began with the publication in 1924 of André Breton's *Manifesto of Surrealism*. The

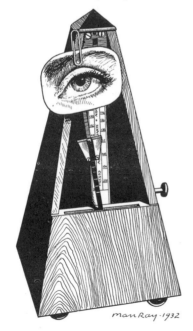

MAN RAY. OBJECT OF DESTRUCTION. 1932.
INDIAN INK.

same year, there appeared in December the first number of the review, *La Révolution Surréaliste*.

1925 – First group exhibition at the Galerie Pierre, with Arp, Chirico, Ernst, Klee, Man Ray, Masson, Miró, Picasso and Pierre Roy.

1926 – Opening on March 26th of the Galerie Surréaliste, 16 rue Jacques Callot. Exhibitions of Marcel Duchamp and Picabia. Jeanne Bucher publishes Ernst's *Histoire Naturelle*, a collection of 'frottages', prefaced by Arp.

1927 – Magritte arrives in Paris.

1928 – Breton publishes his book on *Surrealism and Painting*. Max Ernst exhibition at the Galerie Bernheim; catalogue prefaced by René Crevel.

1929 – Disagreements appear in the group, as can be seen in Breton's *Second Manifesto of Surrealism*. Ernst's *La Femme 100 Têtes* (collage-novel). First exhibition of Dali at Paris, Galerie Goemans; catalogue prefaced by Breton. Dali and Bunuel make the film, *Le Chien Andalou*.

1930 – Breton founds *Le Surréalisme au Service de la Révolution*, a review whose last number appeared in 1933. Dali publishes *La Femme Visible*, an explanation of his 'paranoic-critical method'. Ernst's *Rêve d'une Petite Fille qui voulut entrer au Carmel* (collage-novel). Aragon publishes *La Peinture au Défi*, as the preface to the catalogue of an exhibition of collages and papiers collés at the Galerie Goemans. Bunuel and Dali make the film, *L'Age d'Or*.

1931 – Object-sculptures by Giacometti.

1933 – Victor Brauner arrives in Paris and exhibits the following year at the Galerie Pierre.

1934 – Ernst's *Une Semaine de Bonté*, collage-novel, published by Jeanne Bucher. Dali illustrates *Les Chants de Maldoror* for Skira.

1935 – Wolfgang Paalen rejoins the Surrealist group. First 'décalcomanies' by Oscar Dominguez.

1935-1938 – The movement now commands an international public and important exhibitions are held at Copenhagen, Prague, Brussels (with Magritte, Camille Bryen, Raoul Ubac), London (on the initiative of Roland Penrose), Japan, Chile.

1936 – Hans Bellmer arrives at Paris and publishes *La Poupée*. Paul Delvaux's first Surrealist paintings. Exhibition of Surrealist objects at the Galerie Charles Ratton, rue Marignan. Ernst publishes his essay, *Au-delà de la Peinture*. Large exhibition on the subject of '*Fantastic Art, Dada*,

DALI. GIRAFFE ON FIRE. 1935.
Kunstmuseum, Basel.

Leopold. Russian painter; born in 1879 in Moscow. Having discovered Matisse in the Shchukin collection, Survage went to Paris in 1908 to attend courses at the Academy that Matisse had just opened in the former Couvent des Oiseaux. But he soon discovered Cézanne's work, and later he made the acquaintance of the Cubists, with whom he exhibited at the Salon des Indépendants in 1912. Although he was not one of the creators of Cubism, he joined the movement when it was still growing and the struggle waged by its followers left the door open to any development. In 1917 he came to the austere initial Cubism that bore the mark of Picasso and the Frenchmen who were its originators, among whom Braque and Léger have remained the most original. There was an element of freshness in his work that recalled his Russian origin, an inclination for imagery and light colours. What he brought to the movement was not naïveté but rather a spontaneity that did not exclude reasoning. Survage was not really a Cubist. His art, in spite of his desire for construction, was domi-

Surrealism' at the Museum of Modern Art, New York.

1937 – Opening of the Galerie Gradiva by Breton in the rue de Seine. Matta arrives at Paris. The review, *Minotaure*, founded by Albert Skira in 1933, supports energetically the movement and includes on the editorial board Breton, Duchamp, Eluard and Mabille.

1938 – International exhibition of Surrealism at the Galerie des Beaux-Arts, organised by Marcel Duchamp, whose idea it was to transform the main room into a curved grotto, hung with 1200 sacks of coal. The floor was carpeted with dead leaves and a pond, decorated with reeds and lilies was made in a dip of the ground.

1941-1944 – The war scattered the group. Breton and Ernst went to the United States, where they published the review, *VVV*, with the help of Marcel Duchamp.

Although since the war, there has been no Surrealist group strictly speaking, two international exhibitions have been held at Paris: one at the Galerie Maeght in 1947, the other at the Galerie Daniel Cordier, from December 1959 to March 1960, with Eros as its subject.

ANDRÉ MASSON. CARRIED BY THE STORM. 1938.
PEN AND INK DRAWING.

nated above all by a very personal concept of space. While French Cubism, also concerned with construction, applied itself chiefly to the analysis and recomposition of objects and their volumes, Survage was more drawn to spatial problems. Thus he was less attracted by still life than by landscape. In his work city streets broke into large planes that folded and unfolded like the panels of a screen. He was also concerned with the presence of man, a mysterious presence that he more often suggested by the shadow of a figure than by the figure itself. The result was a strange solitude, haunted by tranquil phantoms, and created by a close contact between nature, its atmosphere and the order that man imposes upon it.

Later, like the other Cubists, he escaped the too rigorous system to which he had originally adhered, but in all his work the same themes can be found. By temperament he was particularly suited for large decorations. Diaghilev understood this and commissioned settings for the ballet *Mavra* from him. In addition Survage had the opportunity to execute, for the Paris International Exhibition of 1937, large murals in which he was able to give his imagination free rein. On the largest surfaces he succeeds in preserving his qualities of freshness and gaiety, and even in his more recent production, in which he appears to have drifted away from the picturesqueness of his early work, the continuity of his thought can be followed, always directed toward a synthesis of space and movement.   R. C.

SUTHERLAND Graham. English painter; born in London in 1903. After studying at the Goldsmiths' School of Art, he concentrated on etching and produced landscapes and illustrations of a hallucinatory character. His art then underwent the influence of William Blake and of his disciple Samuel Palmer (1805-1881) and of the Surrealists as well. Following a stay he made in the County of Pembroke in 1936, Sutherland's style showed a marked change: Nature had apparently acted as a catalytic agent in bringing about a new and magical concept of art. From that time on, his vision expanded and his work acquired greater expressiveness. He discovered new forms of

SURVAGE. LANDSCAPE. 1932.
Private Collection.

life, tinted with hitherto unknown colours. Strange vegetable and mineral forms, insects metamorphosed into totems look out from his canvases on to a mental universe teeming with hidden forces. Anxious eyes, endowed with beneficent or malevolent powers, recall masks from Polynesia and the New Hebrides. They take possession of the spectator as their strange message slowly filters into his consciousness. In Sutherland's work, art reaches back to its primal nature: it inspires in man a mixture of fear, joy, and ecstasy. At once sign and symbol, the work of art becomes, in the hands of this sorcerer, a vehicle for cosmic forces.

Sutherland is, without doubt, one of the leaders of the contemporary English school of painting. In 1944, asked to decorate a church at Northampton, he created a Christ on the Cross which makes one think of certain Spanish primitives, of totems, and, again, of the works of such an artist as Grünewald. Following this, Sutherland devoted considerable time to portraits but he refused to allow himself to be carried away by the tradition of superficial brilliance which has characterized the evolution of portrait painting in English art. The head of a man calls forth from him the same qualities of analysis and synthesis as the phenomena of nature. Thus a portrait dominated by a pair of shrewd, cruel eyes, even though painted in accordance with all laws of realism, seems, at times, not very far from belonging to the plant world, the insect world or the reptile kingdom.

In 1951 Graham Sutherland was commissioned to paint a large panel for the Festival of Britain on the theme, 'The Origins of the Earth'. In 1952 he represented England at the Biennale in Venice, where he was awarded the acquisition prize of the Museum of Modern Art, São Paulo. His most important commission was for the tapestry of Christ in Majesty, measuring about 14 by 40 ft., for Coventry Cathedral, where it was placed in 1962. Byzantine influence is strongly marked in it. His work is well represented in the collections of the Tate Gallery; also, in the Museums of Modern Art of New York and of Paris.   F. MC E.

SWEDISH BALLET (*see* Ballets Suédois).

SYMBOLISM There are two fundamental modes of artistic experience: image and symbol, direct perception and ideal interpretation. Following the progress of science, the effort of the nineteenth century was directed toward realism. The result was Naturalism in literature and Impressionism in painting. From 1885 on, Symbolism, an idealistic reaction, developed in letters and the plastic arts simultaneously. Painters and poets no longer aimed at a faithful representation of the outside world, but at an imaginative suggestion of their dreams through symbolic allusion and the luxuriant apparel of decorative form. The year 1886, with the appearance of Rimbaud's *Illuminations*, the arrival of Van Gogh in Paris and Gauguin's first stay in Brittany, was a turning point that confirmed the break with Impressionism and marked the official birth on the one hand of Neo-Impressionism, a scientific development of Impressionism, and on the other, and at the opposite pole, of Symbolism, which was first expressed in literature. In the Manifesto he published in the *Figaro* of September 18th that year, the poet Jean Moréas put forth the name Symbolism 'as the only word capable of ade-

quately describing the current tendency of the creative spirit in art'. His principal formula was one that would be valid in all the arts: 'To clothe the idea in a sensitive form'. Soon after, there appeared a number of magazines, which propagated the new aesthetic doctrine and showed, by the space they allotted to painting and illustration, the increasing interaction between the plastic arts and literature that was characteristic of the period: as early as 1886 *La Pléiade, Le Décadent, La Vogue, Le Symboliste*; in 1889 *La Plume*, in 1890 *Le Mercure de France*, and in 1891 *La Revue Blanche*. The *Poésies* of Mallarmé appeared in 1887; in 1889, *Parallèlement* of Verlaine, the *Essai sur les Données Immédiates de la Conscience* of Bergson and the famous work of Edouard Schuré, *Les Grands Initiés*, which advanced the mystical and theosophical current of Symbolism. The same year witnessed the appearance of pictorial Symbolism on the occasion of the exhibition at the Café Volpini of the 'Impressionist and Synthesist Group', that is to say, Gauguin and the School of Pont-Aven (Bernard, Laval, Anquetin, and others). The designation 'Impressionist' had been maintained for publicity's sake, but the aesthetic doctrine of the movement, based on Cloisonnism and Synthes-

SUTHERLAND. HEAD OF THORNS. 1946.
Private Collection, New York.

GUSTAVE MOREAU. SALOMÉ.
Gustave Moreau Museum, Paris.

wide comment: 'The work of art', he proclaimed 'must be: 1. *Ideist*, since its only goal will be expression of the idea; 2. *Symbolist*, since it will express the idea in forms; 3. *Synthetic*, since it will transcribe the forms in a mode of general comprehension; 4. *Subjective*, since the object will never be considered in it as an object, but as the sign of the idea perceived by the subject; 5. (As a consequence) *Decorative*, for decorative painting properly so called, as the Egyptians and very likely the Greeks and the Primitives conceived it, is nothing but a manifestation of an art at once subjective, synthetic, symbolist and ideist'. These characteristics, which put emphasis upon Ideist Symbolism and the tendency toward decorative abstraction, applied in particular to Gauguin and the School of Pont-Aven, as well as to the Nabi group–Bonnard, Vuillard, Roussel, Maurice Denis, Ranson, Valloton–connected with Pont-Aven through Sérusier (*vide* Pont-Aven and Nabis); but they were already evident, in an intuitive and rather literary form, in three isolated artists with whom the Symbolist generation claimed kinship: Gustave Moreau, Puvis de Chavannes, and Odilon Redon.

Gustave Moreau (1826-1898) is in France the exact equivalent of the English Pre-Raphaelites that were discovered at the Universal Exhibition of 1855. Before his fake pictorial jewellery and the immense miscarriage of his mythical imagery, one cannot help thinking of the savage *mot* of Degas: 'He wants to make us believe that the gods wore watch-chains'. But because of the mysteriousness of his life, the prestige of his personality and his idealist intentions, Moreau's influence was widely felt; not only by decadent writers like Huysmans and Jean Lorrain, who maintained a real cult for him, but also by the Nabi painters. 'He, the master sorcerer,' said Jean Lorrain, 'has cast a spell upon his time, bewitched his contemporaries and contaminated with the ideal this sceptical and practical end of a century.'

While the work of Puvis de Chavannes (1824-1898), in spite of its nobility and undeniable harmony, now appears more closely related to an academic allegorism than to authentic Symbolism, its influence also was considerable, and all contemporary artists, from Gauguin to the Nabis, claimed him as a precursor. Albert Aurier and Maurice Denis, in their doctrinal articles, re-

ism, was opposed to that of the Impressionists (and Neo-Impressionists), 'who searched', as Gauguin said, 'round the eye and not in the mysterious centre of thought, and so lapsed into scientific reasoning'. Bernard and Gauguin–here in complete contradiction to Cézanne, who was fanatically faithful to nature, and even to Van Gogh, who never separated symbol from reality– maintained the necessity of painting no longer from life but from memory, not 'before the thing' but 'entertaining it in the imagination' that had taken it in, and, after simplification, had retained its 'synthesis', that is to say, 'idea'.

The young critic Albert Aurier, an enthusiastic admirer of Gauguin, whom he introduced into the famous literary circle of the Café Voltaire, dominated by Moréas and Verlaine, defined Symbolism in painting in an article in the *Mercure de France* for March 1891 that caused

peatedly cited the fruitful example of his art, whose three characteristic innovations the critic Mellerio summed up as follows: 'amendment of direct sensation, simplification of drawing, an ornamental tendency'. Gauguin, while stressing the differences that separated him from Puvis de Chavannes, always acknowledged a debt to him, and his dream was to do 'coloured Puvis de Chavannes'. The unanimous recognition accorded at the end of the century to Puvis was such that a banquet, presided over by Rodin, was given in his honour in January 1895, gathering together 550 artists and writers of the most opposed schools, from Carolus-Duran to Renoir and Gauguin, and from Brunetière to Verlaine and Mallarmé.

Odilon Redon (1840-1916), a contemporary of Impressionism, which he thought 'too low-ceilinged', made friends with Mallarmé and the young Symbolist writers, Gide, Valéry and Francis Jammes, and following the example of Gustave Moreau and Puvis de Chavannes, whom he greatly admired, sought in his works 'human beauty with the prestige of thought'. But whereas the intentions of those two painters were hamstrung by academic formulae, Redon suc-

ceeded in creating the plastic idiom of his dreams. He is the Symbolist painter *par excellence*. This is why the Nabis, Bonnard, Vuillard, Roussel, Sérusier, Maurice Denis, of whom he executed admirable lithographic portraits in black, bistre and sanguine, turned to him with fervour and paid homage to him in a collective exhibition at Durand-Ruel's in 1899. Although the Symbolist movement found its finest expression in France with Mallarmé, it spread all over Europe, like Art Nouveau with which it was sometimes identified (*vide* Jungendstil). It was given distinction in Belgium by personalities, like Verhaeren and Maeterlinck, particularly Maeterlinck whose work, wholly concerned with the mysteries of the cosmos and the inner life of the soul, inspired many an aesthetic reverie at the end of the century. There were hardly any artists who remained untouched by the Symbolist mystique: Eugène Carrière and Fantin-Latour in France, Whistler in England, James Ensor in Belgium, who began painting in the Impressionist manner, but in 1890 discovered in the mask an expression for his fantastic universe and irony. In Germany, where there were still reverberations from the Wagnerian storms, Symbolism was transplanted

GAUGUIN. WOMEN IN A GARDEN, ARLES. CIRCA 1888.
Musée des Beaux-Arts, Reims.

by the poet, Stefan George, and ended by merging with Expressionism, to which it gave a

new profundity, as, for instance, in some of the works of Hodler and Munch.

In short, Symbolism was less a school than the atmosphere of a period and it is significant that all the painters who were more or less attracted to it were jumbled together in the exhibitions, held twice a year from 1891 to 1897 at the Galerie Le Barc de Boutteville. The extent of the movement can be measured in a book by André Mellerio, published in 1896, *The Idealist Movement in Painting*, which distinguished four separate groups in what is sometimes called the 'Symbolist mêlée': the chromo-luminarists, the Neo-Impressionists, the synthetists and the mystics. After Gauguin's departure to Tahiti, the most active group was that of the Nabis (synthetists), supported by the *Revue Blanche (*)*, whose versatile talents were exercised in all the decorative arts.   J. LE.

SYNCHROMISM (*see* Abstract Art).

REDON. ARMOUR. CIRCA 1885.
Metropolitan Museum, New York.

T

TAEUBER-ARP Sophie (1889-1943). Swiss painter; born in Davos; died in Zürich. After studying applied art in Munich and Hamburg, Sophie Taeuber was a teacher at the School or Arts and Crafts in Zürich for thirteen years. She belonged to the Dadaist movement together with Arp, whom she met in 1915 and married in 1921. She executed mural paintings and stained glass in Strasbourg, and in particular decorated several rooms of the restaurant *L'Aubette* (which has since been destroyed). From 1928 to 1940, she lived with Arp in Meudon, near Paris, and participated in exhibitions such as *Cercle et Carré* (1930) and *Abstraction-Création* (1933), always showing abstract works with geometrical forms. She founded the review *Plastique*, four issues of which appeared between 1937 and 1939. During the Second World War she took refuge in Grasse and executed coloured lithographs in collaboration with Arp, Sonia Delaunay and Alberto Magnelli. During a trip to Switzerland, she died of asphyxiation from the fumes of a stove. She has left a great number of gouaches, drawings, water-colours and oil paintings, whose importance resides in their simplicity and at the same time in their richness of invention. She was beyond doubt one of the central figures in Abstract Art *(*)* between the two wars. Her art is occasionally related to Neo-Plasticism (cutouts of 1916 and the decorations of the 'Aubette'); at other times to a Constructivism, optimistic and light in spirit. Her work is an almost inexhaustible catalogue of abstract forms and techniques. The style is sober and of crystalline purity. Her innovations were always directed toward greater simplification, but also toward greater freedom, like exercises on a well-tempered clavichord. M. S.

TAEUBER. GOUACHE. 1932.
Private Collection, Paris.

TAMAYO Rufino (born in 1899 at Oaxaca, Mexico). His parents were Zapotecs, who died when he was eight years old. One of his aunts brought him up and took him to Mexico City. He helped her to sell fruit in the market and began to study commercial subjects, while secretly attending painting classes at the San Carlos Art School. But instead of this ineffective academic teaching, he soon preferred to study the great contemporary art movements, Impressionism, Cubism and Expressionism, on his own. 1921 was a landmark for him; he was appointed head of the ethnographical drawing section of the

TAMAYO. ANIMALS. 1941. *Museum of Modern Art, New York.*

Museum of Anthropology of Mexico which, since the Revolution (1910), had been classifying the material of ancient civilisations. Tamayo worked in the archives at a survey of the multiple art forms of pre-Hispanic cultures, ranging from the metates (maize grinders) sculptured in stone, vases, wicker-work and skulls to clay toys and traditional costumes. In this way he was in direct touch with the origins of Mexican culture.

Even in his first one-man show in 1926 at Mexico City, Tamayo aimed to integrate traditional pre-Columbian forms with the achievements of contemporary painting and give them both the quality of universality. But he came up against the taste of the day that was considerably influenced by the vast mural decoration like huge theatrical sets, sprung from a preoccupation with the past and social ideas of the moment. Tamayo's reality had even then a greater dramatic power, while it remained more intimate through the intensity of its expression. He left the same year for New York, where he lived and exhibited for the next two years. On his return to Mexico City, he was appointed to teach at the School of Art and in 1933 his first fresco was commissioned for the Academy of Music. He made it an opportunity to glorify the rich heritage of his country and the

enthusiasm of the workers for the Revolution. From 1938, his position as a teacher in the Dalton School in New York enabled him to divide his time between the United States, where he was in touch with international artistic life, and Mexico which was the source of his inspiration and strength. During this phase, he exhibited nearly every year, but had to wait till 1950 before he received fresh official commissions for public buildings in Mexico.

It was on his return from his first visit to Europe, after exhibiting at Paris, Brussels, Rome and the Venice Biennale (1950), which was a personal triumph, that Tamayo began work on over 645 square feet of wall in the Palacio de Bellas Artes in Mexico City, where till then only Orozco, Rivera and Siqueiros had been invited to work. He covered them with two frescoes, monumental in size and in their powerful conception that went beyond all figurative conventions (1952-1953). He was awarded the first prize for painting at the São Paulo Biennale in 1953, the international prize of the Guggenheim Foundation in 1960 and executed numerous paintings in Mexico, the United States and Paris (Conference Hall of the UNESCO building, 1958).

At first he was influenced by the popular painters of ex-voto pictures, then he changed from harsh, crude, often aggressive colours to tones that were deeper and more refined, but that had lost nothing of their original freshness or brilliance. The forms culminated, organised themselves and tended to merge into vast movements, evolving and growing according to a natural, continuous logic and gradually opening up their fantastic structures to the impulses of the imaginary. Light softened the colour and dissolved the hieratic manner of his first figures, which were inspired and identified with the giants of another age in their epic conflicts. Man questions the universe, perceives new symbols and shares the creative activity of the elements in his escape from the agony of atomic destruction. In going back to the origins of expressive idiom though an instinctively poetic vision of reality, Tamayo found again, by sheer skill and simplicity, the sincerity of the popular artist. He is in direct line with the great epochs of pre-Columbian art and gives a form to new myths.   R.-J. M.

TANGUY Julien (1825-1894). Père Tanguy started his career in art as a dealer in artists materials in the rue Clauzel, in Montmartre. In 1870 he decided to add the sale of the works of his painter friends to that of his regular stock. He bought Van Goghs but never sold a single one of them. He was not disheartened, though, and moved by an unyielding faith, continued to pile up canvases by Monet, Sisley, Cézanne, Gauguin and Seurat. Tanguy visited the painters in their studios at Moret and Pontoise, bringing them paints (payment for which was generally long deferred), and he haunted the Salons. It was at his place that Vollard discovered Cézanne, and it is interesting to note that, from 1877 to 1893, his shop was the only place in Paris where Cézanne's canvases could be seen. He unfailingly backed the efforts of his friends, in spite of the fact that his means were always modest, and it was to him that many painters owed, at certain critical moments, their ability to continue working.

TANGUY Yves (1900-1955). French painter; born in Paris; died in Connecticut. Of Breton parentage, Tanguy entered the merchant marine. He made several trips, to England, Portugal, Spain, Africa and South America. He became friendly with Jacques Prévert in 1920, then Marcel Duhamel and shared a house with them that Duhamel had bought behind Montparnasse station, 54 rue du Château. In 1923, Tanguy suddenly began to paint, after having seen a picture by Chirico in the window of the Paul Guillaume Gallery. Although he had never touched a brush before or thought of doing so, he discovered that this was his calling; he emerged suddenly into an inner universe independent of the real world. His is a near-unique case of completely autonomous creation. In 1925 he met the Surrealists and joined their group, participating in all their exhibitions in France and abroad. His work espoused the profound aims of the movement in advance and ran the gamut of possible impacts of the psychic upon the physical. Nothing impaired the purity of the messages it transmitted from a mental world, in which the artist lived isolated and whose mystery he succeeded in expressing, if not in explaining: His work has been compared to undersea or extraplanetary scenes. But in reality his vision was purely subjective, populated by forms with no equivalents. If these forms sometimes seem to emerge from the mist of dream or to grow out of the very irregularities of the materials employed they possess, however, a precise structure; they obey an inner logic, and rigorous relations are established between them. This is

TANGUY. COMPOSITION.   *J. Snégaroff Collection, Paris.*

TOBEY. STILL-LIFE, SUMI INK. 1957.
J.-F. Jaeger Collection, Paris.

confirmed by the remarkable drawings which constitute an important part of Tanguy's work. Each of his pictures is like a balcony opening upon the unknown, and André Breton has spoken rightly of 'far expeditions'. Having left for the United States in 1939 and having sojourned in California and Canada, he settled in Woodbury, Connecticut, in 1942. He became an American citizen in 1948 and lived on a farm in the United States, far from the world, where he continued his work without any interruption. This developed a greater sense of precision, but the increasingly complex structure showed the same integrity and inventiveness. About 1950, a sudden change came over it and for the last years of his life he painted large canvases (*Multiplication of Arcs,* 1954) where space, which had been so fluid before, was invaded by heaps of calcareous débris, a sort of stifling magma, suddenly solidified by death.   J. LA.

TOBEY Mark (born 1890 at Centerville, Wisconsin). He is the least American of American painters. His painting depends neither on the violence of gesture or colour, nor on Expressionism. It does not suggest speed of execution, nor does it dignify

carelessness into a method. It is, on the contrary, remarkable for the meticulous care lavished on its execution and the refinement of its colour, which is muted and sometimes tends towards a monochrome tonality, owing to his almost exclusive use of water colours, tempera and pastel mediums. Moreover, while the huge scale (suggestive of the vast spaces of America, just like Melville's epic novels, Whitman's poems or Frank Lloyd Wright's prairie houses) is one of the characteristic aspects of transAtlantic painting, Tobey's art is limited to small surfaces. He has a fondness for sizes less than 8in. × 12in. and some of his most intense compositions have been done on sheets of Japanese vellum, the size of a post-card.

Tobey's work is the culmination of a formative period, during which he developed on his own, and several years of travel. He left his family in 1907 and went to Chicago, where he worked for a firm of fashion publications. While he continued this work, he went to York and settled there in 1912. There he became a popular portrait painter, which enabled him to give up fashion designing. He was talked about as if he were a new Sargent. His first one-man show took place in 1917. In 1922, he went to live in Seattle, which became his home town for the time being and where he taught at the Cornish School. From 1925 to 1926, he travelled in France, Greece and the Near East. He returned to the United States and left again for England in 1931, where he stayed till 1938 and which he left for Mexico (1931), then the Far East (1934). This last voyage during which he studied Chinese calligraphy under Teng Kwei at Shanghai and Zen calligraphy in a Japanese monastery, put the final touch to his formative years. In 1935, when he was over forty-four, he painted *Broadway Norm,* his first 'white writing,' followed shortly by *Broadway* and *Welcome Hero.*

This white writing, evolved from the ideograms of Far Eastern writing stripped of their meaning, consists of outlines in white Chinese ink like calligraphic marks, which are used to reduce the various coloured forms composing the painting to the common denominator of a similar encircling line. Thus in *Broadway Norm* the countless individual trajectories of passersby, vehicles and light appear to merge. The reference to the visible world is quite clear and this painting, more than others that are more abstract, is fairly enlightening on the painters' approach to his subject. Impressionistic in the first stage, it becomes progressively more simplified (there are numerous examples of this in the course of Tobey's work in which there are several pictures of crowds: auction sales, streets of New York, and markets, that illustrate every degree of abstraction and representation). But Tobey did not aim at giving pleasure to the eye alone: he developed a theme and posed a problem, that of the one and the many, of the particular and the general. The wisdom of the East had taught him that the should 'strip away every desire and lose all individuality.' But the experience of a portraitist had on the other hand made him look for what was specific and original in human beings. After his phase of portraiture, he completely avoided this particular approach. Although in the beginning Tobey used the basic form of the western city to pose the problem of sameness and otherness, later on he formulated it with uncompromising severity in groups of paintings, such as the *Meditative Series* of 1954, in which the signs have lost all representational significance. Further examples of this are *Multi Movements in Time* and the *Edge of August* (1953; Museum of Modern Art, New York) which, with some of Wols' paintings, are among the most extraordinary graphic meditations on the flow of time and the approach to its further bounds.

However, Tobey's art was never in danger of ossifying into a formula; he always kept in touch with the world of the senses. Drawing from nature remained a necessary discipline for him and alternated with abstract work. Similarly, he explored various spheres in succession; after the field of cultural activity, he turned to nature. Clusters of people were succeeded by clusters of stones, lichens or stars. His ques-

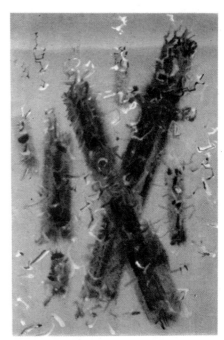

TOBEY. COMPOSITION. 1955.
Galerie Rive Droite, Paris.

tioning gaze fixed with the same intensity on the life of microbes, the surface of a stream or the Milky Way as it had already done on the infinitely small at the limits of the universe. The form of the signs and specially the tonality of the background against which they were set maintained a precarious, but invaluable allusion to actuality. In this way, he succeeded in preserving the reality on which his experience was based, while he went beyond it by rejecting its accidentals. Even in a painting completely covered with apparently identical units, each sign is given an individual treatment by the painter and a close examination shows that it differs from its neighbour by a hardly perceptible inflection of outline or a minute modulation in the colour.

His regular recourse to representational drawing or exercises with sumi inks (a technique of rapid painting with a bamboo brush and Chinese ink, which he learned in the Far East and began practising in 1957); the easy appeal of his abstract paintings and their modest size all helped to conceal for a long time the unity and considerable importance of Tobey's work. Recognition was late in coming, first in Europe at the Venice Biennale of 1958, when he was awarded the International Prize for Painting, then with the retrospective exhibition at the Pavillon de Marsan, Paris, in 1960, and finally the official homage in the United States of an exhibition at the Museum of Modern Art, New York, in 1962.   F. C.

TOMLIN Bradley Walker (1899-1953). American painter; born in Syracuse, N.Y., died in New York. At fourteen he won a scholarship to study painting. Studies at Syracuse University, from which he graduated in 1921 with a Bachelor's degree in painting and a University fellowship for a year's study abroad. Before utilizing it he lived for a year in New York where he did commercial art and had his first one-man show. In Paris (1923) he was especially interested by Cézanne, Van Gogh and Gauguin rather than by Picasso, Matisse or Braque (although the last named was to have a considerable influence on his work). After returning to New York, he again visited Paris in 1926 with his friend the painter Frank London, with whom he shared Rodin's former studio in the Avenue du Maine.

Influenced at first by London and by the 'Immaculatists' (Sheeler, Demuth, Preston Dickinson) to whose architectural severity he however brought a note of fantasy and poetry of his own, he does not find a truly personal style until the late 1930's, possibly as a result of the famous exhibition at the Museum of Modern Art of New York: 'Fantastic Art, Dada and Surrealism' (1936) which he found repellent at first but to which he kept returning, eventually finding other art dull in comparison. But the work of these years takes typically the form of semi-abstract still-lifes suggesting Braque, with however an occasional Surrealist prop (such as the ectoplasmic cat and bust in *Outward Preoccupation* (1939)) visible through a kind of cubist grill. The elegiac note in his work grows deeper and more somber in *To the Sea* (1942) and *Burial* (1942), both montages of abstract forms, architectural details and real objects (a

ship's figurehead, a laurel-crowned athlete's head) and both reflecting his feelings about the war.

Tomlin did not, however, emerge as a truly important and original artist until the last five years before his premature death, when he came under the influence of painters like Pollock, Guston, Motherwell and Gottlieb. It was Gottlieb whose 'pictographs' of the early 1940's first showed Tomlin a way away from the Cubist still-lifes in which, it seems, he had begun to lose conviction. Two important transitional works, *Arrangement* (1944) and *The Armor Must Change* (1946) show the depth of this change as well as its slowness. Both are tautly organized, as usual, and done in a typically restrained palette, but the forms have become looser and less representational, while a new graphism has invaded the canvas, disturbing the subtly ordered arrangements of forms and confounding surfaces, volumes and depths. The ribbon-like outlines of *Number 3* (1948) and especially of *Tension by Moonlight* (1948) which consists of only a half-dozen white bands on black, are the acutest realization of this desire to do away with subtleties and complexities and to establish a new kind of lyricism, strong, free and unreflecting in keeping with the latest developments of Abstract Expressionism.

Interesting as they are, these works are nevertheless not completely typical of Tomlin, who soon returned to the architectural complexities which haunted him but this time using an expanded version of the abstract vocabulary with which he had just been experimenting. The two-dimensional bands, lines and symbols (arrows, triangles or even letters of the alphabet) are now closely organized in a shallow space in which infinitesimal differences in depth are, however, distinctly evident and set up a field of resonance for the increasingly complex counterpoint which cumulates in allover patterns in works like *Number 7* and *Number 18* (1950)— both a kind of architectural and intellectual apprehension of multiple experiences which Pollock was currently translating in another way.

The tremendous tension in these paintings snaps in turn, and in the canvases of his last year, which are his greatest, Tomlin attains the unified lyricism and inward harmony toward which he had perhaps always been working.

Here the angular trajectories dissolve into countless pastel flakes or petals which seem unorganized at first but which on further examination prove to be subtly related through the distribution of their colours and the different directions in which they seem to move. With them Tomlin constructs a new architecture, impalpable but deeply satisfying.

Always unwell in later life, Tomlin died in 1953 in New York after an outing to the country home of his friends the Jackson Pollocks, at the very height of his career. The true extent of the loss to American painting has not yet been fully felt.   J. A.

TOOROP Johannes Theodorus, called Jan (1858-1928). Dutch painter; born at Poerworedjo, Java, died at The Hague. He went to Holland when he was fourteen years old and, after training under Tetar van Elven at the Academy of Fine Arts at Amsterdam (1881), Toorop lived at Brussels and Mechelen from 1882 to 1885. He had already been experimenting for some years with all the new tendencies in

painting that affected his generation. Beginning with Impressionism, he then felt the attraction of Van Gogh, then Signac and he was drawn towards Neo-Impressionism and Divisionism. It was at Brussels too that he made friends with Ensor, the Société des Vingt *(*)* and was in touch with the Symbolists. After a visit to England, he settled at The Hague in 1888 and became one of the best known painters of his time in Holland. His subjects were a vague embodiment of what has been called the 'fin de siècle' malady, with their symmetrical compositions of elongated, androgynous figures, which, like his lithograph posters, made use of all the resources of exuberant, art nouveau ornamentation. Towards the end of his life, his conversion to Catholicism once more brought about a change in his already very varied work. Crowded allegorical scenes frequently appeared in Toorop's work and to the end of his life it reflected his religious faith. Flowing line assumed an even greater importance over colour and tonality. His powerful, simple landscapes of the North Sea and the broad Dutch plains are exceptional in his work.   R.-J. M.

TOMLIN. NUMBER 20. 1949.
Museum of Modern Art, New York.

TORRÈS-GARCIA Joaquin (1874-1949). Uruguayan painter; born and died in Montevideo. The son of a Catalan father and a Uruguayan mother, he went to Barcelona when he was seventeen, studied mural painting there, and executed frescoes at the Palacio de la Deputación. After visiting Paris and Brussels (1910), he returned to Montevideo. In 1920-1922 he stayed in New York and then in Italy. In 1924 he established himself in Paris, where he lived until 1932. During this period, with Michel Seuphor, he founded the review and the group of *Cercle et Carré (*)* and took an active part in the organization of the international exhibition of the same name, which took place in April 1930 and had the participation of the principal abstract painters then alive, notably Kandinsky, Mondrian, Schwitters, Arp,

Pevsner, as well as Léger, Ozenfant and Le Corbusier. Then returning to Montevideo for good, he opened an art school that met with great success and exercised a profound influence upon the new generation. At the same time he continued by himself the review *The Circle and the Square* (*Círculo y Cuadrado*), which became the organ of a school rather than a review of abstract art. He published several works, among them a history of his life (*Historia de Mi Vida*, Montevideo, 1939), and executed numerous decorations in Montevideo as well as an important monument (*Monumento Cósmico*) in the Parque Rodo of the same city. Except for a few works of the Paris *Cercle et Carré* period (1930), the work of Torrès-García remained figurative, although it showed a tendency towards a free improvisation that was peculiar to him. He seems to have learned his deepest lesson from pre-Columbian art, which he contrasted to and

TORRES-GARCIA. COMPOSITION.
J. Ulmann Collection, Paris.

combined with modern European art. His work contains Cubist and Neo-Plastic elements as well as certain aspects of the Klee idiom, all integrated with perfect ease into an ideographic concept that makes of Torrès-García a great Indian artist of our time. M. S.

TOULOUSE-LAUTREC Henri de (1864-1901). French painter, born in Albi; died at the Château de Malromé at Céleyran, one of his childhood haunts. Lautrec was the descendant of a family that traced its origin back to the Counts of Toulouse, defenders of the Albigensian Cathari, and the Viscounts of Lautrec. Count Alphonse, his father, was an original personality, passionately fond of falcon hunting, exotic weapons, horses and carriages. His disguises and games, carried out with the unalterable seriousness of a totally assured man, foreshadowed the wry humour of the painter, his absolute straightforwardness to the point of violence, his stubbornness of will, his wholehearted participation in every act of life. Lautrec's childhood was quite normal. Except for a short period of schooling at the Lycée Condorcet in Paris, it was spent in his family's country house. His studies were directed by his mother. He began drawing very early, filling the margins of his copybooks with caricatures of his parents, his teachers, his cousins, the animals he observed; he showed a special predilection for horses and applied himself to drawing whole sequences of the same subject, to study its variations and different aspects. Two falls, at Albi in 1878, and at Barèges in 1879, in which he broke both legs, left him after months of immobility, completely deformed, his torso supported by two weak and shortened legs. From his convalescences came letters and travel notebooks addressed to cousins or friends, whose gaiety reveals a moving self-control. Not only did he not complain, he even stressed his disability, as if to discourage all compassion in advance. He made every effort to behave like a normal man. In his drawings, based upon remarkable observation, he showed great interest in the vitality and movement of people. Acting upon the advice of the animal painter René Princeteau, a friend of his father, he began painting and discovered a new medium in colour. The influence of this first teacher lasted

TOULOUSE-LAUTREC. SEATED GIRL, BACK VIEW.
1896. *Musée du Louvre, Paris.*

he set up his studio in the Rue Caulaincourt, on the corner of the Rue Tourlaque. He was next door to the Goupil *(*)* print shop, where he encountered Maurice Joyant, his former schoolmate at the Lycée Condorcet, who became the chief defender of his work. Lautrec frequented the ballrooms and cabarets of Montmartre, in particular the 'Mirliton', where Bruant sang his social ballads and greeted his clients with offensive remarks. Lautrec illustrated Bruant's most famous songs: *At Batignolles, At Belleville, At Saint-Lazare*; on the walls of the cabaret he painted dancing scenes, in which La Goulue appeared for the first time (1886); finally, under the influence of Bruant and Raffaelli, he executed realistic works: *Gueule de Bois* (1888-1889), posed by Suzanne Valadon, and *A la Mie* (1891).

Nevertheless, he did not give in to the sentimentality of the slums. He was so intensely interested in the character of his models, whoever they were, that he gave them a remarkable dignity. In the garden of Père Forest, neighbouring his studio, he painted a series of portraits of women out of doors, from Montmartre models and prostitutes whose names or nicknames are barely known: Hélène V., Augusta, Gabrielle, the policeman's daughter, Berthe the Deaf, Casque d'Or, Honorine P., the woman with the gloves. These portraits, rich in psychological and human insight, enabled Lautrec to perfect his pictorial technique. Observing his model in the crude light of day, he accustomed himself to considering it as a whole, without any shadow whatever. He did not think, like the Impressionists, of studying the variations that the time of the day brings to things; he never resorted to chiaroscuro. For him, whose curiosity was concerned with human beings alone, light had only one rôle: to illuminate, not to alter vision or to make changing what is fixed and full. This is why he was led to create the cold and ideal light of which Pierre Mac Orlan speaks, and which enabled him to search the face of man and to strip it of its secrets. Thus he presented the model in a sort of moral and psychological nakedness. He did not paint the representative of a profession or a class, but a being whose destiny appears unique in his attitudes and his face. He rejected everything inessential, sometimes setting the scene precisely, but without ever allowing the setting to capture attention and play more

for two or three years, and in many respects was decisive. Being affected himself by a physical handicap–he was a deaf mute–René Princeteau presumably brought a special comprehension and attention to the formation of the young cripple. In his first works, *Artillerymen and Cuirassiers on Horse-back*, reminiscences of manœuvres that had taken place near his family's estate, Lautrec made use of an abbreviated and flexible technique of small divergent brush strokes, borrowed from his teacher, which was far from the systematic disintegration of tones of Impressionism, but which lent itself to improvisation. In 1882, having received his family's permission to devote himself entirely to painting, he came to Paris to complete his training. He worked at first in the studio of Princeteau and underwent the influence of John Lewis Brown and Forain. In 1883 he entered the École Nationale des Beaux-Arts in the studio of Cormon, a mediocre painter who did prehistoric reconstructions, but was of a tolerant mind, and with whom he worked intermittently until 1887. It was in this studio that he met Emile Bernard, Anquetin and Van Gogh, who impressed him deeply. In 1887, having already lived two years in Montmartre,

TOULOUSE-LAUTREC. JANE AVRIL. 1893.
LITHOGRAPH.

beings whom he found exceptional and applied himself to discovering their unique features. He was the first to follow the idolatrous cult of the star, an exceptional being, a superior animal who attracts all the interest in a show. He brought out the definitive features by emphasizing them; and one can see, for example, a great actress like Yvette Guilbert become the incarnation of Lautrec's representation of her, which deeply shocked her at first.

Even more personal were the solutions Lautrec brought to other spheres of plastic expression. The appeal that theatres had for him caused him to execute, simultaneously with some theatrical settings that have not come down to us, programme covers, and more particularly posters. In these productions he was not less concerned with making a work of art than he was before a canvas. Advertising, which at the beginning resorted only to a rather crude form of art, thus passed to a higher level. Bonnard was the first to have achieved delicate harmonies of shades and subtle design, suggested to him by his taste for Persian fabrics. Chéret created

than the environmental rôle assigned to it. All the persons whose individuality he fixed can be found in the large compositions of dancing at the Moulin de la Galette and the Moulin Rouge. Here he tried to bring out the generic features of his models and to give a collective representation of a milieu. These works obey a rhythm that transfigures them, that of the dance, and the dance itself is personified by La Goulue or Jane Avril. These faces, which haunted him or were familiar to him, took on a special intensity as they touched common life. La Goulue, with her partner Valentin le Désossé, is one of Lautrec's most powerful creations and she inspired him to do a host of drawings and pictures. For Lautrec she represented the perfect identity between the human being and his function. But outside the temple where her cult was celebrated she was no longer anything and went from degradation to degradation. On the other hand the personalities of Jane Avril, Yvette Guilbert, May Belfort, May Milton, and later of the actresses Jeanne Granier, Marcelle Lender, Berthe Bady and many others, unfolded as their art evolved. Thus Lautrec attached himself to

TOULOUSE-LAUTREC. JOCKEY AND TRAINER. 1899.
LITHOGRAPH.

illusion and obsession with lightness and verve. Lautrec's admiration for Japanese prints and the recollection of certain compositions of Degas enabled him to adjust even more completely to mural requirements. He broadened and deepened his pitiless drawing and made it more effective through the arabesque of his foregrounds. His few colours were clear, and applied boldly, and at once established the composition as a whole. Thus in an extreme simplification he gave the silhouette and the movements of his subject the greatest power. The pictures of La Goulue, Bruant, Jane Avril, and Caudieux resulted in a creation of types. The presence that commands attention on the wall with explosive force, Lautrec preserved even in his works of smaller dimensions, almost interior posters, like the pictures of May Belfort and May Milton, the Confetti poster, 'based upon Jeanne Granier's smile', and most of the lithographs in colour. In his black-and-white lithographs, on the contrary, he broke the line and produced a crumbling of form.

Lautrec's interest was not confined to the theatre, music hall, circus, ballroom and bar. With his cousin Gabriel Tapié de Céleyran, who was then a medical student, he frequented the hospital where the famous surgeon Péan operated, capturing his movements with a reporter's curiosity. A few years later, he developed a passion for sporting circles; he followed the training of champions at the Buffalo cycle-racing track, operated by his friend the humorist Tristan Bernard, making sketches of this still unexplored world which he re-created in lithographs and posters. He attended the hearings of great trials. He was extremely fond of travelling and organized his tours with a personal and amusing touch, always dragging along some friend. To go to Bordeaux he embarked every year at Havre and took freighters going to Africa. Once, through admiration for a lady passenger, he went on as far as Lisbon, whence he returned via Toledo, discovering in El Greco the painter who impressed him most, with Cranach and the Japanese. During one of his numerous trips to England, he fell into the midst of the tragedy of Oscar Wilde, whose prodigious swollen night owl's face he drew with a few strokes. In the clearness of his vision, the courage of his analysis, Lautrec renewed all the themes he

TOULOUSE-LAUTREC. YVETTE GUILBERT.
Museum of Western Art, Moscow.

treated. Thus the world of prostitution, which has already inspired Constantin Guys and Degas, furnished him with a completely new repertoire of forms. Besides, he attached the greatest importance to this subject. But he was careful not to create a useless scandal and kept all canvases related to it secret. At his exhibition at the Manzi-Joyant Gallery in 1896, he assembled these pictures in a first-floor room to which he alone had the key, and he showed them only to visitors who asked to see them. Almost all of these works, which remained in his studio, are in the Albi Museum. In them Lautrec depicted the atmosphere of the houses with details of exact truthfulness, but as an almost normal and natural life. He was interested in prostitutes and their way of life, without ever alluding to the profession they exercised; he suggested nothing and dramatized nothing. He who hated professional models and their conventional poses found here an ideal subject of observation: the sight of nudes at liberty, unconstrained. He was interested in the types, the customs, the rules of this world situated outside common morality.

TOULOUSE-LAUTREC. LA PARTIE DE CAMPAGNE. 1897.
LITHOGRAPH.

diluted colours, in his last works he came to paint with thick pastes and construct large planes in conflict with each other.

Toulouse-Lautrec was above all an independent. He had friends but never tried to form pupils or disciples. He hated all artistic theories and participated in no movement; nevertheless, he was completely of his time and succeeded in seizing its fundamental problems by instinct. An implacable enemy of old techniques and traditional recipes, he gave a new vision of reality, in all freedom, unconcerned with influencing anyone, and he always considered young painters like Bonnard, Vuillard or Vallotton as his equals. While he admired Renoir and Monet, he felt infinitely closer to Degas and to Manet, who were more involved in the life of his time. For Lautrec, only the human

He enjoyed the company of this relaxed humanity offered to his analysis. He felt at home in these houses, readily established himself there for several days, receiving friends and working assiduously, living in fraternal sympathy with these beings degraded like himself and alive like himself. This part of his work, alien to all passion or spectator's emotion, is a faithful transcription, accurate beyond all picturesqueness. These personages transcend their condition and partake of the universal.

Beginning in 1898, Lautrec's health deteriorated. Over-indulgence in alcohol extinguished his prodigious vitality; his mood became irritable, the prey of horrible obsessions; he hardly worked at all. In 1899, after an especially serious crisis, he was taken to a nursing home in Neuilly for a cure. He could not bear the loss of freedom, and to prove that he was still himself, he executed from memory, by a tremendous effort of will, the series of coloured-pencil *Circus* drawings, a synthesis of his most precious recollection of the rings he had frequented passionately since his youth. Restored to normal life, he applied himself to perfecting his past work. In a final effort he undertook to renew his technique. Having started from analysis to develop a linear construction so expressive that it needed only a coloured drawing, taking advantage of the natural ground of cardboard or planes of highly

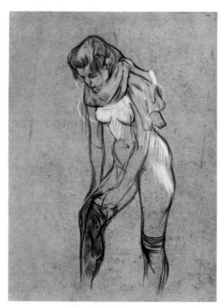

TOULOUSE-LAUTREC. WOMAN PULLING UP HER STOCKING. 1894. *Albi Museum.*

figure counted, and he deplored Monet's early abandonment of the portrait. Later Gustave Moreau would urge his pupils to see a figure by Lautrec, 'all painted in absinthe'. This advice was followed, not only by the Fauves, who, after Lautrec's example, remembered that line is both drawing and colour, but also by a young Spaniard, Pablo Picasso, newly arrived from Barcelona, who would draw from the work of his illustrious predecessor examples to reinforce the melancholy and disenchanted vision he had then formed of the universe. While Lautrec is, then, in his whole work, inseparable from his time, in his last works he had a presentiment of the requirements of the new century, at the dawn of which he died, on September 9th, 1901, at the age of thirty-seven. J. LA.

TSCHUDI Hugo von (1851-1911). As director of the Berlin Nationalgalerie—he was appointed to this important post in 1896—Hugo von Tschudi showed great courage in a difficult struggle before modern art was at last given a place in the state museums. It is true that the situation in Germany was no better than in France, where only official and academic art was paid any honour. The Emperor, William II, had said himself during a reception in 1893: 'Open air painters have a hard time in our country. I rule them with a rod of iron.' In 1886, however, Hugo von Tschudi began to go almost every year to Paris to get a first hand knowledge of its artistic life. The Galerie Durand-Ruel and, a little later on, Ambroise Vollard, received a regular visit from him. In 1899, accompanied by Max Lieberman, he even went to Degas' studio. He was the first French painter to be represented at the Nationalgalerie (1896), followed soon afterwards by the works of Manet, Cézanne, Monet, Pissarro and Sisley. Initiative like this that favoured the new school soon caused complaints and the hostility of official circles forced Tschudi to resign in 1909. The same year, the Bavarian Government invited him to become director of the National Gallery in Munich. His death, two years later, did not put an end to his plans. In 1912, a large still-life by Matisse, which he had ordered for his own collection, was given a place of honour in the museum, while in France

TOULOUSE-LAUTREC. LA CLOWNESSE. 1895.
Musée du Louvre, Paris.

it was not till 1921 that one of his paintings was exhibited at the Musée du Luxembourg. The same year, several art enthusiasts got together to present a number of important works to the Bavarian Government, which were offered as a 'Donation in memory of Hugo von Tschudi' and are still among the riches of the museum.

TYTGAT Edgar (1879-1957). Belgian painter; born and died at Brussels. Although he learned to draw in the studio of his father, who was a lithographer, and began to paint about 1900, it was not till the end of the 1914-1918 War that he formed a style of his own. It was only then that he gave up the impressionist manner of his first phase and became the delightful picture-maker and the spirited narrative painter who for forty years enriched Belgian art with his observation and fantasies. Narrative painters are rare in the twentieth century, since one of the distinctive features of modern art is the lack of importance it attaches to subject matter and its contempt for anecdote. Far from

TYTGAT. CIRCUS IN FLANDRES. 1925.
Mabille Collection, Brussels.

despising the latter, Tytgat made it an essential element in his work. He did not neglect, for all that, its painterly qualities and his naively simplified forms are as attractive as the delicately muted harmonies of his colouring. Both are felicitously combined to create the make-believe atmosphere surrounding his characters; tiny people generally, who belong to a toy world, a little outside the real world and yet who are not strangers to it. Neither love, envy nor sadness are unknown to them. Sometimes they experience drama, or rather dramatic situations, because Tytgat removes any trace of relentlessness from each episode. In spite of everything, his people are too small, their faces are too round and smooth, their gestures too formal ever to allow them to let go their feelings and involve themselves in activities that draw real men into harsh and ruthless conflict. Even when a murderer or executioner does appear, he causes no more suffering than he would in a puppet theatre.

There is a touching sincerity in the meetings of Tytgat's lovers, a sympathetic wonderment and humorous understanding in his descriptions of the circus, merry-go-round horses, stalls and fair grounds. There would be something missing

from Belgian Expressionism if, besides the impetuosity and energy of Permeke, the calmness of Gustave de Smet's compositions and the emotional restlessness of Van den Berghe, there were not also Tytgat's tender ingenuity and malicious, gentle smile.   J.-E. M.

TZARA Tristan. French writer, born in 1896 in Rumania. Tristan Tzara used the word 'Dada' for the first time on February 8th, 1916, at the Meierei café in Zürich, as he would later use the term 'Abstract Art' in one of his lectures at the Kunsthaus in the same city. Coming to Switzerland from Rumania to study mathematics, Tzara met, in 1916, the German poet Hugo Ball, his countryman the painter Marcel Janco, and Hans Arp. With other writers he frequented Meierei's, which later became the Cabaret Voltaire *(*)*. The establishment was situated in the Spiegelgasse, where, at number 17, lived Lenin, who became Tzara's friend. They were soon exchanging both ideas and chessmen. The first event of the group at the Cabaret Voltaire was a concert of Negro music. Poems were recited by Janco, Hülsenbeck and Tzara, who had organized the meeting. In 1917, works of Picasso, Janco, Arp, Delaunay, Kandinsky, Modigliani, Marc, Prampolini, Chirico and others were exhibited there. The review *Dada* appeared in the same year. The first two issues printed compositions by these artists as well as poems, but the general tendency of the magazine did not yet reflect Dadaism properly so called. It was not until the third issue (1918) that the first Dadaist manifesto appeared, signed by Tzara. Needless to say, these events created a scandal in Zürich, but after certain modifications official circles in the city were soon co-operating with the Dadaist trend. However, the war that was going on did not fail to upset the generous feelings of Tzara and his friends. A certain despair invaded their minds and provoked the 'Dadaist disgust', for which there was no remedy other than an anarchistic revolt, destructive of all social, moral, religious, philosophical, literary and artistic entities. Accordingly, in the Dadaist manifesto of 1918 Tzara attacked the plastic arts, opposing them in all their forms, whether traditional or contemporary like Cubism, Futurism or Expressionism. With a vigour coloured by flashes of his imagination and poetic gift, he wrote: 'We have had enough of Cubist and Futurist academies, the laboratories of formal ideas. Is art made to earn money or to soothe the nice bourgeois ? . . . Cubism was born of a simple way of looking at the object: Cézanne painted a cup twenty centimetres below his eyes; the Cubists look at it from above; others complicate appearance by making a perpendicular section and arranging the cup beside it. The Futurist sees the same cup in motion, a succession of objects one next to another, and maliciously adds a few lines of force. This does not prevent the canvas from being a good or a bad painting calculated for the investment of intellectual capital . . . Art has not the importance that we, troopers of the spirit, have been singing for centuries.' He concluded, 'There is a great destructive, negative work to be done: to sweep, to clean'. At the call of this manifesto, the works of the supporters of Dadaism developed in the direction suggested–toward the radical destruction of all conformity, all conventions and routines that generally inspire art, whose very name Tzara wanted to suppress: 'art, a parrot word replaced by Dada, pleiosaurus or handkerchief'. Soon the group gained the support of Marcel Duchamp and Picabia from New York. The vigorous campaign that they had conducted in America consisted fundamentally in transgression of the innumerable rules of art by destroying the barriers which, in their opinion, led it to every decadence. Henceforth they added to their artistic preoccupations the moral disquiet of Dadaism. The link between the two

groups was strengthened and Picabia went to Zurich in 1918 to meet Tzara. The following year, they both decided to go to Paris, where they were given an enthusiastic welcome by Breton, Aragon and Soupault, who had just founded the Littérature group. Violent and provocative shows were immediately organised, first at the Palais des Fêtes in January 1920, then at the Salle Gaveau, where an unforgettable Dada Festival took place. In the fever of revolutionary action, there was complete unity in the movement, but in 1921, disagreements began to appear and the whole-scale destruction, demanded by Tzara, disturbed some of the Dadaists. After a public meeting at the Salle des Sociétés Savantes in May 1921, the aim of which was to bring an accusation against Maurice Barrès and pass judgement on him, Picabia left the group. Breton soon followed while Eluard, Arp and Ribemont-Dessaignes still supported Tzara. But Dada's days were already numbered. Although it attacked the beginnings of Surrealism (*) it was because, still faithful to the spirit of liberty, it only saw in this movement yet another school following the others. Tzara's contribution to what must be in spite of everything called art– and at heart the poet he is has always been sensitive to all forms of plastic expression of value, and has shown a very enlightened interest in them–this contribution has consisted in radically opposing the outdated notions that so dangerously imperiled literature and painting, but in attacking them at their very sources, that is to say their intellectual, moral and political foundations. (*See* also Dada). M. R.

U

UHDE Wilhelm (1874-1947). Uhde was the type of collector who not only is never concerned with the commercial value of a picture but also is prepared to sacrifice everything to acquire the object of his desire. Of German origin, he established himself permanently in Paris in 1904, after having studied in Munich and Florence. When Picasso and Braque were still unknown to most, he bought their canvases: in 1905 his first Picasso, a picture of the Blue Period, for ten francs, and two years later five Fauvist pictures of Braque, also at a very modest price. He was one of the first to discover—as early as 1906—the genius of the Douanier Rousseau, many of whose canvases he bought.

UTRILLO. THE MOULIN DE LA GALETTE.
Private Collection, Paris.

In 1908 he organized a large exhibition of Impressionists in Basel and Zürich, and in the following years several shows of contemporary French painters in Berlin and New York. In 1912, shortly after having published a work on Rousseau, he organized the first great retrospective exhibition of the Douanier. During a stay in Senlis, the same year, he discovered the astonishing Séraphine (*) and became her generous supporter. The author of numerous works, notably on Picasso and Van Gogh, his name remains linked to those whom he called 'primitive masters'–Rousseau, Vivin, Séraphine, Bauchant and Bombois, artists whom he backed and defended, devoting all his energies to making their names known to collectors and public alike. In homage to the memory of this German who contributed so much to the renown of contemporary French painting, relatives and friends have given a collection of 'Primitives of the Twentieth Century' to the Museum of Modern Art in Paris, and the room in which the works are exhibited bears Uhde's name. Thanks to the disinterested help of such people as Uhde, Dr Gachet, and a few dealers, French painting has been able to develop so fruitfully over the last hundred years. A. L.

UTRILLO Maurice (1883-1955). Born in Montmartre, died at Le Vésinet. The illegitimate son of S. Valadon, the travelling acrobat who became the favourite model of Degas and later a painter herself. His father, probably a man named Boissy, disappeared leaving his son no other legacy than a strong penchant for alcohol. In 1891, a Spanish artist, Miguel Utrillo, consented to make the child legitimate. A mediocre and lazy pupil, undisciplined and left to his own devices, the boy thought only of drinking in secret. Expelled from school, he entered a bank but was soon dismissed. Then he was entrusted to the care of his grandmother, at Montmagny. Far from watching him, the old woman let him rove about and get drunk. From this time date the now legendary episodes of Utrillo's life that Francis Carco has recorded in his book, the long drinking bouts followed by nervous crises, the wild nights, the days of stupor, internment at Sainte-Anne hospital, the vain admonitions of his mother, the baneful idleness, the first drawings and the first paintings executed under constraint, submitted to as a remedy;

UTRILLO. BERLIOZ'S HOUSE IN MONTMARTRE. *Private Collection, Paris.*

and then the establishment in Montmartre, the relapse, the return of an ill-repressed passion. Utrillo had now finally resigned himself to the brush that his mother had put into his hand. Forced to paint, and to paint both without a master and without conviction, Utrillo produced works of surprising originality from the outset. At Montmagny, in Montmartre, in the suburbs of Paris, he executed, from 1902 to 1904, some hundred and fifty pictures, which had nothing in common with anything else that could be seen at the time. After a few months of groping, his palette, formerly thick, rough and rather dark, was transformed-under what mysterious influence no one knows. A painter in spite of himself, he began to paint masterpieces. The boozer, the bad lot, the irresponsible man staggering from café to prison, from prison to asylum, from asylum to his desolate mother's; the wretch hooted at by crowds, hunted down by urchins, mauled by prowlers, beaten up by policemen, exploited by amateur art dealers and shopkeepers of Montmartre who hoarded his work; the poor defenceless devil who painted to quench his thirst for alcohol, painted like one inspired, like a master. Ingenuously realistic, he used an amalgam of plaster, sand and glue to render the white of walls. With the minute thoroughness of a mason and the mysticism of a builder of cathedrals he lovingly shaped the dirty, naked façades of tumble-down Montmartre houses and expressed the desperate monotony of rectilinear suburban streets, the melancholy of courtyards and lanes, the rustic peace of small country squares. Gloomy suburbs, empty avenues, small peasant churches, everything in the world that is poor and banal, he transfigured instinctively, seeing it all through the eyes of a child. The humblest chapel became as majestic as a basilica. He needed only a few clouds strewn about a pale sky to convey a feeling of indescribable lightness. The least stone, soiled and cracked, became fascinating under his brush. During the six years of his 'White Period' (1908-1914) he sold for ridiculously low prices pictures that are treasured today in most museums of the world, masterpieces in which objects are invested with a magic splendour that they seem to lack entirely in the eyes of others.

Utrillo's nights of debauchery and drunkenness did not, apparently, prevent him from working regularly in the daytime, with lucidity and fervour. His production was not diminished by the frequency of his fits or by his various sojourns in hospitals and asylums. After numerous internments, notably at Sannois in 1912 and 1914, then again in 1919 and 1921, he finally underwent a very long seclusion in a nursing home at Ivry. Obsessed by alcohol, he was still able to develop coherent logical, carefully executed work, by no means morbid or unwholesome and, as a result of his evangelical sincerity, full of gentleness and freshness. With no masters other than nature and intuition, Utrillo painted with a knowledge of the craft that, although innate, was nevertheless subtle and profound. It is of little consequence, then, if he painted in his Montmartre studio almost exclusively from illustrated post cards as early as 1909. No theory, no academic discipline having blurred his vision, nature freely gave him his means. Utrillo is a constructor: his buildings are firmly set in the ground; his cathedrals rise boldly in the sky. He is an architect: his quays, streets, boulevards stretch out toward the horizon obeying an infallible perspective. He is a colourist: he has an exact notion of the relations between tones, values, atmosphere. His milky whites, singing greys, pale blues, tender greens, glowing reds, velvety blacks defy analysis. For the charming awkwardness of his first canvases he substituted by dint of work a faultless technique and an ease that did not stifle his blissful naïveté. Far

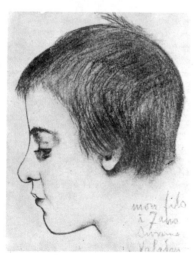

VALADON. MY SON AT THE AGE OF SEVEN. 1891. *Private Collection, Paris.*

from darkening and unbalancing his style, his successive internments seem on the contrary to have strengthened it and enlivened it. It was at the Sannois asylum, in 1912, that his 'white manner' became less gloomy, more sprightly and more sober; *L'Impasse Cottin,* 1910; *Le Lapin Agile,* 1910; the *Church of Saint-Gervais,* 1910; the *Church of Deuil,* 1912; the *Water Tower at Sannois*). It was after his seclusion in 1916 that his forms became separated, his colour burst into flame, his realism was accentuated. But this was already the decline. Utrillo had nothing more to say. From then on he would survive himself to witness his own fame, to collect honours and enjoy the benefits of success. He had participated in the Salon d'Automne in 1909. His first one-man exhibition had taken place in 1913, and at that time he was already known and appreciated. He had admirer–writers like Octave Mirbeau, Élie Faure, Francis Carco. Art dealers sold his works; collectors bought them. In 1925, Diaghilev commissioned the settings and costumes of the ballet *Barabau* from him. In the following year he established himself with Suzanne Valadon and André Utter in a villa that they had built in the Avenue Junot in Montmartre. In 1928 he was made a Chevalier of the Legion of Honour. In 1935 he married Mme Pauwels (Lucie Valore). His exhibitions became more frequent. The price of his pictures went up, as did the number of his imitators. And he who had been strong in his weakness, who had possessed as his sole wealth his poverty and his innocence, he who had never been so great an artist as in the midst of debauchery, destitution and opprobrium, became the frail old man, clean and of regular habits, the good husband and good citizen, the timorous petit bourgeois, submissive, bigoted, the famous painter, valued, decorated, working no longer to create but to produce. As he settled into his ease, his work dried up. Nevertheless the work he accomplished in a mere ten years will forever remain an oasis of peace for men, but an undecipherable enigma also. Utrillo can be situated among those so-called naïve painters or popular painters of reality, right after Henri Rousseau and before all the others, those who have appeared in our century to keep alive a protest of the heart and instinct (*vide* Primitives of Today). F. E.

V

VALADON Suzanne (1865-1938). Born at Bessines; died in Paris. As a young girl Suzanne Valadon reigned for a while over the balls and studios of Montmartre. Beautiful, impudent and lively, she attracted attention among the artists–Renoir admired her lustrous skin, Puvis de Chavannes her slenderness, Lautrec her looks, detecting a hint of sadness and depravity beneath her radiant youth. When she was eighteen, her son Maurice (*vide* Utrillo) was born and she settled down to a calmer life and took to drawing herself instead of

VALADON. BLUE BEDROOM. 1923.   *Musée d' Art Moderne, Paris.*

sitting as model to other artists. She started immediately, as she herself said, 'to work like mad, not to produce beautiful drawings designed to be framed, but good drawings which capture a moment of life in movement–all intensity'. Lautrec, her neighbour, saw these studies and encouraged her, and later Degas was unstinting in his praise and bought some of her work. Suzanne Valadon's aim was to observe rather than to invent, and to express human form within rigid, almost cruel, outlines.

Acknowledging no debt to other painters–for she had nothing in common with those for whom she had sat as model–she admitted only to having been influenced by the technique of Gauguin and his Pont-Aven friends (*see* Nabis)

whose decorative style she had studied at the *Exposition Universelle* in 1889, and gratitude to Degas for the advice he had given her when she started engraving. In 1909 she gave up drawing and engraving, and took to painting. Apart from a few portraits, mainly of her son (*see* page 390), her drawings had been almost entirely of nude figures, for which she chose her charwoman or a servant girl rather than more attractive models. She painted landscapes and still-lifes, though not entirely abandoning nudes and portraits of her friends. In her pictures we find the same power of expression and sharpness of observation as in her drawings, but the colour does not always accord with the emphasis of her line, with the result that often her canvases

VALADON. NUDE DRYING HERSELF. CIRCA 1895.
J. Reiss Collection, London.

give the impression of coloured drawings. But there is no doubt that now and then, when she managed to control her love of crude colours and too obvious contrasts, Suzanne Valadon produced a number of superb oil paintings. She was an unusual artist, who in the feverish hive of Montmartre worked the miracle of developing a style of her own–a vigorous style in which will is the predominating factor.   J. R.

VALLOTTON Félix (1865-1925). Swiss painter; born in Lausanne; died in Paris. He came to Paris at the age of seventeen to study drawing. Enrolled in the Académie Julian (*), he admired Courbet and Manet, and lunched for thirteen *sous* in a modest restaurant of the Faubourg Saint-Denis. The young Vaudois began by exhibiting the *Portrait of M. Ursenbach* at the Salon of 1885. He made copies in the Louvre and executed etchings. He travelled in Austria and Italy. In 1891 he was struck by the works of Lautrec, Van Gogh and the Douanier Rousseau at the Salon des Indépendants. He painted his first important canvases, for which his sitter was Hélène Chatenay, a model with whom he lived. He tried his hand

at the Pointillist manner of Seurat, exhibited at the Salon des Indépendants, worked for the *Revue Blanche (*), Le Rire, Le Courrier Français.* A specialist in the black and white of the woodcut, he illustrated the *Livre des Masques* of Rémy de Gourmont with symbolist portraits (1896). He painted intimate scenes and portraits. 'I dream', he wrote, 'of a great painting stripped of every literal aspect of nature.'

Vallotton has his place among the Nabis (*). But while he was also an intimist, he was a fierce one, a realist after the manner of the novelist Octave Mirbeau, of whom he has left a portrait. Frank, even cynical, his painting oscillated between bitter 'slices of life' lit by the gleam of lamps, and meticulous portraits and still-lifes. His painting sometimes has a dimness, an opaqueness without light that makes the artist the opposite of Seurat: a painter without vibration. Vallotton created an art that reveals both a somewhat dry pungency and a certain taste for invention. A disenchanted realism, which frequently does not shrink from an excessively imitative technique, alternates in his work with rather strange distortions in his nudes. In deliberately naïve and stylized landscapes his work sometimes reveals a taste for simplicity, and even a somewhat summary simplification. All this lacks fervour. Often it is nothing more than a report. It would, however, be a mistake to neglect or even underestimate Vallotton as an artist and as a person. Some of his canvases are of an acid and terrible pessimism. One feels that he had a horror of the pretty, the chalky and the insipid. Having an acute eye and an honest and courageous mind, Vallotton perhaps alone in his generation dared set up his easel before subjects that were then judged too trite for a serious artist–like a sunset over the sea, for example.

Vallotton may have lacked self-confidence and was not always able to maintain a balance between his temptation to reproduce what he saw and his wish to give a transformed and personal vision of things; hence the schematic appearance of some of his landscapes. But he painted portraits and admirable evocations of woods of the Paris region, alive with lovers and Sunday strollers. In these works the hypersensitive person he was arrived at a very personal style, composed of observation, evocation and sad humour. His art is chiefly introspection, and in his successful works he reveals an implacable discipline that is rare in the painting of the last half-century.   P. C.

VALTAT Louis (1869-1952). French painter; born at Dieppe, died at Choisel, in the valley of Chevreuse. After taking the arts course at the Versailles lycée, in 1887 he joined Gustave Moreau's studio at the École des Beaux-Arts in Paris. He began exhibiting in 1889 at the Salon des Indépendants and became one of Jules Dupré's students at the Académie Julian. He visited England and Spain and then met Maillol at Collioure. With Toulouse-Lautrec and Albert André, he designed and painted the sets for the *Terracotta Chariot*, an Indian play of the 4th-5th century. He did drawings and woodcuts for the review, *L'Omnibus de Corinthe* (1897), built himself a studio at Anthéor, stayed at Maganosc with Renoir (1900), travelled in Italy and lived with Signac at Saint-Tropez. That year, 1903, at the first Salon

VALLOTTON. NUDE HOLDING HER NIGHT GOWN. 1904. *Galerie P. Vallotton, Lausanne.*

d'Automne, Valtat exhibited paintings that anticipated the revolt of the Fauves. There is no doubt, in fact, that since 1895 he had been the only painter whose compositions were based on pure colour and linear arabesque, which were fundamental qualities of the great array of Fauve paintings in the Salon d'Automne of 1905. He visited Algeria, became friendly with Paul Valéry (1913), then left the South of France and settled into his studio in the avenue Wagram. In 1918, he carved a stone statue of *Saint Martin* to decorate the portal of the church at Ver-sur-Mer. In 1924, he stayed at Choisel, in the valley of Chevreuse, and paid frequent visits there to the end of his life. He lost his sight in 1948 through glaucoma. Besides exhibiting at several Salons des Indépendants and Salons des Tuileries, the Salon d'Automne held an important retrospective exhibition of his work in 1952, which was a reminder of his technical qualities, the consistency of his style through the widely different subjects and was a revelation of the part he had played as precursor in the development of contemporary painting.   R.-J. M.

VAN DOESBURG Theo. *See* Doesburg.

VAN DONGEN Kees. *See* Dongen.

VAN GOGH Vincent. *See* Gogh.

VELDE Henri-Clemens van de (1863-1957). Belgian painter; born at Antwerp, died in Zürich. He came from a middle-class family and, when he was very young, was interested in the most varied forms of art. He was at first attracted to painting and joined the Academy of Antwerp, then went to Paris to work in Carolus Duran's studio. In 1887, he returned to Belgium to take part in *L'Art Indépendant*, a group of young Antwerp painters with the poet, Max Elskamp, as their secretary. Van de Velde's drive soon made him one of the most active organisers of the group. For the first time, a critic used the term, *art nouveau*, in connection with the Antwerp exhibition of 1887, which consisted of a collection of Neo-Impressionist paintings, at a time when its technique was still unfamiliar and Seurat had only just exhibited his *Grande Jatte*. The term was really coined in connection with Van de Velde's painting that showed a fascination with the intellectual austerity of these scientific theories. He remained faithful to their spirit when he joined the Société des Vingt *(*)* and also when he gave up painting, about 1890, to devote nearly all his energies to the applied arts. He then founded the Belgian, avant-garde review, *Van Nu en Straks*, which enabled him to indulge in some remarkable typographical experiments in the first numbers.

Since 1885, Brussels had been ruled by a socialist government, supported by a powerful group of writers and artists, who wanted to promote an art with a social purpose: Verhaeren, Hankar, Horta, Serrurier, Van Rysselberghe among others. In 1894, the Belgian Socialist Party made Élisée Reclus the head of a new University of the People and Van de Velde inaugurated a course that implied a whole programme of activities in itself, under the title, *Art, Industry, Decoration.* He shared the opening exhibition in 1896 with Vuillard and Maurice Denis at the Galerie Art Nouveau, which he had just finished decorating for Siegried Bing and which became the centre of what was called in France the Modern Style. He planned and furnished throughout the house that he built for himself at Uccle and opened a

workshop that specialised in 'industrial arts, applied arts, and ornamentation'. His activity was tireless and he did all the designing for it himself. This change-over from painting to decorative art was not an isolated phenomenon; the same thing was happening in England under the influence of William Morris (1834-1896) whose theories were propagated by Van de Velde in his lectures and writing. Morris, one of the first English Socialists, considered that easel painting was an anti-social activity, everything should be an occasion of beauty and there should be an 'art for the people by the people.' Towards the end of the century, Van de Velde gave all his time to architecture and abandoned the linear-floral style, which he had helped to create. He worked in Germany from 1899 to 1917; notable among his works were the decoration of the Folkwang Museum at Essen (1900-1902) and the planning of the Werkbund Theatre at Cologne (1914). After various spells in Switzerland and Holland, he returned to Belgium in 1925 to teach at the University of Ghent and found the École de la Cambre, which he ran until 1938. One of his finest achievements was the Kröller-Müller Museum at Otterlo (1937-1954). He spent the last years of his life at Zürich, where an important retrospective exhibition of his work was held in 1958.   R.-J. M.

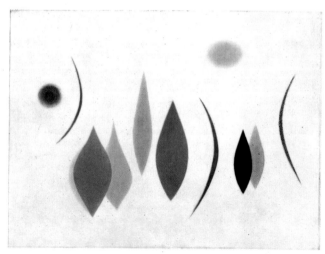

PAULE VEZELAY. COMPOSITION. 1954.
M. S. Collection, Paris.

VEZELAY Paule (born in 1893). English painter, engraver and designer. Educated in London and studied under George Belcher, RA. Moved to Paris in 1926, where she remained until 1939; now lives in London. Attracted by the abstract work of Arp, Miró and others, she undertook her first non-figurative works in 1927-1928. She became a member of Abstraction-Création in 1934 and has been associated with a number of other groups in Paris-the Salon des Surindépen-

VILLON. RACE HORSES. 1922.   *Galerie Louis Carré, Paris.*

dants (1929-1939); the Salon des Réalités Nouvelles from its formation in 1946; the Groupe Espace, Paris, from 1953 and in Britain from 1935, becoming President of the latter in 1957. She is a Fellow of the Society of Industrial Artists.

Paule Vezelay's output, has always shown great diversity. It was as a book illustrator that she first became known and she has continued to practise as such, as well as designing for carpets and textiles. Sculpture, collages, constructions of wire, plastic and string (these date from 1936), engraving, pastels and oils have all at different times formed her mediums. As a painter, she is contemplative rather than exhortatory; discreet and charming rather than dramatic. She uses gentle, subtle colours and flat simple shapes of the utmost clarity, disposing them within the picture frame with elegance and affection. She has been content to remain true to her feminity—never does one sense a straining after a more masculine power—but her style is none the less individual and is crisper and more pure than that of most of her sex and her compatriots, at least of her generation. The titles to her paintings exactly represent their blend of abstract clarity and visual content: for example, *Menacing and Placed Object ; Harmonious Tranquility; Luminous Forms; Dancing Shapes.* A line of Mallarmé has been applied to her: 'musicienne du silence.'

She first exhibited at the Dorien Leigh Gallery in London in 1921. She has since held well over a dozen one-man shows in Paris and London,

and has been widely represented in group and international exhibitions in Europe, America and Asia (Tokyo). Her work has been bought by the Arts Council of Great Britain and is to be found in many private collections, more particularly in France where she is perhaps better known than in England.   M. M.

VILLON Jacques (Gaston Duchamp, 1875-1963). French painter, born at Damville in the Eure; died at Puteaux. The son of a notary and the grandson of Émile Nicolle, a painter and engraver of Rouen, he always saw drawing, painting and engraving practised around him. After his secondary studies he entered a notary's office in Rouen as a clerk. But he attended the courses of the School of Fine Arts more assiduously than he worked at his job. In 1894 he dropped the law and came to Paris. It was then that he took the name of his favourite poet as a pseudonym. Following the example of Forain, Steinlen and especially Lautrec, whom he met every night at the Moulin Rouge, he published satirical and humorous drawings in the papers, notably *Le Rire, Gil Blas, L'Assiette au Beurre* and *Le Courrier Français.* He devoted the first fifteen years of his career to this minor form of art, unable to liberate himself from it. He also did posters for Parisian cabarets and practised engraving, which he has never given up. He exhibited at the Salon d'Automne from the time of its foundation (1904). Toward 1906 he was able to give himself to painting more exclusively. At first influenced by Degas and Toulouse-Lautrec, he seemed at this time to be seized by the contagion of Fauvism. In 1911 he took up Cubism, which met his need for order and discipline. Even then his canvases revealed tendencies and tastes to which he has remained faithful ever since. He organized his compositions carefully and arranged their elements rhythmically around a 'line of intention'. He constructed his forms according to the principle of 'pyramidal vision' formulated by Leonardo da Vinci: an object and its various parts come toward us in pyramids, whose apex is in our eye and whose base is in the object or in a section of the object. He used this procedure with refinement and decisiveness (*The Set Table*, 1912; *Soldiers Marching*, 1913). Finally, under his sponsorhip and in his studio at Puteaux the *Section d'Or (*)* group was constituted: Gleizes, Léger, Metzinger, Kupka, La Fresnaye, Delaunay, Villon's sister, Suzanne Duchamp, and his two brothers, the sculptor Raymond Duchamp-Villon and the painter Marcel Duchamp. If coloured pyramids permit the breakdown of the object or the figure, it has also to be reorganized in a solid and convincing manner. This was why Villon wished to shore up the Cubist methods with strict rules

born of active reflection. The words *Section d'Or* reflected this intellectual requirement, but not the real passion with which he intended to meet it. This method, reinforced and made more flexible, he used for a purpose quite alien to the Cubists' preoccupations. For him the question was less one of transcribing the real in its totality, of accentuating the plastic values of the object, than of taking it apart analytically, giving it more poetry and lyricism, technical skill intervening only to make dream or recollection explicit. Mobilized on August 2nd, 1914, and assigned to the camouflage service, he was discharged in 1919 and eagerly returned to work. From 1919 to 1922, his first abstract period (*Noblesse*, 1920; *Red Equilibrium*, 1921; *The Racehorse*), he tried to render the diversity of values by overlapping planes and sought equivalents capable of expressing the essence of things rather than their exterior attributes. His pictures were painted in a scale of very restricted tones – greys and browns. From 1922 to 1930 he was obliged, in order to live, to devote himself almost entirely to engraving. Capable of creating original and powerful works, he humbly executed a series of coloured reproductions of paintings signed by modern masters–Bonnard, Braque, Picasso, Matisse, Dufy, Utrillo. It was an arid period,

VILLON. DOVECOT IN NORMANDY. 1953.
Private Collection.

painful and depressing. Fortunately, he had several successful exhibitions in New York (Brummer Gallery, 1928) and Chicago (Arts Club, 1933). The American public extended a better welcome to him than his own countrymen. In 1930 he was at last able to go back to his easel. Now very attentive to light, he divided his canvas methodically, superimposing coloured planes according to the laws of the chromatic scale. After another period of abstractionism (*The Leap*, 1932; *Joy*, 1932), he reverted to direct study and also to pure colours, which served to define space and sustain rhythm (*The Draughtsman*, 1935; *The Wrestlers*, 1939). In 1940 he took refuge in the Tarn, and although he had never before shown curiosity for anything but the human figure, he did numerous studies of the surrounding countryside (*Kitchen-garden with Pumpkins*, 1942). After that, he preferred to paint landscape. Since 1944 he has been concentrating all his past experience within the limits of the picture, which comes to us as a complete universe, a paradoxical synthesis of natural phenomena with all the varied, if not contradictory ideas and feelings which characterise the modern man. The masterpieces followed each other: *The Three Orders*, *Castle*, *Church and Countryside* (1944), *Les Grands Fonds* (1945), *The Entrance to the Park* (1948), *Woman Reaping* (1950), *The Black Pigeon-house* (1953), *Orly* (1954), *Cranes near Rouen* (1960).

How does he work? He tells us himself: 'I begin with studies done from nature. From these, I bring out a construction, a play of arabesques and rhythms; in short, I reflect upon nature, which remains my starting point, and I transform it according to a very carefully studied construction of the canvas to be painted. I try to express a space, to find a space in which I can achieve my work. I am also greatly concerned with research in colour and colour values.' His colours are the rarest, the most exquisite: almond greens, pinks, lilacs, oranges, bluish greys. He spreads them with the tip of the brush according to a minutely controlled hierarchy of planes, while preserving the fineness and purity of the line, its dynamic function, and a coherence without heaviness of composition, a unity upon which skill and imagination confer rigour and an inimitable poetry. Villon has always remained faithful to the French tradition. When he accentuates his non-

VILLON. PORTRAIT OF THE ARTIST. 1949.
Louis Carré Collection, Paris.

figurative tendency, he does not betray nature. If he exalts colour, he watches over his drawing even more carefully. In his moments of relaxation or abandon, his delicate architectures remain subject to an unyielding will. Not to sacrifice space to light, solidity to movement, the heart to the intelligence, to express everything and neglect nothing, to remain always open and leave nothing to chance, to be in the vanguard of the struggle and yet revere the masters, paint anecdotal works and yet use only forms and colours, marry Cubism to Impressionism, Abstract Art to Figurative Art–this is an attitude that involves certain risks. Usually by wanting to reconcile everything one finally arrives at compromises. Villon, however, can take pride in incontestable successes. All conquests, all innovations, all presentiments are paradoxically united–and with what ease–in his work. Unlike non-figurative painters, he has practised discredited genres such as the landscape and the portrait; unlike figurative ones he has executed resolutely abstract works. All the tendencies of this century have found their echo in him. He has subscribed to all discoveries, assimilated them and fused them in the melting pot of his own originality. Intelligence and sensibility, reflection and intuition, audacity and humility, his work is a harmonious synthesis of these contrasts. His long career has been made of advances and retreats, of thrusts and resumptions. Yet there has been no hesitation or disquiet: rather precautions, prudent steps, circumspect explorations, subtle allusions. He has developed a conscious and distinguished art, bold but courteous, balanced, shaded, deliciously ambiguous, limpid in spite of its complexity. The art of a free but shy man, of an innovator, agile but careful not to be disconcerting. Less passion than fervour, more implication than assertion, a great nobility in the pleasure given, and thoughtfulness in the effort, so the work appears to us. It is less striking than others more tyrannical or more noisy, but there is no doubt that it goes deeper.   F. E.

VINGT (Les). In 1881, a Belgian lawyer, Octave Maus (1856-1919), who was passionately interested in painting, literature and music, founded the review, *L'Art Moderne*, with the help of his confrère, Edmond Picard (1836-1924). Two years later, when the official jury refused the work of about twenty young painters, with the quip: 'Let them exhibit at home,' Maus, who was an immensely energetic organiser, founded at Brussels with his friends the Association des Vingt (Les XX), a group of twenty Belgian painters and sculptors. Beginning in 1884, they held annual exhibitions to which they invited artists, particularly foreigners, chosen from among the most original, who were often still unknown. So it happened that, before the Société des Indépendants was founded in Paris, these enterprising Belgians found an excellent way of showing the public a representative selection of independent art without having to accept exhibitors indiscriminately. A special committee of three members, chosen annually by lot, was entrusted with deciding whom to invite. The guest artists were chosen consequently by artists who, as the catalogues of the XX prove, were capable of recognising everywhere, in France, England, Germany, Holland, Switzerland and their own

country, the new forces that were to make their mark on the future.

Without the advantage of theories, or a policy or any particular artistic tendencies to unite them, the members of the XX went into battle. Led by their secretary, Octave Maus, eclectic, experienced and above all enthusiastic and tireless, they opened the attack on convention. As a result, for some years Brussels outstripped Paris in an intelligent, sustained and concentrated defence of avant-garde art.

The guest artists, who were generally only invited every other year to avoid repetition or favouritism, presented a choice that was all the more remarkable because most of them had not yet been requested to exhibit anywhere. The most distinguished names among those who have since won world-wide fame were Rodin and Whistler in 1884; Monet, Renoir, Redon and Monticelli in 1886; Morisot, Pissarro and Seurat in 1887; Toulouse-Lautrec and Signac in 1888; Cross, Gauguin, Monet, Pissarro and Seurat in 1889; Cézanne, Redon, Renoir, Signac, Sisley, Toulouse-Lautrec and Van Gogh in 1890; Gauguin, Pissarro, Seurat and Van Gogh (retrospective) in 1891; Cassatt, Maurice Denis, Toulouse-Lautrec and Seurat (retrospective) in 1892. After 1887, Seurat and his friends were regularly represented at Brussels and several members were converted to Divisionism. It was at Brussels, too, that Redon made lasting friendships and found a number of admirers. Finally, it was at the 1890 exhibition that for the first and only time in his life Van Gogh sold a painting.

The periodical, *L'Art Moderne*, now the organ of the XX group, published informed articles on new tendencies and outstanding personalities of contemporary art by Mirbeau, Fénéon, Huysmans, Verhaeren, etc. Besides this, the annual exhibitions were accompanied by lectures given by Catulle Mendès, Villiers de l'Isle-Adam, Mallarmé, Gustave Kahn, Henry van de Velde, Verlaine and there were also concerts. The guest artists often attended the private views: Redon went with his friend, Mallarmé; Seurat, Signac and Toulouse-Lautrec put in an appearance that added to the verve of the artistic scene and brought the young Belgian artists into touch with the intellectual circles of Paris.

The number of members in the group did not always remain at twenty; internal quarrels, resignations and elections changed its composition fairly frequently. Among those who have since won an international reputation were Ensor, de Groux, Knopff, Minne, Rops, Van Rysselberghe and Van de Velde. Towards the end, a few foreigners were elected such as the Dutchman, Toorop, and the Frenchmen, Rodin and Signac. Although all the members of the group cannot claim an outstanding reputation, at least they contributed to a courageous enterprise, which drew together all the vital forces of the day and gave them the chance of an exceptional publicity. Then in 1893, Octave Maus sent a circular letter to the faithful: 'Several members of the Association des XX think that, as avant-garde circles should never continue too long and pay the penalty of decline or retrogression and as the period of ten years, which we have triumphantly reached, should be the limit, have proposed the dissolution of the society.' This dissolution was effectively voted. However, Maus was incapable of remaining inactive, so he then founded on different lines, *La Libre Esthétique*, took charge of it and continued his unflagging efforts in support of modern art.   J. R.

VIVIN. THE LOUVRE. 1930. *Private Collection, Paris.*

VIVIN Louis (1861-1936). French painter; born at Hadol in the Vosges; died in Paris. His is an art of urban character, as though it were made from the tracery of the Eiffel Tower. Held in the net of its tenuous lines, Vivin's painting is one of the valid manifestations of naïve art. There is in general nothing so monotonous as folk art: a transfer of series of identical ideas given the name of a country or a region to differentiate them. From this background, consisting of repeated images of the collective unconscious, there occasionally emerges some more acute art in which a personality is expressed. This is the case with the Douanier Rousseau and Bauchant; it is also the case with Vivin. Drawn stone after stone, block after block, his art is that of a builder. A natural combination of the linear and the pictorial, what he spreads out before our eyes is the most charming world that could be. His sensitive hand wove, as the spider its web, a world of intersecting silk ladders to which, in its best moments, large flat areas, freshly coloured blue, red, brown and green, serve as backgrounds: leaden skies, hulls of barges, shop signs. The painter gives us a portrait of the curiosities of Paris and its suburbs with occasional excursions to harbours and imaginary Venices dreamed from postcards.

Where there are no buildings, no stones to juxtapose, he relapses into the meek and invertebrate style of the usual folk art: bouquets, still-lifes, little scenes of carnage.

When still no more than a child, Vivin covered the doors of his house with drawings. Given a paint box by the village priest, he painted a series of landscapes of his native region. But one has to live, and the boy's father, a teacher, was opposed to a career as a painter for his son. In 1881 Vivin entered the Postal and Telegraph Service, where he later became an inspector. In 1889 he exhibited for the first time in public, showing *The Pink Flamingo* at the postal employees' salon. From then on he lived in a small

VLAMINCK. TUG AT CHATOU. 1906. *Private Collection, U.S.A.*

dusty apartment in Montmartre. From time to time he exhibited out-of-doors at the 'Foire aux Croûtes' near Sacré-Cœur. He was sixty-one when he retired. His days of getting up at five to paint by kerosene lamp before going to his office were over. In 1925 Wilhelm Uhde *(*)* discovered him and gave him encouragement. Paralyzed, the artist had to give up painting during his last years. With his head framed by tousled white hair, a bushy beard, his forehead lined by wrinkles, a rather thick nose, he had the look of a weary observer, a tramp philosopher. A kind of repressed smile, marked with sad humour, radiated from all his features. He was an uneven painter. Some of his canvases have a monotonous quality in the drawing, or a flabby heaviness of stroke. In this respect he was truly a 'Sunday painter'. He did not have the regularity of inspiration that establishes the value of the Douanier Rousseau. In his best works, however, there is a clearness of colour, a vividness, and a limpidity that fully justify his reputation.

P. C.

VLAMINCK Maurice (1876-1958). Born at Paris; died at Rueil-la-Gade-lière, Eure-et-Loir. Vlaminck's father was of Flemish stock and his mother from Lorraine. He spent his childhood in Paris, in the *Halles* district, and later chiefly at Le Vésinet. His parents, both musicians and rather bohemian, seem to have neglected their son's formal education. Vlaminck developed a marked taste for all arts of folk inspiration: sentimental songs, naïve images, small pictures in spun glass, Negro sculpture. His tastes were frankly plebeian: he liked Sunday amusements, picnics, sporting events, walks and bicycle rides. He was happy among the things of the earth. A painter, a writer, a violinist, he was also a farmer. He boasted of never having set foot in the Louvre; he rebelled against the École des Beaux-Arts, the Academy, aesthetes, 'decadent' art forms, precious and refined works. All constraint, all discipline exasperated him: the teacher, the priest, the sergeant, the policeman. He loathed all that limits the personality. He took pride in being a libertarian. Thus he was happy out of doors. As a bicycle racer and later a motoring enthusiast, he craved speed and wide open spaces. Derain, who was born in Chatou, often saw him either participating in a bicycle race, carrying his violin under his arm or lugging his canvases and paintbox. The two young men became friends. They met almost every day, having endless discussions, going to paint on the slopes of Carrières-Saint-Denis or along the banks of the Seine, while tug-boats were passing followed by a line of barges: 'The colour of all this delighted us . . . this was Chatou !' They shared the same studio, in a disused hotel near the island of Chatou, not far from the place that the Impressionists had made famous. Renoir had painted the *Boatmen* there, and Courbet, in 1856, *Les Demoiselles*. Degas had gone there in search of subjects. It was there that Vlaminck and Derain founded the School of Chatou, one of the sources of Fauvism *(*)*. Recalling this period and their friendship, Derain writes: 'We were always intoxicated with colour, with words that speak of colour, and with the sun that makes colour live !' One can imagine, then, the joy with which Vlaminck came into contact with the Fauves of the Académie Carrière (*), and the influence Van Gogh was to exercise upon his work once he had visited the exhibition devoted to the great Dutchman in 1901, and with which he was so enraptured that he exclaimed upon leaving it: 'Van Gogh means more to me than my own father !' A Fauvist: undoubtedly no one has deserved this name more than Vlaminck. No one else had his muscularity, his punch, his vitality. One felt a physical joy in seeing this bragging and jovial giant throw out his chest, flex his calves and lift weights. With his common sense, his noisy enthusiasm, his taste for uproarious practical jokes, his intoxication with colour, his lyrical interpretation of reality, Vlaminck boldly trod the earth ploughed by Vincent. The wild gale, that had shaken the cypresses at Saint-Rémy fifteen years before, developed in his pictures into a storm too violent not to have been consciously expressed. From his thick hands came topsy-turvy forms and frenzied colours, canvases teeming with kinks, thrusts, twistings, freshly squeezed from tubes. The yellow dear to Van Gogh, vermilion, ultramarine, Veronese green, pure white–his favourite tones–he opposed them all and joyfully made them clash. His palette was as exaggerated as his style. Robust, noisy, he shouted and hit hard. But he often hit the mark and persuaded quickly. One swallowed his spiced dishes at a gulp, tired of Impressionist sweets. Monet's evanescent forms and flickering tones were obliterated by the brutal parallels and explosive tones of a picture like *The Red Trees* (reproduced on page 123). No one thought of complaining that the frail regatta of Argenteuil was put to flight by the howling tugboats of Chatou, even if they dragged acrid smells of fried fish in their wake. This Fauve at liberty was a comforting sight, quenching his thirst at the sources of rhythm and browsing on colour in its primal rawness. He painted, discoursed, fulminated, blasphemed, exercised his muscles. Between two pictures he wrote a novel or got on his bicycle, dashed off a newspaper article or hurtled down the roads in his car. Then he returned to his palette and his pipe. In 1905,

VLAMINCK. HOUSE WITH LEAN-TO. 1920.
Musée d'Art Moderne, Paris.

encouraged by Matisse, he exhibited his work for the first time at the Salon des Indépendants and the Salon d'Automne in the famous 'cage of Fauves'. In 1906, he exhibited at the Galerie Berthe Weill and Vollard bought the entire contents of his studio the same year. It was the time when he was friendly with the Bateau-Lavoir group at Montmartre. However in 1908, he painted his last Fauvist canvas, drifted away from Van Gogh and planted his boots in Cézanne's tracks. As he himself has confessed, 'I suffered from not being able to hit harder, from having arrived at the maximum intensity'. It was from 1908 to 1914 that, following the example of Cézanne, Vlaminck sought well-balanced and constructed compositions. He accentuated depth, gave great solidity to volumes, enclosed masses in geometrical contours. Cubism should have attracted him. On the contrary, he turned away from it with rage and was soon denouncing its narrow intellectualism. Around 1915 he broke with Cézannism and settled down comfortably in an expressionism that has, with time, drifted toward an inveterate realism. The Fauvist who let exultant joy burst out in a delirium of crude colours now paints sinister landscapes and faded flowers. Leaden backgrounds, primitive forms, skies slashed with Prussian blue, spinach-green vegetation, dirty-ochre roads, chalky-white walls, trees bent under some unlikely gust of wind–everything in his recent work speaks of his having forgotten his early enthusiasms and his very earthy vision of things. As a landscape painter, he draws on nature very little. As a modern painter, he rejects modern painting and to express himself finds only means borrowed from the old masters of museums: hence the sadness that emanates from the works of his maturity.   F. E.

VOLLARD Ambroise (1865-1939). Coming as a young man to Paris from his native island of Réunion, Ambroise Vollard began as a clerk in a small art gallery. When he became a dealer himself (1893), he prudently began to take interest in 'recognized' painters like Roybet; he told of this later himself with the sly, childish smile that sometimes lit up the usually gruff face made familiar to us by several great painters. To a natural inclination for humour he added penetrating observation. His taste for satire and his horror for routine took on a more concrete significance when, suddenly abandoning Roybet, without transition or half-measure, he adopted Cézanne and in December 1895 organized in his gallery the first great Cézanne exhibition, with a hundred and fifty of his most characteristic canvases. The show created a scandal; the public closed their ranks. Members of the Institut de France who came to the exhibition protested vehemently. Vollard was forced to remove from his window the canvases that provoked the hilarity or hostility of passers-by, but he was beaming; his smile was that of a boy who has played a good trick. Meanwhile real admirers appeared: Auguste Pellerin, Count Camondo, the former King Milan of Serbia, for example. Vollard's shop, his 'cellar', as it was called, became the most brilliant artistic centre in Paris during the first forty years of the century. A drawing by Bonnard, dated 1895, represents him in the midst of the well-known disorder of his shop, surrounded by Rodin, Pissarro, Renoir, Degas and Bonnard himself. No biography of Vollard can omit a rather impressive iconography: Bonnard

BONNARD. PORTRAIT OF VOLLARD.

painted him in 1905, and then in 1915. Cézanne made, in 1899, the famous portrait of him which is now in the Petit Palais, and which took no fewer than a hundred and fifteen sittings. At about the same time Vollard figured in Maurice Denis' *Hommage à Cézanne* (1900). He sat for Renoir four times and one of the paintings shows him quaintly dressed as a torreador (1917). As for Picasso, after painting an admirable Cubist portrait of him, he drew him full-length in 1915, besides two engraved portraits of 1937.

The illustrated book soon became Vollard's main preoccupation and in the period between 1900 and his death about thirty works appeared under his imprint, which are now among the most sought after books of bibliophiles. Fine printing had hardly emerged from a long period of decline, when he published Verlaine's *Parallèlement* in 1900, with lithographs by Bonnard. It is surprising to note that this exceptionally fine book was only moderately successful. Bonnard also illustrated for him *Daphnis et Chloé* (1902) and *Dingo* (1924) by Octave Mirbeau; Rodin: *Le Jardin des Supplices* (1902) by Mirbeau; Maurice Denis: an *Imitation of Christ* (1903) and Verlaine's *Sagesse* (1911); Émile Bernard: Ronsard's *Amours* (1915), *Les Fleurs du Mal* (1916), the *Fioretti* (1928) and the *Odyssey ;* Rouault: *Ubu-Roi* (1918) and *Le Cirque de l'Étoile Filante* (1938); Picasso: Balzac's *Le Chef-d'œuvre Inconnu* (1931); Odilon Redon: Flaubert's *La*

Tentation de Saint Antoine (1937). He used unpublished monotypes by Degas to illustrate an edition of Maupassant's *La Maison Tellier* (1933) and Lucian's *Mimes des Courtisanes* (1935), translated by Pierre Louys. This list would be incomplete if it did not include the books he commissioned from artists, although they did not actually appear until after his death: Buffon's *Histoire Naturelle* (1942), illustrated by Picasso; Gogol's *Les Ames Mortes* (1948) and La Fontaine's *Fables* (1952), both illustrated by Chagall.

Although Vollard's big transaction was with Cézanne, he was none the less interested in artists like the Nabis and Gauguin. He became Gauguin's regular dealer in March 1900 and guaranteed him a monthly allowance in exchange for his paintings. In 1901, Picasso's first exhibition was held at his gallery and he bought from him some thirty canvases for two thousand francs in 1905. The first exhibition of Matisse also took place at Vollard's gallery, in 1904. Vollard had an opportunity to show his fondness for Fauvism by acquiring the whole of Derain's studio in 1905 and Vlaminck's in 1906. Having met Rouault in 1907, he directed him toward ceramics and later toward the illustration of books, eventually installing a studio for him in his own house, where he invited all the artistic and literary élite of Paris for his famous dinners. In addition he brought out bronzes by Rodin, Renoir, Maillol and Picasso. His tremendous activity won him many friendships and enabled people to forgive the redoubtable business man that he was. He had a very original personality and his conversation was extremely lively. A respectful but vigilant observer, he executed portraits himself – literary ones – depicting Cézanne, Renoir and Degas in vivid and colourful books. In 1937 he published his *Souvenirs d'un Marchand de Tableaux* (published first in English, in 1936, as *Recollections of a Picture Dealer*), which will remain an important source for the art history of our time. M. R.

VORTICISM was the most nearly equivalent movement in England to Cubism *(*)* in France and, more comparably, to Futurism *(*)* in Italy. Like them, it was anti-Impressionist; like the latter, it accepted the machine world and sought out machine forms. Those forms, abstracted to the point of non-figuration, were characterized by flat, plan-like systems of arcs and angles organized radially from a particular focal point (the 'vortex'), which had the effect of sucking the spectator into a whirling recession. Vorticism is thus of historical interest as one of the several independent manifestations of the drive to abstraction which became apparent in Europe between the years 1910-1912. Wyndham Lewis *(*)*, its chief protagonist, went so far as to criticize the cubists for basing 'their invention upon the posed model, or the posed Nature Morte, using their models almost to the same extent as the impressionists.'

The movement could be said to have lasted from 1912 to 1915; it was precluded from consolidating its programme and philosophy by the advent of the First World War. Indeed, it is perhaps straining the word to call it a movement at all, for it not merely revolved around the figure of Lewis: it was all but contained by him. His circle included, among others, the writers Ezra Pound (who coined the word 'vorticist' in 1913) and Richard Aldington; T. E. Hulme the anti-romantic philosopher; Epstein and Gaudier-Brzeska the sculptors; William Roberts, Edward Wadsworth *(*)* and C. R. Nevinson the painters. For three years or so, Lewis kept these and others in precarious harness by his own superabundant energy and enthusiasm, while himself contriving polemic enough for several movements. Apart from its purely historical significance, Vorticism is remembered for its generally vitalizing influence in Britain (see also *Blast*).

The 'First' (and last) Vorticist Exhibition took place at the Doré Gallery in June 1915. But, as Lewis was to write nearly a quarter of a century later, 'a bigger Blast than mine had taken the wind out of my sails.' And though a number of painters, in addition to Lewis himself, were subsequently to employ Vorticism's precise, metallic, handwriting to record aspects of the war upon which Europe was embarked—and for which, incidentally, those forms seemed peculiarly fitted—none maintained Vorticism's short-lived pitch of non-figuration. The true sources of abstraction in Britain are to be sought elsewhere but, in a more general sense, the birth of the modern movement in Britain may be found in those years during and immediately after the First World War which were themselves largely shaped by Vorticism. Not only do many of the works by Nevinson, Nash (*), Roberts and Wadsworth (*) retain an intrinsic validity and value; an interesting stylistic echo of Lewis' earlier days was to reverberate through the British neo-romantic movement of the nineteen-forties.

M. M.

VUILLARD Édouard (1886-1940). French painter; born at Cuiseaux, in Saône-et-Loire; died at La Baule. The ways of Vuillard were those of a Parisian petit bourgeois rather than of a provincial. His mother managed a dressmaker's shop. A quiet, orderly, stay-at-home, he spent almost all his life within a small perimeter in Montmartre, in the vicinity of the tiny Square Vintimille, which he has immortaliz-ed, and which ought to bear his name. His beginnings at Le Barc de Boutteville's gallery (1892-1895), his presence at Mallarmé's 'Tuesdays' and the meetings in the editorial offices of the *Revue Blanche* (*), his work as designer at the Théâtre de l'Œuvre–where he learned the technique of tempera–everything brought him near the comrades of his youth: Sérusier, a link with Gauguin; Bonnard, whose studio he shared; K.-X. Rous-

sel, who became his brother-in-law; Vallotton, Maillol and Maurice Denis (*vide* Nabis). Vuillard, who called himself derisively the 'intimist', in his first works skirted realism with extreme caution, as if afraid of frightening it away. A vision of rare subtlety, an innate sense of harmony and layout, made him an heir of Degas and Claude Monet. About 1888 he was painting still-lifes and small portraits that related him to Corot and Chardin; then, toward 1890, influenced like Bonnard, by Gauguin and the Japanese, he gave himself up to a kind of 'Pre-Fauvism'. But he soon abandoned exotic composition and all turbulence of the palette, and reasserted his predilection for minor chords and uncontrasting values. The more modest the setting, the more moving is Vuillard's interpretation. For a long time he painted thinly on grey cardboard, whose uncovered parts played through the touches of colour and contributed to the melancholy charm of the composition. Between 1894 and 1914, he did a number of small decorations which might be called 'apartment frescoes': from the *Gardens of Paris* executed for Alexandre Natanson or *Interiors* (ordered by Dr. Vaquez and today in the Petit Palais) to decorations for the Comédie des Champs-Élysées. The last commissions he received were in 1938 (Palais de Chaillot) and 1939 (League of Nations, Geneva).

Portraits, together with the small interior scenes and decorations, constitute the essential part of his work. When he was alone with his intimates–his mother, who shared his life, and whom we see in so many compositions, reading, sewing, preparing meals, attending to household duties; his friends, who called themselves 'Prophets' or Nabis, Thadée Natanson and Missia, Tristan Bernard, Romain Coolus, Mme Hessel-Vuillard was at his best. He appears less at ease in commissioned por-

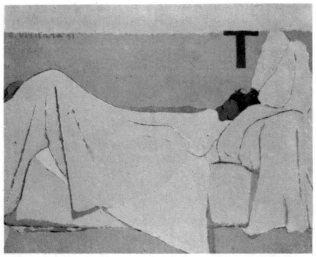

VUILLARD. IN BED. 1891.　　*Musée d'Art Moderne, Paris.*

traits, mostly executed in tempera, in which his sympathy, his amusement go chiefly to the play of light, to exchanges between objects. His comparative failure in painting society people and an atmosphere of wealth was due to an incompatibility of ideals and temperament that he did not always confess to himself, faithful as he was to the sweetness of the simple life and to all that reminded him of his early childhood. In reaction against the vanities and confusion that the twentieth century has seen growing, and even against certain oddities that were part of the charm of the small canvases of the *Revue Blanche* and Symbolist periods, where everything is allusion and whispering, this magician applied, toward the end of his life, his seriousness, his scruples about going beyond these amenities to 'finishing' his canvases, even if he was to move us less. He liked to rely upon the known, an inner and so to speak anterior reality. The role of 'visual memory' is considerable both in his portraits, almost always executed away from the model, and in his still-lifes and decorations. So much rigour in the exquisite, so much precision in enchantment recall the greatest poets of the nuance. The most modest tones are exalted and become precious solely by virtue of

VUILLARD. THE COOK. 1899.
LITHOGRAPH.

their nearness one to another, or of differences that are never discords.   CL. R.-M.

WADSWORTH. SIGNALS. 1942.
Tate Gallery, London.

WADSWORTH Edward Alexander (1889-1949). English painter and engraver; born in Cleckheaton, died in London. The son of a worsted spinner, he studied engineering for a time in Munich before attending art schools there and in England, working finally at the Slade School in London from 1910-1912. He exhibited with the Vorticists(*) and, after service overseas with the Navy between 1915-1917, was engaged upon dazzle camouflage work on shipping at English ports. His interests as a man and as an artist were thus established early: to an over-riding passion for the sea and ships were joined a lively sense of pictorial structure and pattern making, and an instinctive leaning towards precision of expression. In their strong cubist-vorticist formalisation the drawings and prints he made towards the end of and immediately after the First World War—in particular perhaps some small wood engravings done in 1917 and 1918—are genuine documents of their time. In 1920 he published a book of drawings of *The Black Country*, with an introduction by Arnold Bennett, and six years later a book of copper engravings *The Sailing Ships and Barges of the Western Mediterranean and Adriatic*. Thereafter Wadsworth applied himself almost entirely to tempera, a medium which he had first employed some years before but which now, as a result of repeated visits to Italy, he used ever more strictly in the tradition taught by Cennino Cennini. For the rest of his life he developed and refined an idiom in which can be found echoes of Léger and the cubists on the one hand; of de Chirico, Pierre Roy and the surrealists on the other. The typical later Wadsworth comprises a still life of heterogeneous objects, all evocative of ships and shore, hanging silent and motionless before a backdrop of harbour, sea and sky. The clarity of his forms and the lack of rhetoric with which they are displayed may appear to diminish, but in fact seldom entirely destroy, the communication of a genuine ardour. His screws, anchors, sextants, buoys and the rest are assembled and re-assembled with the enthusiasm of the true collector and delineated in obsessive detail with the skill of the engineering draughtsman, but without the emotive undertones and inner conflicts of surrealism proper. Wadsworth was at different times a member of the London Group, X Group, the New English Art Club and Unit One; he was elected an Associate of the Royal Academy in 1943. In 1945 he delivered a paper to the Royal Institute of Civil Engineers, which was subsequently published, on *The Aesthetic Aspect of Civil Engineering Design*. He executed a number of public mural decorations, notably for the Canadian War Museum, RMS *Queen Mary* and the De La Warr Pavilion, Bexhill. His work is represented in the British Museum, the Tate Gallery and the Stedelijk Museum among others. Memorial exhibitions were mounted at the Tate Gallery in 1951.   M. M.

WALCH Charles (1898 - 1948). French painter; born at Thann, in Alsace, died at Paris. When he was very young, he loved exploring the countryside and drawing, all the more because he had been deprived of the use of his left hand since birth. His pencils and brushes were already a means of self-expression and understanding. At eighteen in the middle of the war, he painted, in the Neo-Impressionist manner, some moving water-colours of the ruins of his home town. In 1918, a grant enabled him to live at Paris and study at the École des Arts Décoratifs for four years. He met François Desnoyer there and made friends with him. Then, without any resources, he took over a studio and lived there till the end of his life. In Paris, Matisse and Bonnard and the Italian Primitives at the Louvre taught him how to handle colour. He decorated the

Convent of Sainte-Odile in 1921. From 1923 to 1938, he taught drawing at Sainte-Croix de Neuilly and painted a fresco in the chapel, inspired by the Gospels. His contribution to the Salon d'Automne in 1925 showed the influence of Cubism, but he was soon drawn to Fauvism, which was followed by a monochrome period, then studies of bathers reminiscent of Cézanne. It was not till he was about forty, after a quiet, reflective existence and experiment that showed a sensitive and sincere personality, that Walch reached the full flowering of his powers. Bonnard and Marquet encouraged him and in 1937, when he was thirty-nine, he held his first one-man exhibition. A few years later, he made friends with Rouault.

Nature was always present in his work. If he was not actually painting from nature, he liked to live with it and reflect on it. Out of the splashes of colour, muted at first, then more and more vivid, sprang the landscape of his childhood: the Thur valley, pathways in the Vosges, animals, trees, houses, flowers, children, all fashioned into paint by the same look and the same affectionate attention. A humble humanity, with its awkward, but unaffected attitudes, peopled a countryside, overflowing with flowers and fruit, happiness and the sun, until the day when this 'rustic enchantment', as George Besson called it, burst into bouquets of pure colour. During the war, when he was summoned by the committee of the Salon d'Automne to defend with his friends the 'degenerate' painting that had been branded by the occupying power, Walch did not try to play safe and, in 1944, designed the poster for the first Salon of the Liberation: a tricolour cock brilliant with colour. 'Painting to him meant what it actually is; much more than an aesthetic experience, it was a spiritual and moral activity, without anything dessicated about it,' said Bazaine. The freedom of his brush strokes was never

WALCH. THE SLEDGE.   *Musée d'Art Moderne, Paris.*

WEBER. POT OF GERANIUMS. 1911.
Museum of Modern Art, New York.

exaggerated deliberately, nor the fluidity of his coloured lines that intersected in lively designs, so that his painting might look gayer and more natural. The figures in his paintings have the same transparency as the landscape. Familiar scenes and daily tasks make a vital and luminous imagery in which rich colour and vibrant harmonies count for more than the purely representational element, 'I paint images,' Walch said. His work has the freshness of a bunch of common flowers, a controlled brightness, a spontaneous imagination.   R.-J. M.

WEBER Max (1881-1961). American painter; born in Bialystok, Russia. His parents emigrated with him to America in 1891. After studies in Brooklyn at the Pratt Institute with the famous teacher Arthur Wesley Dow, he went to Paris in 1905, where he studied with J.-P. Laurens at the Académie Julian and for a short time with Matisse. He discovered Cézanne and became friendly with the Douanier Rousseau. Primitive art always had a deep fascination for him: on his return to the United States in 1909 he made an extensive study of American Indian art. His exhibitions at Stieglitz's '291' in 1909 and 1911 were attacked by the critics, but he was invited by Roger Fry to exhibit with the Grafton group in 1913. Weber was a director of the Society of Independent Artists in 1918. Important retrospectives of his work were held in the Museum of Modern Art in 1930 and at the Whitney Museum in 1949.

His early work, influenced by the Fauves, the Cubists, and later the Futurists, took him (1910-1917) to the threshold of abstraction. But several years later he returned to a more frankly expressionistic style related to Fauvism. In spite of his flirtations with abstraction, Weber was never able to renounce for long a basic lyrical streak with overtones of primitive art and of Jewish and Oriental folklore. Again in the middle forties his work approached abstract expressionism in compositions of distorted figures growing out of monochrome planes whose edges suddenly blaze with jewel-like tones. But these tendencies toward formalism are always corrected by a humanistic strain which sets him somewhat apart from prevailing tendencies in postwar American art in which he occupies a position similar to that of Rouault in France.   J. A.

WHISTLER James (1834-1903). American painter; born in Lowell, Massachusetts; died in London. Once, when Vollard showed him a woman's portrait done by Cézanne, Whistler remarked, 'If a ten-year-old child had scrawled that on a slate, his mother—if she was a good mother—would have whipped him'. While the importance of such a quip should not be exaggerated, it does throw some light upon the behaviour of a man who, even though he participated in the revolutionary forays of the Impressionists, generally held back whenever the issue became too disturbing. He was a strange, clever, but timid artist, despite the appearance of liberty he revealed in his more characteristic works. His family traced back to Scotch-Irish ancestors, and his father, a railway construction engineer, was internationally respected. Emulating his father, an Army Major and a West Point graduate, Whistler also enrolled at the military academy, but studies proved too irksome and he was dismissed. At the call of Art he proceeded to Paris, where he soon discovered the Café Guerbois and exchanged ideas with Baudelaire, Manet, Fantin-Latour and Bracquemond. In 1859, he tried to exhibit at the official Salon, but his painting, *At the Piano*, was refused. However it brought him the encouragement of Courbet. In 1863, informed that his *Little White Girl* would not be acceptable for hanging in the Paris Salon, he aligned himself with the other famous rebels in the Salon des Refusés. Determined to oust all influences, whether a traditional classicism or a more recent romanticism–and having been spurred to that end by Courbet–he joined this artist during the summers of 1864 and 1865 at Trouville. Shortly afterwards Whistler embarked for Chile, where he affiliated himself with a band of revolutionary exiles. Later he lived in London with his brother-in-law Seymour Haden, the etcher, and still later was attacked by Ruskin, whom he sued in a celebrated (and successful) court action. He travelled widely and it was only after various visits to Italy, Belgium and Holland, that he finally settled in London in 1880. He was elected to the Society of British Artists and became its president in 1886. He was loaded with decorations and medals, lectured in London, Oxford and Cambridge and enjoyed a brilliant career as a fashionable portrait painter. He died in 1903 after leading a busy and eventful life. Although his works never possessed the force to make of him a major influence (even admitting those followers who had taken note of his flair for the penumbral envelope) he did have his gifts as an improviser who could wed the elegance of his arabesque to a chromatic refinement rightly described as exquisite. Again, whatever the branch of his work, he did commit himself, like the Impressionists, to an unremitting examination of tones, as even his titles emphasize: *Harmony in Grey and Green, Arrangement in Grey and Black, Nocturne in Blue and Green, Symphony in White.* And yet the general trend of his accomplishment did not escape the impersonal. In spite of the sparkle he could impart to his compositions, the underlying substance shows none of that profound humanity invariably present among the other masters of his time. His technical method, while it could be appealing, unsettles and even per-

plexes because of a propensity for the decadent which leaves the suspicion–however involuntary–that he had overlooked the plastic imperatives in painting, and, even more serious, that he simply could not experience that attachment to nature characteristic of his associates among the Impressionists. He is not to be denied his audacity as a technician of the palette and he did concentrate himself upon certain problems–at least those pertaining to 'cuisine'–but even here he fell upon dangerous recipes, and he so diluted his colours in turpentine that eventually they lost their initial intensity. Yet the cause of his quest was his zeal to eliminate

WHISTLER. MISS CICELY ALEXANDER.
HARMONY IN GREY AND GREEN. 1872-1874.
Tate Gallery, London.

all the brightness his sensibility could not accept. He expounded his principles in a witty lecture, 'Ten O'clock', translated into French by Mallarmé. Here he impaled his enemies among the leading contemporary academicians, demonstrating both by aphorism and example that he was the supreme exponent of an atmospheric vision that few of such contemporaries could even understand.　　　　　　　　　　J. M.

WILLUMSEN Jens Ferdinand (1863-1958). Danish painter; born at Copenhagen, died in Cannes. After training at the Academy of Fine Arts in Copenhagen, he went to Paris in 1888 and to Spain in 1889. In July 1890, he went to Pont-Aven, where he met Gauguin, Sérusier and Meyer de Haan. He was stirred by the new Syntheticism and worked in his own manner at decorative paintings of Breton women. He shocked the public of Copenhagen with these paintings a few years later. In 1893, he produced the first sketch for the *Large Relief*, which he hoped would be realised in ceramic, but which was finally executed in gilt bronze with different sorts of marble. As artistic director of the porcelain factory of Bing and Grondal in Copenhagen, his activities were directed to decorative art. When he returned to painting in 1900, it was with the high hopes of the new century. He painted the majesty of the Alps, seashores and beaches with children bathing. Sometimes a panic fear appeared in his painting, as in *After the Storm* of 1905, which revealed an expressionistic Willumsen. His style changed after 1910. He was then living in Spain, afterwards in Algeria and he painted their landscapes in bright colours with a surprising spontaneity. He had seen the work of El Greco and his mannerism influenced his expressionism. It so impressed him that he undertook to edit a two volume work, *The Early Years of El Greco*. The influence of his stay in Spain and admiration for El Greco can be seen in the intense, phosphorescent colours of Willumsen's paintings of Venice

(1929-1930). Living in retirement far from the world, he expressed the isolation of old age in three self-portraits, *The Dying Titian* (1935-1938).　　　　　　　　　　B. L.

WOESTIJNE Gustave van de (1881-1947). Belgian painter; born in Ghent, died at Brussels. When he was eighteen, he went with his brother, Karel, the Belgian poet, to live at Laethem-Saint-Martin, where he knew the painter, Valérius de Saedeler, and the sculptor, George Minne. Like them, he thought they ought to go on from Impressionism, which was victorious in Belgium at the time, and he took the Flemish Primitives, Giotto and Fra Angelico for his models in his efforts to work out his own idiom. He was also influenced by Pieter Bruegel and in 1910, was still hesitating between the easy appeal of the fanciful and realism, which possessed a painful sharpness in spite of certain mannerisms. On the one hand, he could paint an idyllic picture of the countryside, which has an affinity with Maurice Denis (*Sunday Afternoon*); on the other, he painted portraits and particularly peasants' heads that were remarkable for their strained expression and the incisive draughtsmanship. His colour, however, was seldom vigorous and sometimes it was even anaemic.

The 1914-1918 war drove Van Woestijne to take refuge in England, but when peace returned,

WOLS. DRAWING. 1949. INDIAN INK.

WOESTIJNE. THE BEGGAR VIOLONIST. 1920.
Musée des Beaux-Arts, Liège.

he went back to Belgium. In 1925, he was appointed director of the Academy of Mechelen and remained there until 1939. Then he went to Brussels, where he taught at the École de la Cambre. During the 1920's, his art developed a more geometric pattern a harder form, a more forceful colouring and a more dramatic expression. From time to time, he painted religious subjects and whether his Christ was being crucified, or was showing his wounds, or was surrounded by a disordered group of apostles (*The Last Supper*), or was facing the empty desert, his face was always full of anxiety, sometimes it seemed almost panic stricken. In fact, it was when Van de Woestijne was expressing moral conflict and physical suffering after 1919, that his painting was most convincing. It would be more moving if his tendency to use archaic mannerisms did not give it a certain dryness.   J.-E. M.

WOLS (1913-1951). Pseudonym derived from his real name, Wolfgang Schülze. German painter; born in Berlin, died at Paris. He came from a Saxon family of jurists and musicians. He was brought up in Dresden and possessed the most versatile gifts; he was an excellent violonist and was a brilliant pupil of Frobenius at the Institute of African Studies in Frankfurt. After a spell in the Bauhaus, he went to Paris in 1932, where he took up photography and gave German lessons to earn a living. He painted his first watercolours and made friends with Miró, Calder, Tzara and Ernst. In 1933, he was in Spain, and lived in Barcelona until he was deported. He returned to France and lived in great poverty. At the beginning of the war, he was interned as a German citizen in various camps. He was released in 1940 and went to Cassis, then in 1942 to Dieulefit, where Henri-Pierre Roché helped him. The same year, Betty Parsons held the first exhibition of his works in New York. In 1945, he returned to Paris, living in tiny hotel rooms, working in all sorts of conditions, without an easel and almost without light and material, while his wife made hats. On his bed lay nine little musical instruments on which he used to play every day, preferably Bach; a guitar, a mandoline, banjos, a ukelele and harmonicas (his violin had been left in the municipal pawnshop at Barcelona in 1934 and he was never able to buy another). Wols' work is like the unfolding of subjects that overflow the picture area. *Deeply Rooted People, Crowds, Cities* are all swarming with unbounded life or receding in depths. The forms germinate. Wols sought every means to express an inner soliloquy that followed the meanderings of his imagination, or was the result of the automatic association of ideas. As he refused to consider the act of painting a profession or his paintings as merchandise, he would have nothing to do with galleries or critics. René Drouin succeeded in organising two exhibitions; one in 1945 of his gouaches and water-colours, the second in 1947 of his paintings. On the second occasion the critics spoke for the first time of blot painting and, as time passed, it was evident that these exhibitions were the beginning of most of the modern experiments in materials, action and calligraphic painting. Wols also did some remarkable engravings to illustrate various works by Jean-Paul Sartre, Kafka, Jean Paulhan, René de Solier, Antonin Artaud and Camille Bryen (1948-1949). He exhibited at Milan in 1949, then at New York in 1950. He died just when success was beginning to come to him and he can be considered the last of the great 'peintres maudits.'   J. LA.

WOOD Christopher (1901-1930). Born at Knowsley, near Liverpool; died at Salisbury by his own hand. By the charm of his character, the tragedy of his early death, and the extraordinary promise of his painting which burst like a golden rocket in the none-too-bright sky of that post-war decade, 'Kit' Wood has become one of the few legends in British art. On leaving school in 1920 he decided to become a painter. Between 1920 and 1924 his wanderings took him from Inverness to Constantinople, and to the greater part of Europe. Notwithstanding this apparently rootless existence, he formed a wide circle of friends–among them Picasso and Cocteau in France, Ben and Winifred Nicholson in England. It was Picasso who persuaded Diaghilev to commission from him the décor and costumes for a *Romeo and Juliet* ballet, which was, however, later abandoned. His first exhibition was at the Beaux-Arts Gallery in 1926;

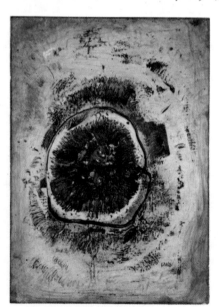

WOLS. PAINTING. 1946.
Jean Paulhan Collection, Paris.

his second at Tooth's in 1929. In 1930 he worked in Paris upon another ballet for C. B. Cochran and his third exhibition at Bernheim's. After two months of furious activity at Tréboul, in Brittany, during the summer, he returned to see his mother at Salisbury on August 21st; later that day he was killed by a train in Salisbury station. It was during this last summer of his life that Wood found himself completely as an artist. Through all his apprenticeship he had always known exactly where he stood; he had accepted influences eagerly, grasped quickly the kernel of truth which they held for him and discarded the husk. From Van Gogh and the old Cornish primitive, Alfred Wallis, he learned, in his last painting, how to express a vision that was entirely personal, of an extraordinary freshness and poetry, and characterized by a remarkable sweetness of colour. By contrasting transparent glazes with the most delicate of opaque tints, he contrived to make the darkest tones of which he was capable 'sing'. His paintings of the Cornish and Breton coasts, with their ink-blue seas, their grey-green jetties and cliffs and cottages, their boats and their fishing nets remain among the most delectable of their time.   M. M.

WOUTERS Rik (1882-1916). Belgian painter; born at Mechelen, died in Amsterdam. He began as a sculptor and continued to sculpture until 1913, so that this work is no less important than his painting. His first notable paintings were produced in 1908, but it was not till 1912 that he produced the work that was to make him one of the most attractive masters of contemporary Belgian painting. He then only had five more years left to work and two of them were years of war, mobilisation, internment in Holland and finally a disease that made him suffer appallingly and ended by impairing his sight. Although he was influenced by Ensor, it was not because he shared his satirical spirit, but because, like him, he was sensitive to light and loved vivid, nacreous tones. His admiration for Cézanne was as great as for Ensor and after a visit to Paris in 1912, he was just as enthusiastic about Renoir. His paintings combined the sensuality of Renoir with Cézanne's concern for structure. His art, however, was more than the result of simple eclecticism: it had a very personal style.

However pure and vivid his colour, his light is less warm than in the French painting. It always seemed as if the northern mists prevented him from being really joyful. There is a strain of melancholy in his works too, not so much in the still-lifes as in the portraits of his wife. He painted her often in her room and although he took pains to record the light, shining on her, he felt too tenderly towards her for us not feel also the sadness and sensitiveness to cold of a sick woman. His art is often delicate; Wouters could combine refinement and brilliance. His composition is sweeping and tempestuous, without being either slip-shod or brutal. All through 1913, the vividness of his colours increased. Although the contrasts became more emphatic, the subtleties of colouring remained. In spite of the illness that was destroying him, he still loved using rich reds and light pinks. His *Self-Portrait* of 1915 is a particularly moving record; the left eye is covered with a bandage and the face is drawn with pain, but he is standing by a curtain, dressed in a triumphant red.   J.-E. M.

WOUTERS. RED CURTAINS. 1913.
Vermeylen Collection, Brussels.

Y - Z

YEATS Jack Butler (1871-1957). Irish painter, illustrator and writer; younger son of the painter John Butler Yeats, Royal Hibernian Academician, and brother of William Butler Yeats the poet. Born in London, he studied there, after a childhood in Sligo, under Frederick Brown at the Westminster School of Art. Nonetheless he was, by every temperamental attachment, wholly Irish in his subject matter and in his approach to it. He began to paint about 1897 and, though his output

as a writer included ten or so books and three plays, as well as a number of ephemera, it is as the great Irish painter of the first half of the twentieth century that his fame has grown. The traveller on the heath, the clown in the music hall, bars, race courses and dripping Irish skies provided him with typical points of departure. If sometimes the images seem to overlap, so that it seems that the clown has donned a cloth cap to go wandering over the mountains or that the traveller has by mistake strayed through the

ZANDOMENEGHI. LE MOULIN DE LA GA-LETTE. *Private Collection, Milan.*

stage door into the pantomime, it is really of no great consequence. Yeats sought to catch the emotional significance of an environment and a moment of time: not its particular surface detail but its undertones of grandeur, or melancholy, or boisterous humour; the turbulence of humanity in a group or the sudden poignancy of a single figure on the skyline.

This moment he spilled on to canvas with a romantic abandon and extravagance that grew with the years. His tool was the palette knife; his sense of form was dubious, of pictorial organisation thin; his colour was dark, the colour of peat and tweed, but shot with wild lights and sudden explosions of riotous intensity. The apparently artless naïveté of his drawing clothed, not the psychological confessions of Germanic or Nordic expressionism, but a fey and feckless romanticism to which his titles often added an additional layer of lyrical obfuscation (perhaps a legacy of the family occultism): *Drive through a City in Fairyland, A Tree Drinking, The Whistle of a Jacket.*

Yeats was a lonely figure who created his own idiom and handwriting on the very perimeter of Europe. But though he stood outside the great movements of contemporary art, in the end the Zeitgeist caught up with him. In his last years the spread of abstract expressionism and tachisme, the revived interest in the matière of painting, gave to his gay and stormy ballads a new sense of topicality, in some senses, a new significance; and brought to their enjoyment, perhaps, a new sympathy. Yeats was Governor and Guardian of the National Gallery of Ireland; he was honoured by the Royal Hibernian Academy and Irish universities; was an Officier de la Légion d'Honneur. He is represented in many galleries in Ireland, Britain and the United States. During the last fifteen years of his life, many exhibitions of his work were shown in Europe and America, including one in 1946, in Edinburgh, which he shared with works by his father.   M. M.

ZANDOMENEGHI Federico (1841-1917). Italian painter; born at Venice, died in Paris. He came from a family of sculptors. He took part in the campaigns of Garibaldi, before joining the Macchiaioli *(*)* in Florence in 1862, whose influence appears in his work. After five years in Florence, he returned to Venice before going to Paris in 1874, where he was friendly with Renoir, Pissarro and Degas. At the instigation of the latter, whose protégé he was, he took part in different exhibitions of the Impressionist group in 1879, 1880, 1881 and 1886. Durand-Ruel gave him his support and he lived his artistic life in the shadow of the great masters. He did some remarkably delicate pastels.   D. F.

ZOLA Émile (1840-1902). French novelist and art critic; born and died in Paris. The powerful personality of Zola deserves to be mentioned in connection with the generous help he gave, at least at the beginning, to the great painters of his time, Manet and Cézanne in particular. His help was so wholehearted and unreserved that one can hardly understand how later he could have so brutally broken the bonds of friendship and esteem that had linked him with most of the Impressionists and denied them any genius. There was a misunderstanding in this, and the deeper reasons are perhaps to be sought elsewhere than in the personality and character of the individuals concerned. In 1857 Zola had known Cézanne at the Collège Bourbon, the future Lycée of Aix-en-Provence. The two schoolboys were of the same age and they took to each other at once. They composed verses and music. Cézanne played the cornet, Zola the clarinet in the college band. When, in 1861, Cézanne obtained leave from his father to go to Paris he lived in lodgings, not far from Zola, in the rue des Feuillantines. At this time Cézanne worked on a portrait of Zola, which they both found bad and which was destroyed. However, relations between the two schoolmates soon became less intimate, although they remained cordial. As a matter of fact, Zola did not have much confidence in Cézanne's painting, particularly after he met Manet, who impressed him more and whose art seemed to correspond in every way to the ordered Naturalism he was dreaming of. At the Café Guerbois *(*)*, which he had been frequenting since 1866, he made the acquaintance of avant-garde critics and the painters who would become the Impressionists. Villemessant, the editor of the newspaper *L'Événement*, having asked him to write a series of articles on the Salon that had just opened, Zola launched, under the pseudonym of 'Claude', a virulent criticism of the selection committee that had rejected the works sent by his new friends, notably *The Fifer* of Manet. The tone of the articles was admirable; it resounded both as a challenge to conformity and a cry of triumph: 'I calmly admit that I am going to admire M. Manet', Zola wrote '. . . I come today to extend a sympathetic hand to the artist whom a group of his colleagues has thrown out of the Salon . . . and who was found unworthy of figur-

ing among the fifteen hundred or two thousand impotents who were received with open arms . . . M. Manet's place is marked in the Louvre like that of M. Courbet . . . It is impossible–impossible, do you hear ?–that M. Manet should not have his day of triumph and not crush the timid mediocrities who surround him.' Such words raised protests from a number of the paper's subscribers and the editor did not hesitate to sacrifice Zola, who did not admit that he was beaten as he published, in the following year, a biographical and critical study on Manet in the *Revue du XIXᵉ Siècle* ('A New Manner in Painting: M. Édouard Manet'). Zola's enthusiasm eventually triumphed: at the Salon of 1868, despite the clamours of the public and the sarcasm of the Press, Manet's famous portrait of him was received. Continuing his campaign for the Impressionists, he wrote another series of articles in *L'Événement Illustré*, the successor to Villemessant's *L'Événement*. He called them 'Naturalists' or 'Actualists'. He praised Pissarro, 'one of the three or four painters of our day . . . never have pictures seemed to me of more masterful breadth'. He was of the opinion, speaking of Manet, that he would 'tame the crowd whenever he should choose to do so', and of Renoir, whom he called Henri, he unreservedly admired *Lise*, 'one of our women, rather one of our mistresses, painted with great truthfulness and a well-rewarded research in the modern idiom'. No doubt Zola was little interested in the Impressionist technique and aesthetic doctrine, but the growing authority of his name and the violence of his colourful style did much to create a favourable attitude toward the new school. Yet his personal opinions were by no means objective. In the same year he already permitted a concern, a doubt to appear about the future of the painting whose apostle he had made himself. He wrote: 'I look into the future and wonder what personality is going to emerge, large enough, human enough to understand our civilization and make it artistic by studying it with the masterly breadth of genius'. These reservations and doubts took on a more serious turn when, in 1880, in *Le Voltaire*, he reproached the Impressionists with neglecting the Salon that he had covered with opprobrium, to adopt the system of private exhibitions. This reproach seems to be a pretext, for with the same violence he had used to defend the Impressionists

ZOLA

he now disowned and attacked them for their
aesthetic intentions, which he seemed finally to
have discovered. It was indeed the very dogmas
of Impressionism that he reproved: 'What an
amazement for the people,' he wrote, 'when they
are put before some canvases painted out-of-
doors, at certain times of day: they are agape
before blue grass, purple earth, red trees, water
bearing all the colours of the spectrum . . . The
great misfortune is that not a single artist of
this group has realized powerfully and definitely
the new formula that all of them have scattered
in their works . . . The formula . . . one finds
nowhere applied by a master . . . They all are
precursors. The man of genius has not been
born.' After having previously written of Monet,
'Here is a man, here is a temperament', he now
reproached him with having been 'fidgeting in a
vacuum for ten years' and with being, like Renoir,
nothing but a 'renegade'. This article appalled
the artists, who retorted by a banquet of protest,
at which Camille Pissarro, Duret, Burty, George
Moore, Mallarmé, Monet, and others were
present. However, Zola once more showed his

ill temper toward the painters by publishing
in 1886 his novel L'Œuvre, in which he represented his former schoolfellow and friend
Paul Cézanne as Claude Lantier, a restless painter
and a failure.

One can easily discern the reasons behind
Zola's behaviour. It was due only to his attachment to realism, which had made him like first
Cézanne and then Manet, in so far as their
tendencies were in line with his own. Fundamentally what he had liked in Monet, Renoir and
Pissarro were the first works, quite evidently
inspired by those of Courbet. The only personal
basis for his partisan enthusiasm was defence of
his Naturalist theories, a fact for which he cannot
be completely reproached, since by remaining
obstinately true to his temperament and his ideas,
be was showing perfect intellectual honesty. Be
this as it may, it cannot be forgotten that his
action, in 1866 and 1868, was courageous and
beneficial, and that it contributed powerfully
to causing at least the name of Manet to be
respected, and thus opened the way to the
future.   M. R.